The Visitations of Bedfordshire, Annis Domini 1566, 1582, and 1634

THE
Publications
OF
The Harleian Society.

ESTABLISHED A.D. MDCCCLXIX.

Volume XIX.

FOR THE YEAR MD.CCC.LXXXIV.

CS
410
H3
v.19

The
Visitations of Bedfordshire,

ANNIS DOMINI 1566, 1582, AND 1634.

MADE BY

WILLIAM HARVEY, ESQ.,
Clarencieulx King of Arms,

ROBERT COOKE, ESQ.,
Clarencieulx King of Arms,

AND

GEORGE OWEN, ESQ,
York Herald,

AS DEPUTY FOR

SIR RICHARD ST GEORGE, KT.,
Clarencieulx King of Arms.

TOGETHER WITH

ADDITIONAL PEDIGREES,
CHIEFLY FROM HARLEIAN MS 1531,

AND AN APPENDIX,

CONTAINING

A LIST OF PEDIGREES ENTERED AT THE VISITATION OF 1669;
ALSO LISTS OF BEDFORDSHIRE KNIGHTS AND GENTRY
TAKEN FROM LANSDOWNE MS 887

EDITED BY

FREDERIC AUGUSTUS BLAYDES.

LONDON:
1884.

Preface.

THE county of Bedford was visited on four different occasions by the officers of the College of Arms for the purpose of recording the pedigrees of the gentry entitled to bear arms. These Visitations were made in the years 1566 by Harvey, 1582 by Cooke; 1634 by George Owen, York Herald, as deputy for Sir Richard St. George, Clarencieux, and 1669 by Bysshe. The last mentioned is the latest Visitation of this county. Three out of the four are now, for the first time, printed in the following pages. I have not been able to discover an available copy of the Visitation of 1669, the only one that I know of is in the College of Arms, MS D 24 I have reason, however, to think that there is a copy of this in some private collection, for I have come across, in what are known as the Dawson MSS.,* a list of Bedfordshire pedigrees comprising (*inter alia*) a list of the pedigrees taken during this Visitation In Gutch's 'Collectanea Curiosa,' vol II, p 212, Oxford, 1781, 8vo, is the following notice of this Visitation: "Sir Ed Bysshe. 1669. 81 B 21, f. 15, Harley" 81 B 21 is the old press-mark of MS Harl. 1405, which does not contain the Visitation of 1669, but only a list of the pedigrees therein, with the arms in trick. Regarding this Visitation Gutch adds the following note· "A copy was at Mr Sheldon's at Weston in 1675, No 139, as appears by 'A Catalogue of MSS, etc., in closet at Weston 1675' (in Mr Sheldon's hand, but no dates mention'd) among Wood's MSS. in Ashm Mus at Oxford, 8578, 116, B. 7" I have appended the list at the end of this volume, as it will probably be of use to those interested in Bedfordshire genealogies Many of the within pedigrees will be found in an extended form in 'The History of the Hundred of Willey,' by W. Marsh Harvey; London, 1872-8; 4to.

* See notes on pages 204, 209, *post*

When I first undertook to edit this volume I had little idea of the amount of work it would entail; for at the very threshold of my investigations I was bewildered by the number of MSS and the want of internal reliable evidence to guide me in selecting the most trustworthy, and assigning them to their respective dates; no two were exactly alike, either as to their contents or as to the number of pedigrees contained in each. After much patient investigation, I have at length been enabled to finish my task, and to evolve something like order out of the chaotic confusion which at first confronted me.

It may be as well for me here to enumerate the various MSS. I have collated and examined. First, amongst the manuscripts in the British Museum Library, the following contain collections of pedigrees relating to this county:

HARLEIAN MSS 1097, 1390, 1531, 2109, 3968, 4600, and 5186. Of these, No 1531, which is in Mundy's handwriting,[*] contains 111 pedigrees; being a collection formed apparently out of the four Visitations. Those which I have not been able to assign to either of the Visitations in the following pages, I have included in this work under the heading "Additional Pedigrees." No 4600 contains 71 pedigrees, with arms in trick, indifferently executed. No. 5867 contains the Visitations of 1566 and 1582, and on the first folio are written the following words: "Comitatus Bedfordie D G. R A. Genealogies 1583." No 2109 contains additions by Challoner and Randal Holme, and apparently formerly belonged to the latter, as attested by the following words on folio 1: "Randle Holme Booke sonne to Randle Holme of ye citty of Chester Alderman 1632 May 15." I have also carefully examined LANSDOWNE MSS. 584, 864, 887, and 888, being the miscellaneous heraldic collections of John Pomfret, Rouge Croix, and John Warburton, Somerset, with notes, etc., relating to Bedfordshire families.

In the Library of QUEEN's COLLEGE, OXFORD, rich in heraldic MSS., I came across one, MS. cxiv, being a manuscript volume of pedigrees in Glover's handwriting. The pedigrees are very neatly written in tabular form in roundles, and the arms carefully tricked. The Index

[*] See page 153

contains 47 pedigrees, which I have extended, for convenience sake, to 51. On one of the fly-leaves is written, "This book formerly belonged to Joseph Williamson."* He was, I believe, the donor of the above-mentioned and other heraldic MSS to this Library. As this is by far the most reliable and authentic manuscript of all I have seen, I have adopted it as the basis of the Visitation of 1566.

Another MS. which I carefully examined is No. 541, article 13, in the Library of CAIUS COLLEGE, CAMBRIDGE. This appears to be a copy of the Visitation of 1566, with a few additions which I have incorporated in "Additional Pedigrees." It is very indifferently written in tabular form, and slightly imperfect at the fore-edges.

In the Library of Sir CHARLES ISHAM, Bart., at Lamport Hall, are two volumes of Bedfordshire genealogies, one of which I made a transcript of; it contains 50 pedigrees, neatly written in narrative form, with the arms carefully tricked, evidently the work of a professional herald. On folio 87 is a note relating to the arms of Butler of Biddenham as follows: "Note—this quarterings be as the were sett forth in the pedegree maid for William Butteler of Kuton in the Parish of Ryddenden [i e Biddenham] co. Bedford by Cooke Clarenceulx and Glouer Somesset A° 1587." This MS. corresponds in nearly every particular with that in the Library of Queen's College, Oxford. The other volume I was unable to see, as it could not be found at the time of my visit.

I have adhered strictly to the original spelling, only departing from this rule in using contractions for the words, "son," "daughter," and "heir." The few footnotes that I have made use of in this Work are chiefly in elucidation of doubtful points, in correction of obvious errors, and to direct those interested to further sources of information. I could have made much freer use of footnotes, as I have collected a great deal of useful material from parish registers, monumental inscriptions, old deeds, wills, etc., which would have enabled me to add considerably to the value of this Work, but in deference to the wish of the Council I have confined myself to the limits above mentioned.

* Sir Joseph Williamson, Secretary of State in the reign of Charles II

In the course of my work I was particularly struck by the similarity which exists between the Visitations of 1566 and 1582, this for a long time puzzled me, and were it not for internal evidence I should have hesitated ere I assigned Harl. MS 5186 to the Visitation of 1582, so exactly alike are the pedigrees which are common to both; but I think the explanation arises from the fact of there being an interval of only sixteen years between the two, and in so short a period it is not likely that many changes could have taken place.

At the same time I am at a loss to account for the fact that the first two Visitations came so close together in point of time, as the average interval between Visitations in other counties appears to be from thirty to forty years, in many cases, indeed, this interval is exceeded; while, on the other hand, in the counties of Bucks and Essex, Visitations appear to have been made so near to each other as to allow of periods of only eight years and six years respectively intervening

I was also struck by the frequent changes that appear to have taken place in the ownership of land in this county. even as between the years 1566 and 1634 the change is remarkably apparent, and still more so in comparing these Visitations with the Domesday of 1875. In the latter I do not think there can be found twelve landowners whose names appear in this volume. Fuller, in his 'Worthies of England,' ed Nuttall, vol. 1., p. 175, after giving the List of Gentry of this county in 12 Hen VI, 1433, quaintly says· "Hungry Time hath made a glutton's meal on this Catalogue of Gentry, and hath left but a very little morsel for manners remaining; so few of these are found extant in this shire, and fewer continuing in a genteel equipage" There is probably scarcely another county in England where land has changed hands so frequently as in this, and if the study of genealogy serves no other purpose, it will at least dispel the illusion prevalent amongst a certain class, that the majority of the present owners of land derive their title from feudal times This county cannot claim to be historically famous, nevertheless, to give it its due, it has produced a few men eminent as statesmen, warriors, etc , as a study of the history of the following noble families will shew Bray, Cheyney, Mordaunt, St John, Wahull, Wentworth The names of

PREFACE. ix

Anderson, Catelyn, Gascoigne, Keeling, Luke, Newdigate, Snagg, Turner, and Winch, are also notable as having attained to high eminence in the legal profession.

Other very important documents relating to the gentilitial history of Bedfordshire are the following:

1. "The Parliamentary Roll" (as it is styled by Mr. Greenstreet), c 1300-15, called N in Papworth's 'Ordinary,' contains a List of Knights, etc., of Bedfordshire, with their arms in blazon. Of this there are several copies, with some variations The Cottonian copy was printed in Palgrave's 'Parliamentary Writs,' i, 413, 1827; and by Sir N. Harris Nicolas, 1828. Rowe Mores's copy was printed by him in 1749; and another copy in 'The Antiquarian Repertory,' ed 1780, iii, 86; ed. 1807, i., 81.

2. The Return of Gentry in 1433 (above referred to), which is entered on the Patent Roll, 12 Hen. VI., pt. 2, memb. 28 Concerning this Mr. GOUGH writes: "The Commons in the Parliament of 1433 (11-12 Hen VI.) having complained that the country swarmed with pilours, robbers, oppressors of the people, and various other evil-doers, it was enacted that certain Commissioners in every county should have power to summon before them all persons of quality, and to administer to them an oath for the better keeping of the peace and observing of the King's laws, both as to themselves and their retainers. Notwithstanding the reason assigned for this proceeding, it can scarcely be doubted that its real purpose was the suppression of the movement which had then set in in favour of the Royal House of York. The first of the Commissioners in every county was the Bishop of the diocese There were generally three others, of whom one was commonly an Earl, or at least a Baron, and the other two the Knights of the shire. The returns exhibit various degrees of completeness; for several counties there are none at all." The Bedfordshire Lists from this and the preceding Roll will be found printed at the end of this Preface.

3. The Register of the Guild or Fraternity of the Holy Trinity in the Church of Luton, a manuscript in the possession of the MARQUIS OF BUTE, K.T. It extends from 1475 to 1546. This Register, together with

the Accounts of the Guild from 1526 to 1547, has been printed, under the editorial care of Mr. HENRY GOUGH, and will be published as soon as the Introduction and some supplementary materials are completed. This Register contains the names of some thousands of persons belonging to Bedfordshire, with the dates, approximately, of their admission to the Guild, and sometimes of their death, with other genealogical facts.

4. The Lists of Knights and Gentry of Bedfordshire taken in 1667-8, from the Lansdowne MSS in the British Museum, which will be found printed in the Appendix.

It will perhaps be within recollection that when this Work was first included in the list of "Proposed Publications," the name of Mr HENRY GOUGH was appended as the Editor. Owing, however, to pressure of engagements, this gentleman was unable to undertake the work, and I was asked to act as co-editor with him; subsequently Mr GOUGH intimated that as he was so fully engaged he could not spare the time, and the task of editing this Work was finally left entirely in my hands. I think it due to Mr GOUGH to state this fact, and to express my great regret that I was deprived of his valuable assistance; and at the same time I take this opportunity of expressing my gratitude for the many valuable hints he has given me, and for the loan of some of his MSS.

My thanks are also due to Sir CHARLES ISHAM, Bart., and to the Librarians of Queen's College, Oxford, and Caius College, Cambridge, for the courteous manner in which they aided me by giving me ready access to the MSS in their libraries. Without this assistance I could not have completed my task.

In conclusion, I may add that I have taken every care to guard against error; every pedigree has been carefully collated and re-read several times: nevertheless in works of this kind it can hardly happen otherwise than that some errors may have been overlooked.

F. A. BLAYDES.

BEDFORD
December, 1884.

NAMES AND ARMS OF KNIGHTS OF BEDFORDSHIRE,

Temp. Edw I.

From an ancient Roll, printed in 'The Parliamentary Writs collected and edited by Francis Palgrave' London 1827, 4to, p 413

Bedffordeshire

Sire JOHN DE PABENH'M barre de azure e de argent de vj peces, a une bende de goules a iij moles de or

Sire JOHN sun Filz meisme les armes, od les moles perces

Sire   DE TRAILY de or, a une crois de goules e iij merelos de goules

Sire JOHN RIDEL palee de argent e de goules, a une bende de sable

Sire WALTER DE BAA de goules, a un cheveron e iij rouwels de argent

Sire JOHN DE SOUTHBURI de ermyne, od le chef de goules a iij roses de or

Sire   DE BEUCHAMP de goules, fiette de argent

Sire RICHARD LE ROUS quartile de argent e de sable, a une bende de sable

Sire JOHN CONQUEST quartile de argent e de sable, a un label de goules

Sire ROB'T DE HOO quartile de argent e de sable, a une bende de or

Sire JOHN PEYVRE de argent a un cheveron de goules a iij flures de or

Sire RAFF* PEROT quartile de or e de azure endente

Sire WILL'M YNGEE de or, a un cheveron de vert

Sire ROGER DE HEYHAM pale de argent e de azure, od le chef de goules a iij escalops de or

Sire JOHN DE MORTEIN de ermyne, od le chef endente de goules

Sire DAVID DE FLITTEWIK de argent, a ij lup[ard]s passauz de sable

Sire RAUF DE GOLDINGTONE de argent a ij lions passanz de azure

Sire   DE WALHULLE † de or, a iij cressanz de goules

Sire PERES LORING quartile dargent e de goulys, a une bende de goulys

Sire ROGER PEYVERE dargent, a un chev[er]oun [de] azure a iij flures dor

Sire ROB'T DE HOTTOT ‡ dazure, a une c[ro]ys patee dermyne a iij rosses dor §

---

* "Raff" inserted from another copy

† "Wahull" in E Rowe Mores's copy Oxon 1749, 4to

‡ "Hotot" E R M

§ The last three names from another copy They are in E. R. M, with variations of spelling

RETURN OF GENTRY IN BEDFORDSHIRE,
12 Henry VI.

The Commissioners for this county were William [Grey], Bishop of Lincoln, John de Faunhope, Chivaler and John Wenloke and John Gascoyne, Esquires, Knights of the shire (Of these, Sir John Cornwall, K G 1410, was created Baron of Fanhope, co Hereford, 1433, Baron of Milbroke, co Bedford, 1442, and died next year, and Sir John Wenlok, K G 1460, was created Baron Wenlok in 1461, and slain ten years later) The list of names returned is as follows; the last column, shewing the residences, or presumed residences of the persons named, being now added

Patent Roll, 12 Hen VI, pt 2, m 28

Abbatis de Woborne et soun Celerer	Woburn
Abbatis de Wardon	Warden
Prioris de Dunstable	Dunstable
Prioris de Chekesonde	Chicksand
Prioris de Nunham	Newenham, in Goldington
Prioris de Caldewell	Caldwell, in St Mary's, Bedford
Prioris de Buschemede	Bushmead, in Eaton-Socon
Simonis Fylbrygge, Chivaler [K G, ob 1442]	Felbrigg, co Norfolk
Henrici Brounflete, Chivaler [Baron Bromflete, or de Vesci, 1449–68]	Wimington
Thome Wauton, Chivaler	Bassmead, in Eaton-Socon.
Thome Manyngham	Luton
Thome Hoo [K G 1445, Baron Hoo and Hastings, 1447–55]	Luton-Hoo.
Johannis Broughton	Toddington
Willelmi Loudesope (Ludsoppe).	
Johannis Enderby	Stratton, in Biggleswade
Roberti Mordaunt	Turvey
Johannis Hertushorne	Northill.
Henrici Godfrey [ob 1444]	Northill.
Johannis Boteler de Northzele	Northill.

Humfridi Acworthe	Luton
Johannis Ragon	Bromham
Thome Ragon	Bromham
Johannis Fitz Geffrey	Gt Barford
Johannis Radewell	Radwell, in Felmersham
Johannis Fyse (Fitz)	Pulloxhill
Johannis Coldington (Goldyngton)	Lidlington
Christofori Preston	
Stephani Crwker (Cruker) [? Crevequer]	Crekars, in Gt Barford
Thome Roxstone (Rokestone)	Roxton
Willelmi Launcelyne (Launceleyne)	Cople
Henrici de Lye	
Johannis Conquest (de Houghton)	Houghton-Conquest
Thome Lounde	
Walteri Lounde	
Johannis Lounde	
Richardi Merstone	
Johannis Pekke, junioris	Cople
Thome Pekke	
Willelmi Pekke	
Johannis Glove, junioris	
Johannis Turvey de Turvey (Johannis Turvey)	Turvey
Johannis Ferrour (Feron') de Bedford	Bedford
Johannis Gerveys de Maldon	Maulden
Henrici Etewell	
Roberti Bolloke	
Willelmi Wale	
Nicholai Ravenhull	
Nicholai Lowe	
Valentini Bailly de Litton [sic]	Luton.
Willelmi White de eadem	Luton
Johannis Boughton.	
Hugonis Hasseldene	Goldington
Thome Bailly de Houghton	Houghton-[? Regis]
Willelmi Trought.	
Henrici Mauntell	
Roberti Valence	
Johannis atte Hay	Luton.
Willelmi Yppyng	Luton.
Johannis Petyfer [i e Pied-de-fer]	

Thome Purvey
Willelmi Purvey
Johannis Shotfolde - - - - - Stotfold
Willelmi Wyngate - - - - - Sharpenhoe, in Streatley
Willelmi Kene
Thome Stokker - - - - - Wyboston, in Eaton-Socon
Ade Alforde
Johannis Morton - - - - - Potsgrave
Thome Morton - - - - - Potsgrave
Thome Stratton
Thome Chamburleyne - - - - - Tilsworth
Radulfi Clerke
Mathei Stepeyng - - - - - Luton
Nicholai Hardyng - - - - - Aspley-Guise
Willelmi Marham - - - - - Barton-le-Clay
Richardi Sampson - - - - - Maulden
Roberti Warner
Johannis Coke de Craweley - - - - Husborn-Crawley
Willelmi Syleham - - - - - Luton
Willelmi Purvey
Willelmi Rede
Thome Blondell - - - - - Harlington
Willelmi Milwarde
Roberti Ratele
Johannis Kyggyll de Todyngton - - - Toddington.
Johannis Pestell de Nunham - - - - Newenham, in Goldington
Thome Chopper de Turvey - - - - Turvey
Johannis Marram - - - - - Barton-le-Clay
Thome Jakes - - - - - - Luton
Johannis Pykot - - - - - Biggleswade, or L Gravenhurst
Willelmi Molso - - - - - Dunstable
Johannis Sewell - - - - - Sewell, in Houghton-Regis
Henrici Sewell - - - - - Sewell, in Houghton-Regis
Radulfi Falwell
Hugonis Byllyngdon - - - - - Billington, in Leighton-Bosard
Johannis Baldoc - - - - - Holwell
Willelmi Palmer
Roberti Davy, junioris
Johannis Stanlowe.
Richardi Lincolne
Walteri Taillarde - - - - - Wrestlingworth

RETURN OF GENTRY IN BEDFORDSHIRE, 1433

Thome Spencer de Geton
Johannis Spencer
Johannis Kynge de Harowdon - - - Hariowden, in Cardington
Johannis Wayte - - - - - Renhold
Willelmi Bochell
Thome William
Roberti Ratull
Roberti Warner de le Hethe - - - - Leighton-Bosard
Johannis Potter
Johannis Greeell
Willelmi Bocher de Henlowe - - - - Henlow
Willelmi Halle de Chitlyngdone - - - Shitlington
Johannis Halle

[After this many of the above names are repeated, with occasional variations, which are in this printed list given within parentheses. Amongst them is the name following:]

Johannis Mepurshale [ob 1440] - - - Mepshall

The Visitation of Bedfordshire, 1566.

THE ARMES OF THE TOWNE OF BEDFORD
Per pale argent and gules, a bend azure.

THE SEALE OF THE SAME TOWNE
An eagle displayed looking to the sinister with wings inverted sable, ducally crowned or, on the eagle a large castle surmounted by two more one above the other or.

Alway

[of Streatley].

ARMS (TWO SHIELDS) —I, *Or, a talbot passant sable, on a chief of the second three martlets of the field,* ALWAY, II, ALWAY, *impaling, Sable, three unicorns courant in pale argent,* FARINGDON

CREST —*On a wreath argent and sable a hind's head argent between two holly-branches vert, fructed gules*

John Alway of faringdon = daughter of . ffaringdon
in com Devon gent — de com Devon gent

John Alway of Stretley = Mary daughter of = [Edmond Wyngate of Shar-
in com Bedf gen sonne | Belfelde* of Studham | penhoe in com Bedfford
and heire | (? *Standon*) in com Hertf | 2 husband]
| gen.

John Alway . | Rauf second sonne [of Channons = [Dorathye d of John Rudall
eldest sonne † | in the p'ish of Shenley in com | (? *Unedall*) of Linfford in com
[ob s p] | Hertfford ob 22 March 1621] | Bucks]
A

* " Sable, three vnicorns currant argent lynes and collar or " (MS. 541, Caius Coll Cambs)
† Harl MS 4600 places here " Richard Alway of Stretley heir to his brother "

B

THE VISITATION OF BEDFORDSHIRE.

A

[Mary 16 yeres old 1621 ux Edward Wingate of Lockley in ye p'ish of Willan in com Hertford]

[Anne 14 yere old 1621 marid to Thomas Bearde sonn of Myles Bearde of Gateley in com Norffolk]

[Dorothy 13 yere old 1621 ux Richard Bernard of Petsoledg in com Bucks]

[Elizabeth died yong]

Anscell
[of Barford Magna].

ARMS (THREE SHIELDS) — I, *Gules, on a saltire or between four bezants a mascle of the field*, ANSCELL, II, *Quarterly*—1 *and* 4, ANSCELL—2 *and* 3, *Sable, two hands conjoined proper, supporting a heart or*, WHEATLEY, III, ANSCELL, *impaling* WHEATLEY.

John Anscell al's Anstell neere Exeter in com Devon = daughter of

Edward Anscell al's Anstell of Westmounton and Tawnton in com Som gen. sonne and heire. = Welthlyan, daughter of Appowell in Wales

John second sonne

Robert Wheateley al's Quytlawe of Joneby in com Cumberland gen = Catherine daughter of Richard ffyssher of Pavenham in com Bedf gen

Nicholas second sonne dyed sans yssue

Thomas Auscell alias Anstell of Barforde in com Bedf sonne and heire = Elizabeth daughter and heire

Mary [ux Will'm Carter of Kempston in com. Bedfford]

Agnes [ux John Bromhall of Stevington in com Bedfford]

Rose [1 ux Wolnich of 2 to Hurlestone]

in com

Temperance [ux Neatley of in com Sussex]

[Ursula d of 1 wiffe] = Wheatley Anscell eldest sonne [of Barfford in com Bedfford]. = [Elizabeth d of Henry Beecher of Fotheringay in com Northampton]

Anne [ux S[r] George Fitz Geffrey of Crekers in the p'ish of Barfford in com Bedford].

[Catherin ux John Allen of Moger Anger in the p'ish of Blonham in com Bedfford]

[Dorathey ux John Cockayne of Shingay in com Cambridge]

[1 Thomas Anscell]

[2 George Auscell]

[Elizabeth]

[Alexander Anscell]

[Mary]

[Anna Anscell]

THE VISITATION OF BEDFORDSHIRE. 3

Arderne

[of Hawnes].

ARMS —*Gules, three cross-crosslets pitchée or, on a chief of the second a martlet azure.*
CREST —*On a wreath or and gules a plume of three ostrich-feathers surmounted by a similar plume argent, charged with a martlet azure*

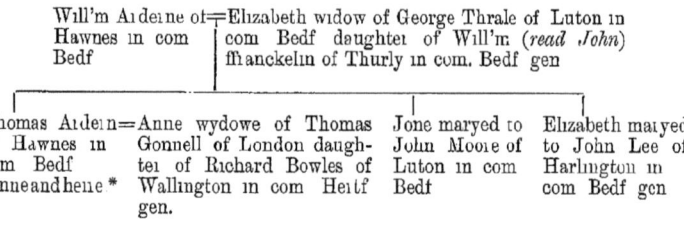

Will'm Arderne of = Elizabeth widow of George Thrale of Luton in
Hawnes in com | com Bedf daughter of Will'm (*read John*)
Bedf | ffranckelin of Thurly in com. Bedf gen

Thomas Ardein = Anne wydowe of Thomas | Jone maryed to | Elizabeth maryed
of Hawnes in | Gonnell of London daugh- | John Moore of | to John Lee of
com Bedf | ter of Richard Bowles of | Luton in com | Harlington in
sonne and heire * | Wallington in com Hertf | Bedf | com Bedf gen
 | gen. | |

Astry

[of Harlington].

ARMS —*Barry wavy of six argent and azure, on a chief gules three bezants*
CREST —*On a wreath or and azure a demi-ostrich argent, wings endorsed gules, in the beak a horse-shoe of the third.*

[Geffrey Astrey of Hitchin in com Hertfford]

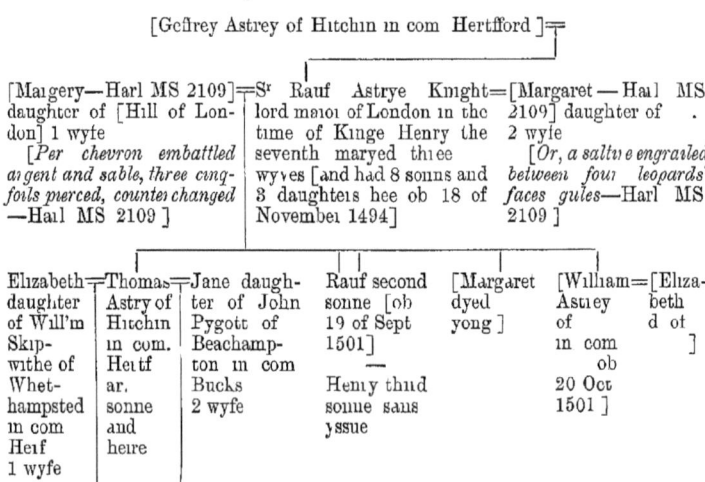

[Margery—Harl MS 2109] = Sr Rauf Astrye Knight = [Margaret — Harl MS
daughter of [Hill of Lon- | lord maior of London in the | 2109] daughter of .
don] 1 wyfe | time of Kinge Henry the | 2 wyfe
[*Per chevron embattled* | seventh maryed three | [*Or, a saltire engrailed*
argent and sable, three cinq- | wyves [and had 8 sonns and | *between four leopards'*
foils pierced, counterchanged | 3 daughters hee ob 18 of | *faces gules*—Harl MS
—Harl MS 2109] | November 1494] | 2109]

Elizabeth = Thomas = Jane daugh- | Rauf second | [Margaret | [William = [Eliza-
daughter | Astry of | ter of John | sonne [ob | dyed | Astrey | beth
of Will'm | Hitchin | Pygott of | 19 of Sept | yong] | of | d of
Skip- | in com. | Beachamp- | 1501] | | in com |]
withe of | Hertf | ton in com | — | | ob |
Whet- | ar. | Bucks | Henry third | | 20 Oct |
hampsted | sonne | 2 wyfe | sonne sans | | 1501] |
in com | and | | yssue | | |
Herf | heire | | | | |
1 wyfe | | | | | |
A | **B** | | | | |

* ' And by her hathe no issue." (Isham MS)

4   THE VISITATION OF BEDFORDSHIRE.

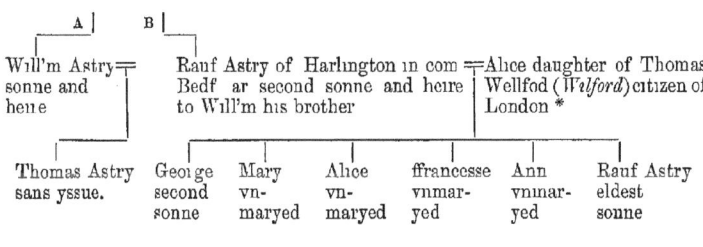

A | Will'm Astry = sonne and heire

B | Ranf Astry of Harlington in com Bedf ar second sonne and heire to Will'm his brother = Alice daughter of Thomas Wellfod (*Wilford*) citizen of London *

Thomas Astry sans yssue.

George second sonne

Mary vnmaryed

Alice vnmaryed

ffrancesse vnmaryed

Ann vnmaryed

Ranf Astry eldest sonne

Barnardiston

[of Northill].

ARMS —[*Azure, a fesse dancettée ermine between six cross-crosslets argent*, BARNARDISTON]

[Sir] Thomas Barnardeston of Kiddington in com Suff ar [Knt] = Elizabeth daughter of John [Roger] Newporte of Pelham in com Herf.

Sr Thomas Barnardeston Knight sonne and heire [of Ketton in com. Suff vide idem].=

A daughter mar to [Thom] Lorde Awdeley Chancellor of England

[Elizabeth] maryed to George ffitzwilliam of Lincolnshire

. maryed to Jenney of Norf gen

George Barnardeston of Norrell in com Bedf ar second sonne = Elizabeth daughter and sole heire of Thomas Burlye [Burley—Harl. 5867] of Lynne in com. Norfl. ar.

[John 3 son a preest.]

. maryed to .. Ayre of .. gent

John Barnardeston of Norrell in com Bedf. ar only sonne and heire. = Joane daughter of Thomas Mylles [Miller —Harl. 5867] of Lynne merchant

George Barnardeston sonne and heire

Christopher second sonne

Thomas third sonne

John fourth sonne

Sigismond fifte sonne

Edward sixt sonne.

Elizabeth vnmaryed

Margaret vnmaryed

Suzan vnmaryed.

Sare vnmaryed.

* " Widow to Tho Rotheram." (MS 341, Caius Coll Cambs)

Bawde

[of Harrold].

ARMS —*Quarterly—1 and 4, Gules, three chevrons argent,* BARHAM , *2 and 3, Gules, three marlions' wings or,* BAWDE
CREST —*On a wreath argent and sable a Satyr's head in profile sable, with wings to the side of the head or, the tongue hanging out of his mouth gules*

Thomas Bawde of Haddam in com Harf. ar =. daughter of .

Thomas Bawde of London = Anne daughter of Sir John ffortescue of Punesborough ar sonne and heire. | in com Herf. Knight

John Bawde of Harwolde = Elizabeth daughter of John Noireys of Stevennage in com. Herf. ar | Anne maryed to Thomas Shefield of Temesford in com Bedf ar

John Bawde of Bedford ar sonne and heire = Elizabeth daughter of Silvester Danvers of Dauncey in com Wilt ar. | Thomas second sonne. — George third sonne. | Elizabeth eldest daughter — Jane third | Margaret second daughter maryed to ThomasStaveley of Bygnell in com. Oxon gen.

fferdinand Bawde sonne and heire.

Bosgrave

[of Renhold].

ARMS (TWO SHIELDS) —I , *Argent, on a cross engrailed sable a griffin segreant of the field,* BOSGRAVE , II (*sinister side*), *Per pale argent and gules, on a chevron between three trefoils slipped all counterchanged a luce naiant or,* PYKE *
CREST —*On a wreath argent and sable a boar's head erased argent, between two oak-branches vert, fructed or*

John Bosgrave of Godmanstone = Margaret daughter of . . . in com Som gen. | Dawnce de com Glouc

A

---

* Papworth (p 51) assigns this coat to Pitts of co Bedf

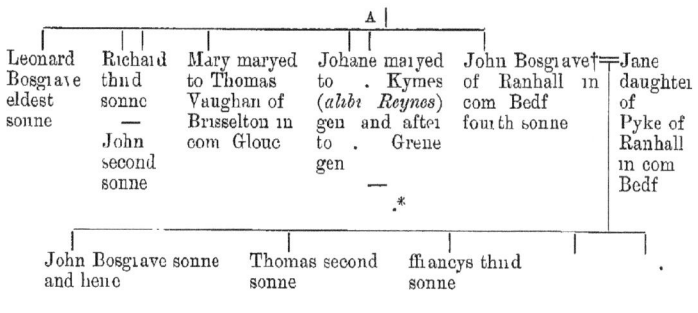

Boteler

[of Biddenham]

ARMS —*Argent, a fesse counter-compony or and azure between six crosses formée sable*
CREST —*Out of a mural crown gules a boar's head argent, armed or*

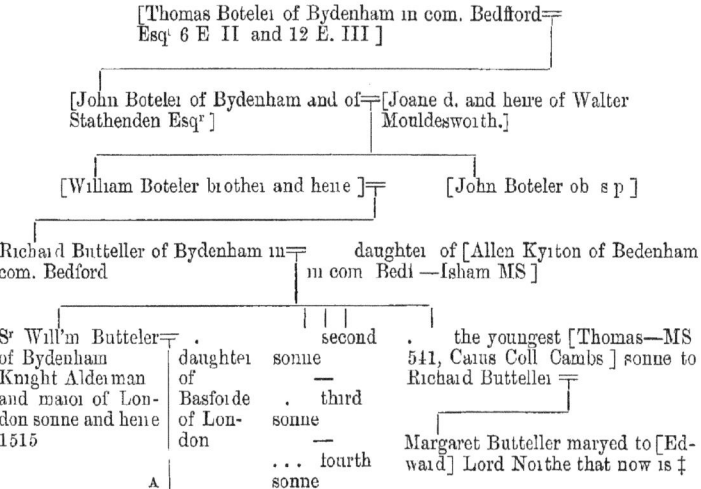

* Harl. 5867 gives another daughter. Anne, MS. 541, Caius Coll Cambs, calls her Agnes.
† In Harl 5867 called both Thomas and John
‡ According to Harl MS 1531 she was also wife successively of Andrew Frances, Sir David Brooke, Knt, and Robert Chertsey

THE VISITATION OF BEDFORDSHIRE.

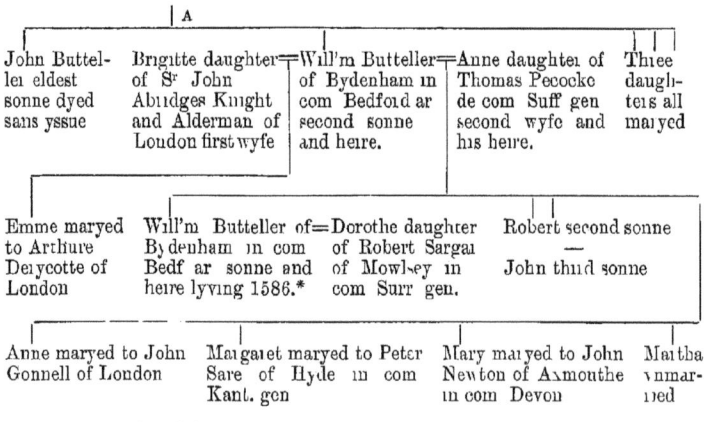

| A |

| John Butteller eldest sonne dyed sans yssue | Brigitte daughter of Sʳ John Abridges Knight and Alderman of London first wyfe | =Will'm Butteller of Bydenham in com Bedford ar second sonne and heire. | =Anne daughter of Thomas Pecocke de com Suff gen second wyfe and his heire. | Three daughters all maryed |

| Emme maryed to Arthure Derycotte of London | Will'm Butteller of Bydenham in com Bedf ar sonne and heire lyvyng 1586.* | =Dorothe daughter of Robert Sargar of Mowlsey in com Surr gen. | Robert second sonne — John third sonne |

| Anne maryed to John Gonnell of London | Margaret maryed to Peter Sare of Hyde in com Kant. gen | Mary maryed to John Newton of Axmouthe in com Devon | Martha unmarried |

Be it remembered that Alane Kryton of Bydenham in the Countie of Bedford had issue Walter Kyrton that dyed sans vssue, and a daughter called Grace that was maryed to Thomas Boteller Which Grace was sister and heire to Walter her brother and by the said Thomas Boteller her husband had issue Richard Boteller father to this Richard here first mentioned

---

Burgoyne

[of Sutton].

ARMS.—*Gules, a chevron or between three talbots argent, on a chief embattled of the last as many martlets azure,* BURGOYNE *impaling, Argent, on a chevron between three boars' heads sable as many escullops or, within a bordure vert bezantée,* BOWLES

CREST.—*A talbot sejant or, ears sable, and plain collared gules.*

| John Burgoyne of Sutton in com Bedf ar | =Jone daughter of . Byll of Ashwell in com. Hertford gen |

| Thomas Burgoyne of Sutton in com Bedf ar sonne and heire | =Anne daughter of John Bowles of Wallington in com Herff ar | Robert second sonne |

| John Burgoyne of Sutton in com Bedf ar sonne and heire not yet maryed [ob s p] | Robert second sonne |

---

* 'This Will'm hath to his second wyfe Vrsula the daughter of Thomas Smith of Ostinghanger in Kent by whome he hath yssue Thomas Boteler a sonne, and Alice a daughter now living 1586" (See Pedigree in MS 541, f 3ᵇ, Caius Coll. Cambs, which does not accord with this)

8 THE VISITATION OF BEDFORDSHIRE.

Bury

[of Toddington].

ARMS (TWO SHIELDS) —I., *Quarterly of four*—1 and 4, *Sable, a chevron engrailed or between three plates each charged with a cross pattée gules*, BURY, 2, *Argent, on a chief indented sable three leopards' faces or*, LICHFIELD, 3, *Argent, a chevron between three lions' heads erased sable*, DRIFFIELD II., BURY, impaling, *Vert, three bucks trippant or*, ROTHERAM

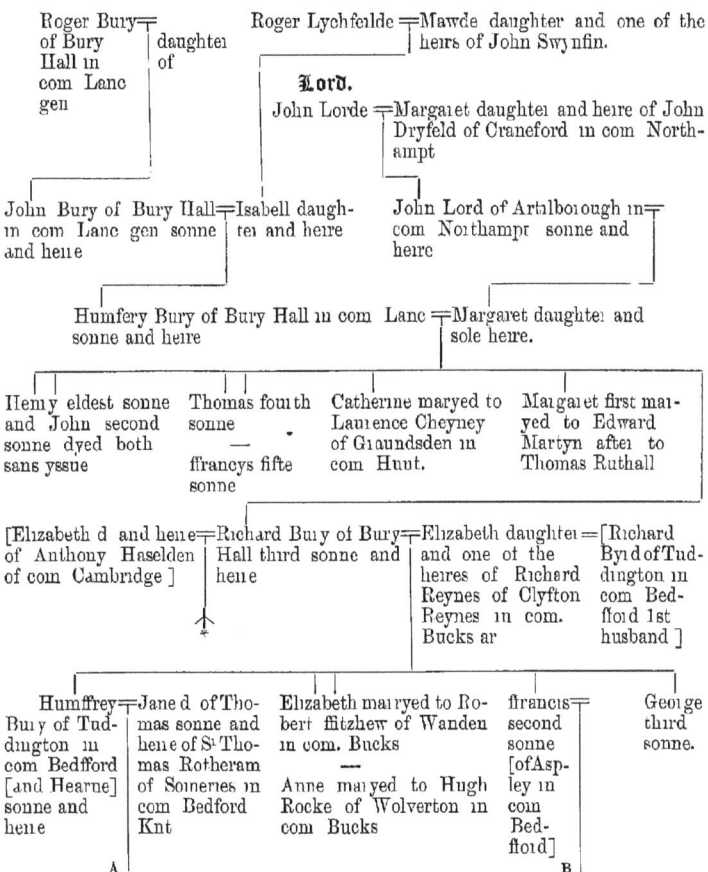

* In Harl MS 1531 there are several further descents from this match, but as they are not connected with the county I have omitted them.

THE VISITATION OF BEDFORDSHIRE.

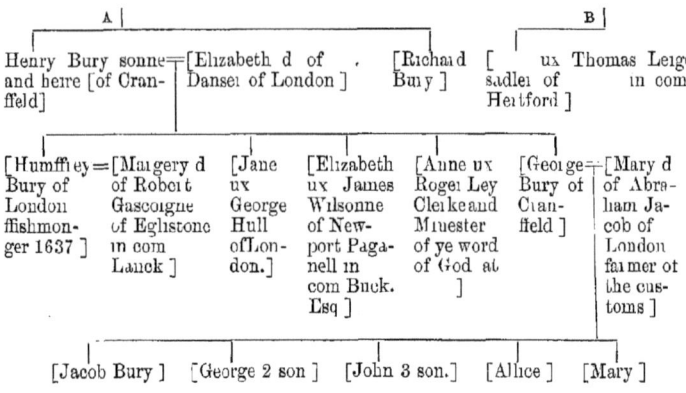

Butler

[of Sharnebrook].

ARMS (TWO SHIELDS).—1, *Quarterly*—1 *and* 4, *Argent, on a chief indented sable three covered cups or*, BUTLER, 2 *and* 3 (*not ticked*) II, BUTLER, *impaling*. *Quarterly of nine*—1, *Argent on a chief gules two mullets pierced or*, ST JOHN. 2, *Argent, a fesse between six cinqfoils gules*, UMFREVILLE, 3, *Azure, a bend argent, coused or, between six martlets of the second*, DELABERE, 4, *Ermine, on a fesse azure three crosses pattée or*, PAVELEY, 5, *Argent, a lion rampant, queue fourché, charged on the shoulder with a cross pattée or*, STURREY 6, *Gules, a fesse between six martlets or, a mullet sable for difference*, BEAUCHAMP, 7, *Argent, a fesse sable between three crescents gules*, PATESHULL, 8, *Ermine, a lion rampant purpure, ducally crowned or*, BROYE, 9, *Paly of six argent and azure, on a bend gules three eagles displayed or*, GRANDISON, *over all a bar sinister*

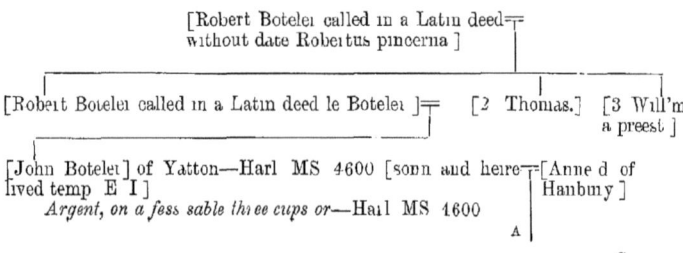

THE VISITATION OF BEDFORDSHIRE.

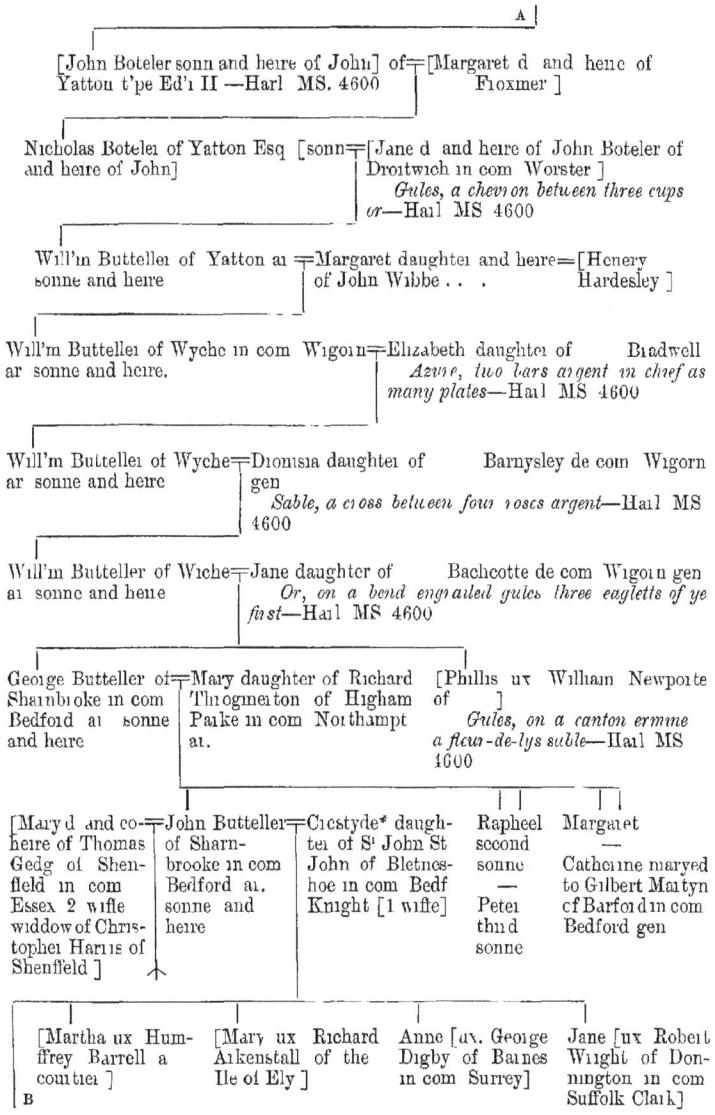

* According to Harl MS 1531, she was an illegitimate daughter by Anne, daughter of Thomas Nevell of Cotterstock, in com. Northampton, 2 sonn of Will'm Nevell of Holte in com Lester.

THE VISITATION OF BEDFORDSHIRE   11

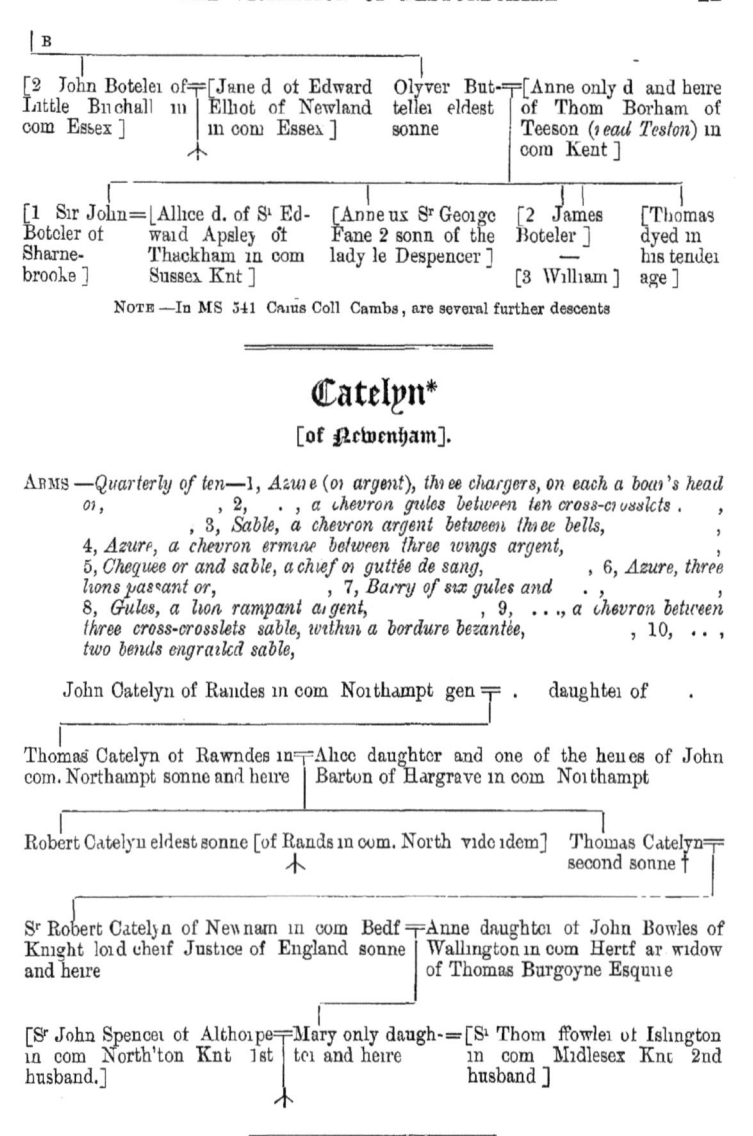

| B

[2 John Boteler of = [Jane d of Edward   Olyver But- = [Anne only d and heire
Little Buchall in Elliot of Newland   teller eldest   of Thom Borham of
com Essex]   in com Essex]   sonne   Teeson (*read Teston*) in
                                                     com Kent]

[1 Sir John = [Alhce d. of S^t Ed- [Anne ux Sr George   [2 James   [Thomas
Botcler of   ward Apsley of   Fane 2 sonn of the   Boteler]   dyed in
Sharne-   Thackham in com   lady le Despencer]   —   his tender
brooke]   Sussex Knt]   [3 William] age]

NOTE —In MS 541 Caius Coll Cambs, are several further descents

Catelyn*
[of Newenham].

ARMS —*Quarterly of ten*—1, *Azure (or argent), three chargers, on each a boar's head or,   , 2, . . , a chevron gules between ten cross-crosslets . ,
    , 3, Sable, a chevron argent between three bells,   ,
4, Azure, a chevron ermine between three wings argent,   ,
5, Chequee or and sable, a chief or guttée de sang,   , 6, Azure, three
lions passant or,   , 7, Barry of six gules and . . ,   ,
8, Gules, a lion rampant argent,   , 9, . . ., a chevron between
three cross-crosslets sable, within a bordure bezantée,   , 10, . . ,
two bends engrailed sable,*

John Catelyn of Randes in com Northampt gen = .   daughter of   .

Thomas Catelyn of Rawndes in = Alice daughter and one of the heues of John
com. Northampt sonne and heire   Barton of Hargrave in com Northampt

Robert Catelyn eldest sonne [of Rands in com. North vide idem]   Thomas Catelyn =
                                                                  second sonne †

Sr Robert Catelyn of Newnam in com Bedf = Anne daughter of John Bowles of
Knight lord cheif Justice of England sonne Wallington in com Hertf ar widow
and heire   of Thomas Burgoyne Esquire

[Sr John Spencer of Althorpe = Mary only daugh- = [St Thom ffowler of Islington
in com North'ton Knt 1st   ter and heire   in com Midlesex Knt 2nd
husband.]   husband]

* *Cf* Le Neve's 'Pedigrees of Knights, Harl Soc , vol viii , p 161
† In Harl MS 1531 this *Thomas* is omitted, and *Sir Robert* is made brother of *Robert.*

Charnocke

[of Pulcote].

ARMS (TWO SHIELDS)—I, *Quarterly*—1 and 4, *Argent, on a bend sable three crosses botonée of the field, a crescent for difference,* CHARNOCKE 2 and 3, *Argent a cross engrailed gules,* II, CHARNOCKE, *impaling, Quarterly*—1 and 4, *Argent crusily fitchée sable, a stork of the last,* PUTTENHAM, 2 and 3, *Chequy or and azure*

Robert Charnocke of Holcott=ffrancesse daughter of Ackworthe in com Bedf ar. | of Tuddington in com Bedf.

Richard Charnocke of=Mary daughter of Robert   ffiorence maryed to Syracke
Holcott in com Bedf | Puttenham of Shirvill in   Pettyte of Boughton vnder
ar. sonne and heire. | com. South   Bleane in Kent *

John Charnocke sonne and heire.   Ambrose second sonne.   ffiorence.

Cheyney

[of Toddington].

ARMS (TWO SHIELDS)—I, *Quarterly of twenty*—1, *Azure, six lions rampant argent a canton ermine,* CHENEY, 2, *Ermine, a chief indented per pale argent and gules, charged on the dexter side with a rose of the last,* SHOTISBROOKE, 3, *Argent, a chevron between three mullets gules,* BROUGHTON, 4 *Azure, three men's heads couped argent,* ? BEARD, 5, *Sable, a chevron ermine between three arrows or,* FORSTER, 6, *Argent, on a chief gules three fleurs-de-lys or,* PEYVRE, 7, *Quarterly argent and gules, a bend of the second,* LORING, 8, *Gules, a bend vair argent and azure between six escallops or,* BEWPLE, 9, *Sable, a saltire engrailed argent,* BLOYON, 10, *Gules, on a chief argent a lion passant sable,* NANSCUIT, 11, *Quarterly per fess indented or and azure,* PERROTT, 12, *Ermine a chief indented gules,* MORTEYNE, 13, *Sable, on a cross or five escallops gules,* STONHAM † 14, *Paly of six argent and sable,* BURGAII, 15, *Argent, a horse barnacle sable,* BARNACKE, 16, *Or, a cross engrailed vert,* NOONE, 17 *Gules, a fesse dancettée between six cross-crosslets or,* ENGAYNE; 18, *Gules three fusils in fesse argent in chief a fleur-de-lys of the second,* DAWBNEY, 19, *Azure, two lions passant-guardant or,* DENSTONE, 20, *Argent, on a chevron sable a fleur-de-lys of the field,* WANTON II (*sinister side*), *Quarterly of twenty-four*—1, *Sable, a chevron between three leopards' faces or,* WENTWORTH, 2, *Quarterly argent and gules, in the second and third quarters a fret or, on a bend sable three mullets of the first,* SPENCER; 3, *Or three chevronells gules,* CLARE, 4 *Barry of six or and azure, a canton ermine,* GAWSELL 5, *Quarterly per fesse indented argent and gules,*

---

* Called Francisca and made daughter to Richard, Harl MS 5186
† According to Papworth the blazon should be, Argent, on a cross sable five escallops of the first

FITZWARINE; 6, *Azure, semée of cross-crosslets or, three luces haurient argent,* FOLKE DE OYREY, 7, *Or, on a chief gules three plates pierced,* CAMOYS 8, *Argent, a saltire engrailed gules,* TIPTOFTE, 9, *Barry of ten argent and azure, an orle of martlets,* CHAWORTH, 10, *Argent, a fesse between two bars gemelles gules,* BADLESMERE, 11, *Azure, a bend engrailed, cotised argent,* FORTESCUE, 12, *Azure, two bars dancettée or, a chief argent,* STONOR, 13, *Or three roses gules,* HARNEHALL, 14 *Azure, six lions rampant argent, a canton ermine,* CHENEY, 15, *Azure, a fesse between three leopards' faces or, an annulet for difference,* DELAPOOLE, 16, *Gules, a saltire argent,* NEVILL, 17, *Argent, three fusils in fesse gules,* MONTACUTE, 18, *Or, an eagle displayed vert, membered and beaked gules,* MONTHERMER, 19, *Gules, a cross engrailed argent,* INGLETHORPE, 20, *Azure, a fesse between three leopards' faces or,* DELAPOOLE, 21, *Argent, on a canton gules a rose or,* BRADESTONE, 22, *Argent, a saltire engrailed gules,* TIPTOFTE, 23, *Gules, three leopards passant in pale within a bordure argent,* HOLLAND 24, *Or, a lion rampant gules,* ? CHARLTON

CREST—*On a wreath or, gules, and vert a bull's scalp argent.*

Broughton.

Sr Rowland Broughton Knight sonne and heire *⊤

Roger Broughton sonne and heire =

Robert Broughton sonne and heire =

William Broughton sonne and heire =

Sr Robert Broughton Knight sonne and heire =

Matthew Broughton sonne and heire =

Forster. Lorynge

Rauf= Broughton sonne and heire	Hugh fforster daughter of Sr John Boyland Knight.	Hugh fforster ot Stony Stratford in com Bucks Kt =	Sr Peter=Joane da. Lorynge and heire Knight of sonne Mor- and teigne heire	Allen= . . da Bloyon and heire of in com St Pierse Corn Nanscutt Kt of Cornw Knight
Robert= Broughton sonne and heire A	da and heire of Bearde	John fforster sonne and heire. B	Sr Roger=Cassander Lorynge da and sonne and heire of heire Reignold Perrott C	Sr Raph=Elizabeth da Bewple and heire of Kt St Allen Bloyou of Cornwall Knight. D

* "NOTE—This Sir Rowland Broughton, Knight, came oute of Denmarke with Kinge Aldridus in the yere of our Lord God 633 He built the towne of Broughton, and was called Baron of Broughton" (*Ita se habet textus*)

THE VISITATION OF BEDFORDSHIRE.

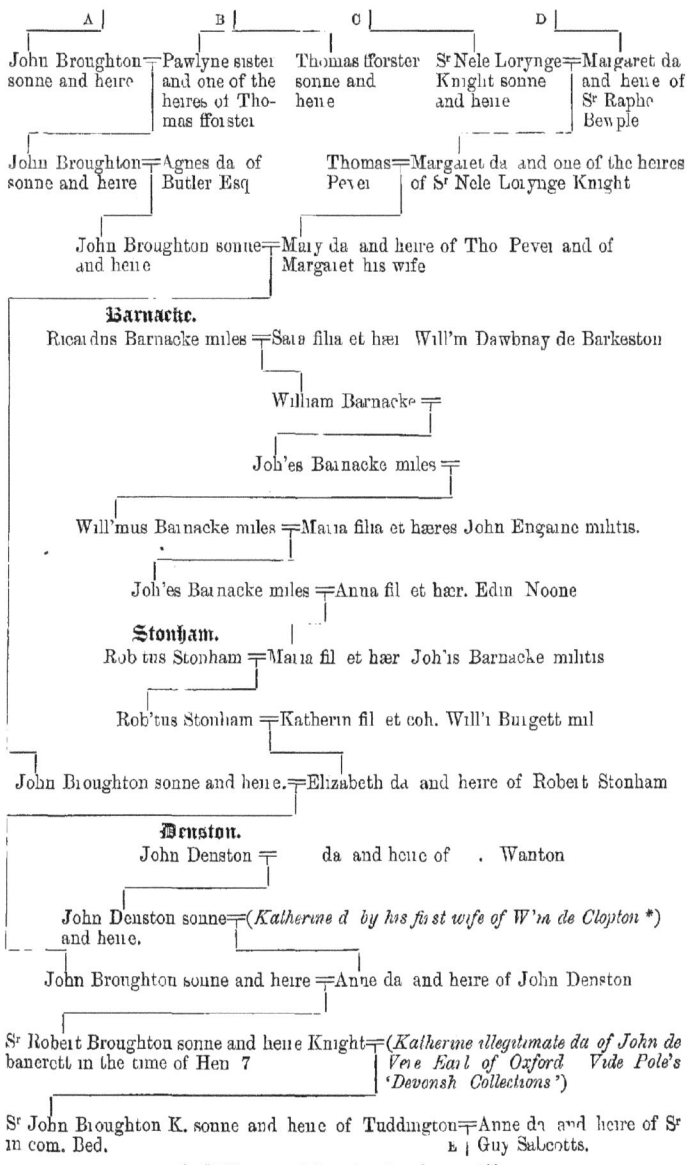

```
   A |              B |              C |              D |
John Broughton=Pawlyne sister  Thomas fforster  Sʳ Nele Lorynge=Margaret da
sonne and heire │ and one of the  sonne and       Knight sonne  │ and heire of
                │ heires of Tho-  heire           and heire      │ Sʳ Raphe
                │ mas fforster                                   │ Bewple

John Broughton=Agnes da of           Thomas=Margaret da and one of the heires
sonne and heire │ Butler Esq         Pevel  │ of Sʳ Nele Lorynge Knight

        John Broughton sonne=Mary da and heire of Tho Pevel and of
        and heire            │ Margaret his wife
```

Barnacke.

Ricardus Barnacke miles =Sara filia et hær Will'm Dawbnay de Barkeston

William Barnacke =

Joh'es Barnacke miles =

Will'mus Barnacke miles =Maria filia et hæres John Engaine militis.

Joh'es Barnacke miles =Anna fil et hær. Edm Noone

Stonham.

Rob'tus Stonham =Maria fil et hær Joh'is Barnacke militis

Rob'tus Stonham =Katherin fil et coh. Will'i Burgett mil

John Broughton sonne and heire.=Elizabeth da and heire of Robert Stonham

Denston.

John Denston = da and heire of . Wanton

John Denston sonne=(Katherine d by his first wife of W'm de Clopton *)
and heire.

John Broughton sonne and heire =Anne da and heire of John Denston

Sʳ Robert Broughton sonne and heire Knight=(Katherine illegitimate da of John de
banerett in the time of Hen 7   │ Vere Earl of Oxford   Vide Pole's
                                          │ 'Devonsh Collections')

Sʳ John Broughton K. sonne and heire of Tuddington=Anne da and heire of Sʳ
in com. Bed.   │ Guy Salcotts.

* Cf. 'Topog and Genealogist, vol ii, p 402.

Cheyney.

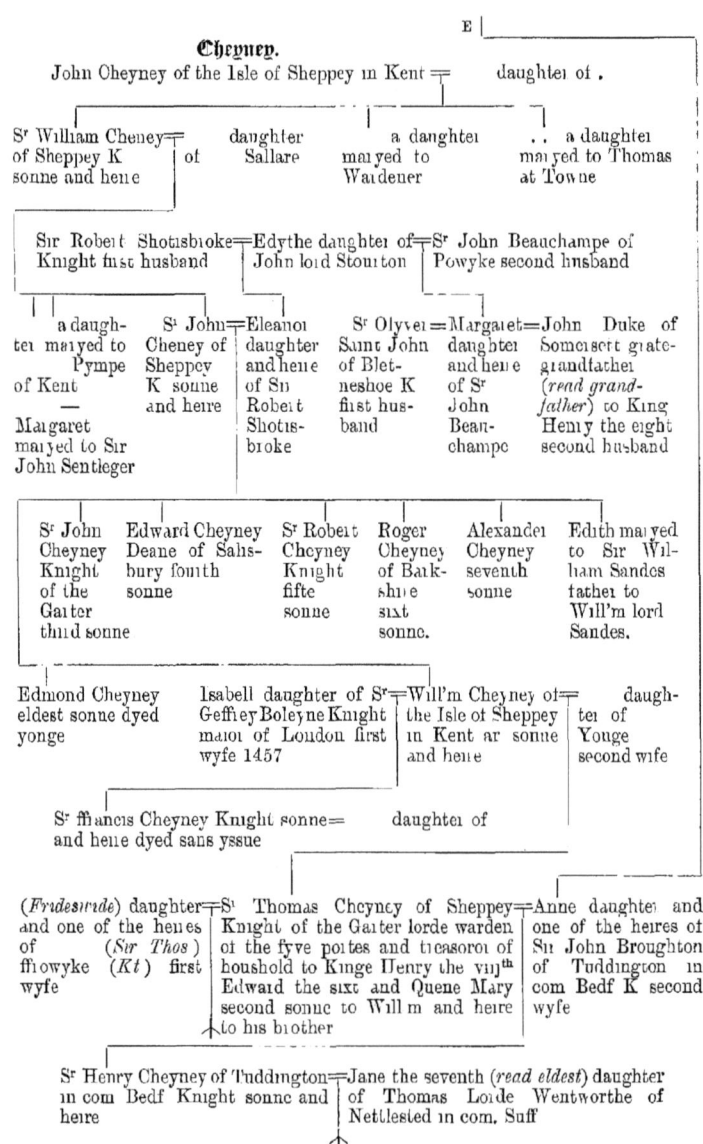

* Cf 'Miscellanea Genealogica et Heraldica,' N S, vol. iv, p 340

Chybnale
[of Felmersham].

ARMS.—*Quarterly—1 and 4, Azure, two lions passant-guardant or between as many flaunches ermine,* CHIBNALL; *2 and 3, Argent, a griffin segreant sable,* GODFREY; *impaling, Gules, on a fesse between three crescents or as many escallops azure,* ELLIS.

[CREST.—*On a wreath or and azure a dragon's head erased sable, ducally gorged or.*]

Thomas Chybnale of Astwoode in com. Bucks, gen. = daughter of ——

Richard Willoughby of Grendon in com. Northampt. gen. = [Elizabeth—Isham MS.] daughter and heire of Richard Godfrey of Norrell in com. Bedf. ar.

John Chybnale of Astwoode in com. Bucks, sonne and heire = Elizabeth daughter of Richard Willoughby of Grendon and of his wyfe the daughter and heire of Richard Godfrey.

- Richard Chybnale eldest sonne sans yssue
- John third sonne sans yssue
- William fourth sonne sans yssue
- Amy maryed to Thom's Leylam de com. Northampt.
- ffrancesse maryed to Richard Wyllymott of Brystowe
- Anne maryed to Henry Ireland of Hardmeade in com. Bucks gen.

Thomas Chybnale of ffelmersham in com. Bedf. second sonne. = Elizabeth daughter of Anthony Ellys of Greate Pavonton in com. Linc. gen.

- Wyborowe unmaryed
- Mary maryed to Henry Cartwright of Astwood in com. Bucks gen.
- Elizabeth and Alice vnmaryed

- Richard Chybnale sonne and heire
- Robert second sonne
- John third sonne
- George fourth sonne
- Anthony John and Thomas died all three yonge
- ffrancesse
- Judith

Cobbe†
[of Sharnebrooke].

ARMS.—*Gules, a chevron wavy between three luces naiant argent, on a chief of the second two shovellers sable, beaked and membered or.*

Will'm Cobbe of Sharnebroke in com. Bedf. gen. ‡ = Alice daughter of Thomas Lecke§ of ffelmersham in com. Bedf.

A

---

* MS. 541, Caius Coll. Cambs., gives a fifth son Anthonie, also mentioned in Isham MS. as having died young.
† This pedigree is not in the Isham MS.
‡ Harl. MS. 1531 gives four earlier generations of "Cobbe of Sentringham in com. Norff.," the immediate ancestors of William Cobbe who heads this pedigree.
§ Harl. MS. 5867 reads "Leche," probably Leach.

THE VISITATION OF BEDFORDSHIRE   17

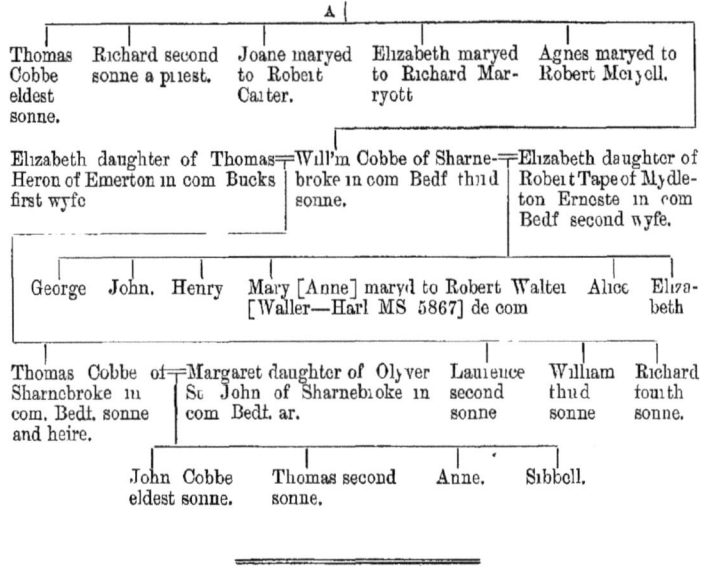

Cokayne

[of Hatley-Port].

ARMS (TWO SHIELDS).—1, *Argent, three cocks gules, membered and beaked azure*, COKAYNE II. (*sinister side*), *Quarterly*—1 and 4, *Argent, a bugle-horn, stringed sable, tasselled or*, LUKE, 2 and 3, *Gules, a fleur-de-lys argent*, LAUNCELYN *

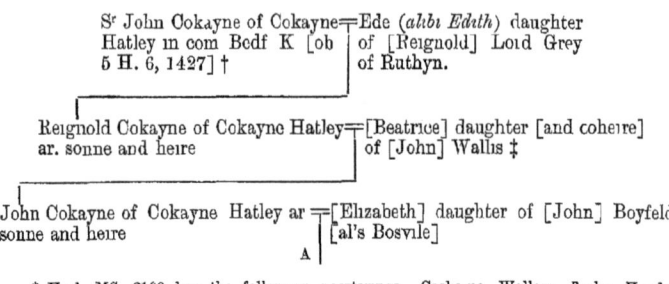

* Harl MS 2109 has the following quarterings Cockaine, Wallers, Turke, Kendall, Colville, Bond, Cobham, Boyvill
† Harl MS 2109 has nine generations earlier, of 'Cockayne de Ashbourne'
‡ Through this match came in the Wallis, Turke, Kendall, and Colville quarterings

D

THE VISITATION OF BEDFORDSHIRE.

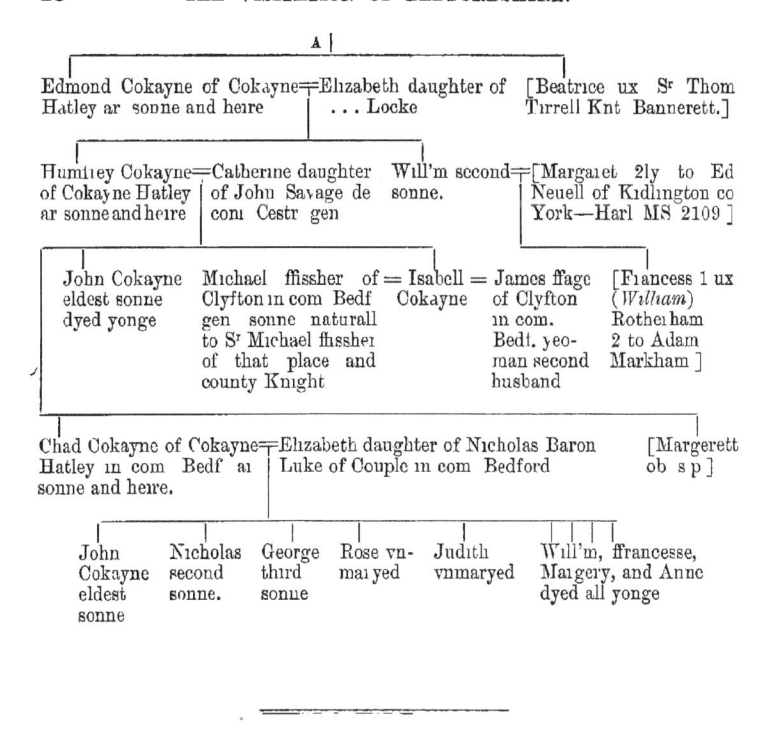

A

Edmond Cokayne of Cokayne = Elizabeth daughter of [Beatrice ux S⟨r⟩ Thom
Hatley ar sonne and heire ... Locke Tirrell Knt Bannerett.]

Humfrey Cokayne = Catherine daughter Will'm second = [Margaret 2ly to Ed
of Cokayne Hatley of John Savage de sonne. Neuell of Kidlington co
ar sonne and heire com Cestr gen York—Harl MS 2109.]

John Cokayne   Michael ffissher of = Isabell = James ffage   [Francess 1 ux
eldest sonne   Clyfton in com Bedf   Cokayne   of Clyfton   (Wilham)
dyed yonge   gen sonne naturall   in com.   Rotherham
               to S⟨r⟩ Michael ffissher   Bedf. yeo-   2 to Adam
               of that place and   man second   Markham]
               county Knight   husband

Chad Cokayne of Cokayne = Elizabeth daughter of Nicholas Baron   [Margerett
Hatley in com Bedf ar   Luke of Couple in com Bedford   ob s p]
sonne and heire.

John   Nicholas   George   Rose vn-   Judith   Will'm, ffrancesse,
Cokayne   second   third   maryed   vnmaryed   Margery, and Anne
eldest   sonne.   sonne   dyed all yonge
sonne

Colbecke

[of Tempsford].

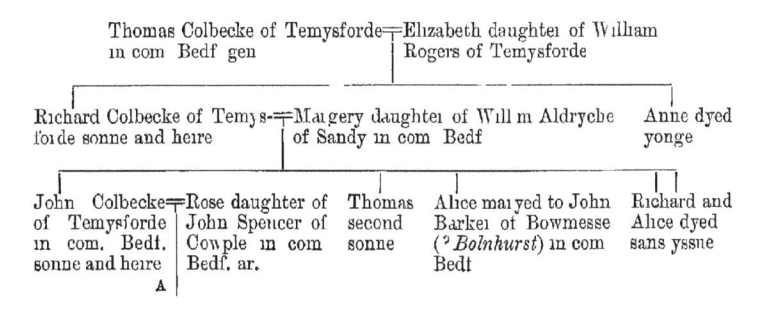

Thomas Colbecke of Temysforde = Elizabeth daughter of William
in com Bedf gen   Rogers of Temysforde

Richard Colbecke of Temys- = Margery daughter of Will m Aldryche   Anne dyed
forde sonne and heire   of Sandy in com Bedf   yonge

John Colbecke = Rose daughter of   Thomas   Alice maryed to John   Richard and
of Temysforde John Spencer of   second   Barker of Bowmesse   Alice dyed
in com. Bedf. Cowple in com   sonne   (? Bolnhurst) in com   sans yssue
sonne and heire Bedf. ar.   Bedf
A

                    A |

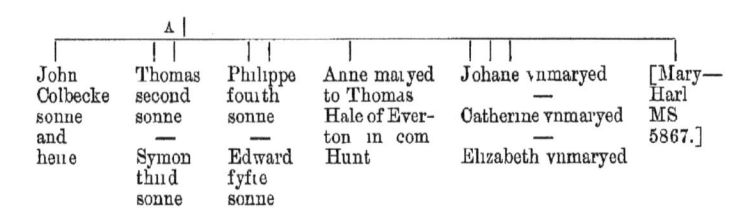

| John Colbecke sonne and heire | Thomas second sonne — Symon third sonne | Philippe fourth sonne — Edward fyfte sonne | Anne maryed to Thomas Hale of Everton in com Hunt | Johane vnmaryed — Catherine vnmaryed — Elizabeth vnmaryed | [Mary—Harl MS 5867.] |

Conquest

[of Poughton Conquest].

ARMS —*Quarterly of six—*1, *Quarterly argent and sable, in chief a label of three points gules,* CONQUEST, 2, *Ermine, a chief bendy of six azure and or,* DABETOT (or FITZ RICHARD); 3, *Argent, a fesse engrailed gules between three bulls' heads cabossed sable,* , 4, *Ermine, a chief indented gules, an annulet argent for difference,* BUTTON, 5, *Sable, a fesse argent between three dexter hands couped or,* BATTE, 6, *Gules, two swords in saltire azure, hilted or,* JELLIBRONDE

CREST —*On a wreath argent and sable a holly-tree vert, fructed gules.*

John Conquest of Houghton = . . daughter of
Conquest in com Bedf. ar. | Batte.

Richard Conquest of Houghton Conquest = Isabell daughter of . . . .
ar sonne and heire | Gamage of Wales

Richard Conquest of Houghton Conquest = . daughter of   Mallet of . . . .
ar. sonne and heire | *Azure, three escallops or*—Harl
                                        | MS. 5867

Richard Conquest of Houghton Conquest = Elizabeth daughter of . . .
ar sonne and heire | Jellybronde.

Edmond Conquest of Houghton Conquest = Joane daughter of William Button of
in com Bedf ar sonne and heire. | Amptell in com. Bedf.

A

                                          Δ
┌─────────────────┬─────────────┬──────────┬──────────┬──────────────────────────┐
Edmond Conquest of   Richard   Will'm   George   Elizabeth maryed to Philippe
Houghton Conquest   second   third   fourth   Kinge of Wornoll in com
ar sonne and heire   sonne   sonne   sonne   Oxon

┌─────────────────┬──────────────────┬──────────────────────┬──────────────┐
Dorothe maryed to John   Anne maryed to   Cicely maryed to Roger   ffrancesse
Rowse of Stewkeley in   Robert Newde-   Duncombe of Bryckhill   vnmaryed
com Hunt gen.   gate of Hawnes   in com Bucks
                         in com Bedf. ar.

Creke

[of Bolnhurst].

William Creke of Rickmesworth=Margaret daughter and heire of   . .
in com. Hertf ar. | Cromer de com Glouc* ar

Thomas Creke of Ryckmesworth ar. sonne and heire = daughter of Saint John
                                                 | of Kent ar

William Creke of Ryckmesworth ar sonne=Alice daughter of Thomas Asheby of
and heire | Harvylde in com Midd ar.

John Creke of Ryckmesworth=Jone daughter of   . Hunte of Coventry in com
sonne and heire | War. gen

┌──────────────┬──────────────────────┬─────────────────────┬──────────────┐
William Creke   Stephen Creke of Boulene-=Olyve daughter of   Bonaventer
eldest sonne   hurst in com Bedf 2 sonne | Will'm Cordall of   third sonne
sans yssue   and heire | St John Strete in   dyed sans
                                            | London   yssue

┌──────────────────┬──────────────────┬──────────────┬──────────────┐
Martyn Creke eldest sonne   Edward second   John third   Anne vnmaryed.
                            sonne   sonne.

---

* "Glouc" in Harl. MS 5867, but "Worc." in MS 541 Caius Coll, Cambs.

Dyve

[of Bromham].

ARMS (TWO SHIELDS) —I , *Quarterly of nine*—1, *Gules, a fesse dancettée or between three escallops ermine*, DYVE , 2, *Vair argent and azure, three bendlets gules*, BRAY , 3, *Gules, on a bend argent three martlets sable*, QUYNTON , 4, *Sable, a chevron between three bees (? three butterflies) volant or*, SAYWELL , 5, *Argent, a chevron sable, on a chief of the second three martlets of the field*, WYLDE , 6, *Argent, a chevron sable fretty or between three stags' heads couped gules*, RAGON , 7, *Argent, a fesse and canton gules*, WOODVILLE , 8, *Argent, a maunch sable, a mullet for difference*, HASTINGS , 9, *Argent, on a fesse azure three boars' heads couped or, in chief a lion passant gules*, AP RICE
II (*sinister side*), *Quarterly*—1 and 4, *Sable, three escallops argent*, STRICKLAND , 2 and 3, *Argent, a fesse dancettée between ten billets sable, four, three, two, and one*, DEYNCOURT

CREST —*On a wreath argent and gules a wyvern with wings addorsed gules*

Henry* [Sʳ Richard] Dyve of Wyke Dyve in com Northampt. Knight † ═ Elizabeth daughter of Thomas Raynes of Clyfton Raynes in com. Bucks ar *Chequy or and gules a canton ermine*

[Henry‡ Dyve eldest sonne.]

Will'm‡ Dyve of Brampton in com Bedf ar. sonne and heire. ═ [Dorothe] daughter of Wassy in com Cornub. gen.

Robert Dyve§ of Brampton [Holwell] ar sonne and heire [to Henry—Harl MS 5867] ═ .... daughter of Rauf Eldercare of Reisby in com Ebor ar

Rauf Dyve of Brampton [Holwell] ar sonne and heire ═ Mawde [Jone] daughter of Henry Mantell of Hayforde in com. Northampt. ar *Argent, a cross engrailed between four martletts sable.*

Δ

* ' Be it noted that this Henry Dyve kylled a servant of Sʳ Robert Trogeant, by reason wherof all his lands wer confiscate and his lyft was at the Kinge's pleasure which was in the tyme of Kinge Stephen, who gave the sayde Henry Dyve body landes and goodes vnto the sayd Sʳ Robert Trogeant, knight, chamberleyne to the sayd kinge And the sayd Trogeant did gyve vnto the sayd Henry Dyve haulf of Brampton Parva and no more " (*Ita se habet textus*)

† Harl MS 2109 commences thus

Simon brother to Alan   Allan de Diue ═   Rob't brother to Alan.

Sir Richard.═Elizabeth.

‡ In Isham MS Henry is called eld s. and husb of Dorothy Wassey, and Will'm 2nd son ; also in Harl MSS 2109 and 5867

§ ' Rob't Dyve m 1st Agnes, d and h of Roger Alwolde of Rothwell, and hath issue Ralf Dyve his eld sonne After, the said Rob't m to his 2nd w Maude da of Sʳ Roger Whelton, Kt , and hath issue Henry 2nd son," (Isham MS. and Harl. MS. 5867) So also Harl MSS 1531, 5186, and MS 541, Caius Coll Cambs

THE VISITATION OF BEDFORDSHIRE.

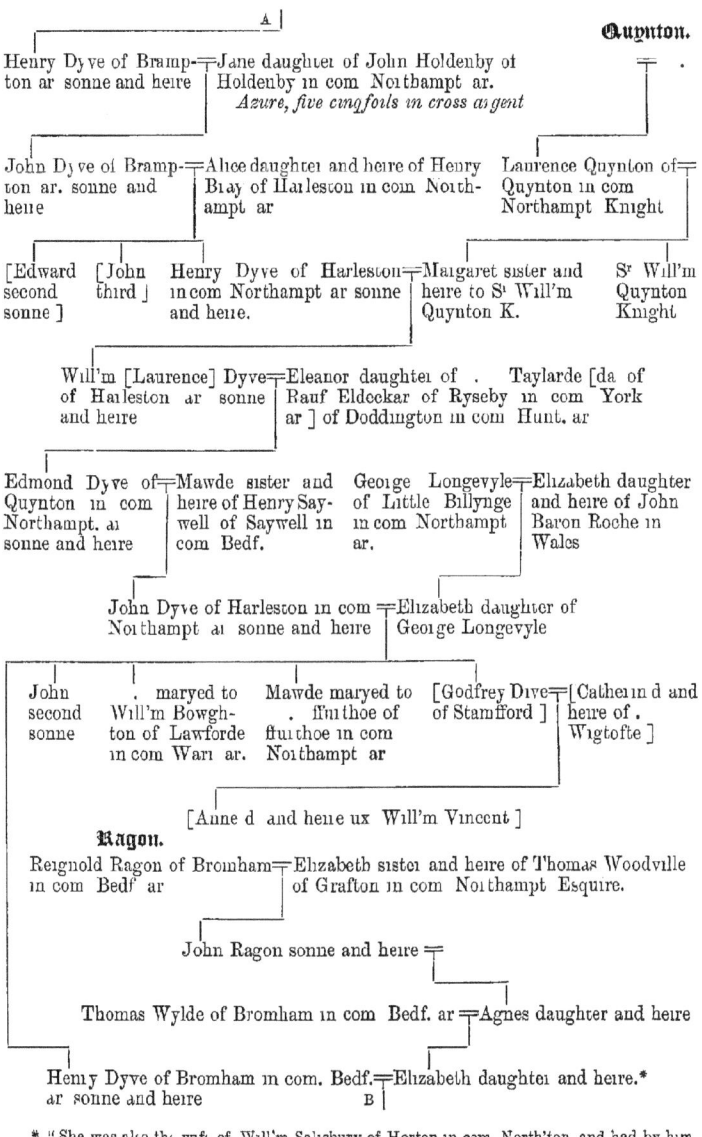

Quynton.

Henry Dyve of Brampton ar sonne and heire === Jane daughter of John Holdenby of Holdenby in com Northampt ar.
Azure, five cingfoils in cross argent

John Dyve of Brampton ar. sonne and heire === Alice daughter and heire of Henry Bray of Harleston in com Northampt ar

Laurence Quynton of Quynton in com Northampt Knight ===

[Edward second sonne] [John third] Henry Dyve of Harleston in com Northampt ar sonne and heire === Margaret sister and heire to Sr Will'm Quynton K. Sr Will'm Quynton Knight

Will'm [Laurence] Dyve of Harleston ar sonne and heire === Eleanor daughter of Rauf Eldeckar of Ryseby in com ar] Taylarde [da of York of Doddington in com Hunt. ar

Edmond Dyve of Quynton in com Northampt. ar sonne and heire === Mawde sister and heire of Henry Saywell of Saywell in com Bedf.

George Longevyle of Little Billynge in com Northampt ar. === Elizabeth daughter and heire of John Baron Roche in Wales

John Dyve of Harleston in com Northampt ar sonne and heire === Elizabeth daughter of George Longevyle

John second sonne

. maryed to Will'm Boughton of Lawforde in com Wari ar.

Mawde maryed to . ffinthoe of ffinthoe in com Northampt ar

[Godfrey Dive of Stamfford] === [Catherin d and heire of . Wigtofte]

[Anne d and heire ux Will'm Vincent]

Ragon.

Reignold Ragon of Bromham in com Bedf ar === Elizabeth sister and heire of Thomas Woodville of Grafton in com Northampt Esquire.

John Ragon sonne and heire ===

Thomas Wylde of Bromham in com Bedf. ar === Agnes daughter and heire

Henry Dyve of Bromham in com. Bedf. ar sonne and heire === Elizabeth daughter and heire.*
B

---

* "She was also the wife of Will'm Salisbury of Horton in com North'ton, and had by him, Mary, ux Will'm Lord Par of Horton, Elizabeth, ux. John Enderby of Stratton in com. Bedfford." (Harl MS. 1531)

THE VISITATION OF BEDFORDSHIRE. 23

B

Sʳ John Dyve of Bromham Knight, sonne and heire == Isabell daughter and one of the heires of Sʳ Rauf Hastinges Knight *

- Will'm Dyve of Bromham in com Bedf ar sonne and heire == Anne daughter and heire of Lewys Appryce of Hansloppe in com Bucks ar
- John Dyve second sonne
- Dorothe maryed to Richard Wake of Hartwell in com Northampt ar

  - Christopher second sonne
  - Thomas† third sonne
  - John fourth sonne
  - George fifte sonne
  - William sixte sonne
  - Henry seventh sonne

  - Isabell maryed to Anthony Wood of Collingtroughe in com Northampt gen
  - Anne dyed yonge
  - Eleanor maryed to George Clapton of Sudbury in com Suff gen

  - Lewis Dyve of Bromham ar. sonne and heire == Mary daughter of Sʳ Walter Strickland of Sycer in com Ebor K
  - Elizabeth maryed to ffrancys Downes of Ramplingham in com Norff gen
  - Catherine maryed to George Downes of Bromham in com Bedf gen

    - [John Lord Digby Erle of Bristol 2 husband.] == [Beatrix d of Charles Walcott of Walcott in com. Sallop 2 wiffe] == John Dyve of Bromham in com Bedt sonne and heire. == Douglas daughter of Sʳ Anthony Denny of Cheston in com. Hertf Knight Grome of the Stole to Kinge Henry the eight ‡

      Honor Dyve dyed yonge

      - Lewys second sonne dyed yonge
      - Elizabeth dyed yonge.
      - [Humffrey Dive]
      - Anne dyed yonge
      - Catherine dyed yonge
      - Mary now lyvinge

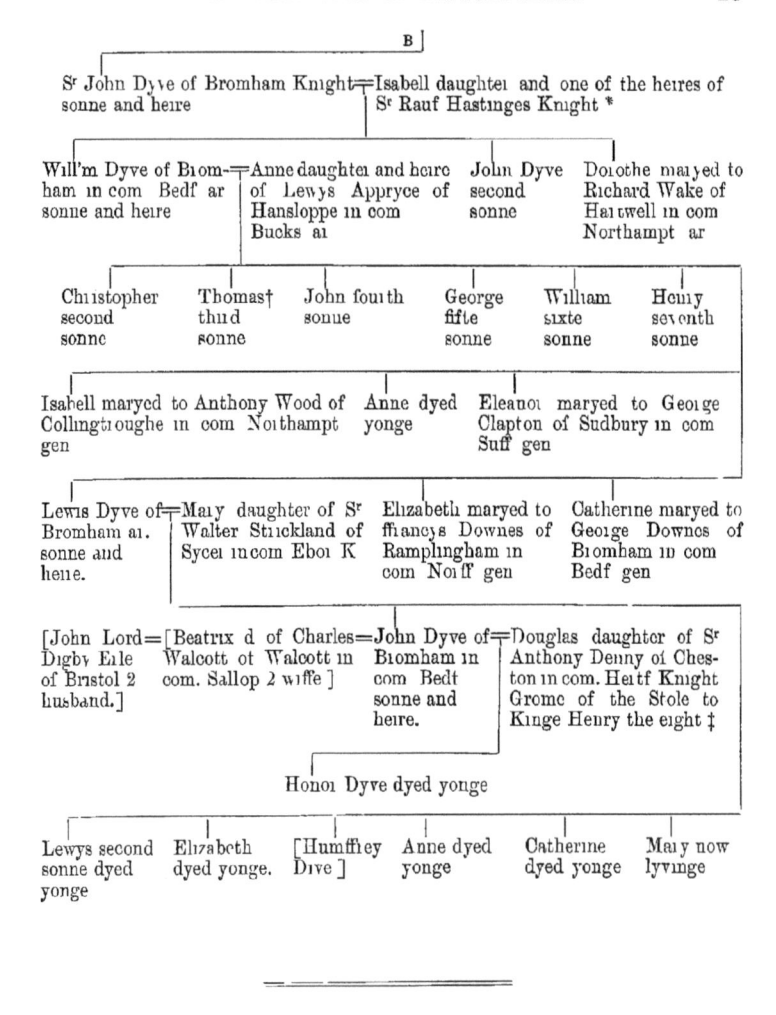

* 'This Sʳ Rauf Hastinges Knight, was capitayne of the castell, towne, and Countye Guynes, and was third brother to Willm Hastinges, Lord Chamberleyne to Kinge Edward the fourthe." (*Ita se habet textus*)
† ' Thomas, m Elizabeth, widow of John West the elder and da to Will'm Borne of Bedford, and by her had issue Honor Dyve, who died young." (Harl MS 5867)
‡ ' And by her hath no issue living (Harl MS 5867)

Eston

[of Holme].

ARMS —(TWO SHIELDS) —I *Or, a fesse gules, in chief a spaniel courant, in base a cock sable,* ESTON—Harl MS 5186   II (sinister side), *Quarterly of four*— 1 and 4, *Argent, a bend cotised sable, a bordure of the second bezantée,* WESTCOTT, 2, *Argent, a chevron between three escallops sable,* LITTLETON, 3, *Argent, a fesse between three dexter hands couped gules,* ? QUATERMAYNE

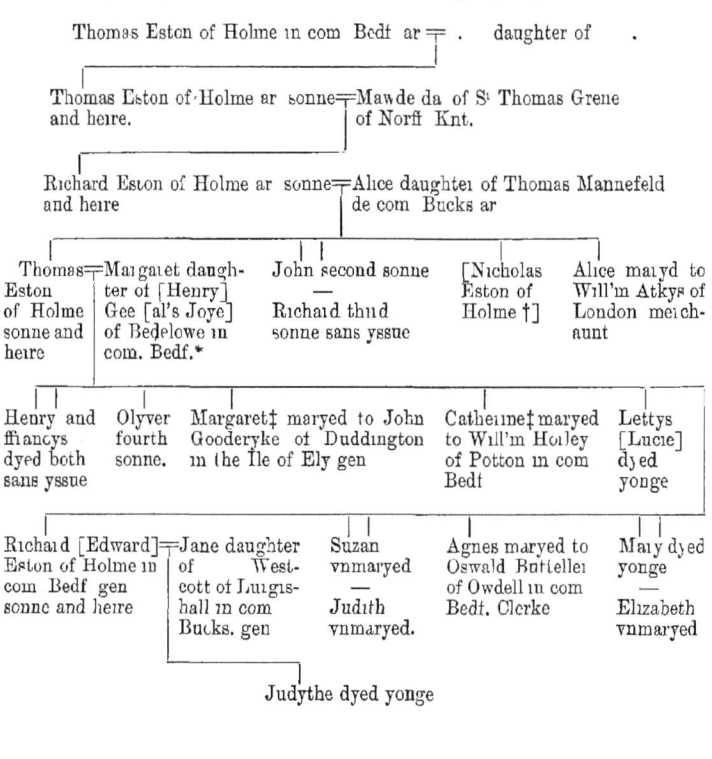

Thomas Eston of Holme in com Bedf ar =╤= . daughter of .

Thomas Eston of Holme ar sonne =╤= Mawde da of S⟨t⟩ Thomas Grene of Norff Knt.
and heire.

Richard Eston of Holme ar sonne =╤= Alice daughter of Thomas Mannefeld
and heire | de com Bucks ar

| Thomas =╤= Margaret daughter of [Henry] Gee [al's Joye] of Bedelowe in com. Bedf.* | John second sonne — Richard third sonne sans yssue | [Nicholas Eston of Holme †] | Alice maryd to Will'm Atkys of London merchaunt |

| Henry and ffrancys dyed both sans yssue | Olyver fourth sonne. | Margaret‡ maryed to John Gooderyke of Duddington in the Ile of Ely gen | Catherine‡ maryed to Will'm Horley of Potton in com Bedf | Lettys [Lucie] dyed yonge |

| Richard [Edward] Eston of Holme in com Bedf gen sonne and heire =╤= Jane daughter of Westcott of Luigishall in com Bucks. gen | Suzan vnmaryed — Judith vnmaryed. | Agnes maryed to Oswald Butteller of Owdell in com Bedf. Clerke | Mary dyed yonge — Elizabeth vnmaryed |

Judythe dyed yonge

---

* ' Renupta Nicho' Pigott de Holme pr'd gen." (Harl MS 5186)
† MS 51), Caius Coll Cambs
‡ Isham MS omits Catherine and makes Margaret wife of W'm Horley

Everarde
[of Biggleswade].

ARMS —*Gules, on a fesse engrailed between three estoiles argent as many torteaux*

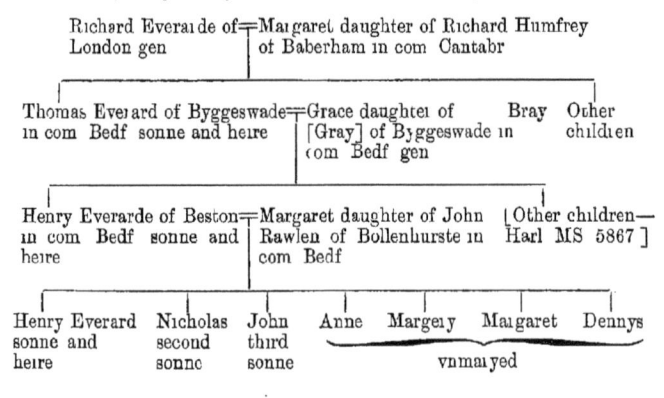

Richard Everarde of London gen = Margaret daughter of Richard Humfrey of Baberham in com Cantabr

┃

Thomas Everard of Byggeswade in com Bedf sonne and heire = Grace daughter of [Gray] of Byggeswade in com Bedf gen | Bray | Other children

┃

Henry Everarde of Beston in com Bedf sonne and heire = Margaret daughter of John Rawlen of Bollenhurste in com Bedf | [Other children— Harl MS 5867]

┃

| Henry Everard sonne and heire | Nicholas second sonne | John third sonne | Anne | Margery | Margaret | Dennys |

Anne, Margery, Margaret, Dennys — vnmaryed

FitzGeffrey
[of Barford and Thurleigh].

ARMS —*Sable, a bull passant or*
CREST —*Out of a ducal coronet a demi-bull rampant or*

daughter ... of ... first wyfe = Will'm ffitzGeffry of Blackborne in com Bedf ar = Elizabeth daughter of .... Wannton of Bashme (? *Bushmead*) in com Bedf at. second wyfe

┃

| John ffitzJeffrey eldest sonne. | Thomas second sonne | William third sonne | John fourth sonne * | Will'm fifte sonne | Edward sixte sonne. | Clement seventh sonne |

| Elizabeth first maryed to John Massam of Bedf. after to Nicholas ffletam of Stowe in com Northampt | Anne first maryed to Gerard Gonnell of St Needes in com Hunt after to Will'm Hall of Everton in com Bedf. | Margaret maryed to Edmond Bendowe of Everton in com Bedf | Cicely maryed to Roger Hibberdine [Hillersden] de com Oxon [Exon — MS 541] | Catherine vnmaryed. | Brigitt maryed to Robert Sha [Sackvele of Riseley in com Bedf gent] |

* Isham MS. and MS. 541 give John eldest son, and John fourth son by second wife.

THE VISITATION OF BEDFORDSHIRE.

Jane daughter of John Baptiste of St Mary Overey in Southwerke first wyfe = George ffitzJeffrey of Blackborne hall in com Bedf eight sonne = Goodith [Edith—Isham MS] daughter of Richard Throgmerton of Higham Parke second wyfe * | Mary maryed to Olyver Saint John of Shainbrooke in com. Bedf ar

[Sr George FitzGeffrey eldest sonne] | [Robert ffitzGeffrey 2 sonne of Blackborne ob s p.] | [Nicholas 3] — [Olyver fforthe.] | [William fifte] [Gerard sixt]

FitzGeffrey
[of Clapham].

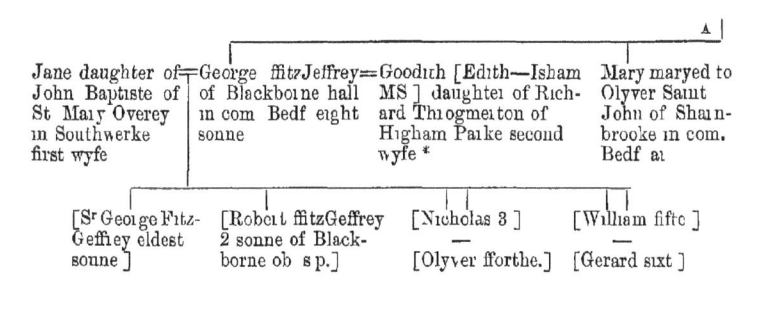

ARMS —*Sable, a bull passant or.* (Isham MS.)

John ffitzJeffrey of Clapham in com. Bedf. ar. = Johane daughter of John Green of Samforde in com Essex Knight.

ffrancis ffitzGeffrey of Clapham sonne and heire. = Elizabeth daughter of . . Catesey of Leigers Ashby in com Northampt. ar.

Leonard ffitzGeffrey of Clapham in com Bedf sonne and heire = Margaret daughter of Edward Bugges of Hallowe in com Essex gen | John second sonne. Alexander third sonne

George ffitzGeffrey eldest sonne | ffrancys second sonne | Elizabeth | Joane

Fitzhugh
[of Wilden].

ARMS —*Quarterly*—1 and 4, *Ermine, on a chief gules three martlets or,* FITZHUGH; 2 and 3, *Argent, three chevrons sable, each charged with a bezant,*

Will'm ffitzhewe of Wylden in com Bedf third sonne to . . = Catherine daughter of . . Byll of Ashwell in com Herf. gen

---

* "And by her hath no yssue" (Isham MS)

```
                                            A
     │                │              │         │                    │              │  │  │
William ffitz-    John fourth     Robert══*[Elizab d of         Mary maryed    Cicely
hewe eldest      sonne [of       fifte   Rich Bury of           to Thomas       ―
sonne.           Wavenden        sonne   Tuddington in          Nokes† of       Jane
  ―              in com                  com Bedd ]             Hatfelde        ―
Thomas dyed      Bucking-                                       Brode Oke in    Anne
sans yssue       ham, vide                                      com Essex.
                 idem]
                                    │              │
                               [Mary 1 da]    [Frances 2 da]
```

                    Nicholas ffitzhewe of Wylden══Grace daughter of Richard Stokes
                        third sonne.   of White Notley in com Essex

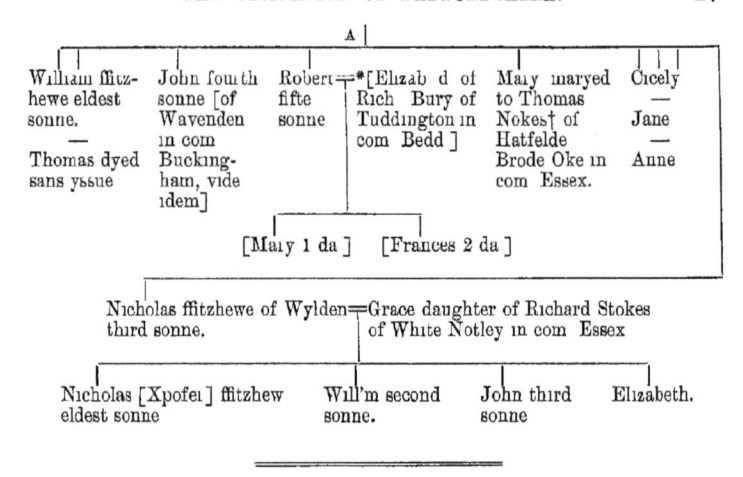

```
    │                    │              │              │
Nicholas [Χροfeι] ffitzhew   Will'm second    John third    Elizabeth.
eldest sonne                sonne.           sonne
```

𝔉𝔦𝔱𝔷𝔴𝔦𝔩𝔩𝔦𝔞𝔪‡
[of 𝔎𝔢𝔪𝔭𝔰𝔱𝔬𝔫].

ARMS (TWO SHIELDS)—I, *Quarterly of fifteen*—1, *Lozengy argent and gules*, FITZWILLIAM ; 2, *Chequy or and azure*, WARREN , 3, *Ermine, a fesse gules*, BERNACKT , 4, *Argent, a chief gules, over all a bend azure*, CROMWELL , 5, *Argent, three cinqfoils and a canton gules*, DRIBY , 6, *Chequy or and gules, a chief ermine*, TATTERSHALL, 7, *Gules, a lion rampant or*, DAWBIGNEY , 8, *Azure, three garbs or*, CHESTER , 9, *Azure, a wolf's head erased argent*, E OF CHESTER , 10, *Argent, a cross engrailed gules*, GREEN ; 11, *Chequy or and azure, a bordure gules*, , 12, *Gules, three water-bougets argent*, , 13, *Quarterly or and gules within a bordure bezantée*, , 14, *Gules, an eagle displayed or*, , 15, As No 1 II , FITZWILLIAM, *impaling, Argent, a chevron between three trefoils slipped sable*, RUFFORD
CREST.—*Out of a ducal coronet or a panache of ostrich-feathers argent.*

```
        Sr Will'm ffitzwilliam lorde of Emley in══[Emma] daughter of [Golabis
        com Ebor. K came in with Wm the        │  of Normandy—Harl MS
        Conqueror and was his marshall            5867§]
                            │
Sr Will'm ffitzwill'm of Emley K ══[Ella—Harl MS 5867] daughter of [William
sonne and heire ||                  —Harl MS 5867] Eile Warren ¶
                              A
```

* In a different hand
† "Tho Nokes de Ashwell in com. Hertf" (Harl MS 5186)
‡ *Cf* 'Visitations of Essex,' Harl Soc , vol xiii , p 198, and 'Visitation of Yorkshire,' Harl. Soc , vol xvi., p. 122   There appear to be several generations omitted in the early portion of this pedigree
§ In a different hand
|| Harl MS 5867 places here "Sr William Fitzwilliam Knight, sonne and heire married Elianore, d and h to Sr John Emley, Lord of Emley"
¶ ' In this woman's right came Warren Hall " (Harl. MS. 5867.)

THE VISITATION OF BEDFORDSHIRE.

A

[Sᵣ Wᵐ] ffitzwill'm of Emley [eld] sonne and heire [Lord of Sprotburgh—Harl MS. 5867] = Albreda daughter of Edmond Lacy Erle of Lincoln *

[Roger ffitzwilliam 2 sonne to whom Wᵐ Earle Warren his vncle gave the Lordshippe of Gretwell—Harl MS 5867.]

[Sʳ Wᵐ] ffitzwill'm of Emley sonne and heire [Lord of Sprotburgh etc.—Harl. MS 5867]. = [Agnes] daughter of the lord Grey of Wilton [Codnor—Harl MS 5867]

Sʳ William ffitzwill'm of Emley Knight sonne and heire = [Maude] daughter of [William—Harl MS 5867] Deyncourte.

Sʳ John ffitzwill'm of Sprotborough in com Ebor K sonne and heire = Elizabeth daughter of the lord Clinton Erle of Huntingdon.

| Edmond second sonne. | John, Richard, and Thomas dyed all three sans issue | Mary maryed to Henry Hastinges of Pykeringlythe | maryed to Edmond Perpoynt Knight | maryed to Sʳ Bryan Thornell [Chorvile—Isham MS] Knight. |

Sʳ Will m ffitzwill'm of Sprotborough K sonne and heire = Mawde daughter of Rauf Cromwell lorde of Tattersall

| Sʳ John ffitzwill'm of Sprotborough Knight sonne and heire = Eleanor daughter of Sir Henry Grene Knight † | Reignolde [Rafe—Harl. MS 5867] second sonne sans yssue | Elizabeth maryed to ‡ Rockley Esquire | Jane maryed to [Sir —Harl MS 5867] Henry Suthill of Suthill |

| Nicholas second sonne = [Margaret daughter (and heire —Harl MS 5867) of John Tansley of Nottingham—Isham MS] | Raufe third sonne [m (Johan—Harl MS 5867) da of Boulton—Isham MS] | Will'm fourth sonne [m Eliz da of Sʳ Wᵐ Chaworth —Isham MS] | John fifte sonne |

John ffitzwill'm of Gaynspark hall in com Essex and of Melton in com Northampt ar § = Helene daughter of Will'm Villers of Brokisby ar

B

---

* Harl MS 5867 calls her "da and heire to Robert Lord Lizures, and heire to Robert Lacy Earle of Lincolne'
† In a different hand—"of Drayton, co North, K" (Harl MS 5867)
‡ In a different hand—"Sʳ Robert of Rockley Hall Kᵗ" (Ibid)
§ Harl MS 5867 has "Robert fourth son was seised of lands in Bentley, Cusworth, and Doncaster William fifth sonne died at Plomtree w'thout yssue John ffitzwilliams sixte sonne of Greensnorton'

THE VISITATION OF BEDFORDSHIRE.   29

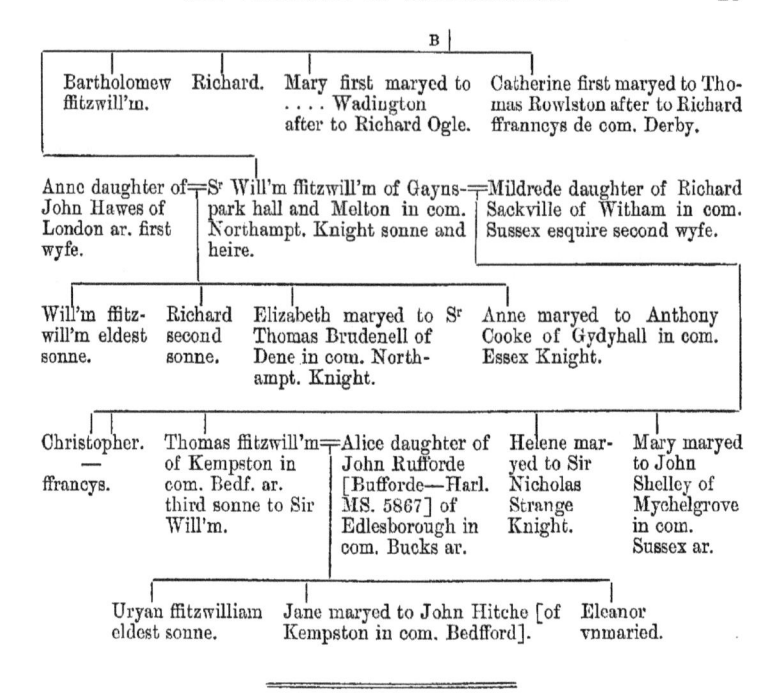

B

Bartholomew ffitzwill'm. | Richard. | Mary first maryed to .... Wadington after to Richard Ogle. | Catherine first maryed to Thomas Rowlston after to Richard ffranncys de com. Derby.

Anne daughter of John Hawes of London ar. first wyfe. =⊤= Sʳ Will'm ffitzwill'm of Gaynspark hall and Melton in com. Northampt. Knight sonne and heire. =⊤= Mildrede daughter of Richard Sackville of Witham in com. Sussex esquire second wyfe.

Will'm ffitzwill'm eldest sonne. | Richard second sonne. | Elizabeth maryed to Sʳ Thomas Brudenell of Dene in com. Northampt. Knight. | Anne maryed to Anthony Cooke of Gydyhall in com. Essex Knight.

Christopher. — ffrancys. | Thomas ffitzwill'm of Kempston in com. Bedf. ar. third sonne to Sir Will'm. =⊤= Alice daughter of John Rufforde [Bufforde—Harl. MS. 5867] of Edlesborough in com. Bucks ar. | Helene maryed to Sir Nicholas Strange Knight. | Mary maryed to John Shelley of Mychelgrove in com. Sussex ar.

Uryan ffitzwilliam eldest sonne. | Jane maryed to John Hitche [of Kempston in com. Bedfford]. | Eleanor vnmaried.

Fowler

[of Tilsworth].

ARMS* (TWO SHIELDS).—I., *Quarterly of six*—1, *Azure, on a chevron argent between three lions passant-guardant or as many crosses moline sable*, FOWLER ; 2, *Barry of six argent and gules, on a chief or a lion passant azure*, EGLESFIELD ; 3, *Argent, three wolves' heads erased gules within a bordure azure, charged with eight castles or*, FOWLER ; 4, *Argent, a chief ermine, on a canton gules an owl of the first*, BARTON ; 5, *Vair argent and gules*, ? GRESLEY ; 6, As No. 1.   II., FOWLER, *impaling, Quarterly*—1 and 4, *Argent, a fesse indented componée sable and gules between three mullets of the last*, MOORE ; 2 and 3, *Argent, a fesse between three annulets gules*, .
CREST.—*On a wreath argent and azure an owl, ducally crowned and membered or.*

[Sʳ Jo. ffowler Kt.]=⊤=[.... da. and sole heire to .... Loueday.]

[Sʳ Henry ffowler Kt.]=⊤=[.... sister and heire to John Barton.]
A

---

* Harl. MS. 5867 has the quarterings thus : 1, Fowler ; 2, Englefield ; 3, Visdeloup ; 4, Barton ; 5, Grysley ; 6, Ferrers.

THE VISITATION OF BEDFORDSHIRE.

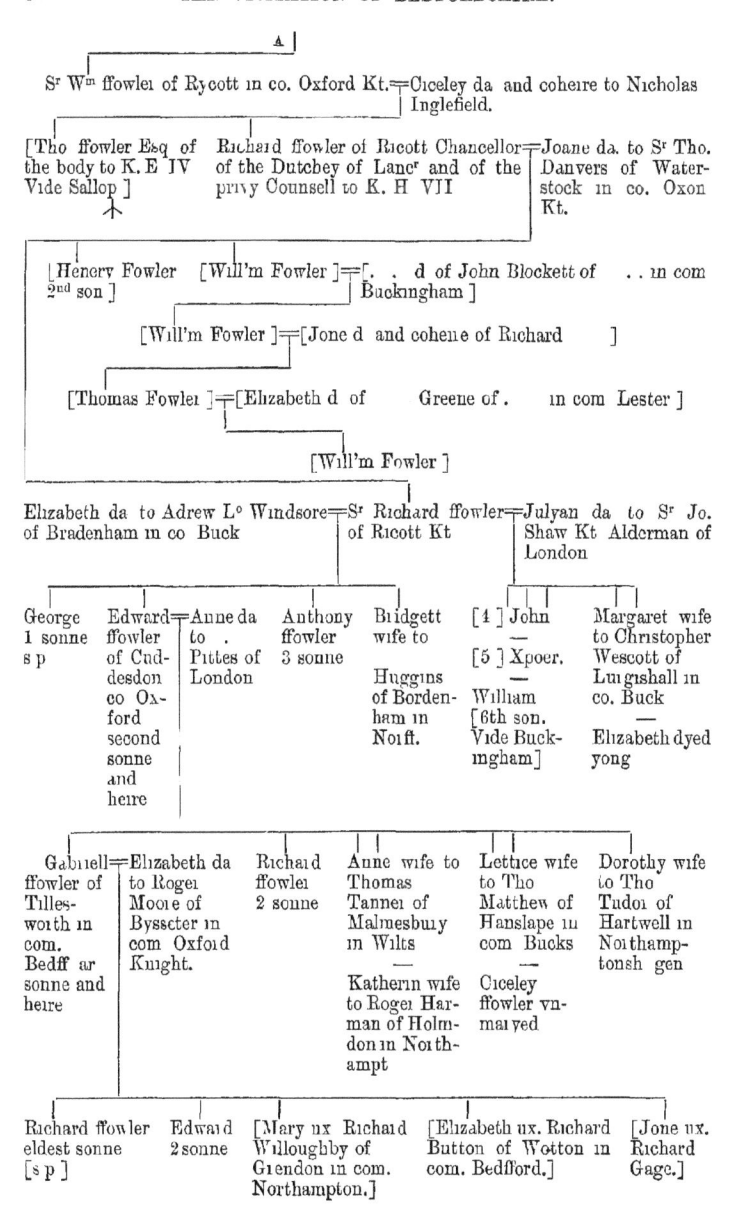

Sʳ Wᵐ ffowler of Rycott in co. Oxford Kt.=Ciceley da. and coheire to Nicholas Inglefield.

[Tho. ffowler Esq of the body to K. E. IV Vide Sallop.]

Richard ffowler of Ricott Chancellor of the Dutchey of Lancʳ and of the privy Counsell to K. H. VII = Joane da. to Sʳ Tho. Danvers of Waterstock in co. Oxon Kt.

[Henery Fowler 2ⁿᵈ son]

[Will'm Fowler] = [. . d of John Blockett of Buckingham]

[. . in com . .]

[Will'm Fowler] = [Jone d. and coheire of Richard]

[Thomas Fowler] = [Elizabeth d of Greene of . . in com Lester]

[Will'm Fowler]

Elizabeth da to Adrew Lᵒ Windsore of Bradenham in co Buck = Sʳ Richard ffowler of Ricott Kt = Julyan da to Sʳ Jo. Shaw Kt Alderman of London

George 1 sonne s p

Edward ffowler of Cuddesdon co Oxford second sonne and heire = Anne da to . . Pittes of London

Anthony ffowler 3 sonne

Bridgett wife to Huggins of Bordenham in Norft.

[4] John
[5] Xpoer.
William [6th son. Vide Buckingham]

Margaret wife to Christopher Wescott of Lurgishall in co. Buck — Elizabeth dyed yong

Gabriell ffowler of Tillesworth in com. Bedff ar sonne and heire = Elizabeth da to Roger Moore of Bysseter in com Oxford Knight.

Richard ffowler 2 sonne

Anne wife to Thomas Tanner of Malmesbury in Wilts — Katherin wife to Roger Harman of Holmdon in Northampt

Lettice wife to Tho Matthew of Hanslape in com Bucks — Ciceley ffowler vnmaryed

Dorothy wife to Tho Tudor of Hartwell in Northamptonsh gen

Richard ffowler eldest sonne [s p]

Edward 2 sonne

[Mary ux Richard Willoughby of Grendon in com. Northampton.]

[Elizabeth ux. Richard Button of Wotton in com. Bedfford.]

[Jone ux. Richard Gage.]

Franklin

[of Thurleigh].

ARMS (TWO SHIELDS) —I , *Argent, on a bend engrailed between two lions' heads erased gules a dolphin naiant between as many martlets or*, FRANKLIN II (*sinister side*), *Argent, a cross moline sable, in the first quarter a fleur-de-lys gules*, COPLEY
CREST —*On a wreath argent and azure a dolphin's head or, erased gules, between two branches vert.*

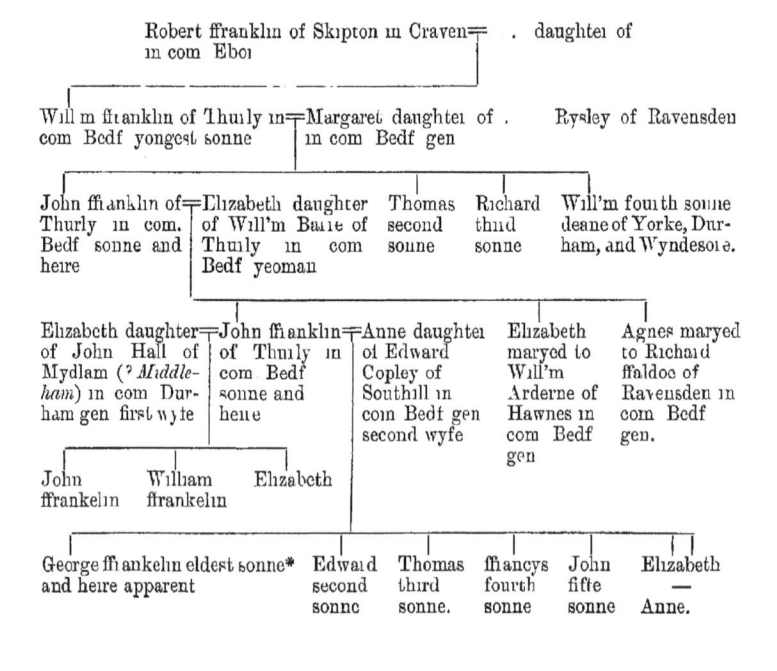

Robert ffranklin of Skipton in Craven in com Ebor == . daughter of

Will'm ffranklin of Thurly in com Bedf yongest sonne == Margaret daughter of . Rysley of Ravensden in com Bedf gen

John ffranklin of Thurly in com. Bedf sonne and heire == Elizabeth daughter of Will'm Baire of Thurly in com Bedf yeoman | Thomas second sonne | Richard third sonne | Will'm fourth sonne deane of Yorke, Durham, and Wyndesore.

Elizabeth daughter of John Hall of Mydlam (? *Middleham*) in com Durham gen first wyfe == John ffranklin of Thurly in com Bedf sonne and heire == Anne daughter of Edward Copley of Southill in com Bedf gen second wyfe | Elizabeth maryed to Will'm Arderne of Hawnes in com Bedf gen | Agnes maryed to Richard ffaldoe of Ravensden in com Bedf gen.

John ffrankelin | William ffrankelin | Elizabeth

George ffrankelin eldest sonne* and heire apparent | Edward second sonne | Thomas third sonne. | ffrancys fourth sonne | John fifte sonne | Elizabeth — Anne.

---

* "By his 2 wyfe,' (MS 541)

Gostwicke*
[of Willington].

ARMS.—*Quarterly of sixteen†—1, Argent, a bend gules cotised sable between six Cornish choughs proper, beaked and membered of the second,* GOSTWICKE; 2, *Gules, a chevron ermine between three heads in profile proper in helmets argent,* OWEN, 3, *Gules, a chevron between three lions passant-guardant or,* ————; 4, *Or, a cross azure,* BOHUN, 5, *Argent, a bend gules, on a chief of the last two mullets or,* ST JOHN, 6, *Sable, a chevron ermine between three maidens' heads couped at the shoulders argent, hair dishevelled or,* ESTFIELD, 7, *Vair, a canton gules,* FILIOL; 8, *Paly of six or and gules, on a chief argent three mascles of the second,* WILKES, 9, *(Azure,) a bend (argent) cotised between six lions rampant (or),* BOHUN, 10, *Gules, a bend between three mullets argent,* HANSARD, 11, *Ermine, a fesse counter-componée or and azure,* ————, 12, *Barry nebulée of eight or and sable,* BLOUNT, 13, *Vair argent and azure,* ————; 14, *Argent, two leopards sable within a bordure semée de torteaux,* ————, 15, *Or, a triple-tower azure,* BLOUNT, 16, *Azure fretty argent,* ————

CREST.—*A griffin's head between two wings expanded gules, semée de roundles of the last*

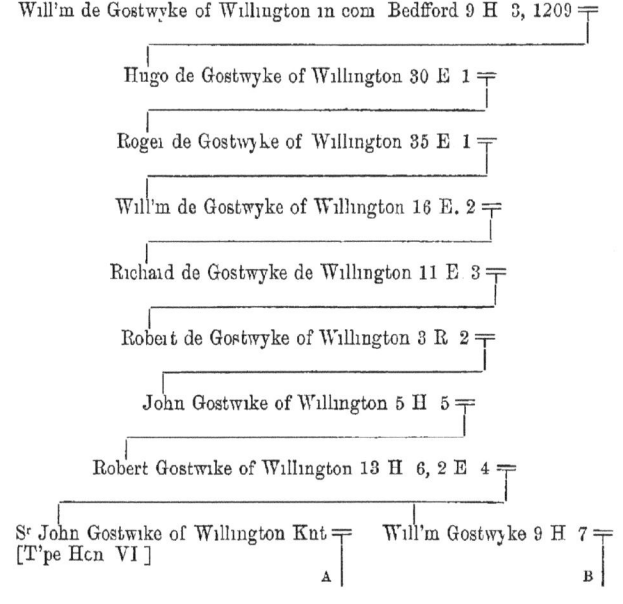

Will'm de Gostwyke of Willington in com Bedford 9 H 3, 1209 ⊤
|
Hugo de Gostwyke of Willington 30 E 1 ⊤
|
Roger de Gostwyke of Willington 35 E 1 ⊤
|
Will'm de Gostwyke of Willington 16 E. 2 ⊤
|
Richard de Gostwyke de Willington 11 E 3 ⊤
|
Robert de Gostwyke of Willington 3 R 2 ⊤
|
John Gostwike of Willington 5 H 5 ⊤
|
Robert Gostwike of Willington 13 H 6, 2 E 4 ⊤
|
Sr John Gostwike of Willington Knt ⊤   Will'm Gostwyke 9 H 7 ⊤
[T'pe Hen VI]
    A   B

---

* I have preferred to give this pedigree from Harl MS. 1531, as all the others are so meagre, and because there is no pedigree of the family entered in the subsequent Visitations
† Harl MS 5867 gives the following quarterings 1, Gostwicke, 2 Owen of Medhurst, 3 ————, 4, Bohun, 5, St John, 6, Estfield, 7, Filiol, 8, Wilkes, 9 ————, 10, ————, 11, ————, 12, Blount,

THE VISITATION OF BEDFORDSHIRE

```
                         A                              B
        ┌────────────────┴────────────┐                 │
 Edward Gostwyke =      Edmond Gostwike =     Elizebeth ux    Com-
                                               maunder of London
   ┌──────┬──────┐         ┌──────┬──────┬──────┐
 John   William  Will'm = Robert  John    Mary ux
 Gostwyke  —    Gostwyke Gostwyke Gostwyke. Miller.
         Thomas                            Dorathey ux
                                             . King

 ┌──────┬──────┬──────┬──────┬──────┐
Roger  Mary  Edward  Jane  Thomas  George
Gostwyke Gostwyke Gostwyke Gostwyke Gostwyke Gostwyke
```

Will'm Gostwike of = Anne d of   Pyke of   Sʳ John Gostwike Knt * Threaseror
Willington   Ranhall in com Bed-   of the first Fruits and Rents to
                    fford   H 8

1 Robert Gostwike of Marston = Margarett d of John   2 John.   3 Thomas
                                Taylor

    1 Will'm Gostwike   2 John Gostwike   Gertrude

4 Edward Gostwike of Shefford in =   d of   . Saunders of   in com
com Bedfford.   Surrey

Catherin d of = Will'm Gost- = Martha d of   Anne ux. Will'm   Allice ux
George Had-   wike of Shef-   Sʳ Humfrey   Clarke of Rain-   Will'm Ashwell
ley of Bark- ford   Radcliff of   wold in com   of Dunstavill
way in com   Elstow in   Bedfford   in com Bed-
Hartfford   com Bed-   fford
1 wiffe   fford.

    5 Edmond Gostwicke of Will- = Anne d of Nicholas   6 Robert   Elizebeth
    ington [of Southill in co Beds | Harding of Norwell
    —Harl MS 4600]   in com Bedfford

        1 John Gostwike of = Elizebeth d of Sʳ John Peeter   2 Will m Gostwike
        Willington   of (*Ingatestone*).
  C D   E

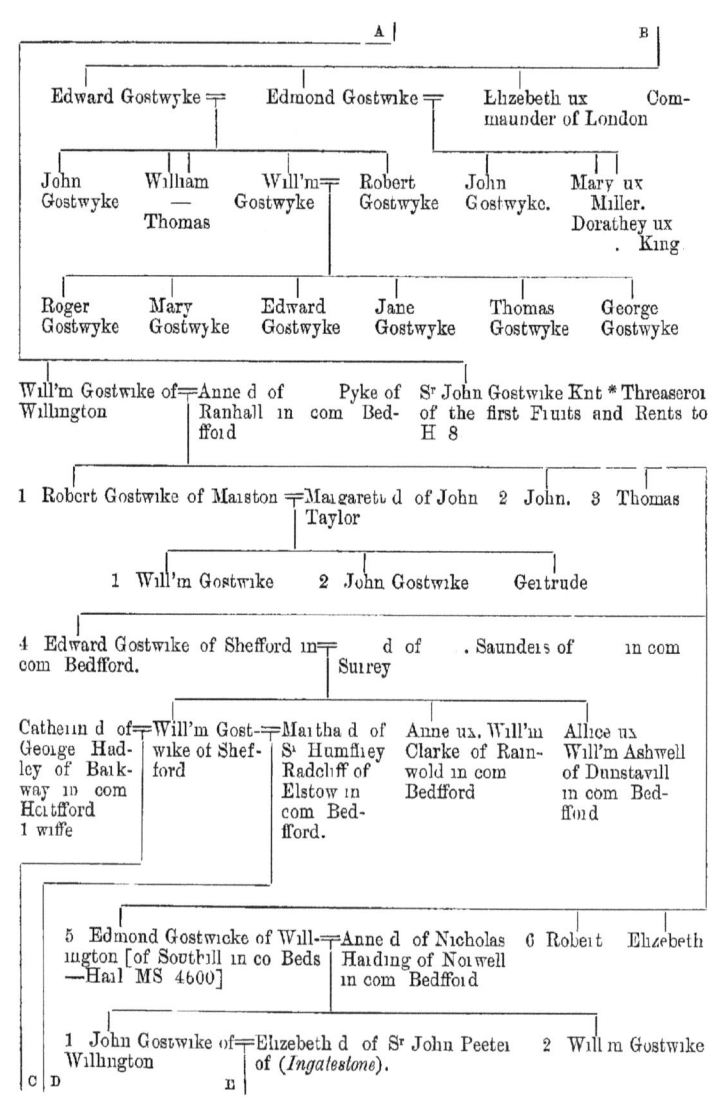

* He married Margaret, dau of Oliver, Lord St John (who remarried Francis, Earl of
Bedford) He was Master of the Horse to Cardinal Wolsey; "wherefore he haue yᵉ horses' heads
in yᵉ cheifc" (Harl MS 5867)

F

THE VISITATION OF BEDFORDSHIRE.

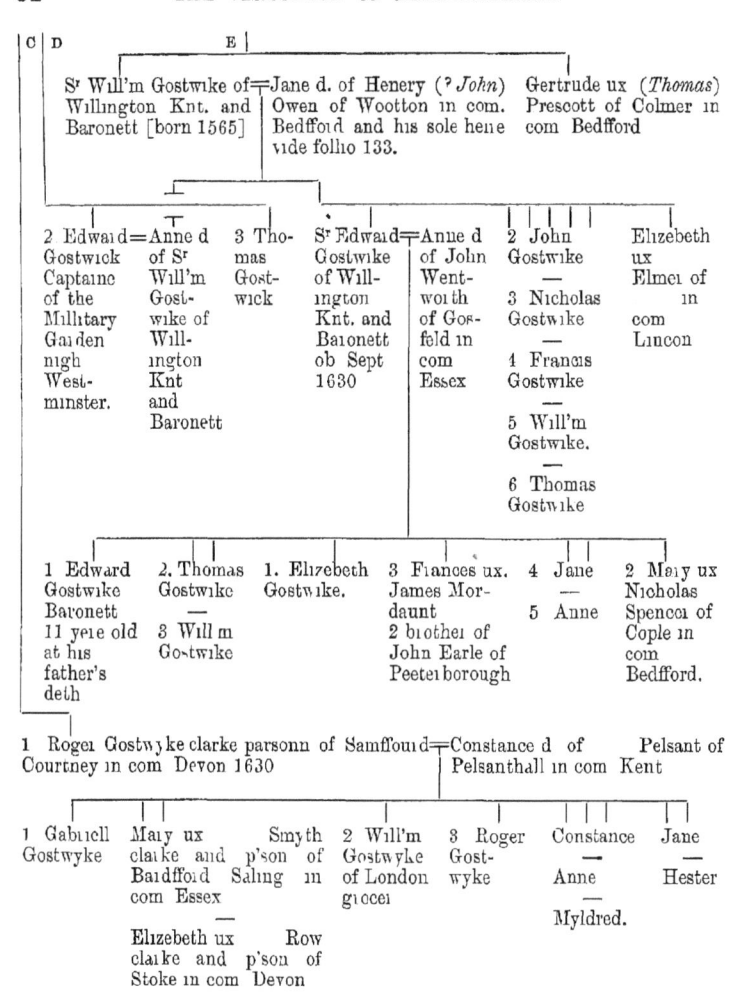

| C | D | E |

Sᵣ Will'm Gostwike of Willington Knt. and Baronett [born 1565] = Jane d. of Henery (? John) Owen of Wootton in com. Bedfford and his sole heire vide follio 133. — Gertrude ux (Thomas) Prescott of Colmer in com Bedfford

2 Edward Gostwick Captaine of the Millitary Garden nigh Westminster. = Anne d of Sʳ Will'm Gostwike of Willington Knt and Baronett

3 Thomas Gostwick

Sʳ Edward Gostwike of Willington Knt. and Baronett ob Sept 1630 = Anne d of John Wentworth of Gosfeld in com Essex

2 John Gostwike
—
3 Nicholas Gostwike
—
4 Francis Gostwike
—
5 Will'm Gostwike.
—
6 Thomas Gostwike

Elizebeth ux Elmer of in com Lincon

1 Edward Gostwike Baronett 11 yere old at his father's deth

2. Thomas Gostwike
—
3 Will m Gostwike

1. Elizebeth Gostwike.

3 Frances ux. James Mordaunt 2 brother of John Earle of Peeterborough

4 Jane
—
5 Anne

2 Mary ux Nicholas Spencer of Cople in com Bedfford.

1 Roger Gostwyke clarke parsonn of Samfford Courtney in com Devon 1630 = Constance d of Pelsant of Pelsanthall in com Kent

1 Gabriell Gostwyke

Mary ux Smyth clarke and p'son of Bardfford Saling in com Essex
—
Elizebeth ux Row clarke and p'son of Stoke in com Devon

2 Will'm Gostwyke of London grocer

3 Roger Gostwyke

Constance
—
Anne
—
Myldred.

Jane
—
Hester

Grey

[of Segenhoe].

ARMS (TWO SHIELDS).—I., *Argent, a bend vert, cotised dancettée gules*, GREY
II, *Or on a fesse vert a bull passant argent*, WOODE
CREST.—*On a wreath argent and sable a demi-woman couped at the waist argent, hair flottant or, holding above her head a wreath vert.*

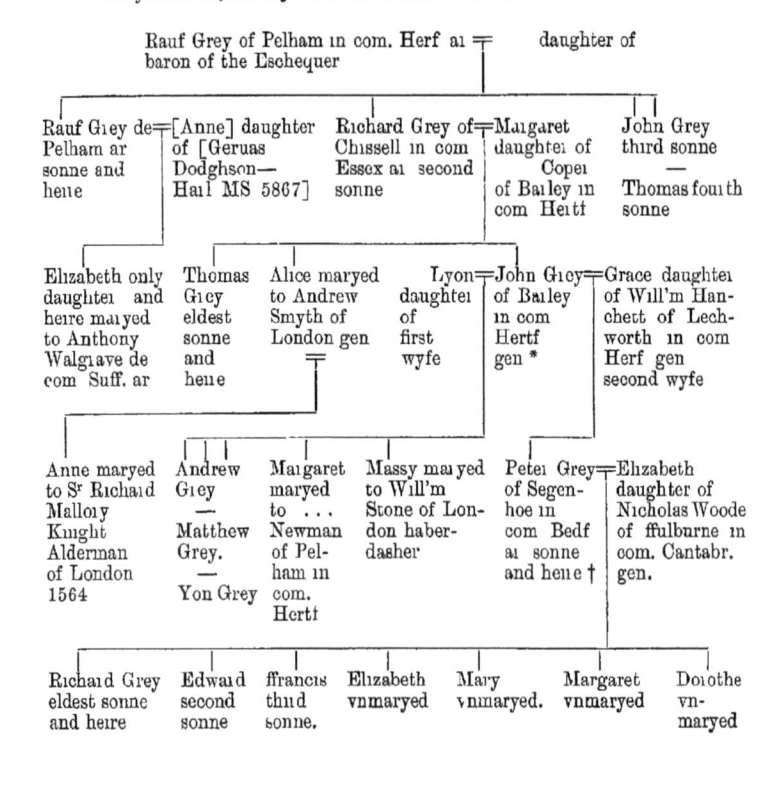

Rauf Grey of Pelham in com. Herf ar = daughter of
baron of the Eschequer

- Rauf Grey de = [Anne] daughter of [Geruas Dodghson—Harl MS 5867]
  Pelham ar sonne and heire
- Richard Grey of = Margaret daughter of Coper of Bailey in com Hertf
  Chissell in com Essex ar second sonne
- John Grey third sonne
- Thomas fourth sonne

- Elizabeth only daughter and heire maryed to Anthony Walgrave de com Suff. ar
- Thomas Grey eldest sonne and heire
- Alice maryed to Andrew Smyth of London gen =
- Lyon daughter of first wyfe
- John Grey of Bailey in com Hertf gen *
- = Grace daughter of Will'm Hanchett of Lechworth in com Herf gen second wyfe

- Anne maryed to Sr Richard Mallory Knight Alderman of London 1564
- Andrew Grey — Matthew Grey. — Yon Grey
- Margaret maryed to ... Newman of Pelham in com. Hertf
- Massy maryed to Will'm Stone of London haberdasher
- Peter Grey of Segenhoe in com Bedf ar sonne and heire †
- = Elizabeth daughter of Nicholas Woode of ffulburne in com. Cantabr. gen.

- Richard Grey eldest sonne and heire
- Edward second sonne
- ffrancis third sonne.
- Elizabeth vnmaryed
- Mary vnmaryed.
- Margaret vnmaryed
- Dorothe vnmaryed

---

* "Naturalis filius Richardi" (Harl MS 5867, in a different hand.)
† In Harl MS 5867 and Lsham MS Peter is made son by the *first* wife, the other children by the *second* wife.

Hervy

[of Thurleigh].

ARMS (TWO SHIELDS)—I, *Quarterly of four*—1 *and* 4, *Gules, on a bend argent three trefoils slipped vert*, HERVY, 2 *and* 3, *Sable, a lion rampant argent within a bordure gobony of the second and first*, NEYRNUTE II (*sinister side*), *Quarterly of ten*—1, *Gules, a saltire ermine*, NEVILL, 2, *Or fretty gules, on a canton per pale ermine and or a ship sable*, NEVILL, 3, *Gules billetée or, a lion rampant of the second*, BULMER, 4, *Gules, three bendlets vert, over all a chevron ermine*, , 5, *Or, two bars counter-nebulée sable, a canton ermine*, , 6, *Azure, a fleur-de-lys argent*, , 7, *Or, a chevron gules, a canton ermine*, , 8, *Or, a chevron gules, a chief indented vert*, , 9, *Argent, a saltire gules, a mullet for difference*, , 10, *Azure, a cross fleury or*,

CREST—*A leopard passant sable, spotted or, collared gules, holding a trefoil vert*

[Henery Harvey lived temp R 1]=
    |
[Henery Harvey lived 2 K John]=[Ciceley]
    |
[Osbert de Hervey ob 7 K. John]=
    |
[Adam Hervey 8 H 3]=[Julian d and heire of John Fitzhugh.]
    |
[John Hervey of Thirley in com Bedfford ob 25 E 1]=[Joane d of John Harman of Thirley in co Bedford Esq—Vol XIV, p 735.]
    |
[Will'm Harvey of Thirley ob 50 E 3]=[Mary d and heire of Richard Folliot]
    |
[Sr] John Harvy of Thurly in com Bedf ar [Knt]=[Margaret] (*read Joanne*) daughter and one of the heires of Sr John Neyrnute of ffletemaison in com Bucks Knight
    |
[John Harvey of Thirley Esq]=[Margery d of Sr Will'm Calthrop Knt ob. 5 H 6]
    |
[Thom Harvey of Thurley Esq]=[Jane d. of Will'm Paston]
    |
Thomas [John] Hervy of Thurly in com Bedf ar sonne and heire=Christian daughter of John Chicheley Chamberleyn of London

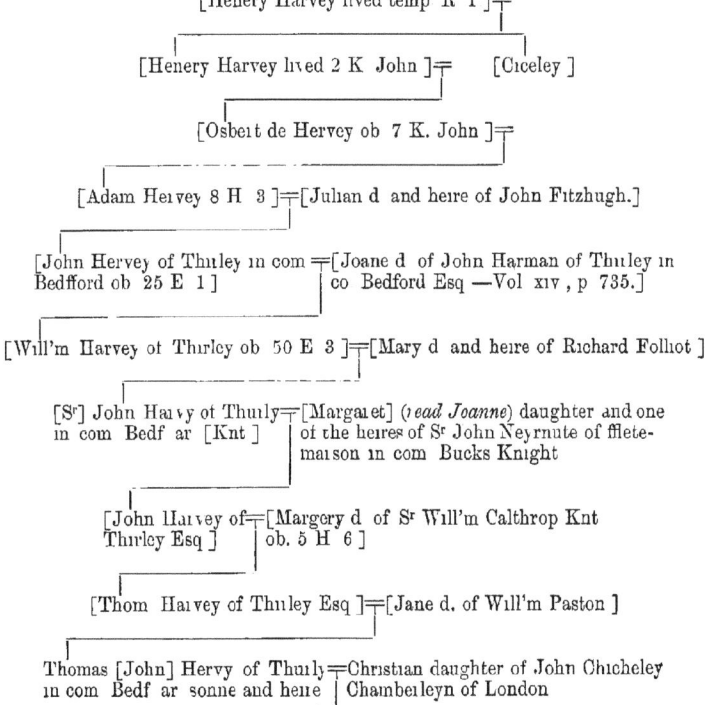

A

THE VISITATION OF BEDFORDSHIRE.

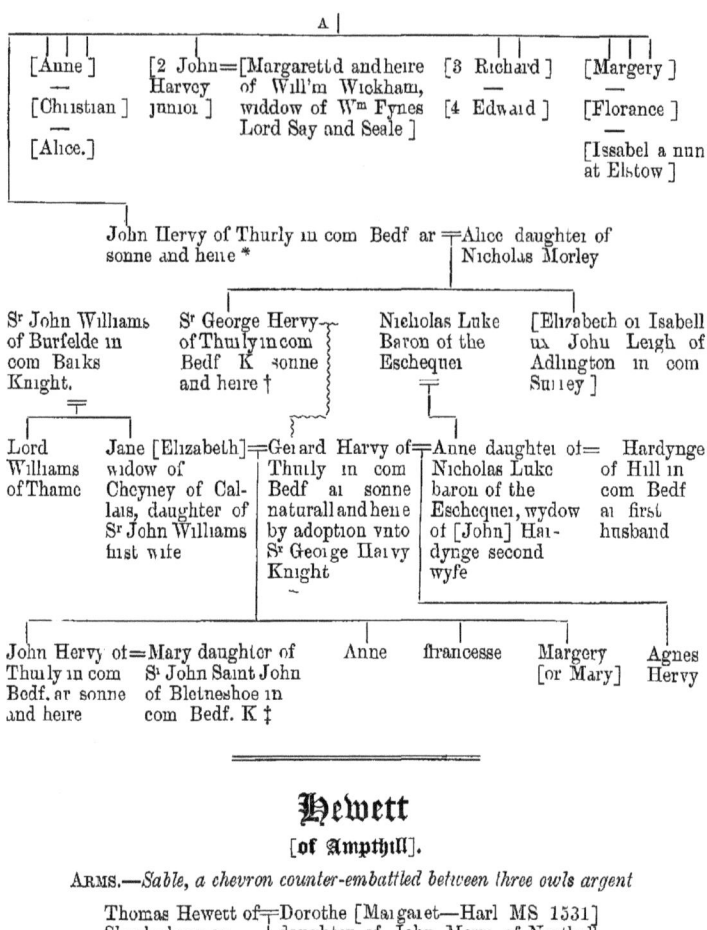

A

| [Anne] [Christian] [Alice.] | [2 John = [Margarett d and heire Harvey of Will'm Wickham, junior] widdow of Wm Fynes Lord Say and Seale] | [3 Richard] [4 Edward] | [Margery] [Florance] [Issabel a nun at Elstow] |

John Hervy of Thurly in com Bedf ar = Alice daughter of
sonne and heire *   Nicholas Morley

Sr John Williams of Burfelde in com Barks Knight. — Lord Williams of Thame

Sr George Hervy of Thurly in com Bedf K sonne and heire †

Jane [Elizabeth] widow of Cheyney of Callais, daughter of Sr John Williams first wife

= Gerard Harvy of Thurly in com Bedf ar sonne naturall and heire by adoption vnto Sr George Harvy Knight

Nicholas Luke Baron of the Escheqner

= Anne daughter of Nicholas Luke baron of the Escheqner, wydow of [John] Hardynge second wyfe

[Elizabeth or Isabell ux John Leigh of Adlington in com Surrey]

= Hardynge of Hill in com Bedf ar first husband

John Hervy of Thurly in com Bedf. ar sonne and heire

= Mary daughter of Sr John Saint John of Bletneshoe in com Bedf. K ‡

Anne   ffrancesse   Margery [or Mary]   Agnes Hervy

Hewett
[of Ampthill].

ARMS.—*Sable, a chevron counter-embattled between three owls argent*

Thomas Hewett of Shenleybury in com Herff ar

= Dorothe [Margaret—Harl MS 1531] daughter of John Merry of Northall in com Hertf gen

Robert Hewett of Ampthell in com Bedf ar sonne and heire
A

= Margery daughter of Tylton de com Cestr.

---

* *A quo* the Harveys of Ickworth in Suffolk *Cf* 'Visitations of Suffolk,' p 39 (ed W C Metcalfe, 1882), and 'Visitations of Essex, Harl Soc vol xiii, p 214
† Harl MS 1531 states that he married " Elizabeth (*or Margaret*) d and coheire of John Stamfford of   "
‡ See note, *ante*, p 10

THE VISITATION OF BEDFORDSHIRE

A

- Will'm Hewett of Mylbrooke in com Bedf ar sonne and heire unm
- Edmond second sonne
- Arthure third sonne
- Robert fourth sonne
- Anne maryed to Thomas Awdeley of Hovghton Conquest in com Bedf. gen

- [Margaret ux Robert ffaldo of Malden in com Bedford Esqr]
- Dorothe maryed to Richard Conquest of Hovghton Conquest in com Bedf gen.
- Elizabeth vnmaryed.

Hunte
[of Chalverston].

ARMS —*Argent, on a chevron within a bordure bezantée gules an annulet or.*
CREST —*On a wreath or and azure a talbot sejeant sable, collared and lined or, in front of an oak-tree azure, fructed or*

Roger Hunte of Chalversterne in com Bedff == daughter ar Baron of the Eschequer — of

Roger* Hunte of Chalversterne == Elizabeth daughter of ——— Taylarde sonne and heire † | of Diddington in com Hunt ar

Roger Hunte of Chalversterne == Mary daughter of Thomas Wauton sonne and heire ‡ | of Basmey in com Bedf ar.

- Thomas Hunte of Chalversterne sonne and heire == Alice daughter of Will'm Hill of Maldon in com. Bedf gen
- Roger second sonne
- Gregory third sonne
- Edward fourth sonne

- Will'm Hunte of Chalversterne in com Bedf sonne and heire § == Jane daughter of John Russell of Lynslade in com Buck
- Saxburge maryed to Thomas Kynge of Rocksonne in com Bedf
- Anne maryed to John Walker of Mylton in com Rutland
- Barbara maryed to Robert Gray of Stapelhoe in com Bedf

- [Joane ux Tho. Wright of Chalversterne]
- [2 Mary]
- [3 Margaret]
- [4 Joane]
- [Roger Hunt eld. s and heire]
- [Thomas 2 sonne]

---

* MS 541, Caius Coll Cambs, omits this generation.
† "Sonne and heire Esqr, ob 28 H 6" (Harl MS 4600)
‡ "Esqr, a° 8 Hen 7 et 1° R 3" (*Ibid*)
§ "Fil et her 2° Eliz" (*Ibid*)

Luke
[of Copley].

ARMS (TWO SHIELDS) —1, Quarterly-quartered First and Fourth Grand Quarters—1 and 4, Argent, a buglehorn sable stringed of the same, tasselled or, LUKE; 2 and 3, Gules, a fleur-de-lys argent, LAUNCELYN; Second and Third Grand Quarters—1 and 4, Argent, a chevron sable, in the dexter chief quarter an annulet of the second for difference, WAUTON; 2 and 3, Sable crusily fitchée, three lions rampant argent, two in chief, one in base, PRFUX II (sinster side), Quarterly of four—1 and 4, Sable, a chevron between three bulls' heads cabossed argent, BULKELEY; 2 and 3, Quarterly-quartered—1 and 4, Argent on a chief gules two stags' heads cabossed or, . 2 and 3, Gules bezantee, a chevron argent,

CREST —On a wreath argent and sable a bull's head azure, ringed or

Sr Walter Luke of Coupley = Anne daughter and one of the heires = [Will m in com Bedford Knight of [Sr Thos —MS 541] Launcelyn of Oxenbridg one of the Judges of the the same place and countie ar [She 1 husband] Kinges benche was nurse to H VIII and ob 1538]

Nicholas Luke of Coupley a baron = Cicely daughter and one of the heires of the Exchequer [only—Hail MS of Sr Thomas Wawton of Basney in 5867] sonne and heire com Bedf Knight

Walter Luke = Anne wydow to	John Luke	Jane maryed Will'm	[Elizabeth
of Coupley in	Thomas Spencer,	eldest sonne	Bulkeley of Burgett	ux Chad
com Bedf	daughter of	and heire †	in com South ar.	Cockayne
gen second	Robert Boulkeley	—	—	of Hatley
sonne *	of Burgett in	Powle third	Anne maryed to John	in com
	com South ar	sonne ‡	Hardynge of Norrell	Bedfford]
	[1 wifle]		in com Bedf gen	

Olyver Luke sonne and heire [ob s p] — [Elizabeth d of Simon Scudamore of Finchley in com Middlesex] = Nicholas second sonne [of Payton (? Paxton) parva in com Hunt]. = [Elizabeth d of Thom Crompton of Lound in com Sallop] — [3 Edward Luke]

[Anne] [Oliver]

[Anne ux Edward Collins of London] — [Elizabeth ux Will'm Francis of Abbotesley in com. .] — [Mary ux Edward Bernard of Barnett.] — [Oliver Luke] — [Nicholas Luke] — [Scudamore Luke ob s p quere whet sonn he was 1 or 3]

---

* According to Hail MS 1531 ne m for his second wife "Bridgitt d of Thom. Parris of Hitchin in com Hertford widow of Will'm Walton,' and had issue by her
† A quo Luke of Woodend, see Additional Pedigrees post
‡ Cf Visitation of Huntingdonshire,' Camd Soc, p 60

Martyn

[of Crekers].

ARMS (TWO SHIELDS)—I, *Quarterly of four*—1 *and* 4, *Per pale argent and gules, on a chevron between three mullets as many talbots, all counterchanged*, MARTYN, 2 *and* 3, *Argent, on a bend between two lions rampant sable a wyvern, wings expanded of the field*, RUDING II (sinister side), *Quarterly*—1 *and* 4, *Argent, on a chief indented sable three covered cups or*, BUTLER, 2 *and* 3 (not blazoned)

```
John Martyn of Wiche === Margaret daughter and one of the heires of Humfrey
in com Wigorn gen         Rudinge of Wiche in com Wigorn ar
        |
 ┌──────┴────────────────────────┐
Gilbert Martyn of Crekers === Catherine daughter of George    John second sonne
in com Bedford sonne and     Butteller of Sharnbroke in       [sans yssue—Harl.
heire                        com Bedf. ar.                    MS 5867]
        |
 ┌──────┬───────────┬──────────┬──────────┬──────────────┐
Robert Martyn  George second  Clement third  John fourth  John the yonger
sonne and heire.  sonne.       sonne.         sonne        fifte sonne
        |
 ┌──────┬──────┬─────────┬──────────┐
Margaret  Jane  Anne  Crestide.  Catherine *
```

Mordaunt†

[of Turvey].

ARMS—*Quarterly of eight*—1, *Argent, a chevron between three estoiles sable*, MORDAUNT, 2 *Quarterly per pale indented or and gules, in the first and fourth quarters five lozenges in cross counterchanged*, DANXO, 3, *Argent on a bend sable a hawk's lure, the line wavy in bend or*, BROOKE, 4, *Quarterly per fesse indented or and azure, in the first quarter a crescent for difference*, PYROTT, 5, *Or, a cross lozengy argent, in the first quarter on an escutcheon of the second an eagle displayed gules*, ARGENTYNE 6, *Gules, an eagle displayed argent within a bordure engrailed or* LESTRANGE, 7, *Gules, a cross patoncée or*, LATYMER, 8, *Quarterly-quartered*—1 *and* 4, *Argent, a cross engrailed sable*, DRAYTON, 2 *and* 3, *Chequy or and azure, a bordure gules*, MAUDUIT *impaling, Quarterly of four*—1, *Argent, three boars' heads erect and erased sable*, BOOTH; 2, *Argent, a chevron gules between three leopards faces sable*, FROWICKE, 3, *Gules, three cinqfoils argent*, FARINGTON, 4, *Argent, a cross engrailed sable between four torteaux*, CLAYTON

* "All vnmarved" (Harl. MS 5867.)
† On ff. 27ᵇ and 28 is another pedigree of Mordaunt but, as all is included within this, I have not thought it worth while to insert it here—ED. Cf. 'Visitations of Essex,' Harl. Soc., vol xiii, p 253

THE VISITATION OF BEDFORDSHIRE.

CREST.—*On a wreath or and azure a Blackamoor's head affrontée, couped at the shoulders, vested sable, bordered or, banded with a wreath round the temples or and gules, and ribbons of the same*

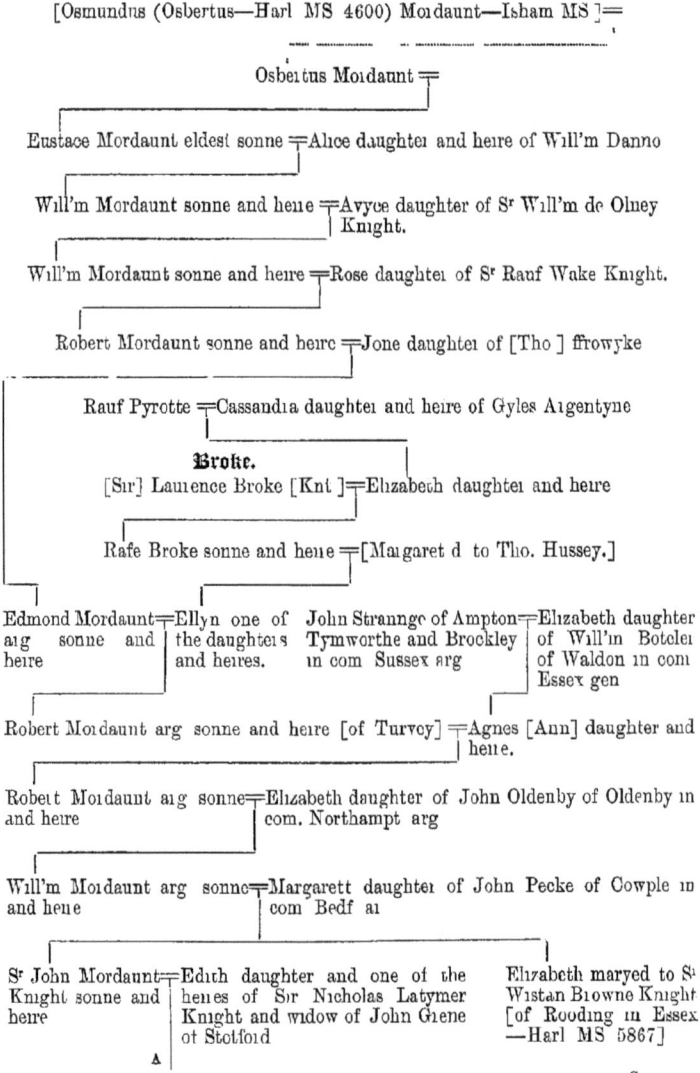

[Osmundus (Osbertus—Harl MS 4600) Mordaunt—Isham MS]=

Osbertus Mordaunt =

Eustace Mordaunt eldest sonne = Alice daughter and heire of Will'm Danno

Will'm Mordaunt sonne and heire = Avyce daughter of S⁰ Will'm de Olney Knight.

Will'm Mordaunt sonne and heire = Rose daughter of S⁰ Rauf Wake Knight.

Robert Mordaunt sonne and heire = Jone daughter of [Tho.] ffrowyke

Rauf Pyrotte = Cassandra daughter and heire of Gyles Argentyne

Broke.
[Sir] Laurence Broke [Knt.] = Elizabeth daughter and heire

Rafe Broke sonne and heire = [Margaret d. to Tho. Hussey.]

Edmond Mordaunt = Ellyn one of   John Strannge of Ampton = Elizabeth daughter
arg   sonne   and   the daughters   Tymworthe and Brockley   of Will'm Botcler
heire   and heires.   in com Sussex arg   of Waldon in com
                                                               Essex gen

Robert Mordaunt arg sonne and heire [of Turvey] = Agnes [Ann] daughter and heire.

Robert Mordaunt arg sonne = Elizabeth daughter of John Oldenby of Oldenby in
and heire   com. Northampt arg

Will'm Mordaunt arg sonne = Margarett daughter of John Pecke of Cowple in
and heire   com Bedf ar

S⁰ John Mordaunt = Edith daughter and one of the   Elizabeth maryed to S⁰
Knight sonne and   heires of Sir Nicholas Latymer   Wistan Browne Knight
heire   Knight and widow of John Grene   [of Rooding in Essex
                   of Stotfold   —Harl MS 5867]

                                    A
                                    |
John Lord Mordaunt==Elizabeth daughter and   Will'm   Jane maryed to Gyles
of Turvey in com | one of the heires of,   second   Strangways of Hynd-
Bedf | Henry Veer of greate   sonne *   forde in com Dorsett
                  | Adington in com North-   arg
                  | ampt arg

Edmond	Edith maryed to	Margaret maryed	Etheldred a nonne	Wynvfride
[alibi	John Elmys of	to Edmond ffeti-	at Barkinge	maried to
Edward]	Lyleford in com	place of Besilles		John
second	Northampt arg	Lye in com	Elizabeth maryed	Cheyney of
sonne	—	Berks arg.	to Silvester Dan-	Chesham
sans	Anne first	—	vers of Dawntesey	Boyse in
yssue	maryed to John	Dorothie maryed	in com Wilt arg	com
—	ffisshar of Clifton	to Thomas More		Bucks arg
George	in com Bedf ar	of Whaddon in		
fourth	after to John	com Cantebridge		
sonne.†	Rodney de com	arg [Bampton in		
	Som'sett gen	com Oxon]		

ffarington.

S' Henry ffarington of ffarington in==   John Clayton of Clayton Hall in==
com Lancastr. Knight | com. Lanc arg |
                              | |
                              |_____|
                                                      |
Will'm ffarington of ffarington in com Lanc. arg ==Isabell daughter and heire
sonne and heire

Booth.

Charles Bouthe of the Bisshopricke of Durham arg ‡==Jane daughter and sole
                                                    | heire

John Lord Mordaunt==Ela daughter and heire   William Mordaunt of==Agnes
of Turvey in com | of Richard ffitzlewys of Okeley in com Bedf | daughter
Bed § sonne and | Thornton in com Es-   arg third sonne to | and heire
heire | sex [nenupt S' Thos   John Lord Mordaunt
                  | Kemp of . Knt]

Lewys Mordaunt eldest   Edmond Mordaunt   Jane   Awdrey   Anne
sonne and heire ap-   eldest sonne ||
parannt.   Elizabeth

_____

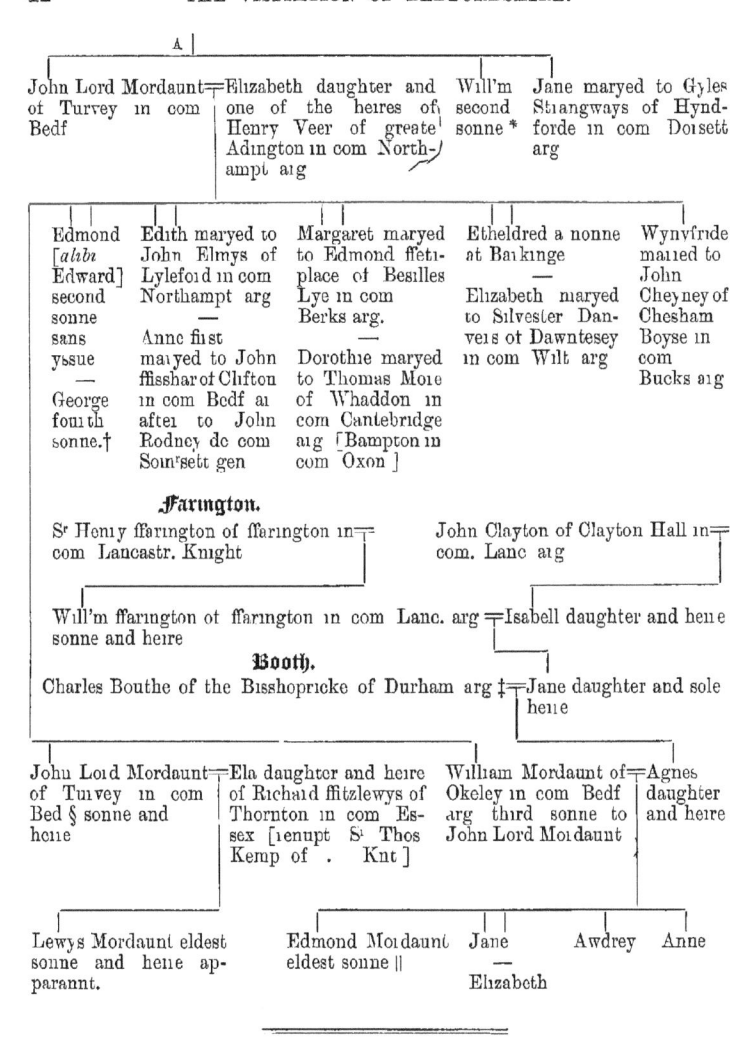

* *A quo* the Mordaunts of Norfolk *cf* Harl MS 4600
† *A quo* the Mordaunts of Thunderley in Essex, *cf* Harl MS 4600 and the Mordaunts of
Northill, *cf* Visitation of 1634, *post*
‡ "The aforesaid Charles Boothe was brother and heire to John Boothe, brother to Thomas
Boothe, sonne and heire to Roger Boothe of Sawleferrye in com Darbye, Esquire." (Isham MS)
§ ' Of Thornton in com Essex " (Harl MS 5867)
|| *A quo* the Mordaunts of Oakley, see Additional Pedigrees, *post*

Neyle

[of Drane].

ARMS (TWO SHIELDS) —I , *Per pale sable and gules, a lion passant-guardant argent*, NEYLE II (sinister side), *Per saltire argent and azure, in pale two moorcocks of the first, in fesse as many escallops or*, MORE

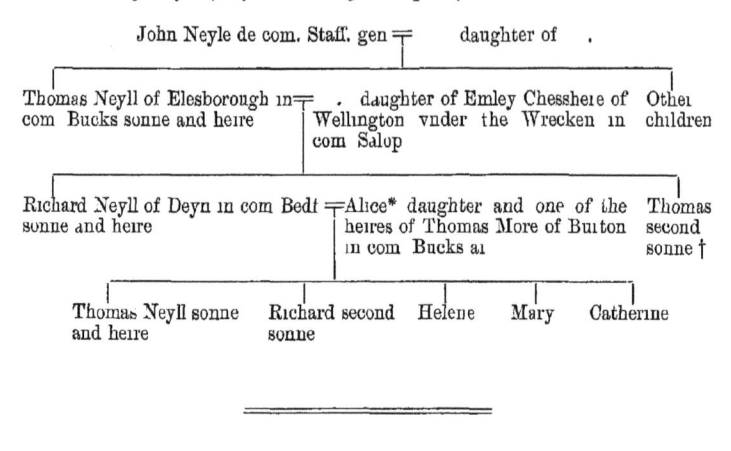

John Neyle de com. Staff. gen = daughter of .

- Thomas Neyll of Elesborough in com Bucks sonne and heire = . daughter of Emley Chesshere of Wellington vnder the Wrecken in com Salop
- Other children

- Richard Neyll of Deyn in com Bedf sonne and heire = Alice* daughter and one of the heires of Thomas More of Burton in com Bucks ar
- Thomas second sonne †

  - Thomas Neyll sonne and heire
  - Richard second sonne
  - Helene
  - Mary
  - Catherine

Neyll

[of Yielden].

ARMS (TWO SHIELDS) —I , *Per pale sable and gules, a lion passant-guardant argent, a crescent for difference*, NEYLL II (sinister side), *Quarterly of four— 1 and 4, Azure, three covered cups or*, BUTLER , *2, Gules fretty argent, a fesse azure*, , *3, Argent, three cocks in fesse sable, armed gules*, .
CREST —*A demi-lion argent, collared and chained sable.* (Isham MS.)

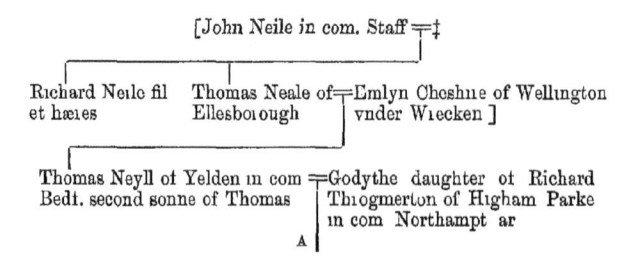

[John Neile in com. Staff = ‡

- Richard Neile fil et hæres
- Thomas Neale of Ellesborough = Emlyn Cheshire of Wellington vnder Wrecken]

  - Thomas Neyll of Yelden in com Bedf. second sonne of Thomas = Godythe daughter of Richard Throgmerton of Higham Parke in com Northampt ar
    A

---

* " Q're si Alicia non fuit vx Tho. et mat librorum p' eund'm Thomam " (Harl. MS. 5186.)
† See next pedigree.   ‡ In a different hand.

THE VISITATION OF BEDFORDSHIRE.

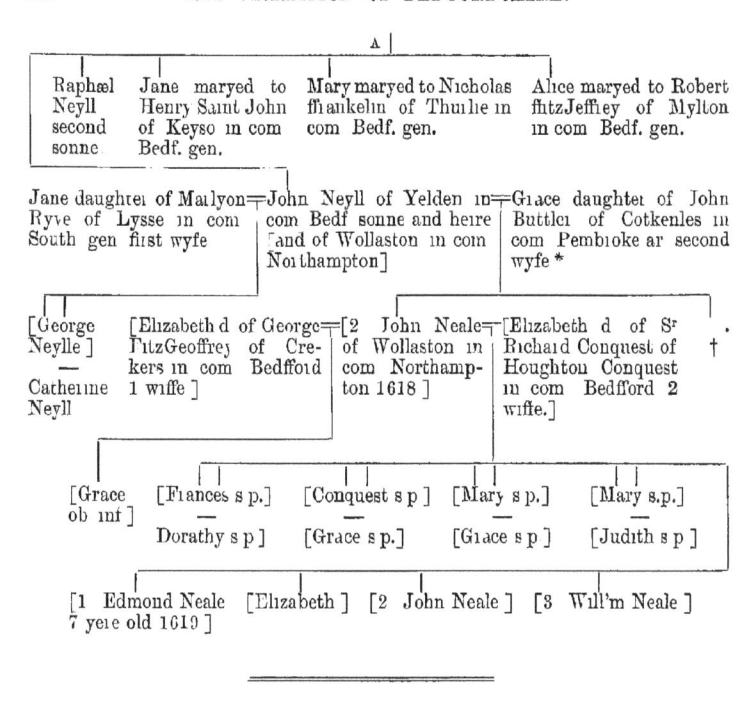

Raphæl Neyll second sonne —|— Jane maryed to Henry Saint John of Keyso in com Bedf. gen. —|— Mary maryed to Nicholas ffrankelin of Thurlie in com Bedf. gen. —|— Alice maryed to Robert fitzJeffrey of Mylton in com Bedf. gen.

Jane daughter of Marlyon Ryve of Lysse in com South gen first wyfe = John Neyll of Yelden in com Bedf sonne and heire [and of Wollaston in com Northampton] = Grace daughter of John Buttler of Cotkenles in com Pembroke ar second wyfe *

[George Neylle] — Catherine Neyll | [Elizabeth d of George FitzGeoffrey of Crekers in com Bedfford 1 wiffe] = [2 John Neale of Wollaston in com Northampton 1618] = [Elizabeth d of Sr Richard Conquest of Houghton Conquest in com Bedfford 2 wiffe.] †

[Grace ob inf] | [Frances s p.] — Dorathy s p] | [Conquest s p] — [Grace s p.] | [Mary s p.] — [Grace s p] | [Mary s.p.] — [Judith s p]

[1 Edmond Neale 7 yere old 1619] [Elizabeth] [2 John Neale] [3 Will'm Neale]

Page

[of Arlesey].

ARMS (TWO SHIELDS)—I (sinister side), Argent, on a cross engrailed per pale gules and sable five escallops or, BROOKE II, Quarterly of four—1 and 4, Or, a fesse dancettée between three martlets azure, PAGE, 2, Azure, three bucks trippant or, a bend sinister argent, GREENE, 3, Gules, a cross fleurée or, LATIMER

CREST—On a wreath or and azure a demi-horse per pale dancettée or and azure, crined or

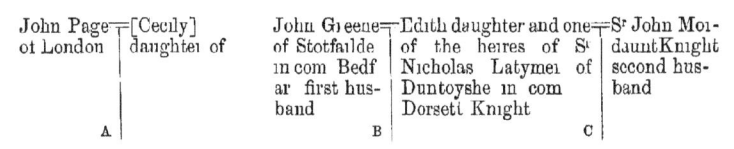

John Page of London =|= [Cecily] daughter of | John Greene of Stotfailde in com Bedf ar first husband =|= Edith daughter and one of the heires of St Nicholas Latymer of Duntoyshe in com Dorsett Knight =|= Sr John Mordaunt Knight second husband

A | B | C

* "And by her at this tyme had no yssue" (Harl MS 5867)
† In Harl MS 1531 several other children and descents are given, for which see Additional Pedigrees *post*

THE VISITATION OF BEDFORDSHIRE.

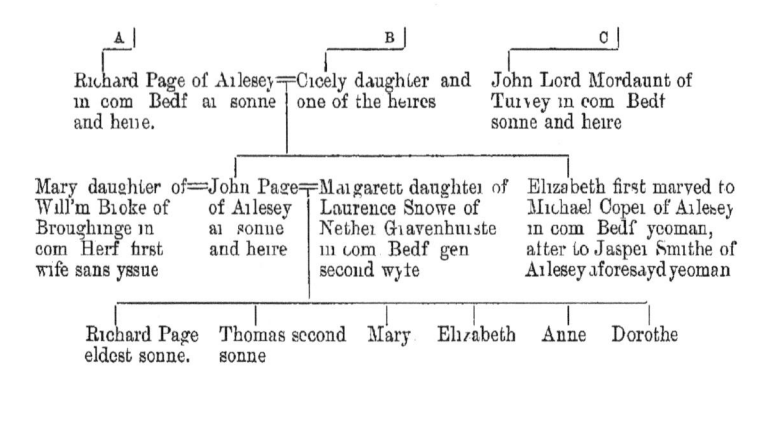

A | Richard Page of Ailesey in com Bedf ar sonne and heire. = B | Cicely daughter and one of the heires   C | John Lord Mordaunt of Turvey in com Bedf sonne and heire

Mary daughter of Will'm Broke of Broughinge in com Herf first wife sans yssue = John Page of Ailesey ar sonne and heire = Margarett daughter of Laurence Snowe of Nether Gravenhurste in com Bedf gen second wyfe   Elizabeth first marved to Michael Coper of Ailesey in com Bedf yeoman, after to Jasper Smithe of Ailesey aforesayd yeoman

Richard Page eldest sonne. — Thomas second sonne — Mary — Elizabeth — Anne — Dorothe

Penn
[of Litlington].

ARMS —*Quarterly*—1 *and* 4, *Argent, on a fesse gules, between three pavones proper, a lion passant-reguardant or between two small tooth-combs of the field,* PENN ; 2 *and* 3, *Or, three nags' heads couped sable, bridled argent,* CHEVALL
CREST —*On a wreath argent and azure a demi-lion rampant gules, in his paws a small tooth-comb azure*

John Penn of Coddecott in com Herff ar grome of the chamber to Kinge Henry the eight and his cheif barbo^r = Lucy daughter and heire of Edmond Chevall of Coddycott in com Herff ar.

Robert second sonne — John third sonne — Helene maryed to .. Barre — Elizabeth vnmaryed — Dorothe vnmaryed

Thomas Penn of Litelington in com Bedf ar sonne and heire = Margery daughter of Thomas Saunders of Agmondesham in com Bucks gen

John Penne eldest sonne and heire — Suzan — Mary — Alice [Lucy]

Pudsey
[of Stotfold].

ARMS.—*Vert, a chevron between three mullets or, a mullet of the second for difference.*
CREST.—*A cat passant proper*

John Pudsey of Rygton in com Ebor = Margaret daughter of Thomas Dickson of third sonne to John Pudsey gen | Stayneborne in com Essex.*

- Richard second sonne
- John third sonne
- Margaret maryed to Thomas Smyth yeoman
- Jone maryed to Thomas [John—Isham MS] ffowler of Rigton in com Ebor yeoman

Thomas Pudsey of Stotfolde in com = Catherine daughter of John Butler
Beds gen sonne and heire | of Waresley in com Hunt gen

John Pudsey eldest sonne and heire.

Pygott
[of Stratton and Holme].

ARMS (TWO SHIELDS)—I, *Quarterly—1 and 4, Sable, three pickaxes argent*, PYGOTT, *2 and 3, Argent, three bugle-horns, stringed sable, a crescent gules for difference,* FORSTER II (dexter side), *Quarterly—1 and 4,* PYGOTT *2 and 3, Argent, three bars dancettée sable, in chief a pale ermine, a crescent for difference,* ENDERBY
CREST.—*On a wreath or and azure a greyhound couchant sable, collared argent, charged on the breast with three millpicks of the fourth*

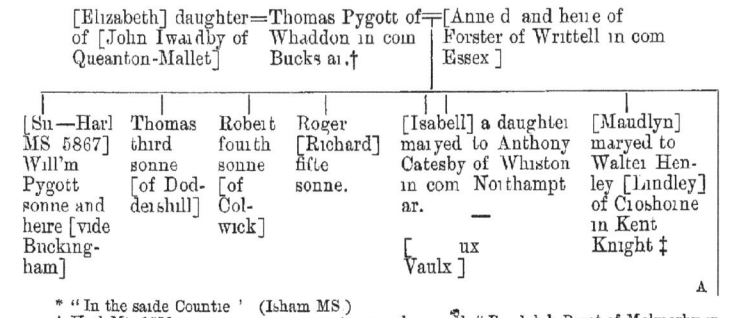

[Elizabeth] daughter = Thomas Pygott of = [Anne d and heire of
of [John Iwardby of | Whaddon in com | Forster of Writtell in com
Queanton-Mallet] | Bucks ar.† | Essex]

- [Sir—Harl MS 5867] Will'm Pygott sonne and heire [vide Buckingham]
- Thomas third sonne [of Dodershill]
- Robert fourth sonne [of Colwick]
- Roger [Richard] fifte sonne.
- [Isabell] a daughter maryed to Anthony Catesby of Whiston in com Northampt ar.
  —
  [ux Vaulx]
- [Maudlyn] maryed to Walter Henley [Lindley] of Croshorne in Kent Knight ‡

A

* " In the saide Countie " (Isham MS)
† Harl MS 1531 commences six generations earlier, with " Randolph Pigot of Melmarby in com York temp E III " Cf ' Genealogist,' II , 294
‡ In Harl MS 1531 Maudlyn is said to have married, 1,   Cotton of com Cambridge , 2 to Sir Walter Lyndley of Kent, 3, to   Warden of Kent, 4, to . . . . Roberts of Sussex.

THE VISITATION OF BEDFORDSHIRE. 47

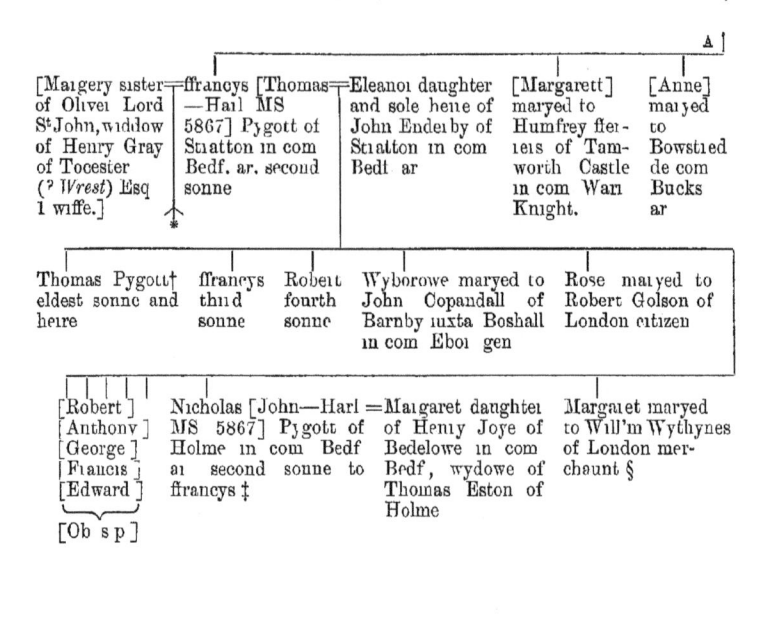

```
                                                                                    A
[Margery sister=ffrancys [Thomas=Eleanor daughter   [Margarett]      [Anne]
of Oliver Lord  —Harl MS       and sole heire of   maryed to        maryed
St John, widdow 5867] Pygott of John Enderby of    Humfrey fler-    to
of Henry Gray   Stratton in com Stratton in com    iers of Tam-     Bowstred
of Tocester     Bedf. ar. second Bedf ar           worth Castle     de com
(? Wrest) Esq   sonne                              in com War       Bucks
1 wiffe.]                                          Knight.          ar

Thomas Pygott†   ffrancys  Robert   Wyborowe maryed to     Rose maryed to
eldest sonne and third     fourth   John Copandall of      Robert Golson of
heire            sonne     sonne    Barnby iuxta Boshall   London citizen
                                    in com Ebor gen

[Robert ]     Nicholas [John—Harl =Margaret daughter    Margaret maryed
[Anthony]     MS 5867] Pygott of   of Henry Joye of     to Will'm Wythynes
[George ]     Holme in com Bedf    Bedelowe in com      of London mer-
[Francis ]    ar second sonne to   Bedf, wydowe of      chaunt §
[Edward ]     ffrancys ‡           Thomas Eston of
                                   Holme
[Ob s p ]
```

Radcliffe

[of Elstow].

ARMS —*Quarterly of eight*—1, *Argent, a bend engrailed sable*, RATCLIFFE , 2, *Or, a fesse between two chevronells gules*, FITZWALTER 3, *Argent, a lion rampant sable, crowned or, within a bordure azure*, BURNELL , 4, *Or, a saltire engrailed sable*, BORETOURT , 5, *Gules, three lucies hauriant argent*, LUCYE 6, *Argent, three bars gules*, MULTON 7, *Or, semée of fleurs-de-lys sable*, ? MORTYMER 8, *Argent, an eagle sable, membered gules, standing on a child proper, lying in a cradle vert, swaddled or*, COULCHEIFE

    * See Additional Pedigrees, *post*
    † 'Sr Tho Pigott eldest son and h , was of Stratton, Kt, high shreife of Bedd mar to his 1t wife Ann, da of Sr Richard Riche, Lord Chaunceler of England, and had issu Mickells of com 1594, 1t son, Oliuer, John, and other children , and by his 2d wife he had issu Lewis, John and daughters
    Mickell, 1t son, had issu Tho 1 Geo 2, Beniamin 3d, Eustace 4 Rich 5, Clement 6, and 5 daughters' (Harl MS 5867, in Randle Holme's hand)
    ‡ ' And ov her hath no yssue " (Isham MS)
    § 'William Withers of London p'ronathery at Law ' (Harl MS 1531)

THE VISITATION OF BEDFORDSHIRE.

[Sr] John [Radcliffe] Lord ffitzwalter.

- Elizabeth daughter of [Hen Stafford] Duke of Buckingham first wyfe
- Robert Lord ffitzwalter first Erle of Sussex
- Margaret sister to th' Erle of Derby second wyfe
- Mary daughter of Sr John Arundell of Lanherne in com Cornub. third wyfe

Children:
- Anne maryed to Sr Thomas Wharton
- Mary maryed to Sr Anthony Browne Knight after Viscount Montague
- Sr John Radclift Knight now lyvinge = [(Ann) d. of (Thomas) Bennolte]

- Henry [Humffrey] Erle of Sussex eldest sonne
- George second sonne dyed sans yssue.
- Sr Humfrey* Radcliff of Elstowe in com. Bedf Knight third sonne = Isabell daughter and heire of Edmond Hervy [of Elstow by Margaret d. of Sr Gyles Wentworth Knt] fourth son to Will'm Hervy.

- Thomas Radcliff eldest sonne [ob s p]
- Edward second sonne
- Mary ffrancesse
- Elizabeth mar to Henry Owen of Wotton in com Surr † arg. sonne and heire to third sonne to Sr Davy Owen Knight
- Martha Owen

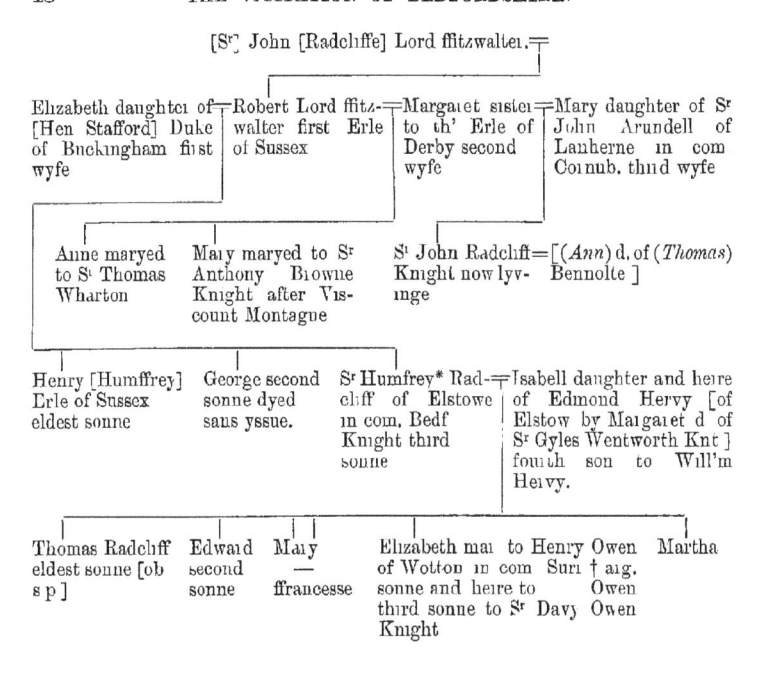

Randes

[of Radwell in Felmersham].

[Note that this man standeth vpon his further tryall, for his Armes are vncertaine and not yet knowen.—Harl MS 5867 and Isham MS ‡]

Radwell.

John Radwell =

- Thomas Randes of Radwell in com Bedf gen. **A**
- Margery cousin and heire to Thomas Radwell
- John Radwell sonne and heire. **B**

---

* Harl MS 1531 erroneously calls him 'Edward.'
† Sic in Harl MS 5867 MS 541 has 'Potton in com Bedf.' It should be *Wootton* in com Bedf
‡ In Burke's 'General Armory' the arms assigned to Randes are Sable, a chevron ermine between three cross crosslets fitchée argent

THE VISITATION OF BEDFORDSHIRE. 49

A | Edward [Edmond—Harl. MS 5867] Randes of Radwell gen sonne and heire =Catherine d of . Grey of Staple in com Bedf.
B | Thomas Radwell sonne and heire sans yssue

Will'm Randes of Radwell gen sonne and heire =Agnes daughter of Will'm Cousin.

Thomas Randes of Radwell gen sonne and heire. =Jane daughter of John Joyce of Renhall in com. Bedf

John Randes of Radwell sonne and heire =Joane daughter of Edward Slade [Chad] of Kimolton in com Hunt.
Elizabeth Alice Margery
all vnmaryed

Edward Randes eldest sonne | George second sonne | Thomas third sonne | John fourth sonne | Jane maryed to Will'm Cullycke [Colbeck— MS 541]. | ffrancesse

Rotheram
[of Farley in Luton].

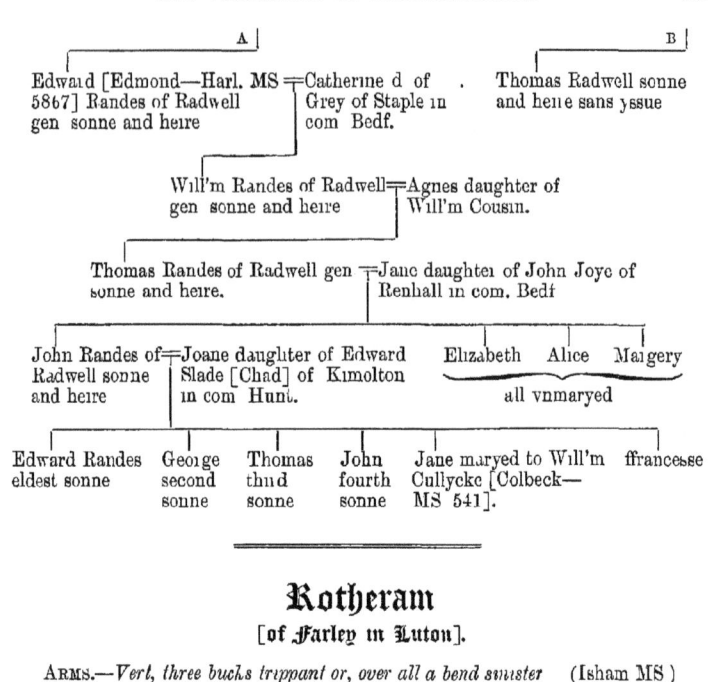

ARMS.—*Vert, three bucks trippant or, over all a bend sinister* (Isham MS.)

[Scott of Rotheram in com Yorke]=

[Thomas Scott al's Rotheram Bishop of lincon, Archbishop of Yorke and Chancellor of Ireland (*read England*), ob at Cawood 1500.]
[S^r] John Rotheram Esquire [Knt] (Lord of Someries in com Bedford—Harl MS 4600). =Alice daughter of Beckett.

Sr Thomas Rotheram Knight eldest sonne =
*
George Rotheram of ffarley in com Bedf second sonne

George Rotheram of ffarley in com. Bedf sonne naturall to George. =Alice daughter of Weltche.

Jane maryed to Will'm Catlyn of Lygrave in com Bedf. gen.
A
| Elizabeth maryed to John Grene of Chiltern Grene in com Bedf | Julyan vnmaryed | Mary vnmaryed. | Awdrey vnmaryed

* See next pedigree

H

THE VISITATION OF BEDFORDSHIRE.

[A]

George Rotheram of ffarley in com Bedf sonne and heire * = Elizabeth daughter of Edmond Bardolf of Harpeden in com. Hertf gen. | William second sonne. | John third sonne

[Joane d of al's Squire (?Spnʋer)—Harl MS 1547.] = George Rotheram eldest sonne. = Elizabeth [Wallop —Ibid] | [Elizabeth—Harl MS 5867]

[George, of Henston—Ibid] | [Thomas Rotheram of Farley living 1634—Ibid] = [Talbott d of Luke Norton of Offley, Hants—Ibid]

Rotheram

[of Someries in Luton].

Sr John Rotheram Kt = Alice da to Beckett

Sr Thomas Rotheram Kt † = Katherin da to . Lord Gray of Ruthen | George Rotheram 2 sonne of ffarly in com Bedfford

Sr Thomas Rotheram Kt = Elizabeth da to Sr John St John of Bletneshoe in com Bedfford Knt | Elizabeth | George Rotheram of ffarley in com Bedfford

Thomas Rotheram = Alice da to Thomas Wellefford | [Elizabeth Rotheram—Harl MS 4600]

Tho died young | Richard Hare of London 1 husb = Elizabeth da to Ric Barnes of Lond Mercer. 3dly to Sr Geo Peryn Kt died 1599 | George Rotheram of Someries died 1599 | Jane da to Christopher Smith, Clerk of the pipe, of Annables in com. Hertfford | Jane wife to Humphry Bury of Tuddington in com Bedfford

Edward Rotheram — Hugh Rotheram | 2 Sr Thomas Rotheram a captayne and knighted in ye ffeld | Agnes ux Thomas Snagg | 1 Sr John Rotheram Kt = Agnes d. of Thom. Snagg Serjeant-at-law

A | B

---

* In Luton Church is a brass to George Rotheram of Farley Esq, 1593, and two wives 1 Elizabeth, d of Bardolfe (with children George, Ralph and Elizabeth), and 2 Anne, d of William Gower Esq (with children, Isaac Edmond, and Anna)

† "✠ Orate pro animabus Thome Rotheram militis d'ni de Luton in Com Bedford et D'ne Catherine vxoris eius qui quidem Thomas obiit xxv die mensis Maii Anno D ni Mill'imo ccccc quarto et predicta D'na Catherina obiit — mensis — A° v° quarum aiabus propicietur Deus "

In Harl MS 1097, fo 43, is the foregoing inscription (incompletely given in Nichols' 'Bib Topog Brit.' vol viii pp 15 and 36) There is also a pen-and-ink sketch depicting four shields, *Rotheram* and *Gray*, etc , and effigies of Sir Thomas Rotheram, Lady Catherine (da of Anthony, Lord Grey de Ruthyn), and four children The blanks were, apparently, never filled in

THE VISITATION OF BEDFORDSHIRE 51

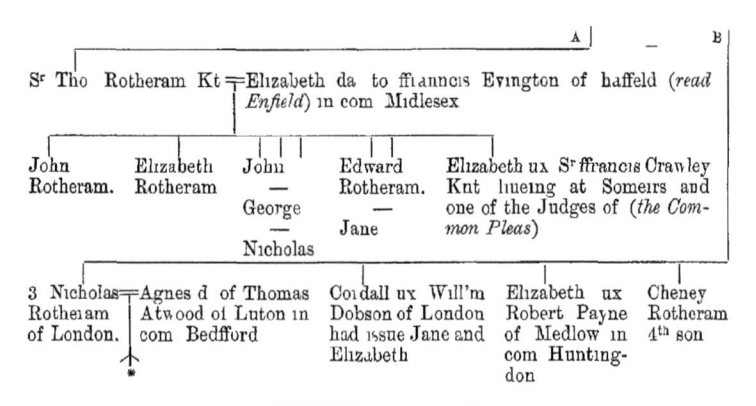

A | — B |

Sr Tho Rotheram Kt =Elizabeth da to ffrancis Evington of haffeld (*read Enfield*) in com Midlesex

| John Rotheram. | Elizabeth Rotheram | John — George — Nicholas | Edward Rotheram. — Jane | Elizabeth ux Sr ffrancis Crawley Knt liueing at Someirs and one of the Judges of (*the Common Pleas*) |

| 3 Nicholas Rotheram of London. ↓ * | =Agnes d of Thomas Atwood of Luton in com Bedfford | Cordall ux Will'm Dobson of London had issue Jane and Elizabeth | Elizabeth ux Robert Payne of Medlow in com Huntingdon | Cheney Rotheram 4th son |

St. John†
[of Bletshoe].

ARMS —*Quarterly of nine*—1 *Argent, on a chief gules two mullets pierced or* ST JOHN, 2, *Argent, a fesse between six cinqfoils gules,* UMFREVILLE ; 3, *Azure, a bend argent cotised or, between six martlets of the second,* DELABERE, 4, *Ermine, on a fesse azure three crosses pattee or,* PAVELEY, 5, *Argent, a lion rampant queue fourché purpure, charged with a cross pattee or,* STURREY, 6, *Gules a fesse between six martlets or, a mullet sable for difference* BEAUCHAMP, 7, *Argent, a fesse sable between three crescents gules,* PATSHULL, 8, *Ermine a lion rampant purpure, ducally crowned or,* BROYE, 9, *Paly of six argent and azure, on a bend gules three eagles displayed or,* GRANDISON impaling, *Quarterly of four*—1, *Argent, on a cheviron between three demi-lions rampant gules as many plates,* FISHER, 2, *Azure, a cheviron between three leopards' faces or,* IROWYKE 3, *Azure, three sturgeons naiant in pale or, fretty gules,* STURGEON, 4, *Argent, on a bend gules three martlets vert, legged or,* DANVERS

SUPPORTERS —*Dexter A monkey or Sinister An asprey argent, armed or*

CREST —*On a wreath argent and gules a mount vert, on which a falcon rising or, belled of the last, ducally gorged gules*

Will'm Seint John of ffanmon in com = . daughter of . Glamorgan in Wales Knight

| Henry Seint John eldest sonne sans issue | Sr John Saint John of ffanmon Knight second sonne and heire to his brother | =Beatrix daughter of [Jo Broye— Isham MS] |

Alexander Seint John of ffanmon =Elizabeth daughter and one of the heires of ar sonne and heire | Sr Henry Humfrevyle of Penmarke in com A | Glamorgan Knight

* See Additional Pedigrees, *post*
† In Harl MS 5867 there are five lines of cypher at the end of this pedigree —ED
Cf 'Visitation of Huntingdonshire 1613,' p 2, Camd Soc

THE VISITATION OF BEDFORDSHIRE

A

Sr John St John of ffanmon in com Glamorgan K sonne and heire = Isabell daughter and heire of John Paveley of Paveleys Pury in com Northampt Knight

Sr Olyver Saint John of ffanmon in com Glamorgan K sonne and heire = Elizabeth daughter and one of the heires of Sr John Delabere Knight

Sr John Saint John of ffanmon K sonne and heire = Elizabeth daughter of .

Beauchamp.

Patıshull.

[Wm—Isham MS] Beauchamp baron of Emley father to the Erle of Warwyke and to Sr Walter [William— Harl MS 5867] Beauchamp of Powyke. =

John Patyshull de com Bedford ar = Mabill one of the sisters and heires of Otho Lord Grandson

Sr Walter Beauchampe of Powyke third sonne and brother to the Erle of Warwyke =

Will'm Patyshull sonne and heire =

Sr Roger Beauchampe third sonne to Sr Walter of Powyke and chamberleyn to King Edward the third = Sibell daughter and heire

Sr Roger Beauchampe sonne and heire =

Sr John Beauchamp of Bletneshoe in com Bedford K sonne and heire = Edyth daughter of John Lord Stourton

Sr Olyver Saint John of Bletneshoe in com Bedf Knight sonne and heire = Margaret daughter and heire = [John Beaufford Duke of Somersett 2 husband]

Sr John Saint John of Bletneshoe in com Bedf K sonne and heire = Alice daughter of Sr Thomas Bradshawe of Hawe in com Lanc K

Olyver Saint John of Wiltshire second sonne

[Agnes ux (Sir) David Malpas]

[Mary ux (Sir) Richard Tregonnell]

Edyth maryed to Sr Gefferey Poole Knight =

Sr Richard Poole Knight maryed Margaret daughter and heire of George Duke of Clarence

Elizabeth first maryed to William Lord Zouche, after to the Lord Scroope

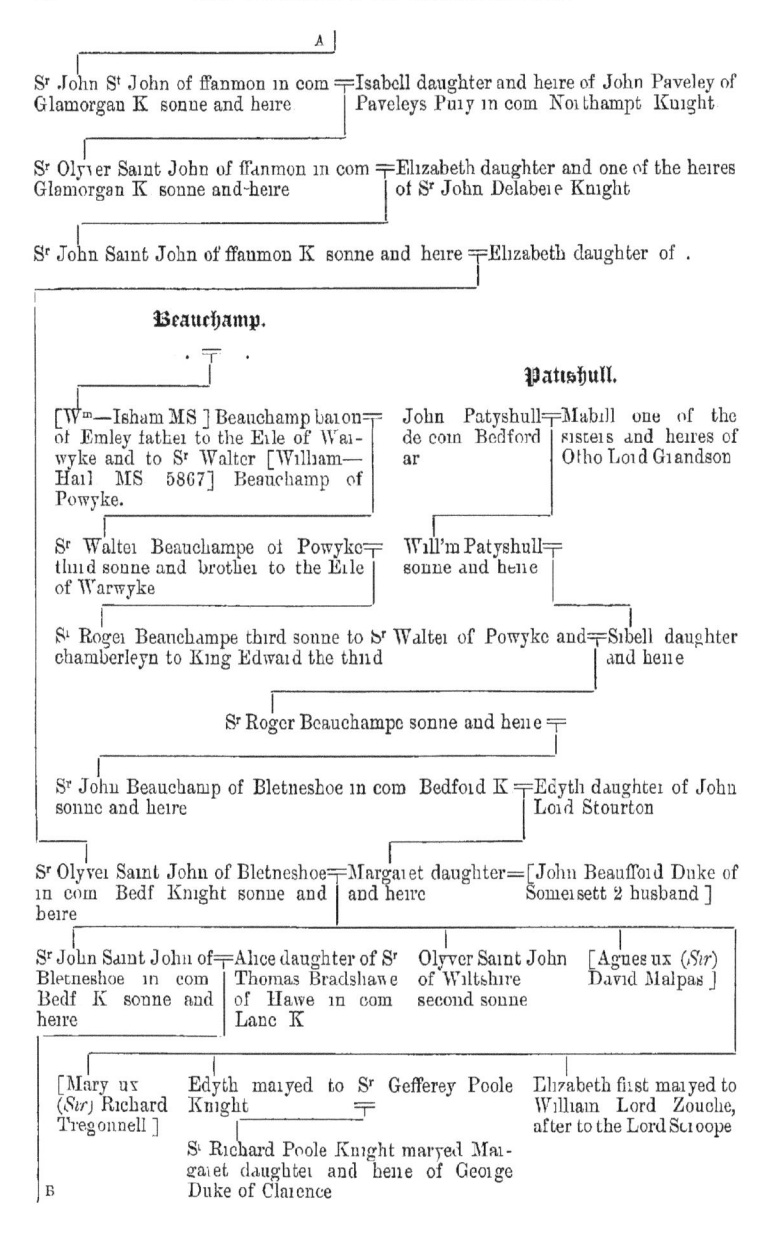

B

THE VISITATION OF BEDFORDSHIRE. 53

| B

Anne maryed to Henry Lord Clifforde. | Eleanor maryed to Sʳ John Southe [Zowche] of Codnore. | Margarett Abbesse of Shaftesbury 1459.

Sʳ John Saint John of Bletneshoe⹀Sibell daughter of [Rice ap] Morgan ap Jenkyn ap Philippe. K. sonne and heire.* | Morys second sonne.

| Alice [Anne] second daughter maryed to Henry Parker Lord Morley. | Margaret third daughter maryed to Sʳ Thomas Gamage of Coyte in Wales Knight. | Elizabeth fourth daughter maryed to Sʳ Thomas Rotheram of Somerics in com. Bedf. K. | Sibill maryed to Sir Robert Kirkham of Warmington in com. Northampt. Knight. |

| Olyver Saint John of Shernbroke second sonne (see p. 54). | Alexander Saint John of Thurley in com. Herf. third sonne (see p. 55). | Catherine eldest daughter first maryed to Sʳ Gryffith Ryce of Wales K., after to Sʳ Richard [Peter] Edgecombe of Mount Edgecombe in com. Devon K. |

[Anne d. of Thomas Nevell of Cotterstock in com. Northampton 2 sonn of Will'm Nevell of Holte in com. Lester.] } Sʳ John Saint John of Bletneshoe K. sonne and heire. ⹀ Margaret daughter of Sʳ Wᵐ Walgrave of Smallbridge [Buers Sᵗ Maryes] in com. Suff. Knight.

| [Charles Sᵗ John.] | [Cressyd ux. John Boteler of Sharnbrooke in com. Bedfford.] | [Jane ux. John Gascoigne of Carington in com. Bedfford.] | [Mary ux. John Harvye of Thirlye in com. Bedfford.] | [.... a daughter.] |

| Margery maryed to Henry Grey sonne and heire of Sʳ Henry Grey, brother to Richard Grey Erle of Kent [2 to Francis Pigott of Whaddon in com. Buck.]. | Anne second daughter maryed to Richard Dennys of Dereham in com. Glouc. | Margaret third daughter maryed to [Sʳ John Gostwick of (Willington) in com. Bedfford, 2] ffrancys Erle of Bedford. | Alice fourth daughter maryed to Edmond Elmes of Lylford in com. Northampt. ar. |

ffrowike.

[Henry Frowike Lord of Gonholsbery—Harl. MS. 5867.]⹀

Sʳ Thomas ffrowyke sonne and heire of Sʳ Henry ffrowyke lord of Gonholesbury maryed Jane daughter and heire of .... Sturgeon. ⹀ [Jane da. and heire of .... Sturgeon— Harl. MS. 5867.]

Sʳ Henry ffrowyke of Gonholesbury in com. Mydd. K. sonne and heire. ⹀ Joane daughter and one of the heires D | of Sʳ Henry Danvers Knight.
| C

* "Maria, filia Davidis Mathew, quæ ob. s.p., vxor 2ᵃ." (Harl. MS. 5186.)

Fisher.

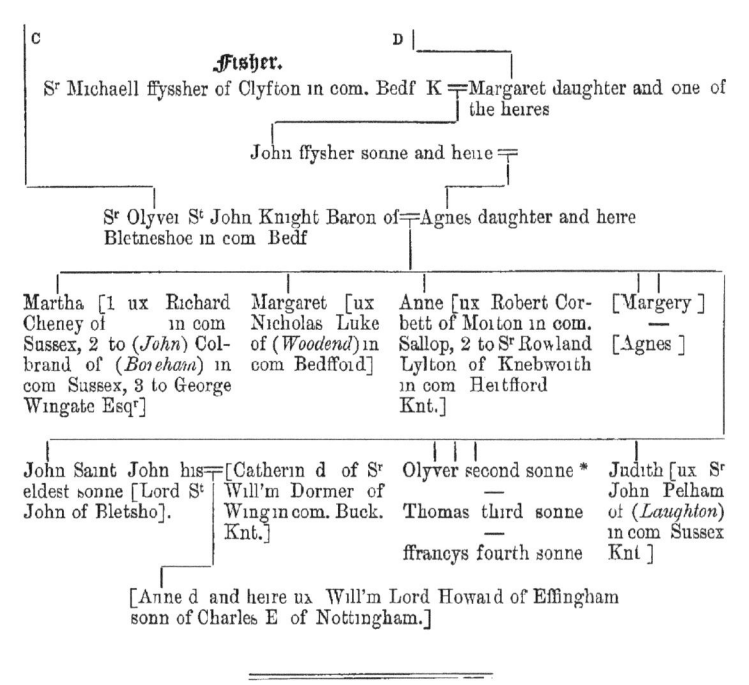

Sr Michaell ffyssher of Clyfton in com. Bedf K = Margaret daughter and one of the heires

John ffysher sonne and heire =

Sr Olyver St John Knight Baron of Bletneshoe in com Bedf = Agnes daughter and heire

- Martha [1 ux Richard Cheney of in com Sussex, 2 to (*John*) Colbrand of (*Boreham*) in com Sussex, 3 to George Wingate Esqr]
- Margaret [ux Nicholas Luke of (*Woodend*) in com Bedfford]
- Anne [ux Robert Corbett of Morton in com. Sallop, 2 to Sr Rowland Lylton of Knebworth in com Hertfford Knt.]
- [Margery]
- [Agnes]

- John Saint John his eldest sonne [Lord St John of Bletsho]. = [Catherin d of Sr Will'm Dormer of Wing in com. Buck. Knt.]
- Olyver second sonne *
- Thomas third sonne
- ffrancys fourth sonne
- Judith [ux Sr John Pelham of (*Laughton*) in com Sussex Knt]

[Anne d and heire ux Will'm Lord Howard of Effingham sonn of Charles E of Nottingham.]

St. John
[of Sharnebrook].

ARMS (TWO SHIELDS) —*The first as in* ST JOHN OF BLETSOE II, *Argent, on a chief gules two mullets pierced or, a crescent for difference,* ST JOHN, *impaling, Sable, a bull passant or,* FITZGEOFFREY

Olyver St John of Shernbroke in com Bedford arg second sonne to Sr John St John of Bletneshoe = Mary daughter of (*William*) ffitzGeffrey of Thurly in com. Bedf arg

- John St John dyed sans yssue
- George second sonne
- Henry third sonne
- Thomas fourth sonne
- ffrancys fifte sonne

- Margaret eldest daughter maryd to Thomas Cobbe of Shernbrooke.
- Alice 2 d mar to Anthony Pollard vncle to Sr John Pollard Knight
- Elizabeth third daughter mar to Will'm Goodfellow of Pavenham in com Bedf.
- Margery fourth daughter vnmaryed

* See Additional Pedigrees, *post*

St. John
[of Thurleigh].

ARMS —*Argent, on a chief gules two mullets pierced or, a mullet for difference*, ST JOHN, *impaling, Gules, two crescents in pale or, a canton ermine*, DALYSON

Alexander S⁺ John of Thurley in com Herf (*read Bedf*) Esquire third sonne to S⁺ John S⁺ John Knight =┬= Jane d of George Dalyson of Cranesley in com Northampt arg wydow of Thomas Lenthroppe of Shinglehall in com. Hertf arg

Olyver S⁺ John eldest sonne of Thurly in com Hertf (*read Bedf*) Esquire [as yet unm —Harl MS 5867]* =[Margaret d of Thomas Eston of Holme in com Bedford]† = [John Gooderick of Doddington in the Ile of Ely 1 husband] | Alice maryed to John Clopton of . com Bedf and dyed sans yssue

Spencer‡
[of Cople].

[ARMS —*Quarterly Or and gules, in the second and third quarters a fret or, on a bend sable three fleurs-de-lis argent.*]

Robert Spencer of Southmylles in com Bedf. gen. =┬= Anne daughter and heire of . . . Pecke of Couple in com. Bedf gen.

John Spencer of Patenham in com [Bedf] gen sonne and heire. =┬= Anne daughter and heire of . Arnoldes of S⁺ Needes in com Hunt gen | Alice maryed to Thom's Dyckons of Wylshamsted in com Bedf. gen. | Johane maryed to Battell

Thomas Spencer of Couple in com Bedf. sonne and heire =┬= Anne daughter of Robert Bowlkeley of Burgate in com South ar. | Elizabeth maryed to John Slade of S⁺ Needes in com Hunt | Rose maryed to John Colbecke of Tempesforde in com Bedf ar.

Robert Spencer of Couple in com Bedf ar sonne and heire as yet vnmaryed | William second sonne. | Elizabeth maryed to Robert [Thomas—Harl MS 5867] Parrys of Kychen in com Cantabrige gen | Anne vnmaryed

---

* In Harl MS 5186 Olyver S⁺ John is styled one of the Auditors of the Exchequer, and is stated to have married Margaret, dau of   Eston of . co Bedf, and to have been the *father* of Alice whom John Clopton.
† Harl MS 4600 calls her ' relict of John Gostwick "
‡ This pedigree is not in the Isham MS *Cf* Visitation of 1634, *post*

The Visitation of Bedfordshire 1582.*

Visitatio Comitatus Bedd · fca A Dni: 1582, 23 Eliz Extract' e li. W G
(In the handwriting of Sr Thomas Jekyll the Essex Collector)

Figuræ Pag.
A   Arma.
C   Crista.
D.   Descensus

A TABLE TO THIS BOOKE OF VISITATION OF BEDFORDSHIRE OF THE NAMES OF THE NOBILITY & GENTRY WITH THEIR COATES OF ARMES CRESTS & NUMBER OF DESCENTS

Name	Pag.	D.	Name	Pag.	D.
Ailway	4	3 d	FitzGeoffrey	27 A C	5 d
Ardern	5 A C	2 d	FitzHugh	25 A	3 d
Astrie	6 A C	6 d	† Fortescue	3 A C	7 d
Auncell	7 A.	5 d	Fowler	42 A	6 d.
Barnardiston	9 A	4 d	Francklyn	36 A	5 d
Bawde	8 A	5 d	Gostwicke	35 A.	3 d
Bosgrave	32 A. C	3 d	Gray	21 A C	6 d
Boteler	11 A.	7 d	Harvy	28 A	6 d
Boteler	10 A	4 d	Hewett	37 A	3 d
† Briscoe	52 A C	8 d	Hunt	39 A	6 d
Broughton	12	15 d	† Lions	51 A	7 d
Burgoyne	31 A	3 d	Luke	24 A	4 d
Bury	15 A.	6 d	Martin	18 A	3 d
Catleyn	46 A	4 d	Neyle	40 A	4 d
Charnock	16 A	3 d	Nicholls	49	6 d
Cheney	13	6 d	Page	23 A C	4 d
Chetwood	55 A C	21 d	Penn	41 A C	3 d
Chibnall	33 A	4 d	Pigott	38 A.	3 d
Cokaine	17	6 d	Poole	14 A	6 d
Colbeck	20	4 d	† Prannell	43 A C	2 d
Conquest	26 A	8 d	Pudesey	44 A.	4 d
Creeke	34	6 d	Radcliffe	53 A	5 d.
† Crew	57 A	6 d	Randes	45	6 d
Dyve	19 A	14 d	Rotheram	47 A	5 d
Eston	48 A	5 d	Seint John	22 A	4 d
Everard	30 A	4 d	Teringham	52 A C	13 d
FitzGeoffrey	27	4 d	Wahull al's Woodhall	59 A	18 d

* As most of the Pedigrees in this Visitation are identical with those recorded in the previous Visitation of 1566, I have only given those which are not to be found in the latter excepting those marked †, which do not appear to have any connection with the County Additions and corrections in brackets are, unless otherwise expressed, from Harl MS 1097.—ED

THE VISITATION OF BEDFORDSHIRE.

Baronetti de hoc Comitatu

25 Novem Will's Gostwick de Willington ar 10 Jacobi
21 Maij seu 24 Sept 11 Jacobi, Rob'tus Nappei al's Sandy de Luton Howe, Miles

Fo. 1.—A Visitation of the gentry of Bedfordshire made by . A° D'ni 1582, A° 24 Elizabethæ R'næ

This County hath 116 paryshes in 9 Hundreds—10 Market Townes

Hundred of	Barford. Biggleswade Clifton fflitt Manshead Redbornstoke Stoddon Willy Wixho'mtree	Market Towns 10	in Red. Ampthill on „ Willy Bedford on „ Big Bigleswade on „ Man Dunstable on „ Man · Leighton on „ fflitt Luton on „ Bigg Potton on „ Clyft Shefford on „ Man^d Tuddington on „ Man Wobuine

CASTLES—Ampthill an Honor, Eaton, Temsford

An Abstract of such religious howses as were in the said county with their valuac'ons as the same are expressed in Speed's Chronicle & recorded in the office of the first fruits & tenths.

	li	s	d
Abbey of Wardon	442	11	11
Priory of Wobuine	430	13	11 ob
„ of Dunstable	402	14	7 ob
Nunnery of Elstow	325	2	1 q
Priory of Newenham	343	15	5
Nunnery of Margate, a priores	325	2	1 ob
„ of Chicksand	230	3	4 ob
Priory of Caldwell	148	15	10
Nunnery of Bisco nere Mergate	113	18	3
Priory of Bushmead	81	13	5 ob
Nunnery of Harwald al's Harwood	47	3	2
Hospitall of Sanctingfield nere Whitsand	61	5	8 ob
„ of Sct John in Bedford	21	0	8
„ of Sct Leonard in Bedford	10	6	8
Colledge of Sct Trinity in Sct Andrewe's Church in Bigleswade	7	0	0
Colledge of Corpus Christi in Eaton	7	16	0
„ in Northile not valued	0	0	0
ffriory or Brotherhood in Dunstable	9	8	7
ffriory or Howse of fryers in Dunstable	4	18	4
ffriery in Bedford	5	0	0

Fo 2 —The Armes of the Corporate Townes of this County of Bedford

Knights of Bedfordshire elected for the parliam^t begun 3rd of november 1640
  Sr Oliver Luke, Knight   [to the Parliam^t
Only the towne & borough of Bedford in Bedfordshire sendeth Burgesses
  O^r S^{ct} John Beauchamp Knight

Astry

[of Harlington].

ARMS.—*Barule of vj wave Ar and az, on a cheife gu 3 bezants*
CREST.—*A demy Ostrich wings open gu, in the beake a horse-shooe ar.*

Galfr'us Ostrich al's Astrie de Hitchin in com Hertf =

Margeria filia = Rad'us Astrie miles Prætor Ciuitatis London 1493 = Margareta
ob 10 Martij 1492 | A° 9 H 7 ob 18 Novembris 1494 sepult^s in eccl'ia | filia .
vxor 2^a. | s'c'i Martini in le Vintrie London. | vxor 1^a

2 Rad'us Astrie ob | Jana filia = 1 Thomas Astrie = Elizabeth filia | 3 Henricus
in juventute 19 | Joh is | de Hitchin in | Will'i Skipwith | [died
Sept 1501 sepult^s | Pigot de | com Hertf ar | de Wethamsted | young].
vbi pat. | co Bucks | | in co Hertf
 | ob. s p | | gen. vxor 1^a
 | vx 2^a |

Will's Astrie = | Rad'us Astrie heres f'tris 1583 de = Alicia filia Thomæ Wilford
 | Harlington in co Bedd ar | [of London] rel'c a Tho
 | | Rotheram ar

Thomas Astrie [s p].

Maria | Elizabeth = 1 Rad'us | Francisca vxor | [Anne mar to | 2 George = Lora
 | filia Petri | Astrie de | Petri Mallory | John Wal- | Astry | filia
 | Gray de | Harlington | de Shelton in | leys of Brack- | | .
 | com | ar 1599 | co Bedd | ford in com | | Row-
 | Bedd ar | | | Bedf] | | ley

1. Henricus Astry   2 Rad'us Astry.

Chetwood[*]

[of Hockliffe].

ARMS.—*Quarterly Ar & gu, 4 crosses patée counterchanged*, CHETWOOD
CREST.—*A demy Manticher or mantiger saliant ar out of a crescent gu*

Joh'es Chetwood d'us de Chetwood in com. Buck. fundator Prioratus =
ib'm vbi corpus eius sepultu' fuit
A

---

[*] Cf 'Miscellanea Genealogica et Heraldica, Second Series, vol. i., p. 69 (May, 1884), where there is an elaborate pedigree of this family

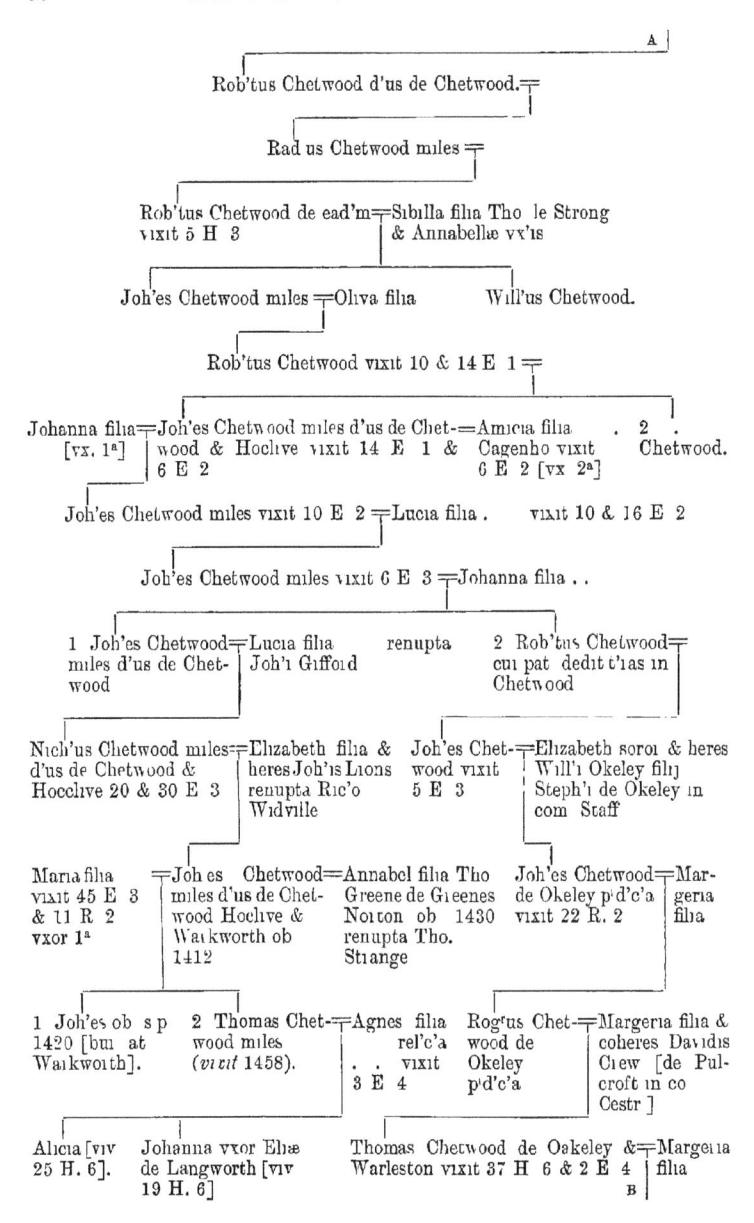

THE VISITATION OF BEDFORDSHIRE.

A

Rob'tus Chetwood d'us de Chetwood.

Rad'us Chetwood miles

Rob'tus Chetwood de ead'm === Sibilla filia Tho. le Strong
vixit 5 H. 3 & Annabellæ vx'is

Joh'es Chetwood miles === Oliva filia   Will'us Chetwood.

Rob'tus Chetwood vixit 10 & 14 E 1

Johanna filia === Joh'es Chetwood miles d'us de Chet- === Amicia filia   2.   .
[vx. 1ª] | wood & Hocclive vixit 14 E 1 & | Cagenho vixit   Chetwood.
6 E 2   6 E 2 [vx 2ª]

Joh'es Chetwood miles vixit 10 E 2 === Lucia filia .   vixit 10 & 16 E 2

Joh'es Chetwood miles vixit 6 E 3 === Johanna filia ..

1 Joh'es Chetwood === Lucia filia   renupta   2 Rob'tus Chetwood ===
miles d'us de Chet- | Joh'i Gifford   cui pat' dedit t'ias in
wood   Chetwood

Nich'us Chetwood miles === Elizabeth filia &   Joh'es Chet- === Elizabeth soror & heres
d'us de Chetwood & | heres Joh'is Lions   wood vixit | Will'i Okeley filij
Hocclive 20 & 30 E 3 | renupta Ric'o   5 E 3 | Steph'i de Okeley in
                     Widville   com Staff

Maria filia   === Joh'es Chetwood === Annabel filia Tho   Joh'es Chetwood === Mar-
vixit 45 E 3 | miles d'us de Chet- | Greene de Greenes   de Okeley p'd'c'a | geria
& 11 R 2 | wood Hocclive & | Norton ob 1430   vixit 22 R. 2 | filia
vxor 1ª | Warkworth ob | renupta Tho.
               1412   Strange

1 Joh'es ob s p 2 Thomas Chet- === Agnes filia   Rog'us Chet- === Margeria filia &
1420 [bur at   wood miles | rel'c'a   wood de | coheres Davidis
Warkworth].   (vixit 1458). | . . vixit   Okeley | Crew [de Pul-
                                   3 E 4   p'd'c'a | croft in co
                                                              Cestr.]

Alicia [viv   Johanna vxor Eliæ   Thomas Chetwood de Oakeley & === Margeria
25 H. 6].   de Langworth [viv   Warleston vixit 37 H 6 & 2 E 4 | filia
              19 H. 6]   B

THE VISITATION OF BEDFORDSHIRE.

Rog'us Chetwood fil & heres intra=Helena filia & heres Will'i de Ree ar & Eliz
no'iatoru' Thomæ & Margeriæ vixit | vx'is eius filiæ & coh. Will'i Rowley & Mar-
3 R 3 & 11 H 7 | g'eta ux'is eius filiæ & heredis Rici Hen-
hull de co Cestr ai.

Helena filia Tho Berisford=Thomas Chetwood de Wai-=Helena fil Joh'is Spur-
de Bentley in com Derb | leston in com Cestriæ fil | stow de Spurstow in com.
vxor 1ª | & heres. | Cestr ai vxoi 2ª

Rog'us Chetwood=Helena filia Tho. Musterson de   Joh'es   Ranulphus   Helena
vixit 27 H 8. | Namptwich in co Cestr ar   ‾‾‾‾‾‾‾‾‾‾‾‾‾‾‾‾‾‾‾‾‾‾‾‾
                                                        obierunt s p

Margeria 1 Jacobus=Catherina 2. Joh'es 3 Ric'us=Agnes filia Helena vxor
ob s p   Chetwood | filia Ph'i Chet-   Chet- | & he   1° Jo
          de Okeley| Hulso   wood.   wood. | Ant'ij   Hanky de
          & Wailes-| ——— | Barons de Churtock
          ton p'd' 28   4 Rog'us | Woodhall   in co. Cestr
          H 8   Chetwood. | quæ ob 18
                                                  | Eliz R'næ

Anna filia=Thomas=Anna filia Will'i Jana filia=Ric'us Chet-=Dorothea filia
& her. | Chet- | Bulkley de   [Will i] | wood miles Nodham
Joh'is | wood. | Halghton in   Diuiy | vixit A°   de Shaventon
Leech de | | com Cestr   mil. | 1603   in com. Salop
Nampt-   ar.
wich.

Will's ob infans 1 Catherine vxor   2 Elizabeth   Ric'us=Anna filia &
———   Will i Skevington ———   Chet- | heres Valen-
2. Thomas Chet-   de Skevington in 3 Anna vxor   wood | tini Knight-
wood   com Leic   Egidij Bi ay de fil & | ley mil.
                                      Barrington mil heres

1 Dorothea   3 Catherina   5. Elizabeth   1 Knightleius*   3 Valentinus*

2 Anna   4 Jana   6 Susanna   2 Ric'us*

4 Francisca 6 Dorothea   8. Gracia   10 Beatrix   3 Rob'tus   5. Joh'es.

5. Maria   7 Jana   9 Abigal.   4 Thomas   6 Tobias

———

* There appears to be an error here, these three sons are probably the issue of Richard
Chetwood by Dorothy, d of Nodham.—ED

Gray

[of Segenhoe in Ridgmont].

ARMS —*Ar , a bend vert cotized indented gu ,* GRAY
CREST —*On a torce ur & gu halfe a mayden cowpie at the brest gu haire expanded, a coronet on her head ar , a chaine of gold about her neck & a tablet hanging at yt supporting with both her hands a garland vert*

Rad'us Graye de Pelham in com Hertf gen^r vnus Baronum Curiæ Scacarij.

Rad'us Gray de ead'm gen^r

Rad'us Gray de ead'm gen. [qre *]

2 Ric'us Gray de Chissell in com Essex.

Margareta filia Cooper de Bailey in com Hertf

Elizabeth vxor Anth'ij Walgrave de in com Suff

3 Joh'es —
4 Thomas

1 Thomas Gray

Gracia filia Will'i Hanchett de Sigenhoe† in com. Bedd vxor 2^a.

Joh'is Gray de Bailey p'd'.

filia Lions vxor 1^a

Alicia vxor Andreæ Smyth de London

Anna vxor Ric'i Mallory de London Al'dri

Margeria vxor Newman de Pelham in com. Hertf

Maseia vxor Will'i Stone de London Hab'dasher

4 Joh'es Gray

3 Matheus Gray

2 Andreas Gray

Petrus Gray de Sigenhoe in com Bedd gen

[Elizabeth da. to Nicholas Wood of ffullborne in co Cambridge gent]

Ed'rus Gray.

Francisca ‡

Elizabeth.

Margareta. — Dorothea

Maria vxor Joh'is S^{ct} George de [Hatley St George] in com Cantabi ar.

---

* Harl MS 1097 makes Elizabeth, wife of Anth Walgrave, da to Ralph Gray, brother of Richard
† "Of Letcheworth in co Hertf" (Harl MS 1097)
‡ "ffrancys." (*Ibid*)

Nicholls*
[of Ampthill].

ARMS.—*Az, 6 crosse crosselets fitche or, on a bend engr cotized or 3 eaglets ar (qre),* NICHOLS
CREST.—*A falcon wings displ or, supporting in her right foote a crosse croslet patée fitche sa*
MOTTO.—FIDE SED CUI VIDE

Arma confirmata fuerunt p' Will'm Seagar Norroy A° 44 Eliz 1602

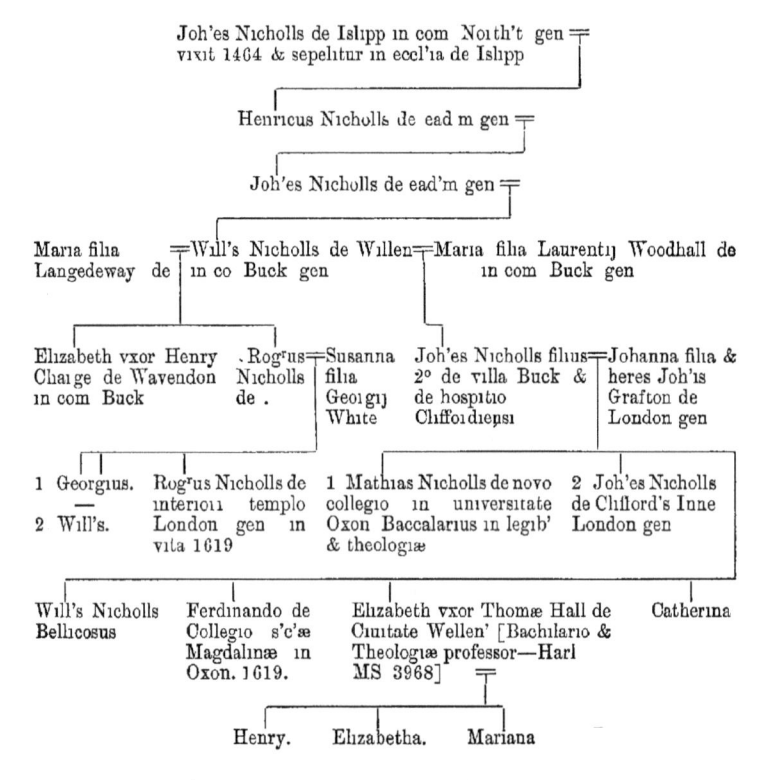

Joh'es Nicholls de Islipp in com North't gen —
vixit 1464 & sepelitur in eccl'ia de Islipp

Henricus Nicholls de ead m gen —

Joh'es Nicholls de ead'm gen —

Maria filia = Will's Nicholls de Willen = Maria filia Laurentij Woodhall de
Langedeway de | in co Buck gen | in com Buck gen

Elizabeth vxor Henry | Rog'rus = Susanna | Joh'es Nicholls filius = Johanna filia &
Charge de Wavendon | Nicholls | filia | 2° de villa Buck & | heres Joh'is
in com Buck | de . | Georgij | de hospitio | Grafton de
 | | White | Clifforidiepsi | London gen

1 Georgius.   Rog'rus Nicholls de   1 Mathias Nicholls de novo   2 Joh'es Nicholls
—   interiori templo   collegio in universitate   de Cliford's Inne
2 Will's.   London gen in   Oxon Baccalarius in legib'   London gen
               vita 1619   & theologiæ

Will's Nicholls   Ferdinando de   Elizabeth vxor Thomæ Hall de   Catherina
Bellicosus   Collegio s'c'æ   Ciuitate Wellen' [Bachilario &
                   Magdalinæ in   Theologiæ professor—Harl
                   Oxon. 1619.   MS 3968] —

                                   Henry.   Elizabetha.   Mariana

* *Cf* 'Topographer and Genealogist,' vol iii, p 533

Poole

[of (?)].

ARMS—POOLE *Az., a lyon rampt ar betw 10 flowre de lizes or*
PENDRED *Ar., on a chevron gu 3 flowre de lizes or*

Thomas Poole de Poole in com Cestria miles vixit 24 H 6 =

Thomas Poole miles de ead'm A° 1 E 4 =

Will's Poole miles de ead'm =

Thomas Poole de ead'm ar = Maria filia Joh'is Talbot de Grafton mil

Joh'es Poole = Catherina filia Joh'is Minshull de Mynshull in co Cesti | Elizabeth vxor Joh'is Butler de Peggesden* in com Bedd gen | Joh'es Pendred maritus 2°

Margareta. Maria. Joh'es Poole. Rob'tus Pendred.

Radcliffe

[of Elstow].

ARMS—*Ar., a bend engr sa*, RADCLIFFE

Joh'es Radcliffe miles submersus apud Heiry Bridge 1461 A° 1 E 4. = Elizabeth filia & heres Walt'i d'ni Fitzwalter de Woodham Walter in com. Essex.

Joh'es Radcliffe miles† d n's Fitzwalter Burnell Boutetort & Egremont = Anna filia Ric'i Weheathill de villa Calisiæ in Gallia militis

[Margarett da to Stanley Earle of Derby 2 wife] = Rob'tus Radcliffe (*primus comes Sussex‡*) miles d n's Fitzwalter Egremont & Burnell s'c'us vicomes Fitzwalter 17 H 8 & comes Sussex 21 H 8 [He mar 3 Mary da of S'r Jo Arundell of Lanheine in Cornwall] = Elizabeth filia Hen. Stafford Ducis Buck.

[S'r John Ratcliff Knight]

A   B

* A hamlet in the parish of Shillington   † Harl MS 1097 commences here
‡ In a different hand

THE VISITATION OF BEDFORDSHIRE

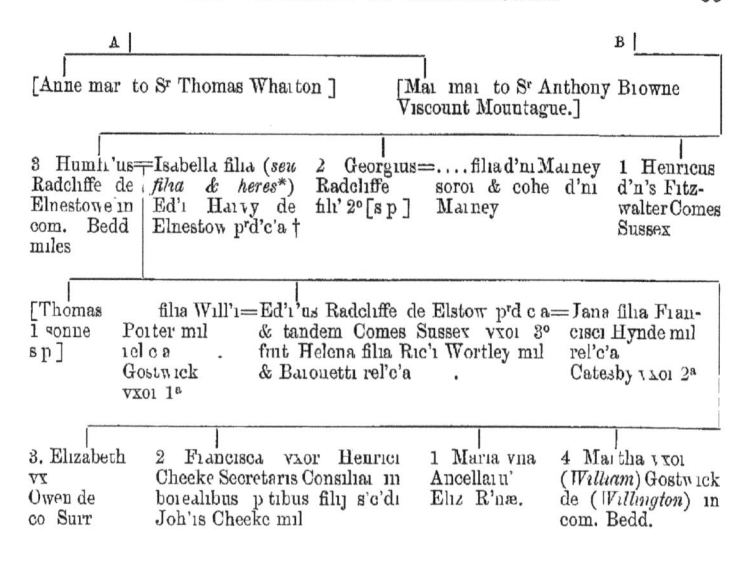

A | B |

[Anne mar to Sʳ Thomas Whaɪton] | [Maɪ maɪ to Sʳ Anthony Bɪowne Viscount Mountague.]

3 Humfr'us=Isabella filia (*seu* | 2 Georgius=....filia d'nɪ Maɪney | 1 Henricus
Radcliffe de | *filia & heres**) | Radcliffe | soroɪ & cohe d'nɪ | d'n's Fitz-
Elnestowe in | Ed'ɪ Haɪvy de | fili' 2°[s p] | Maɪney | walter Comes
com. Bedd | Elnestow p'd'c'a † | | | Sussex
miles

[Thomas | filia Will'ɪ=Ed'ɪ'us Radcliffe de Elstow p'd c a=Jana filia Fɪau-
1 sonne | Poɪter mil | & tandem Comes Sussex vxoɪ 3° | cisci Hynde mil
s p] | ɪel c a | fint Helena filia Ric'ɪ Wortley mil | rel'c'a
 | Gostwick | & Baɪouetti rel'c'a | Catesby vxoɪ 2ᵃ
 | vxoɪ 1ᵃ

3. Elizabeth | 2 Francisca vxoɪ Henrici | 1 Maria vna | 4 Maɪtha vxoɪ
vx | Cheeke Secretaɪɪs Consiliaɪ in | Ancellaɪu' | (*William*) Gostwick
Owen de | boɪealibus p tibus filij s'c'dɪ | Eliz R'næ. | de (*Willington*) in
co Surr | Joh'ɪs Cheeke mil | | com. Bedd.

𝕿iringham‡

[of 𝕳inwick and 𝕱arndish].

ARMS.—1 *Az, a saltier engɪ aɪ*, TERINGHAM
   2. *Az., a frett or seu aɪ*
   3 *Az, 3 water-bougetts ar*
   4. *Az billettée of* 10 oɪ 4, 3, 2, 1
   5 *Ar, a fesse gu within a bordure engr sa*
   6 *Barrulée of 6 ar & az, on a bend gu 3 mulletts oɪ*, PABENHAM
   7 *P'ty p' pale oɪ & gu, a lion rampᵗ & 3 flouɪs de lizes couuterchanged, 2 in cheɪfe the 3ᵈ in the base point*
   8 *Ar, a saltier boɪɪy bendée gu & or betw 4 escallops gu*
   9 *P'ty pɪ chevron gu & er, 2 greyhovnds combatant ar., a bordure sa charged with 14 floure de lizes oɪ*
   10 *Aɪ, a cɪane sa beaked & legged gu*
   11 *Sa, a fesse betw 2 trefoyles in cheife & a libbart's head in base or*
   12 *As the 7th, therefoɪe I think these last vj are but an Impalcd coat.*
CREST.—*A Talbott's head cowpie billettée or*

 * In a different hand
 † And of his wife Margaret, da. of Sʳ Giles Wentworth wᶜʰ Edm waˢ 4 sonn of Wᵐ eldest sonn to Tho 2 sonn of Jo Harvey of Thurley in com Bedford." (Harl MS 1097)
 ‡ *Cf* 'Visitation of Huntingdonshire, A D 1613, ed Camd Soc., p. 115, which differs materially from this, also Additional Pedigrees, *post*

THE VISITATION OF BEDFORDSHIRE.

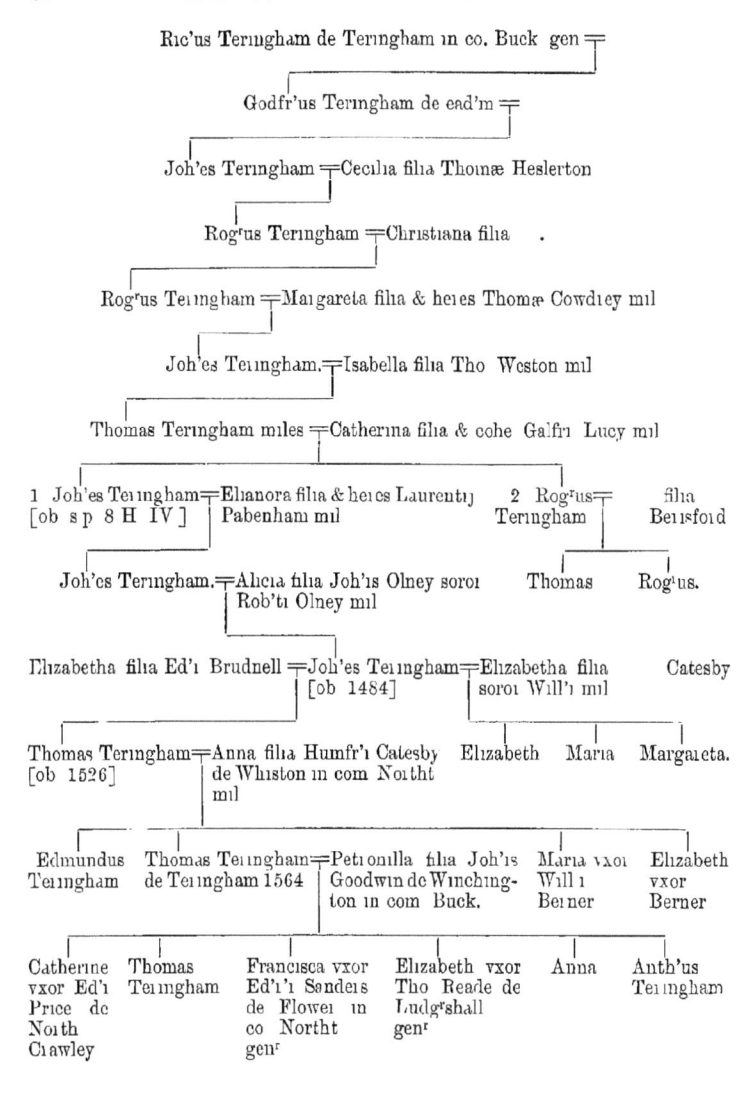

Ric'us Teringham de Teringham in co. Buck gen =

Godfr'us Teringham de ead'm =

Joh'es Teringham =Cecilia filia Thomæ Heslerton

Rog'us Teringham =Christiana filia .

Rog'us Teringham =Margareta filia & heres Thomæ Cowdrey mil

Joh'es Teringham.=Isabella filia Tho Weston mil

Thomas Teringham miles =Catherina filia & cohe Galfri Lucy mil

1 Joh'es Teringham=Elianora filia & heres Laurentij   2 Rog'us=   filia
[ob s p 8 H IV] | Pabenham mil   Teringham   Berisford

Joh'es Teringham.=Alicia filia Joh'is Olney soror   Thomas   Rog'us.
| Rob'ti Olney mil

Elizabetha filia Ed'i Brudnell =Joh'es Teringham=Elizabetha filia   Catesby
| [ob 1484] | soror Will'i mil

Thomas Teringham=Anna filia Humfr'i Catesby   Elizabeth   Maria   Margareta.
[ob 1526] | de Whiston in com Northt
| mil

Edmundus   Thomas Teringham=Petronilla filia Joh'is   Maria vxor   Elizabeth
Teringham   de Teringham 1564 | Goodwin de Winching-   Will i   vxor
                                         | ton in com Buck.   Berner   Berner

Catherine   Thomas   Francisca vxor   Elizabeth vxor   Anna   Anth'us
vxor Ed'i   Teringham   Ed'i Sanders   Tho Reade de   Teringham
Price de   de Flower in   Ludg'shall
North   co Northt   gen'
Crawley   gen'

Wahull* or Woodhall
[of Odell].

ALL THE COATES BELONGING TO THE FAMILIES IN THE PEDIGREE OF THE
CHETWOODS & WAHULL al.'s WOODHALL

BERISFORD   Or, a beare saliant sa., collared & cheyned or
BRAYBROKE   Ar, 8 mascles gu, 3, 3, 2
BULKELEY   Sa, a chev betw 3 bulls' heads ar., a mullet ar for a diff^{ce}
CHETWOOD   Quart'ly ar & gu, 4 crosses patée counterchanged
CREW   Az fretty or, betw every fret a cinqfoyle ar
COTES: Gu, on a cher ar 2 barres gemelles gu betw 12 torteauzes betw 3 leopards' heads ar
DRURY .   Ar, on a cheife vert 2 mullets or, a crescent ar. p' diff
ETWALL
FOXCOTT   Ar, on a crosse az 5 flowre de lizes (? escallops) or
GRAY   Barry of 6 ar & az, a lable of 3 points gu
HANKY   Per pale az. & gu, a wolfe saliant or, vulned gu
HENHULL   Quart'ly ar & sa, on the 2^d & 3^d quart's a buck's head caboshed or
HULSO   Ar 3 piles in point sa
HOBBY   Ar, a fesse betw. 3 hawks sa, bells & leggs or
FITZPETER, Comes Essex   Quart'ly or & gu
FITZWARIN   Quart ly per fess ind. ar & gu
KNESWORTH   Er, a chev battelée count' gu. betw. 3 greyhounds pass^t sa
KNIGHTLEY   Quart'ly er & patée of vj gu and or.
GRIFFIN   Sa, a griffin sergreant ar
GRENE   Az, 3 bucks tripping or
LANGWORTH   Or, 3 dragons' heads coupie sa
LEECH   Er, on a cheife ind gu an annulet ar betw 2 crownes or
LEWSON   Az, a fesse nubile ar & sa betw 3 okeleaves or.
LIONS   Ar, a lion ramp't gu
LUDSUP   Ar, a greene-leaved branch & bordure engr sa, on a canton gu a dragon in bend or
MASTERTON   Er, a chev az betw 3 garbes sa
NEEDHAM   Ar, a chev engr az betw 3 bucks' heads sa
OKELEY †   Sa, fretty or & a fes er, on a cheife ar 3 leopards' heads gu.
PARRE, Baro' Ar, 2 barres az & a bord. engr. sa.
PRAERS   Gu, a fess betw. 4 barres gemewes ar.
RAGON   Ar, a crosse gu, a bend az
REE   Az, a plate betw 3 crescents or.
RALEIGH   Ar, a crosse moline gu betw 9 [   ] sa
ROWLEY   Or, on a bend gu cotized sa. 3 crescents or
SKEVINGTON Ar, 3 bulls' heads erased sa, attired or
SMYTH   Ar, on a bend sa 6 flowre de lizes or, on a cheife az. a lyon pass^t gard^t or
SPURSTON   Az, 3 spurrerowells of vj points or
STRANGE   Gu., 2 lyons pass^t ar
TRACY   Or, 2 bends gu
TRESHAM   P'ly per salter sa & ar, 6 trefoils or, a crescent or. for a diff ———
VIUONIA   Ar, on a cheife gu a label of 3 points or
WIDEVILLE   Ar, a fesse & quart gu
WOODHALL al.'s WAHULL   Or, 3 crescents gu.

CHETWOOD CREST.—A demy mantiger saliant ar, out of a crescent gu., horned or

* Cf 'Bib Topog Brit' No 44 p 15
† "Or fretty sable a bar ermine, on a chief gules three leopards' faces or, SOUNDE"
('N.Y. Gen and Biog. Record,' vol 1, No 4)

𝔚𝔞𝔥𝔲𝔩𝔩 al's 𝔚𝔬𝔬𝔡𝔥𝔞𝔩𝔩, 𝔅𝔞𝔯𝔬𝔫𝔢𝔰.

Or, 3 crescents gu

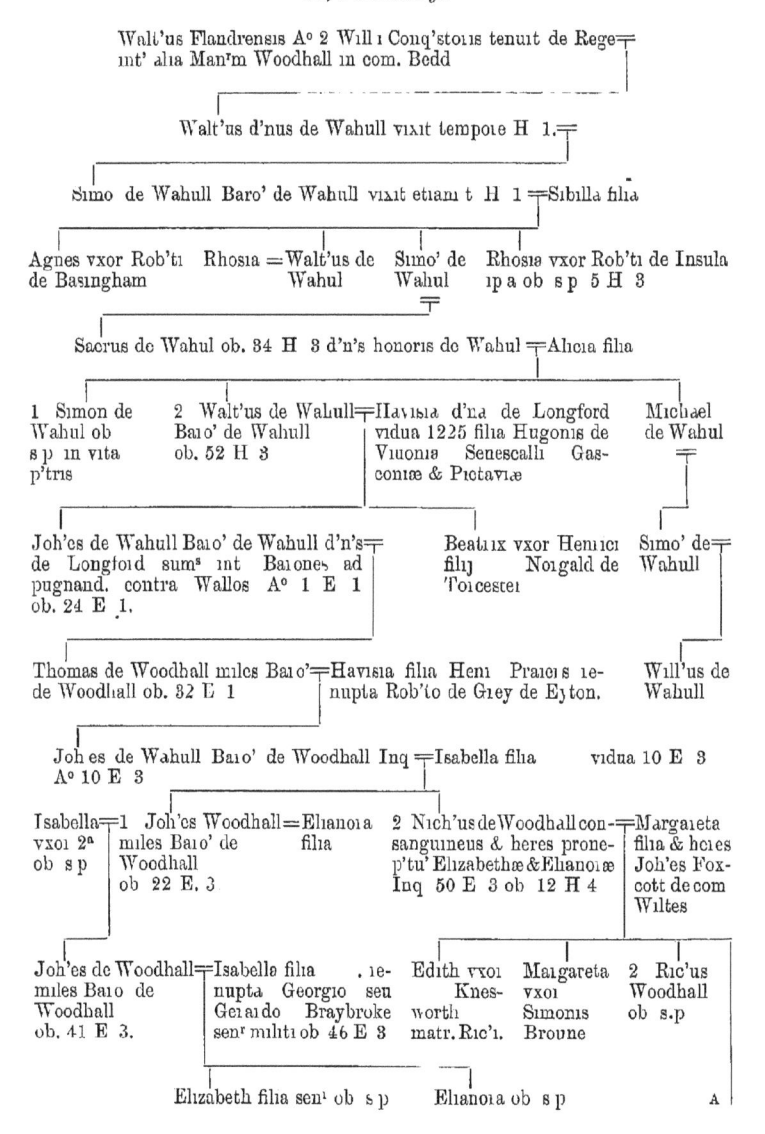

Walt'us Flandrensis A° 2 Will i Conq'storis tenuit de Rege=⊤
int' alia Man'rm Woodhall in com. Bedd

Walt'us d'nus de Wahull vixit tempore H 1.=⊤

Simo de Wahull Baro' de Wahull vixit etiam t H 1 =⊤= Sibilla filia

Agnes vxor Rob'ti | Rhosia =Walt'us de | Simo' de | Rhosia vxor Rob'ti de Insula
de Basingham | Wahul | Wahul | ip a ob s p 5 H 3
 | | =⊤= | |

Sacrus de Wahul ob. 34 H 3 d'n's honoris de Wahul =⊤= Alicia filia

1 Simon de | 2 Walt'us de Wahull =⊤= Havisia d'na de Longford | Michael
Wahul ob | Baro' de Wahull | vidua 1225 filia Hugonis de | de Wahul
s p in vita | ob. 52 H 3 | Viuonia Senescalli Gas- |
p'tris | | coniæ & Pictaviæ | =⊤=

Joh'es de Wahull Baro' de Wahull d'n's =⊤= | Beatrix vxor Henrici | Simo' de =⊤=
de Longford sum⁵ int Barones ad | filij Norgald de | Wahull
pugnand. contra Wallos A° 1 E 1 | Torcester |
ob. 24 E 1. | |

Thomas de Woodhall miles Baro' =⊤= Havisia filia Heni Praters re- | Will'us de
de Woodhall ob. 32 E 1 | nupta Rob'to de Grey de Eyton. | Wahull

Joh'es de Wahull Baro' de Woodhall Inq =⊤= Isabella filia   vidua 10 E 3
A° 10 E 3

Isabella =⊤= 1 Joh'es Woodhall = Elianora | 2 Nich'us de Woodhall con- =⊤= Margareta
vxor 2ᵃ | miles Baro' de | filia | sanguineus & heres prone- | filia & heres
ob s p | Woodhall | | p'tu' Elizabethæ & Elianoræ | Joh'es Fox-
 | ob 22 E. 3 | | Inq 50 E 3 ob 12 H 4 | cott de com
 | | | | Wiltes

Joh'es de Woodhall =⊤= Isabella filia   re- | Edith vxor | Margareta | 2 Ric'us
miles Baro de | nupta Georgio seu | Knes- | vxor | Woodhall
Woodhall | Geraldo Braybroke | worth | Simonis | ob s.p
ob. 41 E 3. | sen' militi ob 46 E 3 | matr. Ric'i. | Broune

Elizabeth filia sen¹ ob s p   Elianora ob s p   A

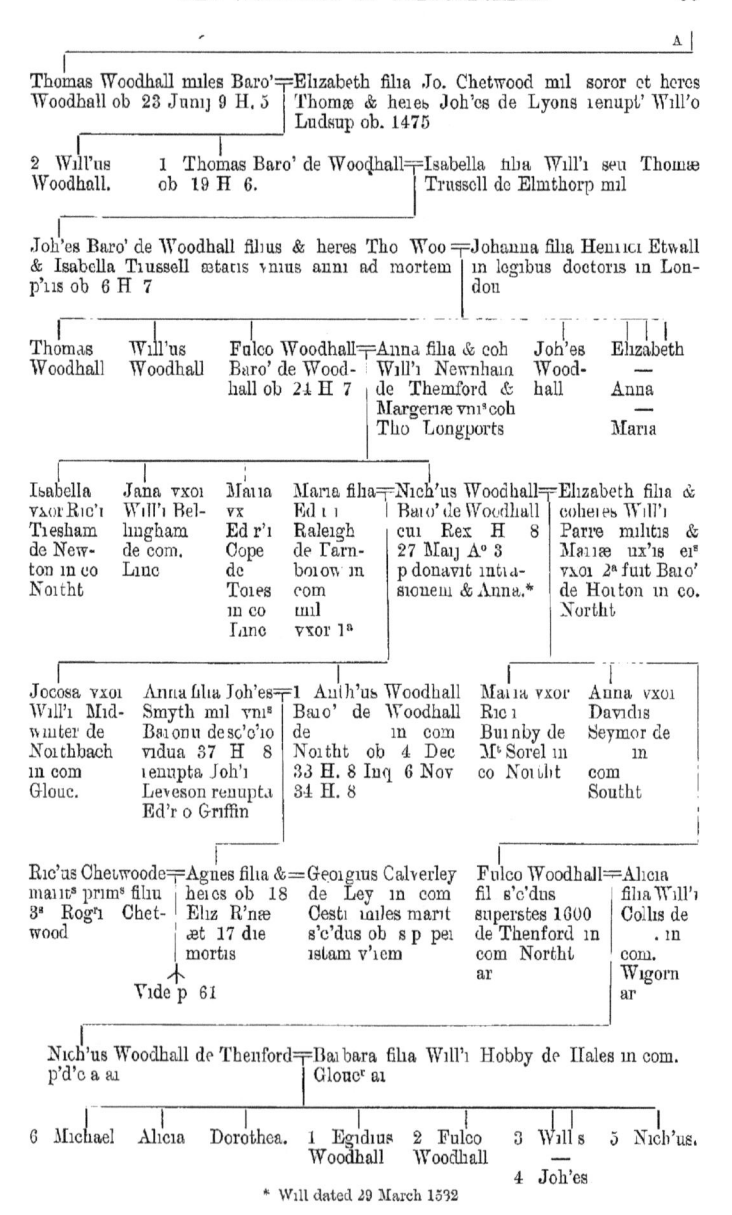

THE VISITATION OF BEDFORDSHIRE.

Thomas Woodhall miles Baro' = Elizabeth filia Jo. Chetwood mil soror et heres
Woodhall ob 23 Junij 9 H. 5 | Thomæ & heres Joh'es de Lyons renupt' Will'o
 | Ludsup ob. 1475

2 Will'us Woodhall. | 1 Thomas Baro' de Woodhall = Isabella filia Will'i seu Thomæ
 | ob 19 H 6. | Trussell de Elmthorp mil

Joh'es Baro' de Woodhall filius & heres Tho Woo = Johanna filia Henrici Etwall
& Isabella Trussell ætatis vnius anni ad mortem | in legibus doctoris in Lon-
p'ris ob 6 H 7 | don

Thomas Woodhall | Will'us Woodhall | Fulco Woodhall Baro' de Wood- = Anna filia & coh Will'i Newnham de Themford & Margeriæ vni° coh Tho Longports | Joh'es Woodhall | Elizabeth — Anna — Maria
 | | hall ob 24 H 7 | | |

Isabella vxor Ric'i Tresham de New- ton in co Northt | Jana vxor Will'i Bel- lingham de com. Linc | Maria vx Ed r'i Cope de Tores in co Linc | Maria filia = Nich'us Woodhall = Elizabeth filia & Ed i i | Baro' de Woodhall | coheres Will'i Raleigh | cui Rex H 8 | Parre militis & de Tarn- | 27 Maij A° 3 | Mariæ ux'is ei° borow in | p donavit intra- | vxor 2ª fuit Baro' com | sionem & Anna.* | de Horton in co. mil | | Northt vxor 1ª | |

Jocosa vxor Will'i Mid- winter de Northbach in com Glouc. | Anna filia Joh'es = 1 Anth'us Woodhall Smyth mil vni° | Baro' de Woodhall Baronu de sc'o'ro | de in com vidua 37 H 8 | Northt ob 4 Dec renupta Joh'i | 33 H. 8 Inq 6 Nov Leveson renupta | 34 H. 8 Ed'r o Griffin | | Maria vxor Ric i Burnby de M° Sorel in co Northt | Anna vxor Davidis Seymor de in com Southt

Ric'us Chetwoode = Agnes filia & = Georgius Calverley mariti° prim° filiu | heres ob 18 | de Ley in com 3ª Rog'ri Chet- | Eliz R'næ | Cesti miles marit wood | æt 17 die | s'c'dus ob s p per | mortis | istam v'iem Vide p 61 | Fulco Woodhall = Alicia fil s'c'dus | filia Will'i superstes 1600 | Collis de de Thenford in | . in com Northt | com. ar | Wigorn | ar

Nich'us Woodhall de Thenford = Barbara filia Will'i Hobby de Hales in com.
p'd'c a ar | Glouc' ar

6 Michael | Alicia | Dorothea. | 1 Egidius Woodhall | 2 Fulco Woodhall | 3 Will s | 5 Nich'us.
 | | | | | 4 Joh'es

* Will dated 29 March 1532

The Visitation of Bedfordshire
1634.*

THE VISITATION OF THE COUNTY OF BEDFORD taken in the xth yeare of the raigne of o[r] dread Soueraigne Lord King Charles by vertue of his Ma[ties] Commission under the greate Seale of England directed to S[r] Richard S[t] George Knight Clarenceux and S[r] John Borowgh knight Norroy Kings of Armes, who deputed for the execution thereof George Owen Esq[r] Yorke Herald and Henry Lilly Rouge-rose Pursuivant, officers of Armes

---

THE COMMON SEALE OF YE TOWNE OF BEDFORD

Argent, an eagle displayed looking to the sinister with wings inverted sable, ducally crowned or, on the eagle a large castle surmounted by two more, one above the other, of the third

Which Towne was incorporated in the leauenth yeare of King Henry the second with all such Customes and Priuiledges as ye sayd Burgesses held in the tyme of King Henry his Grandfather That is to saye with such Priuiledges as ye Burgesses and Cittizens of Oxford enioyed being also confirmed by King Richard the first, King Richard the second Henry ye fourth, Henry the sixt, Edward the fourth, Henry the seauenth, Henry the eight, Queene Mary, Queene Elizabeth, and King James of blessed memory The which Towne is Incorporated by the name of Mayor, Bayliffs, Burgesses, and Comunalty of the sayd Corporacion And at this present visitac'on is Mayor Thomas Hawes, The Right Ho[ble] Oliuer Earle of Bollinbrooke Recorder whoe executeth the same Office by his Deputy Richard Taylor Esq Justice of ye Peace for the County of Bedford, William Warren al's Waller, Robert Bamford Thomas Spencer, William Faldo, Thomas Waller, and Thomas Paradine associates to the saide Maior and haue been Maiors, Simon Becket and Robert Hawes Baliffes, John Beckett Chamberlain A° 1634

THO HAWES, maior
SIMON BECKETT, ROBERT HAWES, JOHN BECKETT, Baliffes

---

* Additions in brackets [ ], except where otherwise stated, are from Harl Ms 1097 Words in italics in parentheses ( ) the Editor is responsible for

TOWNE & BOROUGH OF BEDFORD

ARMS —*Per pale argent and gules, a fesse azure.*

These armes are of anncientie belonging & apperteyning to ye towne & boroughe of Bedford tyme out of mynd

WILL'M HERUY al's Clarenceux King of Armes

These armes here depicted ar belonginge & apperteyning to ye Maior, Balyffes, Burgesses & comunalty of ye towne & boroughe of Bedford wch Armes I Clarenceulx King of Armes of the South East & Weste parties of England haue not onlie ratified & confirmed ye same vnto ye Maior Balyffs burgisses & comunalty of ye towne & bororghe of Bedford but also recorded ye same in ye registers of my visitation now made within ye county of Bedford &c And at this p'sent visitation was Robert Paradyne Mayor, Sr John Gascoigne Knight recorder Henry Albanye, Thomas Leigh, William Bull, Richard Lawrence, Humfrey Lawrence, Henry Lawrence, Symond Beckett, & Alexander Hunt assotiate to ye saide Maior who haue been Mayors, Edward Smyth & Robert Goodalle Bayllyffs George Huxley & William Ladd Chamberleynes In wittness whereof I haue heerevnto subscribed my name ye 7th of June 1566

WILLIAM HERVEY al's Clarenciulx King of Armes

Abbis
[of Bedford].

ARMS —*Gules, a fesse lozengy between three escallops argent*

Thomas Abbis of Bedford three seuerall times Maior of the same Towne and in Commission for the Peace there

William Abbys of the Towne of Bedford in Commission for the Peace there seuerall yeares, Maior of the same Towne of Bedford = Cicely d of William Yarway of Willington in com Bedf.

William Abbys now maior of the Towne of Bedford this third of Nouember A° 1634 for the following yeare = Alice d of Geo Edwards of Emerton co Bucks

Thomas Abbys of Queen's Coll Cambs 2 son

Sciceley eld da.   2. Alice.   3. Anne

WILL'I ABBIS

Albanye*
[of Bedford].

ARMS —*Ermine, on a fesse between three cinqfoils gules a greyhound courant or, collared azure* †
CREST —*Out of a ducal coronet gules a demi-dolphin hauriant or*

Albaney first of London after of the Towne of Bedford

Robert Albanye of Bedford = Elizabeth d of Oliuer St John of Sheinebrooke in com Bedf relict of Wm Goodfellow of Pauenham

John Albanye of Bromham co Bedford A° 1634 = Elizabeth dau'r of Tho. Webb of Roxton com Bedf

John Albaney eld son and heire, aged 11 yeares A° 1634

2 Edward.
3 Robert.

Elizabeth
Mary

Anne

JOHN ALBANYE

---

* *Cf* 'Visitation of London 1568 ' p 48, ed Harl Soc —ED
† "The field should bee argent and not ermen as yt will appeere in the last Visitation of Surrey made 1623 " "Vide the Vis of Surrey for the difference"
Notes respecting grants of arms, in inverted commas are in the original MS —ED

L

Alston

[of Odell].

ARMS.—I, *Azure, ten étoiles or, four, three, two, and one, a martlet for difference,* ALSTON. II, *Quarterly per fesse indented or and azure, over all a bend gules,* BLUNVILLE.

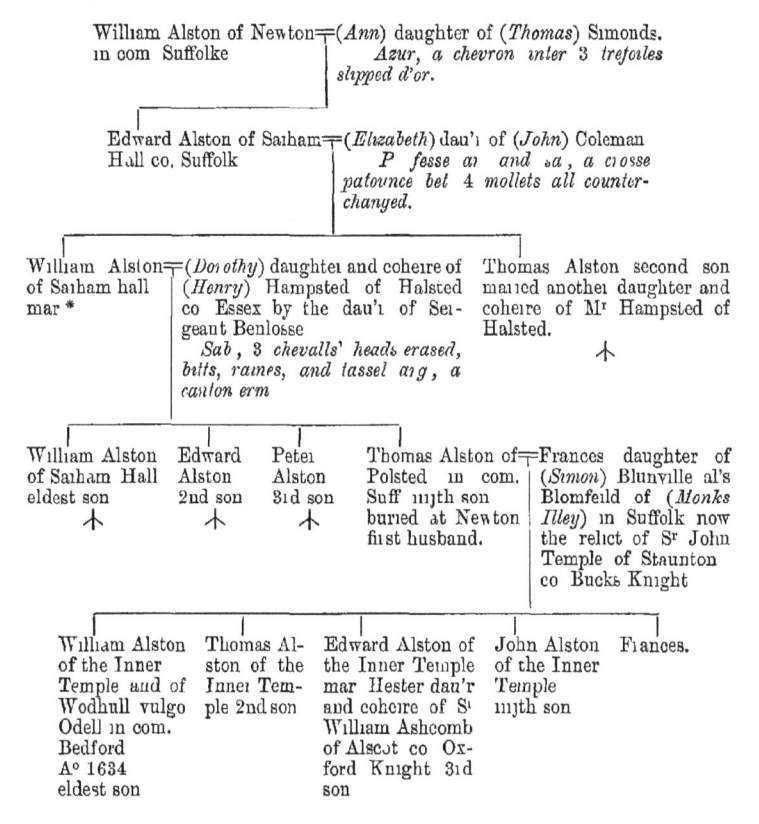

William Alston of Newton=(*Ann*) daughter of (*Thomas*) Simonds.
in com Suffolke │ *Azur, a chevron inter 3 trefoiles slipped d'or.*

    Edward Alston of Sarham=(*Elizabeth*) dau'r of (*John*) Coleman
    Hall co. Suffolk │ *P fesse ar and sa, a crosse patounce bet 4 mollets all counterchanged.*

William Alston=(*Dorothy*) daughter and coheire of   Thomas Alston second son
of Sarham hall │ (*Henry*) Hampsted of Halsted   married another daughter and
mar * │ co Essex by the dau'r of Sergeant Benlosse   coheire of Mr Hampsted of Halsted.
│ *Sab, 3 chevalls' heads erased, bitts, raines, and tassel arg, a canton erm*

William Alston   Edward   Peter   Thomas Alston of=Frances daughter of
of Sarham Hall   Alston   Alston   Polsted in com. │ (*Simon*) Blunville al's
eldest son   2nd son   3rd son   Suff mjth son │ Blomfeild of (*Monks*
                                                                buried at Newton │ *Illey*) in Suffolk now
                                                                first husband. │ the relict of Sr John Temple of Staunton co Bucks Knight

William Alston   Thomas Alston   Edward Alston of   John Alston   Frances.
of the Inner   of the Inner Temple   the Inner Temple   of the Inner
Temple and of   2nd son   mar Hester dau'r   Temple
Wodhull vulgo   and coheire of Sr   mjth son
Odell in com.   William Ashcomb
Bedford   of Alscot co Oxford Knight 3rd son
A° 1634
eldest son

                                                                                                            WILL'M ALSTON

---

* 'The three upp discents of this pedegree togeather wth this Coate and the three matches were set forth on Collons by Rafe Brooke Yorke Herald "

Anderson

[of Epworth].

ARMS.—*Quarterly—1 and 4, Argent, a chevron between three crosses fleuries sable,* ANDERSON , 2 *and* 3,   , *five étoiles   ,*
CREST.—*A water-spaniel passant or*

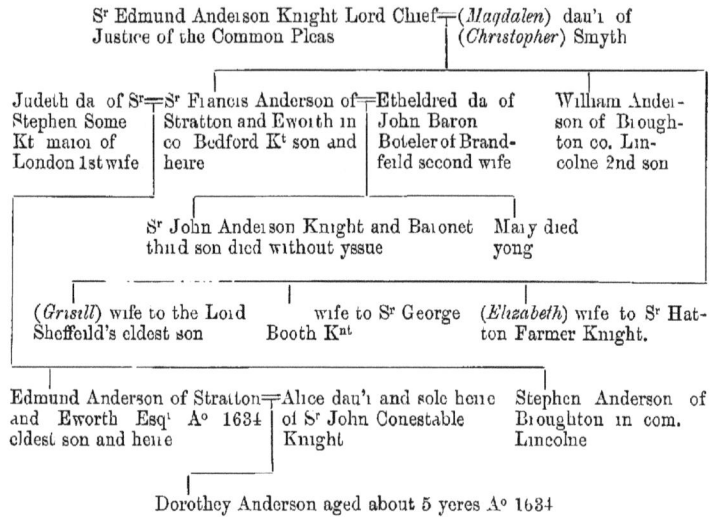

Sr Edmund Anderson Knight Lord Chief = (*Magdalen*) dau'r of Justice of the Common Pleas | (*Christopher*) Smyth

Judeth da. of Sr = Sr Francis Anderson of = Etheldred da. of   William Anderson of Broughton co. Lincolne 2nd son
Stephen Some | Stratton and Eworth in | John Baron
Kt. maior of | co. Bedford Kt son and | Boteler of Brand-
London 1st wife | heire | feild second wife

Sr John Anderson Knight and Baronet third son died without yssue   Mary died yong

(*Grisill*) wife to the Lord Sheffeild's eldest son   wife to Sr George Booth Knt   (*Elizabeth*) wife to Sr Hatton Farmer Knight.

Edmund Anderson of Stratton = Alice dau'r and sole heire   Stephen Anderson of Broughton in com. Lincolne
and Eworth Esqr Ao 1634 | of Sr John Conestable
eldest son and heire | Knight

Dorothey Anderson aged about 5 yeres Ao 1634

WILLIAM WELDON, servant to Mr EDMUND ANDERSON.

Anthony

[of Bedford].

ARMS.—*Argent, a leopard's head gules between two flaunches sable, a crescent for difference*

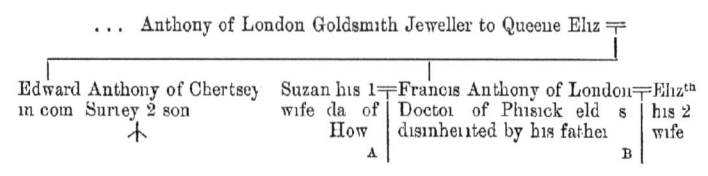

... Anthony of London Goldsmith Jeweller to Queene Eliz =

Edward Anthony of Chertsey in com. Surrey 2 son
A

Suzan his 1 = Francis Anthony of London = Elizth his 2 wife
wife da. of | Doctor of Phisick eld s |
How | disinherited by his father |
A   B

THE VISITATION OF BEDFORDSHIRE.

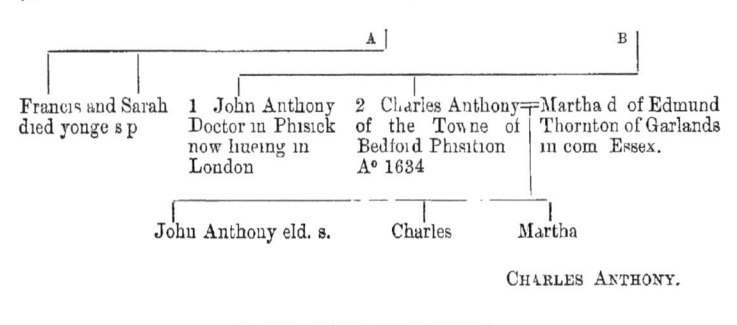

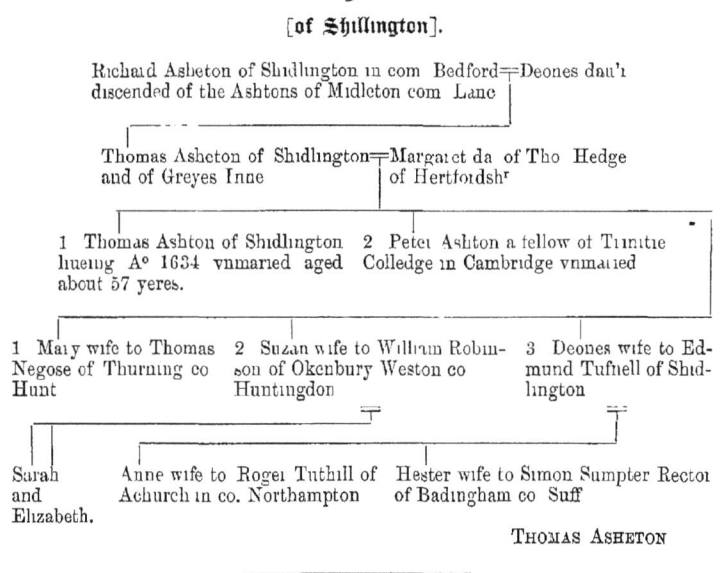

```
                        A                              B
    ┌───────────────────┼───────────────┐              │
Francis and Sarah   1 John Anthony   2 Charles Anthony=Martha d of Edmund
died yonge s p      Doctor in Phisick   of the Towne of│Thornton of Garlands
                    now liueing in      Bedford Phisition│in com Essex.
                    London              Aº 1634
                                        ┌───────────┼───────────┐
                                  John Anthony eld. s.   Charles      Martha
```

CHARLES ANTHONY.

Asheton
[of Shillington].

Richard Asheton of Shidlington in com Bedford=Deones dau'r discended of the Ashtons of Midleton com Lanc

Thomas Asheton of Shidlington=Margaret da of Tho Hedge
and of Greyes Inne   of Hertfordsh'r

1 Thomas Ashton of Shidlington   2 Peter Ashton a fellow of Trinitie
liueing Aº 1634 vnmaried aged   Colledge in Cambridge vnmaried
about 57 yeres.

1 Mary wife to Thomas   2 Suzan wife to William Robin-   3 Deones wife to Ed-
Negose of Thurning co   son of Okenbury Weston co   mund Tufnell of Shid-
Hunt   Huntingdon   lington

Sarah   Anne wife to Roger Tuthill of   Hester wife to Simon Sumpter Rector
and   Achurch in co. Northampton   of Badingham co Suff
Elizabeth.

THOMAS ASHETON

Ashton
[of Tingrith].

Robert Ashton descended from the Ashtons of Leauer=Alice da of
in com Lancaster gentleman of the horse to Fr'ncis│ . Furneys
yᵉ good Earle of Beford
                                          A

A

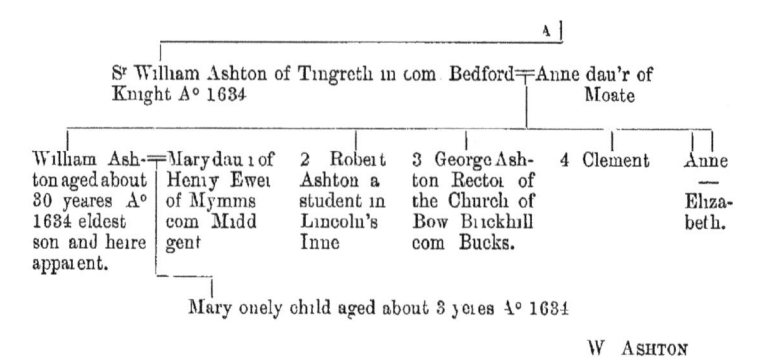

Sr William Ashton of Tingreth in com Bedford = Anne dau'r of Moate
Knight A° 1634

- William Ash-=Mary dau r of | 2 Robert | 3 George Ash- | 4 Clement | Anne
  ton aged about | Henry Ewer | Ashton a | ton Rector of | — | —
  30 yeares A° | of Mymms | student in | the Church of | | Eliza-
  1634 eldest | com Midd | Lincoln's | Bow Brickhill | | beth.
  son and heire | gent | Inne | com Bucks. | |
  apparent.

Mary onely child aged about 3 yeres A° 1634

W Ashton

Astry

[of Harlington].

ARMS —*Barry wavy of six argent and azure, on a chief gules three bezants* [*]
CREST —*On a wreath or and azure a demi-ostrich proper, beaked and feathered gules, in its beak a horse-shoe of the second*

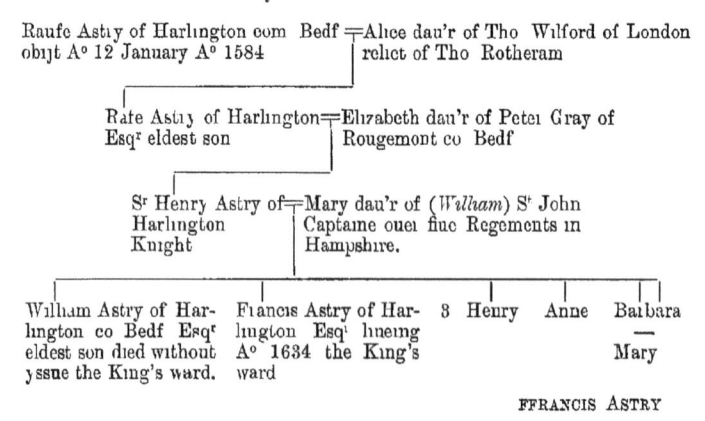

Raufe Astry of Harlington com Bedf = Alice dau'r of Tho Wilford of London
obijt A° 12 January A° 1584 | relict of Tho Rotheram

Rafe Astry of Harlington = Elizabeth dau'r of Peter Gray of
Esqr eldest son | Rougemont co Bedf

Sr Henry Astry of = Mary dau'r of (William) St John
Harlington | Captaine ouer fiue Regements in
Knight | Hampshire.

- William Astry of Har- | Francis Astry of Har- | 3 Henry | Anne | Barbara
  lington co Bedf Esqr | lington Esqr lineing | | | —
  eldest son died without | A° 1634 the King's | | | Mary
  yssue the King's ward. | ward

FFRANCIS ASTRY

---

[*] "Exemplified by Tho Clarenceulx principall hereauld and King of Armes at the south pte of thes Realme of England otherwyse called Tho Holme Kt to Ralphe Astry Citizen of London and borne in ye County of Hertford dated ye xijth of September in the 2d yeare of ye Raigne of our Sou'ragne Lord ye King'

Audley

[of Houghton-Conquest].

ARMS —*Quarterly per pale indented or and azure, on a bend of the second between two eagles displayed a fret or* *
[CREST —*On a chapeau gules, turned up ermine, a wyvern azure with wings addorsed or, charged on the breast with a mullet argent*]

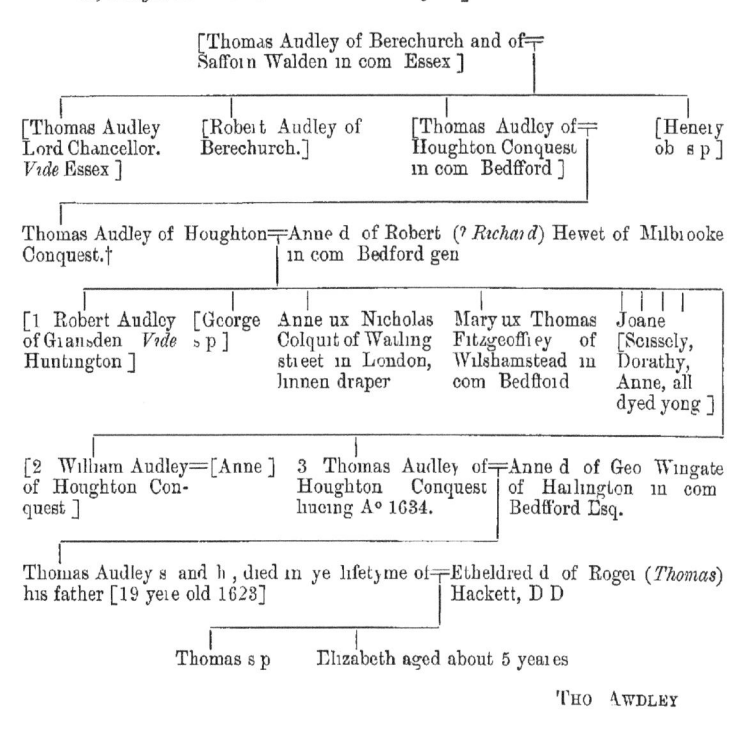

[Thomas Audley of Berechurch and of Saffron Walden in com Essex]

- [Thomas Audley Lord Chancellor. *Vide* Essex]
- [Robert Audley of Berechurch.]
- [Thomas Audley of Houghton Conquest in com Bedford]
- [Henery ob s p]

Thomas Audley of Houghton Conquest.† = Anne d of Robert (? *Richard*) Hewet of Milbrooke in com Bedford gen

- [1 Robert Audley of Gransden *Vide* Huntingdon]
- [George s p]
- Anne ux Nicholas Colquit of Watling street in London, linnen draper
- Mary ux Thomas Fitzgeoffrey of Wilshamstead in com Bedford
- Joane [Scissely, Dorathy, Anne, all dyed yong]

- [2 William Audley of Houghton Conquest] = [Anne]
- 3 Thomas Audley of Houghton Conquest liueing A° 1634. = Anne d of Geo Wingate of Harlington in com Bedford Esq.

Thomas Audley s and h, died in ye lifetyme of his father [19 yere old 1623] = Etheldred d of Roger (*Thomas*) Hackett, D D

- Thomas s p
- Elizabeth aged about 5 yeares

THO AWDLEY

---

* "The exemplification of these Armes and Crest vnder the hand of Will'm Segar Gartar principall of Armes and are remayning ir the hand of Mr Robert Awdley of Gransden in y^e County of Huntingdon Mr Thomas Awdley of Houghton Conquest in ye County of Bedf is third brother to the atoresaid Robert whose armes and his is with the due difference RICHARD MUNDAY"

† 'Visitation of Essex' Harl Soc, vol xiii, p 139, makes Thomas Audley son of Henry, which I think is right, as I do not think Henry had two brothers named Thomas

Bagshaw

[of Bushmead].

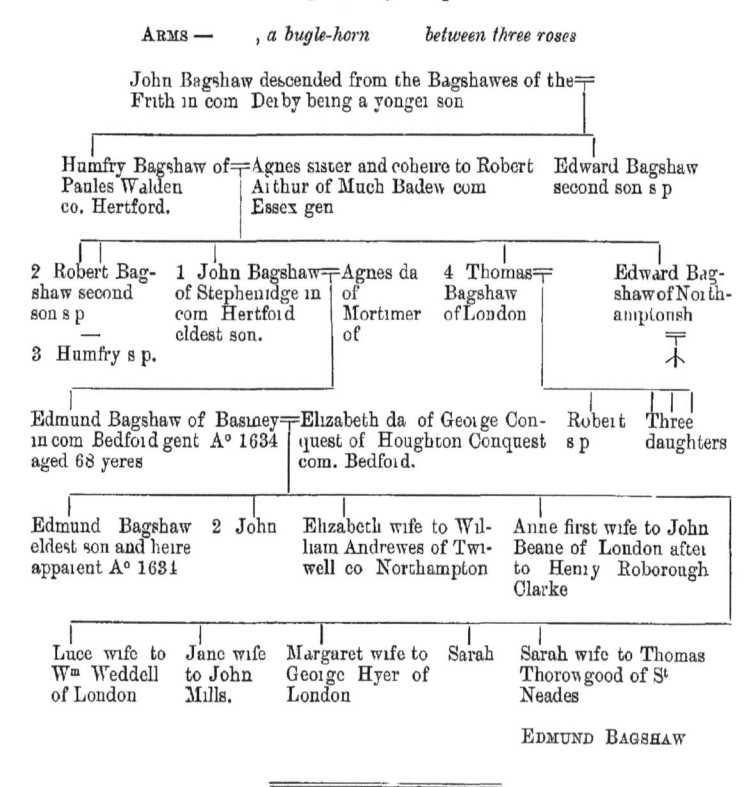

ARMS — , a bugle-horn between three roses

John Bagshaw descended from the Bagshawes of the Frith in com Derby being a yonger son

- Humfry Bagshaw of Paules Walden co. Hertford. = Agnes sister and coheire to Robert Arthur of Much Badew com Essex gen
- Edward Bagshaw second son s p

- 2 Robert Bagshaw second son s p
- 3 Humfry s p.
- 1 John Bagshaw of Stephenidge in com Hertford eldest son. = Agnes da of Mortimer of
- 4 Thomas Bagshaw of London
- Edward Bagshaw of Northamptonsh

Edmund Bagshaw of Basmey in com Bedford gent A° 1634 aged 68 yeres = Elizabeth da of George Conquest of Houghton Conquest com. Bedford.
Robert s p
Three daughters

- Edmund Bagshaw eldest son and heire apparent A° 1634
- 2 John
- Elizabeth wife to William Andrewes of Twiwell co Northampton
- Anne first wife to John Beane of London after to Henry Roborough Clarke

- Luce wife to Wm Weddell of London
- Jane wife to John Mills.
- Margaret wife to George Hyer of London
- Sarah
- Sarah wife to Thomas Thorowgood of St Neades

EDMUND BAGSHAW

Barnardiston

[of Northill].

ARMS —*Azure, a fesse dancetlée ermine between six cross-crosslets argent, a crescent for difference*
[CREST —*Out of a mural crown gules a (?) boar's head argent, tusked or*]

George Barnardiston of Norrill second son of Sr Thomas Barnardiston of Kedington in com Suff = Elizabeth daughter and sole heire of Tho Burley of Lynn

A

THE VISITATION OF BEDFORDSHIRE.

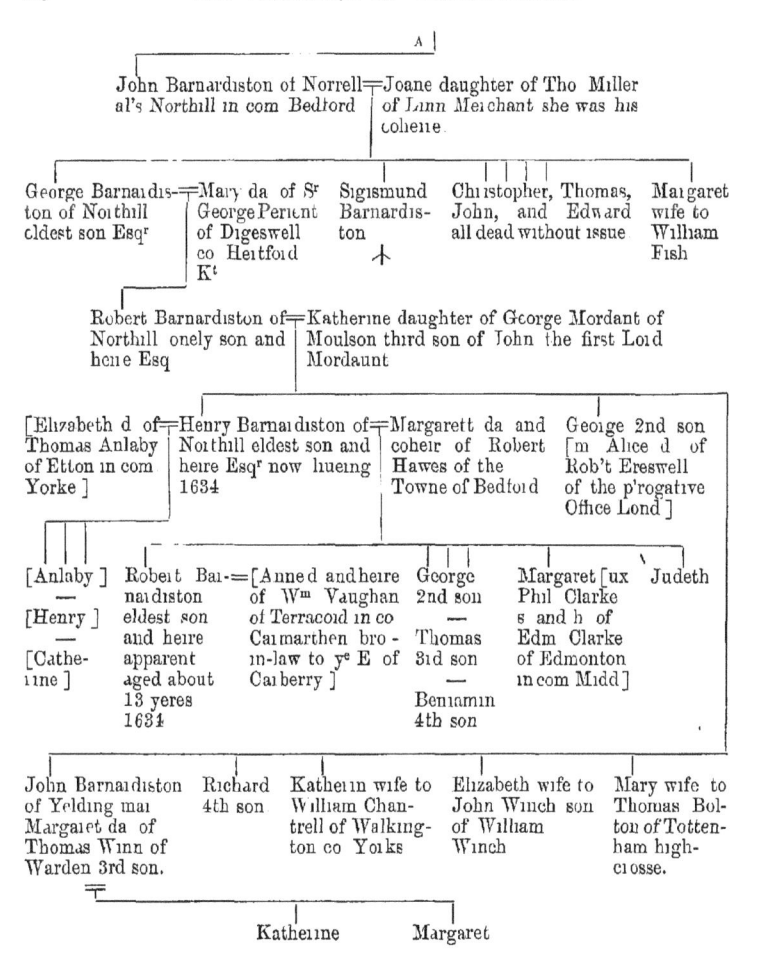

John Barnardiston of Norrell = Joane daughter of Tho Miller
al's Northill in com Bedford   of Linn Merchant she was his
                               coheire.

George Barnardis- = Mary da of S[r]   Sigismund   Christopher, Thomas,   Margaret
ton of Northill   George Perient   Barnardis-   John, and Edward   wife to
eldest son Esq[r]   of Digeswell   ton   all dead without issue William
                    co Hertford   Fish
                    K[t]

Robert Barnardiston of = Katherine daughter of George Mordant of
Northill onely son and   Moulson third son of John the first Lord
heire Esq   Mordaunt

[Elizabeth d of = Henry Barnardiston of = Margarett da and   George 2nd son
Thomas Anlaby   Northill eldest son and coheir of Robert   [m Alice d of
of Etton in com heire Esq[r] now lueing Hawes of the   Rob't Ereswell
Yorke]   1634   Towne of Bedford   of the p'rogative
                                                              Office Lond]

[Anlaby]   Robert Bar- = [Anne d and heire   George   Margaret [ux   Judeth
—   nardiston   of W[m] Vaughan   2nd son   Phil Clarke
[Henry]   eldest son   of Terracord in co —   s and h of
—   and heire   Carmarthen bro-   Thomas   Edm Clarke
[Cathe-   apparent   in-law to y[e] E of 3rd son   of Edmonton
rine]   aged about   Carberry]   —   in com Midd]
            13 yeres   Benjamin
            1634   4th son

John Barnardiston   Richard   Katherin wife to   Elizabeth wife to   Mary wife to
of Yelding mar   4th son   William Chan-   John Winch son   Thomas Bol-
Margaret da of   trell of Walking-   of William   ton of Totten-
Thomas Winn of   ton co Yorks   Winch   ham high-
Warden 3rd son.   crosse.

            Katherine   Margaret

HENFRY BARNARDISTON

Beechar

[of Howbury in Renhold].

ARMS (TWO SHIELDS) —I, *Vair argent and gules, on a canton or a stag's head caboshed sable,* BEECHER * II, *Azure, a chevron or between two lions passant-guardant argent,* RICHE †

CRESTS —I, *A demi-lion erased argent, girded round the waist with a ducal coronet or* ‡ II, *On a wreath argent and sable a buck's head pellettée erased or, gorged with a ducal coronet gules* * III, *Out of a ducal coronet argent a demi-lion issuant ermine,* RICHE †

Henry Bechar of Bishops Morchard in com Deuon gent. 1564 yongest son of eleuen sons, and was heire to all their lands wch they had in gauel kind in Kent == dau'r of Sr Nicholas Heron of Edgecombe in com Kent Kt §

- Bartholomew Bechar 5 son
- Edward Becher Esqr for the body of Queene Eliz mar da of the Lo Cobham
- 4 William Bechar
- 3 Margaret wife to Sr Richard Dabridgecourt Knight
- 2 Mary wife to Chedeoke Warder, mother of St Edward Wardom Kt

Sr William Bechar Clarke of ye Counsell

- 1 Elizabeth wife to John Kelke of London
- Fane Becher 3 son.
- 4 Mabel wife to Richard Norton Kt
- Henry Becher of London Esquire A° 1569, 11° Eliz, sometime Alderman of London, eldest son == Judeth dau'r and sole heire of John Riche of London gent, son and heire of Thomas Riche of Marston co Bedf

- Sr William Bechar of Howbury in the p'sh of Renhall co Bedford Knight A° 1634 == Elizabeth eldest sister of Oliuer Lord St John, Earle of Bullingbrooke.
- 2 Edward Bechar of Peterborow.
- 3 George Bechar of Clauering co. Essex

- 2 Henry
- 3 William
- 4 St John
- 5 Francis
- 6 Howard
- 7 John

---

* 'This Creast was given and this auntient Coate of this ffamelie exemplified by l'res pattents from Wm Harucy Clarenceulx King of Armes dated A° 1564 to Henry Bechar of Bishops Morchard'

† 'Clarenceulx Cooke made an exemplificac'on of this Coat and crest to John Riche of London gen son and heire of Thomas Riche of Marston in com Bedf gent dated A° 1573, 16th Eliz'

‡ "Clarenceulx Cooke exemplefied and graunted to Hen Becher of London Esq this Creast by l'res pattent dated 11° Eliz A° 1569'

§ *Cf* 'Visitation of London, 1568' ed Harl Soc, where the wife is described as "Alice d of Thomas Heron of Croydon 1 wife"

Oliuer Bechar of Howbury Esqr eldest son and heire apparent liueing Aº 1634. =⸻ Elizabeth dau'r of Sr William Tate of Delapree in co. Northampton Kt. | Dorothey wife to William Cogniers of Walthamstow co. Essex Esqr. | Anne wife to Edmund Harding of Aspley in co. Bedford gent. | 3. Elizabeth. — 4. Judeth. — 5. Katherin.

William Bechar* eldest son aged about 6 years Aº 1634. | 2. Oliuer. | 3. Edward. | 4. John s.p. | Elizabeth.

O. BECHAR.

Beverley†

[of Eaton Socon].

ARMS.—*Argent, a fesse dancettée between three leopards' heads sable.*

Thomas Beauerley of Selby com. Yorke. =⸻ Alice d. and coh. of John Stocke.

2. James Beauerley of .... com. Yorke. =⸻ Anne d. of George Gilpin. | John Beuerley eld. s., of Selby. | Walter. | Robert Beverley of Eaton co. Bedf., Clarke of the Kitchin to Queen Eliz., s.p. | Thomas Beuerley of Eaton s.p.

1. James Beuerley of Eaton Socon co. Bedf., sometime high shreife of this county, liueing Aº 1634. =⸻ Jane d. of Sr Richard Conquest of Houghton Conquest co. Bedf. | Ellis Beuerley Rector of Tortworth.

James Beuerley eld. s. and h., one of the Justices of the peace in co. Bedf. gent. 1634. =⸻ Elizabeth d. of Tho. Docwray of Putridge co. Hertf. Esqr. | 2. William. | 3. Thomas. | Robert.

James Beuerley eld. s. and heire aged about 5 yeres Aº 1634. | 2. Thomas. | 3. Nathaniell. | 4. William.

JAMES BEVERLEY iu.

---

* For continuation of pedigree *cf.* 'Le Neve's Knights,' p. 118, ed. Harl. Soc.
† *Cf.* 'Le Neve's Knights,' p. 92, ed. Harl. Soc.

Bletsoe

[of Wymington].

ARMS.—*Or, on a bend sable between three escallops azure as many garbs of the first, all within a bordure gules*
CREST.—*A wolf's head couped or, semée of hurts and gorged with a mural crown azure*

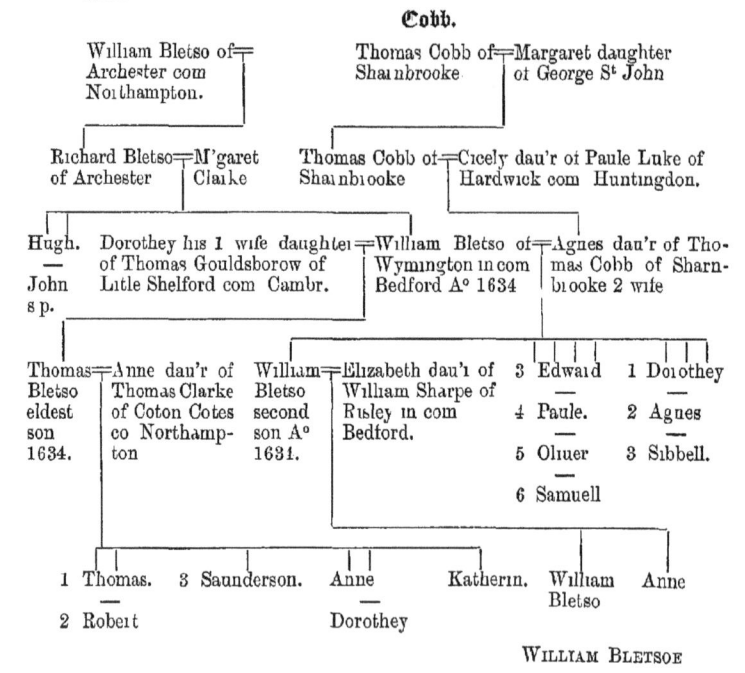

Cobb.

William Bletso of Archester com Northampton. =

Thomas Cobb of Sharnbrooke = Margaret daughter of George St John

Richard Bletso of Archester = M'garet Clarke

Thomas Cobb of Sharnbrooke = Cicely dau'r of Paule Luke of Hardwick com Huntingdon.

Hugh. — John s p.

Dorothey his 1 wife daughter of Thomas Gouldsborow of Litle Shelford com Cambr. = William Bletso of Wymington in com Bedford A° 1634 = Agnes dau'r of Thomas Cobb of Sharnbrooke 2 wife

Thomas Bletso eldest son 1634. = Anne dau'r of Thomas Clarke of Coton Cotes co Northampton

William Bletso second son A° 1631. = Elizabeth dau'r of William Sharpe of Risley in com Bedford.

3 Edward — 4 Paule. 5 Oliuer 6 Samuell

1 Dorothey — 2 Agnes 3 Sibbell.

1 Thomas. 2 Robert 3 Saunderson. Anne Dorothey Katherin. William Bletso Anne

WILLIAM BLETSOE

Bolsworth

[of Leighton-Bussard].

ARMS.—*Azure, three boars' heads couped argent* [*]

Robert Bolsworth of Leighton Buzard in com Bedf., = Rhose he died A° 1541

A

[*] "Respit for proof of these Armes till the Terme"

Bolsworth pedigree

```
                                                    A
    |                           |                   |                    |
John Bolsworth   Edmund Bolsworth of = Anne d. of           Child
ob. s p          Leighton Buzard        of Thickford.

    |                 |                      |                    |            |
  John      Robert Bolsworth of = Joane d. of John     George      Anne.
            Leighton Buzard, he   Ganderie of           —           —
            ob 1624                Pitchcote          Banester.    Alice

    |                                |                 |            |         |
Edmund Bolsworth of = Elizabeth d of John Ire-    Banester     Anne.     Joane
Leighton liveing A°   monger of Stanbridge          —            —          —
1634                                                Robert      Rhose     Suzan

         |          |        |          |          |
      Thomas    Edmund    Sarah     Elizabeth    Ann
```

EDM BOLSWORTH

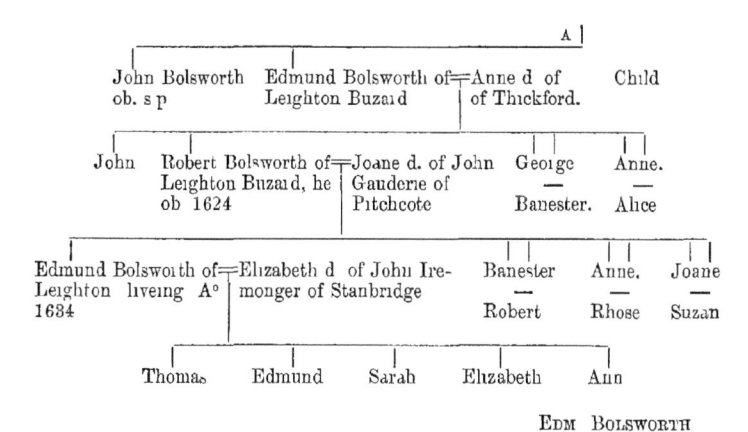

Boteler

[of Biddenham].

ARMS.—*Quarterly*—1, *Gules, a fesse chequée argent and sable between six cross-crosslets or*, BOTELER ; 2, *Gules, an escutcheon vair argent and azure between six cross-crosslets or*, MOLLSWORTH ; 3, *Azure, a fesse, and a chevron in chief gules*, KIRTON ; 4, *Gules, a chevron between three peacocks in their pride argent*, PEACOCK.*

CREST.—*Out of a mural crown gules a boar's head argent, tusked or*

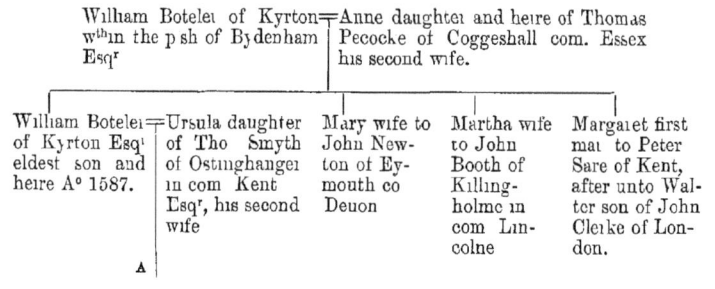

```
William Boteler of Kyrton = Anne daughter and heire of Thomas
w^{th}in the p'sh of Bydenham   Pecocke of Coggeshall com. Essex
Esq^r                           his second wife.

    |                    |              |              |
William Boteler = Ursula daughter   Mary wife to   Martha wife   Margaret first
of Kyrton Esq^r   of Tho. Smyth     John New-      to John       mar. to Peter
eldest son and    of Ostinghanger   ton of Ey-     Booth of      Sare of Kent,
heire A° 1587.    in com. Kent      mouth co.      Killing-      after unto Wal-
                  Esq^r, his second Deuon          holme in      ter son of John
                  wife                             com. Lin-     Clerke of Lon-
                                                   colne         don.
    |
    A
```

* "Certafied thus in a pedegree vnder the hands of clarenceulx Cooke and Glou^r Somerset made for Will'm Boteler of Kyrtons in Bydenham Co. Bedf. Esquier A° D'ni 1587."

Boteler pedigree

Sr Thomas Boteler of Kirton Kt. = Anne daughter and heire of Francis Farrar of Harwood com. Bedford Esqr.

Alice the eldest daughter a twynn born wth Tho. Boteler, maried to Edward Osborne of the Inner Temple Esqr.

Katherin wife to John Kinersley of Wardend co. Warw. gen.

Elizabeth wife to Richard Taylor of Lincolnes Inn Esqr.

William Boteler of Kirton in Bydenham Esqr lineing Aº 1634. = Hellen dau'r of George Nodes of Shephalbury in com. Hertf. gen.

Thomas Boteler of Lincolnes Inne 2nd son.

Francis Boteler 3rd son. — John 4th son.

Martha wife to John Keeling of the Inner Temple Esqr.

Anne.

Thomas Boteler eldest son and heire apparent lineing Aº 1634 aged about 5 yeres.

Helen aged about 3 yeres eld. dan'r.

Anne aged about one yere 2nd dau'r.

William Boteler.

Captain Oliuer Boteler of Bornend in the p'sh of Wooton com. Bedf. second son. He is in comission of the peace. = Judeth dau'r and coheire of Robert Hawes of Bedford Towne Alderman.

1. George Boteler eldest son and heire apparent Aº 1634 aged about 13 yeres.
2. Oliuer.
Ursula.

W. BOTELER.   OLIUER BOTELER.

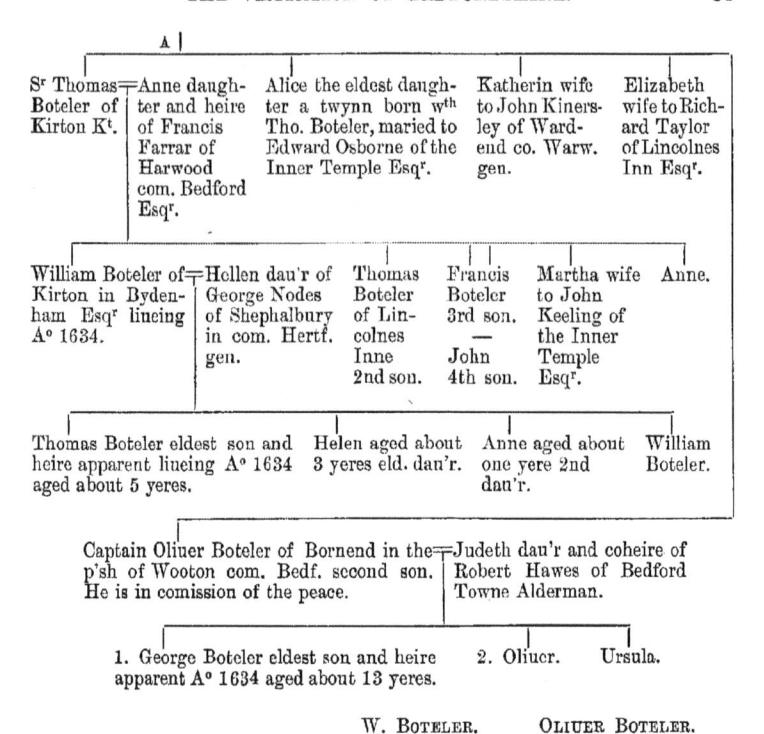

𝕭𝖗𝖊𝖘𝖘𝖊𝖞

[of 𝖂ootton].

ARMS.—*Quarterly per fesse indented sable and argent, in the first quarter a martlet of the second, a mullet for difference or.*

CREST.—*Out of a mural crown sable, purfled or, a demi-eagle displayed argent, beaked gold.**

Edmund Bressey Cittizen of London younger brother of ye Bresseys in Cheshire. = Katherin da. of .... Anderson.

---

* "L'res Pattentes exemplified from Sr Wm Segar Garter to Edmund Bressy, son and heire of Edmund Bressy of Netledon, com. Bucks, Esqr, dated 11th of King James."

THE VISITATION OF BEDFORDSHIRE.

```
                                        A
    ┌───────────────────────────────────┴──┐
    Edmund Bressey of Wootton in ═ Constance da of Thomas Shepard of
    com Bedf gen                   Molden in com Bedford
```

| Thomas Bressey 2d sonn of London | John Bressey 3d sonn | Robert Bressey 4th sonn | Edmund Bressey of Wootton in com Bedford gen now liueing 1634 eldest sonn ═ Elizab da of Reynes Lor of Clifton in com Buck Esq | Ralph Bressey 5th sonn | 1 Lucretia. — 2 Hemphilles |

| 1 Constance. 2. Mary. | 3 Elizabeth 4 Martha | Edmund Bressey eldest sonn aged about 8 yeers at ye tyme of this visitac'o 1634 | Henry 2d sonn | John 3d sonn | Francis 4th sonn. |

EDMUND BRESSEY

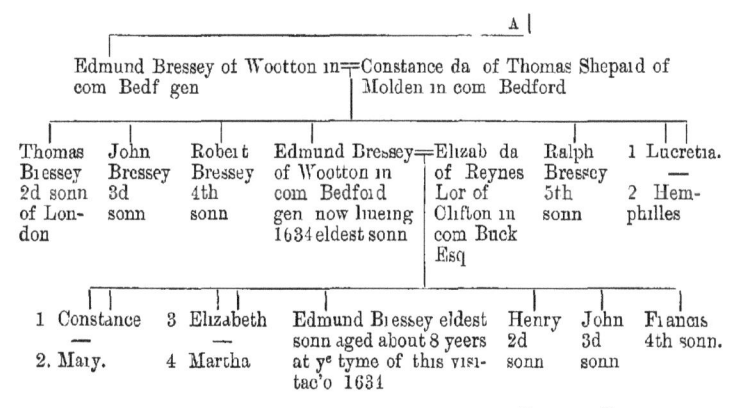

Briers

[of Pulloxhill].

ARMS.—*Azure, a chevron fleurie counterfleurie between three mullets pierced argent*
CREST.—*A demi-leopard rampont-guardant erased azure, gorged with a collar argent, charged with three mullets pierced gules*

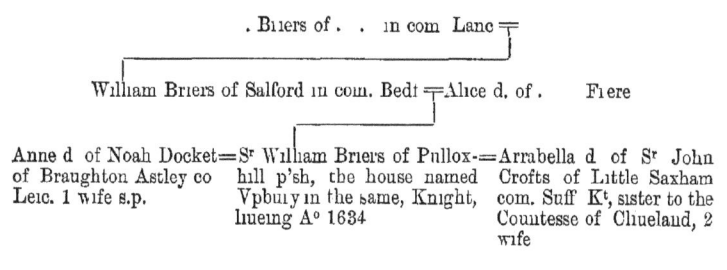

```
            . Briers of . .  in com Lanc ═┐
                     │
    William Briers of Salford in com. Bedf ═ Alice d. of .    Fiere
```

| Anne d of Noah Docket of Braughton Astley co Leic. 1 wife s.p. ═ | Sr William Briers of Pullox-hill p'sh, the house named Vpbury in the same, Knight, liueing A° 1634 | ═ Arrabella d of Sr John Crofts of Little Saxham com. Suff Kt, sister to the Countesse of Clueland, 2 wife |

WILL'M BRIERS.

Bromhall
[of Stevington].

ARMS (TWO SHIELDS)—I, *Sable, a lion rampant or,* BROMHALL   II, *Azure, a chevron between three hanks of cotton argent,* COTTON
CREST.—*A demi-lion or, holding between the paws a cross pommée fitchée sable*
MOTTO.—CALCAR VIRTUTIS HONOR

John Bromhall of Stevington in=Agnes da. of Thom Aunsell of
com Bedford gent | Barford co Bedford gent

1 Robert Bromhall=[Joane] da of [Robert] * 2 Lewes Brom-=[Anne
of Stevington gent. | Throgmorton [of Elling- hall of London | da of
liueing A° 1634 | ton in com. Hunt.] 2 son 1634 | .]

[1 Oliver ob at 18 Sᵗ John Bromhall eldest Robert [Elizebeth] [Anne.]
yeres of age 21 of sonn and hʳ aged about Bromhall dau'r mar to
November 1624] 24 yeres A° 1634 2 sonn Boul-
  ton Clark

3 Oliuer Brom-=[. Katherin ux. Ann Vrsula un- [Elizabeth ux.
hall of Gutford widdow Richard Bass maryed maryed[ux Robert Tay-
[in the p'ish of of [of London to Tho- Edward lor of Steving-
Sandy in] com Tayler] an Attorney mas Charde of ton in com
Bedford gent in the King's Mayhew London] Bedfford]
A° 1634 Bench]
  OL BROMHALL.

Burgoyne
[of Sutton].

ARMS—*Gules, a talbot or, on a chief embattled argent three marllets azure* †

[John Burgoyne of Sutton in=[Joane d of   Bill of Ashwell in
com Bedfford] | com Hertfford]

[Thomas=[Anne d of John Bowles=[Sʳ Robert Catlin Knt. Lord [Robert
Burgoyne | of Wallington in com. Cheefe Justice 2nd husband] Burgoyne
of Sutton] | Hertford] 2nd son]

[John Burgoyne [Robert Burgoyne of Sutton=[Elizabeth d and coheire of Thom
ob s p] and of Wattonhall in com | Munden of Wattonhall in com.
 Hertfford 2nd son] Hertfford Esqʳ]
  A

---

* Harl MS 1097 places here another son, "2 John Bromhall"
† "This coate was granted to John Burgoyn of Sutton in com Bedfford by Sʳ Christopher Barker Knt al's Garter principall kinge of Armes, wᶜʰ John is the first in this descent here sett downe.' (Harl, MS 1097)

THE VISITATION OF BEDFORDSHIRE

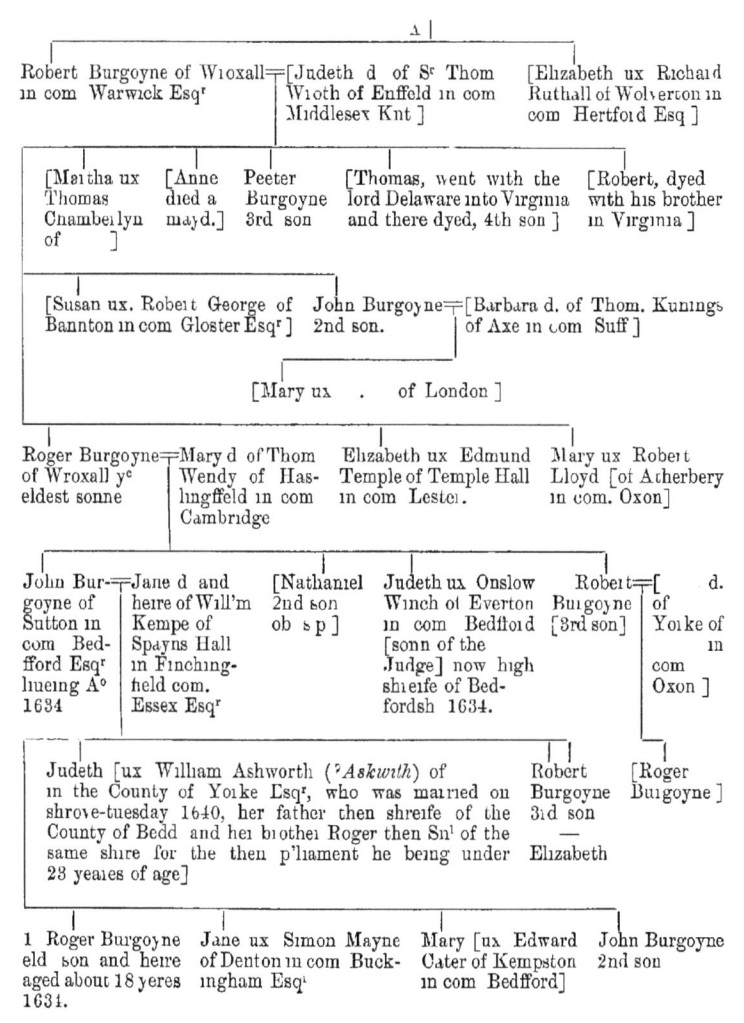

A

Robert Burgoyne of Wroxall = [Judeth d of Sr Thom [Elizabeth ux Richard
in com Warwick Esqr | Wroth of Enffeld in com Ruthall of Wolverton in
 | Middlesex Knt] com Hertford Esq]

[Martha ux | [Anne | Peeter | [Thomas, went with the | [Robert, dyed
Thomas | died a | Burgoyne | lord Delaware into Virginia | with his brother
Chamberlyn | mayd.] | 3rd son | and there dyed, 4th son] | in Virginia]
of]

[Susan ux. Robert George of | John Burgoyne = [Barbara d. of Thom. Kunings
Bannton in com Gloster Esqr] | 2nd son. | of Axe in com Suff]

[Mary ux . of London]

Roger Burgoyne = Mary d of Thom | Elizabeth ux Edmund | Mary ux Robert
of Wroxall ye | Wendy of Has- | Temple of Temple Hall | Lloyd [of Atherbery
eldest sonne | lingffeld in com | in com Lester. | in com. Oxon]
 | Cambridge

John Bur- = Jane d and | [Nathaniel | Judeth ux Onslow | Robert = [d.
goyne of | heire of Will'm | 2nd son | Winch of Everton | Burgoyne | of
Sutton in | Kempe of | ob s p] | in com Bedford | [3rd son] | Yorke of
com Bed- | Spayns Hall | | [sonn of the | | in
fford Esqr | in Finching- | | Judge] now high | | com
liueing Ao | field com. | | sheife of Bed- | | Oxon]
1634 | Essex Esqr | | fordsh 1634.

Judeth [ux William Ashworth (?Askwith) of | Robert | [Roger
in the County of Yorke Esqr, who was married on | Burgoyne | Burgoyne]
shrove-tuesday 1640, her father then shreife of the | 3rd son
County of Bedd and her brother Roger then Snr of the | ———
same shire for the then p'liament he being under | Elizabeth
23 yeares of age]

1 Roger Burgoyne | Jane ux Simon Mayne | Mary [ux Edward | John Burgoyne
eld son and heire | of Denton in com Buck- | Cater of Kempston | 2nd son
aged about 18 yeres | ingham Esqr | in com Bedfford]
1634.

ROBT PHILLIPS,
servant to Mr JO BURGOYNE.

Button

[of Ampthill and Wootton].

ARMS.—*Ermine, a fesse gules*
CREST.—*On a wreath argent and gules a wyvern sable*

James Button* Controller of y⁰ King's howshold =┬=

├── William Button of Ampthill.=┬=. d to Frogmorton of Wescot in com Buck
│   │
│   ├── Margaret m to (Thos) Huet of Ampthill
│   ├── Joane m to (Edm) Conquest of Houghton Conquest
│   └── Wᵐ Button of Ampthill =┬= Margaret d of John Rouse of Rouseleach in com Worc
│   │
│   ├── 1. Dorathey.   3 Anne
│   │   2. Elizabeth   4 Jane
│   ├── James Button of Ampthill s and h =┬= Ann d of Richard Fisher of Bedlowe in com. Bedf
│   │   │
│   │   ├── Elizabeth m. to Wᵐ Snagg of Leachworth in com Hartf. Esq
│   │   ├── Rich Button of Wootton in com Bedf gent liueing Aº 1634 =┬= Elizabeth d and coh of Gabriell Fowler of Tilsworth in com Bedf Esq
│   │   │   │
│   │   │   ├── Richard Button s and h ob s p
│   │   │   └── Edm Wingate of Ampthill in com Bedf gent =┬= Elizabeth d and heire, widow of William Trooche of London gent =┬=
│   │   │   │
│   │   │   ├── Button Wingate.
│   │   │   ├── Edmund
│   │   │   ├── Roger
│   │   │   ├── Anne
│   │   │   ├── James
│   │   │   └── Elizabeth
│   │   │   EDM WINGATE.
│   │   └── Anne m to Edmund Conquest s and h of George Conquest of Houghton Parke Esq
│   ├── 2 William
│   ├── 3 Edmund
│   ├── 4 Humfrey
│   ├── 5. George.
│   └── 6 John

Cater

[of Kempston].

ARMS.—*Sable, a chevron ermine between three salmon hauriant argent* †

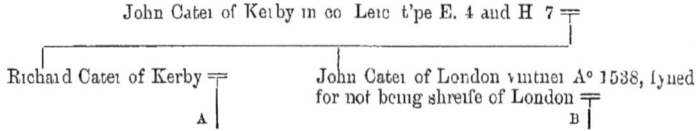

John Cater of Kerby in co Leic t'pe E. 4 and H 7 =┬=

├── Richard Cater of Kerby =┬=
│   A
└── John Cater of London vintner Aº 1538, fyned for not being shreife of London =┬=
            B

---

* "This James Button, Controwler of yᵉ King's houshould lyeth Buryed in yᵉ Church of Sᵗ Martin's in yᵉ fuilds iuxta London"
† "The auntient Armes of the Auncestor of Cornelius Cater of London gent, son of John Cater of the same place, according to a declaration testified vnder the hand and seale of Clarencculx Cooke dated the xvjth yeere of the raigne of Queene Eliz 1584."

THE VISITATION OF BEDFORDSHIRE.

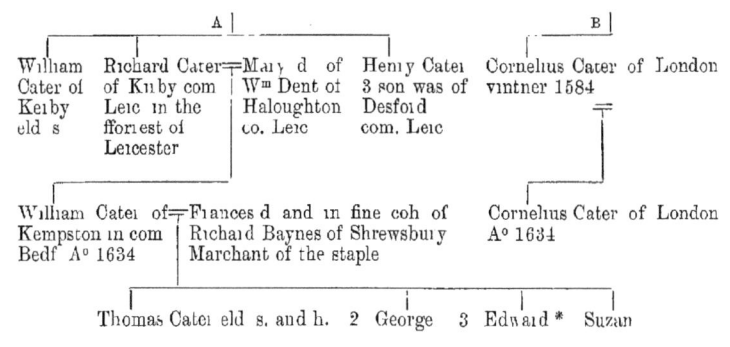

A | | B

William Cater of Kerby eld s. — Richard Cater of Kirby com Leic in the fforrest of Leicester = Mary d of Wm Dent of Haloughton co. Leic — Henry Cater 3 son was of Desford com. Leic   Cornelius Cater of London vintner 1584 =

William Cater of Kempston in com Bedf A° 1634 = Frances d and in fine coh of Richard Baynes of Shrewsbury Marchant of the staple   Cornelius Cater of London A° 1634

Thomas Cater eld s. and h.   2 George   3 Edward *   Suzan

THO PALMER, for my master WILL'I CATER
THOMAS CATER

Carter
[of Kempston].

ARMS —*Azure, a talbot passant between three round buckles or.*
CREST —*Out of a mural crown or and azure a demi-talbot proper* †

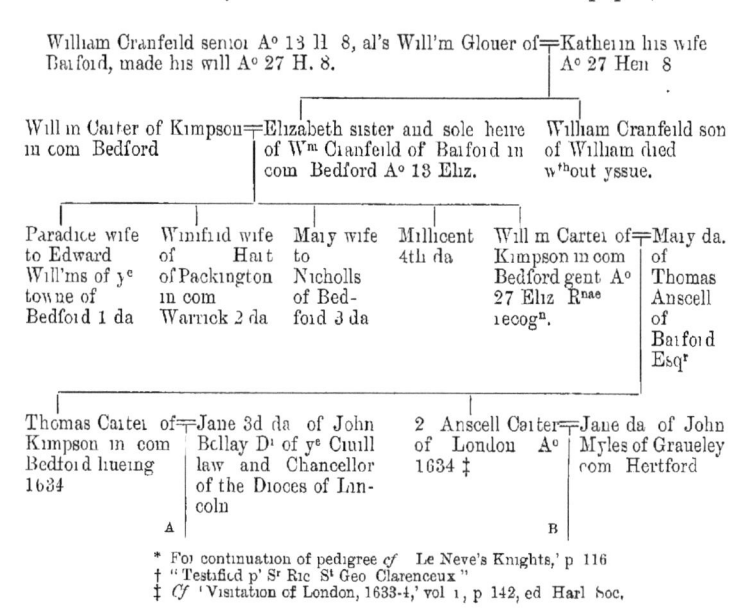

William Cranfeild senior A° 13 H. 8, al's Will'm Glouer of Barford, made his will A° 27 H. 8. = Katherin his wife A° 27 Hen 8

Will'm Carter of Kimpson in com Bedford = Elizabeth sister and sole heire of Wm Cranfeild of Barford in com Bedford A° 13 Eliz.   William Cranfeild son of William died w^thout yssue.

Paradice wife to Edward Will'ms of y^e towne of Bedford 1 da | Winifrid wife of Hart of Packington in com Warrick 2 da | Mary wife to Nicholls of Bedford 3 da | Millicent 4th da | Will'm Carter of Kimpson in com Bedford gent A° 27 Eliz R^nae recog^n. = Mary da. of Thomas Anscell of Barford Esqr

Thomas Carter of Kimpson in com Bedford liueing 1634 = Jane 3d da of John Bellay D^r of y^e Ciuill law and Chancellor of the Dioces of Lincoln
A | 2 Anscell Carter of London A° 1634 ‡ = Jane da of John Myles of Graueley com Hertford
B

* For continuation of pedigree *cf* Le Neve's Knights,' p 116
† "Testified p' Sr Ric St Geo Clarenceux"
‡ *Cf* 'Visitation of London, 1633-4,' vol 1, p 142, ed Harl Soc.

THE VISITATION OF BEDFORDSHIRE. 91

A |

1 Elizabeth. — 2. Jane — 3 Suzan

Will'm Carter of Barford eldest sonn =Anne da and coheire of Tho Emmery of Alridgesey al's Earlscy in com Bedf

Thomas 2 sonn apprentice in London.

B |

1 George — 2 John. — 3. Anscell — 4 William

Jane

Thomas Carter aged 1 yere et amplius at y° tyme of this visitacon 1634

Anne

William Carter borne since the taking this s'vey

THO CARTER

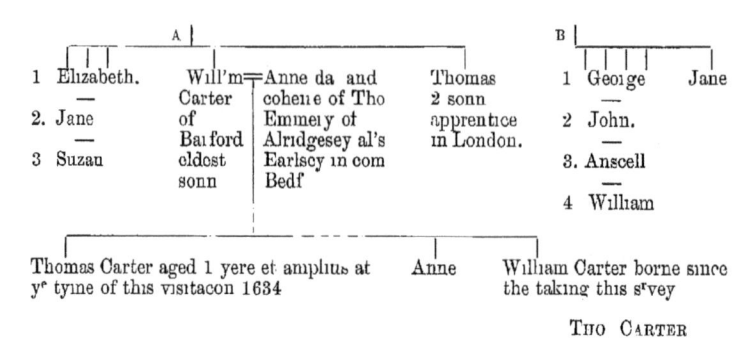

Cheney

[of Sundon].

ARMS —[*Chequée or and azure, a fesse gules fretty ermine*]

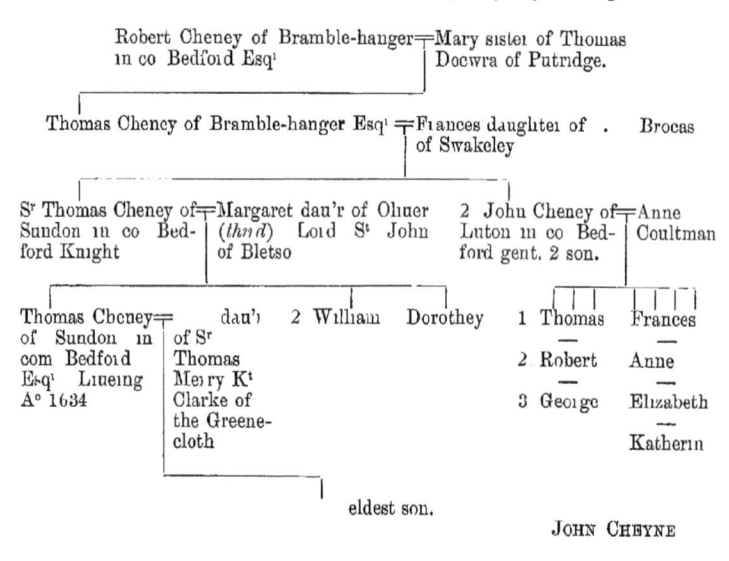

Robert Cheney of Bramble-hanger in co Bedford Esq¹ = Mary sister of Thomas Docwra of Putridge.

Thomas Cheney of Bramble-hanger Esq¹ = Frances daughter of . Brocas of Swakeley

S' Thomas Cheney of Sundon in co Bedford Knight = Margaret dau'r of Oluer (third) Lord S' John of Bletso

2 John Cheney of Luton in co Bedford gent, 2 son. = Anne Coultman

Thomas Cheney of Sundon in com Bedford Esq¹ Liueing A° 1634 = dau'} of S' Thomas Merry K' Clarke of the Greenecloth

2 William

Dorothey

1 Thomas — 2. Robert — 3 George

Frances — Anne — Elizabeth — Katherin

eldest son.

JOHN CHEYNE

Chernocke*

[of Pulcote].

ARMS —*Quarterly*—1 and 4, *Argent, on a bend sable three cross-crosslets of the field*, CHERNOCKE, 2 and 3, *Argent, a cross engrailed gules*,
CREST —*A lapwing proper*.

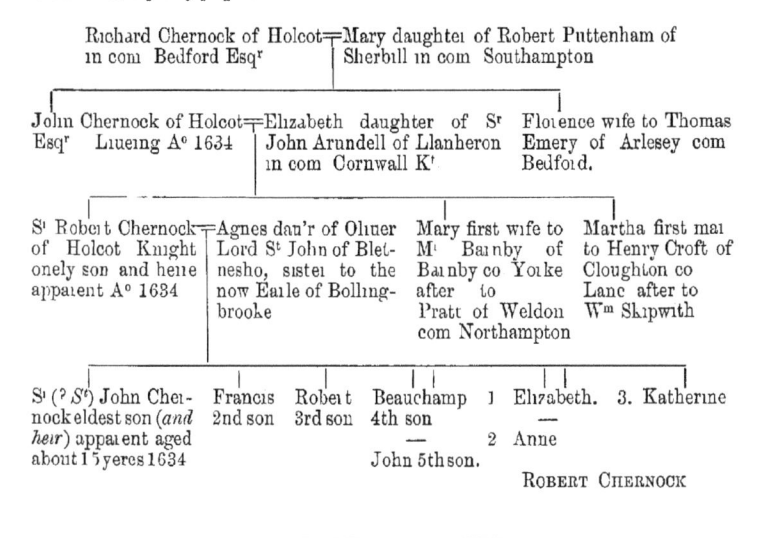

Richard Chernock of Holcot = Mary daughter of Robert Puttenham of in com Bedford Esqr | Sherbill in com Southampton

- John Chernock of Holcot Esqr Liueing A° 1634 = Elizabeth daughter of Sr John Arundell of Llanheron in com Cornwall K^t
- Florence wife to Thomas Emery of Arlesey com Bedford.

- St Robert Chernock of Holcot Knight onely son and heire apparent A° 1634 = Agnes dau'r of Oliuer Lord St John of Bletnesho, sister to the now Earle of Bollingbrooke
- Mary first wife to Mr Barnby of Barnby co Yorke after to Pratt of Weldon com Northampton
- Martha first mar to Henry Croft of Cloughton co Lanc after to Wm Shipwith

- S^t (? S^r) John Chernock eldest son (*and heir*) apparent aged about 15 yeres 1634
- Francis 2nd son
- Robert 3rd son
- Beauchamp 4th son — John 5th son.
- 1 Elizabeth — 2 Anne 3. Katherine

ROBERT CHERNOCK

Child

[of Poddington].

ARMS —*Quarterly*—1 and 4, *Gules a chevron engrailed ermine between three eagles close argent, a crescent for difference*, CHILD, 2 and 3, *Sable, on a chevron between three bezants or as many fleurs-de-lys of the field*, PAYNE †
CREST —*An eagle wings expanded argent, enveloped round the neck with a snake proper*

	Payne.
William Child descended of the family surnamed Child of Worcestershire at Northwick A	William Payne of Bedley in com Worcester B

---

* For detailed account of this family *cf* Burke's 'Extinct and Dormant Baronets,' p 108, ed 1844
† "An escocneon deliuered vnto him by Mr Vincent according to this trick'

THE VISITATION OF BEDFORDSHIRE.

A |
Richard Child of Wrington = Katherine dau'r of Wroynon co. Somerset.
in com. Somerset

B |
Daniell Payne of = Anne
Poddington com ...
Bedford

William Child = Margaret one of the sisters and heires of Will'm Payne
of Wrington.

Wilham Payne eld. son s p

Francis Payne second son died in the lifetime of William Payne his brother.

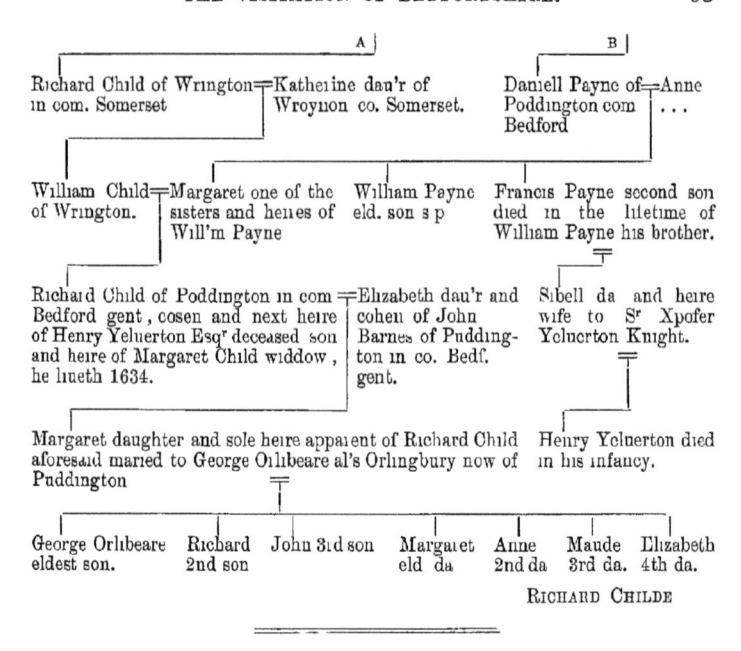

Richard Child of Poddington in com = Elizabeth dau'r and cohen of John Barnes of Puddington in co. Bedf. gent.
Bedford gent, cosen and next heire of Henry Yelverton Esq' deceased son and heire of Margaret Child widdow, he liueth 1634.

Sibell da and heire wife to S' Xpofer Yelverton Knight.

Margaret daughter and sole heire apparent of Richard Child aforesaid maried to George Orlibeare al's Orlingbury now of Puddington

Henry Yelverton died in his infancy.

George Orlibeare eldest son. | Richard 2nd son | John 3rd son | Margaret eld da | Anne 2nd da | Maude 3rd da. | Elizabeth 4th da.

RICHARD CHILDE

Chishull
[of Newtonbury].

ARMS.—*Argent, three bars nebulee azure, on a bend sable as many escallops or, a crescent for difference*
CREST.—*Three chisels or, one in pale and two per saltire.*

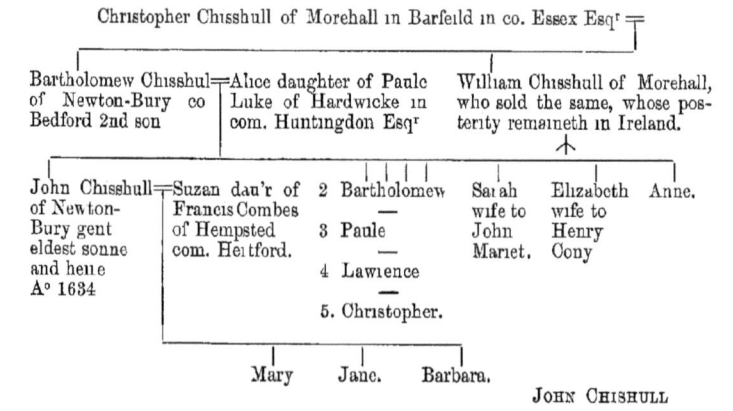

Christopher Chisshull of Morehall in Barfeild in co. Essex Esq' =

Bartholomew Chisshul = Alice daughter of Paule Luke of Hardwicke in com. Huntingdon Esq'
of Newton-Bury co Bedford 2nd son

William Chisshull of Morehall, who sold the same, whose posterity remaineth in Ireland.

John Chisshull = Suzan dau'r of Francis Combes of Hempsted com. Hertford.
of Newton-Bury gent eldest sonne and heire A° 1634

2 Bartholomew
—
3 Paule
—
4 Lawrence
—
5. Christopher.

Sarah wife to John Mariet.

Elizabeth wife to Henry Cony

Anne.

Mary   Jane.   Barbara.

JOHN CHISHULL

Claver

[of Bedford].

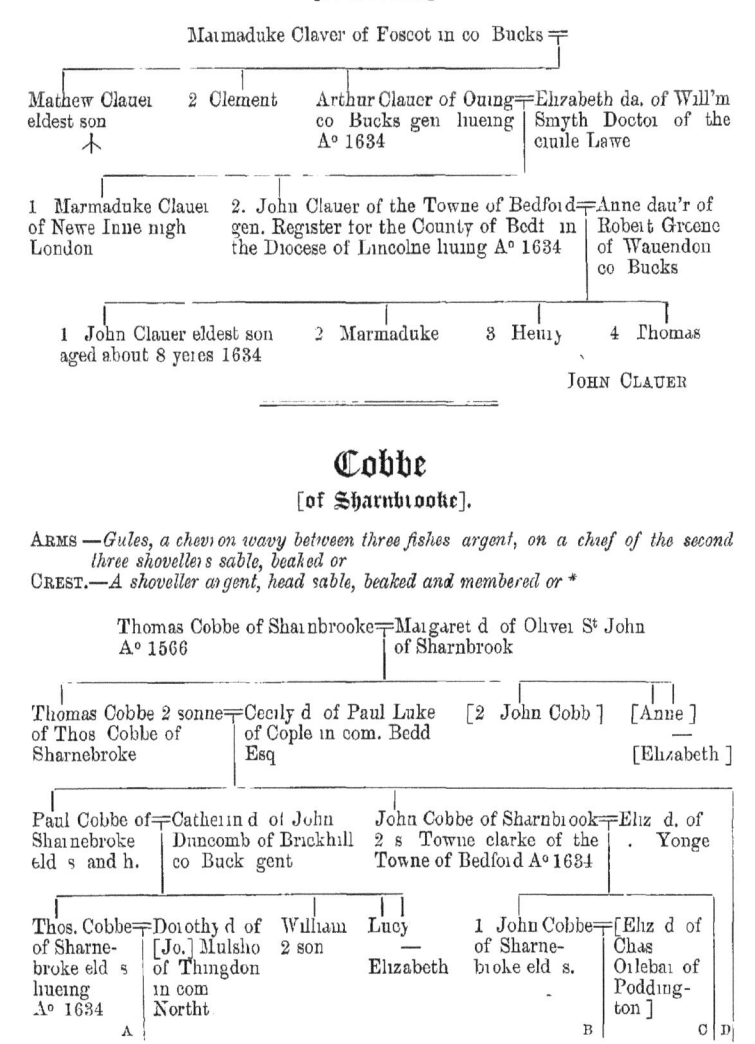

Marmaduke Claver of Foscot in co. Bucks =

- Mathew Clauer eldest son 人
- 2 Clement
- Arthur Clauer of Ouing co. Bucks gen. liueing A° 1634 = Elizabeth da. of Will'm Smyth Doctor of the ciuile Lawe

  - 1 Marmaduke Clauer of Newe Inne nigh London
  - 2. John Clauer of the Towne of Bedford gen. Register for the County of Bedf. in the Diocese of Lincolne liuing A° 1634 = Anne dau'r of Robert Greene of Wauendon co. Bucks

    - 1 John Clauer eldest son aged about 8 yeres 1634
    - 2 Marmaduke
    - 3 Henry
    - 4 Thomas

      JOHN CLAUER.

Cobbe

[of Sharnbrooke].

ARMS.—*Gules, a chevron wavy between three fishes argent, on a chief of the second three shovellers sable, beaked or*
CREST.—*A shoveller argent, head sable, beaked and membered or* *

Thomas Cobbe of Sharnbrooke A° 1566 = Margaret d. of Oliver St. John of Sharnbrook

- Thomas Cobbe 2 sonne of Thos Cobbe of Sharnebroke = Cecily d. of Paul Luke of Cople in com. Bedd Esq
- [2 John Cobb]
- [Anne]
- [Elizabeth]

  - Paul Cobbe of Sharnebroke eld s. and h. = Catherin d. of John Duncomb of Brickhill co. Buck gent
  - John Cobbe of Sharnbrook 2 s Towne clarke of the Towne of Bedford A° 1634 = Eliz d. of . Yonge

    - Thos. Cobbe of Sharnebroke eld s hueing A° 1634 = Dorothy d of [Jo.] Mulsho of Thingdon in com Northt
      A
    - William 2 son
    - Lucy — Elizabeth
    - 1 John Cobbe of Sharnebroke eld s.
      B
    - [Eliz d of Chas Oreban of Poddington]
      C | D

* "Wm Hervy al s Clarenceux King of Armes A° 1566 to Tho Cobb of Sharnbrooke, co Bedford"

```
A |                              B |                C | D |
  |                                |
[William]   [George.]         [John]    [Paul]
[Edward]    [Thomas*]         [George]  [Oliver]
```

```
   |                    |
  Anne      2 Paul Cobbe ═ [Mary d. of        Gardiner]
                 |
            [Paul]   Anne   [Samuel]
```

| Sibell wife to John Whitaker of the Towne of Bedford gent | Margaret youngest d. wife to John Fitzgeoffrey of Wymington | Oliuer Cobbe of Bedford Commissary and official for the Counties of Beds and Bucks in the diocese of Linc 1634 | Mary d of John Smith Batchellor of Lawe and Commissary and official of p'te of the Diocese of Lincoln | Agnes wife to W[m] Bletsoe of Wimyngton in com Bedf |

```
         |          |
       Oliuer     Cicely
```

JOHN COBBE
OL COBB

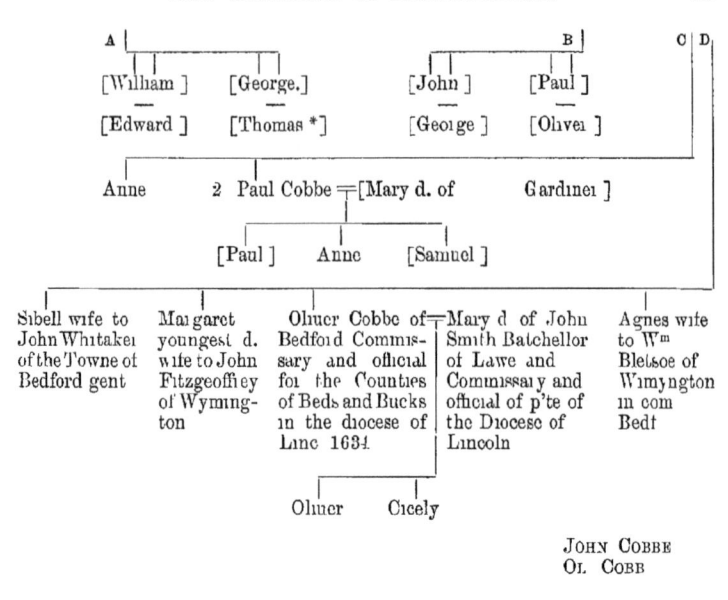

Cokayne

[of Cokayne=Hatley].

ARMS —*Argent, three cocks gules, combs and spurs sable, a crescent on a crescent for difference*
CREST —*A cock's head erased gules, charged with a crescent on a crescent*

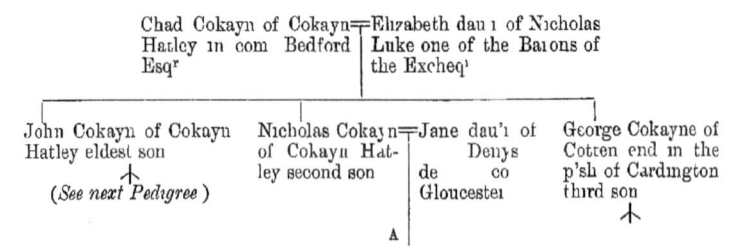

```
Chad Cokayn of Cokayn ═ Elizabeth dau r of Nicholas
Hatley in com Bedford   Luke one of the Barons of
Esqr                    the Excheqr
```

| John Cokayn of Cokayn Hatley eldest son ↑ (See next Pedigree) | Nicholas Cokayn ═ Jane dau'r of of Cokayn Hatley second son / Denys de co Gloucester | George Cokayne of Cotten end in the p'sh of Cardington third son ↑ |

A

* Harl MS 4600 calls Thomas "son and heire," and gives other issue, viz, John, Paul, Dorothy, Ann, Rebecca, and Mary

THE VISITATION OF BEDFORDSHIRE.

△

Charles Cokayne of London goldsmith

Elizabeth wife to George King of Bugden in co Huntingdon

Margaret wife to John Haynes of Hunspill co Somerset.

Oliuer Cokayne eldest son

Dorothey

Nicholas Cokayne of Souldrop in co Bedford Esq[r] of the Bath to S[t] Powlet S[t] John 2nd son =

Katherine da of John Duncombe of Great Brickhill com Bucks Esq.

S[t] John Cokayn eldest son and heire apparent A° 1634 aged about 7 yeres

Nicholas 2nd son

Oliuer 3rd son

Sibell

Katherin

Elizabeth. —
Arabella

Jane

NICHOLAS COKAYN.

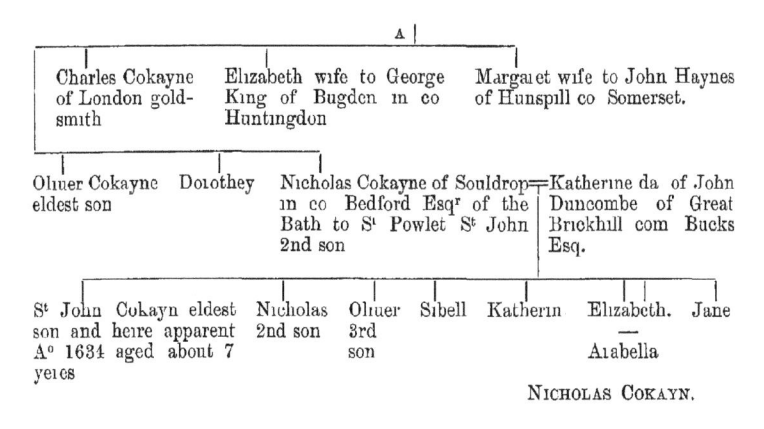

Cokayne.

John Cokayn of Cokayne Hatley Esq eldest son and heire of Chad Cokayne of Cokayn Hatley co Bedford by Eliz Luke his wife = Elizabeth daughter of . Stacy

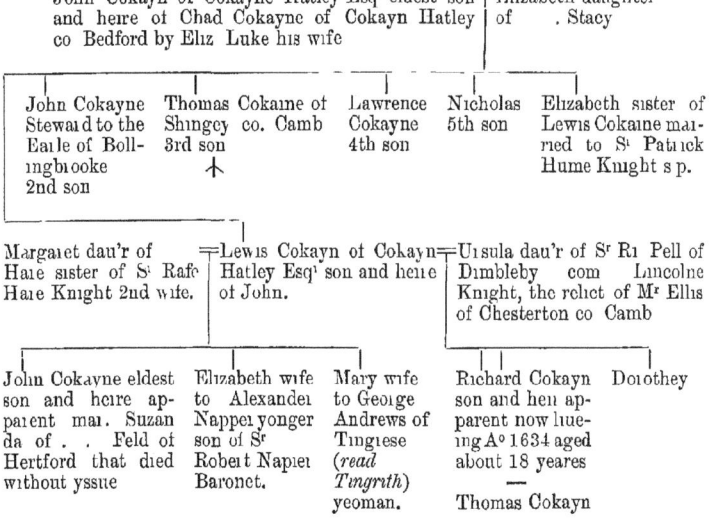

John Cokayne Steward to the Earle of Bollingbrooke 2nd son

Thomas Cokaine of Shingey co. Camb 3rd son ⚔

Lawrence Cokayne 4th son

Nicholas 5th son

Elizabeth sister of Lewis Cokaine married to S[t] Patrick Hume Knight s p.

Margaret dau'r of Hare sister of S[t] Rafe Hare Knight 2nd wife. =

Lewis Cokayn of Cokayn Hatley Esq[r] son and heire of John. =

Ursula dau'r of S[r] Ri Pell of Dimbleby com Lincolne Knight, the relict of M[r] Ellis of Chesterton co Camb

John Cokayne eldest son and heire apparent mar. Suzan da of . . Feld of Hertford that died without yssue

Elizabeth wife to Alexander Napper yonger son of S[r] Robert Napier Baronet.

Mary wife to George Andrews of Tingiese (read Tingrith) yeoman.

Richard Cokayn son and heir apparent now liueing A° 1634 aged about 18 yeares —
Thomas Cokayn

Dorothey

OLIUER COKAYN kinsman to the foresaid LEWIS.

Conquest

[of Houghton Conquest].

ARMS —*Quarterly argent and sable, a label of three points gules*
CREST —*A bay-tree (alibi a holly-tree) vert, fructed gules*

Edm Conquest of Houghton=Joane d. of Wm Button of Ampthill
Conquest in com Bedf Esq | in com. Bedf Esq

- Edm Conquest of Houghton Conquest eld s ob s p
- Sr Richard Conquest of Houghton Conquest Kt brother and heire male of Edmond =Dorothy d of Robert Hewet of Ampthill in com Bedf Esq

Children:
- Elizth wife to John Neale of Wollaston co Northt
- 3. Lewes Conquest m Mary d of John Leigh of Caldwell co Bedf
- Anne wife to Francis Clarke of Houghton Conquest Kt
- Dorothey first m. to Ellis Walcot 2 to Francis Edes of (*Sewell*)
- Frances wife to John Feild of

Judeth wife to Frances Theobald of

Jane wife to James Beneiley of Clophill in com Bedf Esq

Mary wife to Henry Sandys of Eaton

- Sr Edm Conquest of Houghton Conquest Kt. ob. May 1634. =Elizth d of Myles Sandys of Eaton Bray in com Bedf Esq
- 2 Sr Richard Conquest of Houghton Conquest Kt =Sarah d and coh of Edw Snow of Chicksands in com Bedf

Emma

- 4. John.
- 5. Charles
- Hester Conquest wife to Rob't Taylor of Stevington in com Bedf
- Elizabeth wife to John Gascoigne of Oldhurst in com. Hunt Esq.
- Jane s p.
- Dorothy
- Bridgit

- Richard Conquest of Houghton Conquest Esq liueing A° 1634 =Elizth d of Richard Thimelby of Irnham in com. Lincoln Esq one of the ladies of the Priuie Chamber to the Queene
- Myles Conquest 2 son
- William Conquest m. for his 1 wife d of Mr Nutting of Child's Hill co Midd his 2 wife was Dorothy d of Miller sister of Sr John Miller of Islington com. Midd Kt

- John Thimelby Conquest s. and heire aged about 7 years A° 1634.
- Richard
- Elizabeth.
- Jane Conquest by 1st wife
- William Conquest by 1st wife

RICH. CONQUEST.

Crawley

[of Luton].

ARMS —*Quarterly—1 and 4, Or, on a fesse gules between three storks proper as many cross-crosslets of the field,* CRAWLEY,* *2 and 3, Argent, on a chevron between three cinqfoils gules as many bezants,* EDGERLEY

CREST —*A crane proper, holding in the dexter talon a cross-crosslet or.*†

Edgerley.

Katherine da to Thomas Belson of Rowant in com Oxon gent. 1 wife = Robert Edgerley of Milton in com Oxford. = Anne da. of Wm Seycoll of Stanton Harcourt 2d wife

John Crawley of Luton in com Bedford = Dorothey — Elizabeth

John Edgerley of Milton in com. Oxon. =

Robert.

Thomas Crawley of Luton sonn and heir = Dorothey da. and coheire of John Edgerley of Milton in com Oxon.

Florence wife to Wm Smyth Doctor of ye Ciuill Law

Frances wife to John Grover of Leicestersh.

Mary wife to Wm Lambert of Buck. and after to Sr Edward Richardson

Sr Francis Crawley of Luton Kt one of the Justices of ye Comon Pleas 1634 = Elizabeth da of St John Rotheram of Luton Kt

Thomas Crawley 2d sonn

Dorothey wife to William Warren of Buck and after to Mathew Browne.

Francis 2 sonn

Thomas 3 sonn

Robert 4 sonn

John Crawley Esq sonn and heir liueing Aº 1634. = Mary da and heir of Will'm Lambert of Buck

Ann.

FFR CRAWLEY

Daniell

[of Flitton].

Stephen Daniell of Newbury in Flitton in com Bedf. = Elizabeth dau'r of Robert Huet of Ampthill.

A

---

* ' A vellom scochion in mettal thus subscribed These Armes and Creast belong to the Auntiant name and ffamily of Crawley of Bedfordshire from whom Thomas Crawley of Luton in the seyd Countye is descended Exemplified and Confifirmed by me Wm Segar Garter principall King of Armes "

† ' Or a fleur-de-lys or—the creast thus sett out by Sr Henry St George "

THE VISITATION OF BEDFORDSHIRE.   99

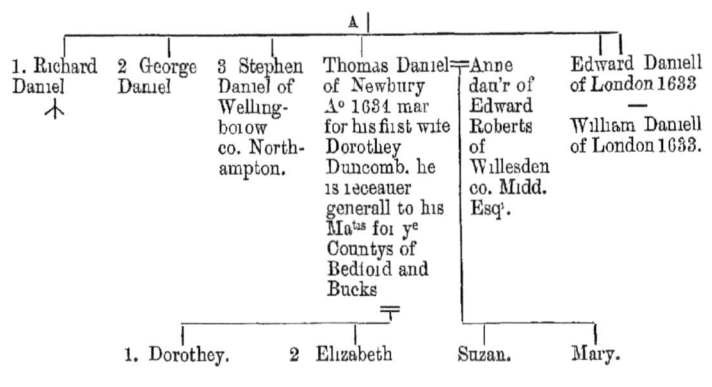

A

| 1. Richard Daniel | 2 George Daniel | 3 Stephen Daniel of Wellingborow co. Northampton. | Thomas Daniel of Newbury Aº 1634 mar for his first wife Dorothey Duncomb. he is receaver generall to his Ma^{tas} for y^e Countys of Bedford and Bucks = Anne dau'r of Edward Roberts of Willesden co. Midd. Esqr. | Edward Daniell of London 1633. — William Daniell of London 1633. |

1. Dorothey.   2 Elizabeth.   Suzan.   Mary.

THO. DANIELL.

Daye
[of Thurleigh].

ARMS.—*Gules, flanched ermine, on a chief azure three suns in splendour or*
CREST.—*A greyhound's head erased argent, collared and chained gules* *

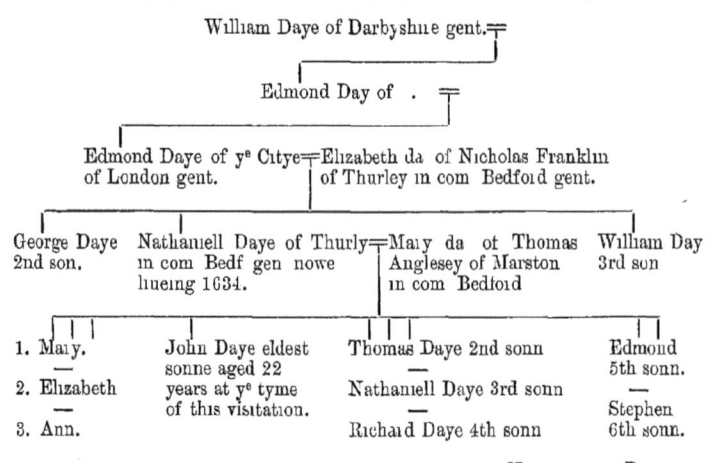

William Daye of Darbyshire gent.=

Edmond Day of . =

Edmond Daye of y^e Citye=Elizabeth da of Nicholas Franklin
of London gent.   of Thurley in com Bedford gent.

| George Daye 2nd son. | Nathaniell Daye of Thurly in com Bedf gen nowe lueing 1634. = Mary da of Thomas Anglesey of Marston in com Bedford | William Day 3rd son |

1. Mary.   John Daye eldest   Thomas Daye 2nd sonn   Edmond
—   sonne aged 22   5th sonn.
2. Elizabeth   years at y^e tyme   Nathaniell Daye 3rd sonn   —
—   of this visitation.   Stephen
3. Ann.   Richard Daye 4th sonn   6th sonn.

NATHANIELL DAY.

---

* "A graunt of Creast by Sr Will'm Dethick Garter principal King of Armes vnto Edmond Day of London sonn of Edmond sonn of Will'm Day of Darbyshire dated the 20th day of March Aº 1582."

Dudley

[of Harrold].

ARMS.—*Quarterly—1 and 4, Azure, a chevron or between three lions' heads erased argent* DUDLEY, *2 and 3, Azure, a cross pattée or between four cingfoils argent,* HUTOST. *In the fesse point a crescent for difference*

CREST.—*On a ducal coronet or a woman's head with a helmet thereon, hair dishevelled, throat-latch loose proper.*

Will'm Dudley of Clopton Esq == [Elizebeth] d of [Augustin] Porter [of Belton in com. Lincon]

Thomas Dudley of Clopton in com Northampton Esq. == Mary d of M[r] [Richard] Watson [of Liddington in com. Rutland] aunt to S[r] Edward Watson of Rockingham Castle Kt.

Edward Dudley of Clopton Esq eld son == Margery d of Kenelm Digby of Stoke Dry in com Rutland

Edward Dudley of Clopton [1618] Esq eld son

2 Thomas Dudley of Harwold in com Bedfford [1618] gen A° 1634 == Margarett d. of Robert Wood of Lamley in com Nottingham [sister of Elizabeth]

[Mountague Dudley 15 yeare old 1618]

1 Edward Dudley eld son and heire A° 1634 aged about 24 yeres == Elizabeth d of Geo Edwards of Emmerton in com Bucks

2 Thomas Dudley 2 son.

[Allice.]

Lettice wife to Thomas Temple of Staughton in com Hunts

Thomas Dudley eldest son   Elizabeth.

THO. DUDLEY.

Duncombe

[of Battlesden].

ARMS.—*Per chevron engrailed gules and argent, three talbots' heads erased counterchanged.*

CREST.—*Out of a ducal coronet or a horse's hind-leg couped at the thigh sable, shoe argent*

(Mary da and coh of Richard Reynes) 1 wife == Will'm Duncombe of Aston Ivinghoe in com. Bucks Esq == (Alice da of William Watton of Woodstock co. Oxon) 2 wife

THE VISITATION OF BEDFORDSHIRE.

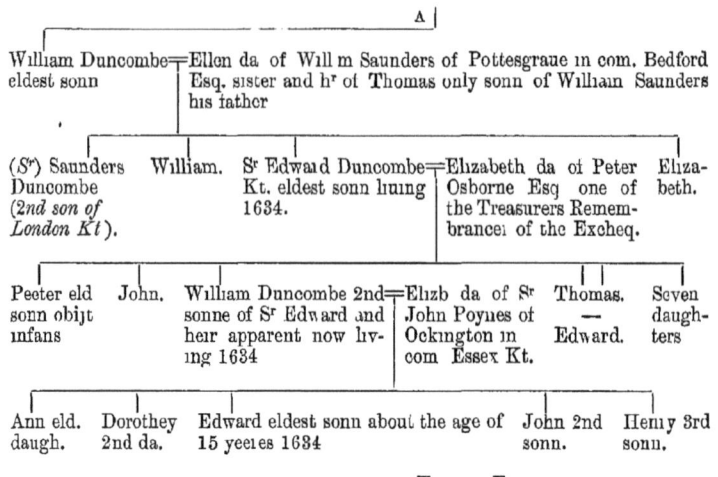

A |

William Duncombe=Ellen da. of Will m Saunders of Pottesgraue in com. Bedford
eldest sonn | Esq. sister and h' of Thomas only sonn of William Saunders his father

(S') Saunders Duncombe (2nd son of London Kt). — William. — S' Edward Duncombe=Elizabeth da of Peter Osborne Esq one of the Treasurers Remembrancer of the Excheq. — Elizabeth.
Kt. eldest sonn liuing 1634.

Peeter eld sonn obijt infans — John. — William Duncombe 2nd sonne of S' Edward and heir apparent now liuing 1634 = Elizb da of S' John Poynes of Ockington in com. Essex Kt. — Thomas. — Edward. — Seven daughters

Ann eld. daugh. — Dorothey 2nd da. — Edward eldest sonn about the age of 15 yeeres 1634 — John 2nd sonn. — Henry 3rd sonn.

THOMAS ELTHAM
for my master S' EDW DUNCOMBE by his direction.

Edwards*
[of Henlow].

ARMS —*Per bend sinister sable and ermine, a lion rampant or*
CREST —*A helmet proper, garnished or, thereon on a wreath a plume of feathers argent* †

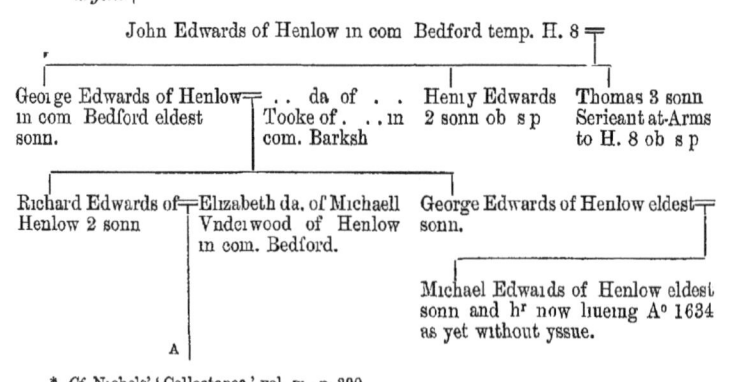

John Edwards of Henlow in com Bedford temp. H. 8 =

George Edwards of Henlow in com Bedford eldest sonn. = .. da of .. Tooke of . . . in com. Barksh — Henry Edwards 2 sonn ob s p — Thomas 3 sonn Serieant-at-Arms to H. 8 ob s p

Richard Edwards of Henlow 2 sonn = Elizabeth da. of Michaell Vnderwood of Henlow in com. Bedford. — George Edwards of Henlow eldest sonn. =

Michael Edwards of Henlow eldest sonn and h' now liueing A° 1634 as yet without yssue.

A

---

* *Cf* Nichols' 'Collectanea' vol vi , p 290
† "This Coate and Creast is testified under y" hand of S' Richard b' George Clarenceux unto Rich. Edwards of Henlow in com Bedford A° 1632"

THE VISITATION OF BEDFORDSHIRE.

A |

Elizabeth mar to Christopher Halleleigh of Hackney in co. Midlesex gen.

Thomas Edwards eldest sonn and hr = Constance d. of George Smyth of Marum in com Salop gent.

Richard Edwards 2 sonn Register of the Chancery liueing A° 1634. = Elianor d of Thomas Manfeild of Spaldwik in com. Hunts

Ann mar to Joh Halleleigh.

2. George.

Richard Edwards eldest son and hr. = Dorothey da of Rob. Dorington of Stow in com Huntington gen.

1 Elizabeth 2. Mary 3 Elianor

Richard Edwards eldest sonn and hr. = Katherine da of Sr Henry Whitehead of Normans Court in com Southampt.

Thomas Edwards 2 sonn mar Anne one of ye das of Thomas Hewson

3. John.
4 Jasper.
—
5. Laurence
—
6 Francis vnmaried

1. Elizabeth mar. to Rob Page of Henningford in co. Huntington Barrester.

2 Mary mar. to Rob. Deuenish of London.
—
3. Elianor.

Richard eldest son and hr aged about 5 yeers A° 1634.

Henry 2 sonn.

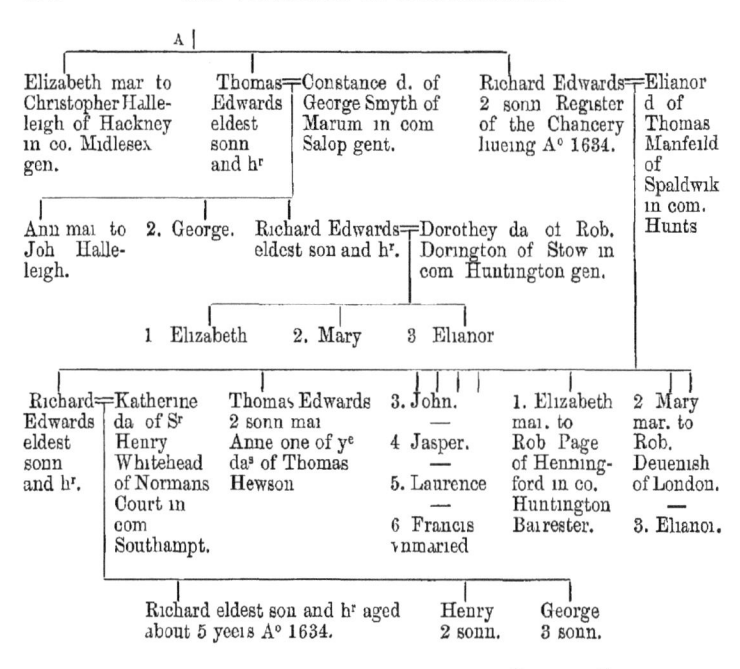

George 3 sonn.

RICHARD EDWARDS.

Eedes

[of Sewell].

ARMS.—*Azure, a chevron engrailed between three lions' faces argent*

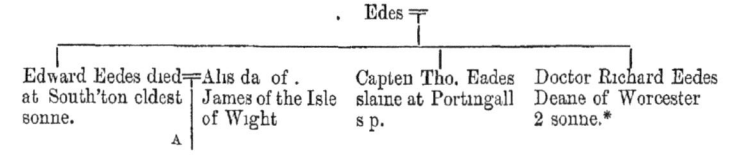

. Edes ⊤

Edward Eedes died at South'ton eldest sonne. = Alis da of . James of the Isle of Wight

A

Capten Tho. Eades slaine at Portingall s p.

Doctor Richard Eedes Deane of Worcester 2 sonne.*

---

* There is a monument to RICHAPD EEDES, Dean of Worcester, ob 1604, in Worcester Cathedral with these Arms Az , a chev eng between three leopards' faces ar. Crest A lion's foot ar out of a laurel vert. (Burke's 'Armory.')

THE VISITATION OF BEDFORDSHIRE.   103

A

Francis Eedes of Reding in com. Berks and of Sewell com. == Dorothey dau'r of Sr Richard Conquest of Houghton-Conquest Knight.
Bedford A° 1634 mar Joane his first wife dau'r of Richard Llewehn of Barton co Heref. gent. one of the heires of the Lady Hawkins ==

Margaret 1 wife to Richard Stafford of Thornbury co Gloc^r Esqr, secondly she married to Willm Wroth of Heauenend co Hertford

Richard Eedes onely son and heire apparent A° 1634

RICHARD EEDES

Everard

[of Beeston in Biggleswade].

ARMS —*Gules, on a fesse between three estoiles argent as many torteaux*

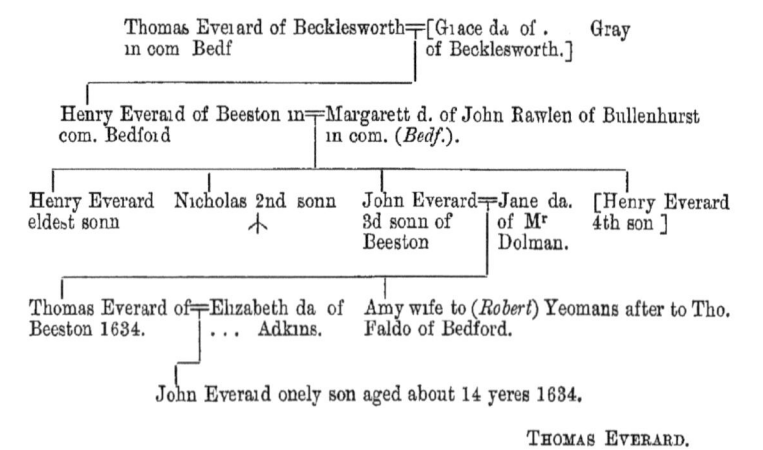

Thomas Everard of Becklesworth == [Grace da of . . . Gray of Becklesworth.]
in com Bedf

Henry Everard of Beeston in == Margarett d. of John Rawlen of Bullenhurst
com. Bedford   in com. (*Bedf.*).

Henry Everard eldest sonn   Nicholas 2nd sonn 人   John Everard 3d sonn of Beeston == Jane da. of Mr Dolman.   [Henry Everard 4th son]

Thomas Everard of == Elizabeth da of . . . Adkins.   Amy wife to (*Robert*) Yeomans after to Tho. Faldo of Bedford.
Beeston 1634.

John Everard onely son aged about 14 yeres 1634.

THOMAS EVERARD.

Ewer

[of Luton].

ARMS.—*Or, a tiger statant sable, on a chief gules three crosses pattée argent,* EWER *impaling, Sable, three covered cups argent,* SYMONDS
CREST.—*A pheon or, headed argent, mounted on a broken dart gules, environed with a snake proper.**
MOTTO.—HONOS ARTES.

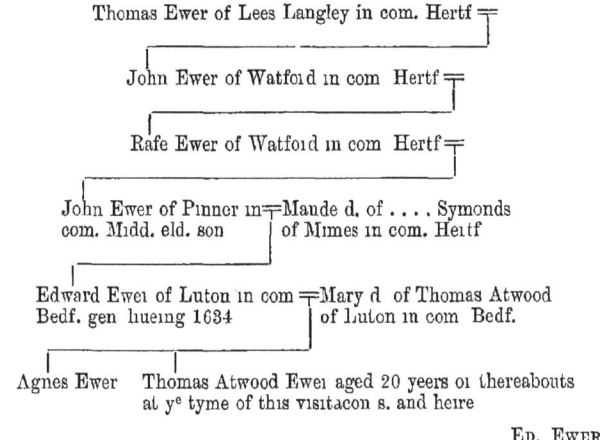

Thomas Ewer of Lees Langley in com. Hertf =
|
John Ewer of Watford in com Hertf =
|
Rafe Ewer of Watford in com Hertf =
|
John Ewer of Pinner in com. Midd. eld. son = Maude d. of .... Symonds of Mimes in com. Hertf
|
Edward Ewer of Luton in com Bedf. gen liueing 1634 = Mary d of Thomas Atwood of Luton in com Bedf.
|
— Agnes Ewer
— Thomas Atwood Ewer aged 20 yeers or thereabouts at ye tyme of this visitacon s. and heire

ED. EWER

Faldo†

[of Goldington].

ARMS.—*Gules, three stags' heads cabossed or, attired argent, a fleur-de-lys of the second for difference*

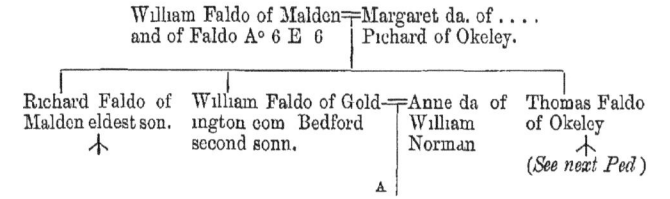

William Faldo of Malden and of Faldo A° 6 E 6 = Margaret da. of .... Pichard of Okeley.
|
— Richard Faldo of Malden eldest son. ⚭
— William Faldo of Goldington com Bedford second sonn. = Anne da of William Norman
— Thomas Faldo of Okeley ⚭ (*See next Ped*)

A

---

* "The Cote and Crest of Ewer together wth this impalement are exemplified by two pattents dated A° 1572 and in ye 14th yeare of Elizabeth from Robert Cooke Claren King of Armes to John Ewer of Pinner gent, s and h of Raphe Ewer of Watford, s and h. of John Ewer of Watford, com Hertf, s and h of Tho. Ewer of Leet Langley in the county aforesaid gent,"

† See Additional Pedigrees, *post*

THE VISITATION OF BEDFORDSHIRE.

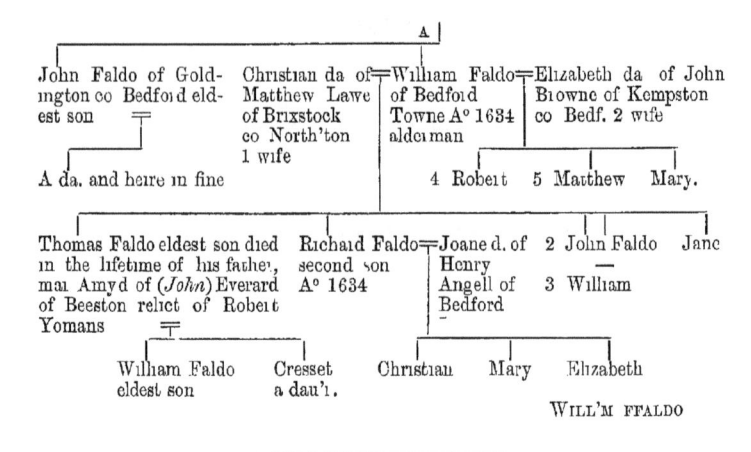

A

John Faldo of Goldington co Bedford eldest son = A da. and heire in fine

Christian da of Matthew Lawe of Brixstock co North'ton 1 wife

William Faldo of Bedford Towne A° 1634 alderman = Elizabeth da of John Browne of Kempston co Bedf. 2 wife

4 Robert   5 Matthew   Mary.

Thomas Faldo eldest son died in the lifetime of his father, mar. Amy d of (John) Everard of Beeston relict of Robert Yomans

Richard Faldo second son A° 1634 = Joane d. of Henry Angell of Bedford

2 John Faldo — 3 William

Jane

William Faldo eldest son

Cresset a dau'r.

Christian   Mary   Elizabeth

WILL'M FFALDO

==========

ᚠaldo

[of Oakley].

ARMS —*Same as Faldo of Goldington, a mullet for difference*

William Faldo of Malden and of Faldo A° 6 E 6 = Margaret d of Pichard of Okeley.

Thomas Faldo of Okeley co Bedf. 3 son of William = Margaret d of [Will'm*] Barber

[Mary ux . Morgan of London]

Richard Faldo of Okeley eldest son

2 John Faldo of Okeley second son = Jane da of ... Walsingham.

Robert Faldo of Okeley eldest son, heire masle to his unckle Richard after the death of Richard son of the saied Richard, he liueth A° 1634 = Frances da of .. Booth of Lincolnshire.

Rafe Faldo eldest son and heire aged about 6 yeres 1634

Suzan   Elizabeth

RO FFALDO

==========

* "Robert"—Harl. MS 4600

Fishe*

[of Biggleswade].

ARMS —*Azure, a fesse argent, over all on a bend gules five mullets or*
[CREST —*A lion rampant argent, holding in the dexter paw a mullet sable*]

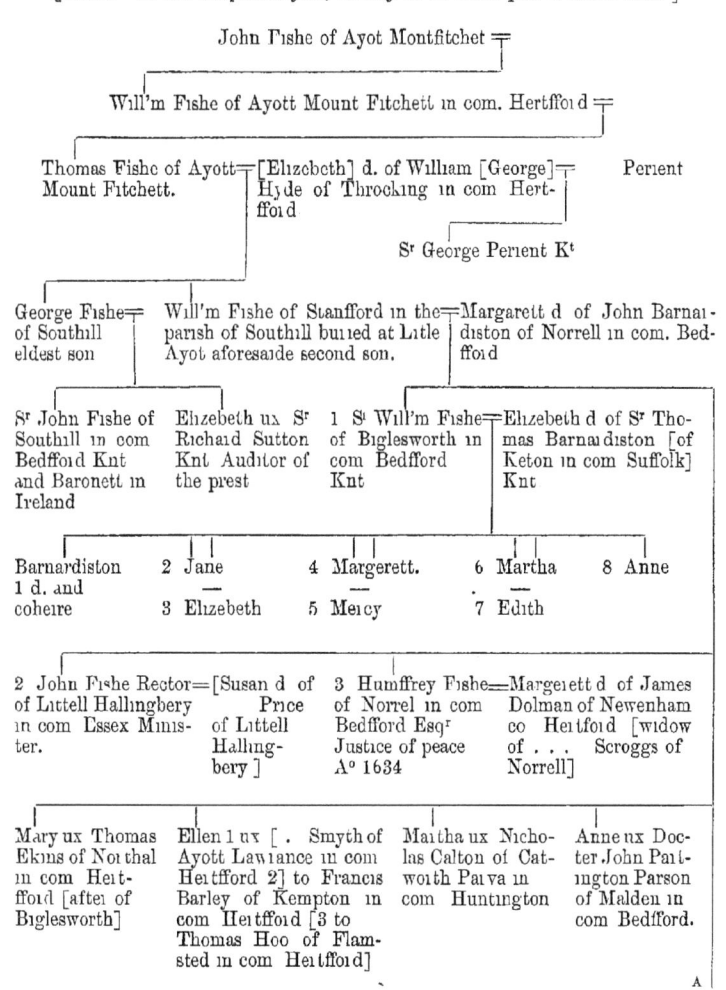

John Fishe of Ayot Montfitchet =

Will'm Fishe of Ayott Mount Fitchett in com. Hertfford =

Thomas Fishe of Ayott Mount Fitchett. = [Elizebeth] d. of William Hyde of Throcking in com Hertfford

[George] = Perient
Sr George Perient Kt

George Fishe of Southill eldest son =

Will'm Fishe of Stannford in the parish of Southill buried at Litle Ayot aforesaide second son. = Margarett d of John Barnardiston of Norrell in com. Bedfford

Sr John Fishe of Southill in com Bedfford Knt and Baronett in Ireland

Elizebeth ux Sr Richard Sutton Knt Auditor of the prest

1 Sr Will'm Fishe of Biglesworth in com Bedfford Knt = Elizebeth d of Sr Thomas Barnardiston [of Keton in com Suffolk] Knt

Barnardiston 1 d. and coheire

2 Jane

3 Elizebeth

4 Margerett.

5 Mercy

6 Martha

7 Edith

8 Anne

2 John Fishe Rector of Littell Hallingbery in com Essex Minister. = [Susan d of Price of Littell Hallingbery]

3 Humffrey Fishe of Norrel in com Bedfford Esqr Justice of peace Ao 1634 = Margerett d of James Dolman of Newenham co Hertford [widow of . . . Scroggs of Norrell]

Mary ux Thomas Ekins of Northal in com Hertfford [after of Biglesworth]

Ellen 1 ux [. Smyth of Ayott Lawrance in com Hertfford 2] to Francis Barley of Kempton in com Hertfford [3 to Thomas Hoo of Flamsted in com Hertfford]

Martha ux Nicholas Calton of Catworth Parva in com Huntington

Anne ux Docter John Parington Parson of Malden in com Bedfford.

A

* See Additional Pedigrees, *post*

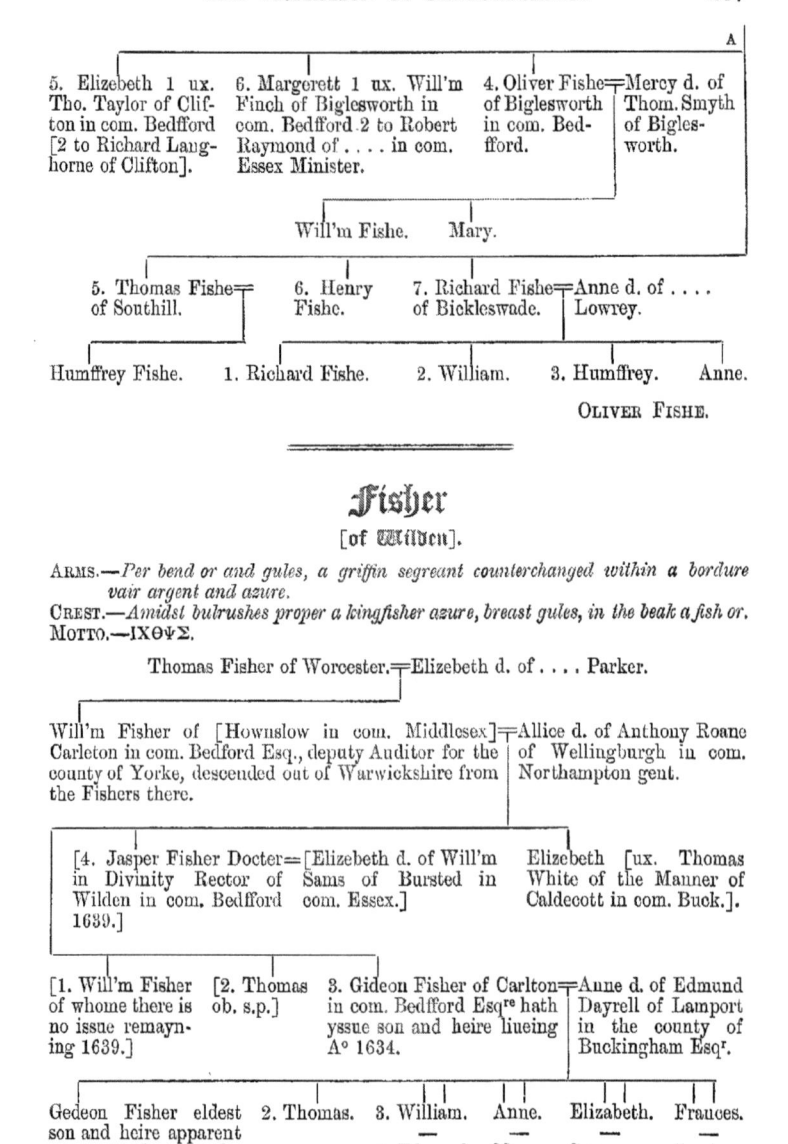

5. Elizebeth 1 ux. Tho. Taylor of Clifton in com. Bedfford [2 to Richard Langhorne of Clifton]. | 6. Margerett 1 ux. Finch of Biglesworth in com. Bedfford. 2 to Robert Raymond of .... in com. Essex Minister. | 4. Oliver Fishe of Biglesworth in com. Bedfford. = Mercy d. of Thom. Smyth of Biglesworth.

Will'm Fishe.   Mary.

5. Thomas Fishe of Southill. =   6. Henry Fishe.   7. Richard Fishe of Bickleswade. = Anne d. of .... Lowrey.

Humffrey Fishe.   1. Richard Fishe.   2. William.   3. Humffrey.   Anne.

OLIVER FISHE.

Fisher
[of Wilden].

ARMS.—*Per bend or and gules, a griffin segreant counterchanged within a bordure vair argent and azure.*
CREST.—*Amidst bulrushes proper a kingfisher azure, breast gules, in the beak a fish or.*
MOTTO.—ΙΧΘΨΣ.

Thomas Fisher of Worcester. = Elizebeth d. of .... Parker.

Will'm Fisher of Carleton in com. Bedford Esq., deputy Auditor for the county of Yorke, descended out of Warwickshire from the Fishers there. [Hownslow in com. Middlesex] = Allice d. of Anthony Roane of Wellingburgh in com. Northampton gent.

[4. Jasper Fisher Docter in Divinity Rector of Wilden in com. Bedfford 1639.] = [Elizebeth d. of Will'm Sams of Bursted in com. Essex.]   Elizebeth [ux. Thomas White of the Manner of Caldecott in com. Buck.].

[1. Will'm Fisher of whome there is no issue remayning 1639.]   [2. Thomas ob. s.p.]   3. Gideon Fisher of Carlton in com. Bedfford Esqre hath yssue son and heire liueing A° 1634. = Anne d. of Edmund Dayrell of Lamport in the county of Buckingham Esqr.

Gedeon Fisher eldest son and heire apparent now a student in the Vniuersity of Oxford A° 1634.   2. Thomas.   3. William. Anne. Elizabeth. Frances.
                                                                                        4. Edmund. Mary. Suzan. Sarah.

GEDEON FISHER.

Fitzgeoffrey[*]

[of Blackborne Hall].

ARMS —*Sable, a bull passant or, a crescent for difference*
CREST —*Out of a ducal coronet a demi-bull or*

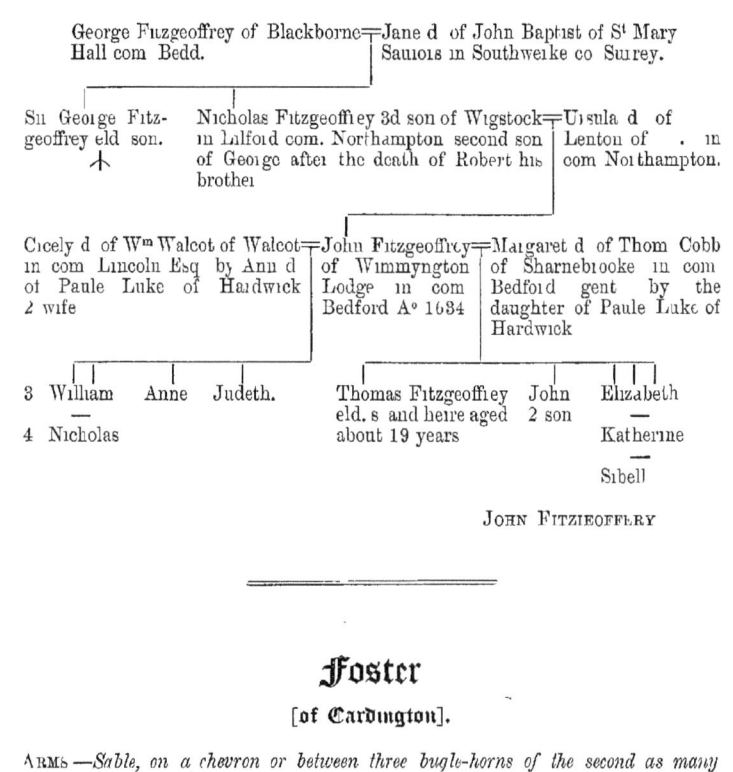

George Fitzgeoffrey of Blackborne = Jane d. of John Baptist of St Mary
Hall com Bedd. | Sauiois in Southwerke co Surrey.

- Sir George Fitzgeoffrey eld son. ┼
- Nicholas Fitzgeoffrey 3d son of Wigstock in Lilford com. Northampton second son of George after the death of Robert his brother = Ursula d. of Lenton of . . in com Northampton.

Cicely d of Wm Walcot of Walcot in com Lincoln Esq by Ann d of Paule Luke of Hardwick 2 wife = John Fitzgeoffrey of Wimmyngton Lodge in com Bedford A° 1634 = Margaret d of Thom Cobb of Sharnebrooke in com Bedford gent by the daughter of Paule Luke of Hardwick

- 3 William
- 4 Nicholas
- Anne
- Judeth.
- Thomas Fitzgeoffrey eld. s and heire aged about 19 years
- John 2 son
- Elizabeth
- Katherine
- Sibell

JOHN FITZGEOFFREY

Foster

[of Cardington].

ARMS —*Sable, on a chevron or between three bugle-horns of the second as many pheons azure* [†]
CREST —*A stag's head couped sable gouttée d'or, collared azure*

Thomas Foster of Wellen in com Hertford =

Henry Foster of Cardington in com Bed = A

---

[*] See Additional Pedigrees, *post*
[†] "L'res Pattents exem by Sr Richard St George Knight Clarenceux King of Armes dated A° 10° Car Regis 1634 to Will'm Foster of Cardington in com, Bedford."

THE VISITATION OF BEDFORDSHIRE.   109

William Foster of Card-=Elizabeth daughter of Michael Shawler of Riseley in com
ington in com | Bedford son of Gabriell son of Walter Shawler of Riseley
Bedford 1634 | and of Jane his wife daughter and sole heire in fine of
| Simon Sackuille of Riseley

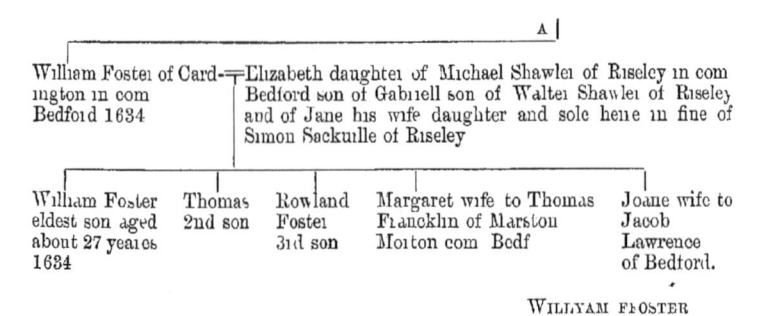

William Foster | Thomas | Rowland | Margaret wife to Thomas | Joane wife to
eldest son aged | 2nd son | Foster | Francklin of Marston | Jacob
about 27 yeares | | 3rd son | Morton com Bedf | Lawrence
1634 | | | | of Bedford.

WILLYAM FFOSTER

Fountaine

[of Kempston].

ARMS —*Quarterly*—1 *and* 4, *Argent, a fesse gules between three elephants' heads crased sable*, 2, *Sable, a bend between three lilies argent, stalked and leaved vert*, 3, *Sable, three fishes naiant in pale or*, *a martlet or for difference*

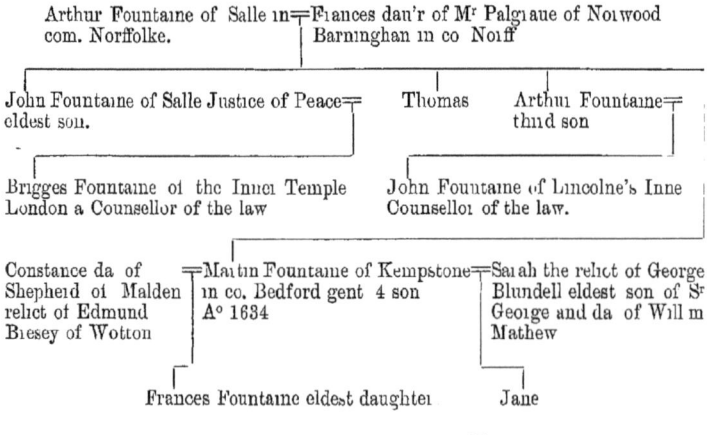

Arthur Fountaine of Salle in=Frances dau'r of Mr Palgraue of Norwood
com. Norffolke. | Barningham in co Norff

John Fountaine of Salle Justice of Peace=   Thomas   Arthur Fountaine=
eldest son. | | third son |

Brigges Fountaine of the Inner Temple   John Fountaine of Lincolne's Inne
London a Counsellor of the law. Counsellor of the law.

Constance da of =Martin Fountaine of Kempstone=Sarah the relict of George
Shepherd of Malden | in co. Bedford gent 4 son | Blundell eldest son of Sr
relict of Edmund | Aº 1634 | George and da of Willm
Bresey of Wotton | | Mathew

Frances Fountaine eldest daughter   Jane

MARTYNE FFOUNTEYN.

Francklyn*
[of Bolnhurst].

ARMS.—*Argent, on a bend engrailed between two lions' heads erased gules a dolphin naiant between as many martlets or*
CREST.—*A dolphin's head per fesse or and gules between two branches vert*

| Elizabeth da. of John Hall of Milham in the Bishopricke of Durthme 1 wife | = | John Francklyn of Thurley in com Bedford. | = | Anne his second wife daughter of Edward Copley of Southill com Bedford |

Children:
- John Franckln eld son
- William 2nd son.
- Elizabeth.
- George Francklyn of Maborne al's Mavorne co Bedford = [Anne] daughter of Edmond Style of Langley in com. Kent.

Children of George:
- Edmond Francklin of Mavorne Esqr lueing Aº 1634 eldest son — George Francklin 2nd son
- Nicholas 3rd son. — John 4th son
- Anne wife to Richard Gery of Bishmead co Bedford Esqr
- Elizabeth wife to Thomas Bosse of Burton in co. Bucks gent
- Margaret wife to Thomas Bacon of Earles Barton co. Northampton gent

JOHN NEGUS for EDMOND FFRANKLIN my Mr

Gery
[of Bushmead in Eaton-Socon].

ARMS (TWO SHIELDS).—I, *Gules, two bars argent charged with three mascles of the field, on a canton or a leopard's face azure,*† GERY   II, *Per fess nebulée argent and azure, three antelopes' heads counterchanged, attired gules,* SNOW ‡
CRESTS.—*An antelope's head erased quarterly argent and sable, charged with four mascles counterchanged, attired or,* GERY   *An antelope's head erased per pale nebulée argent and azure, attired or,* SNOW

Thomas Gery of Royston in the county of Hertford gentleman 1503 =

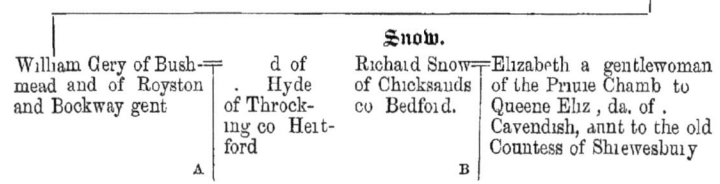

| William Gery of Bushmead and of Rockway gent = d. of . Hyde of Throcking co Hertford [A] | **Snow.** Richard Snow of Chicksands co Bedford = Elizabeth a gentlewoman of the Priuie Chamb to Queene Eliz, da. of . Cavendish, aunt to the old Countess of Shrewesbury [B] |

---

* *Cf* 'Le Neve's Knights,' p 300, and Additional Pedigrees, *post*
† "L'res Pattents exemplified by Thomas Wriothesley Garter and Tho. Benolt Clarenceux Aº 1503"
‡ "Lettres Pattents exemplified by Thomas Hawlay al's Claren' King of Armes to Richard Snow of Chicksand in ye County of Bedford gent graunted at London ye xith day of Febru, in yº xxxviijth yeare of King Hen. viijth."

THE VISITATION OF BEDFORDSHIRE.

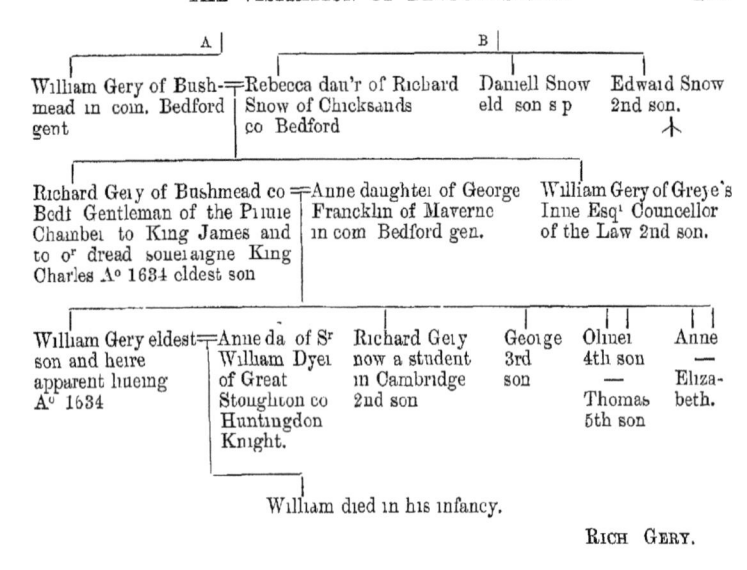

A |
William Gery of Bush-=Rebecca dau'r of Richard | Daniell Snow | Edward Snow
mead in com. Bedford | Snow of Chicksands | eld son s p | 2nd son.
gent | co Bedford

B |

Richard Gery of Bushmead co =Anne daughter of George | William Gery of Greye's
Bedf Gentleman of the Privie | Francklin of Maverne | Inne Esq' Councellor
Chamber to King James and | in com Bedford gen. | of the Law 2nd son.
to o' dread soveraigne King
Charles Aº 1634 oldest son

William Gery eldest=Anne da of S' | Richard Gery | George | Oliver | Anne
son and heire | William Dyer | now a student | 3rd | 4th son | —
apparent liveing | of Great | in Cambridge | son | — | Eliza-
Aº 1634 | Stoughton co | 2nd son | | Thomas | beth.
| Huntingdon | | | 5th son
| Knight.

William died in his infancy.

RICH GERY.

Goddard

[of Carlton].

ARMS.—*Quarterly*—1 and 4, *Gules, a chevron vaire argent and azure between three crescents of the first*, GODDARD of Wilts, 2 and 3, *Azure, five fusils in fesse gules between three eagles' heads erased or*, GODDARD of Hants
CREST.—*A stag's head couped at the neck affrontée gules, attired or.*

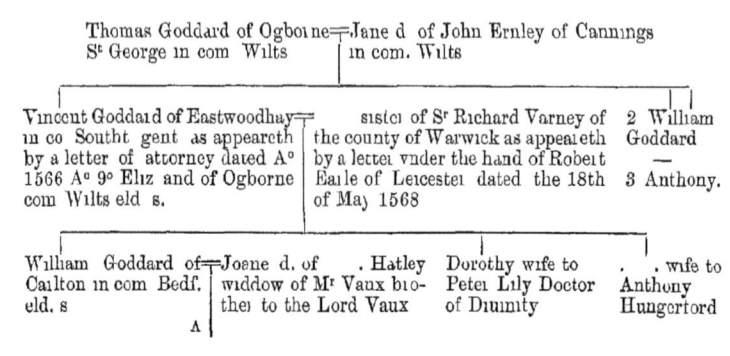

Thomas Goddard of Ogborne=Jane d of John Ernley of Cannings
S' George in com Wilts | in com. Wilts

Vincent Goddard of Eastwoodhay= sister of S' Richard Varney of | 2 William
in co Southt gent as appeareth | the county of Warwick as appeareth | Goddard
by a letter of attorney dated Aº | by a letter vnder the hand of Robert | —
1566 Aº 9º Eliz and of Ogborne | Earle of Leicester dated the 18th | 3 Anthony.
com Wilts eld s. | of May 1568

William Goddard of=Joane d. of . Hatley | Dorothy wife to | . . wife to
Carlton in com Bedf. | widdow of M' Vaux bro- | Peter Lily Doctor | Anthony
eld. s | ther to the Lord Vaux | of Divinity | Hungerford
A

THE VISITATION OF BEDFORDSHIRE.

▲

Vincent Goddard of Carleton = Edith d of . Pawlet brother to Sr Amyas Pawlet eld s | of Hinton St George com. Somersett Kt

William Goddard of Carleton co Bedf = Mary d. of Lewis gent eld s liveing 1634 | Richardson of .

Vincent Goddard aged about 7 yeres A° 1634 eld. s and heire — Henry — John — Katherin

WILLIAM GODDARD

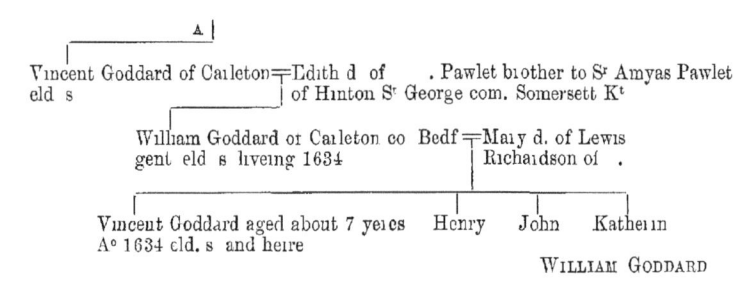

Gray
[of Pertenhall].

ARMS.—*Argent, a bend vert cotised dancettée gules*
CREST.—*A demi-woman couped at the waist proper, hair flottant, holding in her hands a wreath vert*

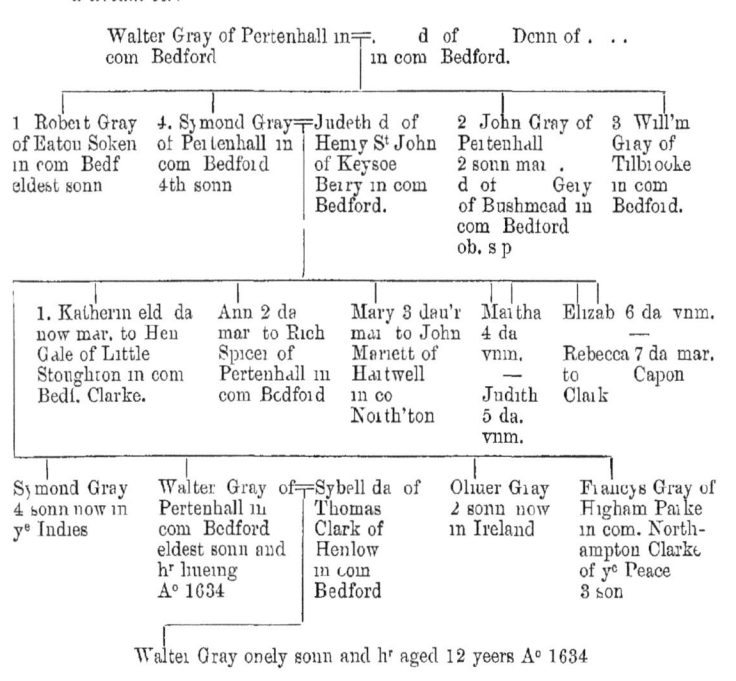

Walter Gray of Pertenhall in = . d of Denn of . . . com Bedford | in com Bedford.

1 Robert Gray of Eaton Soken in com Bedf eldest sonn

4. Symond Gray = Judeth d of of Pertenhall in | Henry St John com Bedford | of Keysoe 4th sonn | Berry in com Bedford.

2 John Gray of Pertenhall 2 sonn mar. d of Gery of Bushmead in com Bedford ob. s p

3 Will'm Gray of Tilbrooke in com Bedford.

1. Katherin eld da now mar. to Hen Gale of Little Stoughton in com Bedf. Clarke.

Ann 2 da mar to Rich Spicer of Pertenhall in com Bedford

Mary 3 dau'r mar to John Mariett of Hartwell in co North'ton

Martha 4 da vnm. — Judith 5 da. vnm.

Elizab 6 da vnm. — Rebecca 7 da mar. to Capon Clark

Symond Gray 4 sonn now in ye Indies

Walter Gray of = Sybell da of Pertenhall in | Thomas com Bedford and | Clark of hr liueing | Henlow A° 1634 | in com | Bedford

Oliuer Gray 2 sonn now in Ireland

Francys Gray of Higham Parke in com. Northampton Clarke of ye Peace 3 son

Walter Gray onely sonn and hr aged 12 yeers A° 1634

WALTER GRAY

Griffin

[of Cockayne-Hatley].

ARMS —*Sable, a griffin segreant argent, fore-legged or.*

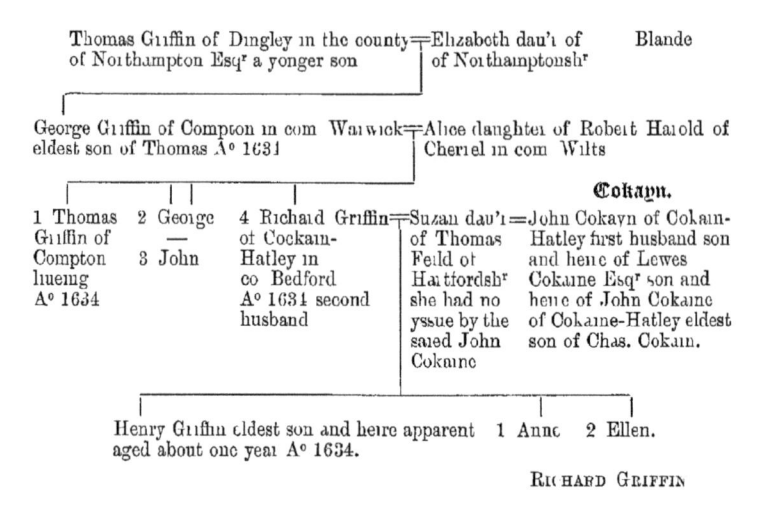

Thomas Griffin of Dingley in the county of Northampton Esqr a yonger son = Elizabeth dau'r of Blande of Northamptonsh^r

George Griffin of Compton in com Warwick eldest son of Thomas A° 1634 = Alice daughter of Robert Harold of Cheriel in com Wilts

Cokayn.

1 Thomas Griffin of Compton liueing A° 1634

2 George — 3 John

4 Richard Griffin of Cockain-Hatley in co Bedford A° 1634 second husband = Suzan dau'r of Thomas Feild of Hartfordsh^r she had no yssue by the saied John Cokaine = John Cokayn of Cokain-Hatley first husband son and heire of Lewes Cokaine Esqr son and heire of John Cokaine of Cokaine-Hatley eldest son of Chas. Cokain.

Henry Griffin eldest son and heire apparent aged about one year A° 1634.

1 Anne 2 Ellen.

RICHARD GRIFFIN.

Hale*

[of Clifton].

"Noueint universi p' presentes me Johannem Hale de Aspley Gyse in com Bedds recepisti et habuisse die confectionis presentium de Mathe Hale de Hexton in com Hartford tratri meo xxvij li vj s viij d in plenam solutionem pro monibus, &c Dat' quarto die mensis Aprilis A° Regni Henrici Octavi dei gracia Angliæ & Franciæ Regis fidei defensoris et dni Hiberniæ vicessimo primo"

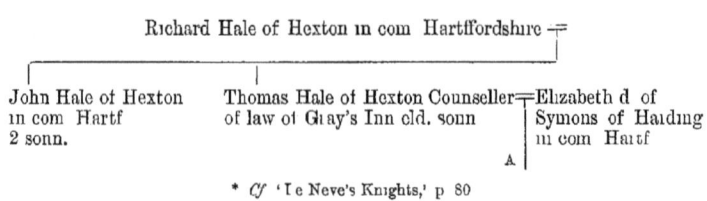

Richard Hale of Hexton in com Hartffordshire =

John Hale of Hexton in com Hartf 2 sonn.

Thomas Hale of Hexton Counseller of law of Gray's Inn eld. sonn = Elizabeth d of Symons of Harding in com Hartf

A

* Cf 'Te Neve's Knights,' p 80

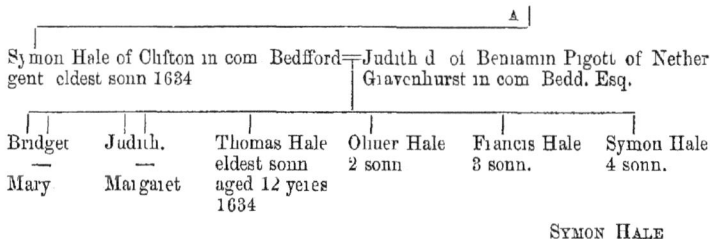

Symon Hale of Clifton in com Bedfford = Judith d. of Beniamin Pigott of Nether
gent eldest sonn 1634 | Gravenhurst in com Bedd. Esq.

- Bridget — Mary
- Judith — Margaret
- Thomas Hale eldest sonn aged 12 yeres 1634
- Oliuer Hale 2 sonn
- Francis Hale 3 sonn
- Symon Hale 4 sonn

SYMON HALE

Harding

[of Aspley].

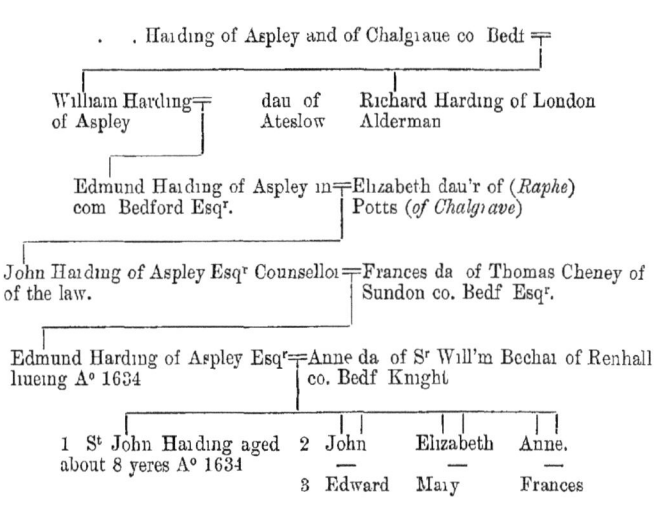

. . Harding of Aspley and of Chalgraue co. Bedf =

- William Harding of Aspley = dau of Ateslow
- Richard Harding of London Alderman

Edmund Harding of Aspley in = Elizabeth dau'r of (*Raphe*)
com Bedford Esq'. | Potts (*of Chalgrave*)

John Harding of Aspley Esq' Counsellor = Frances da. of Thomas Cheney of
of the law. | Sundon co. Bedf Esq'.

Edmund Harding of Aspley Esq' = Anne da. of S' Will'm Bechar of Renhall
liueing A° 1634 | co. Bedf Knight

- 1 S't John Harding aged about 8 yeres A° 1634
- 2 John
- 3 Edward
- Elizabeth
- Mary
- Anne
- Frances

EDMUND HARDINGE.

Haselden
[of Goldington].

ARMS —*Argent, a cross patonce sable*

"Pateat Vniversis p present' me Thomam de Hasulden att'nasse & loco meo posuiste dilt m michi in xpo Joh'em rueborough fidelem att'uam meu' ad delib and' Will mo de Sneycale de Wakefeld Ric Oult' de Wakefeld Joh'i Marchaund de Feribrigge capell'o & Joh'i de Ardern de com Ebore et In cuius iei testimon' p'sent Sigillu' meu' apposui Datu' apud London die Lune p'y'n ante festu' nat' S'c'i Joh Bapt' ct rcgni Regis Edwardi tertii post conquestu' quadragesimo 3 tio '*

"Ego Thomas Haselden de Waketeild dedi concessi et uac presenti carta mea confirmaui D'ne Johanne Marchunt de Feribrigge capell'o Joh i Mille de Waketeild capell'o John de Brecherton capell'o Henrico Parbon'e de Stepilmordon capell'o Ric'o Bulter & Ric'o de Holoud Maneriu' de Goldington cu' Redditib' & p'c'is past' & pastur' cu' Ward' Maritag Relev' Escaet' & cum omnibus aliis suis p'tin' p'd c o Maneriis quomismodo Spectantib' Hend' & tenend' p'd'c'm maneriu cu' Redd & s'uic' p'c'is past' et past' cu' Ward et In cuius rei testimoniu' hui P'senti carta Sigillu' meu apposui Hijs testib Joh'ne Maieyu' Thomu' Gyldespynde Hamonc Flan ville Gi'b'to Drye Thom Juidu aliis Dat' ap d Goldington quartodecimo die Mensis Maii A° regni Regis Ric'i S'c di post conquestu' quarto "

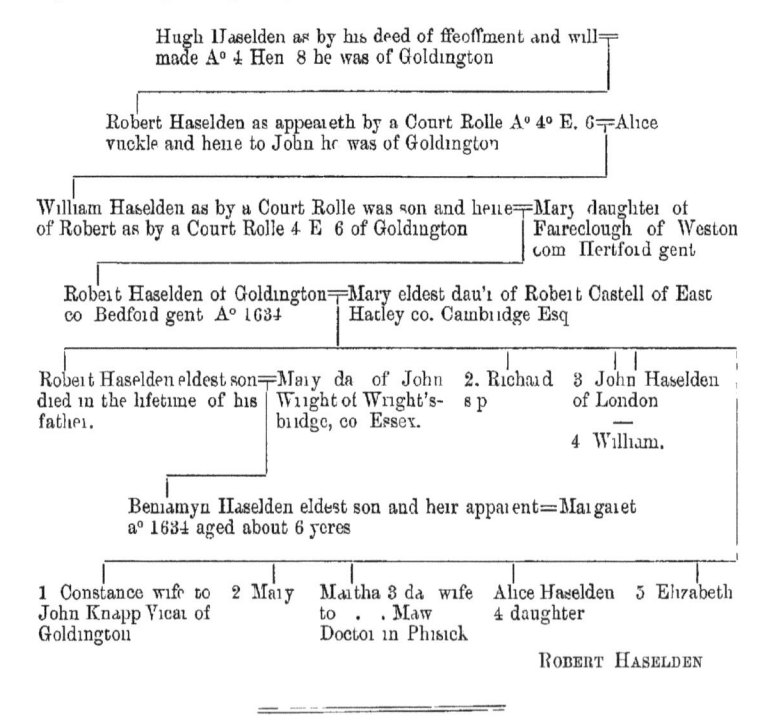

```
Hugh Haselden as by his deed of ffeoffment and will
made A° 4 Hen 8 he was of Goldington
    |
Robert Haselden as appeareth by a Court Rolle A° 4° E. 6 = Alice
vuckle and heire to John he was of Goldington
    |
William Haselden as by a Court Rolle was son and heire = Mary daughter of
of Robert as by a Court Rolle 4 E 6 of Goldington       Faireclough of Weston
                                                        com Hertford gent
    |
Robert Haselden of Goldington = Mary eldest dau'r of Robert Castell of East
co Bedford gent A° 1634         Hatley co. Cambridge Esq
    |_____
    |                            |              |
Robert Haselden eldest son = Mary da of John   2. Richard   3 John Haselden
died in the lifetime of his  Wright of Wright's- s p        of London
father.                      bridge, co Essex.
                                                            4 William.
    |
Benjamyn Haselden eldest son and heir apparent = Margaret
a° 1634 aged about 6 yeres
    |_____
    |           |         |                |              |
1 Constance wife to  2 Mary  Martha 3 da wife   Alice Haselden  5 Elizabeth
John Knapp Vicar of          to . . Maw        4 daughter
Goldington                   Doctor in Phisick
```

ROBERT HASELDEN

---

* Underneath the copy (or abstract?) of above deed is an ink sketch of a circular seal having a shield charged with a cross patonce and having the legend "Sigillum   omam de hasulden"

Hervy
[of Thurleigh].

ARMS.—*Quarterly of ten*—1, *Gules on a bend argent three trefoils slipped vert*, HERVY, 2, *Sable, a lion rampant argent within a bordure gobony of the second and first*, NERNUITE, 3, *Argent, on a pale sable a conger's head erect couped or*, GASCOIGNE, 4, *Gules, three pickaxes argent*, PICOT 5, *Azure, two bars or, in chief three plates*, WAKE, 6, *Quarterly or and gules, a bend gules*, BEAUCHAMP, 7, *Ermine, a lion rampant sable*, VINTER or UNTER, 8, *Ermine, a saltire engrailed gules*, SCARGILL, 9, *As No. 7*, 10, *As No 8*

Gascoigne.

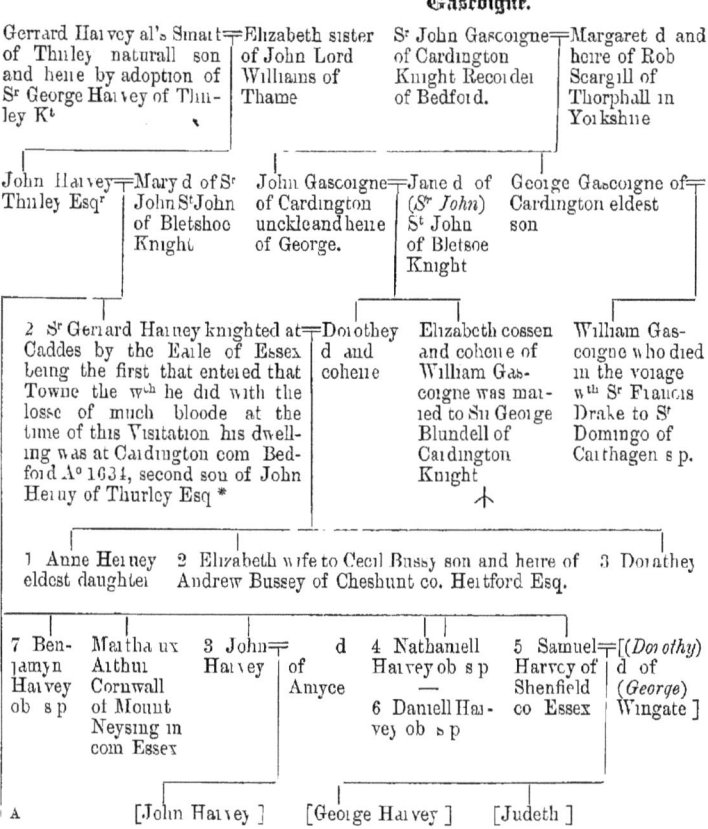

Gerrard Harvey al's Smart of Thurley naturall son and heire by adoption of Sr George Harvey of Thurley Kt = Elizabeth sister of John Lord Williams of Thame

Sr John Gascoigne of Cardington Knight Recorder of Bedford. = Margaret d and heire of Rob Scargill of Thorphall in Yorkshire

John Harvey of Thurley Esqr = Mary d of Sr John St John of Bletshoe Knight

John Gascoigne of Cardington unckle and heire of George. = Jane d of (Sr John) St John of Bletsoe Knight

George Gascoigne of Cardington eldest son =

2 Sr Gerard Harvey knighted at Caddes by the Earle of Essex being the first that entered that Towne the wch he did with the losse of much bloode at the time of this Visitation his dwelling was at Cardington com Bedford Ao 1634, second son of John Heruy of Thurley Esq * = Dorothey d and coheire

Elizabeth cossen and coheire of William Gascoigne was maried to Sir George Blundell of Cardington Knight

William Gascoigne who died in the voiage wth Sr Francis Drake to St Domingo of Carthagen s p.

1 Anne Hervey eldest daughter   2 Elizabeth wife to Cecil Bussy son and heire of Andrew Bussey of Cheshunt co. Hertford Esq.   3 Dorothey

7 Benjamyn Harvey ob s p
Martha ux Arthur Cornwall of Mount Neysing in com Essex
3 John Harvey = d of Amyce
4 Nathaniell Harvey ob s p — 6 Daniell Harvey ob s p
5 Samuel Harvey of Shenfield co Essex = [(*Dorothy*) d of (*George*) Wingate]

A [John Harvey]   [George Harvey]   [Judeth]

* "Sr Gerard Heruy Kt sometime serjant Maior of Ostend Vnder the Gouernment of Sr Edw Naris than to Cades voiage then luictenant Cornett wth Sr Arthur Sauage into France from thence returned to Ostend and there continued vntill my Lord of Essex went into Ireland where he was .. maior of the Army imploied in Conogh"

THE VISITATION OF BEDFORDSHIRE. 117

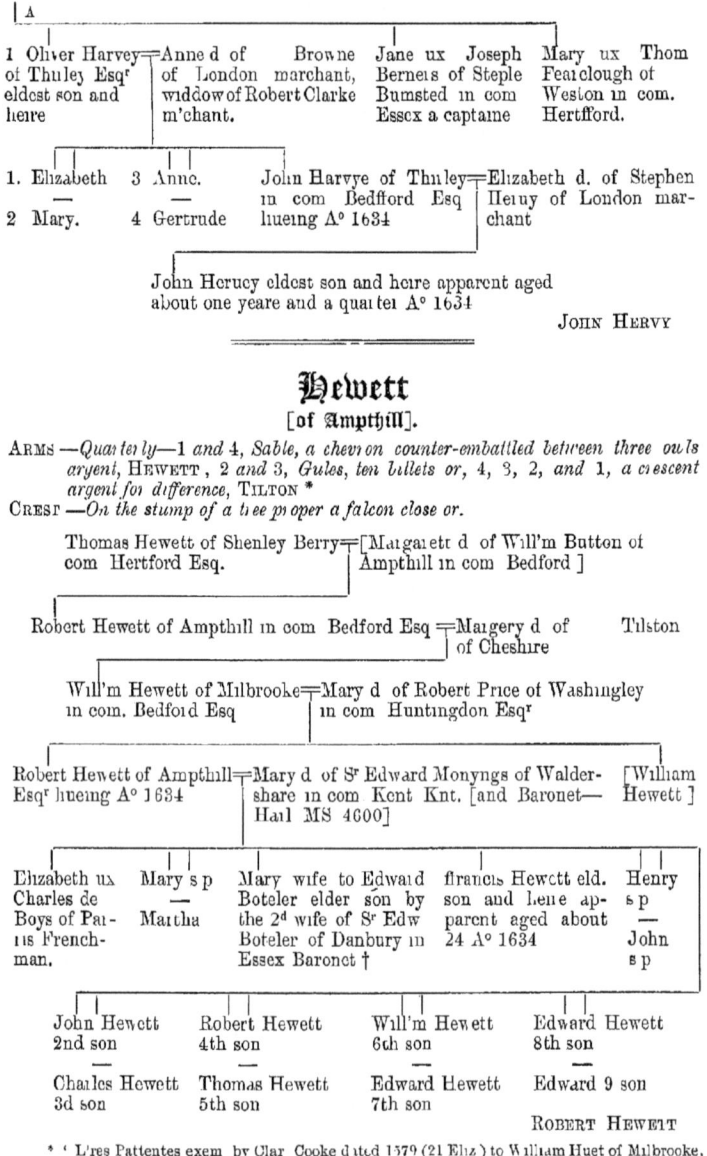

| A

1 Oliver Harvey=Anne d. of Browne of London marchant, widdow of Robert Clarke m'chant. — of Thuley Esqr eldest son and heire.

Jane ux Joseph Berners of Steple Bumsted in com Essex a captaine.

Mary ux Thom Fearclough of Weston in com. Hertfford.

1. Elizabeth
2 Mary.
3 Anne.
4 Gertrude

John Harvye of Thuley=Elizabeth d. of Stephen Henry of London marchant — in com Bedfford Esq hueing A° 1634

John Hervey eldest son and heire apparent aged about one yeare and a quarter A° 1634

JOHN HERVY

Hewett
[of Ampthill].

ARMS —*Quarterly*—1 *and* 4, *Sable, a chevron counter-embattled between three owls argent,* HEWETT, 2 *and* 3, *Gules, ten billets or,* 4, 3, 2, *and* 1, *a crescent argent for difference,* TILTON *

CREST —*On the stump of a tree proper a falcon close or.*

Thomas Hewett of Shenley Berry=[Margarett d. of Will'm Button of Ampthill in com Bedford] com Hertford Esq.

Robert Hewett of Ampthill in com Bedford Esq =Margery d. of   Tilston of Cheshire

Will'm Hewett of Milbrooke=Mary d. of Robert Price of Washingley in com. Bedford Esq   in com. Huntingdon Esqr

Robert Hewett of Ampthill=Mary d. of Sr Edward Monyngs of Walder-   [William Esqr hueing A° 1634   share in com Kent Knt. [and Baronet— Hewett] Harl MS 4600]

Elizabeth ux Charles de Boys of Paris Frenchman.

Mary s p
—
Martha

Mary wife to Edward Boteler elder son by the 2d wife of Sr Edw Boteler of Danbury in Essex Baronet †

francis Hewett eldest son and heire apparent aged about 24 A° 1634

Henry s p
—
John s p

John Hewett 2nd son
Charles Hewett 3d son

Robert Hewett 4th son
Thomas Hewett 5th son

Will'm Hewett 6th son
Edward Hewett 7th son

Edward Hewett 8th son
Edward 9 son

ROBERT HEWETT

* ' L'res Pattentes exem by Clar Cooke dated 1579 (21 Eliz) to William Huet of Milbrooke, com Bedford Esq "   † In another hand

Hill
[of Silsoe].

ARMS —*Sable, a chevron ermine between three cats argent, a crescent for difference.*

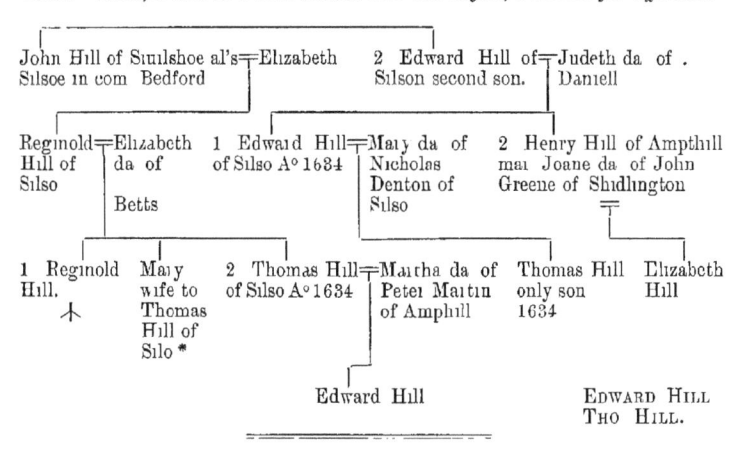

- John Hill of Stnilshoe al's Silsoe in com Bedford == Elizabeth
  - Reginold Hill of Silso == Elizabeth da of Betts
    - 1 Reginold Hill.
    - Mary wife to Thomas Hill of Silo *
  - 1 Edward Hill of Silso A° 1634 == Mary da of Nicholas Denton of Silso
    - 2 Thomas Hill of Silso A° 1634 == Martha da of Peter Martin of Amphill
      - Edward Hill
- 2 Edward Hill of Silson second son == Judeth da of . Daniell
  - 2 Henry Hill of Ampthill mar Joane da of John Greene of Shidlington
    - Thomas Hill only son 1634
    - Elizabeth Hill

EDWARD HILL
THO HILL.

Hunte
[of Chalversterne].

ARMS —*Argent, on a chevron within a bordure bezantée gules an annulet or.*
CREST —*On a mound vert an oak-tree proper, fructed or, at the base a talbot couchant argent, collared or*

William Hunte of Chalversterne in com Bedf s. and h of Thomas Hunte A° 2° Eliz whose auncestrs used the titles of Esquires as appeareth by severall Court Rolles remaining at Chalverston == Jane d. of John Russell of Lynslade in com Buck

- [Joane ux Tho Wright of Chalver- sterne]
- [2 Mary — 3 Mary — 4. Joane]
- Roger Hunt of Chal- uerston gent. filius et hæres 38 Eliz Rnne 1596 == Mary d of Wm Goodfellow of Pavenham in com Bedf
- Thomas 2 filius of Kempston Hardwick co Bedford second son

Tho Hunt of Chauls'ton gent sonne and heire of Roger liueing A° 1634 == Rhose d. of Euerton in com Hunt Hale of

- James Hunt eldest son and heire apparent liueing A° 1634 aged about 24 yeres
- Tho Hunt of second son.
- == [Margaret d. of]
- Mary

THOMAS HUNT, Senior

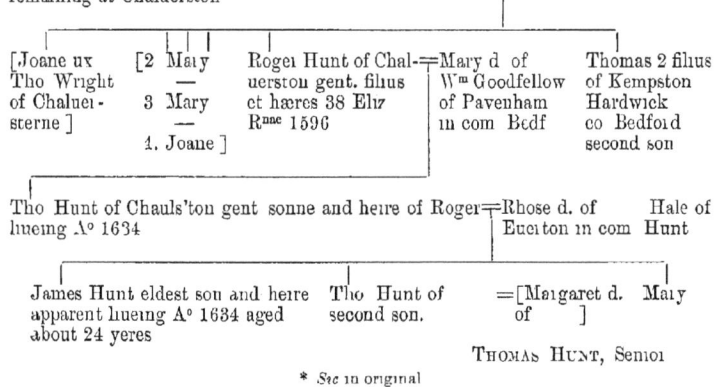

* Sic in original

𝕳𝕪𝕟𝕥𝕠𝕟
[of 𝕰𝕧𝕖𝕣𝕤𝕙𝕠𝕝𝕥].

ARMS.—*Per fesse indented sable and or, five fleurs-de-lis, 3 and 2, counterchanged* *

Robert Hynton of Flitton in com Bedford buried in the same church, branched out of Shropshire
│
George Hynton of Euersholt
│
Thomas Hynton of Euersholt in co Bedford = Francis daughter of   Decons
│
George Hynton of Euersholt g' maried and is liueing = Mary da. of Geo Foster of Fleetwick in com Bedf
A° 1634
│
George Hynton eldest son and heire apparent   Mary.   Frances.   Dorothey
liueing A° 1634 aged about 11 yeres

GEORGE HYNTON

𝕵𝕠𝕙𝕟𝕤𝕠𝕟[†]
[of 𝕮𝕙𝕒𝕝𝕘𝕣𝕒𝕧𝕖 𝕒𝕟𝕕 𝕸𝕚𝕝𝕥𝕠𝕟=𝕭𝕣𝕪𝕒𝕟𝕥].

ARMS.—*Argent, on a pile azure three leopards' heads erased of the field*
CREST.—*On a cap of maintenance gules, turned up ermine, a leopard's head erased argent, spotted sable* ‡

(Thomas) Johnson of the North.
│
Thomas Johnson of Chalgrave = Mary da. of Mr Potts sister of
co Bedford.   Nicholas Potts Esq
│
Nicholas Johnson of Milton = Elizabeth da of Richard Spicer   Francis 2nd son.
Brian co Bedford gent liue- al's Uelder of Tingre co Bed-   —
ing A° 1634   ford.   William 3rd son
│
Nicholas Johnson aged about 10 yeres 1634   William 2nd son   Elizabeth   Mary

NICHOLAS JOHNSON

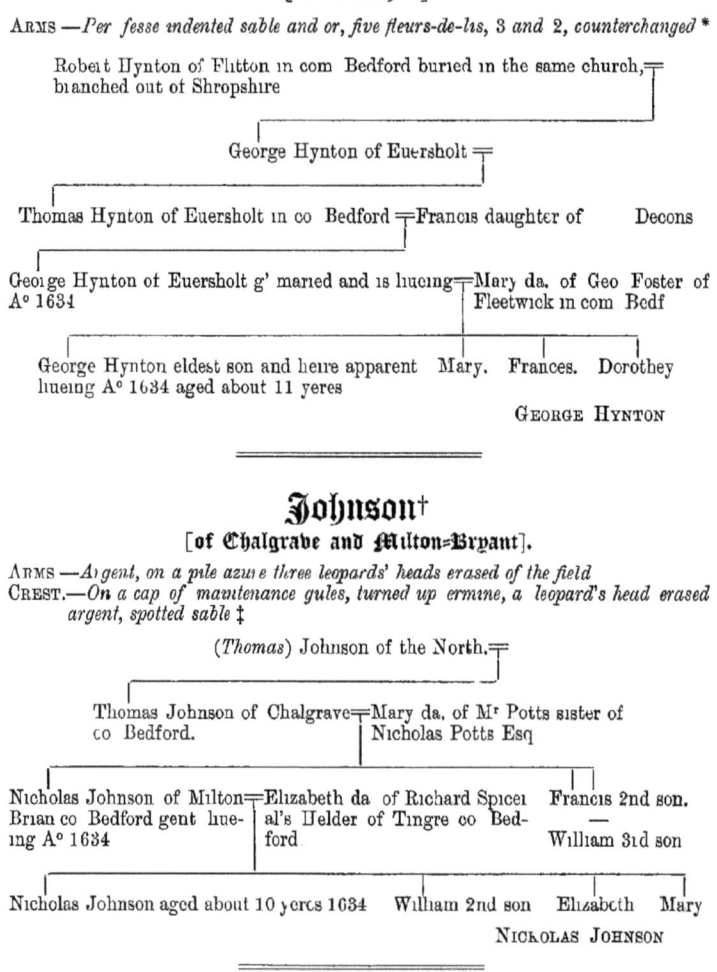

* "By certificate vnder the hand of Mr Tauerner and Mr Wyngate, who veiwed the euidences and monuments of this family"

† *Cf* 'Miscellanea Genealogica et Heraldica, vol II, New Series, p 122

‡ "L'res Pattents exemplified by Sr Richard St George Knight Claren' King of Armes to Nicholas Johnson of Milton Brian co Bedford and to Francis Johnson and William Johnson brothers of the saide Nicholas and to their seuerall descendants. Dated the viijth day of May An'o D ni 1632 8° Car Regis"

Jones

[of Litlington].

ARMS.—*Azure, a cross between four pheons or, a martlet gules for difference*
CREST.—*On a chapeau azure, turned up or, an armed arm embowed, tasselled gules, holding in the hand proper a spear-staff of the fourth, armed of the second* †
MOTTO.—CALILUS MIHI VIVES

[Henery Jones of Midleton in com Lanck]

- Sr Roger Jones Knt Alderman and Shreeve of London = Anne [Jane] d of Thomas Hackett of London sister to Sr Cuthbert Hackett Knight sometime maior of London.
- [Thomas Jones Archbishop of Dublyn and Chancellor of Ireland]

Children:

1. Thomas Jones [of Lambeth in com Surrey] eldest son and heire = [Sarah d of Sr Thomas Hays Knt Lord Maior of London]
2. Henery Jones [liveing in Ireland] = [Jane d of Henery Peers of Ireland]
3. John Jones = [Catherin d of Samwell Hare of London]
4. Roger [Robert] Jones [a Captaine] ob s p = [Elizebeth d. of John Lacye of Melton Mowbrey in com Lester widdow of Peeter Bostock of London]
5. Richard Jones of Litlington in com Bedfford A° 1634 = Christian d. of Roger Hackett Doctor in Divinity elder brother to the said Sr Cuthbert Hacket Knight
6. Hugh Jones
7. Peter
8. Robert
— Anne Duppa
— Margaret Stubbs
— Hester Estington

Children of Richard:

1. Roger Jones eldest son and heire aged about 15 yeres A° 1634
2. Richard
3. William
4. Thomas
— Elizabeth
— Christian
— Margaret
— Anne.

RICHARD JONES

---

* *Cf* 'Visitation of London, 1633-4' vol ii, p 20, ed Harl Soc
† "Letters pattents exemplifyed to Thomas Jones of London Esq eldest sonn of Sr Roger Jones Kt sometymes shreif and senator of London elder brother to the right reverend father in god Thomas Jones first lord Bishop of Meath in Ireland then Arch Bishop of Dublyn then also lord Chancellor of Ireland Father to ye right hoble sr Roger Jones Kt Viscount Ranelergh in ye County of Wicklow and Baron of Nauan in ye County of Eastmeath which Sr Roger Jones was sonn of Henry Jones gent discended Lineally from a right worshipfull family of the TREOWENS in ye County of Monmouth in Wales All which was exemplified by Sr Wm Segar Kt Garter vnto ye sayd Thomas Jones Esqr and his posterity and all ye rest of ye Children of ye sayd Sr Roger Jones for euer Dated 1628 A° 4 King Charles'

Keynsham

[of Tempsford].

ARMS —*Per pale argent and azure, three roses counterchanged*
CREST —*A greyhound's head couped or, barry of six argent and vert, gouttée d'eau*

Richard Keynsham of Brixton in com. Deuon =⸺ Elizabeth dau'r of . . Parker of Plumpton com. Deuon

- Thomazen da of John Leech of Sowtham in com Deuon first wife = John Keynsham of Brixton in com Deuon eldest sonne = Thomazenda of Iscomb 2nd wife.
- George Keynsham of Temesford in ye county of Bedford 2nd sonn of Richard sometime high shreife co Bedford. = Elizabeth daughter of . . Alpert
- Alice m to . . Payne.

Children:
- Richard Keynsham sanz issue.
- George Keynsha' sonn and heire.
- John Keynsha' sanz issue.
- Stephen Keynsham of Temesford in com Bedford = Anne daughter of Edmund Lee of Pitston in com Bucks Esq'

[Elizabeth] — [Joane.] — George Keynsham of Tempesford com Bedford Esq' A° 1634 sometime high shreife for the county of Bedford. = Frances daughter of S' Richard Chitwood of Chitwood com Buckingham Knight

Anne daughter and sole heire apparent aged about 10 yeres

GEORGE KEYNSHAM.

Lake

[of Pulloxhill].

ARMS —*Quarterly or and azure, four crescents counterchanged.*[*]
CREST —*A cross formée fitchée or and azure in a crescent or*

Richard Lake of Pulloxhill in com Bedfford =. . . d of . . Man.

Thomas Lake of Pulloxhill in com Bedfford liueing 1634 = Annis d of . . Reding

- Liuia 1 da.
- Elizab. 2.
- Sarah 3.
- Mary 4.
- Constance 6.
- Suzan 7.
- Thomas Lake eldest sonne.
- Lidia 5 da m. to Edward Smith of Ampthill

THOMAS LAKE

[*] "Certified by M' Cambden in an escocheon vnder his hand"

ately in source...

Mallory

[of Shelton].

ARMS —*Or, a lion rampant queue fourchée gules, within a bordure of the second*
CREST —*A horse's head couped gules, charged with a fleur-de-lys*

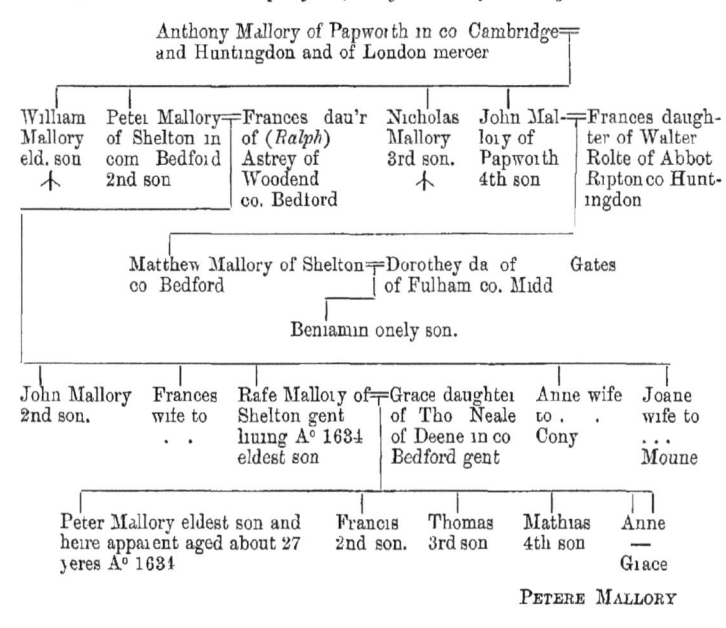

Anthony Mallory of Papworth in co Cambridge
and Huntingdon and of London mercer

- William Mallory eld. son ⚔
- Peter Mallory of Shelton in com Bedford 2nd son = Frances dau'r of (Ralph) Astrey of Woodend co. Bedford
- Nicholas Mallory 3rd son ⚔
- John Mallory of Papworth 4th son = Frances daughter of Walter Rolte of Abbot Ripton co Huntingdon

Matthew Mallory of Shelton co Bedford = Dorothey da of of Fulham co. Midd   Gates

Benjamin onely son.

- John Mallory 2nd son.
- Frances wife to . .
- Rafe Mallory of Shelton gent living A° 1634 eldest son = Grace daughter of Tho Neale of Deene in co Bedford gent
- Anne wife to . . Cony
- Joane wife to . . . Moune

- Peter Mallory eldest son and heire apparent aged about 27 yeres A° 1634
- Francis 2nd son.
- Thomas 3rd son
- Mathias 4th son
- Anne — Grace

PETERE MALLORY

Manley

[of Wilshamstead].

ARMS —*Quarterly—1 and 4, Argent, a dexter hand couped and erect sable, a bordure engrailed of the last,* MANLEY, *2 and 3, Vert, a bend ermine,* ? WETTENHALL

CREST —*On a wreath or and azure a Saracen's head affrontée proper, wreathed with a fillet vert*

' MEMORAND It appeareth by the Last Will and Testament of the first person named in this descent taken in the Visitation of Bedfordshire A° 1634 that his Christian name was Edward Manley and not Robert which will and Testament mentioneth his wife and children as are expressed and is registered in the booke called Arundell 2° fo 39—remayning in the Prerogative Office   Ita Testor, Will m's Dugdale Norroy necnon Fran Sandford Rouge Diagon "

THE VISITATION OF BEDFORDSHIRE. 123

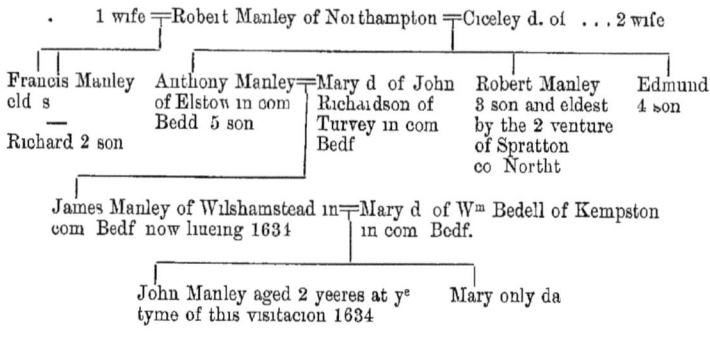

1 wife =Robert Manley of Northampton= Ciceley d. of ... 2 wife

- Francis Manley eld s
- Richard 2 son
- Anthony Manley of Elstow in com Bedd 5 son =Mary d of John Richardson of Turvey in com Bedf
- Robert Manley 3 son and eldest by the 2 venture of Spratton co Northt
- Edmund 4 son

James Manley of Wilshamstead in com Bedf now lueing 1634 =Mary d of Wm Bedell of Kempston in com Bedf.

John Manley aged 2 yeeres at y^e tyme of this visitacion 1634

Mary only da

JOHN MANLEY.

Monoux*

[of Wootton].

ARMS —*Argent, on a chevron sable between three oak-leaves vert as many bezants, on a chief gules a martlet between two anchors of the first*

CREST —*A turtle-dove azure, winged or, membered and beaked purpure, holding in the beak an oak-branch vert, acorned gold* †

[Thomas Monoux of Walthamstow in com Essex] =[Anne da of John Turbevile of in com Dorsett]

- George Monoux of Walthamstow in com Essex heire male to Sir George Monoux K^t of London alderman =Elizebeth da of John Lord Mordaunt of Turvey sister of Lewis Lord Mordaunt
- [William ob. s p]
- [Anne ux Thomas Carpenter of in com Gloster and hath yssue Richard, Mary, and Anne]

Humffrey Monoux [of Wootton in com Bedfford] eldest son and heire =Anne da of Edward Walgrave of Lawfford in com Essex Esqr

- [Dowglas ux Habel Fickman]
- [Anne ux John Birch of London Vintner at the Star in Cheapside 1634]
- [Elizabeth ux John Pariat of]
- [Lucy.]

A

---

* *Cf* Visitations of Essex,' pp 78 9, 253, ed Harl Soc
† ' A patent of this Armes and Creaste to George Monox Cossen and heire to Sr George Monox Knt lord maior of London by William Harvey Clarenceulx King of Armes 1561, the 3 of Queene Elizabeth "

124   THE VISITATION OF BEDFORDSHIRE.

Jane da of Henry Birch of Oldcombe co Som 2 wiffe == Lewes Monoux of Wootton in com Bedfford Esqr == Elizabeth da [and coheire] of Thomas Walshe of [Waldeine] in com Sussex 1 wiffe   [George]   [Walgrave] [Humffrey]

Humffrey Monoux of Wootton Esqr liueing Ao 1634 | Frances — [Elizabeth] | Anne wife to Thomas Perrot of Shitlington | 2 Thomas Monoux. — [3 William Monoux] | [Margarett]

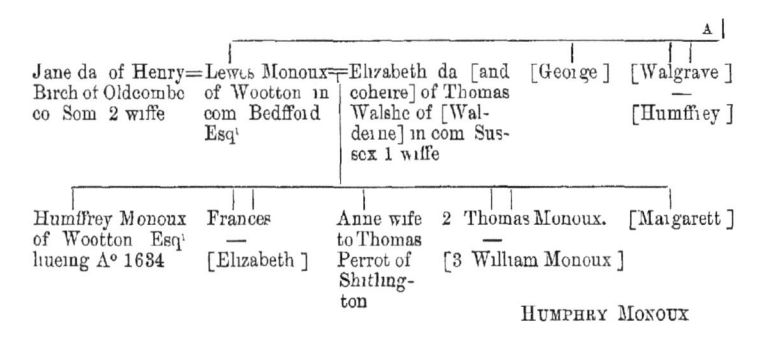

HUMPHRY MONOUX

Moore
[of Colmworth].

"Proofe of the armes to bee made in the tearme of Godfrey moore No proofe made therefore the descent struck out and the fee repaied"

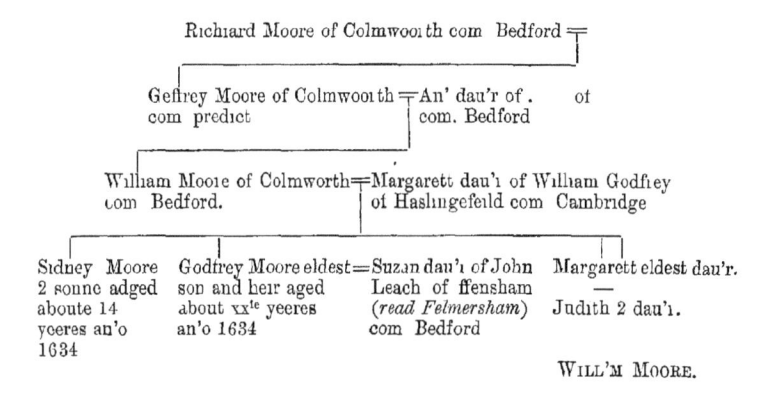

Richard Moore of Colmwooith com Bedford ==

Geffrey Moore of Colmwooith com predict == An' dau'r of . . . of . . . com. Bedford

William Moore of Colmworth com Bedford. == Margarett dau'r of William Godfrey of Haslingefeild com Cambridge

Sidney Moore 2 sonne adged aboute 14 yeeres an'o 1634 | Godfrey Moore eldest son and heir aged about xxte yeeres an'o 1634 == Suzan dau'r of John Leach of ffensham (*read Felmersham*) com Bedford | Margarett eldest dau'r. — Judith 2 dau'r.

WILL'M MOORE.

Mordaunt
[of Northill].

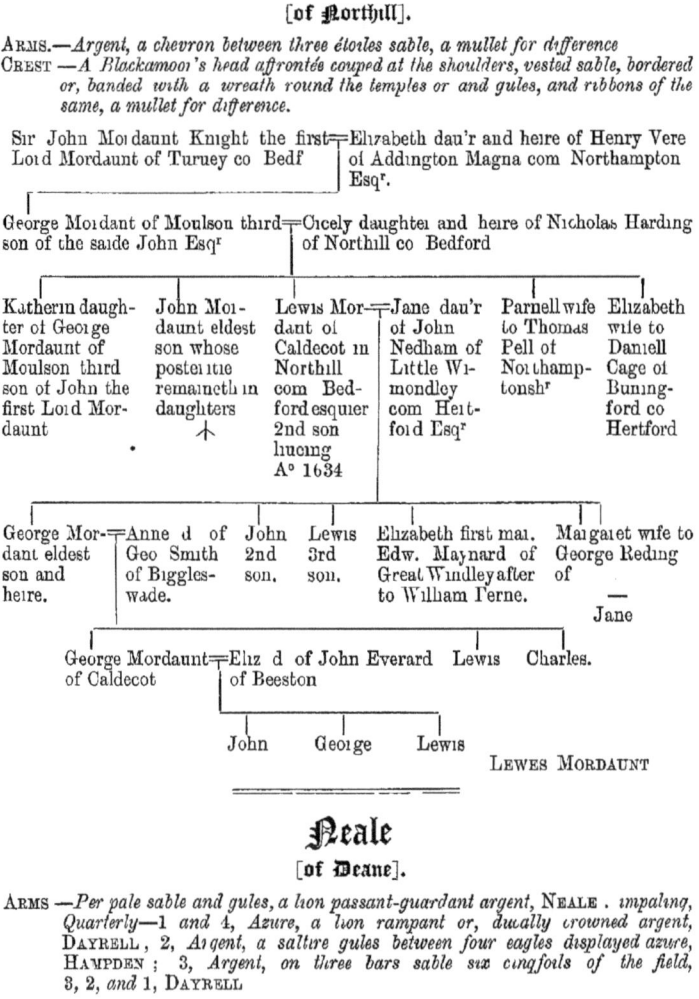

ARMS.—*Argent, a chevron between three étoiles sable, a mullet for difference*
CREST.—*A Blackamoor's head affrontée couped at the shoulders, vested sable, bordered or, banded with a wreath round the temples or and gules, and ribbons of the same, a mullet for difference.*

Sir John Mordaunt Knight the first = Elizabeth dau'r and heire of Henry Vere Lord Mordaunt of Turvey co Bedf | of Addington Magna com Northampton Esq'.

George Mordant of Moulson third = Cicely daughter and heire of Nicholas Harding son of the saide John Esq'r | of Northill co Bedford

| Katherin daughter of George Mordaunt of Moulson third son of John the first Lord Mordaunt | John Mordaunt eldest son whose posteritie remaineth in daughters | Lewis Mordant of Caldecot in Northill com Bedford esquier 2nd son liueing Aº 1634 | = Jane dau'r of John Nedham of Little Wimondley com Hertford Esq'r | Parnell wife to Thomas Pell of Northamptonsh'r | Elizabeth wife to Daniell Cage of Buningford co Hertford |

| George Mordant eldest son and heire. | = Anne d of Geo Smith of Biggleswade. | John 2nd son. | Lewis 3rd son. | Elizabeth first mar. Edw. Maynard of Great Windley after to William Ferne. | Margaret wife to George Reding of — Jane |

George Mordaunt = Eliz d of John Everard   Lewis   Charles.
of Caldecot | of Beeston

John   George   Lewis

LEWES MORDAUNT

Neale
[of Deane].

ARMS.—*Per pale sable and gules, a lion passant-guardant argent,* NEALE. *impaling,* Quarterly—1 and 4, *Azure, a lion rampant or, ducally crowned argent,* DAYRELL; 2, *Argent, a saltire gules between four eagles displayed azure,* HAMPDEN; 3, *Argent, on three bars sable six cinqfoils of the field,* 3, 2, *and* 1, DAYRELL

John Neale de com Stafford =

Thomas Neale of Ellesborough = [. . d of . . . Chicshire of Willington in com Buck | in com Salop]
A

THE VISITATION OF BEDFORDSHIRE.

A

Richard Neale of Deane in com. Bedfford. =ː= Allice da. and heire of Thomas Moore of Burton in com. Buckingham.

Thomas Neale of Yelden in com. Bedfford.

Thomas Neale son and heire of Richard Neale of Deane in com. Bedf. aged 91 yeares A° 1634. =ː= Anne da. of ffrancis Dayrell of Lamport co. Bucks.

[Ellen.] — [Mary.]

Richard Neale 2 sonne.

[Catherin.]

1. John Neale of Deane eldest son and heire apparent. =ː= Bridgit da. and sole heire of John More of Layton in com. Bedford.

2. Peter Neale of Deane. =ː= Ann da. of Wm Cave of Bagrave co. Leic.

3. Paule Neale mar. Elizabeth da. of . . . . Bennet of Swinsted.

Grace wife to Raph Mallory of Shelton co. Bedf.

1. Noah Neale of Deane. =ː= [Ennis da. of Sam. (? Tho.) Wade.]

2. Samuell. — 3. Thomas.

4. Beniamyn. — 5. James.

Thomas. — Isaake. Grace.

[Noah.]

1. John Neale of Deane son and heire. =ː= [. . . . da. of . . . . Cromwell of Upwood in com. Hunt.]

2. Timothy. — 3. Joseph.

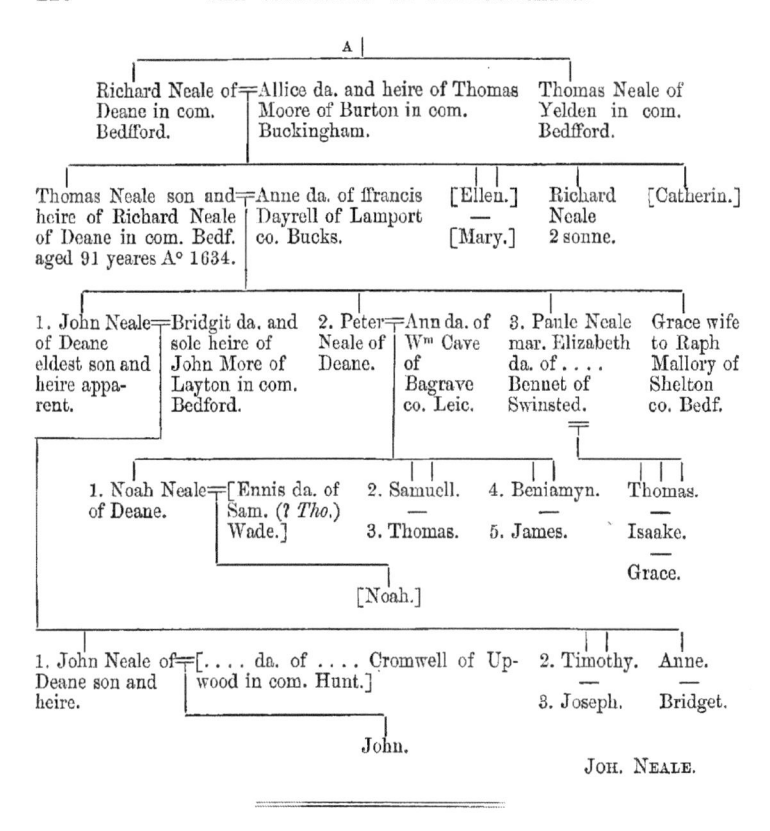

Anne. — Bridget.

John.

JOH. NEALE.

Newman
[of Langford].

ARMS.—*Azure, three lions rampant argent gouttée de sang.*
CREST.—*A demi-lion rampant erased argent gouttée de sang and holding between the paws a cross pattée gules.*

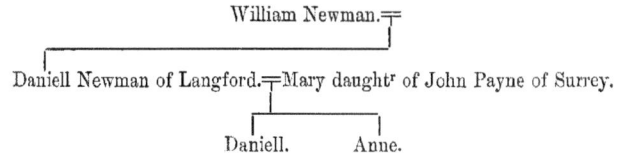

William Newman. =ː=

Daniell Newman of Langford. =ː= Mary daught^r of John Payne of Surrey.

Daniell. Anne.

ANTHONY CASLETON for DANIEL NEWMAN.

𝔑ewton
[of 𝔅iddenham].

ARMS.—*Quarterly*—1 *and* 4, *Argent, three lozenges conjoined in fesse azure each charged with a garb or,* NEWTON ;* 2 *and* 3, *Gules, on a canton or a bend of the field, a mullet for difference,* GODFREY
CREST.—*Two arms counter-embowed dexter and sinister, vested azure, holding up in the hands proper a garb or*

John Newton of Axmouth in com. Deuon = d. of . . . Fry of Deuonshire

William Newton of Axmouth = Joane d. of Will'm Mallock of Axmouth
s and heire. | in com. Devon Esq[r]

John Newton of = Mary d of W[m] Boteler of Biddenham . . wife
Axmouth s. and | in com Bedd. Esq s of S[r] William to . .
heire Osborne

| Anne wife to Tho Layton of Lynn marchant. | William Newton of Biddenham in com. Bedf gent hueing A° 1634 eld sonn | =Frances d of John Godfrey of Bedford Towne gent *Arg., a gryffin seg pass. sa* | Humphrey Newton of Ondle in co Northt. 2 s. m. Dorothy d. of Edw Saunders of Flowre co. Northt. | =Sibell d of S[r] Anthony Tryngham of Tryngham Knt 2 wife |

| William Newton eld. s and heire hueing A° 1634 | =Joane d. and sole heire to Edward (*alibi Gregory*) Miller of Gillingham in Kent. | Mary wife to Phillip Willoughby of Grendon co Northt. | Anne — Elizabeth. | Humfrey. — Edward | John Thomas — Mary and another dau'r |

Thomas Newton eld. s. aged about   1 Frances   2 Ellen   Anne.
7 yeres and 4 months A° 1634   —
                                      3. Mary
                                                    W[I] NEWTON, Jun[r]

𝔑odes
[of 𝔗empsford].

[ARMS —*Sable, on a pile argent three trefoils slipped of the first*
CREST —*Two lions' gambs sable, holding a garb or*]

William Nodes of Stevenedge in com = Joane his wife suruiued him
Hert. gent A° 1533 et A° 12° H 8 | his relict A° 25° H. 8.
et de London gen   A

* "Exemplified the xiij[th] day of Decemb A° D'ni 1615, annoq' Regni regis Jacobi Decimo tertio By mee Will'm Segar principall King of Armes"

128   THE VISITATION OF BEDFORDSHIRE.

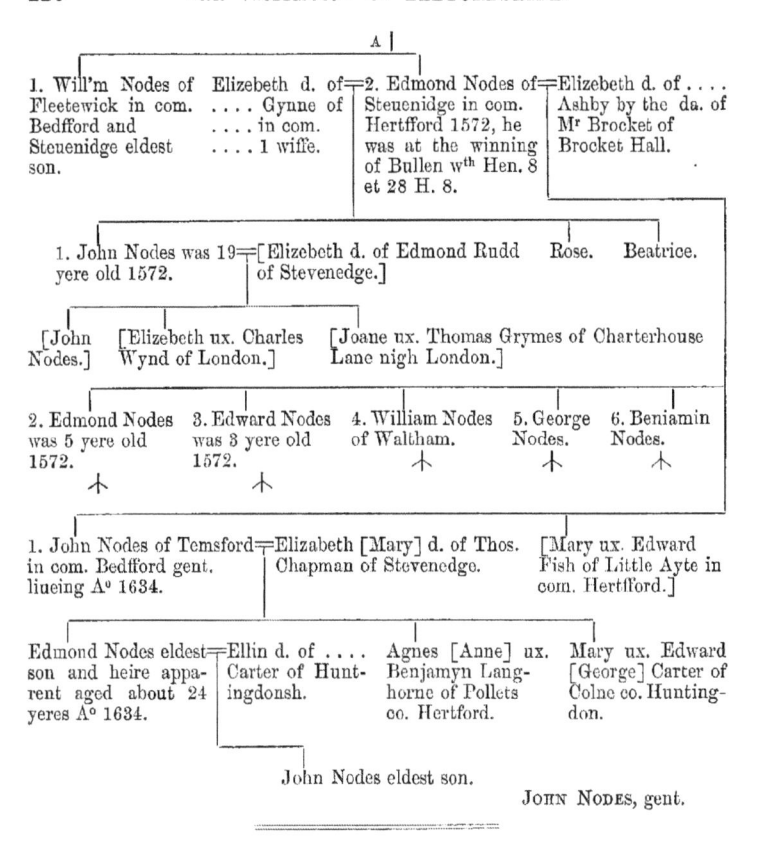

A

1. Will'm Nodes of Fleetewick in com. Bedfford and Steuenidge eldest son. = Elizebeth d. of .... Gynne of .... in com. .... 1 wiffe. | 2. Edmond Nodes of Steuenidge in com. Hertfford 1572, he was at the winning of Bullen wth Hen. 8 et 28 H. 8. = Elizebeth d. of .... Ashby by the da. of Mr Brocket of Brocket Hall.

1. John Nodes was 19 yere old 1572. = [Elizebeth d. of Edmond Rudd of Stevenedge.]   Rose.   Beatrice.

[John Nodes.]   [Elizebeth ux. Charles Wynd of London.]   [Joane ux. Thomas Grymes of Charterhouse Lane nigh London.]

2. Edmond Nodes was 5 yere old 1572. ⋏   3. Edward Nodes was 3 yere old 1572. ⋏   4. William Nodes of Waltham. ⋏   5. George Nodes. ⋏   6. Beniamin Nodes. ⋏

1. John Nodes of Temsford in com. Bedfford gent. liueing A^o 1634. = Elizabeth [Mary] d. of Thos. Chapman of Stevenedge.   [Mary ux. Edward Fish of Little Ayte in com. Hertfford.]

Edmond Nodes eldest son and heire apparent aged about 24 yeres A^o 1634. = Ellin d. of .... Carter of Huntingdonsh.   Agnes [Anne] ux. Benjamyn Langhorne of Pollets co. Hertford.   Mary ux. Edward [George] Carter of Colne co. Huntingdon.

John Nodes eldest son.

JOHN NODES, gent.

Norton
[of Sharpenhoe in Streatley].

ARMS.—*Quarterly*—1 and 4, *Gules, a fret argent, a crescent for difference, over all a bend vair or and gules,* NORTON al's NERUILE ; 2 and 3, *Sable, a cross pointed argent, charged with a crescent,* GRAVELEY.

.... Norton of Sharpenhoe co. Bedford. =

Thomas Norton of Sharpenhoe co. Bedford Esqr Counsellor at Law. ⋏   Luke Norton one of the m^rs of the Chauncery dwelt at Offley in com. Hertford Esqr and Councellor of the Law of the Inner Temple. = Lettice d. and sole heire of George Graueley of Hitchin com. Hertford a yonger brother of Graueley of Graueley com. Hertford.

A

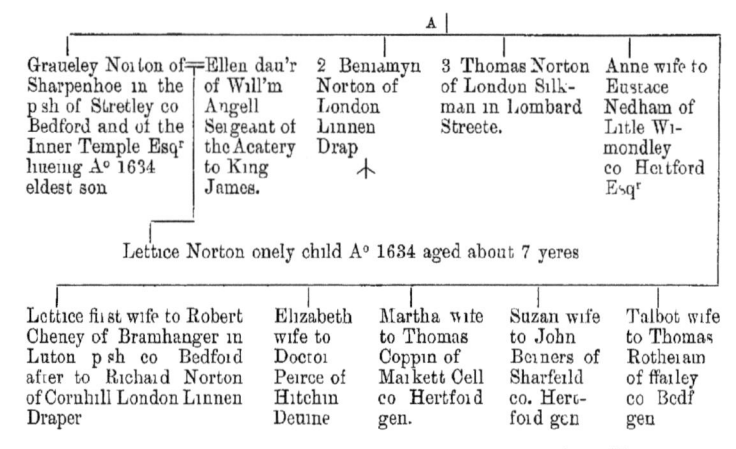

THE VISITATION OF BEDFORDSHIRE   129

A

Graueley Norton of Sharpenhoe in the p sh of Stretley co Bedford and of the Inner Temple Esq[r] liueing A° 1634 eldest son = Ellen dau'r of Will'm Angell Serjeant of the Acatery to King James.

2 Beniamyn Norton of London Linnen Drap

3 Thomas Norton of London Silkman in Lombard Streete.

Anne wife to Eustace Nedham of Litle Wimondley co Hertford Esq[r]

Lettice Norton onely child A° 1634 aged about 7 yeres

Lettice first wife to Robert Cheney of Bramhanger in Luton p sh co Bedford after to Richard Norton of Cornhill London Linnen Draper

Elizabeth wife to Doctor Peirce of Hitchin Deune

Martha wife to Thomas Coppin of Markett Cell co Hertford gen.

Suzan wife to John Berners of Sharfeild co. Hertford gen

Talbot wife to Thomas Rotheram of ffarley co Bedf gen

GRA NORTON

Osborne
[of Northill].

ARMS.—*Quarterly*—1, *Quarterly ermine and azure, a cross or*, OSBORNE, 2, *Barry of five argent and gules, on a canton of the second a cross of the first*, EITON, 3, *Argent, a chevron vert between three torteaux*, SINGLETURNE, 4, *Azure, on a fesse fleurie counterfleurie or between three lions passant argent as many lapwings proper*, HEWETT *in the fesse point a crescent for difference*

CREST.—*An heraldic tyger passant or, tufted and maned sable, charged with a crescent of the second.*

Richard Osborne of Ashtford in com Kent ⊤

S[r] Edward Osborne Knt Lord = Alice d and sole heire of S[r] Will'm Hewett Knt
Maior of London 1583   Lord Maior of London 1559

1 S[r] Hewett Osborne knighted by the Earle of Essex in Ireland father to the Baronet *Vide* London

Anne wife to Robert Offley of Grace Street London

Jane wife to Jo Welby of Tidd S[t] Giles in the Isle of Ely

Alliced of W[m] Butler of Bidenham in com Bedfford 1 wiffe = 2 Edward Osborne of Norrell in com Bedfford and of the Inner Temple a Bencher. = Frances d of James Harvey of Dagenham in com. Essex 2 wiffe *Vide* London

Allice ux S[t] John Payton of Isleham co Cambridge Knt and Baronett

A   B

S

130 THE VISITATION OF BEDFORDSHIRE.

A — | B —

1 Edward Osborne of Northill and of the Inner Temple liueing A° 1634 | Ursula ux Will'm Buckby (or Buckley) bacheler of Divinity | Anne ux Ellis Yong of the Chequer office — 2 Will'm Osborne | [Elizebeth ob. yong.] — [Elizebeth ob yong] — [James ob yong]

EDWARD OSBORNE

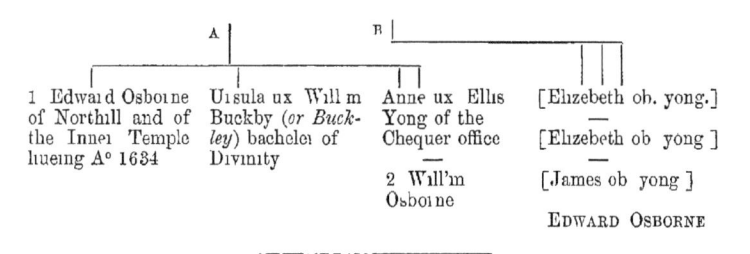

Palmer*
[of Hill in Warden].

ARMS —*Argent, two bars gules charged with three trefoils of the field, 2 and 1, in chief a greyhound courant sable, collared or*

CREST —*On a mound vert a greyhound sejeant sable, collared or, on the shoulder a trefoil argent.*

Thomas Palmer of Marston in com. Stafford descended of a Familie of that S'name in Yorksh'

3 William Palmer of London m'chaunt | Robert Palmer of Hill in com Bedfford gent = Mary dau'r of Walt'r Craddocke of Staffordshire

Will'm Palmer of Hill in com Bedfford Esq' one of the Justices of the Peace in y° saide County A° 1634 = Dorothey daur of S' John Bramston Knight the King's serieant | 2. John Palmer incumbent of the church of Stafford | Tho Palmer of Marston in com Stafford

John Palmer eldest son and heire apparent A° 1634 aged about 3 yeares | Mary | Dorothey | Bridget

WILL PALMER

Paradyne
[of Bedford].

ARMS.—*Sable, two bars ermine between three (?) eagles' heads erased or, two in chief and one in base*

CREST —*On a wreath or and sable a mound vert, upon which a wolf argent, tusked or, crined sable, holding in its dexter paw an escutcheon or* †

---

* "A patt ffeb. 1634 p. S Rich S' George " (Harl MS 5867)
† "An exemplification of these Armes and guift of this Crest w'th a Cressant to George Paradyne of London gent son of Robert Paradyne of Bedford gent by Rob't Cooke al's Clarenceu' King of Armes the 4'th of Septemb' A° D ni 1581, in the xxiij'th yeare of the Raigne of Queene Elizabeth,'

THE VISITATION OF BEDFORDSHIRE. 131

Robert Paradyne of Bedford gent. three seuerall yeares Maior of Bedford =⊤=

- 2 George Paradyne of London gent of the society of the Grocers in London died without yssue
- William Paradyne of Bedford eldest son =⊤= Dorothey dau'r of R West of Bedford
- 3 Thomas Paradyne of London third son of Robert he was a marchant his wiues name was Eliz Leigh of Caldwell co. Bedf. =⊤=

- Robert Paradyne of Bedford =⊤= Mary dau'r of William Goodwin of Greenefeild
- Peter Paradyne of London gent.
- Robert Paradyne of Essex second sonne

Thomas Paradyne of Bedford gent thrice Maior of =⊤= Anne dau'r of Matthew Child of Potton in com Bedford
the same Towne liueing A° 1634.

| 1 Robert Paradyne eldest son and heire apparent 1634 | 2 Thomas — 3 Richard | 4 William — 5 Matthew | 6. George | Mary — Anne | Elizabeth |

THOMAS PARADYNE.   ROBERT PARADINE

Parkinson
[of Ampthill].

ARMS.—*Gules, on a fesse between three ostrich-feathers argent as many escallops sable*

James Parkinson of   in com York =⊤= .. da of ...

John Parkinson of Lincoln's Inn =⊤= Margery da. of Will'm Dimock
Remembrancer of the duchyland | of Chester gent

- Edward Parkinson Counsellor at law at Lincoln's Inne 2d sonne
- John Parkinson Captaine of a foote Company in y^e viage to Cales the Ile of Ree and Rochell now of Ampthill Esq 1634 eldest sonn =⊤= Francis da of John Graunt of ... in com Sussex gent by the dau'r of Sr Edward Watson of Rockingam Castle com North'ton

James Parkinson eldest sonne aged 4 yeeres et amplius at the tyme of this visitation 1634
Thomas Parkinson second sonn.

JOHN PARKINSON

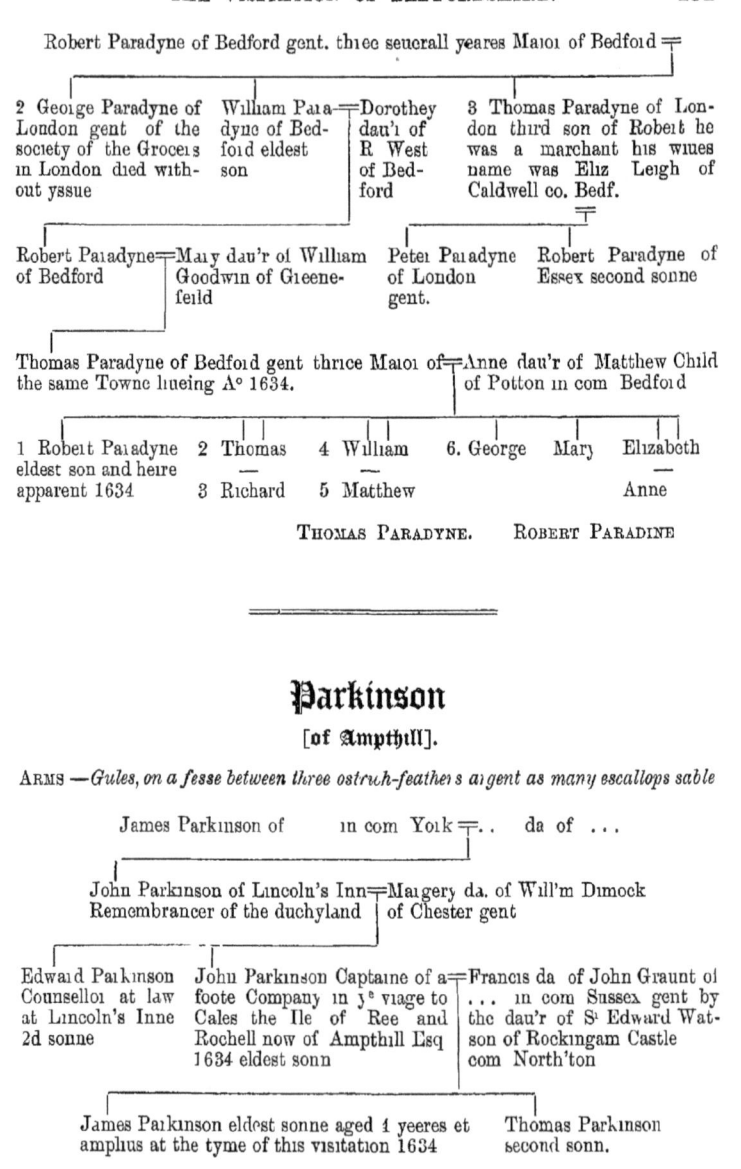

Pigott

[of Gravenhurst].

ARMS —*Sable, three pickaxes argent, a mullet for difference*
CREST —*An arm couped at the wrist barry undee or and vert, cuffs argent, in the hand proper a pickaxe of the third*

Agnes [Anne] da and heire of Mr Forster of Writtell in com Essex first wyfe == Thom Pigott of Harwood and Whaddon in com. Buckingham made serjeant of Law A° 2 H 8 == Elizabeth da. of John Iwardby of Swainton Mallet. == [Will'm Elmes]

1 William Pigott *Vide* Buckingham

Margery sister of Oliver Lord St John of Bletsoe == 2 Francis Pygott of Stratton in com Bedford == [Ellinor d and sole heire of John Enderby of Stratton] *

Winiffrid da and sole heire of Ambrose Dormer widdow of Sr Will'm Hawtrey of Chakers Knt 2 wiffe == John Pigott of Grays Inn an aprentice to the Law was of Edlesburgh in com Buck == Winiffrid da and heire of Thomas Sankey of Edlesburgh in com Buckingham 1 wiffe

Catherin borne 3 July

Margarett borne 13 July 1597
—
Anne borne 1 June 1598

1. Thomas Pigott
  1 Thomas
  2 Francis

2. Henry Pigott
  Winiffrid
  Mary
  —
  Margery

Margery ux Oliver Styles of Eaton.
—
Allice ob a mayd
—
Frances ux Henry Bruges

Anne d and coheire of Thos Wiseman of Essex second wife == 2 Benjamyn Pigott of Grauenhurst in com Bedford A° 1588 == Mary d of Raffe Astry of Woodend in com Bedford widow of (*Francis*) Markham of Luton in com Bedf == Bridget 3 wife da of John Nedham of Wimlie com Hertf

1 Henry Pigott of Gauenhurst in co Bedford Esqr A° 1634

2 Oliuer Pigott s p
—
[A daur]

Children dyed

3 John Pigott of

Anne ux Edward Wright Counsellor of the Lawe.
—
Judeth wife to Simon Hale of Hexton co Hertf gen

Bridgit.
—
Talbot
—
Mary
—
Suzan

HEN PIGOTT

* See Additional Pedigrees, *post*

Randes
[of Radwell in Felmersham].

ARMS.—*Sable, a chevron ermine between three cross-crosslets fitchée argent*
CREST.—*A lion's head erased . . ducally crowned*

Thomas Randes of Radwell in com Bedford = Jane dau'r of John Joye of Renhall

John Rands of Radwell eldest son = Jane dau'r of Edward Slade of Kimbalton.

Edward Randes of Radwell eldest son = Judeth dau'r of Thomas Kirby of the province of Huntingdon.

Oliuer Rands of Radwell eldest son and heire liueing A° 1634 = Sciceley dau'r of Edmond Blofeild of ffleetwick co Bedford

- Giles Randes eldest son and heire aged about 20 yeres A° 1634.
- William 2nd son
- Oliuer 3rd son
- Edward 5th son
- Frances wife to Christopher Hall of Radwell 4.
- Cicely 6

OLIUER RANDES

Rolte*
[of Milton-Ernest].

ARMS.—*Argent, on a bend sable three dolphins of the field, crowned or* †

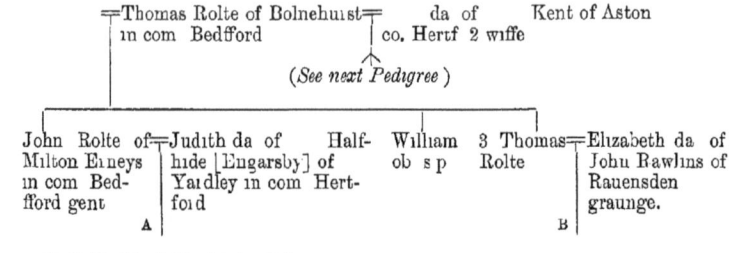

= Thomas Rolte of Bolnehurst in com Bedford = da of ... co. Hertf 2 wiffe — Kent of Aston

(See next Pedigree.)

- John Rolte of Milton Erneys in com Bedfford gent = Judith da of Halfhide [Engarsby] of Yardley in com Hertford A
- William ob s p
- 3 Thomas Rolte = Elizabeth da of John Rawlins of Rauensden graunge. B

* *Cf* 'Le Neve's Knights,' p 366
† "Mʳ Camden exemplifieth this coate to Edward Rolt of Greys Inne Esq now of Putenhall in com Bedf, wᶜʰ Edward was son of Edward Rolt of the same county Esq, wᶜʰ was son of Thomas Rolt of the same county gent wherein he certifieth that their auntient and lawtull coate armor is Argent, a bend sables charged with three dolphins of the first crowned or the Creast A griffin gules membered and beaked or sitting on a broken launce argent, holding the head thereof in his beake, wᶜʰ creast he grannteth to the saide Edward and Henry Rolt onely dated A° 1623.'

THE VISITATION OF BEDFORDSHIRE.

A │ ─────────────────── B │
 1. Stephen Rolte of Thurley co. Bedf. eld. son   2. Will'm Rolte.
 m. Dorothy d. of Edmund Day.

Stephen Rolt eld. sonn.   Thomas 3 son.   John   Sara.
Will'm 2 son.   Edward 4 son.   Samuel.

[Judith ux. William Port-   [Sarah ux. Thomas   Mary ux. Sʳ Will'm Hartop
ington of .... in   Rudd of Higham in   of Burton Lazars in
com. Leicester.]   com. Northampton.]   com. Lester Knt.

[Rebecka.]   Thomas* Rolte of Milton=Catherin d. of Thomas Staueley of West
 Erneys in com. Bedfford │ Langton in com. Leic. [Bignell in com.
 Esq. one of the Justices │ Oxon] Esqʳ by the da. of .... Brooke
 of the Peace for this │ Esqʳ of Greate Oakley co. Northᵗ.
 county Aº 1634.

Judith ux. Tho-   Katherin.   1. John Rolte eld.   2. Edward.   5. Walter.
mas Medwell of   —   s. and heire ap-   3. Charles.   6. Richard.
Gedington in   Elizebeth.   parent Aº 1634   —
com. North-   —   aged about   4. Thomas.
ampton gent.   Ellen.   18 years.

                    THO. ROLT.   STEPHEN ROLTE.

Rolt
[of Pertenhall].

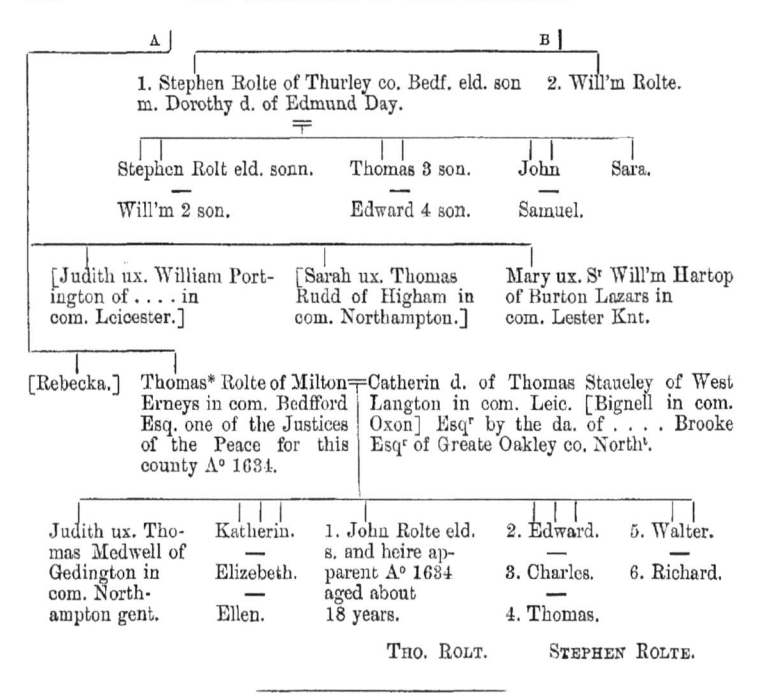

Same Arms as ROLT of Milton-Ernest, *a crescent argent for difference.*†

Edward Rolte of Pertenhall in com. Bedfford=Jane d. of John Baldwin of Much
Counsellor at Law Justice of Peace and Recorder │ Stoughton in com. Huntington
of the towne of Bedfford eldest s. of Tho. Rolt │ gent. sister to Thomas Baldwin now
of Bolnehurst by the d. of Kent of Aston. │ of Stoughton Magna Esqʳ.

Jane ux. Robert   Elizebeth [ux. Richard   Martha [ux.   Lora ux. Michael
Guill'm of Fother-   Todd of Pertenhall in   Robert Kings].   Style of Baynton
ingay in com.   com. Bedfford].   —   co. North.
Northampton.   Mary.

A
---
* "Edward." (Harl. MS. 5867.)
† "L'res pattent exemplified by learned Camden clarenceulx of this Coate and Creast wᵗʰout
difference to Edward Rolt of Grays Inne Esqʳ son and heire of Edward Rolt of Pertenhall co.
Bedf. Esqʳ who was s. of Thomas Rolt of the same county gen. to whom the saide Camden
graunted the said Creast and also to Henry Rolt of Sᵗ Margarets in Kent with their seuerall
differences wᶜʰ pattent beareth date the eighth day of September Aº 1623, Aº 21 Jac. Regis.
This difference being a cressant was assigned to the said Edward Rolt with his consent in
this visitation."

THE VISITATION OF BEDFORDSHIRE.   135

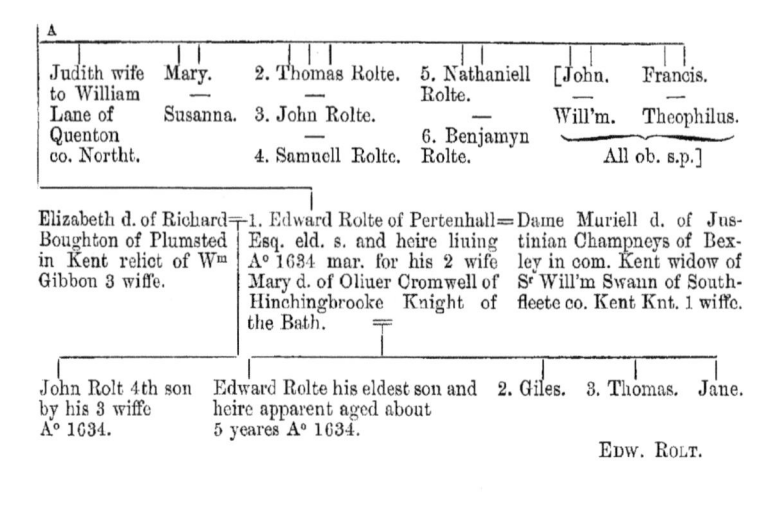

A
|
Judith wife to William Lane of Quenton co. Northt. — Mary. — Susanna. | 2. Thomas Rolte. — 3. John Rolte. — 4. Samuell Rolte. | 5. Nathaniell Rolte. — 6. Benjamyn Rolte. | [John. — Will'm. | Francis. — Theophilus. All ob. s.p.]

Elizabeth d. of Richard Boughton of Plumsted in Kent relict of Wm Gibbon 3 wiffe. = 1. Edward Rolte of Pertenhall Esq. eld. s. and heire liuing A° 1634 mar. for his 2 wife Mary d. of Oliuer Cromwell of Hinchingbrooke Knight of the Bath. = Dame Muriell d. of Justinian Champneys of Bexley in com. Kent widow of Sr Will'm Swann of Southfleete co. Kent Knt. 1 wiffe.

John Rolt 4th son by his 3 wiffe A° 1634. Edward Rolte his eldest son and heire apparent aged about 5 yeares A° 1634. 2. Giles. 3. Thomas. Jane.

EDW. ROLT.

Rotherham

[of Farley in Luton].

ARMS.—*Vert, three bucks trippant or, over all a bend sinister argent.*

George Rotherham of Farley in co. Bedford 1566. = Elizabeth da. of Edm. Bardolfe of Harpden co. Hertford.

George Rotherham of Farley eldest sonne and heire. = Joane da. of Richard Helder al's Spicer of Lilly in com. Hertford.

1. George Rotherham of Farley eldest son liueing A° 1634. = Ollife da. of Henry Morton of Olney in co. Buck.   2. Thomas.

Anne.   Mary.

GEORGE ROTHERHAM.

Sadleir

[of Aspley-Guise].

ARMS —*Or, a lion rampant per fesse azure and gules, a crescent sable for difference.*
CREST —*A demi-lion azure, ducally crowned* .

Sʳ Ralphe Sadler Knt Baronett lord of the mannor of Stondon in com = Margaret
Hertfford Chancellor of the Dutchey of Lanck and one of the privy | Mitchell
councell to H 8 Ed 6 and Queene Elizabeth [ob 30ᵗʰ of March 1587
buried at Stondon]

| [Anne ux George Horsey of Digswell in com Hertfford] | [Mary ux. Thomas Bolls of Wallington in com Hertfford] | [Jane ux Edward Bash of Stanstedbury in com Hertfford] | [Dorathey ux Edward Elrington of Byrchall in com Essex] | [Mary d. of Edward Gilbert of Everley in com Wilts 1 wiffe] = Henery Sadler of Everley nere Hungerfford in com Wilts | = [Ursula d of John Gill of Wydyhall in com Hertfford 2 wiffe] |

[Thomas Sadler] [Gertrude] [Dorathey] [Grace] [Ellyn]

| [Ursula d of Sʳ Henry Sherington of . in com... Knt 1 wiffe] = 1 Sʳ Thomas Sadler of Stondon Knt | = [Gertrud d of Thomas Markham of Cotham in com Nottingham 2 wiffe] | 2 Edward Sadler of Temple Dionesley in com Hertfford and of Aspley co Bedf Esqʳ | = Anne d and coheire of Sʳ Richard Leigh of Sopwell nigh Sᵗ Albans in com Hertfford Knt. |

| 1 Raphe Sadler of Stondon Esqʳᵉ A° 1634 | = [Anne d of Sʳ Edward Cooke Knt lord cheefe Justice of England] | [Gertrud ux. Sᵗ Walter Aston Knt of the Bath and Baronett] | [Mary ux Thomas Connyngsby of . in com] | 2 Richard* Sadler of Sopwell | = [Joyce d of Robert Honywood of Charing in com Kent] | 3. Edward Sadler of Lottestord. — 1 Thomas Sadler |

| [Mary ux. .. Thompson of .. in com Kent] | [Dorathey ux. James Ellis of Sᵗ Albans in com Hertfford] — [Margarett] | [7 Henery] — [6 Blount] — [5 Edward] | [1. Robert Sadler 18 yere old 1623] [2 Raphell] | [3 Richard] — [4 Thomas] — [5 Edward— Harl 5867] |

* 'Edward." (Harl MS 5867)

```
                    ┌──────────────────────────────────────┐
    1 Leigh Sadler of Temple══Elizebeth d of Will'm Paschall of Preston
      in com Hertfford      │  [Southamingffeld] in com Essex
```

| Anne wife to Edward Aston second brother to Walter Lord Aston. | Thomas Leigh Sadler of Temple══Frances d and heire of Dionesley and of Aspley Hall in com Bedfford Esqr hueing Aº 1634 | Francis Bury of Beckering Parke [Aspley Hall] in com Bedfford |

| Thomas Sadleir eldest son and heire apparent Aº 1634 aged about 15 yeres | 2 Edwin
3 Rafe
4 Leigh
5 Edward | 6 William
7 Richard
8 Robert. | 1. Elizabeth
2. Francis
3 Anne | 4 Jane
5 Sarah |

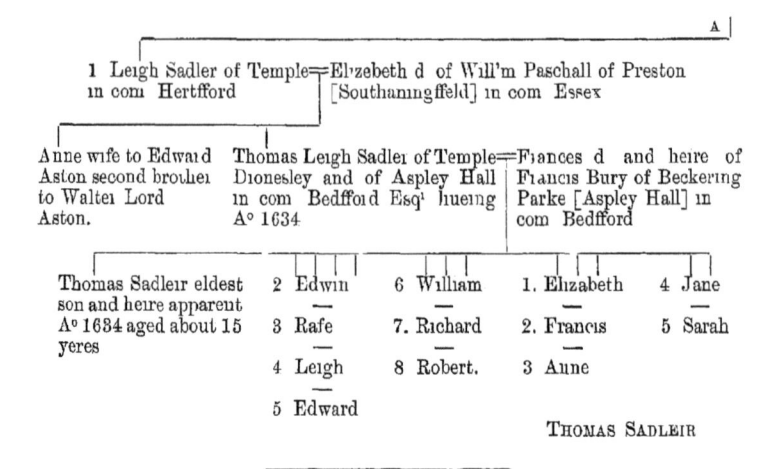

THOMAS SADLEIR

Saunders
[of Pottesgroue].

ARMS.—[*Per chevron argent and sable, three elephants' heads erased counterchanged*]
CREST.—[*An elephant's head erased sable*]

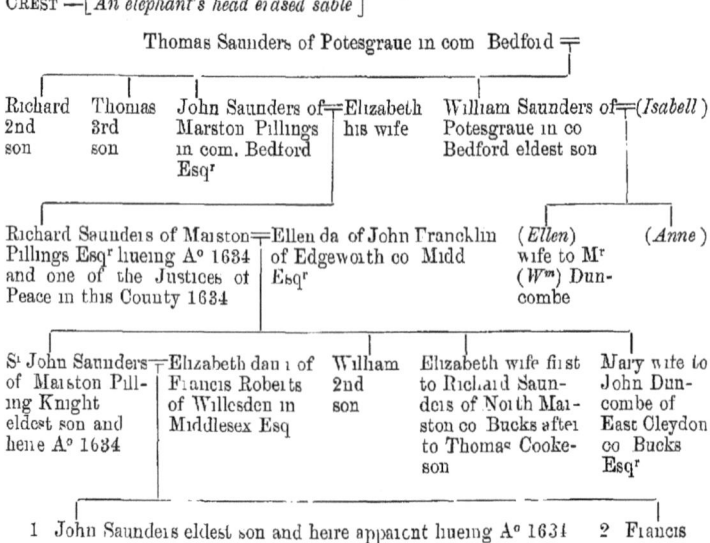

Thomas Saunders of Potesgraue in com Bedford ══

| Richard 2nd son | Thomas 3rd son | John Saunders of══Elizabeth Marston Pillings his wife in com. Bedford Esqr | William Saunders of══(Isabell) Potesgraue in co Bedford eldest son |

| Richard Saunders of Marston══Ellen da of John Francklin Pillings Esqr hueing Aº 1634 of Edgeworth co Midd and one of the Justices of Esqr Peace in this County 1634 | (*Ellen*) wife to Mr (*Wm*) Duncombe | (*Anne*) |

| Sr John Saunders══Elizabeth dau r of of Marston Pill- Francis Roberts ing Knight of Willesden in eldest son and Middlesex Esq heire Aº 1634 | William 2nd son | Elizabeth wife first to Richard Saunders of North Marston co Bucks after to Thomas Cookeson | Mary wife to John Duncombe of East Cleydon co Bucks Esqr |

1 John Saunders eldest son and heire apparent hueing Aº 1634   2 Francis

JOHN SAUNDERS

Savage

[of Cardington].

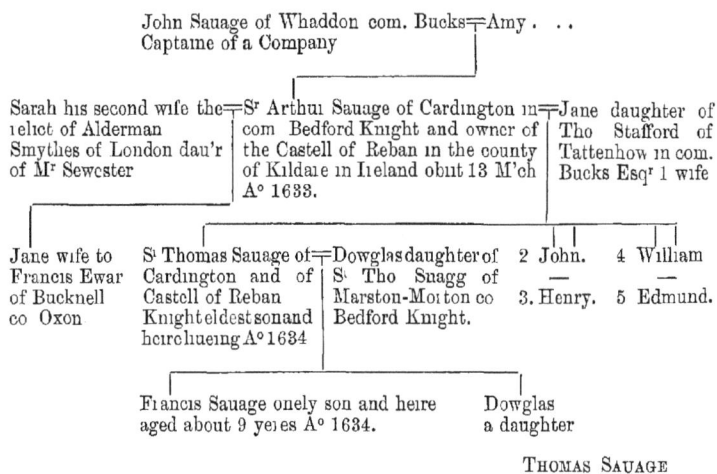

John Sauage of Whaddon com. Bucks == Amy . . .
Captaine of a Company

Sarah his second wife the relict of Alderman Smythes of London dau'r of M{r} Sewester == S{r} Arthur Sauage of Cardington in com Bedford Knight and owner of the Castell of Reban in the county of Kildare in Ireland obiit 13 M'ch A° 1633. == Jane daughter of Tho Stafford of Tattenhow in com. Bucks Esqr 1 wife

Jane wife to Francis Ewar of Bucknell co Oxon

St Thomas Sauage of Cardington and of Castell of Reban Knight eldest son and heire liueing A° 1634. == Dowglas daughter of Sr Tho Snagg of Marston-Morton co Bedford Knight.

2 John.
3. Henry.
4 William
5 Edmund.

Francis Sauage onely son and heire aged about 9 yeres A° 1634.

Dowglas a daughter

THOMAS SAUAGE

Sheppard

[of Maulden].

ARMS.—*Azure, on a chevron or between three fleurs-de-lys argent as many étoiles gules*

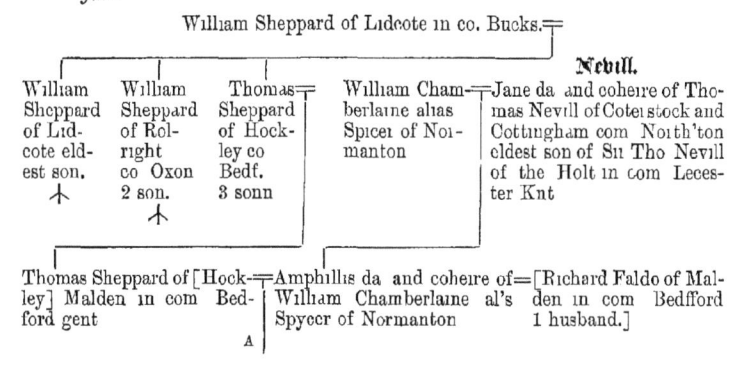

William Sheppard of Lidcote in co. Bucks. ==

William Sheppard of Lidcote eldest son. ⊥

William Sheppard of Rolright co Oxon 2 son. ⊥

Thomas Sheppard of Hockley co Bedf. 3 sonn

William Chamberlaine alias Spicer of Normanton == Jane da and coheire of Thomas Nevill of Coterstock and Cottingham com North'ton eldest son of Sir Tho Nevill of the Holt in com Leicester Knt **Nevill.**

Thomas Sheppard of [Hockley] Malden in com Bedford gent == Amphillis da and coheire of William Chamberlaine al's Spycer of Normanton == [Richard Faldo of Malden in com Bedfford 1 husband.]

A

A

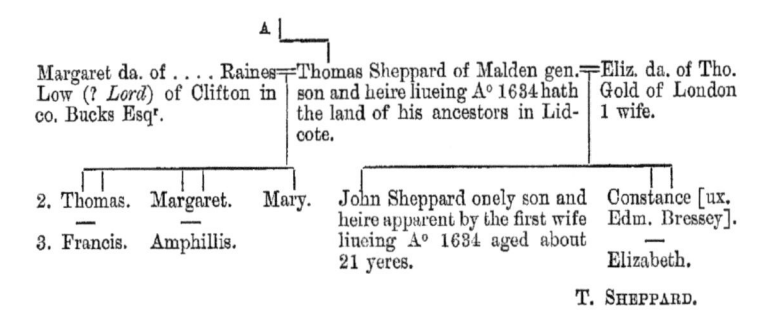

Margaret da. of .... Raines=Thomas Sheppard of Malden gen.=Eliz. da. of Tho.
Low (? *Lord*) of Clifton in | son and heire liueing A° 1634 hath | Gold of London
co. Bucks Esqr. | the land of his ancestors in Lid- | 1 wife.
| cote.

2. Thomas.   Margaret.   Mary.   John Sheppard onely son and   Constance [ux.
——   heire apparent by the first wife Edm. Bressey].
3. Francis. Amphillis.   liueing A° 1634 aged about   ——
                                 21 yeres.   Elizabeth.

T. SHEPPARD.

Slingesby
[of Husborne-Crawley].

Edmond Slingesby of Abbots Wooburne in com. Bedf.=
whose auncestors came out of Yorkshire.

Robert Slingesby of Husband=Abiath d. of Mathias Cony of Apwell
Crawley in com. Bedf. | in com. Camb.

Edmond Slingesby of Husband   Hezekiah Slingesby artiu'   Marke Slingesby
Crawley eld. s. now liueing   magistr' Aule Cat'r' 2 son. 3 son.
1634.

HEZ. SLINGESBY.

Smyth
[of Woburn].

ARMS.—*Per pale or and azure, a chevron ermine between four lions passant-guardant counterchanged.*
CREST.—*A leopard's head argent pellettée, murally gorged sable, lined gules and ringed of the second.*

Will'm Smyth of Woborne in com. Bedfford Esqr A° 3 E. 6.=

George Smyth of Bickleswade in com. Bedfford Esqr 3 Q. Eliz.=

Thomas Smyth=Mary d. of Thom. Parratt of Shitlington
of Bickleswade. | in com. Bedfford.
A

THE VISITATION OF BEDFORDSHIRE

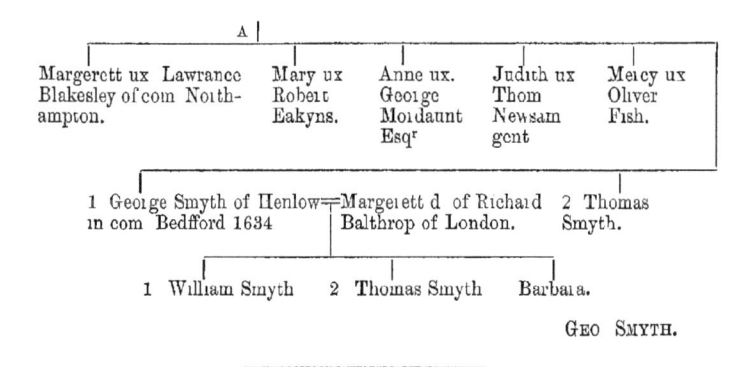

A

- Margerett ux Lawrance Blakesley of com Northampton.
- Mary ux Robert Eakyns.
- Anne ux. George Mordaunt Esqr
- Judith ux Thom Newsam gent
- Mercy ux Oliver Fish.

1 George Smyth of Henlow in com Bedfford 1634 = Margerett d of Richard Balthrop of London. | 2 Thomas Smyth.

1 William Smyth | 2 Thomas Smyth | Barbara.

GEO SMYTH.

Snagge
[of Marston=Mortaine].

ARMS — *Quarterly* —1, *Argent, three pheons sable*, SNAGG ; 2, *Or, a chevron gules fretty of the field between three roses azure slipped vert*, DICKONS , 3, *Chequée or and gules, a canton ermine*, REYNES , 4, *As No* 1

CRESTS —1, *Out of a ducal coronet or a demi-horse argent* , 2, *A demi-antelope ermine, attired or*

Dicons.

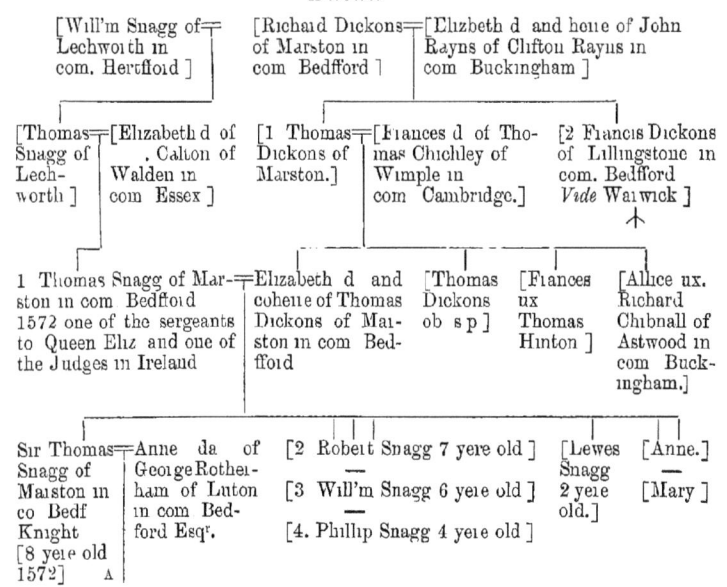

[Will'm Snagg of Lechworth in com. Hertfford] | [Richard Dickons of Marston in com Bedfford] = [Elizbeth d and heire of John Rayns of Clifton Rayns in com Buckingham]

[Thomas Snagg of Lechworth] = [Elizabeth d of . Calton of Walden in com Essex] | [1 Thomas Dickons of Marston.] = [Frances d of Thomas Chichley of Wimple in com Cambridge.] | [2 Francis Dickons of Lillingstone in com. Bedford *Vide* Warwick]

1 Thomas Snagg of Marston in com Bedfford 1572 one of the sergeants to Queen Eliz and one of the Judges in Ireland = Elizabeth d and coheire of Thomas Dickons of Marston in com Bedfford | [Thomas Dickons ob s p] | [Frances ux Thomas Hinton] | [Alice ux. Richard Chibnall of Astwood in com Buckingham.]

Sir Thomas Snagg of Marston in co Bedf Knight [8 yere old 1572] = Anne da of George Rotherham of Luton in com Bedford Esqr. | [2 Robert Snagg 7 yere old] — [3 Will'm Snagg 6 yere old] — [4. Phillip Snagg 4 yere old] | [Lewes Snagg 2 yere old.] | [Anne.] — [Mary]

A

THE VISITATION OF BEDFORDSHIRE.   141

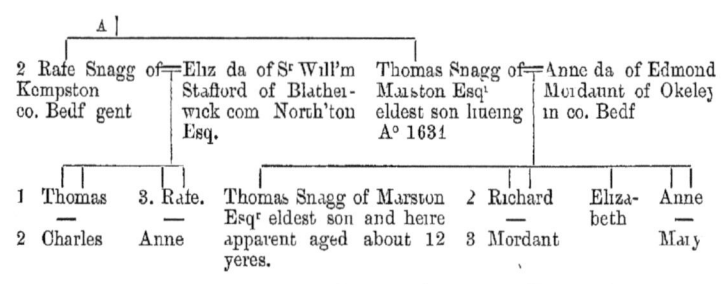

2 Rafe Snagg of=Eliz da of Sr Will'm   Thomas Snagg of=Anne da of Edmond
Kempston | Stafford of Blather-   Marston Esq¹ | Mordaunt of Okeley
co. Bedf gent | wick com North'ton   eldest son liueing | in co. Bedf
             | Esq.   A° 1634

1 Thomas   3. Rafe.   Thomas Snagg of Marston   2 Richard   Eliza-   Anne
—   —   Esqʳ eldest son and heire   —   beth   —
2 Charles Anne   apparent aged about 12   3 Mordant   Mary
                     yeres.

                                    RALPHE SNAGGE.   THOMAS SNAGGE.

Spencer
[of Cople].

ARMS.—*Quarterly*—1, *Quarterly or and gules, in the second and third quarters a fret of the first, on a bend sable three fleurs-de-lys argent,* SPENCER. 2, *Argent, three pickaxes sable,* PECK, 3, *Sable, two lions passant or,* ARNOLD, 4, *blank*
CREST —*Out of a ducal coronet gules a griffin's head argent, collared or, between two wings expanded of the third, charged on the breast and on each wing with a fleur-de-lys sable, and on the neck a crescent*

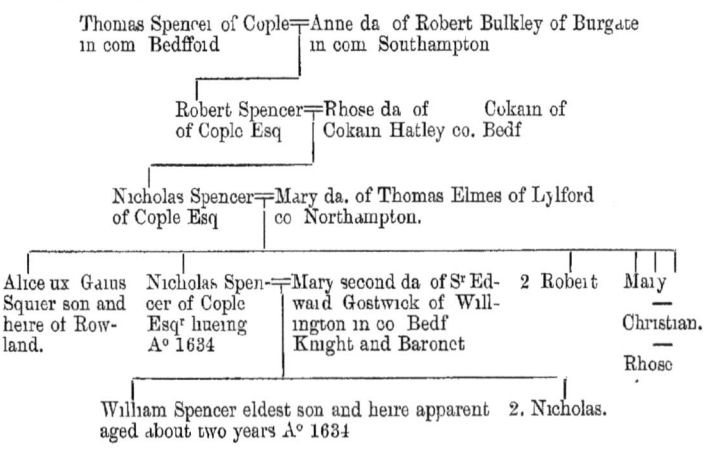

Thomas Spencer of Cople=Anne da of Robert Bulkley of Burgate
in com Bedfford | in com Southampton

        Robert Spencer=Rhose da of   Cokain of
        of Cople Esq | Cokain Hatley co. Bedf

        Nicholas Spencer=Mary da. of Thomas Elmes of Lylford
        of Cople Esq | co Northampton.

Alice ux Gaius   Nicholas Spen-=Mary second da of Sr Ed- 2 Robert   Mary
Squier son and   cer of Cople | ward Gostwick of Will-   —   —
heire of Row-   Esqʳ liueing | ington in co Bedf   Christian.
land.   A° 1634 | Knight and Baronet   —
                                                                    Rhose

        William Spencer eldest son and heire apparent   2. Nicholas.
        aged about two years A° 1634
                                                    NICHOLAS SPENCER.

Squier

[of Eaton-Socon].

ARMS.—*Sable, a chevron engrailed between three swans' heads erased argent, a crescent gules for difference.*
CREST.—*An elephant's head erased argent, tusked, eared, and gorged with a crest coronet or.**

William Squier son and heire of Richard.=Joane daughter of .... Ferne.

William Squier son and heire.=Joane daughter of Robert Burton of London.

Thomas Squier eldest son. ⋏

Rowland Squier of Eaton-Soken in co. Bedf. gent. 1634. =Elizabeth dau'r of Tho. Rufford of Butlers in com. Bucks Esqr.

Mary wife of Jo. Taylo^r of Bickerto' in co. Ebor.

Gaius Squier onely son and heire apparent liueing 1634. =Alice da. of Nicholas Spencer of Cople in com. Bedford Esqr.

Mary Squier aged about 4 yeres 1634.

GAIUS SQUIER.

Staunton

[of Birchmore in Woburn].

ARMS.—*Vair argent and ermines, a canton gules.*
CREST.—*A demi-lion couped vair argent and ermines, ducally crowned or.*

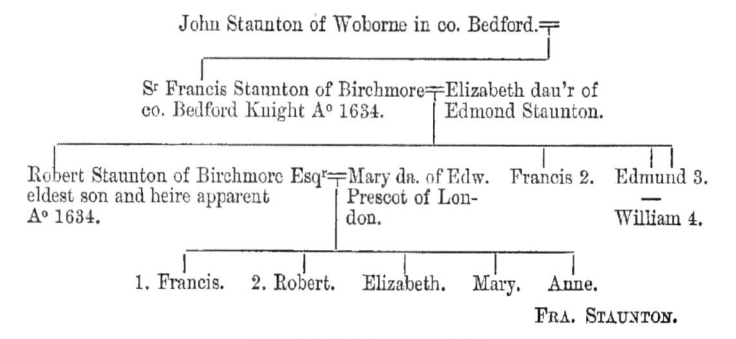

John Staunton of Woborne in co. Bedford.=

Sr Francis Staunton of Birchmore co. Bedford Knight A° 1634. =Elizabeth dau'r of Edmond Staunton.

Robert Staunton of Birchmore Esqr eldest son and heire apparent A° 1634. =Mary da. of Edw. Prescot of London.

Francis 2.

Edmund 3.
—
William 4.

1. Francis. 2. Robert. Elizabeth. Mary. Anne.

FRA. STAUNTON.

---

* "Exemplified vnder the hand and seale of Cla. Cooke to Will'm Squier of London gent. dat. A° 23 Eliz. 1581."

THE VISITATION OF BEDFORDSHIRE. 143

Stocker

[of Wyboston in Eaton-Socon].

"Johannes Stockker filius et haeres Thomae Stockker filij et haered' Henrici Stockker nuper de Wyboston in com Bedf sal'tem in D no sempiternam cum Ricardus Day servinand' ad legem et Margaret uxor eius nuper uxor Gulhelmi Stockker militis habeant et teneant in jure ipsius Margaret un,am mesuag,um cum   p'tinentiis in p'ochia S^{ti} Michaelis in Cornhull in civitat' London' in quo Johan' Saunders nuper inhabitauit necnon aliud mesuagium in quo Reginaldus Rutter modo inhabitat cum tribus priis tenements eidem mesuagio adiascent' pro termino vitae ipsius Margaretae reversione inde post decessum praefat' Margaretae mihi praefat' Johanni Stockker et haered' meis spectantibus &c   Dat 7º die mensis Augusti Aº 4º R 7"

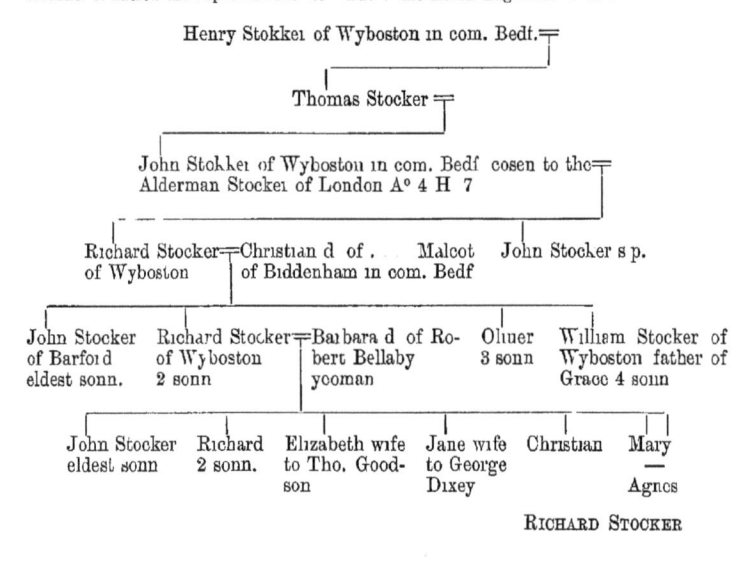

Henry Stokker of Wyboston in com. Bedf.=

Thomas Stocker =

John Stokker of Wyboston in com. Bedf cosen to the= Alderman Stocker of London Aº 4 H 7

Richard Stocker=Christian d of . . Malcot   John Stocker s p.
of Wyboston   of Biddenham in com. Bedf

John Stocker   Richard Stocker=Barbara d of Ro-   Oliuer   William Stocker of
of Barford   of Wyboston   bert Bellaby   3 sonn   Wyboston father of
eldest sonn. 2 sonn   yeoman   Grace 4 sonn

John Stocker Richard   Elizabeth wife Jane wife   Christian Mary
eldest sonn   2 sonn.   to Tho. Good-   to George   —
                        son   Dixey   Agnes

RICHARD STOCKER

Stone

[of Segenhoe in Ridgemont].

ARMS —*Argent, three cingfoils sable, a chief azure*
CREST —*Out of a dual coronet or a griffin's head argent between two wings expanded or*

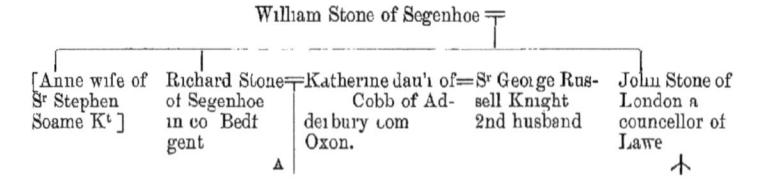

William Stone of Segenhoe =

[Anne wife of   Richard Stone=Katherine dau'r of=Sr George Rus-   John Stone of
Sr Stephen   of Segenhoe   Cobb of Ad-   sell Knight   London a
Soame K^t]   in co Bedf   derbury com   2nd husband   councellor of
                 gent   Oxon.   Lawe

[Stone continued]

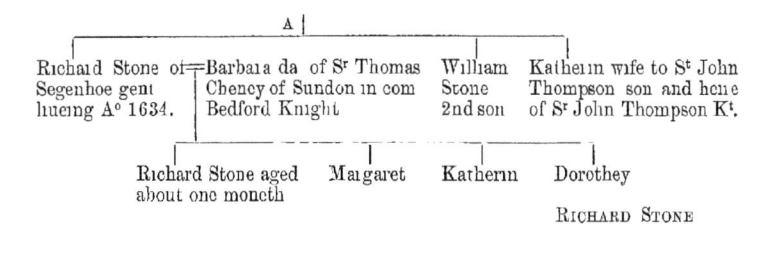

```
                                      A
   ┌──────────────────────┬──────────────────┬──────────────────┐
Richard Stone of=Barbara da of Sr Thomas  William    Katherin wife to St John
Segenhoe gent   Cheney of Sundon in com   Stone      Thompson son and heire
liueing Ao 1634. Bedford Knight           2nd son    of Sr John Thompson Kt.
   ┌──────────────┬──────────┬──────────┐
Richard Stone aged  Margaret  Katherin   Dorothey
about one moneth
                                           RICHARD STONE
```

Style
[of Steppingley].

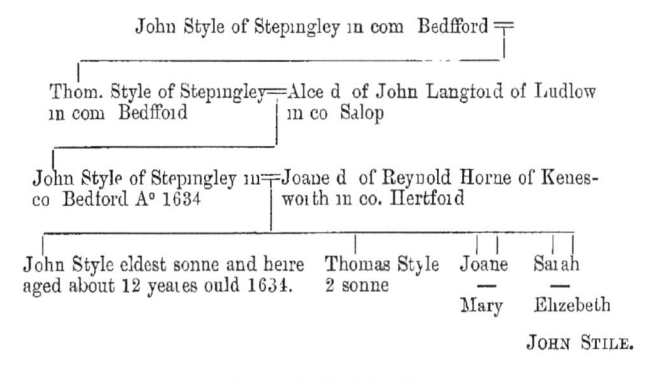

```
John Style of Stepingley in com Bedfford =

Thom. Style of Stepingley = Alce d of John Langford of Ludlow
in com Bedfford            in co Salop

John Style of Stepingley in = Joane d of Reynold Horne of Kenes-
co Bedford Ao 1634          worth in co. Hertford

┌─────────────────────────┬──────────────┬──────┬──────┐
John Style eldest sonne and heire  Thomas Style  Joane  Sarah
aged about 12 yeares ould 1634.    2 sonne       —      —
                                                 Mary   Elizebeth
```
JOHN STILE.

Taylor
[of Litlington and Clapham].

ARMS—*Ermine, on a chief dancettée sable a ducal coronet or between two escallops argent* [*]

CREST—*A demi-lion rampant ermine, holding between the paws a ducal coronet or*

```
Thomas Taylor of Litlington in com Bedford gen =     dau'r of       Hale
who built the North Ile together with the church   of Euerton in com Hunt-
porch of the saide church of Litlington             ingdon and of Bedford.
                                       A
```

[*] "An exemplification of this Coate and Crest to Richard Taylor of Grymsbury in the p'ish of Bolnhurst in ye County of Bedford Esqr, one of his Ma'ties Justices of the peace wth the sd County and also one of the Auntients or Benchers of Lincolns Inn London, graunted by Sr Richard St George Clarencieulx King of Armes vnder his hand and seale of Office Dated the 15 of July 1624."

THE VISITATION OF BEDFORDSHIRE.   145

Thomas Taylor of Grymesbury = Elizabeth dau'r of Wm King of Chaluerston and of Sexbridge by the daughter of Wm Hunt of Chaluerston Esqr
in the p'sh of Bolneherst in com Bedf gent

Richard Taylor of Grymesbury and of Clapham in co Bedford Esqr one of his Maties Justices of Peace in the saide County A° 1634 one of the Benchers of Lincolns Inne. = Elizabeth daughter of Wm Boteler of Biddenham com Bedford Esqr

Joyce wife to Parr Parrs of Longstow com Huntingdon

Margaret wife to Jo Francklin of Great Stoughton co Huntingdon

Richard Taylor eldest son and heire apparent aged about 14 yeres A° 1634

Humfry 2nd son
—
William 3rd son

Oliuer 4th son
—
John 5th son

Samuel 6th son
—
Simon 7th son.

Ursula aged about 18 yeres 1634

Cicely
—
Elizabeth

RICH TAYLOR.

Taylor

[of Stebington].

ARMS.—*Azure, a saltire voided between four stags' heads cabossed or*

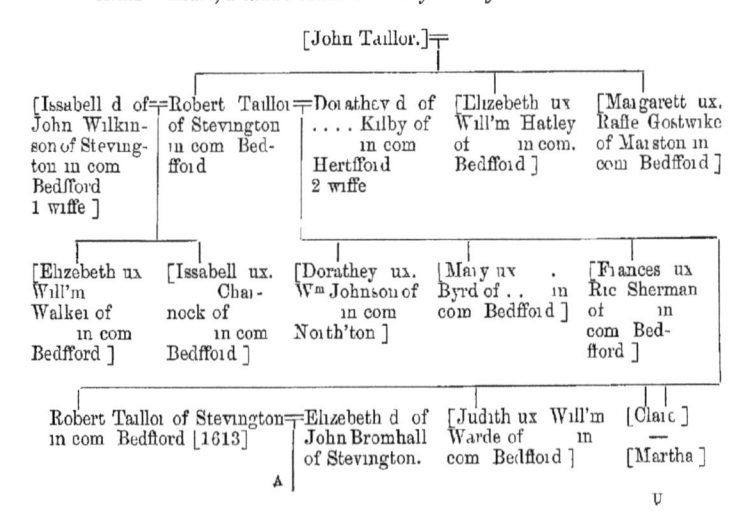

[John Taillor.]

[Issabell d of John Wilkinson of Stevington in com Bedfford 1 wiffe] = [Robert Taillor of Stevington in com Bedfford] = Dorathey d of .... Kilby of in com Hertfford 2 wiffe

[Elizebeth ux Will'm Hatley of in com. Bedfford]

[Margarett ux. Rafle Gostwike of Marston in com Bedfford]

[Elizebeth ux Will'm Walker of in com Bedfford]

[Issabell ux. Charnock of in com Bedfford]

[Dorathey ux. Wm Johnson of in com North'ton]

[Mary ux Byrd of .. in com Bedfford]

[Frances ux Ric Sherman of in com Bedfford]

Robert Taillor of Stevington in com Bedfford [1613] = Elizebeth d of John Bromhall of Stevington.

[Judith ux Will'm Warde of in com Bedfford]

[Clare]
—
[Martha]

U

146   THE VISITATION OF BEDFORDSHIRE.

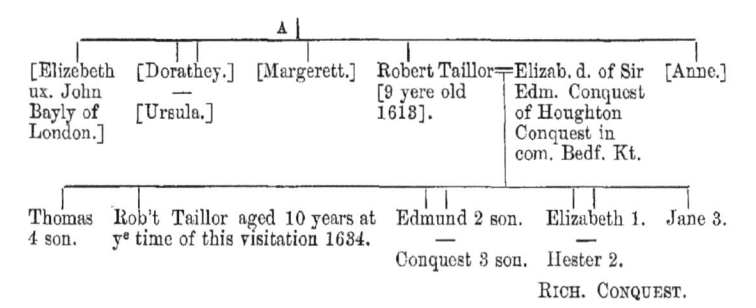

A

[Elizebeth ux. John Bayly of London.] — [Dorathey.] [Ursula.] — [Margerett.] — Robert Taillor [9 yere old 1613].=Elizab. d. of Sir Edm. Conquest of Houghton Conquest in com. Bedf. Kt. — [Anne.]

Thomas 4 son. — Rob't Taillor aged 10 years at ye time of this visitation 1634. — Edmund 2 son. Conquest 3 son. — Elizabeth 1. Hester 2. — Jane 3.

RICH. CONQUEST.

Thomson

[of Husborne=Crawley].

ARMS.—*Quarterly*—1, *Azure, a lion passant-guardant or,* THOMPSON; 2, *Or, a fesse between three martlets sable,* CHADWORTH; 3, *Sable, a fesse ermine between three crescents argent,* GLOVER; 4, *Argent, a fesse dancettée between three roses gules,* SMYTH.

[Richard Thomsonn of Laxton in com. York gent. usher to H. 4.]=

[Will'm Thomsonn.]=[.... d. and heire of .... Chadworth.]

[Richard Thomsonn.]=[Agnes d. of Hugh Gedney. *Vert,* 3 *eagles splayd a.*]

[2. Thomas Thomsonn. *Vide* Lincon.] — [Allice d. and heire of Robert Glover.]=[John Thomsonn.]=[Allice d. of .... Harvye.] — [3. Will'm Thomsonn. *Vide* Lincon.]

Will'm Thomson of Wellinger in com. Lincon.=Catherin d. and coheire of Robert Smyth. — [Thomas Thomson a preest.]

John Thomsonn one of the Auditors to Q. Elizebeth.=Dorathy d. of Ric. Gilbert. — [Margery ux. Will'm Clarke.] — [Allice ux. John Page.]

Robert Thomson of Husborne-Crawley in com. Bedford Esqr.=Jane da. of .... Coningesby sister of Sr Rafe Conyngesby Knight.
A — [1. John Thomsonn.] — [Elizebeth.] — [2. Henery Thomsonn.] — [3. Francis Thomsonn.]

THE VISITATION OF BEDFORDSHIRE.   147

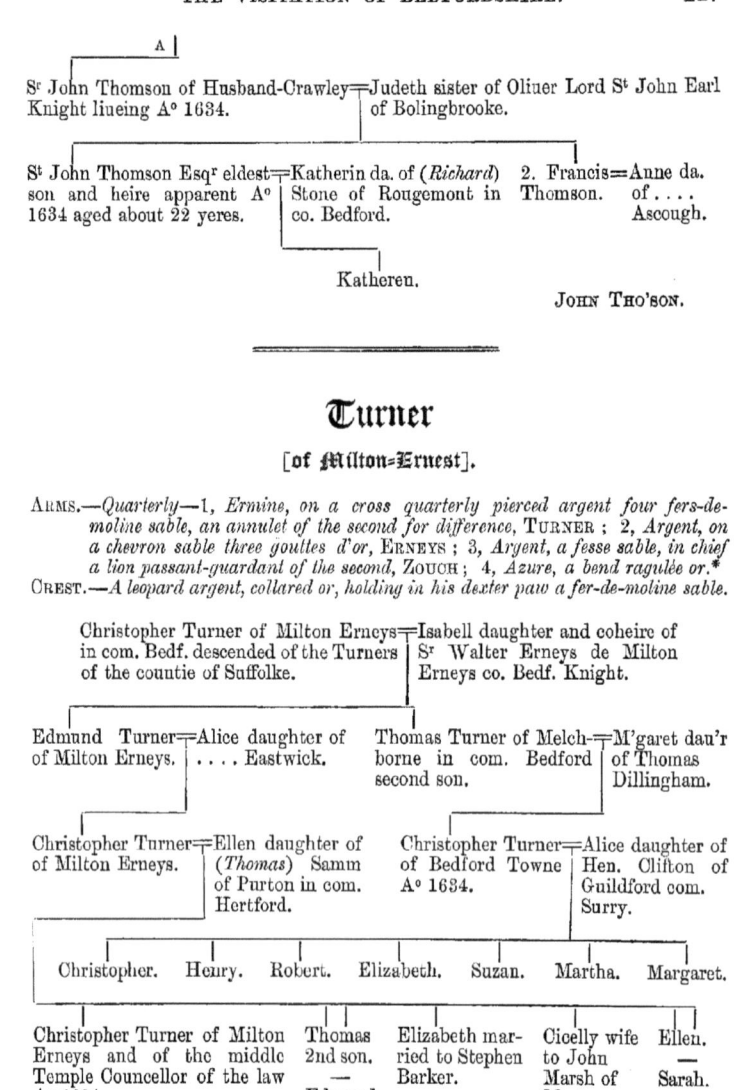

A |

Sr John Thomson of Husband-Crawley=Judeth sister of Oliuer Lord St John Earl
Knight liueing Aº 1634. | of Bolingbrooke.

St John Thomson Esqr eldest=Katherin da. of (*Richard*)   2. Francis=Anne da.
son and heire apparent Aº | Stone of Rougemont in   Thomson. of . . . .
1634 aged about 22 yeres. | co. Bedford.   Ascough.

Katheren.

JOHN THO'SON.

𝔗urner

[of 𝔐ilton=𝔈rnest].

ARMS.—*Quarterly*—1, *Ermine, on a cross quarterly pierced argent four fers-de-moline sable, an annulet of the second for difference*, TURNER ; 2, *Argent, on a chevron sable three gouttes d'or*, ERNEYS ; 3, *Argent, a fesse sable, in chief a lion passant-guardant of the second*, ZOUCH ; 4, *Azure, a bend ragulée or.**
CREST.—*A leopard argent, collared or, holding in his dexter paw a fer-de-moline sable.*

Christopher Turner of Milton Erneys=Isabell daughter and coheire of
in com. Bedf. descended of the Turners | Sr Walter Erneys de Milton
of the countie of Suffolke. | Erneys co. Bedf. Knight.

Edmund Turner=Alice daughter of   Thomas Turner of Melch-=M'garet dau'r
of Milton Erneys. | . . . . Eastwick.   borne in com. Bedford | of Thomas
                                        second son. | Dillingham.

Christopher Turner=Ellen daughter of   Christopher Turner=Alice daughter of
of Milton Erneys. | (*Thomas*) Samm   of Bedford Towne | Hen. Clifton of
                  | of Purton in com.   Aº 1634. | Guildford com.
                  | Hertford. | Surry.

Christopher. Henry. Robert. Elizabeth. Suzan. Martha. Margaret.

Christopher Turner of Milton   Thomas   Elizabeth mar-   Cicelly wife   Ellen.
Erneys and of the middle   2nd son. ried to Stephen to John   —
Temple Councellor of the law   —   Barker.   Marsh of   Sarah.
Aº 1634.   Edmund   Marton in
                               3rd son.   Kent.

CHRISTOPHER TURNER.

* "Vnder the hand of Clar, Cooke."

Vaux
[of Whipsnade].

ARMS (TWO SHIELDS)—I, *Argent, a bend chequée or and gules, a crescent for difference*, VAUX. II, *Vert, a chevron argent gouttee de sang between three pheons or*, HOLMAN *

CREST—*On a wreath argent and vert a bow and arrow drawn or, the arrow fesseways between two wings expanded gules*, HOLMAN †

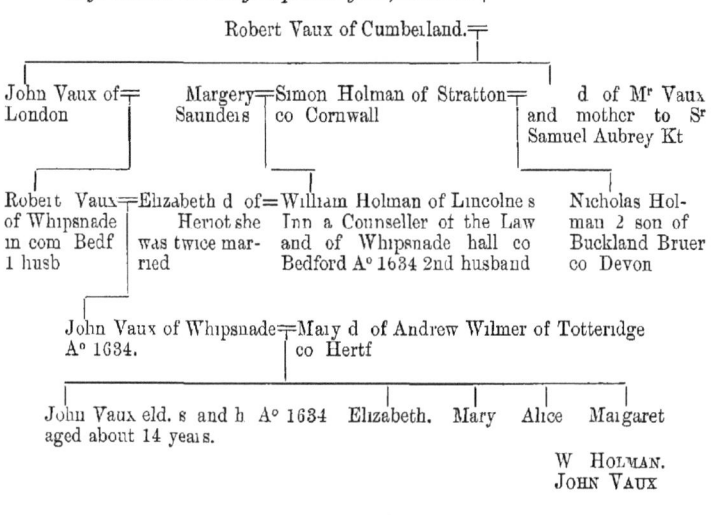

Robert Vaux of Cumberland.=

- John Vaux of London =
- Margery Saunders = Simon Holman of Stratton co Cornwall =
- d. of Mr Vaux and mother to Sr Samuel Aubrey Kt

- Robert Vaux of Whipsnade in com Bedf 1 husb = Elizabeth d of Heriot she was twice married = William Holman of Lincolne s Inn a Counseller of the Law and of Whipsnade hall co Bedford A° 1634 2nd husband
- Nicholas Holman 2 son of Buckland Bruer co Devon

John Vaux of Whipsnade A° 1634. = Mary d of Andrew Wilmer of Totteridge co Hertf

- John Vaux eld. s and h A° 1634 aged about 14 years.
- Elizabeth.
- Mary
- Alice
- Margaret

W HOLMAN.
JOHN VAUX

Ventris
[of Campton].

ARMS—*Azure, a dolphin naiant or between two bendlets wavy argent*

[CREST—*A sword erect argent, hilt and pommel or, between two wings expanded of the second*]

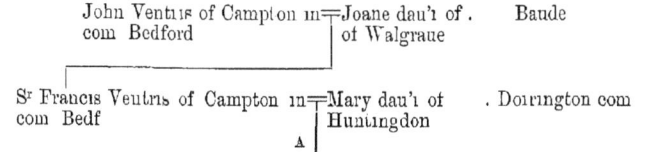

John Ventris of Campton in com Bedford = Joane dau'r of . Baude of Walgraue

Sr Francis Ventris of Campton in com Bedf = Mary dau'r of . Dorrington com Huntingdon

A

---

* " Certif by Mr Philpot Som^rset "
† " An escocheon vnder the hand of Mr Camden to William Holman of Lincolne's Inn, son of Simon Holman of Stratton in Cornwall "

THE VISITATION OF BEDFORDSHIRE. 149

A

Francis Ventris Esqr eldest son died without yssue | Charles Ventris of Campton Esqr brother and heire masle of Francis hueing A° 1634 === Mary dau'r of Sr Lewes Pemberton of Rushdon com Northampton K^t. | Henry Ventris third son.

John Ventris eldest son and heire aged about 4 yeres A° 1634   Mary

CHARLES VENTRIS

𝔚arren al's 𝔚aller
[of 𝔅edford].

Robert Warren al's Waller of Bedford descended of a branch === Mary dau'r of (W^m) of the Warrens al's Wallers of Ashwell co Hertford This   Cobb of Shernbrooke Robert was three times maior of Bedford   com. Bedford

1 Robert Warren al's Waller   2. Thomas   3 William Warren al's === Elizabeth dau'l of Michael Waller three seuerall times maior of Bedford hueing A° 1634.   Vnderwood of Henlow com Bedford

WILLIAM WARREN alias WALLER

𝔚ateson
[of 𝔄mpthill].

ARMS —*Argent, a fesse gules, in chief two crosses botonnée of the second*
CREST —*An arm embowed in armour proper, garnished or, holding in the gauntlet a broken fetter-lock sable.*

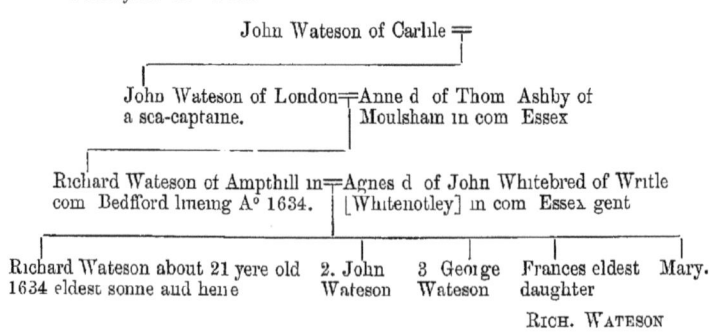

John Wateson of Carlile ===

John Wateson of London === Anne d of Thom Ashby of
a sea-captaine.   Moulsham in com Essex

Richard Wateson of Ampthill in === Agnes d of John Whitebred of Writle
com Bedfford lineing A° 1634.   [Whitenotley] in com Essex gent

Richard Wateson about 21 yere old 1634 eldest sonne and heire | 2. John Wateson | 3 George Wateson | Frances eldest daughter | Mary.

RICH. WATESON

Whitaker

[of Bedford].

ARMS—*Argent, a chevron between three mascles azure* *

James Whitaker of Altham in co. Lancaster

Christopher Whitaker of Walshay in co. Lanc = Alice dau'r of ... Ormerod of Huncote com. Lanc.

John Whitacre of the Towne of Bedford gent. liueing A° 1634 = Sibell dau'r of Tho. Cobb of Sharnebrooke com. Bedf. gent.

2 Richard Whitaker rector of Gluuias and Beaudoke co. Cornwall

Jane wife to . Jackson

3 James Whitaker Batchelor of Diuinity = Joyce dau'r of Sr Edward Greule Knight.

1 Edward   2 John Whitaker now of London   3 Thomas

JOHN WHITAKER

Wilkes

[of Leighton-Bussard].

ARMS—*Per pale or and argent, a chevron between three eagles' heads erased sable* †
CREST—*On a mount vert a cross-bow erect or*
MOTTOES—IN DEO SALUS MEA. ARCUI MEO NON CONFIDO.

John Wilkes of Layton Buzard in com. Bedford

Mary mar. to George Bates of Milton Mowbray in com. Buckingham

Edward Wilkes of Layton Buzard in com. Bedford now liueing 1634 = Jane da of .... Besouth Clark of Common (*Corner*) Hall in com. Harts

Martha mar. to John Sedgwick of Southwick iuxta London bruer to King Charles

Matthew Wilkes Ironmonger of London eldest sonn

Mark 2nd sonn.

Luke 3rd sonn.

Thomas 4th sonn

Joane 2nd da

LUKE WILKES

---

* " Ex sigillo res for furth proofe"
† They also bear the following arms Paly of eight or and gules, on a chief argent three lozenges of the second (another—three roses gules, seeded or). All these arms are depicted on the mural tablets set up to Luke Wilkes and Edward Wilkes in the chancel of Leighton-Bussard Church.—ED

Wingate

[of Ampthill].

ARMS (TWO SHIELDS)—1, *Sable, a bend ermine cotised between six martlets or,* WINGATE II, *Quarterly*—1 and 4, WINGATE, 2 and 3. *Azure, a fesse between three gouttes d'or,* BELVERGE *In the centre point an escutcheon Ermine, on a fesse a mullet gules,* BUTTON
CREST—1, *A greyhound's head or, gorged with two bars-gemelles sable* ; 2, *A gate or, a crescent for difference* *

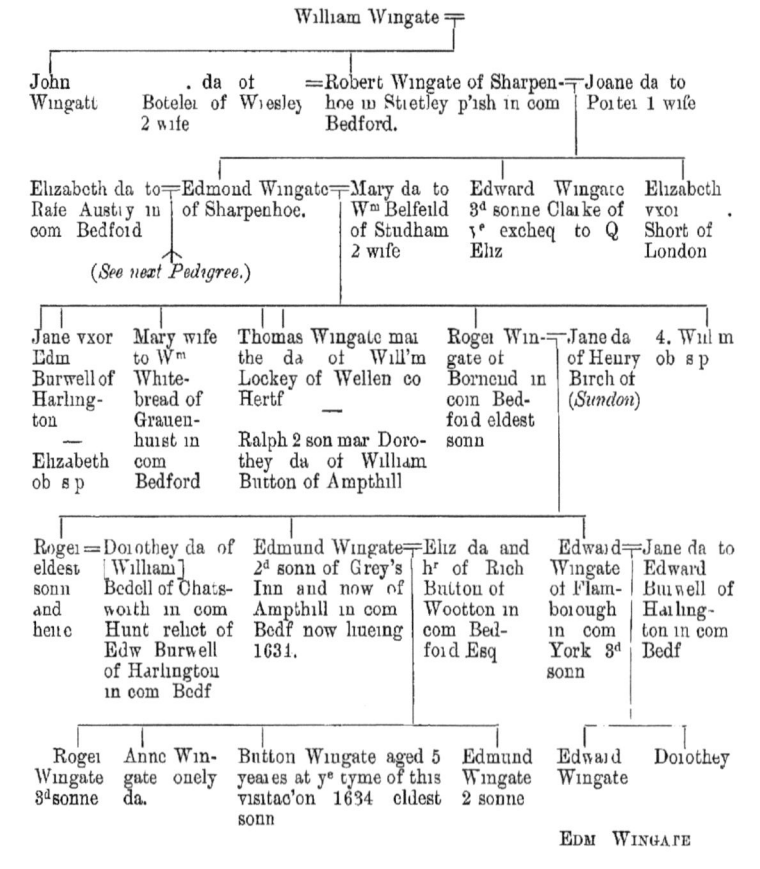

William Wingate =

- John Wingatt . da ot Boteler of Wresley 2 wife = Robert Wingate of Sharpen-hoe in Stretley p'ish in com Bedford. = Joane da to Porter 1 wife

  - Elizabeth da to Rafe Austry in com Bedford = Edmond Wingate of Sharpenhoe. (*See next Pedigree.*) = Mary da to Wm Belfeild of Studham 2 wife
  - Edward Wingate 3^d sonne Clarke of y^e excheq to Q Eliz
  - Elizabeth vxor . Short of London

    - Jane vxor Edm Burwell of Harlington — Elizabeth ob s p
    - Mary wife to Wm Whitebread of Grauenhurst in com Bedford
    - Thomas Wingate mar the da of Will'm Lockey of Wellen co Hertf —
      Ralph 2 son mar Dorothey da of William Button of Ampthill
    - Roger Wingate of Bornend in com Bedford eldest sonn = Jane da of Henry Birch of (*Sundon*)
    - 4. Will m ob s p

      - Roger eldest sonn and heire = Dorothey da of [William] Bedell of Chatsworth in com Hunt relict of Edw Burwell of Harlington in com Bedf
      - Edmund Wingate 2^d sonn of Grey's Inn and now of Ampthill in com Bedf now liueing 1634. = Eliz da and h^r of Rich Button of Wootton in com Bedford Esq
      - Edward Wingate of Flamborough in com York 3^d sonn = Jane da to Edward Burwell of Harlington in com Bedf

        - Roger Wingate 3^d sonne
        - Anne Wingate onely da.
        - Button Wingate aged 5 yeares at y^e tyme of this visitac'on 1634 eldest sonn
        - Edmund Wingate 2 sonne
        - Edward Wingate
        - Dorothey

EDM WINGATE

* "This creast did belong to Edward Wingate Clarke of the Check to him onely and no other of his family"

Wingate

[of Harlington].

ARMS—*Sable, a bend ermine cotised between six martlets or.*

Edmond Wingate=Elizabeth da. to Rafe Astrey in com. Bedford
of Sharpenhoe

Anne dau'r of William Wise-=George Wingate of Sharpenhoe Esq'=Anne dau'r of
man of Canfeild Hall com | one of the Justices of the Peace in | John Belfeild
Essex 2 wife relict of | this County his third wife was | of Studham in
Fitch and mother of S' Wil- | (*Martha*) da of Oliuer Lo S' John | co Hertford
liam Fitch | of Bletneso | 1 wife.

Robert Wingate=Amy da of Roger | 2 Edward Wingate of Lockley mar | Richard,
of Harlington | Warr of Hester- | Margaret da to Peter Tauerner | Rafe and
in com. Bedf. | combe co Somer- | son of Richard Tauerner of | George
Esq'. | set Esq' | Soundes co Oxon | s p

John Wingate of=Alice da of Francis | George Win- | Edward Wingate of Lock-
Harlington Esq' | Smallman of Kin- | gate of the | ley co Hertford mar Mary
one of the Jus- | ersley in co. Here- | Middle | Alway da and coh of
tices of the Peace | ford Esq | Temple ob | Rafe Alway of Cannons
A° 1634. | | s p | com Hertord gent

Robert Wingate eldest sonne   2 Francis   3. George   Hester
and heire apparent aged about
7 yeres A° 1634.   Amy

                                                    JO WINGATE

Wyld

[of Bromham].

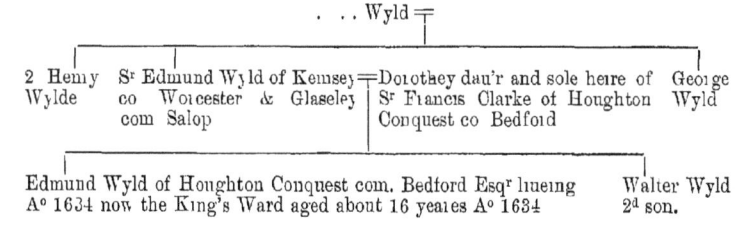

. . . Wyld =

2 Henry | S' Edmund Wyld of Kemsey=Dorothey dau'r and sole heire of | George
Wylde | co Worcester & Glaseley | S' Francis Clarke of Houghton | Wyld
      | com Salop | Conquest co Bedford

Edmund Wyld of Houghton Conquest com. Bedford Esq' liueing   Walter Wyld
A° 1634 now the King's Ward aged about 16 yeares A° 1634   2ᵈ son.

                                                    EDMUND WYLDE.

Additional Pedigrees.

"The vissitation of Bedffordshire made in A° 1566 endeth at ye 90 leaffe in this booke most of wh descents are continued & enlarged by some of ye same ffamilyes and [*one word here illegible*] pedigrees the rest of ye descents flolowing the 90 leaffe are descents of ye same county truly transcribed by me RICHARD MUNDY.

"Noate that I lent this book to George owen yorke herald & henery lilly rouge when they went the vissitation of this county in A° 1634." (Harl MS 1531.)

EDW COPLEY of Southill —Argent, a cross moline gules, in the dexter chief a fleur-de-lys of the second

RADCLIFF of Elstow —Argent, a bend engrailed sable a crescent for difference

NEWDIGATE of Hawns —Gules, a chevron ermine between three lions' jambs argent

SEWELL of Edworth —Argent, on a bend gules three martlets of the field, within a bordure engrailed of the second

MOLYSWORTH —Gules, an inescutcheon vair argent and azure within an orle of cross-crosslets or.

PYNFFOLD of Dunstable.—Azure, a chevron or surmounted of another of the field between three doves proper

    Crest —A pine-tree or, leaved vert, fructed proper, enclosed within pales argent and sable (*Granted* 18 *Oct* 1591.)

JOHN BRENKER —Argent, a fesse gules between six estoiles sable

JUDG or JUG —Or, a chevron vert

BARDOLFFE —Argent, a chevron ermine between three crosses pattée fitchée gules

CLOPTON —Gules, a fesse ermine between six mascles or

BAA —Gules, a chevron argent between three plates

BAA —Gules, a chevron between three mullets argent

FAYREY —Per pale or and azure, a chevron between three eagles all counterchanged, on a chief gules as many fusils ermine.

    [*Crest* —A griffin rampant wielding a sword in the dexter claw.]

FLYTWECKS —Or, two lions passant-guardant sable

    [*Crest* —An arm embowed, vested and cuffed argent, in the hand proper an arrow sable headed and feathered of the first.]

SOMERY.—Or, two lions passant-guardant azure

GOLDINGTON —Or, two lions passant sable.

GUBYON —Gules, a cross pattée argent, over all a label of three points azure.

HARNEYS —Argent, a chevron sable gouttée d'or, a crescent gules for difference

    [*Crest* —A stag's head sable gouttée d'or, attired of the last.]

HENXTON —Gules, a chevron between three leopards' faces argent.
ROGER HEIGHAM —Paly of six argent and azure, on a chief gules three escallops of the first
  [*Crest* —An escallop or, charged with a mullet gules]
PAKINGHAM —Barry of six or and azure (another sable and or), on a bend gules three mullets or
PEVER (*of Toddington*) —Argent, a chevron gules between three fleurs-de-lys or
PYGOTT.—Argent, a bend between six pickaxes sable
ROUS [or ROWSE] —Quarterly argent and sable, a bend of the second
SOMERY —Quarterly or and azure, a bend gules
SLADE —Argent, three horses' heads erased sable, a chief gules
  [*Crest.*—A horse's head erased sable]
TRAYLEY (*of Northill*) —Or, a cross between four martlets gules
STOKES of Carlton —Argent fretty azure, on a canton of the second a boar's head erased or
HUNT —Sable, a fesse between three cinqfoils or.
JACOB —Per chevron or and argent, an eagle displayed sable
JOHN JOHNSON of Goldington —Azure, a chevron between three eagles volant or
HENRY WHITLOCK of Shitlingtonbury —Sable, a fesse embattled between three escallops or
  Crest —Out of a mural crown or a demi-talbot ermine
JUGER —Quarterly—1, Or, a chevron vert ; 2, Gules, a fesse . on a chief argent a lion passant gules ; 3, Gules, a chevron between three horseshoes argent ; 4, Blank
JOHN LANCELOTT —Argent, on a chief azure three fusils or
HUMFFREY WINCH (*of Everton*) —Per pale azure and gules, an escallop or
  Crest —An escallop per fesse or and argent
Sʳ JOHN FOURTHORPE, KNT ; type E I —Ermine, on a chief gules three roses or.
ALEXANDER SCROGGS of Raynold, sonn of Thomas Scroggs of Patmore —Argent, on a bend azure between two greyhounds courant bendways sable three Cornish choughs or
  Crest —A pewit's head argent, collared gules, wings endorsed bendy of four or and sable
THOMAS BEDELL of Wootton — a bend argent, cotised or, between six lions passant-guardant or
PYKE of Ranhall —Per pale or and gules, on a chevron between three trefoils slipped a luce naiant all counterchanged
PATESHULI of Pateshull —Paly of six or and gules, a fesse argent.
RYDELL —Paly of six argent and gules, a bend sable
JOHNSON of Leighton —Argent, a fesse lozengy between three lions' heads erased gules
  Crest —A nag's head sable, gouttée d'or and crined of the last.
JOHN MANLEY of Wilshamstead —Quarterly—1 and 4, Argent, a dexter hand couped and erect within a bordure sable ; 2 and 3, Vert, a bend ermine In the fesse point an annulet for difference
  Crest —A Saracen's head affrontée proper, wreathed about the temples vert.

ADDITIONAL PEDIGREES 155

WM. BLETSHO of Wiminton —Or, on a bend sable between three escallops azure as many garbs of the first, all within a bordure gules

    Crest —A wolf's head or, semée of hurts, and gorged with a mural collar azure

RICHARD WAGSTAFFE of Ravensden —Argent, two bends engrailed gules, the lower one couped at the top, in chief an escallop of the second

Fo 14. In Wouburne Church in com Bedfford in the glasse windows of the same :—
1 Azure, three bars wavy argent, CISTERCIAN ABBEY OF WOBURN
2 Quarterly or and gules, in the first quarter a mullet argent, VERE
3. Quarterly—1 and 4, Or, three bars wavy azure, SANDFORD, 2 and 3, VERE
4. SANDFORD.

In the South Ile —
1 Argent, a chevron sable fretty or between three roses slipped vert,

The armes of the ffather and Mother of Robert Hobbs, Abbot of Woborne —
Sable, a cross engrailed between four martlets or, a chief ermine, , impaling, Azure, on a chief argent three torteaux,

These inscriptions remain in the wall on the north side of the Inner Court there —
    "HIC IACET 𝔚ill'm's 𝔚eston...."
    "𝔥ic jacet 𝔊uido de 𝔙ere...."

On ye old buildings there —
1 SANDFORD
2 Quarterly— and , in the first quarter a mullet, in the second quarter three bars wavy *

The Baron of Sandffoid and the erles of oxfford were ffounders of the Abbey of Wouborne

Fo 21 In Luton Church —
    "𝔍esu 𝔠hrist most of myght
    have mercy on 𝔍ohn le 𝔚enlock knight
    and of his wife 𝔈lizabeth
    wch out of this world is past by death
    wch founded thes chapell here
    helpe them wth your harty praier
    that they may com to that place
    where ever is joy and solace."

ARMS —Quarterly of eight—1, Argent, a chevron between three Blackamoors' heads erased sable, WENLOCK , 2, Quarterly argent and sable, HOO , 3, Sable, a bend between six crosses fitchée or, ; 4, Barry of six ermine and gules, in chief a demi-lion rampant gules, , 5, As No 2 , 6, 7, and 8, Blank

    * The blazon of this shield is clearly wrong It is probably intended to represent *Vere* impaling *Sandford*

" Hic jacet Thomas Rotheram miles et
D'na Katherina uxor eius qui quidem
Thomas obiit .... Die .... Ao D'ni 15 .... qui
quidem Katherina obiit Ao D'ni ...."

ARMS—Vert, three stags trippant or, ROTHERAM, impaling, Barry of six argent and azure, in chief three torteaux, GREY.

In Bletso Church —

" Hic jacet Radulphus lannor quondam Cofferarius et custos
Garderop prin? cum nobilissima Domina Margaret Ducissa
Somersatia ac? Icon D'na Wells qui obiit 18 Die Augusti 1458
Cuius a'ia propt'et, &c."

ARMS (TWO SHIELDS) —I, Quarterly—1 and 4, Azure, three fleurs-de-lys or, a crescent for difference, LANNOR, 2 and 3,   , three lions rampant   ,
? WELLES   II (in an old glasse window), Quarterly—1 and 4, Ermine, three chevrons gules,   2 and 3, Gules, on a bend argent three trefoils slipped vert, HARVEY

ADDITIONAL PEDIGREES 157

Astry

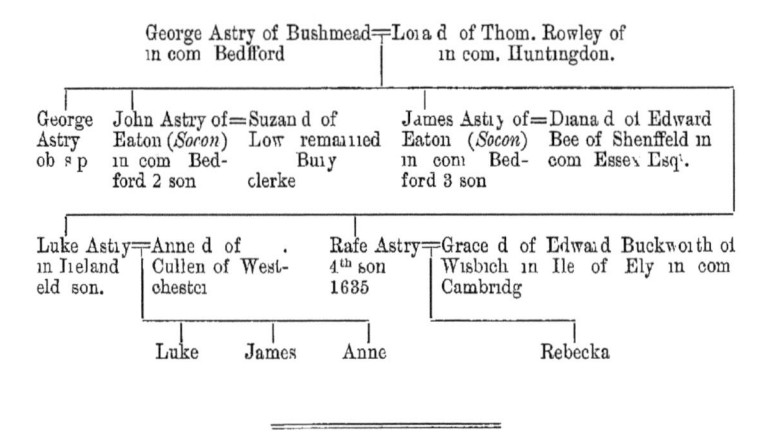

[of Eaton-Socon].

George Astry of Bushmead = Lora d of Thom. Rowley of
in com Bedford — in com. Huntingdon.

- George Astry ob s p
- John Astry of Eaton (*Socon*) in com Bedford 2 son = Suzan d of Low remarried Bury clerke
- James Astry of Eaton (*Socon*) in com Bedford 3 son = Diana d of Edward Bee of Shenffeld in com Essex Esq.

- Luke Astry in Ireland eld son. = Anne d of . Cullen of Westchester
- Rafe Astry 4th son 1635 = Grace d of Edward Buckworth of Wisbich in Ile of Ely in com Cambridg

  - Luke
  - James
  - Anne
  - Rebecka

Banester

[of Bedford].

ARMS —*Argent, a cross fleurie sable, a crescent gules for difference*
CREST —*A peacock sejeant proper, encircled by a snake proper*

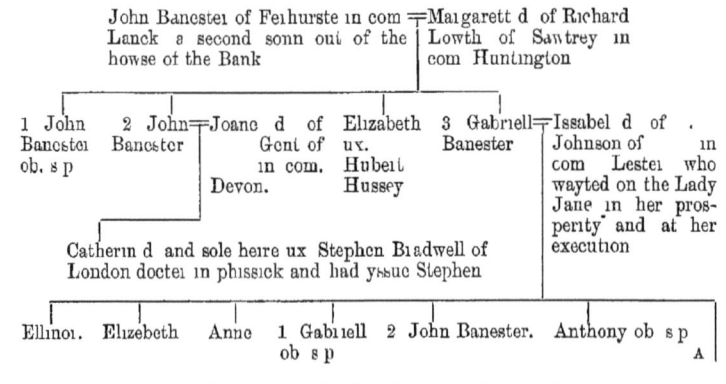

John Banester of Ferhurste in com Lanck a second sonn out of the howse of the Bank = Margarett d of Richard Lowth of Sawtrey in com Huntington

- 1 John Banester ob. s p
- 2 John Banester = Joane d of Gent of ux. in com. Hubert Devon. Hussey
- Elizabeth Banester
- 3 Gabriell Banester = Issabel d of . Johnson of in com Lester who wayted on the Lady Jane in her prosperity and at her execution

Catherin d and sole heire ux Stephen Bradwell of London docter in phissick and had yssue Stephen

- Ellinor.
- Elizebeth
- Anne
- 1 Gabriell ob s p
- 2 John Banester.
- Anthony ob s p

A

* *Cf* Genealogical Memoirs of the Families of Astry,' p 90 by R E Chester Waters

158 THE VISITATION OF BEDFORDSHIRE.

3 Francis Banester of the towne of Bedford == Amy d of Wi'm Carter of Kempton
Docter in Phissick | in com Bedfford

Mary ux. Joseph Lane of Hidgenton in com Buckingham. — Elizebeth ux William Lane of Shaftesbury in com Dorsett.

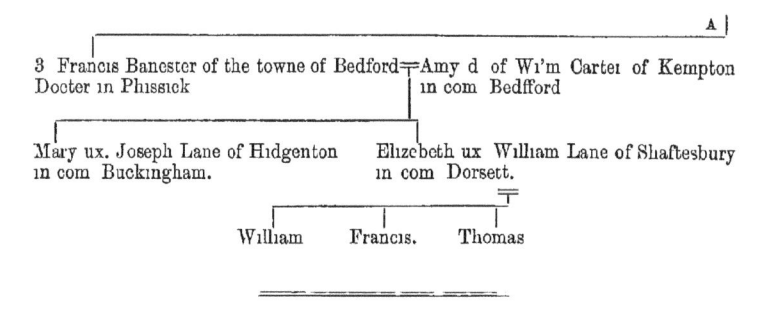

William — Francis. — Thomas

Birch
[of Sundon].

ARMS —*Gules, on a chevron between three griffins' heads erased argent as many lozenges azure, on a chief crenellée or three birch-branches vert*

CREST —*A hare rampant barry or and azure, holding in its paws a branch of filbert-nuts*

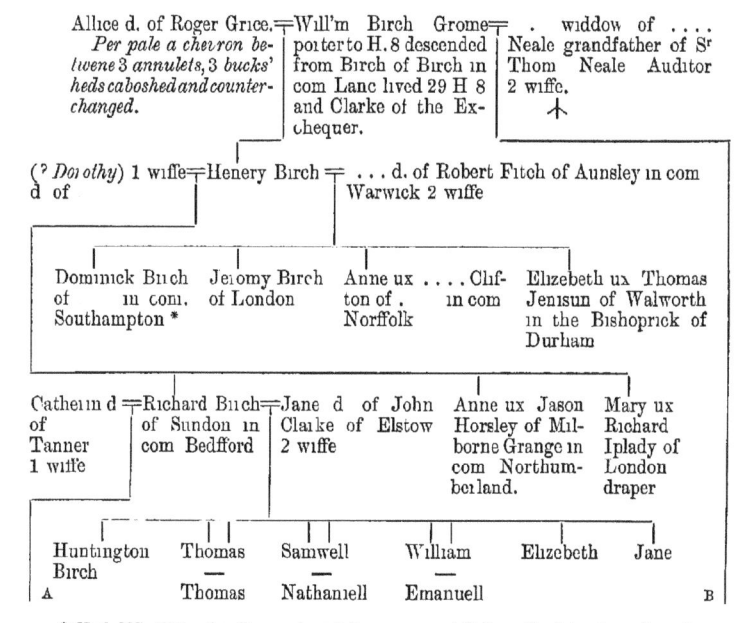

Allice d. of Roger Grice. == Will'm Birch Grome == . . . widdow of . . . .
Per pale a chevron be- | porter to H. 8 descended | Neale grandfather of S'r
twene 3 annulets, 3 bucks' | from Birch of Birch in | Thom Neale Auditor
heds caboshed and counter- | com Lanc lived 29 H 8 | 2 wiffe.
changed. | and Clarke of the Exchequer.

(? *Dorothy*) 1 wiffe == Henery Birch == . . . d. of Robert Fitch of Aunsley in com
d of | Warwick 2 wiffe

Dominick Burch of in com. Southampton * — Jeromy Birch of London — Anne ux . . . . Clifton of . Norffolk — Elizebeth in com — Elizebeth ux Thomas Jenisun of Walworth in the Bishoprick of Durham

Catherin d == Richard Burch == Jane d of John — Anne ux Jason — Mary ux
of | of Sundon in | Clarke of Elstow | Horsley of Mil- | Richard
Tanner | com Bedfford | 2 wiffe | borne Grange in | Iplady of
1 wiffe | | | com Northum- | London
 | | | berland. | draper

Huntington Birch — Thomas — Samwell — William — Elizebeth — Jane
A — Thomas — Nathaniell — Emanuell — B

* Harl MS 4600 makes Dominick and Jeremy sons of William Birch by the widow of Neale, and also makes Judith, Henry, Jane, Priscilla, and Susan issue of Henry Birch by his wife da of Rob t Fitch

ADDITIONAL PEDIGREES. 159

A					B
1. Henery.	3. Richard s p	4 John Buch of London Vintner 1634	=Anne d. of Humffrey Monox of Walt- hamstow in com Essex	5 Nicholas.	Frances ux W'm Barnes of com Dorsett

1 John dyed yong	2 John Birch [14 yeares old July 1634*]	3 Humffrey [8 years old*].	Elizebeth [12 years old*].	Anne [11 years old*]

Jane ux. Roger Wyngate of Barnend in com. Bed- fford †	Priscilla 1 ux John Moore- howse of Comberland 2 to John Carlton‡ of Segston in com York	Susan ux Georg Bedells of Siton in com Buck- ingham

Judith ux Thomas Smyth of Slapham (? *Slapton*) in com Buckingham	2 Henery Buch of Otcomb in com Somersett	=Joane d of Will'm Skipwith of St Albans in com Hert- fford

1 Thomas Buch.	Jane ux Lewes Monox 2 to John Gade a procter of the Civill Law	Elizebeth — Dorathey	Mary.	Grace ux Edmond Iremonger

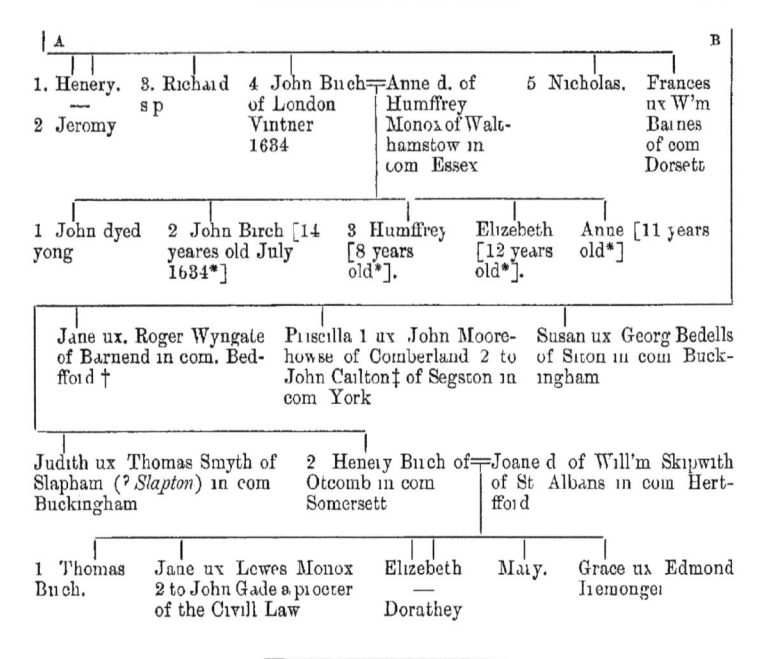

Blenerhasset

[of Blunham].

ARMS —*Quarterly of six*—1, *Gules, a chevron ermine between three dolphins embowed argent,* BLENERHASSET ; 2, *Argent, three escutcheons sable, two and one,* LOWDHAM , 3, *Gules, a pallium inverted ermine,* KELDON , 4, *Azure, a lion rampant argent, crowned or,* , 5, *Azure, a fesse between three fleurs-de-lys or, a crescent for difference,* , 6, *Blank In the fesse point a crescent for difference*

CREST —*A wolf sejeant gules, a crescent on the shoulder.*

Raffe Blenerhasset of Frens in com Norff	=Jane d and heire of Sr John Lowdham of Lowdham in com Suff *vid idem*

Jane d of Thomas Higham of Higham Greene in com Suff. 1 wiffe A	=John Blenerhasset of Trens in Nor- folk.	=Jane d. of Sr Thomas Tyndall of Norff 2 wiffe by whome hee had yssue as in Suff and Norfolk.

* 'Visitation of London,' Harl Soc, vol 1, p 131
† "Widow to " (Harl MS 4600)
‡ "Coulton." (Harl Ms 4600)

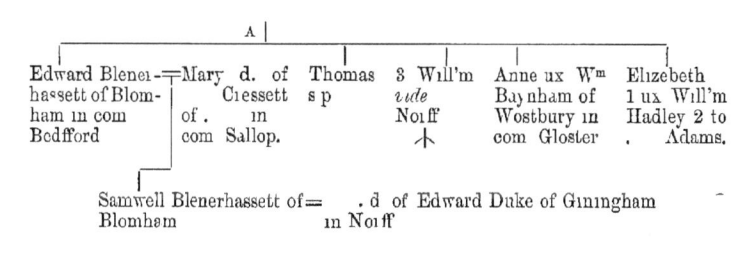

```
                                            A |
Edward Blener-┬-Mary d. of   Thomas   3 Will'm    Anne ux Wm      Elizebeth
hassett of Blom-│  Cressett  s p      ude        Baynham of      1 ux Will'm
ham in com     │  of .  in            Norff      Wostbury in     Hadley 2 to
Bedfford       │  com Sallop.          ⊥         com Gloster  .  Adams.
               │
     Samwell Blenerhassett of=  . d of Edward Duke of Giningham
     Blomham                   in Norff
```

Blundell [*]

[of Cardington].

ARMS.—*Quarterly of six*—1, *Azure, ten billets, four, three, two, and one, and a canton or charged with a raven sable,* BLUNDELL ; 2, *Sable, three lozenges in fesse between as many stags' heads cabossed argent,* BUDOCKSHYDE ; 3, *Argent, three bendlets engrailed sable,* TRAVALARD *alias* MORTON ; 4, *Argent, a chevron surmounted of a cross pattee sable,* GOPHILL ; 5, *Argent, a chevron between three Blackamoors' heads sable,*   , 6, *Blank*

CREST.—*A squirrel sejeant gules, collared and holding a nut or, on the shoulder a crescent for difference*

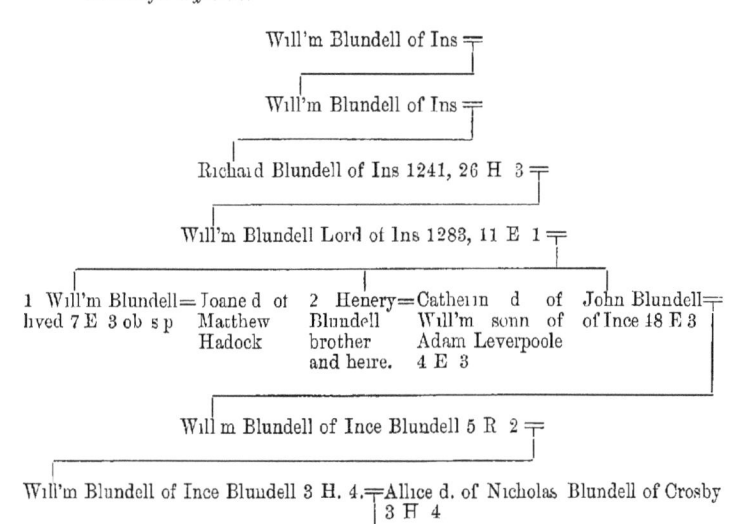

```
                    Will'm Blundell of Ins ⊤
                              │
                    Will'm Blundell of Ins ⊤
                              │
              Richard Blundell of Ins 1241, 26 H 3 ⊤
                              │
              Will'm Blundell Lord of Ins 1283, 11 E 1 ⊤
                              │
   ┌──────────────────────┬──────────────────┬─────────────────────┐
1 Will'm Blundell=Joane d of   2 Henery=Catherin d of    John Blundell⊤
  lived 7 E 3 ob s p  Matthew     Blundell   Will'm sonn of  of Ince 18 E 3
                     Hadock     brother     Adam Leverpoole
                                and heire.    4 E 3
                                                          │
                    Will'm Blundell of Ince Blundell 5 R 2 ⊤
                              │
Will'm Blundell of Ince Blundell 3 H. 4.=Allice d. of Nicholas Blundell of Crosby
                                        │ 3 H 4
                                      A │
```

* *Cf* Le Neve's Knights, p 135, and Burke's 'Extinct and Dormant Baronets' p 600

ADDITIONAL PEDIGREES.

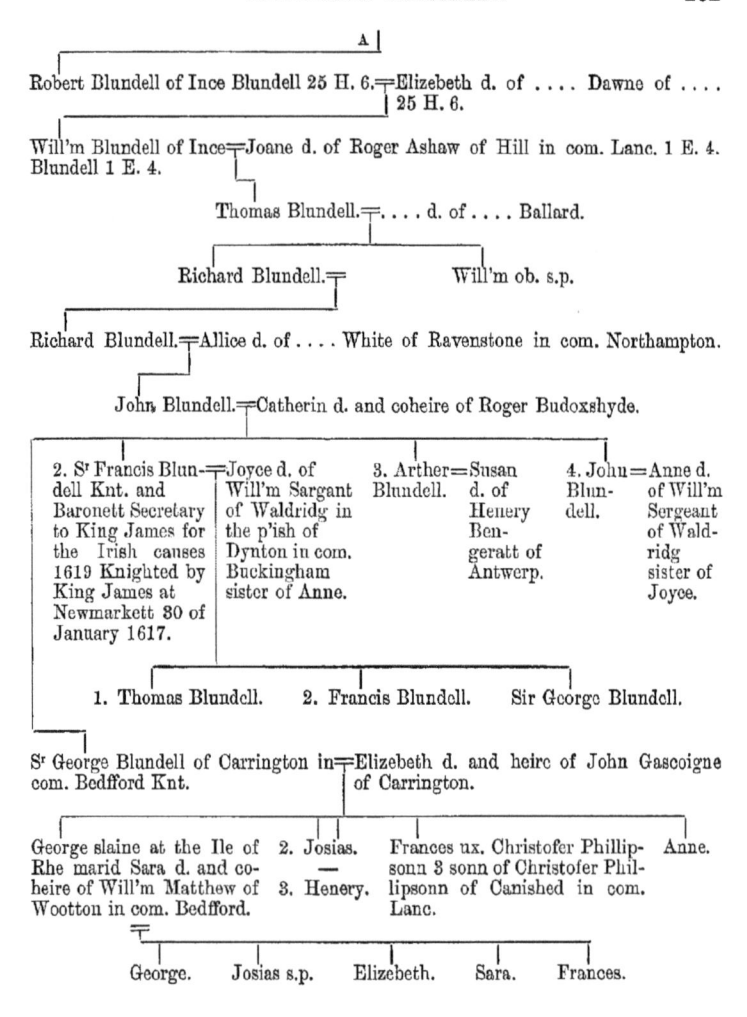

A

Robert Blundell of Ince Blundell 25 H. 6.=Elizebeth d. of .... Dawne of .... 25 H. 6.

Will'm Blundell of Ince=Joane d. of Roger Ashaw of Hill in com. Lanc. 1 E. 4. Blundell 1 E. 4.

Thomas Blundell.=.... d. of .... Ballard.

Richard Blundell.=   Will'm ob. s.p.

Richard Blundell.=Allice d. of .... White of Ravenstone in com. Northampton.

John Blundell.=Catherin d. and coheire of Roger Budoxshyde.

| 2. Sʳ Francis Blundell Knt. and Baronett Secretary to King James for the Irish causes 1619 Knighted by King James at Newmarkett 30 of January 1617. | =Joyce d. of Will'm Sargant of Waldridg in the p'ish of Dynton in com. Buckingham sister of Anne. | 3. Arther=Susan Blundell. d. of Henery Bengeratt of Antwerp. | 4. John=Anne d. Blundell. of Will'm Sergeant of Waldridg sister of Joyce. |

1. Thomas Blundell.   2. Francis Blundell.   Sir George Blundell.

Sʳ George Blundell of Carrington in=Elizebeth d. and heire of John Gascoigne com. Bedfford Knt.   of Carrington.

| George slaine at the Ile of Rhe marid Sara d. and coheire of Will'm Matthew of Wootton in com. Bedfford. | 2. Josias. — 3. Henery. | Frances ux. Christofer Phillipsonn 3 sonn of Christofer Phillipsonn of Canished in com. Lanc. | Anne. |

George.   Josias s.p.   Elizebeth.   Sara.   Frances.

Bray, Lord Bray

[of Eaton Bray].

ARMS.—*Quarterly of nine*—1, *Argent, a chevron between three eagles' legs erased à la quise sable*, BRAY ; 2, *Vair, three bendlets gules*, LONGVALE ; 3, *Argent, on a bend gules three goats passant of the field, armed or*, HALEIWELL ; 4, *Sable, on a chevron between three bulls' heads argent a fleur-de-lys of the field*, NORBURY ; 5, *Gules, a fesse counter-componée argent and sable between six crosses formée fitchée or*, BOTTELER ; 6, *Or, two bendlets gules*, SUDLEY ; 7, *Bendy of ten or and azure*, MOUNTFORT ; 8, *Sable, a cross between four bees erect or*, CROSYER ; 9, *Azure, a chevron or*, DABERNON.

CRESTS.—1, *A lion passant-guardant or between two wings endorsed vair or and azure;* 2, *A flax-breaker or ;* 3, *A ? rabbit gules.*

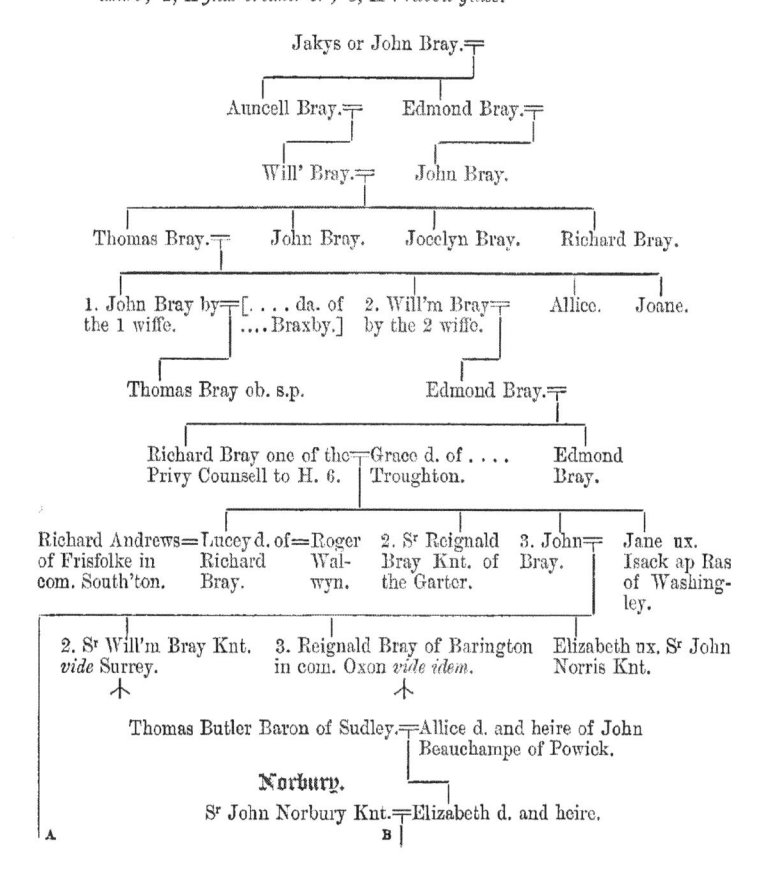

```
                      Jakys or John Bray.=⊤

         Auncell Bray.=⊤           Edmond Bray.=⊤

         Will' Bray.=⊤             John Bray.

Thomas Bray.=⊤   John Bray.   Jocelyn Bray.   Richard Bray.

1. John Bray by =⊤ [.... da. of    2. Will'm Bray=⊤   Allice.   Joane.
   the 1 wiffe.    ....Braxby.]    by the 2 wiffe.

       Thomas Bray ob. s.p.        Edmond Bray.=⊤

              Richard Bray one of the=⊤Grace d. of ....   Edmond
              Privy Counsell to H. 6.  | Troughton.        Bray.

Richard Andrews=Lucey d. of=Roger   2. Sr Reignald   3. John=⊤   Jane ux.
of Frisfolke in  Richard    Wal-    Bray Knt. of    Bray.      Isack ap Ras
com. South'ton.  Bray.      wyn.    the Garter.                of Washing-
                                                                ley.

  2. Sr Will'm Bray Knt.    3. Reignald Bray of Barington    Elizabeth ux. Sr John
  vide Surrey.              in com. Oxon vide idem.          Norris Knt.
       ⋏                         ⋏

       Thomas Butler Baron of Sudley.=⊤Allice d. and heire of John
                                      | Beauchampe of Powick.

                      Norbury.
                Sr John Norbury Knt.=⊤Elizabeth d. and heire.
A                               B
```

ADDITIONAL PEDIGREES.

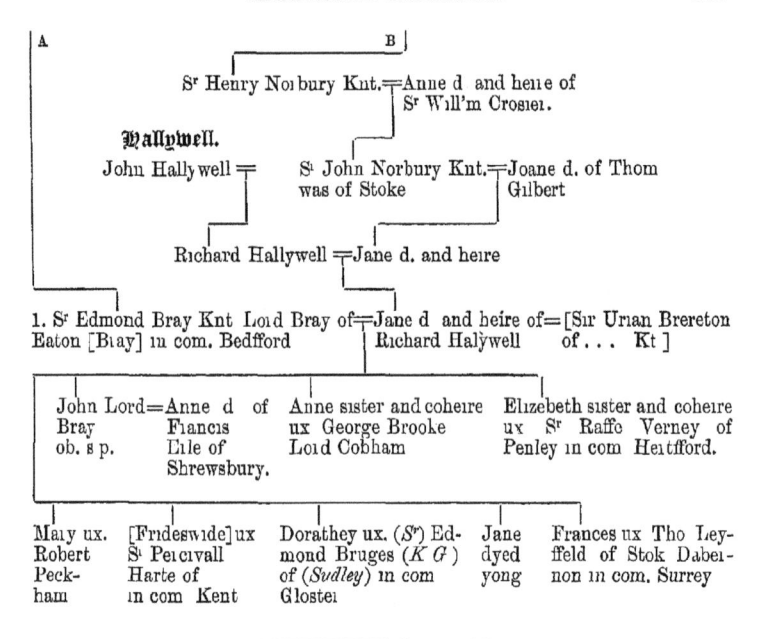

```
A                              B
                    Sr Henry Norbury Knt.=Anne d. and heire of
                                          Sr Will'm Crosier.
        𝕳𝖆𝖑𝖑𝖞𝖜𝖊𝖑𝖑.
        John Hallywell =      St John Norbury Knt.=Joane d. of Thom
                              was of Stoke            Gilbert

              Richard Hallywell =Jane d. and heire

1. Sr Edmond Bray Knt Lord Bray of=Jane d. and heire of=[Sir Urian Brereton
   Eaton [Bray] in com. Bedfford   Richard Halywell     of ... Kt]

   John Lord=Anne d. of    Anne sister and coheire    Elizebeth sister and coheire
   Bray     Francis        ux George Brooke           ux Sr Raffe Verney of
   ob. s p. Erle of         Lord Cobham                Penley in com. Hertfford.
            Shrewsbury.

   Mary ux.   [Frideswide] ux  Dorathey ux. (Sr) Ed-   Jane    Frances ux Tho Ley-
   Robert     St Percivall     mond Bruges (K G)       dyed    ffeld of Stok Daber-
   Peck-      Harte of         of (Sudley) in com.     yong    non in com. Surrey
   ham        in com. Kent     Gloster
```

𝕭𝖗𝖞𝖉𝖎𝖒𝖆𝖓

[of 𝕿𝖎𝖓𝖌𝖗𝖎𝖙𝖍].

ARMS.—*Quarterly of eight*—1, *Argent, on a cross sable five fusils ermine*, BRYDIMAN ; 2, *Sable, a lion rampant-guardant or*, BROCAS ; 3, *Sable, two lions passant-guardant argent*, ROCHES, 4 *Gules, six rayged staves argent, three, two and one*, , 5, *Argent, a cross between four mullets pierced gules*, BANBURY ; 6, *Or, a fesse gules between three mascles azure*, SCOVILL , 7, *Argent, a fesse sable between three bulls' heads gules, horned or*, BODINANT , 8, *Blank*

CREST.—*A wolf's head couped quarterly argent and sable*

```
            George Brydiman of Tingrave =Edith d. and sole heire
            in com. Bedfford.            of John Brockas

1 Edmond Brydi-=Margarett d of St Walter   2 Charles=Margerett d   Margerett
man of Tingrave | Waller of Groomsbridge   Brydiman  of ... Giles  ob. s p
in com. Bedfford.| in com. Kent Knt.       of Tin-   of ... in
                                           graue     com. Hunt.

        Mary d. and sole heire ux. John Cade sonn and heire of St Will'm
        Cade of King's Langley in com. Hertfford Knt
```

Bulkley
[of Odell].

ARMS.—*Quarterly of six*—1, *Sable, a chevron between three bulls' heads argent, armed or, a crescent for difference*, BULKELEY ; 2, *Party per pale or and argent, an eagle displayed sable*, BIRD ; 3, *Azure, on a fesse argent between six cross-crosslets fitchée or three escallops gules*, TITLEY ; 4, *Or, on a bend azure a fret of the field*, WORE ; 5, *Barry of six argent and gules*, MOLTON ; 6, *As No.* 1. *In the fesse point a crescent for difference.*

Robert Bulkley lord of the mannor of Bulkley in com. Cester.

Will'm Bulkley lord of Bulkley.

Robert Bulkley of Bulkley.=(Jane) d. of (S^r W^m) Butler Baron of Warrington.

1. Will'm Bulkley of Bulkley a quo Bulkley of Hayton in com. Cester *vide idem*.

2. Peter Bulkley.=Nichola d. and heire of Thom. Bird by whome hee had land in Alpraham.

John Bulkley.=Ardeene d. and heire of John Titley of Wore in com. Sallop.   Robert.

Hugh Bulkley of Wore.=Hellen d. of Thom. Wilbraham of Woodhey Esqr.

2. Roger Bulkley of Broxton.=Margery d. and heire of John Bird of Broxton.

Humffrey Bulkley of Woore *vid*. Chesh^r *he had issue William who had this Thomas*.=Scissely d. and heire of John Molton of Molton.   Issabell ux. Sr Lawrance Warren of Pointon.   Margarett ux. Thom. Tattenhall.

Thomas Bulkley of Wore.*=Elizebeth d. of Randall Grosvenor of Bellapre in com. . . . . Esqr.

1. Rowland Bulkley of Wore *vide* Sallop.   Margerett ux. Thom. Smyth.   Anne ux. Will'm Greene.   2. Edward Bulkley (*Rector*) of Odell in com. Bedfford Docter of Divinity had 3 sonns and 12 daughters.=Catherin ux. George Baker of Coulshurst.

Peter Bulkley of Odell.†   Nathaniell.   Paule dyed at Cambridge.

---

* In the MS. Thomas is placed as above ; his father William should immediately precede.
† Rector of Odell in 1620 ; ob. at Concord, N. America, 9 March 1658. ('Non-Conformists' Memorial,' ed. 1778, vol. i., p. 505.) For issue of Peter see Harvey's 'Hist. Willey Hundred,' p. 365.

Carter
[of Higham].

ARMS —*Azure, a talbot passant between three round buckles or*
CREST —*Out of a mural crown argent a demi-monkey proper*

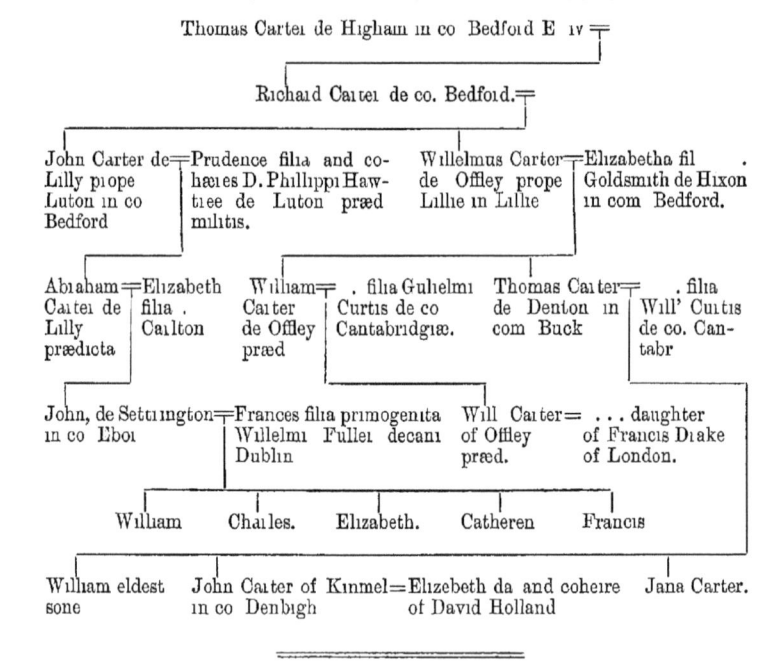

Thomas Carter de Higham in co Bedford E iv =

Richard Carter de co. Bedford. =

- John Carter de = Prudence filia and co-
  Lilly prope | hæres D. Phillippi Haw-
  Luton in co | tree de Luton præd
  Bedford | militis.
- Willelmus Carter = Elizabetha fil
  de Offley prope | Goldsmith de Hixon
  Lillie in Lillie | in com Bedford.

- Abraham = Elizabeth
  Carter de | filia .
  Lilly | Carlton
  prædicta
- William = . filia Guilelmi
  Carter | Curtis de co
  de Offley | Cantabridgiæ.
  præd
- Thomas Carter = . filia
  de Denton in | Will' Curtis
  com Buck | de co. Can-
  | tabr

- John, de Settrington = Frances filia primogenita
  in co Ebor | Willelmi Fuller decani
  | Dublin
- Will Carter = ... daughter
  of Offley | of Francis Drake
  præd. | of London.

William Charles. Elizabeth. Catheren Francis

William eldest John Carter of Kinmel = Elizebeth da and coheire Jana Carter.
sone   in co Denbigh   of David Holland

Chester†
[of Tilsworth].

ARMS —*Quarterly of six*—1, *Per pale argent and sable, a chevron engrailed between three rams' heads erased, horned or, all counterchanged, within a bordure engrailed gules bezantée,* CHESTER, 2, *Azure fretty argent, a mullet for difference,* CAVE , 3, *Gules, three mullets argent*   , 4, *Sable on a bend fleurie counter-fleurie or three escallops gules,* BROMFLEETE 5, *Ermine, on a bend sable three demi-luces argent,*   , 6, *Argent, three moorcocks vert, beaked and membered gules.*
CREST.—*A ram's head couped argent, armed or, charged with a mullet for difference.*

William Chester of London gent. =
A |

* By a later hand   *Cf* 'Le Neve's Knights,' p 65, ed Harl Soc
† *Cf* 'Le Neve's Knights,' p 16

THE VISITATION OF BEDFORDSHIRE.

A |

John Chester of London gent.=Joane d. of .... Hill of London.

- Nicholas Chester of London.
- Elizabeth d. of Thomas Lovett of Astwell in com. Northampton 1 wiffe. =Sʳ William Chester Kⁿᵗ lord maior of London 1561. = Elizabeth d. of Thomas Turner of .... and widdow of Will'm Beswick of London Alderman.

- Richard Chester ob. s.p.
- Frances ux. Wᵐ Robinson of London grocer.
- Jane ux. Richard Offley brother of Sʳ Thomas.
- Emme ux. John Gardiner of London grocer.
- Susan ux. John Trott of London.
- Thomas a bishop in Ireland 2nd son.

- John 3rd son.
- Danyell 4th son.
- Francis 5th son.
  s.p.
- Judith d. and coheire of Anthony Cave of Chichley in com. Buck. 1 wiffe. =William Chester of London Esqʳ eldest son. =Mary d. of [John] ffryer of [London] in com. [Midd.] 2nd wife.

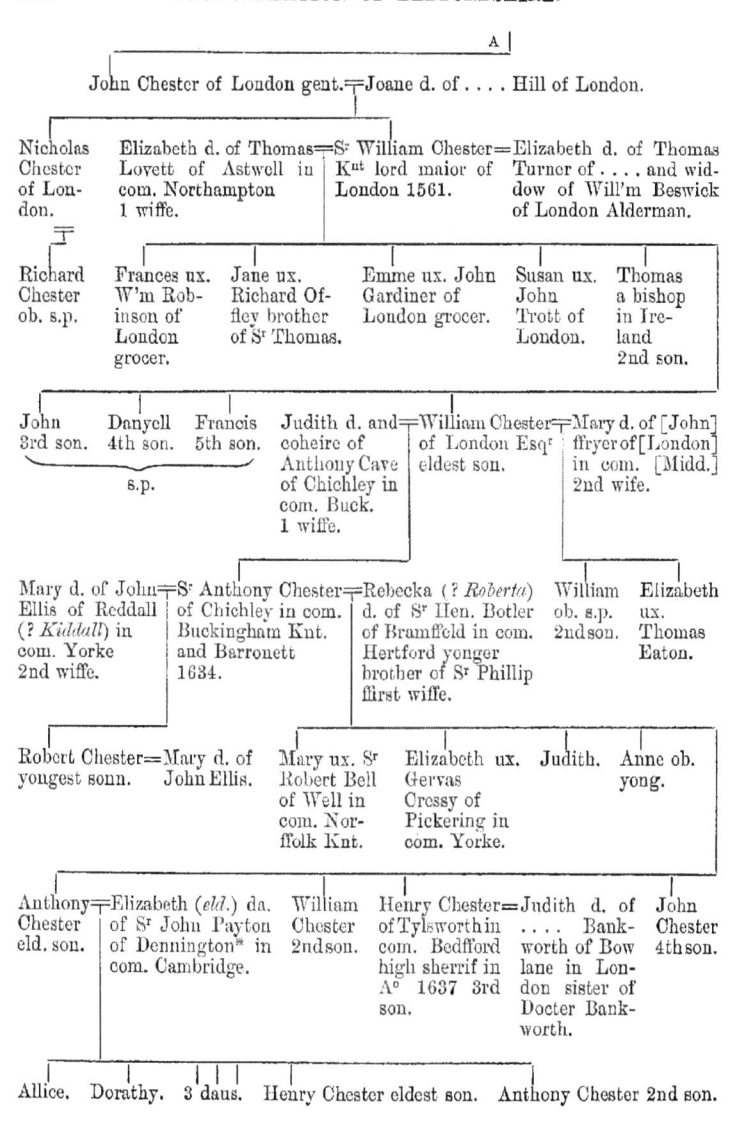

- Mary d. of John Ellis of Reddall (? *Kiddall*) in com. Yorke 2nd wiffe. =Sʳ Anthony Chester of Chichley in com. Buckingham Knt. and Barronett 1634. =Rebecka (? *Roberta*) d. of Sʳ Hen. Botler of Bramffeld in com. Hertford yonger brother of Sʳ Phillip ffirst wiffe.
- William ob. s.p. 2nd son.
- Elizabeth ux. Thomas Eaton.

- Robert Chester youngest sonn. =Mary d. of John Ellis.
- Mary ux. Sʳ Robert Bell of Well in com. Norffolk Knt.
- Elizabeth ux. Gervas Cressy of Pickering in com. Yorke.
- Judith.
- Anne ob. yong.

- Anthony Chester eld. son. =Elizabeth (*eld.*) da. of Sʳ John Payton of Dennington* in com. Cambridge.
- William Chester 2nd son.
- Henry Chester of Tylsworth in com. Bedfford high sherrif in Aᵒ 1637 3rd son. =Judith d. of .... Bankworth of Bow lane in London sister of Docter Bankworth.
- John Chester 4th son.

Allice. Dorathy. 3 daus. Henry Chester eldest son. Anthony Chester 2nd son.

---

* Dodington in the Isle of Ely.

ADDITIONAL PEDIGREES.

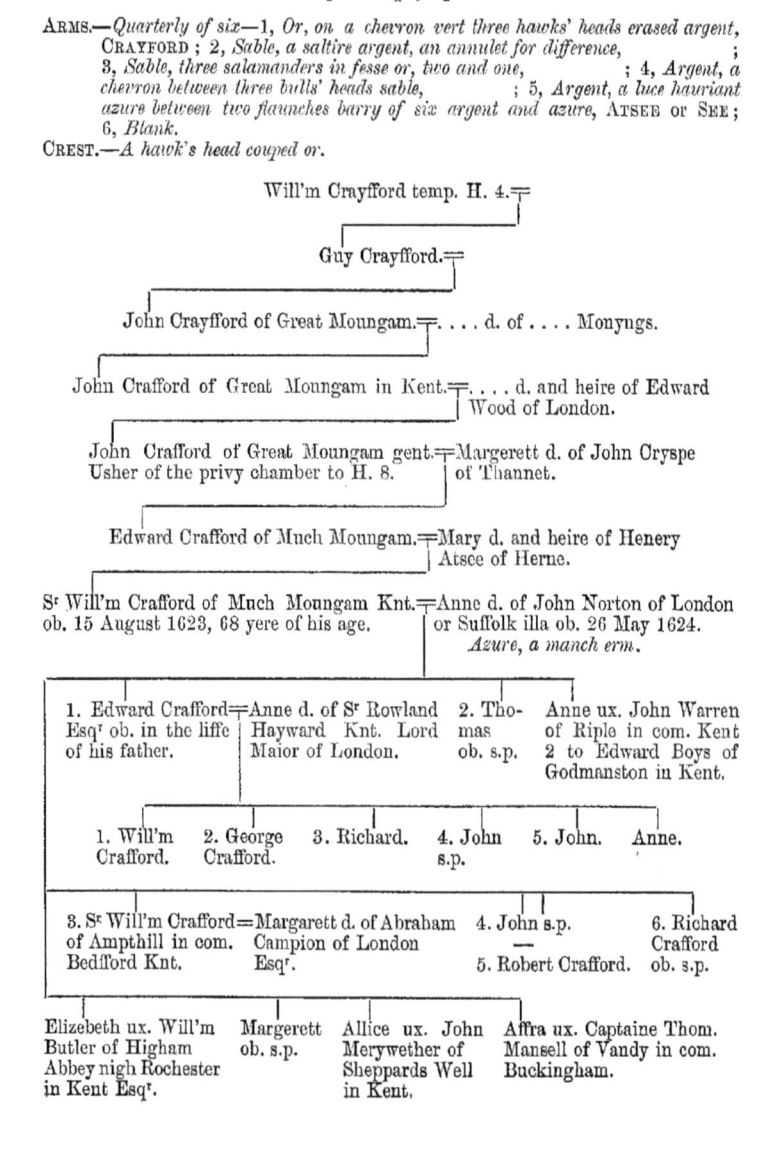

Crayford
[of Ampthill].

ARMS.—*Quarterly of six*—1, *Or, on a chevron vert three hawks' heads erased argent,* CRAYFORD ; 2, *Sable, a saltire argent, an annulet for difference,* ; 3, *Sable, three salamanders in fesse or, two and one,* ; 4, *Argent, a chevron between three bulls' heads sable,* ; 5, *Argent, a luce hauriant azure between two flaunches barry of six argent and azure,* ATSEE or SEE ; 6, *Blank.*

CREST.—*A hawk's head couped or.*

Will'm Crayfford temp. H. 4.=

Guy Crayfford.=

John Crayfford of Great Moungam.= .... d. of .... Monyngs.

John Crafford of Great Moungam in Kent.= .... d. and heire of Edward Wood of London.

John Crafford of Great Moungam gent. Usher of the privy chamber to H. 8. =Margerett d. of John Cryspe of Thannet.

Edward Crafford of Much Moungam.=Mary d. and heire of Henery Atsce of Herne.

S⁣ʳ Will'm Crafford of Much Monngam Knt. ob. 15 August 1623, 68 yere of his age. =Anne d. of John Norton of London or Suffolk illa ob. 26 May 1624. *Azure, a manch erm.*

1. Edward Crafford Esqʳ ob. in the liffe of his father. =Anne d. of Sʳ Rowland Hayward Knt. Lord Maior of London.

2. Thomas ob. s.p.

Anne ux. John Warren of Riple in com. Kent 2 to Edward Boys of Godmanston in Kent.

1. Will'm Crafford. 2. George Crafford. 3. Richard. 4. John s.p. 5. John. Anne.

3. Sʳ Will'm Crafford of Ampthill in com. Bedford Knt. =Margarett d. of Abraham Campion of London Esqʳ.

4. John s.p. —
5. Robert Crafford.

6. Richard Crafford ob. s.p.

Elizebeth ux. Will'm Butler of Higham Abbey nigh Rochester in Kent Esqʳ.

Margerett ob. s.p.

Allice ux. John Merywether of Sheppards Well in Kent.

Affra ux. Captaine Thom. Mansell of Vandy in com. Buckingham.

Faldo

[of Maulden].

ARMS (TWO SHIELDS).—I., *Quarterly*—1, *Gules, three stags' heads cabossed or, attired argent,* FALDO ; 2, *Gules, on a chevron between three escallops or a castle of the field,* CHAMBERLEYN ; 3, *Gules, a saltire ermine,* NEVELL of Rolston ; 4, *Blank.* II., *Quarterly of ten*—1, FALDO ; 2, CHAMBERLEYN ; 3, NEVELL ; 4, *Or fretty gules, on a canton per pale argent and ermine a lymphad sable,* NEVIL of Holt ; 5, *Gules billettée sable, a lion rampant or,* BULMER ; 6, *Bendy of six or and vert, a chevron ermine,* INGLEBERT ; 7, *Argent, two bars nebulée sable, a canton ermine,* ROLLESTON ; 8, *Azure, a fleur-de-lys ermine,* PALMER ; 9, *Bendy of six or and azure, a canton ermine,* BISHOPTON ; 10, *Argent, a chevron gules, a chief indented vert,* FANCOTS.

Faldo is a hamlet in . . . .

"The field is Gules, three stags' heads trunked or, armed or, attired argent. This Coate is borne by the name of Faldo in the county of Bedford, where there are diuerse gentlemen of that name yet remayning, and some of them owners of the said manner (as I take it)." (Guillim, p. 183.)

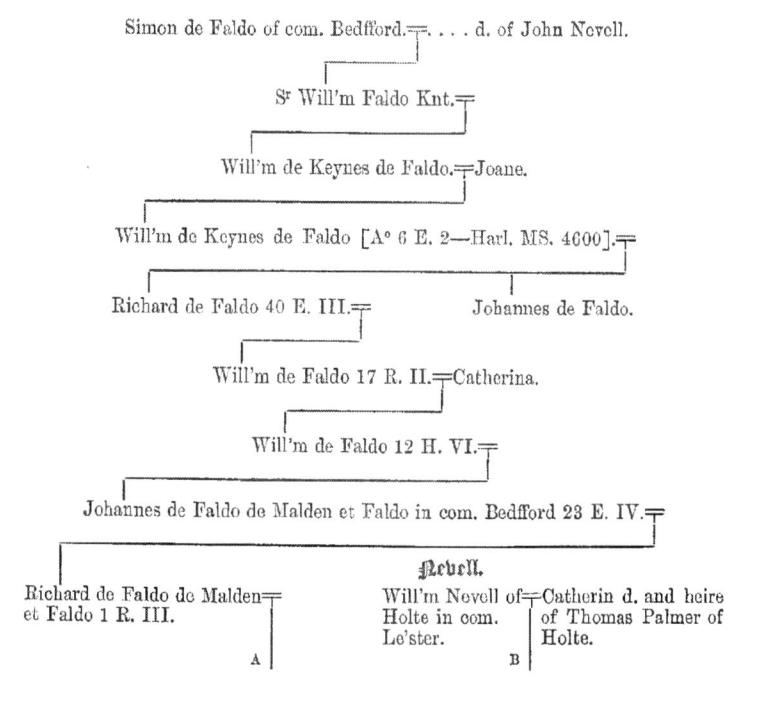

Simon de Faldo of com. Bedfford.=. . . . d. of John Nevell.
 |
Sr Will'm Faldo Knt.=
 |
Will'm de Keynes de Faldo.=Joane.
 |
Will'm de Keynes de Faldo [A° 6 E. 2—Harl. MS. 4600].=
 |
Richard de Faldo 40 E. III.=   Johannes de Faldo.
 |
Will'm de Faldo 17 R. II.=Catherina.
 |
Will'm de Faldo 12 H. VI.=
 |
Johannes de Faldo de Malden et Faldo in com. Bedfford 23 E. IV.=

Nevell.

Richard de Faldo de Malden=   Will'm Nevell of=Catherin d. and heire
et Faldo 1 R. III.   Holte in com.   of Thomas Palmer of
                                                Le'ster.   Holte.
A   B

ADDITIONAL PEDIGREES.

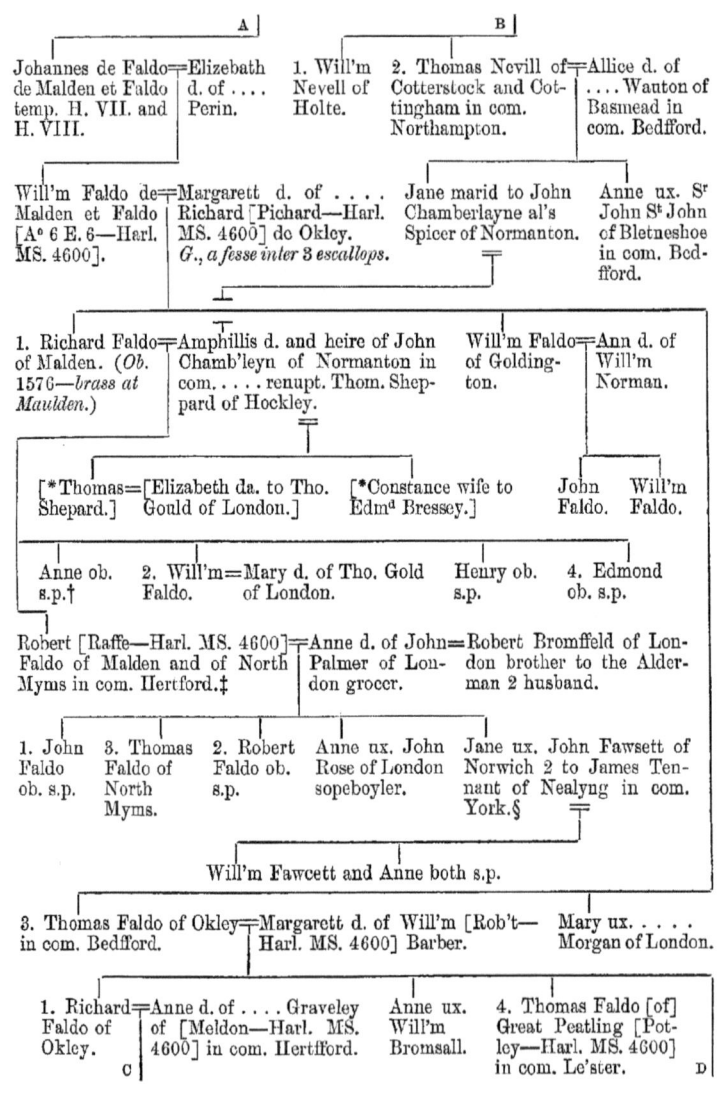

A | **B**

Johannes de Faldo = Elizebath d. of .... Perin. | 1. Will'm Nevell of Holte. | 2. Thomas Nevill of Cotterstock and Cottingham in com. Northampton. = Allice d. of ....Wauton of Basmead in com. Bedfford.

Will'm Faldo de Malden et Faldo [A° 6 E. 6—Harl. MS. 4600]. = Margarett d. of .... Richard [Pichard—Harl. MS. 4600] de Okley. G., *a fesse inter 3 escallops.* | Jane marid to John Chamberlayne al's Spicer of Normanton. | Anne ux. S⁼ John S⁼ John of Bletneshoe in com. Bedfford.

1. Richard Faldo of Malden. (*Ob.* 1576—*brass at Maulden.*) = Amphillis d. and heire of John Chamb'leyn of Normanton in com. .... renupt. Thom. Sheppard of Hockley. | Will'm Faldo of Goldington. = Ann d. of Will'm Norman.

[*Thomas Shepard.] = [Elizabeth da. to Tho. Gould of London.] | [*Constance wife to Edm⁼ Bressey.] | John Faldo. | Will'm Faldo.

Anne ob. s.p.† | 2. Will'm Faldo. = Mary d. of Tho. Gold of London. | Henry ob. s.p. | 4. Edmond ob. s.p.

Robert [Raffe—Harl. MS. 4600] Faldo of Malden and of North Myms in com. Hertford.‡ = Anne d. of John Palmer of London grocer. = Robert Bromffeld of London brother to the Alderman 2 husband.

1. John Faldo ob. s.p. | 3. Thomas Faldo of North Myms. | 2. Robert Faldo ob. s.p. | Anne ux. John Rose of London sopeboyler. | Jane ux. John Fawsett of Norwich 2 to James Tennant of Nealyng in com. York.§

Will'm Fawcett and Anne both s.p.

3. Thomas Faldo of Okley in com. Bedfford. = Margarett d. of Will'm [Rob't—Harl. MS. 4600] Barber. | Mary ux. .... Morgan of London.

1. Richard Faldo of Okley. = Anne d. of .... Graveley of [Meldon—Harl. MS. 4600] in com. Hertfford. | Anne ux. Will'm Bromsall. | 4. Thomas Faldo [of] Great Peatling [Potley—Harl. MS. 4600] in com. Le'ster.

C | **D**

* Harl. MS. 4600.   † Ob. 1594, æt. 18 ; brass in Maulden Church.
‡ In Westham Church, co. Midd., is a monument to Rob't Faldo, Esq., 1613 ; Francis his fifth son, 1632 ; and John Fawcit, gent. (who mar. Jane Faldo), 1625.
§ "Of Westham in com. Essex, A° 1634." ('Visit. of Essex,' p. 500, Harl. Soc.)

THE VISITATION OF BEDFORDSHIRE.

C

John Faldo. — Richard ob. s.p. — Robert Faldo. — Mary [d. and coheir—Harl. MS. 4600] 1 ux. John Birkett of London vintner 2 to Stephen Knight of London vintner.

D

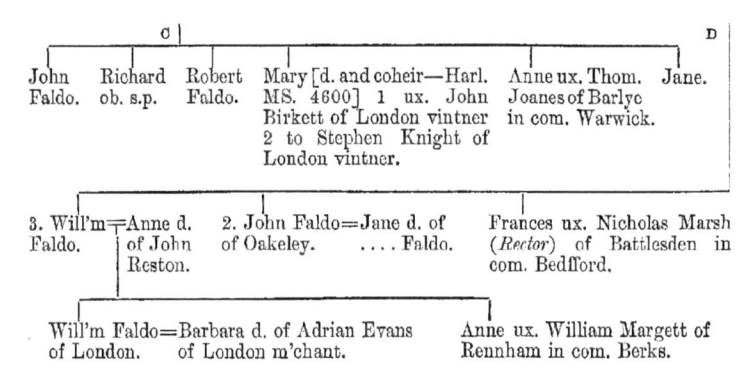

Anne ux. Thom. Joanes of Barlyc in com. Warwick. — Jane.

3. Will'm Faldo. = Anne d. of John Reston.

2. John Faldo = Jane d. of .... Faldo. of Oakeley.

Frances ux. Nicholas Marsh (*Rector*) of Battlesden in com. Bedfford.

Will'm Faldo of London. = Barbara d. of Adrian Evans of London m'chant.

Anne ux. William Margett of Rennham in com. Berks.

Fishe

[of Southill].

ARMS.—*Azure, a fesse argent, over all on a bend gules five mullets or.*
[CREST.—*A lion rampant argent, holding in his dexter paw a mullet sable.*]

Thomas Fishe of Ayott Mount Fitchett. = Elizabeth da. of William [George] Hyde of Throcking in com. Hertfford.

Elizabeth d. of Auditor Thompson 1 wiffe. = George Fishe of Southill eldest son. = Judith d. of John Hamby of London Auditor of the prest 2 wiffe.

Sr John Fishe of Southill in com. Bedfford Knt. and Baronett in Ireland. = Mary d. of Edward Pulter of Bradffeld and Wymondley in com. Hertfford.

Elizabeth ux. Sr Richard Sutton Knt. Auditor of the prest.

Dorothey ux. Docter Michell Boyle Bishop of Waterford in Ireland.

Sr Edward Fishe Knt. and Baronett in Ireland. = Elizebeth d. and coheire of Martin Heton Bishop (*of*) Ely.

Mary ux. John Blundell Brother to Sr Francis.

Anne ux. Sr George Sexton of .... in Ireland Knt.

Edward Fishe 6 yeare ould in May 1635.

1. Allice.

2. Lettice.

3. Anne.

4. Elizabeth.

ADDITIONAL PEDIGREES.   171

FitzGeffrey

[of Wilshamstead].

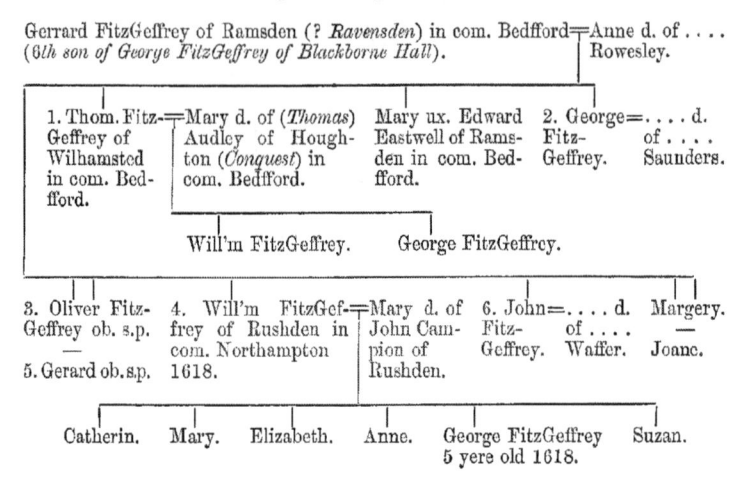

Gerrard FitzGeffrey of Ramsden (? *Ravensden*) in com. Bedfford=Anne d. of ....
(*6th son of George FitzGeffrey of Blackborne Hall*). | Rowesley.

1. Thom. Fitz-=Mary d. of (*Thomas*) Mary ux. Edward   2. George=.... d.
Geffrey of   Audley of Hough-   Eastwell of Rams-   Fitz-   of ....
Wilhamsted   ton (*Conquest*) in   den in com. Bed-   Geffrey.   Saunders.
in com. Bed-   com. Bedfford.   fford.
fford.

            Will'm FitzGeffrey.   George FitzGeffrey.

3. Oliver Fitz- 4. Will'm FitzGef-=Mary d. of   6. John=.... d.   Margery.
Geffrey ob. s.p. frey of Rushden in John Cam-   Fitz-   of ....   —
—   com. Northampton   pion of   Geffrey. Waffer.   Joane.
5. Gerard ob.s.p. 1618.   Rushden.

Catherin.   Mary.   Elizabeth.   Anne.   George FitzGeffrey   Suzan.
                                         5 yere old 1618.

Fitzhenry

[of Campton].

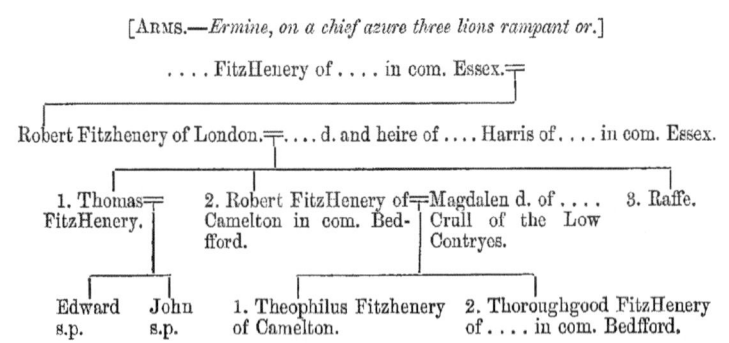

[ARMS.—*Ermine, on a chief azure three lions rampant or.*]

.... FitzHenery of .... in com. Essex.=

Robert Fitzhenery of London.=.... d. and heire of .... Harris of.... in com. Essex.

1. Thomas=   2. Robert FitzHenery of=Magdalen d. of ....   3. Raffe.
FitzHenery.   Camelton in com. Bed- Crull of the Low
              fford.   Contryes.

Edward   John   1. Theophilus Fitzhenery   2. Thoroughgood FitzHenery
s.p.   s.p.   of Camelton.   of .... in com. Bedfford.

Franklyn.*

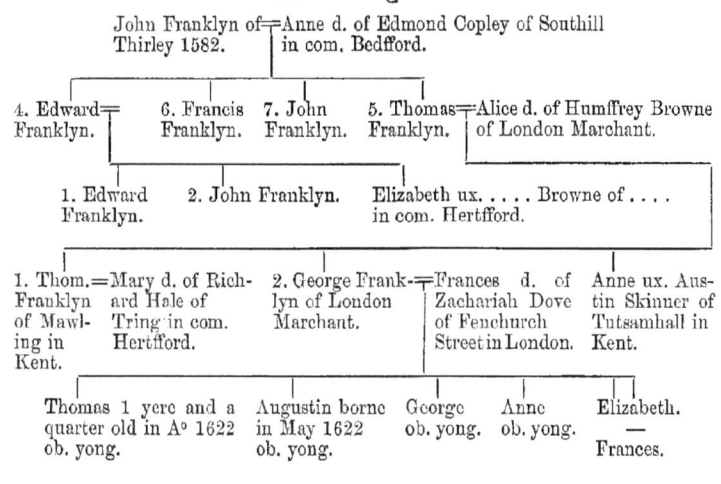

John Franklyn of Thirley 1582. = Anne d. of Edmond Copley of Southill in com. Bedfford.

- 4. Edward Franklyn. =
- 6. Francis Franklyn.
- 7. John Franklyn.
- 5. Thomas Franklyn. = Alice d. of Humffrey Browne of London Marchant.

- 1. Edward Franklyn.
- 2. John Franklyn.
- Elizabeth ux. .... Browne of .... in com. Hertfford.

- 1. Thom. Franklyn of Mawling in Kent. = Mary d. of Richard Hale of Tring in com. Hertfford.
- 2. George Franklyn of London Marchant. = Frances d. of Zachariah Dove of Fenchurch Street in London.
- Anne ux. Austin Skinner of Tutsamhall in Kent.

- Thomas 1 yere and a quarter old in A° 1622 ob. yong.
- Augustin borne in May 1622 ob. yong.
- George ob. yong.
- Anne ob. yong.
- Elizabeth. —
- Frances.

Gascoigne

[of Cardington].

ARMS.—*Quarterly of six*—1, *Argent, on a pale sable a demi-luce erect or*, GASCOIGN; 2, *Gules, three pickaxes azure*, PIGOTT; 3, *Or, three bars azure, in chief three torteaux*, WAKE; 4, *Quarterly or and gules, a bend of the second*, BEAUCHAMP; 5, *Ermine, a lion passant sable*, VINTER [? WITHER]; 6, *Ermine, a saltire gules*, SCARGILL.

CREST.—*A demi-luce's head erect between two ostrich-feathers or.*

Beauchamp.

Will'm Bechamp Baron of (*Bedford*). =

- .... Gascoigne. = ... d. and heire of .... Gawthorpe.
- Will'm Bechamp (*Baron of Bedford*). =

Pigott.

- William Gascoigne. = Elizebeth d. and heire of Will'm Bolton.
  A
- Michell Pigott. = Joane d. and coheire of Will'm Becham Baron of (*Bedford*) in com. Bedfford.†
  B
- Will'm Paynell 2 husband.

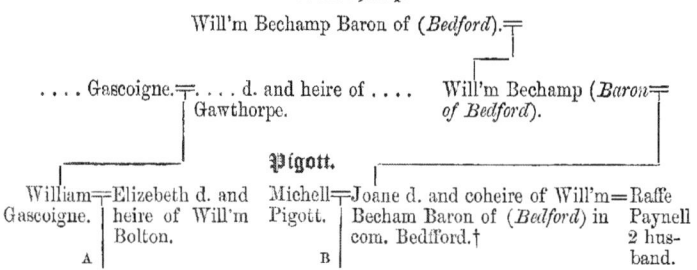

* *Cf.* 'Visitation of London,' vol. i., p. 290, ed. Harl. Soc.
† There is an error here: Joane was daughter of the first-named William, and sister (and coheir with her sisters) of the second-named William.—ED.

ADDITIONAL PEDIGREES.

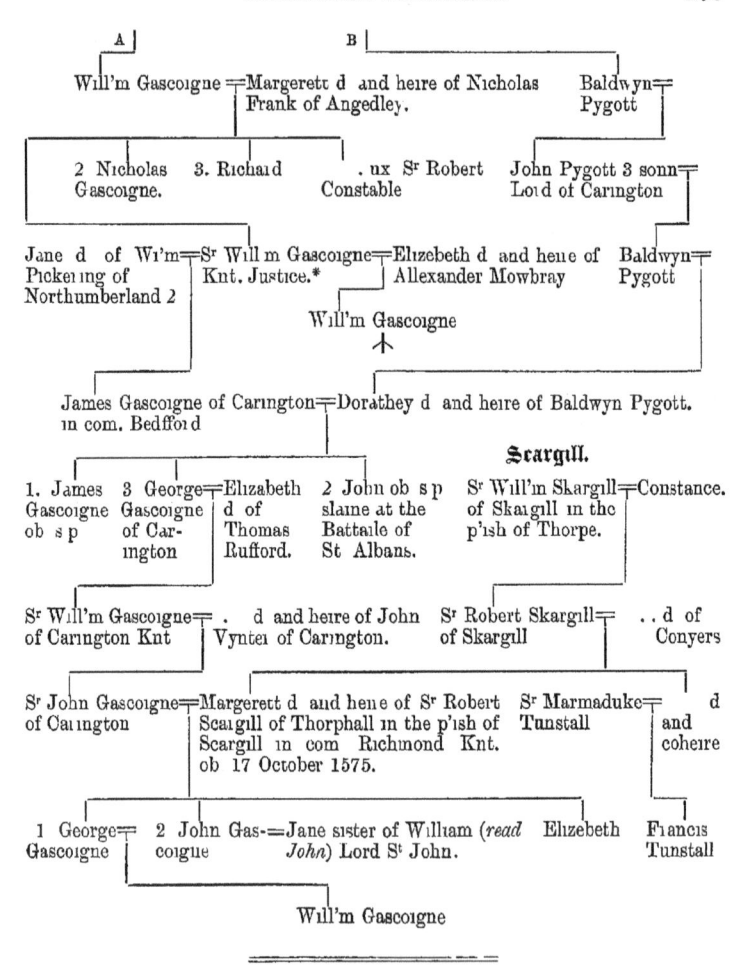

```
         A                              B
Will'm Gascoigne =Margerett d and heire of Nicholas    Baldwyn=
                 Frank of Angedley.                    Pygott

  2 Nicholas   3. Richard    . ux Sr Robert   John Pygott 3 sonn=
  Gascoigne.                 Constable        Lord of Carington

Jane d of Wi'm=Sr Will'm Gascoigne=Elizebeth d and heire of   Baldwyn=
Pickering of   Knt. Justice.*    Allexander Mowbray          Pygott
Northumberland 2
                       Will'm Gascoigne

         James Gascoigne of Carington=Dorathey d and heire of Baldwyn Pygott.
         in com. Bedfford
```

```
                                                    Scargill.
1. James   3 George=Elizabeth   2 John ob s p    Sr Will'm Skargill=Constance.
Gascoigne  Gascoigne  d of      slaine at the    of Skargill in the
ob s p     of Car-    Thomas    Battaile of      p'ish of Thorpe.
           ington     Rufford.  St Albans.

Sr Will'm Gascoigne=  . d and heire of John   Sr Robert Skargill=  ..d of
of Carington Knt      Vynter of Carington.    of Skargill          Conyers

Sr John Gascoigne=Margerett d and heire of Sr Robert   Sr Marmaduke=       d
of Carington     Scargill of Thorphall in the p'ish of Tunstall       and
                 Scargill in com Richmond Knt.                        coheire
                 ob 17 October 1575.

  1 George=  2 John Gas-=Jane sister of William (read   Elizebeth   Francis
  Gascoigne  coigne       John) Lord St John.                       Tunstall

              Will'm Gascoigne
```

𝕲𝖗𝖊𝖞

[of 𝖘𝖊𝖌𝖊𝖓𝖍𝖔𝖊 𝖎𝖓 𝕽𝖎𝖉𝖌𝖒𝖔𝖓𝖙].

John Gray of Barley=Grace d of Will'm Hanchett of Lech-
in com Hertfford.   worth in com. Hertfford. 1 wiffe
        A

* In Cardington Church is a brass to Sir Wm Gascoigne, Comptroller of the Household to Cardinal Wolsey, and his two wives, in heraldic dresses, circa 1540, inscription lost He died in 1412 according to Burke.

THE VISITATION OF BEDFORDSHIRE.

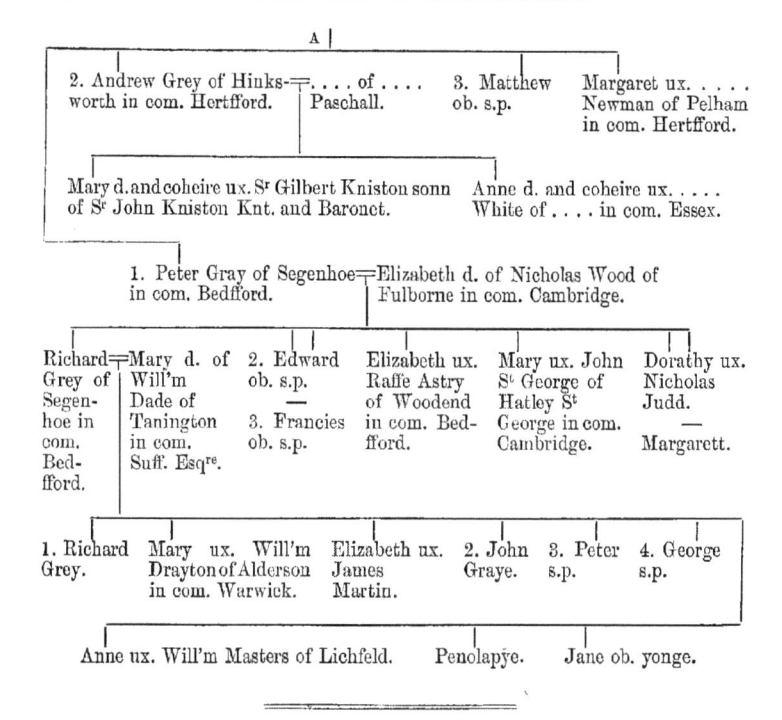

A

2. Andrew Grey of Hinks-=. . . . of . . . .   3. Matthew   Margaret ux. . . . .
worth in com. Hertfford.   Paschall.   ob. s.p.   Newman of Pelham
                                                  in com. Hertfford.

Mary d. and coheire ux. Sr Gilbert Kniston sonn   Anne d. and coheire ux. . . . .
of Sr John Kniston Knt. and Baronet.   White of . . . . in com. Essex.

1. Peter Gray of Segenhoe=Elizabeth d. of Nicholas Wood of
in com. Bedfford.   Fulborne in com. Cambridge.

Richard=Mary d. of   2. Edward   Elizabeth ux.   Mary ux. John   Dorathy ux.
Grey of | Will'm   ob. s.p.   Raffe Astry   St George of   Nicholas
Segen- | Dade of   —   of Woodend   Hatley St   Judd.
hoe in | Tanington 3. Francies in com. Bed-   George in com. —
com. | in com.   ob. s.p.   fford.   Cambridge.   Margarett.
Bed- | Suff. Esqre.
fford.

1. Richard   Mary ux. Will'm   Elizabeth ux.   2. John   3. Peter   4. George
Grey.   Drayton of Alderson James   Graye.   s.p.   s.p.
             in com. Warwick.   Martin.

Anne ux. Will'm Masters of Lichfeld.   Penolapye.   Jane ob. yonge.

Hillersden

[of Elstow].

ARMS.—*Argent, on a chevron sable three bulls' heads of the field, within a bordure engrailed of the second.*

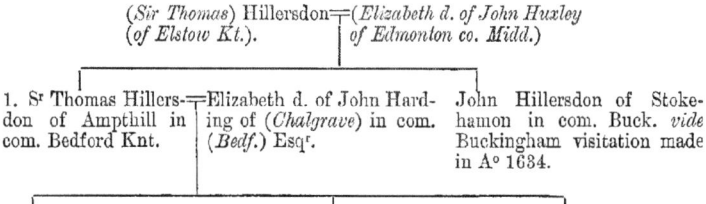

(Sir Thomas) Hillersdon=(Elizabeth d. of John Huxley
(of Elstow Kt.).   of Edmonton co. Midd.)

1. Sr Thomas Hillers-=Elizabeth d. of John Hard-   John Hillersdon of Stoke-
don of Ampthill in   ing of (*Chalgrave*) in com. hamon in com. Buck. *vide*
com. Bedford Knt.   (*Bedf.*) Esqr.   Buckingham visitation made
                                                   in Ao 1634.

Thomas=Allice d. of Sr Will'm   Joane ux. Thomas Baker   Elizabeth ux.
Hillers- Litton of Knebworth   of Smalebridge in com.   Thomas Rouse of
don.   in com. Hertford Knt.   Suffolk.   . . . . in com. . . . . .

Hitch

[of Kempston].

ARMS.—*Or, a bend vair between two cotises indented gules*
CREST.—*An antelope's head erased sable, horned and vulned through the neck with an arrow or, feathered and barbed argent, holding the end in the mouth*

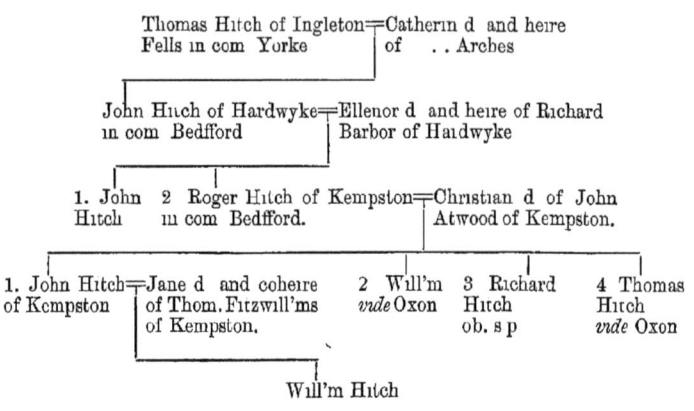

Thomas Hitch of Ingleton Fells in com. Yorke = Catherin d. and heire of . . Arches

John Hitch of Hardwyke in com. Bedfford = Ellenor d. and heire of Richard Barbor of Hardwyke

1. John Hitch
2. Roger Hitch of Kempston in com. Bedfford = Christian d. of John Atwood of Kempston.

1. John Hitch of Kempston = Jane d. and coheire of Thom. Fitzwill'ms of Kempston.
2. Will'm *vide* Oxon
3. Richard Hitch ob. s p
4. Thomas Hitch *vide* Oxon

Will'm Hitch

Hoddesdon

[of Leighton-Buzzard].

ARMS.—*Argent, a bend wavy gules between two horseshoes azure*
CREST.—*A man's head couped at the shoulders proper, vested azure, collared or, on the head a cap of maintenance turned up ermine*

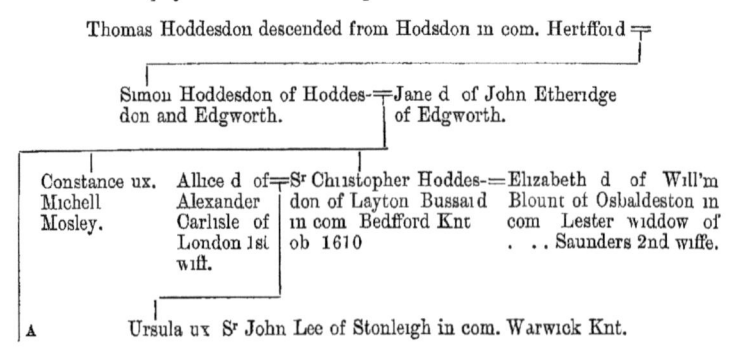

Thomas Hoddesdon descended from Hodsdon in com. Hertfford =

Simon Hoddesdon of Hoddesdon and Edgworth. = Jane d. of John Etheridge of Edgworth.

Constance ux. Michell Mosley.
Alice d. of Alexander Carlisle of London 1st wiff.
= Sr Christopher Hoddesdon of Layton Bussard in com. Bedfford Knt ob 1610
= Elizabeth d. of Will'm Blount of Osbaldeston in com. Lester widdow of . . . Saunders 2nd wiffe.

A
Ursula ux Sr John Lee of Stonleigh in com. Warwick Knt.

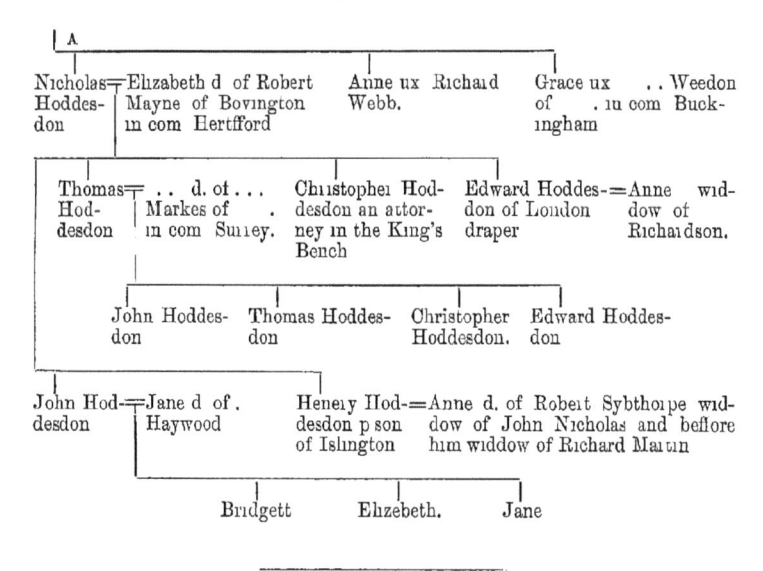

THE VISITATION OF BEDFORDSHIRE.

```
A
├─ Nicholas Hoddesdon == Elizabeth d. of Robert Mayne of Bovington in com Hertffford
├─ Anne ux Richard Webb.
└─ Grace ux .. Weedon of . in com Buckingham
```

Children of Nicholas and Elizabeth:
- Thomas Hoddesdon == .. d. of .. Markes of .. in com Surrey.
- Christopher Hoddesdon an attorney in the King's Bench
- Edward Hoddesdon of London draper == Anne widdow of Richardson.

Children of Thomas:
- John Hoddesdon
- Thomas Hoddesdon
- Christopher Hoddesdon.
- Edward Hoddesdon

- John Hoddesdon == Jane d of . Haywood
- Henery Hoddesdon p son of Islington == Anne d. of Robert Sybthorpe widdow of John Nicholas and beffore him widdow of Richard Martin

Children:
- Bridgett
- Elizebeth.
- Jane

𝔥𝔬𝔡𝔤𝔨𝔦𝔰

[of Ampthill].

ARMS.—*Sable, a chevron or between three griffins' heads erased argent*
CREST.—*A cubit arm erect in a coat of mail argent, garnished or, holding in the hand proper a griffin's head erased of the second, beaked azure.*

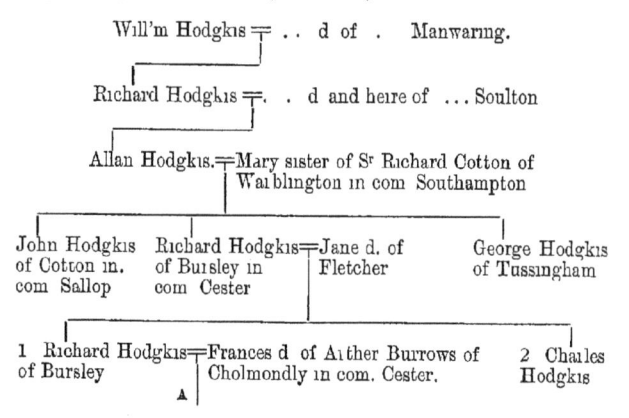

```
Will'm Hodgkis == .. d of . Manwaring.
  │
Richard Hodgkis == . . d and heire of … Soulton
  │
Allan Hodgkis == Mary sister of Sr Richard Cotton of Warblington in com Southampton
  │
  ├─ John Hodgkis of Cotton in. com Sallop
  ├─ Richard Hodgkis of Bursley in com Cester == Jane d. of Fletcher
  └─ George Hodgkis of Tussingham
```

Children of Richard and Jane:
- 1 Richard Hodgkis of Bursley == Frances d. of Arther Burrows of Cholmondly in com. Cester.
- 2 Charles Hodgkis

A

ADDITIONAL PEDIGREES.

A

| 2 Arther Hodgkis of London | 3 Thomas Hodgkis | Elizebeth ux Thom Hill of Sovelsho (*Silsoe*) in com. Bedffoid | 1 Richard Hodgkis of Ampthill in com Bedffoid = Elizebeth d of . . Chapman widdow of Geffrey Palmer of Ampthill |

| Jane ux Will'm Dod of Haithill in com. Cester. | Dorathey ux John Povery of . . in com Cester. | Margerett ux John Dod |

Hurlestone

[of Cardington].

ARMS —*Quarterly*—1, *Argent, four ermine spots in cross sable*, HURLESTONE, 2, *Argent, two bendlets engrailed sable, the upper one couped at the upper extremity*, SCARISBRICK,[*] 3, *Argent, a chevron between three stone-bows sable*, HURLFSTONE, 4, *Blank*

John Hurleston of Hurleston in com. Lanc. [t'pe E. 1] ⚭

Will'm Hurleston of Hurleston in com Lanc ⚭

Nicholas Hurleston of Hurleston. ⚭ Elinor d. of . . Chisnall of . . . . in com. Lanc.

1. Robert Hurleston of Hurleston ⚭ Agnes d of . . Scarsbrike of Scarsbrike   2. Hugh Hurleston   3. Gilbert Hurleston.

1. Humffrey Hurleston of Hurleston ⚭ Issabell d. of Thomas Poole of Poole in com Cester   2 James Hurleston

Thomas Hurleston of Hurleston ⚭ Elizabeth d of Adam Birkenhed of . in com. .   Maud ux Rushton of Lanc   Allice ux. Peter Farington of Littell Farrington

1 Richard Hurleston of Hurleston in com Lanc and of Picton in com Cester *vide* Chester [viv 1566] ⚭ Elizabeth d of James Shalcrosse of Manchester.   2 Randall ⚭ Margarett.   3 Robert

A

[*] In the 'Visitation of Cheshire,' 1580, Harl Soc, vol xviii, p 130, the second coat is assigned to WAGSTAFF

A A

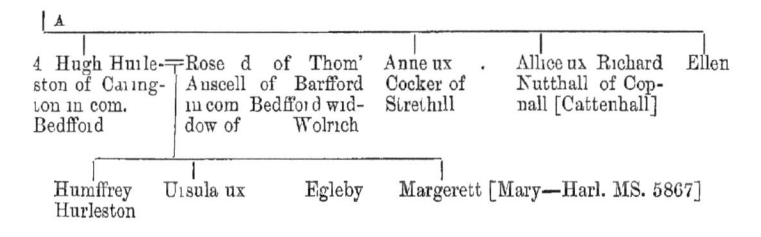

THE VISITATION OF BEDFORDSHIRE

A

4 Hugh Hurleston of Carington in com. Bedfford = Rose d of Thom' Auscell of Barfford in com Bedfford widdow of Wolrich | Anne ux Cocker of Strethill | . | Allice ux Richard Nutthall of Copnall [Cattenhall] | Ellen

Children:
- Humffrey Hurleston
- Ursula ux
- Egleby
- Margerett [Mary—Harl. MS. 5867]

Kent
[of Henlow].

John Kent of Aston in com Hertfford. = Mary d of Thomas Saunders (of) Agmondisham in com. Buckingham.

1 Thomas Kent *vide* Hertfford | 3 Edward Kent of Henlow in com Bedfford = Jane d of John Fareclough of Weston in com Hertfford | 2 John Kent *vide* Hertfford

Edward Kent of Henlow. = . d of . Harding of . . in com Bedfford | 2 John Kent | 3 Thomas Kent | 4 Charles Kent.

Lavinder*
[of Felmersham].

ARMS.—*Per fesse gules and or, a pale and three round buckles of the second, tongues pendent azure* †

Richard Lavinder of Felmersham in com Bedfford = Anne d of . Risley of Risley in com Bedfford

1 Will'm Lavinder of the towne of Bedfford = | 2 John Lavinder of Stewkley in com Huntington | 4 Richard Lavinder of Fellmersham in com Bedfford | Anne maud to Henery Joy of the towne of Bedfford

3 Thomas Lavinder of London Grocer 1634 = Margerett d of Ambrose Salesbery of Ravenston in com Lester

Thomas Lavinder 4 yere old 1634 | Elizebeth | Margerett | Mary | Anne | Sara

---

* *Cf* 'Visitation of London,' 1633-4, ed Harl Soc , vol ii , p 52
† ' A smale vellom escuchion in collers thus subscribed Wm DETHECK, York Herald, 1580."

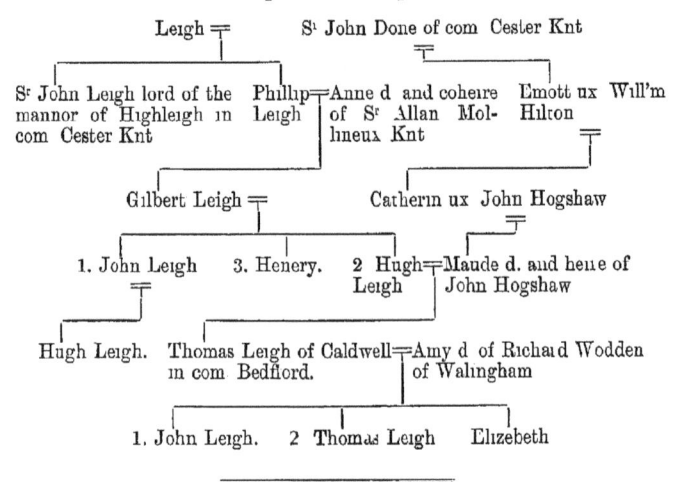

Leigh
[of Cauldwell].

```
Leigh =T= Sᵗ John Done of com Cester Knt
         |
 ┌───────┼───────────────────┬───────────────┐
Sʳ John Leigh lord of the   Phillip=T=Anne d and coheire   Emott ux Will'm
mannor of Highleigh in      Leigh  of Sʳ Allan Mol-        Hilton
com Cester Knt                     lineux Knt
         |
 ┌───────┴───────┐
Gilbert Leigh =T=                Catherin ux John Hogshaw
         |
 ┌───────────────┬──────────────┐
1. John Leigh   3. Henery.    2 Hugh=T=Maude d. and heire of
   =T=                          Leigh    John Hogshaw
   |                                  |
 ┌─┴────┐                  ┌──────────┴────────┐
Hugh Leigh.  Thomas Leigh of Caldwell=T=Amy d of Richard Wodden
             in com Bedfford.           of Walingham
                                  |
                     ┌────────────┼─────────────┐
               1. John Leigh.  2 Thomas Leigh  Elizebeth
```

Luke
[of Woodend in Cople].

ARMS.—*Quarterly of six*—1, *Argent, a bugle-horn sable, stringed gules*, LUKE. 2, *Argent, a fleur-de-lys sable*, LAUNCELIN. 3, *Argent, a chevron between three annulets sable*, WAUTON. 4, *Argent, a chevron between three mullets gules*, . 5, *Sable, semée de cross-crosslets fitchée argent, three lions passant gules*, . 6, *Gules, on a fesse between three mascles or as many escallops of the field, on a bordure of the second eight torteaux*, HEMING.

```
John Luke of Woodend in com Bedfford=T=Anne d and coheire of John Heming of
(eldest son and heir of Nicholas)      Arle(se)y in com Bedfford
                            |
        ┌───────────────────┴──────────────────────┐
1 Nicholas Luke=T=Margarett d of   2 Sʳ John Luke=T=Mary d of      Coningsby
of Woodend ob  | Oliver Lord       of Annabl's in | of North Myms in com
July 1613.†    | Sᵗ John of        com. Hertfford | Hertfford ‡
            A  | Bletsho Knt                    B
```

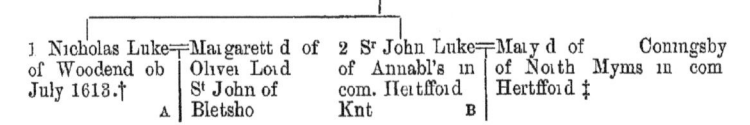

---
* ' This descent is in a booke in the office, on the back of wᶜʰ book is thees Pedegrees E 5 (1634) in this yere I saw it in the office '
" Caldwell is in Derbysh'' and I have seen a Pedigree under Mʳ Wyley the Pursivant's hand with a Lion rampᵗ gules in a field or for this Family Distinguished with a mollet azure.—R D "

† ' This Nicholas Luke Esquire died yᵉ forth of July 1613, and was solemly buried at Copley yᵉ torth day of August Sʳ Oliver Luke his son and heire being chief mourner Sʳ John Luke Knt his brother and Thomas Luke his 2ᵈ son being assistante. York herald officer." (Harl. MS 4600.)

‡ " Jane d of   Collet of Barkshire " (*Ibid*)

THE VISITATION OF BEDFORDSHIRE.

```
A                                          B
│                                          │
```

Sᵣ Oliver=Elizabeth d. and   Anne ux. Sʳ   2. Thomas   Judith   Mary ux.
Luke of   coheire of Sʳ Val- MylesFleet-   Luke.   ux. John   John Mat-
Wood-   lentyn Knightley   wood of   Cooke.   thewe of
end Knt. of [Fawsley] in   .... in   —   Bradden in
          com. Northampton   Knt.   Catherin.   com. North-
          [ob. 1618].   ampton.

[Sʳ] Samuell Luke [of Woodend=[Eliz. d. of Wᵐ   2. [John]   3. Nicholas
in Coupley Knt.].*   Freeman.]   Luke.   Luke.

[Oliver Luke=[Eliz. d. of Onslow Winch of Everton   [John.]   [Samuel.]
of Woodend.] | in com. Bedd.]

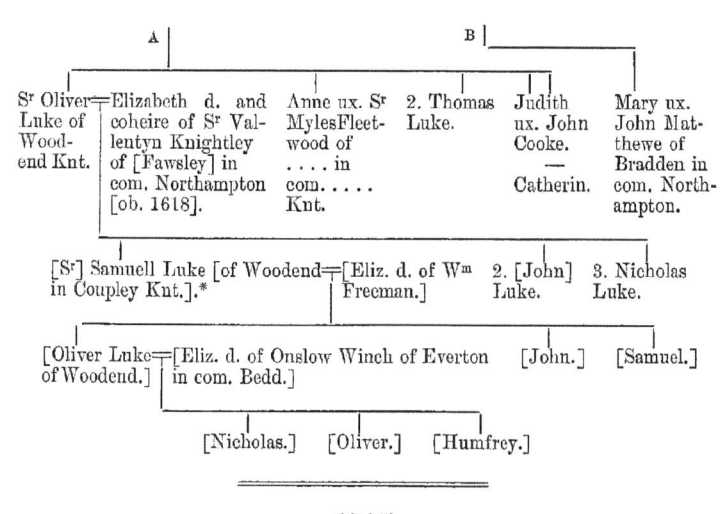

[Nicholas.]   [Oliver.]   [Humfrey.]

Mills
[of ? Toddington].

ARMS.—*Barry of ten argent and vert, over all six escutcheons gules, three, two, and one.*
CREST.—*A wing barry of ten argent and vert.*

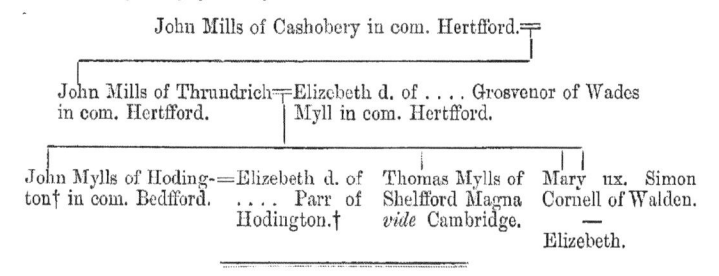

John Mills of Cashobery in com. Hertfford.=

John Mills of Thrundrich=Elizebeth d. of .... Grosvenor of Wades
in com. Hertfford.   Myll in com. Hertfford.

John Mylls of Hoding-=Elizebeth d. of   Thomas Mylls of   Mary ux. Simon
ton† in com. Bedfford. .... Parr of   Shelfford Magna   Cornell of Walden.
                        Hodington.†   *vide* Cambridge. —
                                                            Elizebeth.

Mordaunt
[of Oakley].

Will'm Mordaunt of Okley=Agnes d. and coheire of Charles Booth
in com. Bedfford.   of the Bishoprick of Durham.
        A

---

* For further issue of this match, and issue by Elizabeth his second wife, *cf.* Malcolm's 'Londinium,' vol. ii., pp. 369-70. See also extracts from the registers of Hawnes and Cople, chiefly relating to the family of Luke, in Nichols's 'Collectanea Topographica,' vols. ii., p. 85, and v., p. 362.
† Probably Toddington near Dunstable.—ED.

ADDITIONAL PEDIGREES. 181

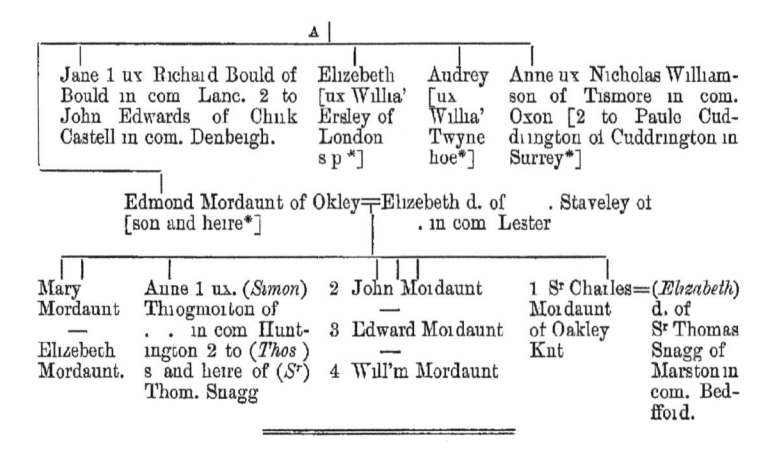

A
|
- Jane 1 ux Richard Bould of Bould in com Lanc. 2 to John Edwards of Chirk Castell in com. Denbeigh.
- Elizebeth [ux Willia' Ersley of London s p*]
- Audrey [ux Willia' Twyne hoe*]
- Anne ux Nicholas Williamson of Tismore in com. Oxon [2 to Paule Cuddington of Cuddrington in Surrey*]

Edmond Mordaunt of Okley=Elizebeth d. of . Staveley of
[son and heire*]   . in com Lester

- Mary Mordaunt — Elizebeth Mordaunt.
- Anne 1 ux. (Simon) Throgmorton of . . in com Huntington 2 to (Thos) s and heire of (Sr) Thom. Snagg
- 2 John Mordaunt — 3 Edward Mordaunt — 4 Will'm Mordaunt
- 1 Sr Charles Mordaunt of Oakley Knt = (Elizabeth) d. of Sr Thomas Snagg of Marston in com. Bedfford.

Napier
[of Luton-Hoo].

ARMS.—*Argent, a saltire engrailed between four roses gules.*
CREST —*A greyhound sejant gules, collared and lined or*
SUPPORTERS.—*Dexter An eagle proper, beaked or Sinister. A greyhound gules, collared and lined or*

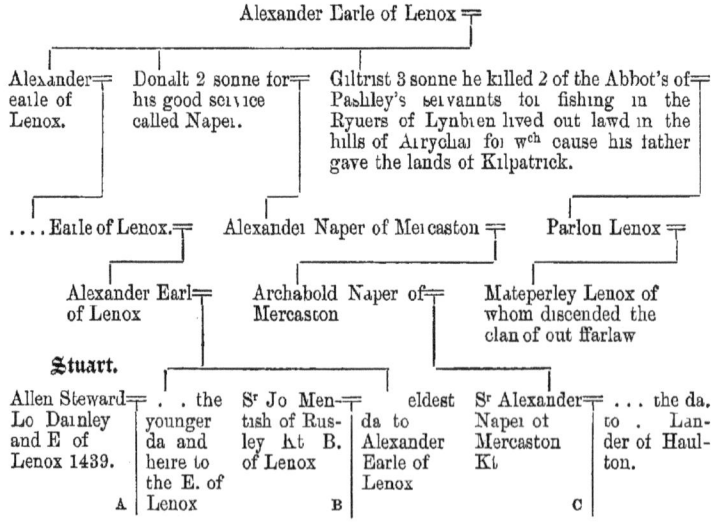

Alexander Earle of Lenox =
|
- Alexander earle of Lenox.
- Donalt 2 sonne for his good service called Naper.
- Giltrist 3 sonne he killed 2 of the Abbot's of Pashley's servannts for fishing in the Ryuers of Lynbren lived out lawd in the hills of Airychar for wch cause his father gave the lands of Kilpatrick.

- .... Earle of Lenox.=
- Alexander Naper of Mercaston =
- Parlon Lenox =

- Alexander Earl of Lenox =
- Archabold Naper of Mercaston =
- Mateperley Lenox of whom discended the clan of out ffarlaw

Stuart.

- Allen Steward Lo Darnley and E of Lenox 1439. =
- . . the younger da and heire to the E. of Lenox
- Sr Jo Mentish of Rusley Kt B. of Lenox =
- eldest da to Alexander Earle of Lenox
- Sr Alexander Naper of Mercaston Kt =
- . . . the da. to . Lander of Haulton.

A | B | C

* Harl MS 4600

THE VISITATION OF BEDFORDSHIRE.

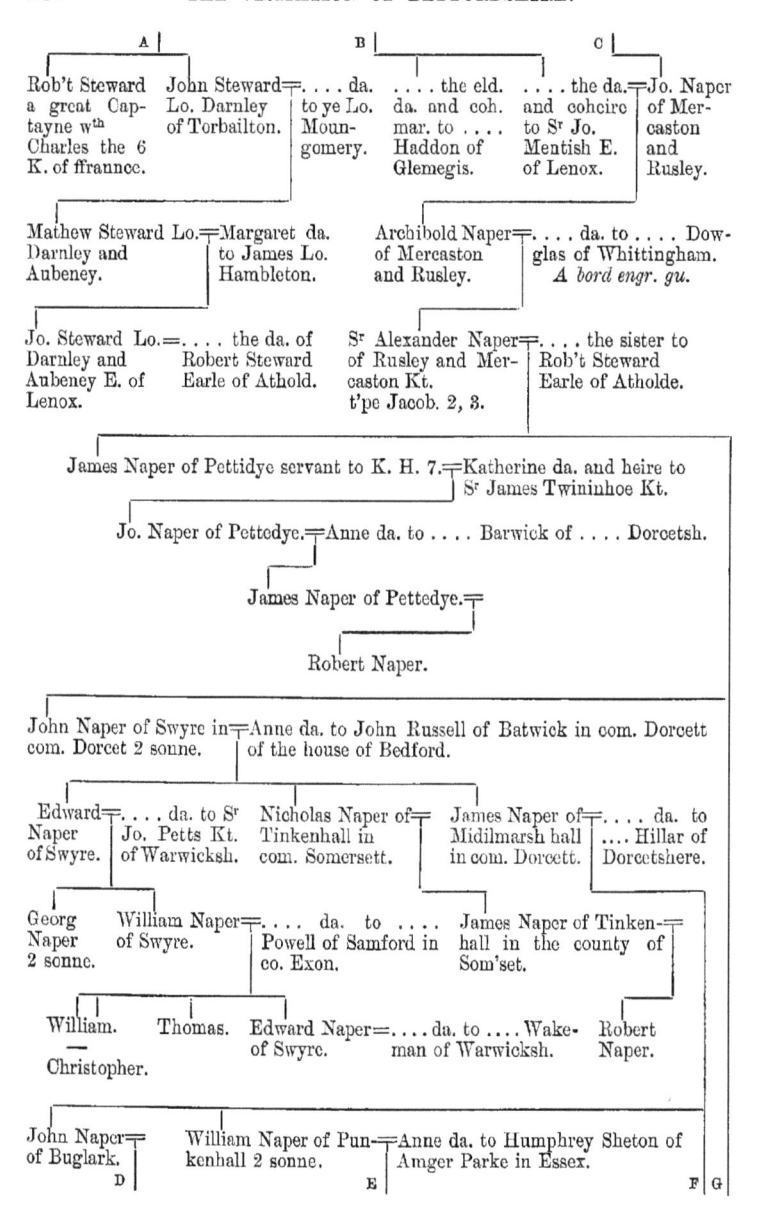

A | B | C |

Rob't Steward a great Captayne wth Charles the 6 K. of ffraunce.

John Steward=.... da. to ye Lo. Moungomery.
Lo. Darnley of Torbailton.

.... the eld. da. and coh. mar. to .... Haddon of Glemegis.

.... the da. and coheire to Sr Jo. Mentish E. of Lenox.

=Jo. Naper of Mercaston and Rusley.

Mathew Steward Lo.=Margaret da. to James Lo. Hambleton.
Darnley and Aubeney.

Archibold Naper=.... da. to .... Douglas of Whittingham.
of Mercaston and Rusley. *A bord engr. gu.*

Jo. Steward Lo.=.... the da. of Robert Steward Earle of Athold.
Darnley and Aubeney E. of Lenox.

Sr Alexander Naper=.... the sister to Rob't Steward Earle of Atholde.
of Rusley and Mercaston Kt. t'pe Jacob. 2, 3.

James Naper of Pettidye servant to K. H. 7.=Katherine da. and heire to Sr James Twininhoe Kt.

Jo. Naper of Pettedye.=Anne da. to .... Barwick of .... Dorcetsh.

James Naper of Pettedye.=

Robert Naper.

John Naper of Swyre in com. Dorcet 2 sonne.=Anne da. to John Russell of Batwick in com. Dorcett of the house of Bedford.

Edward Naper of Swyre.=.... da. to Sr Jo. Petts Kt. of Warwicksh.

Nicholas Naper of Tinkenhall in com. Somersett.=

James Naper of Midilmarsh hall in com. Dorcett.=.... da. to .... Hillar of Dorcetshire.

Georg Naper 2 sonne.

William Naper=.... da. to .... Powell of Samford in co. Exon.
of Swyre.

James Naper of Tinkenhall in the county of Som'set.=

William. — Christopher.

Thomas.

Edward Naper=.... da. to .... Wakeman of Warwicksh.
of Swyre.

Robert Naper.

John Naper=
of Buglark.
D

William Naper of Punkenhall 2 sonne.=
E

Anne da. to Humphrey Sheton of Amger Parke in Essex.
F | G

ADDITIONAL PEDIGREES.

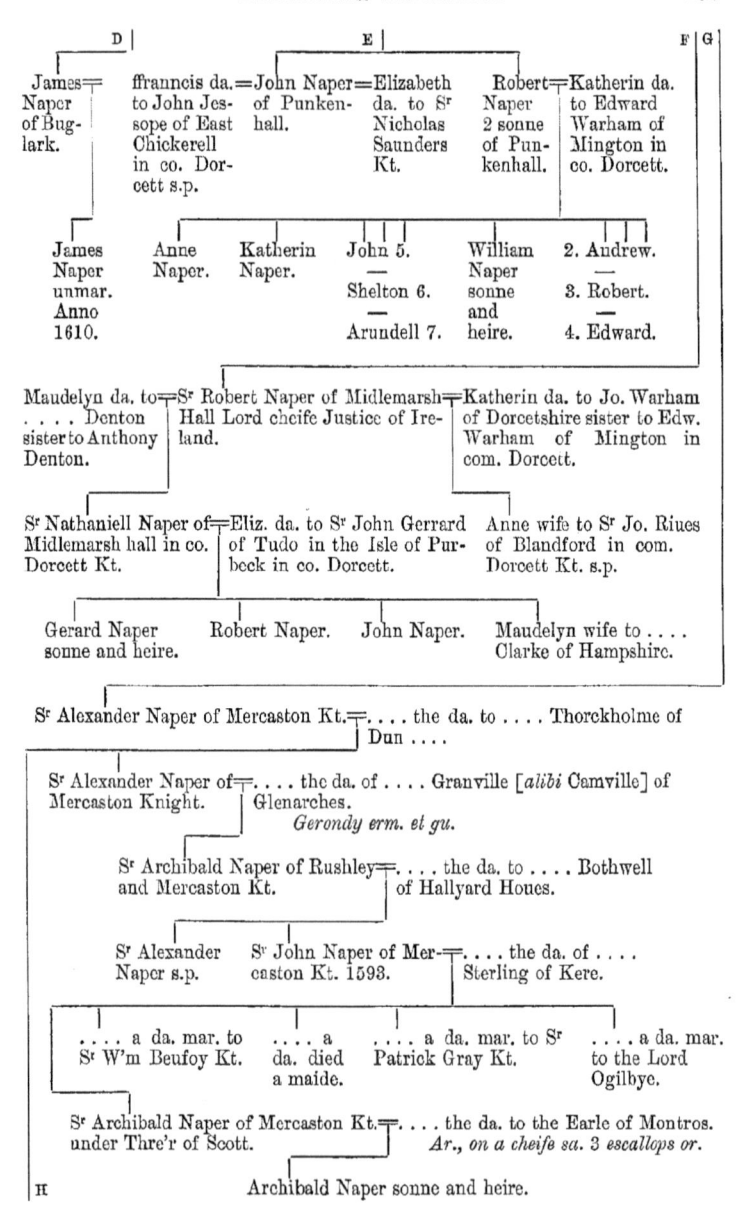

D | E | F | G

James Naper of Buglark.=ffrauncis da. to John Jessope of East Chickerell in co. Dorcett s.p.=John Naper of Punkenhall.=Elizabeth da. to Sr Nicholas Saunders Kt. | Robert Naper 2 sonne of Punkenhall.=Katherin da. to Edward Warham of Mington in co. Dorcett.

James Naper unmar. Anno 1610. | Anne Naper. | Katherin Naper. | John 5. — Shelton 6. — Arundell 7. | William Naper sonne and heire. | 2. Andrew. — 3. Robert. — 4. Edward.

Maudelyn da. to .... Denton sister to Anthony Denton.=Sr Robert Naper of Midlemarsh Hall Lord cheife Justice of Ireland.=Katherin da. to Jo. Warham of Dorcetshire sister to Edw. Warham of Mington in com. Dorcett.

Sr Nathaniell Naper of Midlemarsh hall in co. Dorcett Kt.=Eliz. da. to Sr John Gerrard of Tudo in the Isle of Purbeck in co. Dorcett. | Anne wife to Sr Jo. Riues of Blandford in com. Dorcett Kt. s.p.

Gerard Naper sonne and heire. | Robert Naper. | John Naper. | Maudelyn wife to .... Clarke of Hampshire.

Sr Alexander Naper of Mercaston Kt.=.... the da. to .... Thorckholme of Dun ....

Sr Alexander Naper of Mercaston Knight.=.... the da. of .... Granville [*alibi* Camville] of Glenarches.
Gerondy erm. et gu.

Sr Archibald Naper of Rushley and Mercaston Kt.=.... the da. to .... Bothwell of Hallyard Houes.

Sr Alexander Naper s.p. | Sr John Naper of Mercaston Kt. 1593.=.... the da. of .... Sterling of Kere.

.... a da. mar. to Sr Wm Beufoy Kt. | .... a da. died a maide. | .... a da. mar. to Sr Patrick Gray Kt. | .... a da. mar. to the Lord Ogilbye.

Sr Archibald Naper of Mercaston Kt. under Thre'r of Scott.=.... the da. to the Earle of Montros.
Ar., on a cheife sa. 3 escallops or.

Archibald Naper sonne and heire.

H

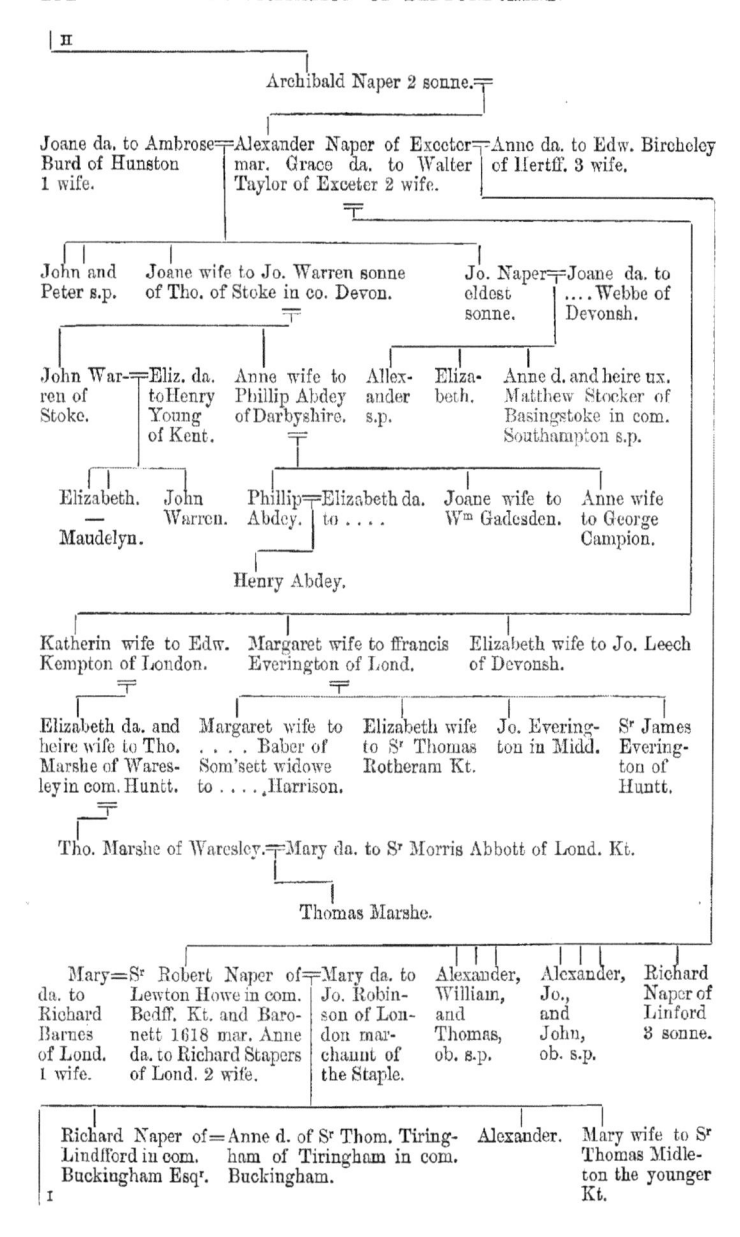

184   THE VISITATION OF BEDFORDSHIRE.

Archibald Naper 2 sonne.

Joane da. to Ambrose Burd of Hunston 1 wife. = Alexander Naper of Exceter mar. Grace da. to Walter Taylor of Exceter 2 wife. = Anne da. to Edw. Bircheley of Hertff. 3 wife.

- John and Peter s.p.
- Joane wife to Jo. Warren sonne of Tho. of Stoke in co. Devon.
- Jo. Naper eldest sonne. = Joane da. to .... Webbe of Devonsh.

- John Warren of Stoke. = Eliz. da. to Henry Young of Kent.
- Anne wife to Phillip Abdey of Darbyshire.
- Allexander s.p.
- Elizabeth.
- Anne d. and heire ux. Matthew Stocker of Basingstoke in com. Southampton s.p.

- Elizabeth. — Maudelyn.
- John Warren.
- Phillip Abdey. = Elizabeth da. to ....
- Joane wife to Wm Gadesden.
- Anne wife to George Campion.

Henry Abdey.

- Katherin wife to Edw. Kempton of London.
- Margaret wife to ffrancis Everington of Lond.
- Elizabeth wife to Jo. Leech of Devonsh.

- Elizabeth da. and heire wife to Tho. Marshe of Waresley in com. Huntt.
- Margaret wife to .... Baber of Som'sett widowe to ...., Harrison.
- Elizabeth wife to Sr Thomas Rotheram Kt.
- Jo. Everington in Midd.
- Sr James Everington of Huntt.

Tho. Marshe of Waresley. = Mary da. to Sr Morris Abbott of Lond. Kt.

Thomas Marshe.

- Mary da. to Richard Barnes of Lond. 1 wife.
- = Sr Robert Naper of Lewton Howe in com. Bedff. Kt. and Baronett 1618 mar. Anne da. to Richard Stapers of Lond. 2 wife.
- = Mary da. to Jo. Robinson of London marchaunt of the Staple.
- Alexander, William, and Thomas, ob. s.p.
- Alexander, Jo., and John, ob. s.p.
- Richard Naper of Linford 3 sonne.

Richard Naper of Lindfford in com. Buckingham Esqr. = Anne d. of Sr Thom. Tiringham of Tiringham in com. Buckingham.
Alexander.
Mary wife to Sr Thomas Midleton the younger Kt.

ADDITIONAL PEDIGREES. 185

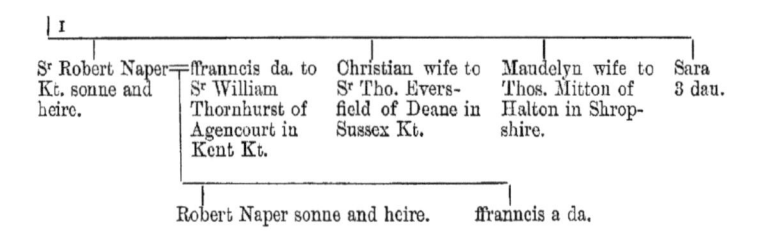

Sʳ Robert Naper=ffranncis da. to   Christian wife to   Maudelyn wife to   Sara
Kt. sonne and   Sʳ William   Sʳ Tho. Evers-   Thos. Mitton of   3 dau.
heire.   Thornhurst of   field of Deane in   Halton in Shrop-
                Agencourt in   Sussex Kt.   shire.
                Kent Kt.

Robert Naper sonne and heire.   ffranncis a da.

Neale

[of Yeldeu].

ARMS.—As in Visitation of 1634.

John Neyle of Yeldon in com. Bedfford=Grace d. of John Butler of Coydkenles
                                      in com. Pembrooke 2 wiffe.
and of Wollaston in com. Northampton.

Elizebeth. Edmond. Jane.   Ellen ux. Stephen   Frances ux. Rob.   Margaret
——   ——   ——   Dryden of   Freeman of   ux. . . . .
Thomas.   Henery. Grace.   Bulwike in com.   Whitton and   Cromer.
            s.p.   North'ton brother   Houghton in com.
                              to Erasmus.   Huntington.

3. Henery Neale of Hanging=Elizabeth d. of   4. Raphell Neale=Jane widdow of
Houghton in com. North'-   Edward Lacon   of Drury Lane in . . . . Forman
ton 1618.   of Willey in   London.   docter of
                           com. Sallop.   phissick.

Lacon Neale   2. Walter.   Lancelot.   Lancelot.   Grace.   James Neale
8 yere old   ——   3 yere old 1618.
1618.   Frances.   s.p.

Newdigate*

[of Hawnes].

Sʳ Robert Newdigate of=Elizebeth d. of Thom. Stutvile
Hawns in com. Bedfford. | of Dalham in com. Suffolk.

1. Will'm Newdigate.   Robert ob. s.p.   Anne.   Dorothy.
                                                                    A

* See extracts from the Parish Registers and Epitaphs at Hawnes in Nichols's 'Collectanea Topographica,' vol. iii., p. 85.

B B

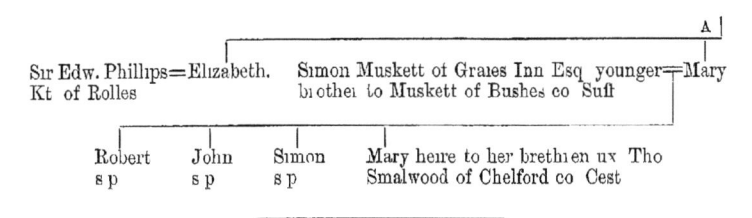

Sir Edw. Phillips=Elizabeth. Simon Muskett of Graies Inn Esq younger=Mary
Kt of Rolles   brother to Muskett of Bushes co Suff

Robert   John   Simon   Mary heire to her brethren ux Tho
s p   s p   s p   Smalwood of Chelford co Cest

Nicholls[*]

[of Ampthill].

ARMS —*Azure, a fesse between three lions' heads erased or*
CREST —*A tiger sejant ermine*

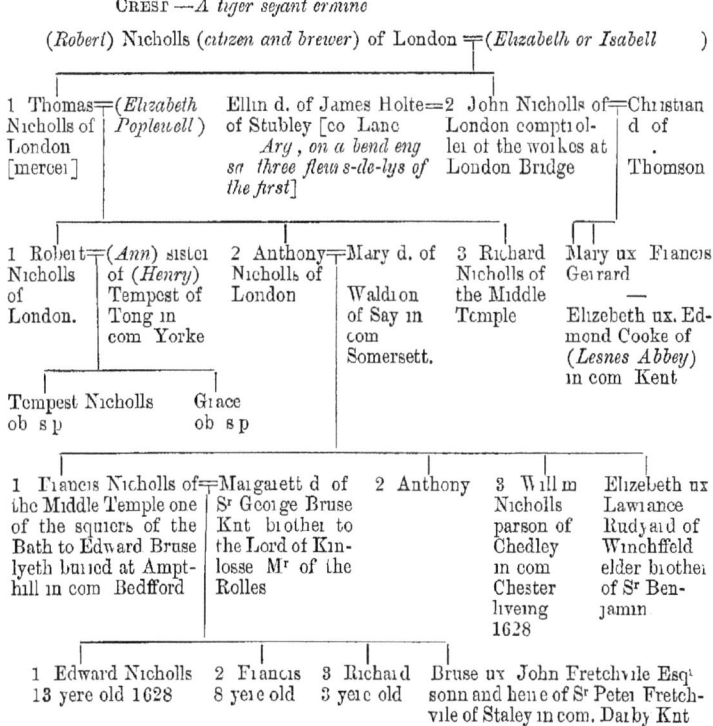

(Robert) Nicholls (citizen and brewer) of London =(Elizabeth or Isabell   )

1 Thomas=(Elizabeth   Ellin d. of James Holte= 2 John Nicholls of=Christian
Nicholls of | Poplewell) of Stubley [co Lanc   London comptrol- | d of
London   *Arg, on a bend eng*   ler of the workes at
[mercer]   *sa three fleurs-de-lys of* London Bridge   Thomson
                          the first]

1 Robert=(Ann) sister   2 Anthony=Mary d. of   3 Richard   Mary ux Francis
Nicholls | of (Henry)   Nicholls of Waldron   Nicholls of   Gerrard
of | Tempest of   London   of Say in the Middle   —
London. | Tong in   com   Temple   Elizebeth ux. Ed-
           com Yorke   Somersett.   mond Cooke of
                                                           (Lesnes Abbey)
                                                           in com Kent

Tempest Nicholls   Grace
ob s p   ob s p

1 Francis Nicholls of=Margarett d of   2 Anthony   3 Willm   Elizebeth ux
the Middle Temple one | Sr George Bruse   Nicholls   Lawrance
of the squiers of the | Knt brother to   parson of   Rudyard of
Bath to Edward Bruse | the Lord of Kin-   Chedley   Winchffeld
lyeth buried at Ampt- | losse Mr of the   in com   elder brother
hill in com Bedfford | Rolles   Chester   of Sr Ben-
                                                     liveing   jamin
                                                     1628

1 Edward Nicholls   2 Francis   3 Richard   Bruse ux John Fretchvile Esqr
13 yere old 1628   8 yere old 3 yere old sonn and heire of Sr Peter Fretch-
                                            vile of Staley in com. Darby Knt

---

[*] For detailed account of this family cf. 'Topographer and Genealogist,' vol iii, p 533,
and 'Visitation of London 1566,' p 66 ed Harl Soc

Over
[of Woburn].

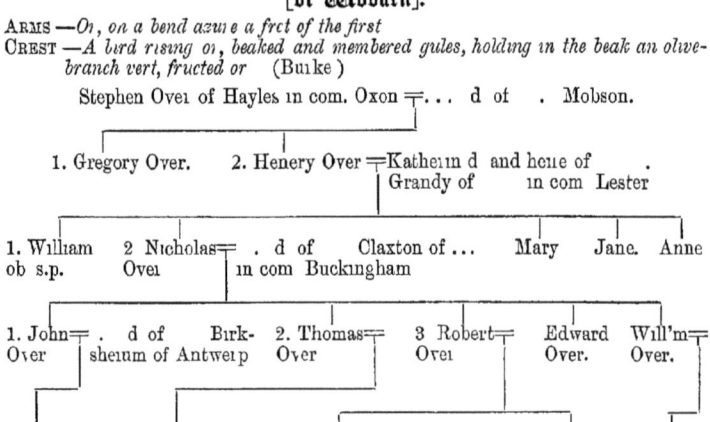

ARMS —*Or, on a bend azure a fret of the first*
CREST —*A bird rising or, beaked and membered gules, holding in the beak an olive-branch vert, fructed or*   (Burke)

Stephen Over of Hayles in com. Oxon =... d of . Mobson.

1. Gregory Over.   2. Henery Over = Katherin d and heire of . Grandy of in com Lester

1. William ob s.p.   2 Nicholas Over = . d of Claxton of ... in com Buckingham   Mary   Jane.   Anne

1. John Over = . d of Birksheium of Antwerp   2. Thomas Over   3 Robert Over   Edward Over.   Will'm Over.

James Over.   Bennett Over of Barking   Edward Over of Oburne in com Bedfford.   John Over.   Timothey Over

Owen
[of Wootton].

ARMS —*Quarterly of seven*—1, [*Gules,*] *a chevron* [*ermine*] *between three esquires' helmets argent*, OWEN TUDOR 2, *Gules, a chevron . between three lions passant-guardant*, , 3, *Vaire argent and azure*,   , 4, *Argent, two leopards sable, a bordure charged with eight saltires gules*, , 5, *Or, a castle azure*, BLOUNT , 6, *Azure fretty argent*,   ; 7,   *a fret* ...

Sr Owen Tudor Knt. =

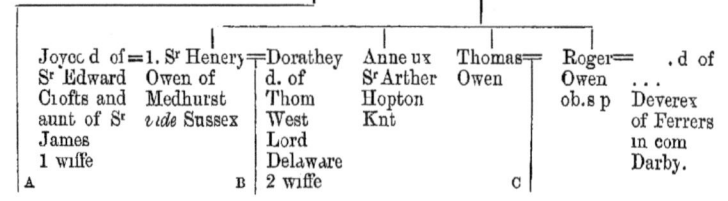

Anne d and coheire of Will'm Blount sonn and heire of Walter Blount 1 Lord Mountjoy 2 wiffe = Sr David Owen of Medhurste in com Sussex* Knt. = Mary d and heire of John Bohun of Medhurste *vide* Sussex 1 wiffe

Joyce d of Sr Edward Crofts and aunt of Sr James 1 wiffe = 1. Sr Henery Owen of Medhurst *vide* Sussex = Dorathey d. of Thom West Lord Delaware 2 wiffe   Anne ux Sr Arther Hopton Knt   Thomas Owen   Roger Owen ob.s p = . d of ... Deverex of Ferrers in com Darby.

A   B   C

* " Of Cowdrey in Surrey, base son to Sr Owen Tudor " (Harl MS 4600) Sir David Owen's will bears date 20th Feb 1529, and contains genealogical notes of value. *Cf* 'Test. Vetust ' p 700.

THE VISITATION OF BEDFORDSHIRE.

```
A                    B                                            C
|                    |                                            |
David Owen      .... ux.      Elizabeth d. and coheire     Will'm=      Thomas=
dyed in         .... Tin-     ux. Nicholas Dering of       Owen.        Owen.
Flaunders       gleton of     Petworth in com. Sussex.
s.p.            Surrey.
```

```
        William Owen.    Benjamyn.    Levy.    Thomas.    William.
```

John Owen of=Elizabeth d. of [Sr—Harl. MS.=John Prestolffe   Henery   Jasper
Wootton in | 4600] Richard Catesby of   2 husband.   Owen.   Owen.
com. Bedfford.| Legers Ashby in com. North-
             | ampton.
             *

Jane d. and sole heire ux. Sr Will'm Gostwike of Willington in
com. Bedfford Knt. and Baronett *vide ante* p. 34.

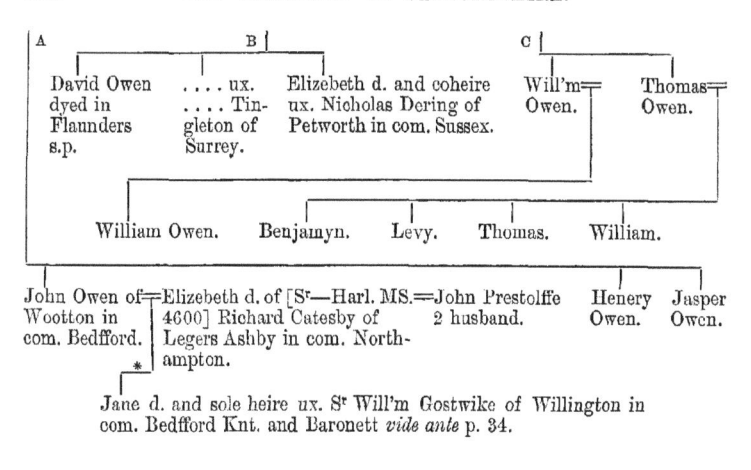

Pigott

[of Stratton].

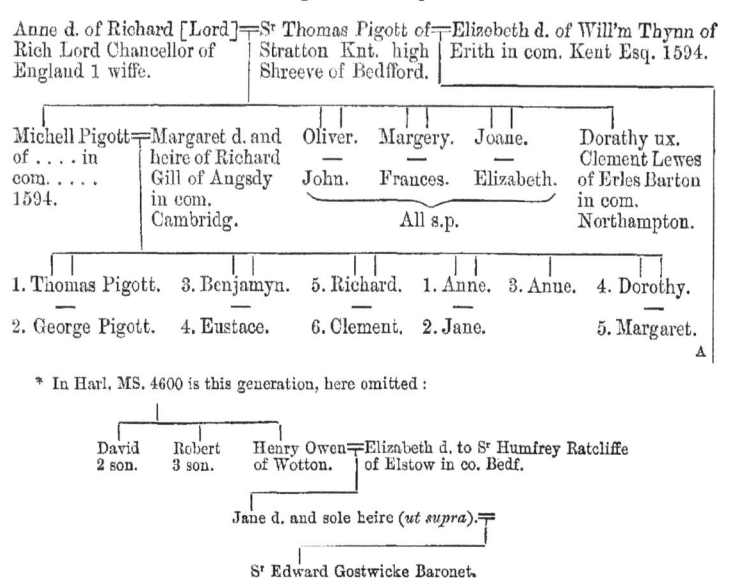

Anne d. of Richard [Lord]=Sr Thomas Pigott of=Elizabeth d. of Will'm Thynn of
Rich Lord Chancellor of | Stratton Knt. high | Erith in com. Kent Esq. 1594.
England 1 wiffe. | Shreeve of Bedford.|

Michell Pigott=Margaret d. and   Oliver.   Margery.   Joane.   Dorathy ux.
of .... in | heire of Richard —   —   —   Clement Lewes
com. .... | Gill of Angsdy   John.   Frances.   Elizabeth.   of Erles Barton
1594. | in com.   in com.
              | Cambridg.   All s.p.   Northampton.

1. Thomas Pigott.   3. Benjamyn.   5. Richard.   1. Anne.   3. Anne.   4. Dorothy.
   —   —   —   —   —   —
2. George Pigott.   4. Eustace.   6. Clement.   2. Jane.   5. Margaret.
                                                                                 A

* In Harl. MS. 4600 is this generation, here omitted :

```
        |
David      Robert      Henry Owen=Elizabeth d. to Sr Humfrey Ratcliffe
2 son.     3 son.      of Wotton. | of Elstow in co. Bedf.
                            |
                  Jane d. and sole heire (ut supra).=
                            |
                  Sr Edward Gostwicke Baronet.
```

ADDITIONAL PEDIGREES. 189

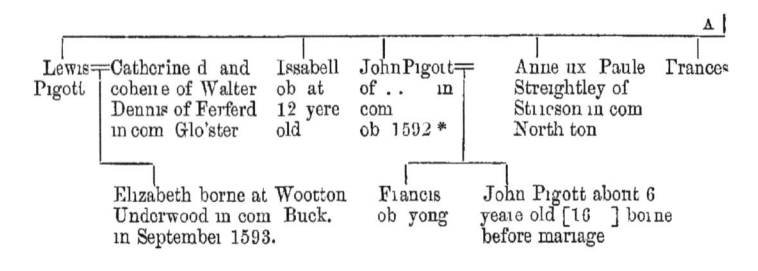

Lewis Pigott =₁ Catherine d and coheire of Walter Dennis of Ferferd in com Glo'ster | Issabell ob at 12 yere old | John Pigott of . . in com ob 1592 * =₁ Anne ux Paule Streightley of Stiicson in com North ton | Frances

– Elizabeth borne at Wootton Underwood in com Buck. in September 1593.
– Francis ob yong
– John Pigott about 6 yeare old [16] borne before mariage

Plomer
[of Hill in Warden].

ARMS —*Vert, a chevron between three lions' heads erased or, on each as many gouttes gules (another four billets)* (Burke.)

Will'm Plomer of Radwell in com Hertfford =₁ Catherin d of . . Moore of . . in com Southampton

– Anne ux George Cockayne of Cockayne Hatley in com. Cambridge.
– Catherin ux. Robert Audley of Gransden in com Huntington
– 2 Thomas Plomer
– 3 Edward Plomer

Mary d of Will'm Godfrey of Lechworth in com Hertfford 1 wiffe =₁ Sʳ Will'm Plomer of Hill in com Bedford High Shreeve of the same 1610 knighted by King James on Monday 23ʳᵈ of September in the same yere in Enffeld Chase =₂ Margerett d of Robert Warren of Elstree in com Middlesex widdow of Richard Balthrop of London brewer.

– 2 Thomas Plomer.
– 3 John Plomer of Grays Inn
– 4 Edward Plomer
– 5 George Plomer
– Rose
– Elizabeth.
– Margerett.†

Will m Plomer of Radwell = Anne d and coheire of Stumpe of Malmesbery in com Wilts
Mary ux. (*Christopher*) Ridley a counsellor of (*the Middle Temple*)

---

* In Edlesborough Church, co Bucks, is a brass to John Pigott and wife, 1592, also inscription to Hen Brugis gent who married Frances Pygott, 1617 —ED
† ' Ellen and Mary." (Harl MS 5867.)

Pooley*

[of Biddenham].

ARMS.—*Quarterly of eight*—1, *Or, a lion rampant sable*, POOLEY; 2, *Argent, on a bend sable three cross-crosslets of the field*, POOLEY; 3, *Sable, a chevron engrailed or between three mullets pierced argent*, BADWELL; 4, *Azure, a saltire or between four billets argent*, LYOSE; 5, *Or, a chevron between three leopards' faces gules*, HERVY; 6, *Ermine, on a cross gules four escallops or*, WEYLAND; 7, *Gules, three fusils in fesse ermine between as many martlets argent*, SHAA; 8, *Blank*.

CREST.—*Or, a lion rampant sable, collared and lined of the first.*

Thomas Pooley of Boxted in com. Suff. had a 2ᵈ wiffe by whome hee had issue as in Suff. =Maude d. and heire of John Gislingham by Maude d. and heire of John Gardevile.

1. Richard Pooley. =Margerett d. of Simon Blyant of Thornham in com. Essex. | 2. John a preest. | Anne ux. Nicholas Lovell. | Rose Pooley.

1. Simon Pooley of Badley in com. Suff. *vide idem.* | 2. John Pooley of Bidenham in com. Bedfford. =Joane d. of John Hynde of Harlington in com. Bedfford. | Margery ob. yong. | Catherin ob. yong.

John Pooley of Bidenham. =Prudence d. of Richard Sheldon. | Thomas ob. s.p. | Barbara ux. .... Darrell of Kent. | Joane ux. Wᵐ Ernest of .... in com Bedfford. | Jane ux..... Baker.

1. John Pooley of Bidenham. = | Margerett. | Jane. | 2. Thomas Pooley of Bidenham. | 3. Nicholas Pooley.

Robert Pooley of Bromham in com. Bedfford. =Jane d. of John Carrisforth of Barnesley in com. York.

John Pooley of .... in com. Cambridge. =Allice d. of John Smyth of Cambridge.

Thomas Pooley.

---

* *Cf.* 'Visitations of Suffolk,' p. 58, ed. W. C. Metcalfe.

Rotheram*

[of Someries in Luton].

ARMS (TWELVE SHIELDS) — 1, (Az.,) a hound passant argent, BURGOYNE, 2, Sable, a fesse componee or and azure between three horses' heads erased argent, HIGHAM, 3, Argent, a bend vert cotised indented gules, GRAY, 4, (Argent,) on a chief gules two mullets (or), a crescent for difference, ST JOHN, 5, Ermine, a lion rampant gules, LEGAT, 6, , a canton ermine, , 7, Argent, ten torteaux, 4, 3, 2, and 1, GIFFORD, 8, Sable, a chevron engrailed between three plates argent, each charged with a pallet gules, DOCWRA, 9, (Gules,) three arrows in pale or, feathered and barbed argent, HALES, 10, a bend engrailed between two ? cinqfoils , 11, Sable, a bend ermine cotised or between six martlets of the last, WINGATE, 12, Argent, a bend lozengy sable, TAVERNER

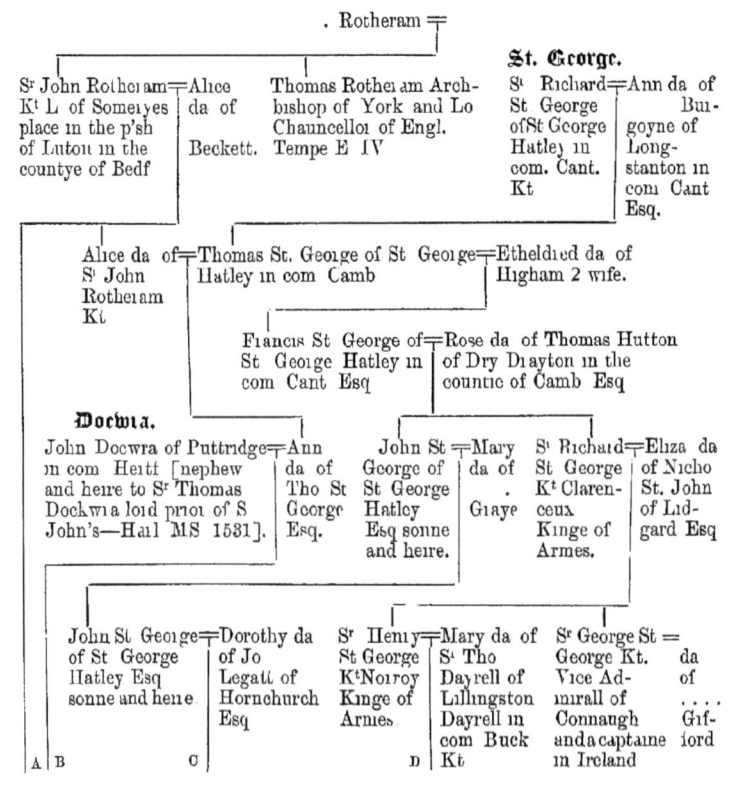

. Rotheram ⊤

Sʳ John Rotheram=Alice | Thomas Rotheram Arch- | **St. George.**
Kᵗ L of Someryes | da of | bishop of York and Lo | Sᵗ Richard=Ann da of
place in the p'sh | Beckett. | Chauncellor of Engl. | St George | Bur-
of Luton in the | | Tempe E IV | ofSt George | goyne of
countye of Bedf | | | Hatley in | Long-
| | | com. Cant. | stanton in
| | | Kt | com Cant
| | | | Esq.

Alice da of=Thomas St. George of St George=Etheldred da of
Sʳ John | Hatley in com Camb | Higham 2 wife.
Rotheram
Kt

Francis St George of=Rose da of Thomas Hutton
St George Hatley in | of Dry Drayton in the
com Cant Esq | countie of Camb Esq

Docwra.

John Docwra of Puttridge=Ann | John St=Mary | Sʳ Richard=Eliza da
in com Hertf [nephew | da of | George of | da of | St George | of Nicho
and heire to Sʳ Thomas | Tho St | St George | | Kᵗ Claren- | St. John
Docwra lord prior of S | George | Hatley | Graye | ceux | of Lid-
John's—Harl MS 1531]. | Esq. | Esq sonne | | Kinge of | gard Esq
| | and heire. | | Armes.

John St George=Dorothy da | Sʳ Henry=Mary da of | Sʳ George St =
of St George | of Jo | Sᵗ George | Sʳ Tho | George Kt. | da
Hatley Esq | Legatt of | KᵗNorroy | Dayrell of | Vice Ad- | of
sonne and heire | Hornchurch | Kinge of | Lillingston | mirall of | ....
| Esq | Armes | Dayrell in | Connaugh | Gif-
| | | com Buck | andacaptaine | ford
A | B C | D Kt | in Ireland

* Pedigree of St. George and Rotheram, in the handwriting of Sʳ Henry St. George, MS. 541, Caius Coll Cambs.

THE VISITATION OF BEDFORDSHIRE.

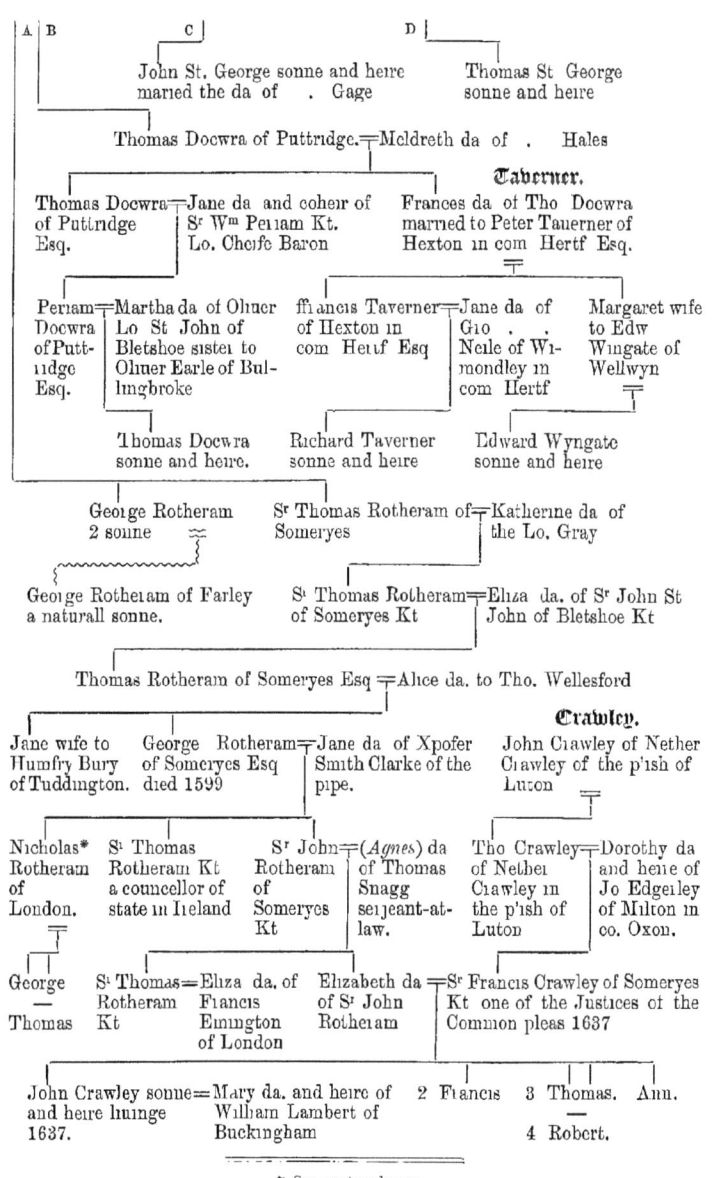

A | B | C | D

John St. George sonne and heire maried the da of . Gage

Thomas St George sonne and heire

Thomas Docwra of Puttridge.=Meldreth da of . Hales

Taverner.

Thomas Docwra of Puttridge Esq. = Jane da and coheir of Sr Wm Periam Kt. Lo. Cheife Baron

Frances da of Tho Docwra married to Peter Tauerner of Hexton in com Hertf Esq.

Periam Docwra of Puttridge Esq. = Martha da of Oliuer Lo St John of Bletshoe sister to Oliuer Earle of Bullingbroke

ffrancis Taverner of Hexton in com Hertf Esq = Jane da of Gio . . Neile of Wimondley in com Hertf

Margaret wife to Edw Wingate of Wellwyn

Thomas Docwra sonne and heire.

Richard Taverner sonne and heire.

Edward Wyngate sonne and heire.

George Rotheram 2 sonne

Sr Thomas Rotheram of Someryes = Katherine da of the Lo. Gray

George Rotheram of Farley a naturall sonne.

St Thomas Rotheram of Someryes Kt = Eliza da. of Sr John St John of Bletshoe Kt

Thomas Rotheram of Someryes Esq = Alice da. to Tho. Wellesford

Crawley.

Jane wife to Humfry Bury of Tuddington.

George Rotheram of Someryes Esq died 1599 = Jane da of Xpofer Smith Clarke of the pipe.

John Crawley of Nether Crawley of the p'ish of Luton

Nicholas* Rotheram of London.

St Thomas Rotheram Kt a councellor of state in Ireland

Sr John Rotheram of Someryes Kt = (Agnes) da of Thomas Snagg serjeant-at-law.

Tho Crawley of Nether Crawley in the p'ish of Luton = Dorothy da and heire of Jo Edgerley of Milton in co. Oxon.

George — Thomas

St Thomas Rotheram Kt = Eliza da. of Francis Emington of London

Elizabeth da of St John Rotheram = Sr Francis Crawley of Someryes Kt one of the Justices of the Common pleas 1637

John Crawley sonne and heire huinge 1637. = Mary da. and heire of William Lambert of Buckingham

2 Francis

3 Thomas.

Ann.

4 Robert.

* See next pedigree.

ADDITIONAL PEDIGREES. 193

Rotherham.

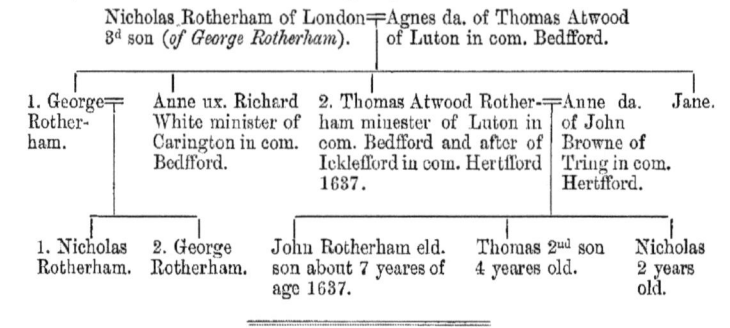

Nicholas Rotherham of London = Agnes da. of Thomas Atwood
3ᵈ son (*of George Rotherham*). of Luton in com. Bedfford.

1. George Rotherham.

Anne ux. Richard White minister of Carington in com. Bedfford.

2. Thomas Atwood Rotherham minester of Luton in com. Bedfford and after of Icklefford in com. Hertfford 1637. = Anne da. of John Browne of Tring in com. Hertfford.

Jane.

1. Nicholas Rotherham.   2. George Rotherham.

John Rotherham eld. son about 7 yeares of age 1637.

Thomas 2ᵘᵈ son 4 yeares old.

Nicholas 2 years old.

Rowe
[of Clapham].

ARMS.—*Argent, on a chevron azure between three trefoils slipped, each per pale gules and vert, as many bezants.*
CREST.—*A stag's head gules, attired or.*

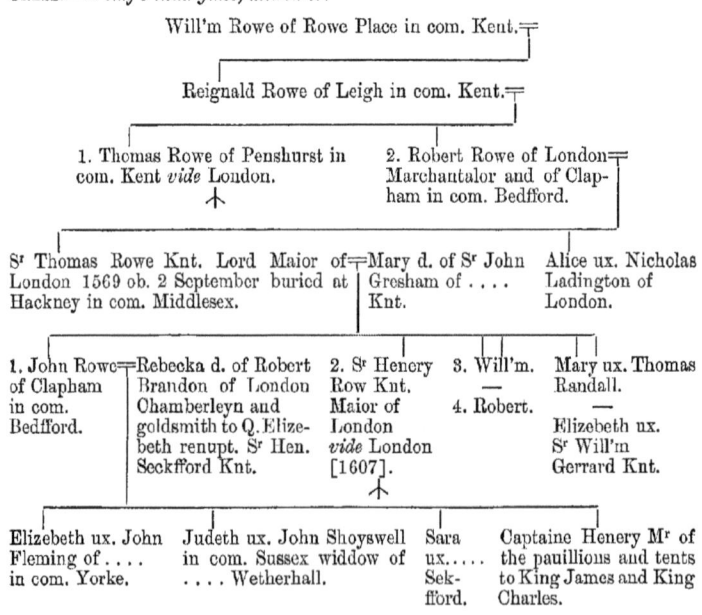

Will'm Rowe of Rowe Place in com. Kent. =

Reignald Rowe of Leigh in com. Kent. =

1. Thomas Rowe of Penshurst in com. Kent *vide* London.

2. Robert Rowe of London Marchantalor and of Clapham in com. Bedfford. =

Sʳ Thomas Rowe Knt. Lord Maior of London 1569 ob. 2 September buried at Hackney in com. Middlesex. = Mary d. of Sʳ John Gresham of .... Knt.

Alice ux. Nicholas Ladington of London.

1. John Rowe of Clapham in com. Bedfford. = Rebecka d. of Robert Brandon of London Chamberleyn and goldsmith to Q. Elizebeth renupt. Sʳ Hen. Seckfford Knt.

2. Sʳ Henery Row Knt. Maior of London *vide* London [1607].

3. Will'm.
4. Robert.

Mary ux. Thomas Randall.
—
Elizebeth ux. Sʳ Will'm Gerrard Knt.

Elizebeth ux. John Fleming of .... in com. Yorke.

Judeth ux. John Shoyswell in com. Sussex widdow of .... Wetherhall.

Sara ux..... Sekfford.

Captaine Henery Mʳ of the pauillions and tents to King James and King Charles.

C C

194   THE VISITATION OF BEDFORDSHIRE.

St. John
[of Bletshoe].

Oliver St John of Ripton Regis in com. = Dorathey d. of John Read of Bodington
Huntington Lord St John of Bletsho. | in com. Gloster.

Margarett ux. Sr Thomas Cheney of (Sundon) in com. (Bed.) Knt.

4. Sr Alexander St John Knt.

Judith ux. Sr John Thompson Knt.

Anne ux. Robert Charnock.

Catherin.

5. Sr Rowland St John.

Dorathey ux. Edward Earle of Bath.

Martha ux. . . . . Dockwray.

6. Sr Henry St John Knt.

7. Sr Beauchamp St John Knt.

8. Dudley St John.

Oliver St John Lord St John and Earle of Bullingbrooke. = Elizabeth d. and heire of Will'm Pawlett of . . . . in com. South'ton.

2. John St John ob. s.p.

3. Sr Anthony St John Knt.

Elizabeth ux. W'm Beecher (of Howbury co. Bedf.).

2. Pawlett St John.
—
3. Francis St John.

Oliver St John Lord St John Earle of Bollingbrooke. = Arabella d. of Sr John Egerton Knt. Earle of Bridgwater.

4. Anthony St John.

Elizabeth.
—
Dorathey.
—
Barbara.

1. Frances.   2. Elizebeth.   3. Arbella.   4. Dorathey.

Sanderson
[of Tempsford].

Lawrance Sanderson of Temsford in com. Bedfford (clerke). = Joane d. of . . . . Mighton of Temsford.

1. Will'm Sanderson of Temsford 1618. = Jane d. of George Astry of Bashmeade in com. Bedfford.

2. John Sanderson of Littell Adington in com. Northampton vide North'ton.

Susan ux. Allexander Eykins of Cheveston and Caldecott in com. Northampton.

1. Lawrance Sanderson.   2. John Sanderson.

Scroggs
[of Renhold].

ARMS.—*Argent, on a bend azure between two greyhounds courant bendways sable three Cornish choughs or.*
CREST.—*A pewit's head argent, collared gules, wings endorsed, bendy of four or and sable*

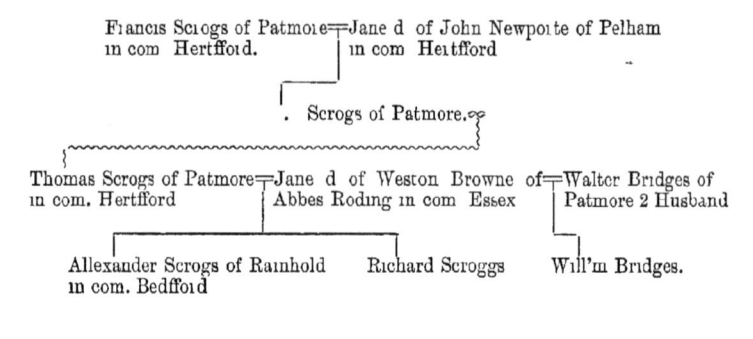

Francis Scrogs of Patmore in com. Hertfford. =Jane d of John Newporte of Pelham in com. Hertfford

. Scrogs of Patmore.

Thomas Scrogs of Patmore in com. Hertfford =Jane d of Weston Browne of Abbes Roding in com. Essex =Walter Bridges of Patmore 2 Husband

Allexander Scrogs of Rainhold in com. Bedfford — Richard Scroggs — Will'm Bridges.

Spencer
[of South-Mills].

ARMS.—*Quarterly or and gules, in the second and third quarters a fret of the first, on a bend sable three fleurs-de-lys argent*
CREST.—*Out of a mural crown per pale argent and gules, a griffin's head, collared or, beaked gules, between two wings expanded, charged on the breast and on each wing with a fleur-de-lys sable, all counterchanged*

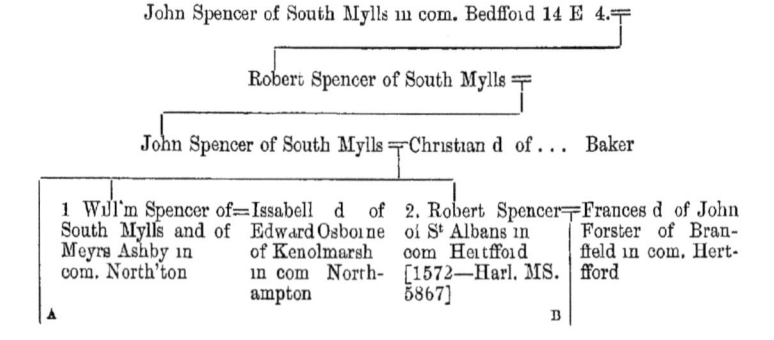

John Spencer of South Mylls in com. Bedfford 14 E 4.=

Robert Spencer of South Mylls =

John Spencer of South Mylls =Christian d of ... Baker

| 1 Will'm Spencer of South Mylls and of Meyrs Ashby in com. North'ton =Issabell d of Edward Osborne of Kenolmarsh in com. Northampton | 2. Robert Spencer of St Albans in com. Hertfford [1572—Harl. MS. 5867] =Frances d of John Forster of Branfield in com. Hertfford |

A   B

A			B	
John Spencer was=Margerett d. of		=Twyfford Wath of	Anne ux.	
10 yere old 1572 Bayly of .... in		Slipton in com.	Gylman of	
hee ob. 6 January com. Hertfford.		Northampton	in com. Hert-	
1622 s.p.		2 husband.	fford.	

John Speneser of London marchant.=Anne d. of .... Clarke of London.

Mary 1 ux. John White	Christian ux. Reignald	Jane ux.	Margerett ux. Law-
of Nordiam in com.	Greene of London.	Richard	rance Greene of
Sussex 2 to Thomas	*B.*, 3 *buck Triping or*	Cockerham	London marchant
Ballard of .... nere	[*a trefoil slipped*] *A.*	of London	free of the Grocers.
Wadehurst in com.	*in cheeffe.*	grocer.	*G.*, *a lyon rampant*
Sussex.			*party per fess A. and*
			sab., crowned or.

Taverner

[of Marston-Mortaine].

ARMS.—*Quarterly*—1 *and* 4, *Argent, a bend lozengy sable, in the sinister chief point a torteau,* TAVERNER; 2 *and* 3, *Ermine, a chevron argent, a marlett for difference,*

Henry Taverner of North Elingham in com. Norffolk descended from Warren=
Le Taverner who lived at North Ellingham temp. H. 2 as apereth by his deed
seald with the seale of his Armes, viz. *A bend fusile.*

Nicholas Taverner of Elingham.=

Allice d. and heire=John Taverner of North Elingham	=Anne d. of .... Crane of
of .... Silvester	ob. 1545 being 88 yeares of age	.... in com. Norffolk
of North Eling-	buried at Brisley in Norffolk.	wth her husband and hath
ham.		yssue as in Norffolk.

1. Richard Taver-	4. Silvester* Taverner=	3. Robert Taverner	2. Roger Taver-
ner of Wood	of Marston in com.	of Artwys (*alibi*	ner of Up-
Eaton in com.	Bedfford a Follower	*Arnoys*) in com.	minster in com.
Oxon *vide* Oxon.	of the Duke of Somer-	Essex *vide* Essex.	Essex *vide*
	sett.		Essex.

1. Silvester Taverner of Marston	2. Thomas Taverner of	3. John	4. ....
in com. Bedfford.	.... in com. Kent.	Taverner.	Taverner.

---

* In Taverner pedigree, 'Visitations of Essex,' App., p. 607, ed. Harl. Soc., *q.v.*, he is called "Gilbert."

Tyringham*
[of Hinwick].

ARMS —*Quarterly of six*—1, *Azure, a saltire engrailed or*, TIRRINGHAM ; 2, *Azure, a fret argent*, DAVILL ; 3, *Azure, three bougets argent*, ROOS ; 4, *Azure, ten billets or, four, three, two, and one*, COWDRAY ; 5, *Argent, a fesse gules, a bordure engrailed sable*, WELSH ; 6, *Barry of six argent and azure, on a bend gules three mullets or*, PABENHAM *In the fesse point a crescent charged with a mullet for difference*

CREST —*A talbot's head couped gules billettée or, on the shoulder a crescent charged with a mullet*

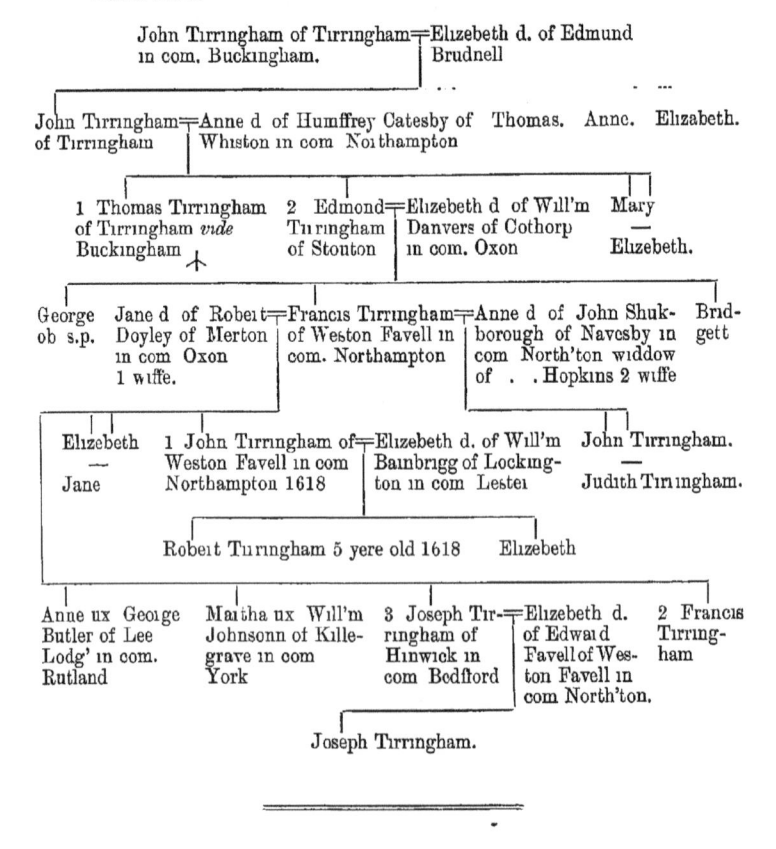

John Tirringham of Tirringham = Elizebeth d. of Edmund in com. Buckingham. Brudnell

John Tirringham of Tirringham = Anne d of Humffrey Catesby of Whiston in com Northampton | Thomas. Anne. Elizabeth.

1 Thomas Tirringham of Tirringham *vide* Buckingham | 2 Edmond Tirringham of Stonton = Elizebeth d of Will'm Danvers of Cothorp in com. Oxon | Mary — Elizebeth.

George ob s.p. | Jane d of Robert Doyley of Merton in com Oxon 1 wiffe. = Francis Tirringham of Weston Favell in com. Northampton = Anne d of John Shukborough of Navesby in com North'ton widdow of .. Hopkins 2 wiffe | Bridgett

Elizebeth — Jane | 1 John Tirringham of Weston Favell in com Northampton 1618 = Elizebeth d. of Will'm Bambrigg of Lockington in com Lester | John Tirringham. — Judith Tirringham.

Robert Tirringham 5 yere old 1618   Elizebeth

Anne ux George Butler of Lee Lodg' in com. Rutland | Martha ux Will'm Johnsonn of Killegrave in com York | 3 Joseph Tirringham of Hinwick in com Bedford = Elizebeth d. of Edward Favell of Weston Favell in com North'ton. | 2 Francis Tirringham

Joseph Tirringham.

---

* *Vide ante,* p 65.

Wauton*

[of ? Eaton-Socon].

ARMS.—*Quarterly*—1, *Argent, a chevron sable, an annulet of the second for difference,* WAUTON; 2, *Gules, a lion rampant vair argent and azure, ducally crowned or,* MARMYON; 3, *Argent, a chevron between three mullets gules,* CRETING; 4, *Sable, on a bend or three goats gules,* CHENDRCOTTS.
CREST.—*A trefoil slipped sable, charged with another argent, a crescent gules for difference.*

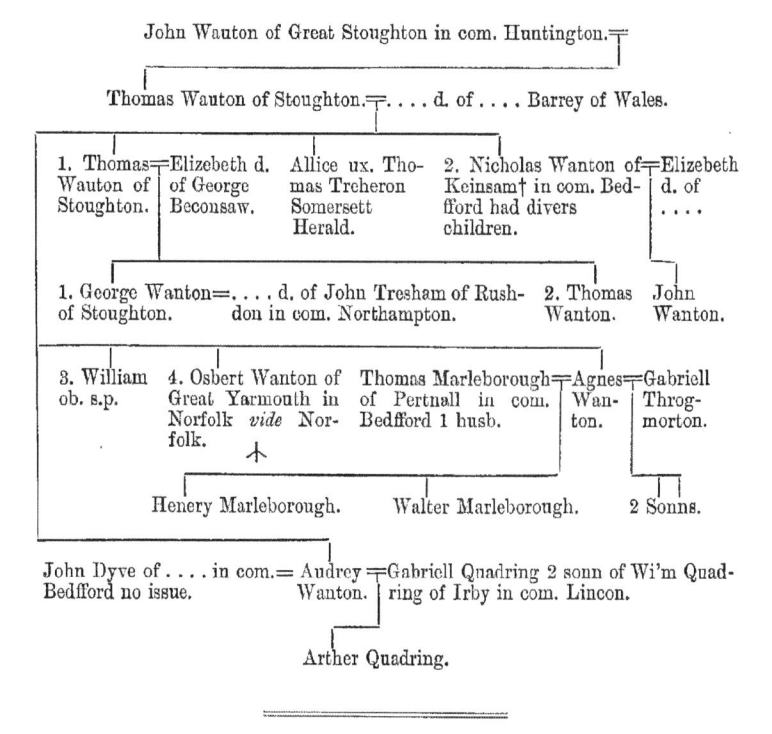

```
John Wauton of Great Stoughton in com. Huntington.=
                              │
        Thomas Wauton of Stoughton.=.... d. of .... Barrey of Wales.
                              │
┌──────────────┬──────────────┼──────────────────┬──────────────┐
1. Thomas=Elizebeth d.   Allice ux. Tho-    2. Nicholas Wanton of=Elizebeth
Wauton of │of George     mas Treheron       Keinsam† in com. Bed- │d. of
Stoughton.│ Beconsaw.    Somersett          fford had divers      │....
          │              Herald.            children.             │
          │                                                       │
┌─────────┴─────────┬──────────────┐              ┌───────────────┴───┐
1. George Wanton=.... d. of John Tresham of Rush-  2. Thomas   John
of Stoughton.    don in com. Northampton.          Wanton.     Wanton.
          │
┌─────────┼──────────────┬─────────────────┬──────────┬──────────┐
3. William  4. Osbert Wanton of   Thomas Marleborough=Agnes=Gabriell
ob. s.p.    Great Yarmouth in    of Pertnall in com.  Wan- │Throg-
            Norfolk vide Nor-    Bedfford 1 husb.     ton. │morton.
            folk.                                          │
                     ↓                                     │
            ┌────────────────────┬──────────────┐          │
            Henery Marleborough.  Walter Marleborough.   2 Sonns.
                                        │
┌───────────────────────┬───────────────┴──────────────────────┐
John Dyve of .... in com.= Audrey =Gabriell Quadring 2 sonn of Wi'm Quad-
Bedfford no issue.         Wanton.  │ring of Irby in com. Lincon.
                                    │
                              Arther Quadring.
```

---

* This name appears to be indifferently spelt WAUTON, WANTON, WAWTON, and WAULTON. This is probably the same family as that mentioned on p. 39, *ante*, as the arms of WAUTON above agree with the impaled arms of WAULTON on the brass to Nicholas Luke (ob. 1563) and "Cecyle his wyffe, one of the doughters and heyre of Sir Thomas Waulton, knyght," in Cople Church. According to Lysons the family of Wauton was seated at Bassmead in the parish of Eaton-Socon, co. Bedford, temp. H. VIII. See also p. 25, *ante*.—ED.

† *Sic* in original, but there is no such place in this county.—ED.

ADDITIONAL PEDIGREES. 199

Winch

[of Everton].

St Humffrey Winch of (*Everton*) in com. Bedfford Knt one of the Justices of the Comon Pleas * = Scissely d. of Richard Onslow of Knowll in com. Surrey [Solicitor General to Q. Elizabeth]

Onslow Winch = Judith d. of Roger of Everton in Burgoyne of Wrox- com. Bedfford all in com. War- wick.	Dorathy ux George Scott of Congherst in com Kent	(*Humphrey ob. inf.*)	(*Hellen ob inf*)
		(*Margaret ob inf*)	

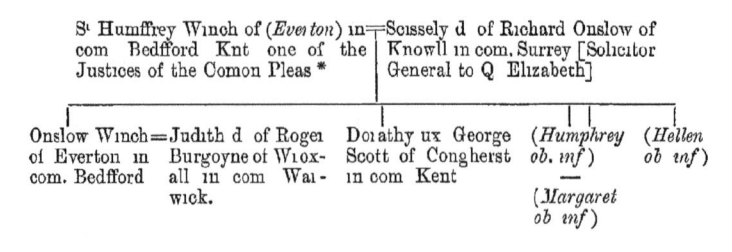

Wingate

[of Sharpenhoe in Streatley, and Harlington].

ARMS.—*Sable, a bend ermine cotised between six martlets or*
CRESTS —1, *A yate or*   MOTTO over "WIN"   2, *A hind's head couped proper*

["William Beleuerge of Sharpenho in the p'sh of Strethe in the Countie of Bedford where he liued about or before the Reigne of Hen. 3 as appeares by antient euidences without date of wch one was sealed by Ailcoyne son of Henry de Albury concerning a house and land in the p'sh of Strethe to wch deed William Beluerge wth others witnesses as also he was witnes to another deede sealed by William de Dene of land in Sharpenhoe"]

Beleverge.

[John Beleuerge of Sharpenho proued by seuerall deeds without date] =

[William Beleuerge of Sharpenho A° 31 E. 1] = [Alice relict of the saide William A° 34 E. 1]
A

---

* "In memory of Sr Humphrey Winch al's De la-Winch, Knt, who in ye 4 yeare of King James Ano Dmii 1606 was sent by him to serve in Ireland, First as Chiefe Baron after as Chiefe Justice and Councillor of State for that Kingdom From whence recalled he served his Maj'tie as one of his justices in ye court of Common Pleas at Westminster and Councillor of State fore Ireland until an apoplexye seized him in his Roabes ye 4 Day of Feb'ry 1624, in ye 71 yeare of his age, whereof in about 24 hours after he died in Chancery Lane, London whose Corps imbalmed was brought down and buried heare belowe He took to Wife Cicely one of ye daughters of Richard Onslow Alias Ondeslow Esq Sollicitor Generall to Queene Elizabeth by whome he had issue 2 sonnes and 3 daughters, viz, Onslow, Humphrey, Margaret Helle' and Dorothy Humphrey, Marg't, and Helle' died in their infancy His wife dame Cicely with Onslow and Dorothy surviving him Onslow married Judeth only daughter of Roger Burgoyne of Sutto' Esq Dorothy married George Scott of Hawkhirst in ye Countie of Kent Esq" (*M I Everton Ch*)—*Lansd MS* 887, *f* 97

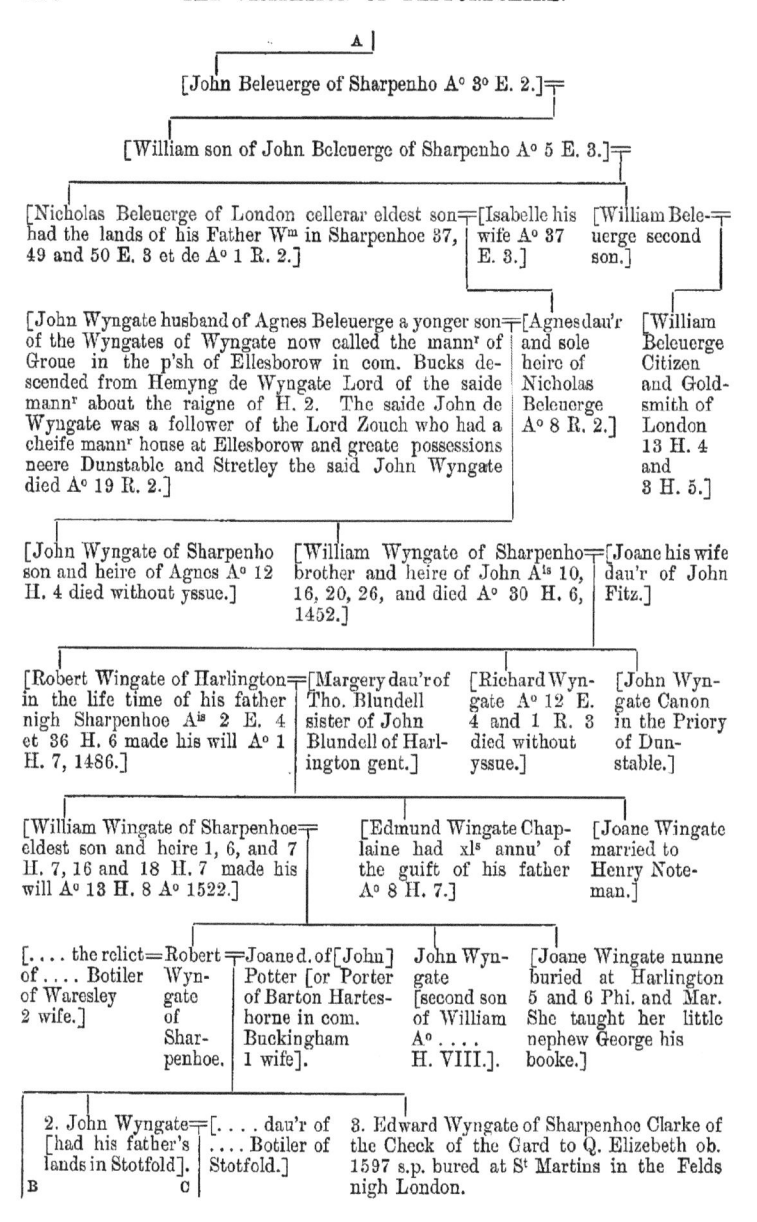

THE VISITATION OF BEDFORDSHIRE.

A |

[John Beleuerge of Sharpenho A° 3° E. 2.]=

[William son of John Beleuerge of Sharpenho A° 5 E. 3.]=

[Nicholas Beleuerge of London cellerar eldest son=[Isabelle his wife A° 37 E. 3.] [William Beleuerge second son.]
had the lands of his Father Wm in Sharpenhoe 37, 49 and 50 E. 3 et de A° 1 R. 2.]

[John Wyngate husband of Agnes Beleuerge a yonger son=[Agnes dau'r and sole heire of Nicholas Beleuerge A° 8 R. 2.] [William Beleuerge Citizen and Goldsmith of London 13 H. 4 and 3 H. 5.]
of the Wyngates of Wyngate now called the mann{r} of Groue in the p'sh of Ellesborow in com. Bucks descended from Hemyng de Wyngate Lord of the saide mann{r} about the raigne of H. 2. The saide John de Wyngate was a follower of the Lord Zouch who had a cheife mann{r} house at Ellesborow and greate possessions neere Dunstable and Stretley the said John Wyngate died A° 19 R. 2.]

[John Wyngate of Sharpenho son and heire of Agnes A° 12 H. 4 died without yssue.]
[William Wyngate of Sharpenho=[Joane his wife dau'r of John Fitz.]
brother and heire of John A{is} 10, 16, 20, 26, and died A° 30 H. 6, 1452.]

[Robert Wingate of Harlington=[Margery dau'r of Tho. Blundell sister of John Blundell of Harlington gent.]
in the life time of his father nigh Sharpenhoe A{is} 2 E. 4 et 36 H. 6 made his will A° 1 H. 7, 1486.]
[Richard Wyngate A° 12 E. 4 and 1 R. 3 died without yssue.]
[John Wyngate Canon in the Priory of Dunstable.]

[William Wingate of Sharpenhoe= eldest son and heire 1, 6, and 7 H. 7, 16 and 18 H. 7 made his will A° 13 H. 8 A° 1522.]
[Edmund Wingate Chaplaine had xl{s} annu' of the guift of his father A° 8 H. 7.]
[Joane Wingate married to Henry Noteman.]

[.... the relict=Robert =Joane d. of [John] Potter [or Porter of Barton Harteshorne in com. Buckingham 1 wife].
of .... Botiler of Waresley 2 wife.] Wyngate of Sharpenhoe.
John Wyngate [second son of William A° .... H. VIII.].
[Joane Wingate nunne buried at Harlington 5 and 6 Phi. and Mar. She taught her little nephew George his booke.]

2. John Wyngate=[.... dau'r of .... Botiler of Stotfold.]
[had his father's lands in Stotfold].
B   C
3. Edward Wyngate of Sharpenhoe Clarke of the Check of the Gard to Q. Elizebeth ob. 1597 s.p. bured at St Martins in the Felds nigh London.

ADDITIONAL PEDIGREES. 201

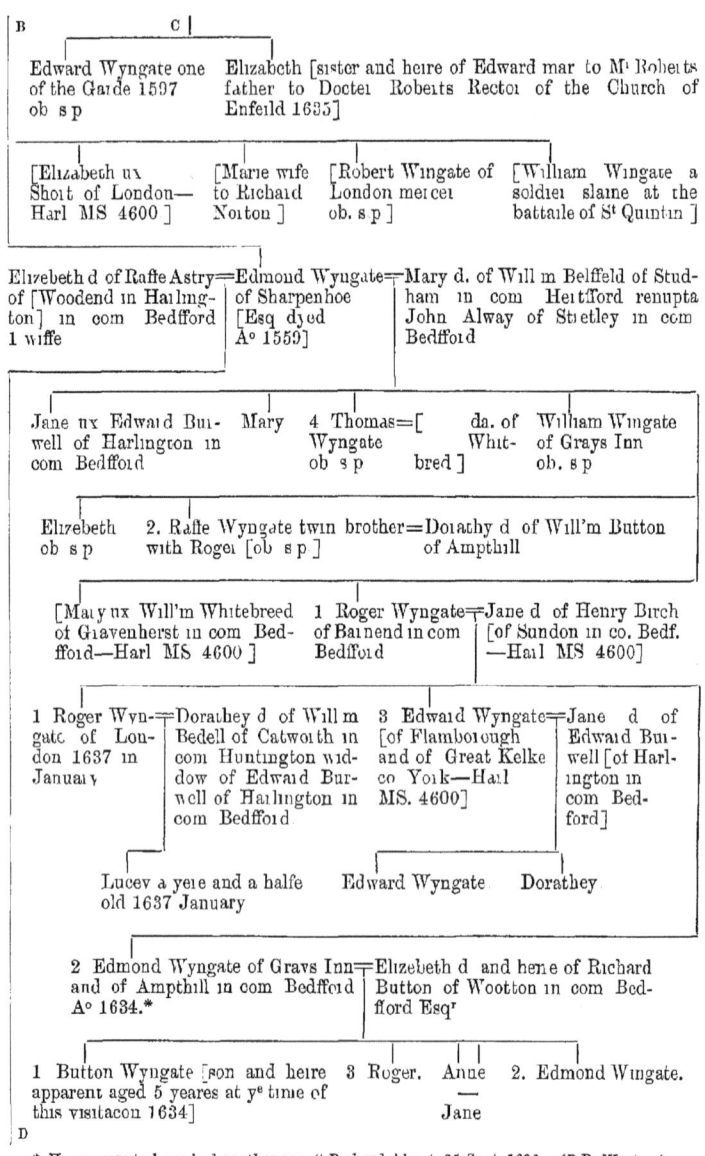

B — C

Edward Wyngate one of the Garde 1597 ob s p —— Elizabeth [sister and heire of Edward mar to Mr Roberts father to Docter Roberts Rector of the Church of Enfeild 1635]

[Elizabeth ux Short of London—Harl MS 4600] — [Marie wife to Richard Norton] — [Robert Wyngate of London mercer ob. s p] — [William Wyngate a soldier slaine at the battaile of St Quintin]

Elizebeth d of Raffe Astry of [Woodend in Harling-ton] in com Bedfford 1 wiffe = Edmond Wyngate of Sharpenhoe [Esq dyed A° 1559] = Mary d. of Will m Belffeld of Stud-ham in com Hertfford renupta John Alway of Stretley in com Bedfford

Jane ux Edward Bur-well of Harlington in com Bedfford — Mary Wyngate ob s p — 4 Thomas=[da. of Whit-bred] Wyngate — William Wingate of Grays Inn ob. s p

Elizebeth ob s p — 2. Raffe Wyngate twin brother=Dorathy d of Will'm Button of Ampthill with Roger [ob s p]

[Mary ux Will'm Whitebreed of Gravenherst in com Bed-fford—Harl MS 4600] — 1 Roger Wyngate=Jane d of Henry Birch of Barnend in com Bedfford [of Sundon in co. Bedf.—Harl MS 4600]

1 Roger Wyn-gate of Lon-don 1637 in January = Dorathey d of Will m Bedell of Catworth in com Huntington wid-dow of Edward Bur-well of Harlington in com Bedfford — 3 Edward Wyngate=Jane d of Edward Bur-well [of Harl-ington in com Bed-ford] [of Flamborough and of Great Kelke co York—Harl MS. 4600]

Lucey a yere and a halfe old 1637 January — Edward Wyngate — Dorathey

2 Edmond Wyngate of Grays Inn=Elizebeth d and heire of Richard and of Ampthill in com Bedfford Button of Wootton in com Bed-A° 1634.* ford Esqr

1 Button Wyngate [son and heire apparent aged 5 yeares at ye time of this visitacon 1634] — 3 Roger. — Anne — 2. Edmond Wingate. — Jane

D

* He appears to have had another son, "Richard," bapt 23 Sept 1636 (P R Wooton)

D D

THE VISITATION OF BEDFORDSHIRE.

[D

Anne d. of John = George Wyngate of [Harlington Esqr = Anne* d. of John
Belffeld of Stud- | A° 41 Eliz. died A° 1604] [mar. (*Martha*) | Wiseman of Canffeld
ham in com. | da. to y^e Lord St John 3 wiffe—Harl. | in com. Essex 2 wiffe
Hertfford [niece | MS. 4600]. (*She mar. 1 Rich. Cheney of* | [relict of Mr Fitch
to Mary Win- | *com. Sussex 2 to .... Colbrand also of* | and mother to S^r W^m
gate] 1 wiffe. | *Sussex.*) | Fitch].

1. Nicholas = ... d. | Dorathy ux. | Judith. | 2. Raffe = Jane d. of S^r | 3. Henry
Wyngate | of S^r | Samwell | | Wyn- | George Fitz | Wyn-
of Harling- | Charles | Harvey of | | gate. | Geffrey of | gate.
ton and of | Corn- | Brentwood | | | [Great Bar-
Hunsdon. | wallis | in com. | | | ford] in
| of .... | Essex. | | | com. Bed-
| Knt. | | | | fford Knt.

[Mary Wyngate.]

Robert Wyngate† = Amye‡ d. of [Roger] Warre of | Mary ux. George | Anne ux.
eldest sonne [died | [Hestercomb] in com. Somer- | Ereswell of Saf- | Thom.
in y^e lifetime of | sett [Esqr and of his wife da. | forn Walden in | Audley of
his father 1603. | of Sr John Popham K^t Cheife | Essex. | Houghton-
| Justice of the Kinges Bench]. | | Conquest.

John Wyngate§ 16 yere = [Alice da. of Francis | George ob. [in ye | [Thomas—
old 1617 [of Harling- | Smallman of Kiners- | Temple—Harl. | Harl. MS.
ton Esqr liueing | ley in co. Hertford | MS. 4600] s.p. | 4600.]
A° 1634]. | Esqr.]

[Robert Wingate eldest son and | [2. Francis.] | [Hester.]
heire apparent aged about 7 | —— | ——
yeres A° 1634.] | [3. George.] | [Amy.]

5. George | [Margery ob. s.p.— | [1. William Wingate | [John died in
ob. s.p. | Harl. MS. 4600.] | died s.p.] | London s.p.]

4. Raffe | [3. Richard— | 2. Edward Wyngate = Margarett d. of Peeter Taverner of
ob. s.p. | Harl. MS. | of Harlington in | Hexstonbury in com. Hertfford
| 4600.] | com. Bedfford [Esqr | [Esqr by his wife da. of Tho.
| | A° 1634]. | Docwray thelder Esqr].
| | E

* In 'Visitation of Essex,' ed. Harl. Soc., vol. i., pp. 51, 129, she is called *Agnes* and *Ellen*.
† He was s. and h. of George Wingate, and ob. v.p. 5 Aug. 1603, æt. 29. (M.I. Leighton.)
‡ She mar. secondly Gifford Long of Rowd Ashton, Sheriff of Wilts 1624.
§ Will dated 19 July, proved 20 Aug. 1642. He mar. 1, Alice, d. of Francis Smallman of Kinnersley, co. Hereford, Esq., and 2, Eliz'th, 3rd da. of Sir Anthony Chester by his first wife Eliz'th Boteler.

ADDITIONAL PEDIGREES.

E

Botiler.

1 EdwardWyngate*=Mary d and coheire of Rafe Alway of Channons in the p'ish of Shenley in com. Hertfford.

of Lockley in the p'ish of Willan in com Hertfford [sonne and heire apparent liueing A° 1634].

Frances Wyngate ux. Eustace Nedham of Wembley in com Hertfford

Jone ux John Botiler sonn and heire of William younger sonn of old Sr John Botiler of Woodhall in com Hertfford

[Rafe Wingate eldest son ob. s p.]

[Edward Wingate son and heire.]

[George Wingate]

[Frances.]

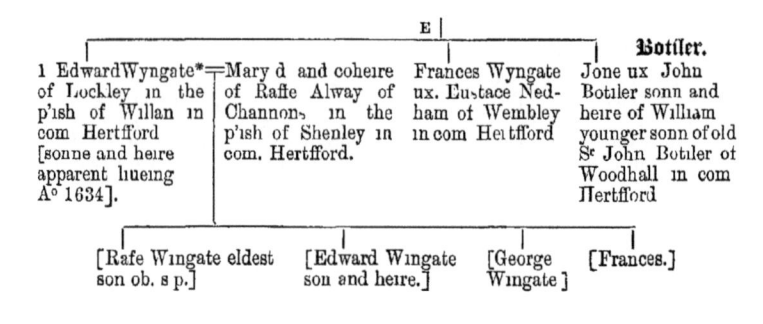

* He had an only da Mary, who mar Sir Jerome Smithson of Stanwick, co York, Bart, and had issue Sir Hugh Smithson, Bart, *ex quo* the Dukes of Northumberland

APPENDIX.

ALPHABETICAL LIST OF PEDIGREES ENTERED AT THE VISITATION OF 1669 (Ex Dawson MSS.*)

1. Abbis of Bedford
2. Aleyn of Blunham
3. Alston of Odell.
4. Armiger of Cople
5. Barnardiston of Northill
6. Bedford of Clifton and Henlow
7. Beecher of Howbury
8. Berkeley of Colworth
9. Blundell of Cardington
10. Boteler of Kirton
11. Bromsall of Beeston.
12. Carby of Everton
13. Carter of Kempston
14. Charnock of Holcutt.
15. Cheyne of Luton and Sundon
16. Cobb of Sharnebrooke.
17. Cockain of Cokayn-Hatley
18. Corbett of Sundon.
19. Crompton of Elstow
20. Daniel of Flitton
21. Day of Thurleigh.
22. Denton of Houghton-Conquest
23. Dimock of Cranfield
24. Edwards of Henlow and Ailesey
25. Fitzgeoffrey of Blackbornhall
26. Francklin of Thurleigh
27. Haselden of Goldington
28. Hastings of London
29. Hunt of Chalversterne
30. Keyling of Southill
31. Longville of Blunham
32. Luke of Cople
33. Manley of Wilshamstead.
34. Mordaunt of Oakley
35. Napier of Luton-Hoo
36. Neal of Deane and Yielden
37. Orlebar of Hinwick
38. Osborne of Chicksands
39. Pemberton of Wootton
40. Smyth of Biggleswade
41. Smythes of Bedford
42. Symcotts of Clifton
43. Vaux of Whipsnade
44. Ventris of Campton

---

* A valuable collection of Bedfordshire notes and sketches collected and made by Mr Dawson of Clapham, co Bedford —Ed

A LIST OF BEDFORDSHIRE KNIGHTS

TRANSCRIBED FROM WARBURTON AND POMFRET'S GENEALOGICAL COLLECTIONS FOR THE COUNTY OF BEDFORD, LANSDOWNE MS 887, IN B M

Knights made—

At the Charterhouse, 11 May 1603, Sir Oliver Luke
At Sir John Fortescue's, June 1603, Sir John Dives, Sir Thomas Snagg, Sir Edmond Conquest
At Sir George Farmour's, July 1603, Sir Richard Conquest
At Whitehall, 3 May 1607, Sir Edward Gostwick
At Whitehall, 27 May 1607, Sir Richard Conquest
At Bletsho, July 1608, Sir Alexander St John
At Whitehall, 7 January 1610, Sir Peter Osborne
At Hounslow 21 July 1612, Sir Robert Napper al's Sandy, Baronet
At Whitehall, 10 March 1616, Sir George Blundell
At Bletshoe. 24 July 1619, Sir Henry St John, Sir Beauchamp St John
At Kirkby, 27 July 1619 Sir William Beecher Sir Robert Charnock
At Whitehall, 19 April 1620, Sir Lewis Dives
At Ampthill, 21 July 1621 Sir William Crawford (*i e Crayford*)
At Bletshoe, 24 July 1621, Sir Francis Stanton
At Whitehall, 30 April 1622, Sir Robert Napper, Junior
At Houghton Lodge, 20 July 1624, Sir Samuel Luke
In the way between Bletshoe and Castle Ashby Sir Francis Clerke de Houghton Conquest, High Sheriff of Bedfordshire

Knights made by Charles I—

At Whitehall, 29 April 1627, Sir William Bryers of Pulloxhill
At Ampthill, 22 July 1627 Sir George Russel de Rougemont
At Ampthill, 23 July 1627, Sir Henry Austry de Woodend
At Theobald's, 19 December 1628, Sir William Ashton of Tingreth
At Whitehall, 1 January 1628, Sir John Bracking of Eaton
At Whitehall, 4 November 1632 Sir Francis Crawley of Luton, Judge
At Windsor, by Charles, Prince of Wales 20 May 1638, Thomas, Earl of Elgin
At Whitehall, 4 July 1641, Sir William Boteler of Biddenham
1641 18 July, Sir Roger Burgoine of Sutton
1641 9 August, Sir John Rolt of Milton
Date ignota, Sir John Duncombe of Battlesden *

CHARLES II

1660 11 July, Sir James Beaverley of Beyneney, co Bedf
1660 16 July, Sir Christopher Turner of Milton Erneys, one of the Barons of the Exchequer
1660 20 October, Sir Henry Piggot of Nether Gravenhurst
1660 6 November, Sir Edward Cater of Kempston
1660 16 November, Sir William Beacher of Howberry
1660 4 December, Sir Samuel Browne of Arlesey, one of the Justices of the Common Pleas
1661 17 April, Sir George Blundell of Cardington
1661 22 December, Sir John Moore, brother of Sir Henry Moore of Fawley.
1661 21 January, Sir John Keling of Southill

* He was knighted in 1648 by King Charles I while a prisoner at Carisbrooke, *cf* Wood's 'Athen Oxon,' vol iv, ii, ed Bliss

1662 16 March, Sir John Huxley of Eaton Park
1668 24 November, Sir William Gostwick of Willington
1671 30 April, Sir Francis Wingate of Harlington
1678 30 August, Sir William Franklin of Malverne *
1678 28 November, Sir William Millard of Houghton Regis
1679 20 October, Sir John Keling of Southill
1683 20 November, Sir James Astrey of Harlington
1700 24 October, Sir Thomas Bromsell
1712 23 June, Sir Samuel Ongley of Warden
1715-16 , Sir George Bing of Southill, Bart, Sir William Smith of Warden

A LIST OF BEDFORDSHIRE GENTRY OF THE SEVENTEENTH CENTURY †

(LANSDOWNE MS 887, In B M)

A Catalogue of the names of Gentlemen of Quality that have sold their Estates and are quite gone out of Bedfordshire within lesse than the space of fifty years and a known truth by Sir Robert Chernocke of Hullcott

Mr Abbiss of Stotfold
,, Ackworth of Limberry in Luton
,, Allen of Moggerhanger
,, Ansell of Barford
,, Ardds of Renhold
Sir Wm Ashen of Tingrith
Mr Astrey of Northill
,, Audley of Houghton Conquest
,, Berry of Cranfeild
Sir James Beverley of Clophill
Mr Bloteild of Flitwick
Lord Boteler of Higham Gubbin.
Mr Bray of Wootton
Sir Wm Bryers of Pulloxhill
Mr Button of Wootton
Lord Capel of Warden Abbey
Mr Catesbye of Roxhill Mannor
, Cator of Renhold
,, Chase of Milton Ernesse
,, Geo Cheyne of Stopsley
Lord Cheyne of Toddington
Mr. Child of Wimmington
Sir Richard Chetwood of Odhill
Mr Clerk of Wootton Pilling
Sir Francis Clerke of Houghton Conquest
The Earl of Cleaveland
Mr Geo Conquest of Houghton Park
,, Sam Cotton of Hinwick Hall
Sir Wm Crawford of Beckerings Park
,, John Crofts of Utberry (Upbury)
,, John Crofts of Toddington
Mr Delaune of Roxton

Mr Duncombe of Lidlington Park
,, Eades of Seawell (Sewell)
,, Richard Edwards of Henlow
,, Emery of Arlesey
,, Estwick of Wootton Woodend.
,, Farrer of Harrold
Sir John Ferris of Caddington
,, Edward Fish of Southill
,, Wm Fish of Carleton
Mr Fitzgeoffery of Crecors
Sir John Fitzwilliams of Kempston
Mr Tho Fowler of Tillsworth
,, Phillip Garroway of Tingrith
,, Gascoyn of Carrington
,, Gostwick of Marston.
,, Grey of Segenho
,, Grigg of Dunstable
,, Hale of Stotfold
,, Harding of Aspley
Sir Gerard Harvey of Fenlake.
Mr Hawkins of Tillbrooke
,, Hewit of Millbrook
,, Hinton of Eversholt
,, Iremonger of Stanbridge
,, Jakeman of Billington
,, Johnson of Brockborough Park.
,, Kempson of Tempsford.
Five Earles of Kent died without issue, only this sixth remaines.
Mr Langford of Sawford
Sir Tho (now Lord) Leigh of Leighton
Mr Ley of Caudwell by Bedford.

* Maverns in the parish of Bolnhurst
† The numerals before the names are so in the original The only alteration I have made is that of arranging the names in alphabetical order to facilitate reference —ED

APPENDIX. 207

Mr Lillingston of Lidlington Towne
,, Lovett of Elstow
,, Marborough of Warden
,, Michael of Totternhoe
,, Middleton of Brocksborough
,, Moore of Leighton
Sir St John Moore
,, Charles Mordaunt of Oakeley
Mr Nicholls of Ampthill Great Park
,, Norton of Sharpenhoe
Sir Robert Nudigate of Hawnes
Mr Paine of Puddington
,, Palmer of the Great Park
,, Paradine of Bedford
,, Piggot of Gravenhurst
Sir Wm. Plummer of Hill
Mr John Potts of Chalgrave
Sir Edward Ratcliffe of Elstow
Mr Ravens of Henlow
,, Rolt of Clifton
,, Rookes of Roxton

Sir John Rotheram of Luton
,, George Russell of Ridgemont
Mr Sadler of Aspley
Sir Beauchamp St John of Tillbrooke
Golden Sandys of Eaton Bray
Sir Arthur Savage of Carrington
Mr Shepherd of Malden
,, Ralph Snag of Kempston
,, Spicers of Marston
,, Robert Staunton of Beckerings
,, Taylor of Steventon
Sir Tho Tirringham of Hinwick Hall
,, Nicholas Trott of Eaton Bray
Mr Vites of Pulloxhill
,, Waller of Knotting
,, Watson of Little Park
,, Waverer of Clapham
Sir Humphrey Winch of Everton
Mr Wingate of Wootton
,, Geo Wyant of Moggerhanger

This list was taken in February 1667-8

Feb 14th, 1667-8, was taken a List of the Gentlemen now remaining —

	Sir Tho Alston of Odhill	3	Sir Lewis Dives of Bromham
	Mr Stephen Anderson of Eyworth	18	Mr Dodsworth of Ridgemont
	,, Astrey of Harlington	1	Sir John Duncombe of Battlesden
	Sir Wm Beecher of Hoobery	4	,, Lodwick Dyer of Colmworth
	,, Geo Blundell of Carrington		Mr Edwards of Arlesey.
17	Mr Boteler of Biddenham		,, Fish of Ickwell
15	,, Bromsall of Biggleswade	16	,, Franklin of Malvern
	Sir Sam Brown, a Judge of the Com'on Pleas	2	Sir Edward Gostwick of Willington
	,, Roger Burgoyne of Sutton		Mr Granger of Shidlington
25	,, Cary of Everton	20	,, Halfpenny of ——
	Sir Edward Cater of Kempston		,, Harvey of Ickwell
	,, St John Chernocke of Hullcott	19	,, Harvey of Thurleigh
	,, Anthony Chester of Lidlington	21	,, Hide of ——
			,, Hillersden of Elstow
6	Mr Cheyne of Bramingham		Sir John Huxley of Eaton
7	,, Cheyne of Sundon.		Mr Johnson of Milton Bryan
	,, Cockaine of Cockaine Hatley	5	Sir John Keiling Lord Chief Justice of Kings B
9	,, Conquest of Houghton Conquest		Mr Leigh of Leighton
26	,, Ben Conquest, Esq, of Hawnes		Sir Sam Luke of Cople Woodend
	,, Coppin of Market Sell, now Pulloxhill		,, Humphrey Monoux of Wootton
27	,, Cotton of Hinwick Hall, now Mr Livesay's		,, John Napier of Luton
			Mr Orlebarr of Harrold
	Sir John Cotton of Stratton		,, Osborn of Chicksand
24	Mr Daniel of Silsoe		Sir William Palmer of Hill
	,, Davies of Goldington.		,, William Palmer of Warden.
	,, Dennis of Kempston		Mr Rolt of Milton Ernys
	,, Denton of Barton	12	,, Saunders of Marston
		22	,, Simcotts of Clifton
			,, Snagg of Marston Park
		29	,, Spencer of Cople

23	Mr Squire of Eaton Socon	11	Mr Thomson of Crawley	
8	„ Stanton of Woburn		„ Vaux of Whipsnade	
28	„ Capt Stone of Brockborough		„ Ventris of Campton	
10	„ Stone of Ridgemont	14	„ Wells of Heath and Reach	
13	„ Taylor of Clapham		„ Wingate of Harlington	

The following have sold their Estates since the List was taken by Sir Robert Chernocke, and they are now in the possession of those Persons I have sett against them in the following List, viz —

Sir John Duncombe to Sir Gregory Page
,, Edward Gostwick to the Duchess of Marlborough
,, Lewis Dives to Lord Trevor
,, Lodwick Dyer to Mr Richard Hillersden
,, John Keiling to Lord Torrington
Mr Cheyne of Brammingham to Mr Crosse a Brewer
,, Cheyne of Sundon to William Clayton, Esq
,, Stanton of Wooborn to Sir Gilbert Pickering's Lady
,, Stone of Ridgemont to Ralph Ratcliffe, Esq
,, Thomson of Crawley to Mr Williamson
,, Saunders of Marston to
,, Taylor of Clapham to Lord Ashburnham
,, Wells of Heath and Reach to
,, Bromsall of Biggleswade to his Granddaughter
,, Franklin of Malvern to
,, Boteler of Biddenham to Lord Trevor
,, Dodsworth of Ridgemont to Francis Lowe, Esq
,, Harvey of Thurleigh to
,, Hide to
,, Simcots of Clifton to his Daughter
,, Squire of Eaton Socon to
,, Daniel of Silsoe to Mr Coghill
,, Cary of Everton to Mr Astell a late S S Director
,, Benjamin Conquest of Hawnes to Sir Pyn. Chernocke
,, Cotton of Hinwick Hall to Mr Livesay
Captain Stone of Brockborough to the Duke of Bedford
Mr Spencer of Cople to Mr Francis Brace, Duchess Dowager of Marlborough
,, Luke of Cople, Woodend, to Duchess Dowager of Marlborough
Edward Snagg, Esq, of Marston to

CORRIGENDA

Page	9	Read [(*Francis*) ux Thomas Leigh Sadler of (*Aspley-Guise*) in com Bedford]
„	86	For "Lor" read 'Lowe' Edmond Brassey and Elizabeth Lowe were mar. 31 Aug 1620 (P R Wootton)
„	137	For "Francis" read "Frances," line 9
,	174	Dele all within ( ) in first generation of HILLERSDEN pedigree and in third generation *after* "Allice read "(*Margaret*)"
	178	*After* "Ursula" *dele* "ux Egleby" It was Ambrose Eghonby who mar Margaret 24 Feb 1611 (P R Cardington) Ursula mar 3 Feb 1611 to "Walter Hill of Alveston in com Glouc" (*Ibid*)
„	207	*After* ' Golden' read "(? *Edwyn*)" in 2nd col, line 5
,	208	It was Edward, eld s of William Duncomb by Jane, only da of Frederick, Lord Cornwallis, who sold the Battlesden Estates, etc to Dame Frances Bathurst, and Allen Bathurst, Esq (afterwards Lord Bathurst of Battlesden), in 1706 and in 1724 the Bathurst family sold the same estates to Sir Gregory Page of Wrickle marsh, Bart, having first obtained a special Act of Parliament enabling them to do so.

APPENDIX.

ALPHABETICAL LIST OF PEDIGREES ENTERED AT THE VISITATION OF 1669 * Extracted from the Dawson MSS,† with Variations in ( ) from MS Harl. 1405, fo 15, and Additions in [ ] chiefly ex inform H Gough

1 ABBIS (W^m) of Bedford (Stotfold) [Arms as in Visitation 1634]
2 ALEYN (W^m) of Blunham (Eyne[son House in Upper Gravenhurst] 2^d brother to Sr Tho Aleyne of London K^t and Bar Sable, a cross potent or, a crescent for difference Crest—A demi-lion rampant or holding in the paws a rudder sable)
‡3 ALSTON of Odell [Azure, ten estoiles or, four, three, two, and one, on a chief argent a crescent reversed gules between two boars' heads sable]
4 ARMIGER§ (Sr Clement) of Cople (K^t Quarterly—1 and 4, Azure, three helmets or between two bars argent, ARMIGER, 2 and 3, Vair, argent and sable, a bend gules, MANCHESTER Crest—On a ducal coronet or a tiger sejant gules, crined and tufted gold)
5 BARNARDISTON (Robert) of Northill (Esq Quarterly—1 and 4, Azure, a fesse dancettée ermine between six cross-crosslets argent, BARNARDISTON, 2 and 3, Argent, a lion rampant collared argent queue fourché gules, HAVERING Crest—An antelope's head argent, charged with a crescent for difference Pedigree signed by Geo Owen and Hen Lilly)
6 BEDFORD (Samuel) of Clifton and Henlow (Esq Argent, three lions' gambs couped within a bordure engrailed sable Crest—A demi-lion rampant erased sable, collared argent)
7 (BEDFORD, the Towne of —Per pale argent and gules, a fesse azure)
8 BEECHER (S^r W^m) of Howbury [in Renhold Arms as in Visitation 1634, surcharged with an escutcheon of pretence—Argent, on a chief gules two mullets pierced or, St JOHN]
9 BERKELEY (John) of Col[m]worth (A younger family of ye Lo Berkley Gules, a chevron ermine between ten crosses pattée argent, an annulet for difference By a discent in writing)
10 BLUNDELL (Sr George) of Cardington (K^t Quarterly of eight—1, BLUNDELL, 2 GASCOYNE, 3 PIGOT, 4 WAKE, 5 BEAUCHAMP, 6 VINIER, 7 SCARGILL, 8 Blank) [Cf pp 160, 172, *ante*]

---

* Since page 201 was in type I have been enabled to identify the MS referred to on page v, *ante*, as '81 B 21,' with Harl MS 1405 in the British Museum On turning to f 15 of same I found a list of Pedigrees entered at the Visitation of 1669 with the arms in trick As this MS contains valuable information not in the former list, I append a transcript of it here The above Names have not been included in the Index, as it was already prepared before the MS was identified, but they will be found on p 204, which is indexed

† A valuable collection of Bedfordshire notes and sketches collected and made by Mr Dawson, late of Clapham, co Bedf —ED

‡ Not in Harl MS 1405   § Cf Le Neve's 'Knights,' ed Harl Soc, page 76

11 BOTELER (W^m) (Butler of Kirton [in Biddenham, Kirton's or Biddenhamford] Esq   Quarterly of six [first four quarters as in Visitation of 1634], 5, Argent on a bend engrailed sable three horseshoes of the field, [FARRER, of Harrold], 6, Blank)

12 BROMSALL* (Tho) of Beeston (Esq, now High Shreef of Bedford, mard and h of John Chase of Milton-Vrnis in co Bedf   2 shields—1, Azure a lion rampant queue fourché or, (?) BROMSALL   II, [Gules,] six crosses 3, 2, and 1, [argent,] on a canton [or] a lion passant [azure] CHASE   By a seale)

13 CAREY (Walter) of Everton (Esq   Argent, on a bend sable three roses of the field, in the sinister chief a swan   )

14 CARTER (Tho) of Kempston   [Arms as in Visitation 1634]

15 CHARNOCK (Villiers) of Holcut (Esq   [Arms as in Visitation 1634, a crescent for difference]   Crest—A lapwing proper)

16 CHENEY (W^m) of Sundon (Cheyne   Quarterly—1 and 4, [Or and azure,] a fesse [gules] fretty [ermine, CHENEY], 2 and 3,   a lion rampant BROCKAS, Bucks)

17 CHEYNE (Tho of Bramblehanger [in Luton]   Same arms, a crescent for difference)

18 COBB (Tho) of Sharnebrooke (and John Cobb of Sharnebrooke, with a crescent)   [Arms as in Visitation 1634]

19 COCKAIN (Tho) of Cockayn-Hatley (Astwick   Argent, three cocks gules   By a discent from Cokeyn Lo Cheife Baron of ye Exchequer)

20 CORBETT (Francis) of Sundon

21 CROMPTON (Robert) of Elstow   (Quarterly of four—1, Argent, on a chief vert three pheons or, CROMPTON   2, Argent a chevron ermine between three crosses formée fitchée sable, BOUGHTON, 3, Gules, three falchions barwise argent, pomelled or, HUDSON, 4, LOUFTT   A scocheon p Rich Lee, Clar 1596)

22 DANIELL (W^m) of (Newbery in ye Parish of) Flitton   Quarterly—1 and 4, a pale fusilée   , 2 and 3,   a unicorn   Crest—A unicorn's head couped   By a seale   Ent^d 1634 without arms)

23 DAY (John) of Thurleigh   [Arms as in Visitation 1634]

24 DENTON (Matthew) of Houghton-Conquest   ([Argent,] two bars [gules], in chief three cinqfoils [sable], a crescent for difference   Lanc)

25 DYMOCK (Charles) of Cranfield   (Sable, two lions passant argent ducally crowned or in the dexter chief a mullet pierced   Linc)

26 EDWARDS (Rich) of Arlesey (Esq)   [Arms as in Visitation 1634] (p Rich St George Clar 27 Aug 1632)

27 FITZGEOFFREY (John) of Blackbornhall (Bedford)   [Arms as in Visitation 1634]

---

* Burke gives these arms s n "Bromhall," but "Bromsall" is undoubtedly right   There is a monument in Biggleswade Church with a curious Latin inscription to Sir Thomas Bromsall, Knt, who died in 1706, aged 63

28 FRANCKLIN (John) of Thurleigh (Bedford) [Arms as in Visitation 1634]
29 (HASELDEN, John, of Clophill)
30 HASELDEN (Benjamin) of Goldington (Argent a cross fleurie sable Ent^d 1634)
31 HASTINGS of London (Argent, a maunch sable, in chief a trefoil slipped gules)
32 HUNT (Tho) of Chalversterne [in Roxton Arms and Crest as in Visitation 1634]
33 KEYLING of Southill *
34 LONGVILLE (Grey) of Chidlington [Shitlington] Esq Quarterly of eight—1, Gules, a fesse dancettée ermine between six cross-crosslets argent [LONGUEVILLE], 2, Azure, an eagle displayed or debruised by a bend gules [WOLVERTON], 3, Or, on a chief gules two dexter-hands argent [MENFELIN, old lords of Wolverton], 4, Gules, three fishes naiant in pale argent [? ROCHE], 5, Quarterly gules and or, in the first quarter a cross patonce argent [MIDDLETON] , 6, Azure [? vert], three lions passant-guardant argent [? LUDLOW] , 7, Sable [? azure], semée de [or an orle of] cross-crosslets argent, three covered cups of the second,   8, Blank A crescent for difference)
35 LUKE (Oliver) of (Woodend in) Cople (Quarterly—1 and 4, LUKE, 2 and 3, LAUNCELYN To Tho Luke of Cowpull in com Bedf, Esqr, p Tho Hawley, Clar , 1 Oct 36 H VIII)
36 MANLEY (W^m) of Wilshamstead [Arms as in Visitation 1634]
37 MORDAUNT (George) of Oakley (Northill, Esq Quarterly—1 and 4, Argent, a chevron between three étoiles sable, MORDAUNT, 2 and 3, Blank Crest [as in Visitation 1634])
38 NAPIER (Sr John) of Luton-Hoo (Baronet)
39 NEAL (John) of Deane (Esq Ent^d 1634)
40 ORLEBAR (Rich) of Hinwick (in Pudington Quarterly—1 and 4, Argent, two bars gules, charged, the upper with as many roses, and the lower with one of the field barbed vert, seeded or [ORLEBAR] 2 and 3, Gules a chevron engrailed between three eaglets close argent [CHILDE] Ent^d the first Coate p St Edw Bysshe, Clar , 1 Apr 1662)
41 OSBORNE (Edw) (of Norrell and of ye Inner Temple) [Arms as in Visitation 1634])
42 PEMBERTON (John) of Wootton (Quarterly—1 and 4, Argent, a chevron between three buckets sable, hoops and handles or [PEMBERTON], 2 and 3, Argent, three dragons' heads erect sable, couped and langued gules [   ] Crest—A dragon's head erect sable, couped and langued gules Hertf , by a scocheon)
43 (SMITH, JOHN, of Old-Warden Sable, on a chevron between six crosses pattée or three fleurs de-lys azure By a scale Crest—A stork's (?) head erased   , in the beak a fish .)

* For arms and pedigree of Le Neve's 'Knights,' page 150

*44 SMYTH of Biggleswade
45 SMYTHES (W^m) of Bedford (grandchild to Alderman Smithes of London   Argent, a chevron azure between three oak-leaves vert, upon each an acorn or   Granted p Wm Camden, Clar , to Alderman Smithes)
46 SYMCOTTS (W^m) of Clifton   (Sable, on a chevron engrailed between three spearheads argent as many annulets gules   By a seale)
47 VAUX (John) of Whipsnade   [Arms as in Visitation 1634]
48 VENTRIS (John) of Campton   [Arms as in Visitation 1634]

* Not in Harl MS 1405

———

[N B —In Richard Blome's 'Britannia,' London, 1673, folio, pages 348-9, is a list of " Nobility and Gentry, which are, or lately were, related unto the County of Bedford with their Seats and Titles by which they are, or have been known "   Browne Willis's 'Notitia Parliamentaria,' London, 1715, contains a list of Knights of the Shire, Borough Members from K Edward I to Q Anne, and the ' Records of the Bedford Corporation,' printed at Bedford, 1883, by order of the Corporation, contains a list of Mayors of the Borough of Bedford from 1647 to 1883 — E<small>D</small>]

INDEX.

Pedigrees are printed in SMALL CAPITALS   Arms in *italics*

A

Abbis, 73
ABBIS, 73, Alice, 73, Anne, 73, Cicely, 73, Thomas 73, William 73, —, 204, 206
Abbott, Mary, 184, Sir Morris, 184
Abdey Anne, 184 Elizabeth, 184, Henry, 184, Joane 184, Philip, 184
Abridges, Bridget, 7, Sir John, 7
Ackworth, Frances, 12, —, 206
Adkins, Elizabeth, 103
Albany, 73
ALBANY, 73, Anne, 73 Edward, 73 Elizabeth, 73, Henry, 72, John, 73 Mary 73, Robert, 73
Albury, Ailcoyne, 199, Henry, 199
Aldrich, Margery, 18, William, 18
Aldridus King, 19
Aleyn, —, 204
Allen, Catherine, 2, John, 2, —, 206
Alpert, Elizabeth, 121
Alston, 74
ALSTON, 74, Anne, 74, Dorothy, 74, Edward, 74, Elizabeth, 74, Frances, 74, Hester, 74 John 74, Peter, 74, Sir Thomas, 207, Thomas, 74, William, 74 —, 204
Alway, 1.
ALWAY 1, Anne 2, Dorothy, 1 2, Elizabeth, 2, John 1, 201, Mary, 1, 2, 152, 201, 203, Ralph, 1, 152, 203, Richard, 1
Alwolde, Agnes, 21, Roger, 21
Amyce, —, 116
Anderson, 75
ANDERSON, 75, Alice, 75, Dorothy, 75, Sir Edmond 75, Edmond, 75, Elizabeth, 75, Etheldred, 75, Sir Francis 75, Grisell, 75 Sir John, 75, Judith, 75, Katherine, 85, Magdalen, 75, Mary, 75, Stephen, 75, 207, William, 75
Andrews Elizabeth 79, George, 96 Lucy, 162, Mary 96, Richard 162, William, 79

Angell, Ellen, 129, Henry, 105, Joane, 105, William 129
Anglesey, Mary, 99, Thomas 99
Anlaby, Elizabeth, 80, Thomas, 80
Ansell, 2
ANSELL *alias* ANSTELL, 2 Agnes, 2, 87, Alexander, 2, Anna, 2, Anne, 2, Catherine, 2, Dorothy, 2, Edward, 2 Elizabeth, 2, George, 2, John 2, Mary, 2, 90, Nicholas, 2, Rose, 2, 178 Temperance 2, Thomas, 2 87, 90, 178, Ursula 2, Welthlyan, 2, Wheatley 2, — 206
Anthony, 75
ANTHONY, 75, Dr Charles, 76, Charles, 76, Edward, 75 Elizabeth, 75, Dr Francis, 75, Francis 76, Dr John, 76, John, 76, Martha, 76, Sarah 76, Susan, 75
Appowell, Welthlyan, 2
Apprice, Anne, 23, Lewis, 23
Ap Rice, 21
Apsley, Alice 11, Sir Edward, 11
Arches, Catherine, 175
Ardds, — 206
Ardern, 3
ARDERN, 3, Anne, 3, Elizabeth, 3, 31, Joane, 3, John, 115, Thomas, 3, William, 3, 31
Argentine, 40
Argentine, Cassandra, 41, Giles, 41
Arkenstall, Mary, 10, Richard, 10
Armiger, —, 204
Arnold, 141
Arnoldes, Anne, 55
Arthur, Agnes, 79, Robert, 79
Arundell, Elizabeth, 92, Sir John 48, 64, 92, Mary, 48, 64
Ascough, Anne, 147
Ashaw, Joanne, 161, Roger, 161
Ashburnham, Lord, 208
Ashby, Alice, 20, Anne, 149, Elizabeth, 128, Thomas, 20, 149
Ashcombe, Hester, 74, Sir William, 74
Ashen, Sir William, 206

ASHTON, 76, Alice, 76, Anne, 77, Clement 77, Dionisia, 76, Elizabeth 77, George, 77, Margaret, 76 Mary 76, 77, Peter, 76, Richard, 76, Robert, 76, 77 Susan, 76, Thomas, 76, Sir William, 77, 205, William 77
Ashwell Alice 33, William 33
Ashworth, or Askwith, Judith, 88, William, 88
Astell, —, 208
Aston Anne, 137, Edward, 137, Gertrude, 136, Walter, Lord, 137, Sir Walter, 136
Astry 3, 59, 77
ASTRY, 3, 59, 77, 157, Alice, 4, 59 77, Anne, 4, 59 77, 157, Barbara, 77, Diana, 157 Elizabeth, 3, 59, 77, 151, 152, 174 201, Frances 4, 59, 122, Francis, 77, Geoffrey 3, 59, George 4, 59 157, 194, Grace, 157, Sir Henry, 77, Henry 3, 59, 77, Sir James, 206, James, 157, Jane 3 59, 194, John, 157, Lora, 59, 157, Luke, 157, Margaret, 3, 59, Mary, 4, 59, 77, 132, Sir Ralph, 3, 59 Ralph, 3, 4, 59, 77, 122 132, 151, 152, 157, 174, 201, Rebecca, 157, Susan 157, Thomas, 3, 4, 59, William, 3, 4, 59, 77, —, 206, 207 *See* Astry
Ateslow, —, 114.
Athole, Earl of, 182
Atkys, Alice, 24, William, 21
Atvee, 167
Atvee, Henry, 167, Margaret, 167
Atwood, Agnes, 51, 193, Christian, 175, John, 175, Mary, 104, Thomas, 51, 104, 193
Aubrey, Sir Samuel, 148
Audley, 78
AUDLEY, 78, Anne 38, 78 202, Catherine, 189, Cicely, 78, Dorothy, 78 Elizabeth, 78, Etheldred, 78, George, 78, Henry, 78, Joane 78, Mary, 78, 171, Robert, 78, 189, Thomas, Lord 4, 78 Tho-

mas, 38, 78 171, 202, William, 78, — 206
Anstry, Sir Henry, 205
Ayre, —, 4

B

Baa, 153
Baber Margaret, 184
Bachcott, 10
Bachcott, Jane, 10
Bacon, Margaret, 110, Thomas 110
Badlesmere. 13.
Badnell, 190
Bagshaw, 79
BAGSHAW, 79, Agnes, 79. Anne, 79, Edmund, 79, Edward, 79, Elizabeth, 79, Humphrey, 79, Jane, 79, John 79, Lucy, 79 Margaret, 79, Robert, 79, Sarah, 79, Thomas, 79
Bainbrigg Elizabeth, 197, William, 197
Baker, Catherine, 164 Christian, 195, George, 164, Jane, 190 Joane, 174, Thomas, 174
Baldwin, Jane, 134, John, 134, Thomas, 134
Ballard Mary, 196, Thomas, 196, —, 161
Balthrop, Margaret, 140, 189, Richard, 140, 189
Bamford Robert, 71
Banbury 163
Banester, 157
BANESTER 157, Amy, 158, Anne, 157, Anthony, 157, Catherine, 157, Eleanor, 157, Elizabeth, 157, 158, Dr Francis, 158, Gabriel, 157, Isabel, 157, Joane, 157, John, 157, Margaret, 157, Mary, 158
Bankworth, Dr, 166, Judith, 166
Baptist, Jane 26, 108, John, 26, 108
Barber, Eleanor, 175, Margaret, 105, 169, Richard, 175, Robert, 169 William 105, 169
Bardolfe, 153
Bardolfe, Edmond, 50, 135, Elizabeth, 50, 135
Barham, 5
Barker, Alice, 118, Sir Christopher, Garter, 87, Elizabeth, 117, John 18, Stephen, 147
Barley Elizabeth, 4, Ellen, 106, Francis, 106, Thomas, 4
Barnacke, 12
Barnacke, Anne, 14 Sir John, 14, Mary, 14, Sir Richard 14, Sarah, 14, Sir William 14, William, 14
Barnardiston, 4, 79
BARNARDISTON, 4, 79, Alice, 80, Anlaby, 80, Anne, 80,

Benjamin, 80, Christopher, 4, 80, Edward, 4, 80, Elizabeth, 4, 79, 80, 106, George, 4, 79, 80, Henry, 80, Joane, 4, 80, John, 4, 80, 106, Judith, 80, Katherine 80, Margaret, 4, 80, 106, Mary, 80, Richard, 80, Robert, 80 Sarah, 4, Sigismond, 4, 80, Susan, 4 Sir Thomas, 4, 79, 106, Thomas, 4, 80, —, 204
Barnby, Mary, 92
Barnes, Elizabeth 50 98, Frances 159, John, 93, Mary, 184, Richard, 50, 184, William 159
Barnesley, 10
Barnesley, Dionisia 10
Barre, Elizabeth 81, Ellen, 45, William, 31
Barrell Humphrey, 10, Martha, 10
Barrey, —, 198
Barton, 29
Barton, Alice, 11, John, 11 29
Barwick, Anne, 182
Basford, —, 6
Bash, Edward, 136 Jane, 136
Basingham, Agnes, 68, Robert, 68
Bass, Katherine, 87, Richard, 87
Bates, George, 150, Mary, 150
Bath, Dorothy, Countess of 194, Edward, Earl of, 194
Bathurst, Allen, Lord, 208, Lady Frances 208
Batte, 19
Batte, —, 19
Battell Joane, 55
Bande, 5
BAWDE 5, Anne, 5 Elizabeth, 5, Ferdinand 5, George 5 Jane, 5, Joane, 148, John 5, Margaret, 5, Thomas, 5
Bayly, Elizabeth, 146, John 146, Margaret, 196
Baynes, Frances, 90, Richard, 90
Baynham, Anne, 160, William 160
Beanc, Anne, 79, John, 79
Beard, 12
Beard, Anne, 2, Miles, 2, Thomas 2, — 13
Beauchamp, 9, 51, 116, 172
Beauchamp, Alice 162, Edith, 15, 52, Isabel, 52, Joane, 172 Sir John, 15, 52, 58, John, 162 Margaret, 15 52, Sir Roger, 52, Sir Walter, 52, William, Baron of Bedford, 172, Sir William, 52, William, 52, —, Earl of Warwick, 52
Beaufort, John, Duke of Somerset, 15, 52 Margaret, Duchess of Somerset, 15 52
Beaufoy, Sir William 183
Beckett, Alice 49, 50, 191, John, 71 Simon, 71 72

Beconsaw, Elizabeth, 198, George, 198
Bedell, 154
Bedell, Dorothy, 151, 201, Mary, 123, Thomas, 154 William, 123, 151, 201
Bedells, George, 159, Susan, 159
Bedford, 1, 71, 72
Bedford, Francis, Earl of, 33, 53, 76, Margaret, Countess of, 33, 53, —, Duke of, 208, —, 204
Bee, Diana, 157, Edward, 157
Beecher, 81
BEECHER, 81, Anne, 82, 114, Bartholomew, 81 Dorothy 82, Edward, 81, 82, Elizabeth, 2, 81, 82, 194 Fane, 81, Francis, 81, George, 81, Henry, 2 81, Howard, 81, John 81, 82. Judith 81, 82, Katherine, 82 Mabel 81, Margaret, 81, Mary, 81, Oliver, 82, St John, 81, Sir William, 81, 114, 205, 207, William, 81, 82, 194, — 204
Beleverge 151
Beleverge, Agnes, 200 Alice, 199, Isabel, 200, John, 199, 200, Nicholas, 200, William, 199, 200
Belfield, 1
Belfield Anne, 152, 202, John, 152 202 Mary, 1, 151, 201, William, 151, 201
Bell Mary, 166, Sir Robert, 166
Bellaby Barbara, 143 Robert, 143
Bellay, Jane, 90, Dr John 90
Bellingham, Jane 69, William, 69
Belson Katherine, 98, Thomas, 98
Bendowe, Edmond, 25, Margaret, 25
Bengeratt Henry, 161, Susan, 161
Beulosse Sergeant, 71
Bennett, Elizabeth, 126
Benolte, Anne 18, Thomas, Clarenceux, 110, Thomas, 48
Beresford, 67
Berisford, Ellen 61, Thomas, 61, —, 66.
Berkeley, —, 204
Bernacke 27
Bernard, Dorothy, 2, Edward 39, Mary, 39, Richard, 2
Berner, Elizabeth, 66, Mary, 66, William, 66
Berners, Jane 117, John, 129, Joseph 117, Susan 129
Berry, —, 206
Besouth, Jane, 150
Beswick Elizabeth, 166, William, 166
Betts, Elizabeth, 118
Beverley, 82
BEVERLEY, 82, Alice, 82, Anne, 82, Elizabeth, 82 Ellis, 82,

INDEX. 215

Sir James, 205, 206; James, 82 97; Jane, 82 97; John, 82; Nathanie¹, 82 Robert, 82; Thomas, 82; Walter, 82; William, 82
Bewple, 12
Bewple, Elizabeth, 13, Margaret, 14; Sir Ralph, 13, 14
Bill, Catherine 26; Joane, 7, 87
Bing Sir George, 206
Birch, 158
BIRCH, 158, Alice, 158, Anne, 123, 158, 159, Catherine 158, Dominick, 158, Dorothy, 158, 159 Elizabeth, 158, 159, Emanuel, 158, Frances, 159, Grace, 159, Henry, 124, 151 158, 159 201, Humphrey, 159, Huntingdon, 158, Jane 124, 151, 158, 159, 201 Jeremy, 158, 159, Joane, 159, John, 129 159, Judith, 158 159, Mary, 158, 159, Nathaniel, 158, Nicholas, 159, Priscilla, 158 159 Richard 158 159, Samuel, 158, Susan 158, 159, Thomas 158 159, William, 158
Bircheley, Anne, 184 Edward, 184
Bird, 164
Bird, Elizabeth 8, John, 164, Margery, 164, Mary, 145, Nichola, 164, Richard, 8 Thomas 164
Birkenhead, Adam 177, Elizabeth 177
Birkett, John, 170 Mary, 170
Birksherum —, 187
Bishopton 168
Blakesley Lawrence, 140, Margaret 110
Bland, Elizabeth 118
Blennerhasset, 159
BLENNERHASSET, 159, Anne, 160, Edward, 160, Elizabeth 160, Jane, 159, John, 159 Mary 160, Ralph 159, Samuel, 160, Thomas, 160, William, 160
Bletsoe, 83, 155
BLETSOE 83, Agnes 83, 95, Anne, 83, Dorothy 83, Edward, 83, Elizabeth, 83, Hugh, 83, Isabella, 83, John 83 Katherine, 83, Margaret, 83 Oliver, 83, Paul, 83, Richard, 83, Robert, 83, Samuel, 83, Saunderson, 83, Thomas, 83, William 83 95, 155
Blockett, John, 30
Blofield, Cicely, 133, Edmund, 133 —, 206
Blount, 32, 187
Blount, Anne, 187, Elizabeth, 175, Walter, Lord Mountjoy, 187 William, 175, 187
Bloyon, 12
Bloyon Sir Allen, 13, Elizabeth, 13

Blundell 160
BLUNDELL, 160, Alice, 160, 161, Anne, 161, Arthur 161, Catherine, 160, 161, Elizabeth, 116, 161 Frances, 161, Sir Francis, 161, 170, Francis, 161, Sir George 109, 116 161, 205, 207, George, 109, 161, Henry, 160 161 Joane, 160, 161, John 160, 161, 170, 200, Josias, 161, Joyce, 161, Margery, 200, Mary 170, Nicholas, 160, Richard, 160, 161 Robert, 161, Sarah, 109 161, Susan, 161, Thomas 161, 200, William, 160, 161, —, 204
Blunville 74
Blunville *alias* Blomfield, Frances, 74, Simon, 74
Blyant, Margaret, 190, Simon, 190
Bodinant, 163
Bohun, 32
Bohun John, 187, Mary, 187
Bold Jane, 151, Richard, 181
Boreyne Sir Geoffrey, 15, Isabel, 15
Bolingbroke, Oliver, Earl of, 71, 81 92, 96, 147, 192 194
Bolsonoth 83
BOLSWORTH, 83, Alice 84, Anne, 84, Banester, 84, Edmund 84, Elizabeth 84, George, 84 Joane, 84, John, 84 Robert, 83, 84, Rose, 83, Sarah 84, Susan, 84, Thomas, 84
Bolton, Elizabeth, 87, 172, Joane, 28 Mary, 80, Thomas, 80, William, 172
Bond, —, 17
Booth, 40
Booth, Agnes 42, 180, Charles, 42, 180, Frances 105, Sir George, 75, Jane, 42, John, 42, 84, Martha, 84, Roger, 42 Thomas, 42
Borham, Anne, 11, Thomas, 11
Borne Elizabeth, 23, William 23
Borough, Sir John, Norroy, 71
Bosgrave, 5
BOSGRAVE, 5 Agnes, 6, Anne, 6, Francis 6 Jane, 6, Joane, 6, John, 5, 6, Leonard, 6, Margaret, 6 Mary, 6, Richard, 6, Thomas, 6
Bosse Elizabeth, 110 Thomas 110
Bostock Elizabeth, 120, Peter, 120
Boteler *See* Butler
Botetourt, 47
Bothwell, — 183
Boughton, Elizabeth, 135, Richard, 135, William, 22
Bowles, 7
Bowles, Anne, 3, 7 11, 87, John 7, 11, 87, Mary, 136, Richard, 3, Thomas, 136

Bowstred, Anne, 47
Boyfield *alias* Bosvile, Elizabeth 17, John, 17
Boyland, Sir John, 13
Boyle, Dorothy, 170, Dr Michael, Bp of Waterford 170
Boys, Anne, 167, Edward 167 *See* De Boys
Brace, Francis, 208
Bracking Sir John, 205
Bradestone, 13
Bradshaw, Alice, 52, Sir Thomas, 52
Bradwell, 10
Bradwell Catherine, 157, Elizabeth, 10, Dr Stephen, 157, Stephen 157
Bramstor, Dorothy, 130, Sir John, 130
Brandon, Rebecca, 193, Robert, 193
Braxby, —, 162
Bray, 21, 162
BRAY, 162, Alice 22 162 Anne, 61, 163, Auncell, 162, Dorothy, 163 Sir Edmund, Lord, 163, Edmund, 162, Sir Egidius, 61, Elizabeth, 162, 163, Frances, 163, Frideswide, 163, Grace, 25, 162 Henry 22, Jane, 162 163, Jaques 162 Joane, 162, Jocelyn, 162 John, Lord 163, John, 162 Lucy, 162, Mary, 163, Sir Reignald 162, Reignald, 162, Richard, 162, Thomas, 162, Sir William, 162, William, 162, —, 206
Braybrooke, 67
Braybrooke, Sir George 68, Sir Gerard, 68, Isabella, 68
Brecherton, John, 115
Brenker, 153
Brenker, John, 153
Brereton, Jane, 163, Sir Urian, 163
Bressey 85
BRESSEY 85, Constance 86, 109, 139, 169, Edmund 85, 86, 109, 139, 169 Elizabeth, 86, Francis, 86, Hemphilles, 86, Henry, 86 John 86, Katherine 85, Lucretia 86 Martha, 86, Mary, 86, Ralph, 86, Robert, 86 Thomas, 86
Bridges Jane, 195, Walter, 195, William, 195
Bridgwater, John, Earl of, 194
Briers 86
BRIERS, 86, Alice, 86, Anne, 86 Arabella 86, Sir William, 86 205, 206, William, 86
Briscoe, —, 57
Bristol, Beatrice, Countess of 23, John, Earl of 23
Brocas 163
Brocas Edith, 163, Frances, 91, John 163
Brocket, —, 128

Bromfield, Alderman 169, Anne, 169, Robert, 169
Bromfleet 165
Bromhall, 87
BROMHALL, 87, Agnes, 2 87 Anne, 87 Elizabeth, 87, 145 Joane, 87, Sir John, 87 John, 2, 87, 145, Katherine, 87, Lewis, 87, Oliver, 87 Robert, 87 Ursula, 87
Bromsall, Anne, 169, Sir Thomas 206 William, 169 —, 204 207, 208
Brooke, 40, 44
Brooke, Anne, 163, Sir David, 6, Elizabeth 41, Ellen, 41, George, Lord Cobham 81, 163, Sir Lawrence 41, Margaret, 6, 41, Mary 45, Ralph York Herald, 74, Ralph, 41, William 45, —, 134
Broughton, 12
Broughton Agnes, 14, Anne 14, 15 Elizabeth, 14 Sir John, 14 15, John, 14, Katherine, 14, Mary 14, Matthew 13, Pauline, 14, Ralph, 13 Sir Robert, 13, 14, Robert, 13 Roger, 13, Sir Rowland, 13, William, 13
Browne, Alice 172 Anne 117, 193, Sir Anthony Viscount Montagu, 48, 65, Dorothy, 98, Elizabeth, 41, 105, 172, Humphrey 172 Jane, 195 John, 105, 193, Margaret, 68, Mary, 48, 65 Matthew, 98, Sir Samuel, 205, 207, Simon 68, Weston, 195 Sir Wistan 41
Broye, 9, 51
Broye, Beatrice, 51, John, 51
Bruce, Edward, 186, Sir George, 186 Margaret 186, —, Lord of Kinloss, 186
Brudenell, Edmund, 66, 197 Elizabeth, 29, 66, 197 Sir Robert, 29
Bruges, Dorothy, 163, Sir Edmund, 163, Frances, 132, 189, Henry, 132, 189
Brydiman, 163
BRYDIMAN 163, Charles, 163 Edith, 163, Edmund, 163, George 163, Margaret, 163, Mary, 163
Bryers *See* Briers
Buckby, or Buckley, Ursula, 130 William, 130
Buckingham, Henry, Duke of, 48 64
Buckworth, Edward, 157, Grace, 157
Budockshyde, 160
Budockshyde Catherine, 161, Roger, 161
Bugges, Edward, 26, Margaret, 26
Bulkeley, 39, 67, 164
BULKELEY, 164 Anne, 39, 55, 61, 141 164, Ardeene, 164,
Catherine 164, Cicely, 164, Dr Edward 164 Elizabeth, 164, Ellen, 164 Hugh 164 Humphrey, 164, Isabel, 164, Jane, 39, 164, John, 164, Margaret, 164, Nathaniel, 164, Nichola, 164, Paul, 164 Peter, 164, Robert, 39, 55, 141, 164, Roger, 164, Rowland, 164, Thomas 164, William 39, 61, 164
Bull, William, 72
Butler 36, 168
Bulter, Richard, 115
Burd, Ambrose 184, Joane, 184
Burgatt, 12
Burgett, Katherine, 14, Sir William, 14
Burgoyne, 7, 87, 191
BURGOYNE, 7, 87, Anne, 7, 11, 87, 88, 191 Barbara, 88, Elizabeth, 87, 88 Jane 88, Joane, 7, 87, John, 7, 87, 88, Judith, 88 199, Martha, 88, Mary, 88, Nathaniel, 88, Peter, 88, Robert, 7, 87 88, Sir Roger, 205, 207, Roger, 88 199, Susan, 88 Thomas, 7, 11, 87 88
Burleigh, Elizabeth 4, 79, Thomas 4 79
Burnby, Mary, 69 Richard 69
Burnell, 47
Burrows, Arthur, 176 Frances, 176
Burton Joane, 142, Robert, 142
Burwell Dorothy, 151, 201 Edmund, 151, Edward, 151, 201, Jane, 151, 201
Bury, 8
BURY, 8, Alice, 9, Anne 8, 9 Catherine 8, Elizabeth 8, 9, 27, Frances, 137, 204, Francis, 8, 137, George, 8, 9 Henry, 8, 9, Humphrey 8 9, 50, 192, Isabel 8, Jacob, 9, June, 8, 9, 50 192, John, 8, 9, Margaret, 8, 9, Mary, 9, Richard, 8, 9, 27, Roger, 8, Susan, 137, Thomas, 8
Bussey Andrew, 116, Cecil, 116, Elizabeth, 116
Butler, 6, 9 10 40, 43. 84, 162
BUTLER or Boteler 6 9, 84, Agnes, 14, 24, Alice, 7, 11, 85, 129 162, Anne 7, 9-11, 84, 85 197, Bridget 7, Catherine 10, 40, 46, 85, Crestyde, 10 53, Dionisia 10, Dorothy 7, Sir Edward, 117, Edward, 117, Elizabeth, 10 41 64, 85, 145, 162, 167, 202, Ellen 85, Emma, 7, Etheldred, 75, Francis, 85, George 10, 40, 85 197, Grace, 7, 44, 185, Sir Henry 166, James, 11, Jane, 10 11, 164, Joane, 6, 203, John, Baron, 75, Sir John, 11, 203,
John, 6, 7, 9 11, 11, 46 53, 64, 85 185 203, Judith, 85 Margaret 6,7 10 84, Martha, 7 10, 84, 85, Mary 7. 10 84, 117 127, Nicholas, 10, Oliver 11 85 Oswald 24, Peter 10, Sir Philip. 166, Phillis, 10, Raphael 10, Rebecca, 166, Richard, 6, 7, Robert 7 9, Roberta 166, Thomas, Baron, of Sudley, 162, Sir Thomas, 85, Thomas 6, 7, 9, 11, 85, Ursula, 7, 84, 85, Sir William, Baron of Warrington 164, Sir William, 6, 127, 205, William, 6, 7, 9-11 41, 84, 85, 127 129 145, 167 203, —, Lord 206, —, 151, 200, 204, 207, 208
Button, 19, 89, 151
BUTTON 89, Anne, 89, Dorothy, 89, 151, 201 Edmund, 89, Elizabeth, 30, 89, 151, 201, George, 89, Humphrey, 89, James 89, Jane, 89, Joane, 19, 89, 97, John 89, Margaret, 89, 117 Richard, 30, 89, 151, 201, William 19, 89, 97, 117 151, 201, — 206
Button, —, 206

C

Cade, John, 163, Mary, 163 Sir William 163
Cage, Daniel, 125, Elizabeth, 125
Cagenho Amicia, 60
Cailton, John, 159, Priscilla, 159
Calthrop, Mary, 36, Sir William 36
Calton, Elizabeth, 140, Martha, 106, Nicholas, 106
Calverley, Agnes, 69, Sir George, 69
Camden, —, Clarenceux, 121, 133, 134, 148
Camoys, 13
Campion, Abraham, 167, Anne, 184, George, 184 John, 171, Margaret, 167 Mary 171
Camville, —, 183
Capel, Lord, 206
Capon, Rebecca, 112
Carberry, Earl of, 80
Carey, —, 204, 207, 208
Carlisle, Alexander, 175 Alice, 175
Carlton, Elizabeth, 165
Carpenter Anne. 123 Mary, 123, Richard, 123, Thomas, 123
Carrisforth Jane, 190, John, 190
Carter 90, 165
CARTER, 90, 165, Abraham, 165, Amy, 158, Anne 91, Aunsell, 90, 91, Catherine, 165, Charles, 165, Edward, 128, Elizabeth, 90, 91, 165, Ellen, 128, Frances, 165,

INDEX. 217

Francis 165, George, 91, 128, Jane, 90, 91 165, Joane 17, John, 91 165, Mary 2 90, 128, Millicent, 90, Paradise, 90, Prudence, 165, Richard, 165, Robert 17, Susan 91, Thomas, 90, 91, 165, William, 2, 90, 91 158, 165, Winifred, 90 —, 204
Cartwright, Henry, 16, Mary, 16
Casleton, Anthony, 126
Castell, Mary 115, Robert, 115
Cater, 89
CATER 89, Cornelius, 89, 90, Sir Edward, 205, 207 Edward, 88, 90, Frances, 90, George 90, Henry, 90, John, 89, Mary 88, 90, Richard, 89 90, Susan, 90, Thomas, 90 William, 90, —, 206
Catesby, Anne, 66, 197, Anthony 46, Elizabeth, 66, 188, Sir Humphrey, 66, 197, Isabel, 46, Jane, 65, Richard, 188, Sir William, 66 —, 206
Catesey, Elizabeth, 26
Catlin, 11
CATLIN 11, Alice, 11 Anne 11, 87, Jane, 49, John 11, Mary, 11, Sir Robert, 11, 87, Robert, 11, Thomas, 11, William, 49
Cave, 165
Cave, Anne, 126 Anthony, 166, Judith 166, William, 126
Cavendish, Elizabeth, 110
Chad, Edward, 49, Joane, 49
Chadnorth, 116
Chadworth, —, 146
Chamberlain, 168
Chamberlain Martha, 88, Thomas, 88
Chamberlain *alias* Spicer, Amphilis, 138, 169, Jane, 138, 169, John, 169, William, 138
Champneys, Justinian 135, Muriel, 135
Chantrell Katherine, 80, William 80
Chapman Elizabeth, 128, 177, Mary, 128, Thomas, 128
Chard, Edward 87, Ursula, 87
Charge, Elizabeth, 63, Henry, 63
Charles VI of France, 182
Charlton, 13
Charnock, 12, 92
CHARNOCK, 12, 92, Agnes, 92 Ambrose, 12, Anne, 92, 194, Beauchamp, 92 Elizabeth, 92, Florence, 12, 92, Frances 12, Francis 92, Isabel, 145, Sir John, 92, John, 12 92, Katherine 92 194, Martha, 92, Mary, 12, 92, Sir Pyn, 208, Richard, 12, 92, Sir Robert, 92, 205, Robert, 12, 92, 194, Sir St John, 207 St John, 92, —, 204
Chase —, 206
Chaworth, 13

Chaworth, Elizabeth, 28, Sir William 28
Cheeke Frances, 65, Henry, 65, Sir John 65
Chendercotts, 198
Cheney, 12, 13 91
CHENEY, 12, 91, Alexander, 15, Anne, 15, 91 Barbara, 144, Catherine, 8, 91, Dorothy, 91, Edith, 15 Edmond 15, Edward, Dean of Salisbury, 15, Eleanor, 15, Elizabeth, 37, 91, Frances, 91, 114, Sir Francis, 15, Frideswide, 15, George, 91, 206, Sir Henry, 15, Isabel 15, Jane, 15, 37, Sir John, 15, John, 15, 42, 91, Lawrence 8, Lettice, 129, Margaret, 15, 91, 194, Martha 54, 202, Mary 91, Richard, 54, 202, Sir Robert, 15, Robert, 91, 129 Roger, 15, Sir Thomas, 15, 91, 144, 194, Thomas, 91, 114, Sir William, 15, William, 15, 91, Winifred, 42, —, Lord, 206, —, 204, 207, 208
Chertsey, Margaret, 6, Robert, 6
Cheshire, Emley, 43, — 125
Chester, 27 165
CHESTER, 165, Alice 166, Anne, 166, Sir Anthony, 166, 202, 207, Anthony 166, Daniel, 166 Dorothy 166, Elizabeth, 166, 202, Emma, 166, Frances, 166 Francis, 166, Henry 166, Jane, 166, Joane 166, John, 166, Judith 166, Mary, 166, Nicholas, 166, Rebecca, 166, Richard, 166, Robert, 166, Roberta, 166 Susan 166 Thomas, 166, Sir William, 166, William 165, 166
Chester, Earl of, 27
Chetwood, 59, 67
CHETWOOD, 59 Abigail, 61, Agnes, 60, 61, 69, Alice 60, Amicia, 60, Annabel, 60 Anne 61, Beatrice, 61, Catherine, 61, Dorothy, 61, Elizabeth, 60 61, 69, Ellen, 61, Frances, 61, 121, Grace, 61, Isabel, 60, James, 61, Jane, 61, Joane, 60, Sir John, 60, 69, John, 59-61, Knightley, 61, Lucy, 60 Margery, 60, 61, Mary, 60, 61 Sir Nicholas, 60, Olive, 60, Sir Ralph 60 Randolph, 61, Sir Richard 61 121, 206, Richard, 61, 69, Robert, 60, 61, Roger 60, 61 69, Susanna 61, Sir Thomas, 60, Thomas 60, 61, 69, Tobias, 61, Valentine 61, William, 60, 61
Cherall, 45
Chevall, Edmond, 45, Lucy, 45

Cheyne *See* Cheney
Chibnall, 16
CHIBNALL, 16, Alice, 16, 140, Amy, 16, Anne 16, Anthony 16 Elizabeth, 16, Frances 16, George, 16, John, 16 Judith, 16, Mary 16, Richard 16, 140, Robert, 16, Thomas, 16, William 16, Wyborow, 16
Chicheley, Christian 36, Frances, 140, John, 36, Thomas, 140
Child 92
CHILD, 92, Anne, 84, 131, Elizabeth, 93, Katherine, 93, Margaret, 93, Matthew 131, Richard 93, William, 92 93, —, 206
Chishull, 93
CHISHULL, 93, Alice, 93, Anne, 93, Barbara 93 Bartholomew, 93, Christopher, 93, Elizabeth, 93, Jane, 93, John 93, Lawrence, 93, Mary, 93, Paul 93, Sarah, 93, Susan, 93, William, 93
Chisnall, Eleanor, 177
Chorvile, Sir Bryan, 28
Clapton, Eleanor, 23, George, 23
Clare, 12
Clarence, George, Duke of, 52
Clarke, Anne, 33 83 97, 117, 196, Dorothy 152, Edmund, 80, Sir Francis, 152, 205, 206, Francis, 97, Isabel, 112, Jane, 158, John 84, 158, Magdalen 183, Margaret, 80, 83, 84, 116, Philip, 80, Robert, 117 Thomas, 83, 112, Walter 84, William, 33, 146, —, 206
CLAVER 94, Anne, 94, Arthur, 94, Clement, 94, Elizabeth, 94 Henry, 94 John 94, Marmaduke, 94, Matthew, 94, Thomas, 94
Claxton, — 187
Clayton, 40
Clayton, Isabel, 42, John, 42
Cleveland, Countess of 86, Earl of, 206
Clifford, Anne, 53, Henry, Lord, 53
Clifton, Alice 147, Anne, 158, Henry 147
Clinton, Elizabeth 28, —, Lord, Earl of Huntingdon 28
Clopton, 153
Clopton, Alice 55 John, 55, Katherine, 14, William, 14
Cobb 16 94
COBB, 16, 94, Agnes 17, 83, 95, Alice, 16, 17, Anne, 17, 94 95, 108 Catherine 94, 148, Cicely, 83, 94, 95, Dorothy, 94 95, Edward, 95, Elizabeth 17, 94, George, 17, 95, Henry, 17, Isabel,

F F

17, 95, 150 , Joane, 17 , John, 17, 94, 95 , Lawrence, 17 , Lucy, 94 , Margaret, 17, 54, 83, 94, 95, 108 , Mary, 17, 95 149 , Oliver 95 Paul, 94, 95 , Rebecca, 95 Richard, 17 , Samuel, 95 , Thomas, 17, 54, 83, 94, 95, 108, 150 , William, 16 17, 94, 95, 149 , —, 204
Cobham, George, Lord, 81, 163 , —, 17
Cockayne, 17, 95
COCKAYNE, 17, 95 , Anne, 18 189 , Arabella, 96 , Beatrice, 17, 18 , Catherine, 18 96 , Chad, 18, 39, 95, 96 , Charles 96, 113 , Dorothy, 2, 96 Edith, 17 , Edmund, 18 , Elizabeth 17, 18, 39, 95, 96 , Frances, 18 , George, 18, 95, 189 , Humphrey 18 , Isabel, 18, 96 , Jane, 95 96 , Sir John 17 , John, 2, 17, 18, 95 96, 113 , Judith, 18 , Lawrence, 96 , Lewis, 96 , 113 , Margaret, 18 96 , Mary, 96 , Nicholas, 18, 95, 96 , Oliver, 96 , Reynold 17 , Richard, 96 , Rose, 18, 141, St Jonn, 96 , Susan, 96 113 , Thomas, 96 Ursula, 96 , William, 18 , —, 204, 207
Cocker, Anne, 178
Cockerham, Jane, 196 , Richard 196
Coghill, —, 208
Cogniers, Dorothy, 82 , William, 82
COLBECK, 18 , Alice, 18 , Anne, 18 19 , Catherine, 19 , Edward, 19 Elizabeth 18 19 , Jane, 49 , Joane 19 , John, 18, 19, 55 , Margery, 18 , Mary, 19 , Philip, 19 , Richard, 18 , Rose, 18, 55 , Simon, 19 , Thomas, 18, 19 , William, 49
Colbrand, John, 54 , Martha, 54, 202
Colman, 74
Coleman, Elizabeth, 74 , John, 74
Collet, Jane, 179
Collins Anne, 39 , Edward, 39
Collis, Alice, 69 , William, 69
Colquit, Anne, 78 , Nicholas, 78
Colville, —, 17
Combes, Francis, 93 , Susan, 93
Commaunder, Elizabeth, 33
Coningsby Jane, 146 , Mary, 136 179 Sir Ralph, 146 , Thomas, 136
Conquest, 19, 97
CONQUEST, 19, 97 , Anne, 20, 89 97 , Benjamin, 207, 208 , Bridget, 97 , Charles, 97 , Cicely, 20 , Dorothy, 20 38, 97, 108 , Sir Edmond, 97, 146, 205 , Edmond, 19, 20, 89, 97 ,

Elizabeth, 20, 44, 79, 97, 146 , Emma 97 , Frances, 20, 97 , George, 20, 79, 89, 206, Hester, 97 , Isabel 19 , Jane, 82 97 , Joane, 19, 89, 97 John, 19, 97 , John Thimelby, 97 , Judith, 97, 108 , Lewis, 97 , Mary, 97 , Miles 97 , Sir Richard 44, 97, 103, 205 , Richard, 19 20, 38, 82, 97 , Sarah, 97 William, 20, 97 , —, 207
Constable, Alice, 75 , Sir John, 75 Robert, 173
Cony, Abian, 139 , Anne, 122 , Elizabeth, 93 , Henry, 93 , Matthias, 139
Conyers, —, 173
Cooke, Anne, 29, 136 , Anthony, 29 , Edmund, 186 , Sir Edward, 136 , Elizabeth, 186 , John 180 , Judith, 180 , Robert Clarenceux, 81, 89, 104, 117, 130, 142, 147
Cookeson, Elizabeth, 137 , Thomas, 137
Cooper, Elizabeth, 45 , Margaret, 35, 62 , Michael, 45
Copandall, John, 47 , Wyborow, 47
Cope, Edward, 69 , Mary, 69.
Copley, 31, 153
Copley Anne, 31, 110, 172 , Edward, 31, 110, 153, 172
Coppin, Martha, 129 , Thomas, 129 , —, 207
Corbett, Anne, 54 , Robert, 54 , —, 204
Cordall, Olive 20 , William, 20
Cornell, Mary, 180 , Simon, 180
Cornwall, Arthur, 116 , Martha, 116
Cornwallis, Sir Charles, 202 Frederick, Lord, 208 , Jane, 208
Cotes, 67
Cotton, 87
Cotton, Sir John, 207 Magdalen, 46 , Mary, 176 , Sir Richard, 176 Samuel, 206 —, 207, 208
Coulcherfe, 47
Coultman, Anne, 91
Coulton John, 159 , Priscilla, 159
Cousin Agnes, 49 , William, 49
Condray, 197
Cowdray, Margaret 66 , Sir Thomas 66
Craddock, Mary, 130 , Walter, 130
Crane, Anne, 196
Cranfield alias Glover Elizabeth, 90 , Katherine, 90 , William, 90
Crawford See Crayford
Cramley. 98
CRAWLEY, 98 , Anne, 98, 192 , Dorothy, 98 192 , Elizabeth 51, 98, 192 , Florence, 98 , Frances, 98 , Sir Francis, 51,

98 192 205 , Francis, 98, 192 , John, 98, 192 Mary, 98, 192 , Robert, 98, 192 , Thomas, 98, 192
Crayford, 167
CRAYFORD, 167 , Afra, 167 , Alice, 167 , Anne, 167 , Edward 167 , Elizabeth, 167 , George 167 , Guy, 167 , John, 167 , Margaret, 167 , Mary, 167 , Richard, 167 , Robert 167 , Thomas, 167 , Sir William, 167, 205, 206 William 167
CREKE, 20 , Alice, 20 , Anne, 20 , Bonaventer, 20 , Edward, 20 , Joane, 20 , John, 20 , Margaret, 20 , Martin, 20 , Olive, 20 , Stephen, 20 , Thomas, 20 , William, 20
Cressett, Mary, 160
Cressy, Elizabeth, 166 , Gervas, 166
Creting 198
Crew, 67
Crew, David, 60 , Margery, 60 , —, 57
Crispe, John, 167 , Margaret, 167
Croft, Henry, 92 , Martha, 92
Crofts, Arabella, 86 , Sir Edward, 187 , Sir James 187 , Sir John, 86, 206 , Joyce, 187 , —, Countess of Cleveland, 86
Cromer, Margaret, 20, 185
Crompton, Elizabeth, 39 , Thomas 39 , —, 204
Cromwell, 27
Cromwell Mary 135 , Maude, 28 , Ralph, 28 , Sir Oliver, 135 , —, 126.
Crosier, 162
Crosier, Anne, 163 , Sir William, 163
Crosse, —, 208
Crull, Magdalen 171
Cuddrington, Anne, 181 , Paul, 181
Cullen, Anne, 157
Cullick, Jane, 49 ; William, 49
Curtis, William, 165

D

Dabernon, 162
Dabetot, 19
Dabridgecourt, Margaret, 81 , Sir Richard 81
Dade, Mary, 174 , William 174
Dalison, 55
Dalison, George, 55 , Jane, 55
Dance, Margaret 5
Dancer, Elizabeth, 9
DANIELL, 98 , Anne, 99 , Dorothy, 99 , Edward, 99 , Elizabeth, 98, 99 , George, 99 , Judith, 118 , Mary 99 , Richard, 99 , Stephen, 98, 99 ,

INDEX

Susan, 99, Thomas, 99, William, 99, —, 204, 207, 208
Denno, 40
Danno, Alice, 41, William, 41
Danvers, 51
Danvers, Elizabeth, 5, 42, 197, Sir Henry, 53, Joane, 30, 53, Silvester, 5, 42 Sir Thomas, 30, William, 197.
Darnley, Lord, 181, 182
Darrell, Barbara, 190.
Davies, —, 207
Davill, 197
Dawbigney, 27
Dawbney, 12
Dawbney, Sarah, 14, William, 14
Downe, Elizabeth, 161
Day, 99
DAY, 99, Anne 99 Dorothy, 134, Edmund, 99, 134, Elizabeth, 99, George, 99, John, 99, Margaret, 143, Mary, 99, Nathaniel, 99, Richard, 99, 113, Stephen, 99, Thomas 99, William, 99, —, 204
Dayrell, 125
Dayrell, Anne, 107, 126, Edmond, 107, Francis, 126, Mary, 191, Sir Thomas, 191
De Boys, Charles, 117, Elizabeth, 117.
Decons, Francis, 119
Delabere 9, 51
Delabere, Elizabeth, 52, Sir John, 52
Delapoole, 13
Delaune, —, 206
Delaware, Thomas, Lord, 187, —, Lord 88
Dene, William, 199
Denn, —, 112
Dennis Anne, 53, Catherine, 189, Jane, 93, Richard 53, Walter, 189, —, 207
Denny, Sir Anthony, 23, Douglas, 23
Deuston, 12
Deuston, Anne, 14, John, 11, Katherine, 14
Dent, Mary, 90, William, 90
Denton, Anthony, 183, Magdalen, 183, Mary, 118, Nicholas, 118, —, 204, 207
Derby, Stanley, Earl of, 48, 64
Dering, Elizabeth, 188, Nicholas, 188
Derycott, Arthur, 7 Emma, 7
Dethick, Sir William Garter, 99, York Herald, 178
Devenish, Mary, 102, Robert, 102
Devereux, —, 187
Deyncourt, 21
Deyncourt, Maude, 28, William, 28
Dickons, 140
Dickons, Alice, 55, 140, Elizabeth, 140, Frances, 110, Francis, 140 Richard, 140, Thomas, 55, 140

Dickson, Margaret, 46, Thomas, 46
Digby, Anne, 10, Beatrice 23, George, 10, John, Lord, Earl of Bristol, 23, Kenelm, 100, Margery, 100
Dillingham, Margaret, 147, Thomas, 147
Dimock, Margery, 131, William, 131, —, 204
Dives, Sir John, 205, Sir Lewis, 205, 207, 208
Dixey, George, 143, Jane, 143
Dobson, Cordall, 51, Elizabeth, 51 Jane, 51, William, 51.
Docket, Anne, 86, Noah, 86
Docwra, 191
Docwra, Anne, 191, Elizabeth, 82, Frances, 192; Jane, 192, John, 191, Martha, 192 191, Mary, 91, Meldreth, 192, Periam, 192, Sir Thomas, 191, Thomas, 82, 91, 192 202
Dodd, Jane, 177, John 177, Margaret, 177, William, 177
Dodgson, Anne, 35, Gervase, 35
Dodsworth, —, 207, 208
Dolman, James, 106, Jane, 108, Margaret, 106
Done, Emott, 179, Sir John, 179
Dorington, Dorothy, 102; Mary, 148, Robert, 102
Dormer, Ambrose, 132, Catherine, 54, Sir William, 54, Winifred, 132
Douglas, 182
Douglas, —, 182
Dove Frances, 172, Zachariah, 172
Downes, Catherine, 23, Elizabeth, 23, Francis, 23, George, 23
Doyley, Jane, 197, Robert, 197
Drake, Sir Francis, 116, Francis, 165
Drayton, 40
Drayton, Mary, 174, William, 174
Driby, 27
Driffield, 8
Driffield, John, 8, Margaret, 8
Drury, 67
Drury, Jane, 61, Sir William, 61
Dry, Gilbert, 115
Dryden, Ellen, 185, Erasmus, 185, Stephen, 185
Dudley, 100
DUDLEY, 100, Alice, 100, Edward, 100, Elizabeth, 100, Lettice, 100, Margaret 100, Mary, 100, Montagu, 100, Thomas, 100, William, 100
Dugdale, William, Norroy, 122.
Duke, Edward, 160.
Duncombe, 100
DUNCOMBE, 100, Alice, 100, Anne, 101, Catherine, 94, 96, Cicely, 20, Dorothy, 99, 101, Sir Edward, 101, Edward, 101, 208, Elizabeth, 101, Ellen, 101, 137, Henry, 101, Jane, 208, Sir John, 205, 207, 208, John, 94, 96, 101, 137, Mary, 100, 137, Peter, 101, Roger, 20, Sir Saunders, 101, Thomas, 101, William, 100, 101, 137, 208, —, 206.
Dyer, Anne, 111, Sir Lodwick, 207, 208, Sir William, 111
Dyre, 21
DIVE 21, Agnes, 21, Alan, 21, Alice, 22, Anne 22, 23, Audrey, 198, Beatrice, 23, Catherine, 22, 23, Christopher, 23, Dorothy, 21, 23, Douglas, 23, Edmond, 22, Edward 22, Eleanor, 22, 23, Elizabeth, 21-23, George, 23, Godfrey, 22, Henry, 21-23, Honor, 23, Humphrey, 23, Isabel, 23, Jane, 22, Joane, 21, Sir John, 23, John, 22, 23, 198, Lawrence, 22, Lewis, 23, Mary, 23, Maude, 21, 22, Ralph, 21, Sir Richard, 21, Robert, 21, Simon, 21, Thomas, 23, William, 21-23

E

Eades *See* Eedes
Eastwell, Edward, 171; Mary, 171
Eastwick, Alice, 147
Eaton, Elizabeth, 166, Thomas, 166
Edgcumbe, Catherine, 53, Sir Peter, 53, Sir Richard, 53
Edgerley, 98
Edgerley, Anne, 98, Dorothy, 98, 192, Elizabeth, 98, John, 98, 192, Katherine, 98, Robert, 98
Edwards, 101
EDWARDS, 101, Alice, 73, Anne, 102, Constance, 102, Dorothy, 102, Eleanor, 102, Elizabeth, 100-102, Francis, 102, George 73, 100-102, Henry, 101, 102, Jane, 181, Jasper, 102, John, 101, 102, 181, Katherine, 102, Lawrence, 102, Mary, 102, Michael, 101, Richard, 101, 102, 206, Thomas, 101, 102, —, 204, 207
Eedes 102
EEDES, 102, Alice, 102 Dorothy, 97, 103, Edward, 102, Francis, 97, 103, Joane, 103, Margaret, 103, Dr Richard, Dean of Worcester, 102, Richard, 103, Thomas, 102, —, 206
Egerton, Arabella, 194, John, Earl of Bridgwater, 194
Egleby, Ursula, 178, 208

Eglesfield, 29
Eglionby, Ambrose, 208, Margaret, 208
Ekins Mary, 106 140, Robert, 140, Thomas, 106 *See* Eykins
Eldercar, Eleanor, 22, Ralph, 21, 22
Elgin, Thomas, Earl of, 205
Elliott Edward, 11, Jane, 11
Ellis, 16
Ellis, Anthony 16, Dorothy, 136, Elizabeth, 16, James 136, John, 166, Mary, 166, Ursula 96
Elmer, Elizabeth, 34
Elmes Alice, 53, Edith, 42, Edmond 53, Elizabeth 132, John, 12, Mary 141, Thomas, 141, William, 132
Elrington, Dorothy 136, Edward, 136
Eltham, Thomas 101
Emery, Anne, 91, Florence, 92, Thomas, 91, 92, —, 206
Emington, Elizabeth, 192, Francis, 192
Emley, Eleanor, 27, Sir John, 27
Enderby, 46
Enderby Eleanor, 47, 132, Elizabeth, 22, John, 22, 47, 132
Engarsby, Judith, 133
Engayne, 12
Engayne, Sir John, 14, Mary, 14
Englefield, 29
Ercswell Alice, 80, George, 202, Mary, 202, Robert, 80
Ernest, Joane, 190, William, 190
Erneys, 147
Erneys, Isabel, 147, Sir Walter, 147
Ernley, Jane, 111, John, 111
Ersley, Elizabeth 181, William 181
Essex, Earl of 116, 129
Estfeld, 32
Eston, 24
ESTON, 24 Agnes 24, Alice 24, Catherine, 24 Edward 24, Elizabeth, 24, Francis, 24, Henry, 24, Jane, 24, John, 24 Judith, 24, Lettice, 24, Lucy, 24, Margaret, 24, 47 55, Mary, 24, Maude, 24, Nicholas, 24, Oliver 24, Richard, 24, Susan, 24, Thomas, 24, 47, 55
Estwick, —, 206
Etaeridge, Jane, 175, John 175
Etton, 129
Etwall, Dr Henry 69, Jane, 69, —, 67
Evans, Adrian, 170, Barbara, 170
Everard 25 103

EVERARD, 25, 103 Amy 103 105, Anne, 25, Dennis, 25, Elizabeth, 103, 125, Grace 25, 103, Henry, 25 103, Jane, 103, John, 25, 103, 105 125, Margaret 25, 103, Nicholas, 25, 103, Richard, 25, Thomas 25 103
Everington Elizabeth, 184 Francis, 184, Sir James, 184, John, 184, Margaret 184
Eversfield, Christian, 185, Sir Thomas, 185
Evington, Elizabeth, 51, Francis 51
Ewer, 104
EWER 104, Agnes, 104 Edward, 77 104, Francis 138, Jane, 138, John, 104, Mary, 77, 104, Maude, 104 Ralph, 104, Thomas, 104, Thomas Atwood, 104
Lykins, Alexander, 194, Susan, 194 *See* Ekins

F

Fage, Isabel, 18, James, 18
Fairclough Jane, 178, John, 178 May, 115, 117, Thomas 117
Fanney, 153
Faldo, 104, 105, 168
FALDO, 104, 105, 168 Agnes, 51, Ampallis, 138, 169, Amy, 103 105, Anne, 104, 169, 170, Barbara 170 Catherine, 168 Christian, 105, Cressit, 105, Edmond, 169, Elizabeth, 105, 169, Frances, 105, 170, Francis 169, Henry, 169, Jane, 105, 169, 170, Joane, 105, 168, John, 105, 168-170, Margaret, 38, 104, 105 169, May, 105, 169, 170, Matthew, 105, Ralph, 105, 169, Richard, 31, 104, 105, 138, 168-170, Robert 38, 105, 169, 170, Simon 168, Susan, 105, Thomas, 103-105, 169, Sir William, 168, William. 71, 104, 105, 168-170, William de Keynes de, 168
Fancotts, 168
Fane, Anne, 11, Sir George 11
Faringdon, 1
Faringdon, —, 1
Farington 40
Farington, Alice, 177, Sir Henry 42, Isabel, 42, Jane, 42, Peter, 177 William, 42
Farmer Elizabeth, 75, Sir Hatton, 75
Farmour, Sir George, 205
Farrer, Anne, 85, Francis, 85, —, 206
Favell, Edward, 197, Elizabeth, 197

Fawcett, Anne, 169, Jane, 169, John, 169, William, 169
Ferne, Elizabeth, 125, Joane, 142, William 125
Ferrers, 29
Ferrers, Humphrey, 47, Margaret, 47
Ferris, Sir John, 206
Fetiplace, Edmond, 42, Margaret, 42
Fickman Douglas, 123 Habel, 123
Field, Frances, 97, John, 97, Susan, 96, 113 Thomas, 113
Filiol, 32
Finch, Margaret, 107, William, 107
Fish, 106, 170
FISH, 106, 170, Alice, 170, Anne, 106, 107, 170, Bernardiston, 106, Dorothy, 170, Edith 106, Sir Edward, 170 206, Edward, 128, 170, Elizabeth, 106, 107, 170, Ellen, 106, George, 106, 170, Henry, 107, Humphrey, 106, 107, Jane, 106, Sir John, 106, 170, John, 106 Judith, 170, Lettice 170, Margaret, 80, 106, 107 Martha, 106, Mary 106, 107, 128 170, Mercy, 106, 107, 140 Oliver, 107, 140, Richard, 107, Susan, 106, Thomas, 106, 107, 170, Sir William 106, 206, William 80, 106, 107, —, 207
Fisher, 51 107
FISHER, 107, Agnes, 54, Alice, 107, Anne, 42 89, 107 Catherine, 2, Edmund 107, Elizabeth, 107, Frances, 107, Gideon, 107 Isabel, 18, Di Jasper 107, John, 42, 54, Margaret 54, Mary, 107, Sir Michael 18, 54 Michael, 18, Richard, 2, 89, Sarah 107, Susan, 107, Thomas, 107 William, 107
Fitch Anne, 152 202, Robert, 158, Sir William 152 202
Fitz Joane, 200, John 200
FitzGeoffrey, 25 26, 54, 108
FITZGEOFFREY, 25, 108 171 Alexander, 26, Alice 44, Anne, 2, 25, 171, Bridget, 25, Catherine, 25, 108, 171, Cicely 25 108, Clement, 25, Edith 26, Edward, 25, Elizabeth, 25, 26 44, 108, 171, Francis, 26, Sir George, 2, 26, 108, 202, George, 26, 44, 108, 171 Gerard, 26, 171, Goodith, 26, Isabel, 108, Jane 26, 108 202 Joane, 26, 171, John 25, 26, 95, 108, 171, Leonard, 26, Margaret, 25, 26, 95 108, 171, Mary, 26 54, 78, 171, Nicholas 26, 108, Oliver, 26, 171, Robert, 26, 44, 108, Susan,

INDEX

171, Thomas, 25, 78, 108, 171, Ursula 108, William, 25, 26, 54, 108, 171, —, 204, 206
FitzHenry, 171
FITZHENRY, 171, Edward, 171, John, 171, Magdalen, 171, Ralph 171, Robert 171, Theophilus, 171, Thomas, 171 Thoroughgood, 171
Fitzhugh, 26
FITZHUGH, 26, Anne, 27, Catherine, 26, Christopher, 27, Cicely, 27, Elizabeth, 8, 27 Frances, 27, Grace, 27, Jane, 27, John 27, 36, Julian, 36, Mary, 27, Nicholas, 27, Robert, 8, 27, Thomas, 27, William, 26, 27
Fitzlewis, Ela, 42, Richard, 42
Fitzpeter, 67
Fitz Richard, 19
Fitzwalter, 47
Fitzwalter, Elizabeth, 64, John, Lord, 48, 64, Robert, Lord, 48, 64, Walter, Lord, 64
Fitzwarien, 13 67
Fitzwilliam, 27
FITZWILLIAM, 27, Agnes, 28, Albreda, 28, Alice, 29, Anne, 29, Bartholomew, 29, Catherine, 29, Christopher, 29, Edmond, 28, Eleanor, 27 29, Elizabeth 4, 28, 29, Ella, 27, Ellen, 28, 29, Emma, 27, Francis, 29, George, 4, Jane, 28, 29, 175, Joane, 28, Sir John, 28, 206, John, 28, Margaret, 28, Mary, 28, 29, Maude, 28, Mildred, 29, Nicholas, 28, Ralph, 28, Reynold, 28, Richard, 28, 29, Robert. 28, Roger, 28, Thomas, 28, 29, 175, Urian 29, Sir William, 27-29, William 28, 29
Flanville, Hamon 115
Fleetwood, Anne, 180, Sir Miles, 180
Fleming, Elizabeth, 193, John, 193
Fletam, Elizabeth, 25, Nicholas 25
Fletcher, Jane, 176
Flitwelks, 153
Folke de Oyrey, 13
Folliot, Mary, 86, Richard 36
Forman, Dr 185, Jane, 185
Forster, 12, 46
Forster, Agnes, 132, Anne, 46, 132, Frances, 195, Sir Hugh, 13, John, 13, 195, Pauline, 14, Thomas, 14
Fortescue, 13
Fortescue, Anne, 5, Sir John, 5, 205, —, 57
Foster, 108
FOSTER, 108, Elizabeth, 109, George, 119, Henry, 108, Joane, 109, Margaret, 109, Mary, 119, Rowland, 109, Thomas, 108, 109, William, 109
Foulthorpe, 154
Foulthorpe, Sir John, 154
Fountain, 109
FOUNTAIN, 109, Arthur, 109, Briggs, 109, Constance, 109, Frances, 109, Jane, 109 John, 109, Martin 109, Sarah, 109, Thomas 109
Fowler, 29
FOWLER 29, Anne, 30, Anthony, 30, Bridget, 30, Christopher, 30, Cicely 30, Dorothy, 30, Edward, 30 Elizabeth, 30, 89 Gabriel 30, 89, George, 30, Sir Henry, 29, Henry, 30, Joane, 30, 46, Sir John 29 John, 30, Julian, 30, Katherine, 30, Lettice, 30, Margaret, 30, Mary, 11, 30, Sir Richard, 30, Richard, 30 Sir Thomas, 11, Thomas, 30, 46, 206, Sir William, 30, William, 30
Foxcott, 67
Foxcott, John, 68, Margaret, 68
Francis, Andrew, 6, Catherine, 29, Elizabeth 39, Margaret, 6, Richard, 29 William, 39
Frank Margaret, 173, Nicholas, 173
Franklin 31 110
FRANKLIN, 31, 110, 172, Agnes, 31, Alice, 172, Anne 31, 110, 111, 172, Augustin, 172, Edmond, 110, Edward 31, 172, Elizabeth, 3 31, 99, 110, 172, Ellen, 137, Frances, 172 Francis, 31, 172, George, 31, 110 111, 172, John, 3, 31, 110, 137, 145, 172, Margaret, 31, 109 110, 145, Mary, 44, 172, Nicholas, 44, 99, 110, Richard, 31, Robert, 31, Thomas, 31, 109, 172, William, Dean of York, Durham, and Windsor, 31, Sir William, 206, William, 3, 31 110, —, 204, 207, 208
Freeman, Elizabeth, 180 Francis, 185 Robert, 185, William, 180
Frere, Alice, 86
Fretchvile, Bruce, 186, John, 186, Sir Peter, 186
Frogmorton, —, 89
Frowicke, 40, 31
Frowicke Frideswide, 15 Sir Henry, 53, Jane, 53, Joane, 41, 53, Margaret 54, Sir Thomas, 15, 53, Thomas, 41
Froxmer, Margaret, 10
Fry, —, 127
Fryer, John, 166, Mary, 166
Fuller Frances, 165, William, Dean of Dublin, 165
Furneys, Alice, 76

Furtho, Maude, 22
Fynes, Margaret, 37, William, Lord Say and Seale, 37

G

Gade, Jane, 159, John, 159
Gadsden, Joane, 184, William, 184
Gage, Joane, 30, Richard, 30, —, 192
Gale, Henry, 112, Katherine, 112
Gamage Isabel, 19, Margaret, 53, Sir Thomas, 53
Gardevile, John, 190, Maude, 190
Gardiner, Emma, 166, John, 166, Mary, 95
Garroway, Philip, 206
Gascoigne, 116, 172
GASCOIGNE, 172, Dorothy, 116, 173, Elizabeth, 97, 116, 161, 172 173, George, 116, 173, James, 173, Jane, 53, 116, 173, Sir John, 72, 116, 173, John, 53, 97, 116, 161, 173, Margaret, 9, 116, 173, Nicholas, 173, Richard, 173 Robert, 9, Sir William, 173, William, 116, 172, 173, —, 206
Gates, Dorothy, 122
Gawdrey, Joane, 84, John, 84
Gansell, 12
Gawthorpe, —, 172
Gedge, Mary, 10, Thomas, 10
Gedney 146
Gedney, Agnes, 146, Hugh, 146
Gee *alias* Joy, Henry, 24, Margaret, 24
Gent, Joane, 157
George, Robert, 88, Susan, 88
Gerrard, Elizabeth, 183, 193, Francis 186, Sir John, 183, Mary, 186, Sir William, 193
Gery, 110
GERY, 110, Anne, 110, 111, Elizabeth. 111, George, 111, Oliver, 111, Rebecca, 111, Richard, 110, 111, Thomas, 110, 111, William, 110, 111, —, 112
Gibbon, Elizabeth, 135, William, 135
Gifford, 191
Gifford, John, 60, Lucy, 60, —, 191
Gilbert, Dorothy, 146, Edward 136, Joane, 103, Mary, 136, Richard, 146, Thomas, 163.
Gildespin, Thomas, 115
Giles Margaret, 163
Gill, John, 196, Margaret, 188, Richard, 188, Ursula, 136.
Gilman, Ann, 196
Gilpin, Anne, 82, George, 82.
Gislingham, John, 190, Maude, 190
Glover, 146

Glover, Alice, 146 , Robert, 146
  See Cranfield
Goddard, 111
GODDARD, 111 , Anthony, 111 ,
  Dorothy, 111 , Edith, 112 ,
  Henry, 112 , Jane, 111 ,
  Joane, 111 , John, 112 ,
  Katherine, 112 , Mary, 112 ,
  Thomas, 111 , Vincent, 111 ,
  112 , William, 111, 112
Godfrey, 16, 127
Godfrey, Elizabeth, 16 , Frances, 127 , John, 127 , Margaret, 124 , Mary, 189 , Richard, 16 , William, 124, 189
Golabis of Normandy, 27.
Goldington, 153
Goldsmith, Elizabeth, 165
Golson, Robert, 47 , Rose, 47
Gonnell Anne, 3, 7 25 , Gerard, 25 , John, 7 , Thomas, 3
Goodall, Robert 72
Goodfellow, Elizabeth, 54, 73 , Mary, 118 , William, 54, 73, 118
Goodrick, John, 24, 55 , Margaret, 24, 55
Goodson, Elizabeth, 143 , Thomas, 143
Goodwin, John, 66 , Mary, 131, Petronilla, 66 , William, 131
Gophill 160
Gostwick, 32
GOSTWICK, 32 , Alice, 33 , Anne, 33, 34 , Catherine, 33 , Constance, 34 , Dorothy, 33 , Edmund, 33 , Sir Edward, 34, 141, 188, 205, 207, 208 , Edward, 33, 34 , Elizabeth, 33, 34 , Frances, 34 , Francis, 34 , Gabriel, 31 , George, 33 , Gertrude 33, 34 , Hester, 34 , Hugh, 32 , Jane, 33, 34, 188 , Sir John, 32 , 33, 53 , John, 32-34, 55 , Margaret, 33, 53, 145 , Martha, 33, 65 , Mary, 33, 34, 141 , Mildred, 34 , Nicholas, 34 , Ralph, 115 , Richard, 32 , Robert, 32-34 , Roger, 32 34 , Thomas, 33, 34 , Sir William, 34, 188, 206, William, 32-34, 58, 65 , —, 65, 206
Gould, Elizabeth, 139, 169 , Mary, 169 , Thomas, 139, 169
Gouldsborough, Dorothy 83 , Thomas 83
Gower, Anne, 50 , William, 50
Grafton, Joane, 63 , John, 63
Grandison, 9, 51
Grandison, Mabel, 52 , Otho, Lord, 52
Grandy, Katherine, 187
Granger, —, 207
Granville, 183
Granville, —, 183
Graunt, Frances, 131 , John, 131
Graveley, 128

Graveley, Anne, 169 , George, 128 , Lettice, 128
Gray, or Grey, 35, 62, 67, 112 156, 191
GRAY, or GREY, 35, 62, 112, 173 , Agnes, 28 , Alice, 35, 62 Andrew, 35, 62, 174 , Anne, 35, 62, 112, 174 , Anthony, Lord, 50 , Barbara, 38 , Catherine, 49, 50, 112, 192 , Dorothy, 35, 62, 174 , Edith, 17 , Edward, 35, 62, 174 , Elizabeth, 35, 59, 62 77, 112, 174 , Frances, 62 , Francis, 35, 62, 112, 174 , George, 174 , Grace, 25, 35, 62, 168, 173 , Hawise, 68 , Sir Henry, 53 , Henry, 47, 53 , Isabel, 112 , Lady Jane, 157 , Jane, 174 , John, 35, 62, 112, 173 174 , Judith, 112 , Lyon, 35 , Margaret, 35, 47, 53, 62, 174 , Martha, 112 , Mary, 35, 62, 112, 174, 191 , Masera, 62 , Massy, 35 , Matthew, 35, 62, 174 , Oliver, 112 , Sir Patrick, 183 , Penelope, 174 , Peter, 35, 59, 62, 77, 174 , Ralph, 35, 62 , Rebecca, 112 , Reynold, Lord, 17 , Richard, 35, 62, 174 , Robert, 33, 68, 112 , Simon 112 , Thomas, 35, 62, Walter, 112 , William, 112, Yon, 35 , —, Lord, 28 192 , —, 206
Green, 27, 44, 67, 196
Green Annabel, 60 , Anne, 94, 164 , Christian, 196 , Cicely, 45 , Edith, 41, 44 , Eleanor, 28 , Elizabeth, 30, 49 ; Sir Henry, 28 , Joane, 6, 26, 118 , John, 26 41, 44, 49, 118 , Lawrence, 196 , Margaret, 196 , Maude, 24 , Reynold, 196 , Robert 94 , Sir Thomas, 24 , Thomas, 60 , William, 164
Gresham, Sir John, 193 , Mary, 193
Gresley, 29
Greville, Sir Edward, 150 , Joyce, 150
Grice 158
Grice, Alice, 158 , Roger, 158
Griffin, 67, 113
GRIFFIN, 113 , Alice, 113 , Anne, 69, 113 , Edward, 69 , Elizabeth, 113 , Ellen, 113 , George, 113 , Henry, 113 , John, 113 , Richard, 113 , Susan, 113 , Thomas, 113
Grigg, —, 206
Grosvenor, Elizabeth, 164, 180 , Randall, 164
Grover, Frances, 98 , John, 98
Grymes, Joane, 128 , Thomas, 128
Gubyon, 153
Guilliam, Jane, 134, Robert, 134
Gynne, Elizabeth, 128

H

Hackett, Anne, 120 , Christian, 120 , Sir Cuthbert, 120 , Etheldred, 78 , Jane, 120 , Dr Roger, 78, 120 , Dr Thomas, 78 , Thomas, 78, 120
Haddon, —, 182
Hadley, Catherine, 33 , Elizabeth, 160 , George, 33 , William, 160
Hadock, Joane, 160 , Matthew, 160
HALE, 113 , Anne, 19 , Bridget, 114 , Elizabeth, 113, Francis, 114 , John, 113 , Judith, 114, 132 , Margaret, 114 , Mary, 114, 172 , Matthew, 113 , Oliver, 114 , Richard, 113, 172 , Rose, 118 Simon, 114, 132 , Thomas, 19, 113, 114 , —, 144, 206
Hales, 191
Hales, Meldreth, 192
Halftide, Judith, 133
Halfpenny, —, 207
Hall, Anne, 25 , Christopher, 133 , Elizabeth, 31, 63, 110 , Frances, 133 , Henry, 63 , John, 31, 110 , Marian, 63 Thomas, 63 , William, 25
Halleleigh, Anne, 102 , Christopher, 102 , Elizabeth, 102 , John, 102
Halliwell, 162
Halliwell Jane, 163 , John, 163 , Richard, 163
Hamby, John, 170 , Judith, 170
Hamilton, James, Lord, 182 , Margaret, 182
Hampden, 125
Hampstead, 74
Hampstead, Dorothy, 74, Henry, 74.
Hanbury, Anne, 9
Hanchett, Grace, 35, 62, 173 , William, 35, 62, 173
Hanky, 67
Hanky, Ellen, 61 , John 61
Hansard 82
Hardesley, Henry, 10 , Margaret, 10
HARDING, 114 , Anne, 33, 37, 39, 82, 114 , Cicely, 125 , Edmund, 82, 114 , Edward, 114 , Elizabeth, 114, 174 , Frances, 114 , John, 37, 39 114, 174 , Mary, 114 , Nicholas, 33, 125 , Richard, 114 , St John, 111 , William, 114 , —, 178, 206
Hare, Catherine, 120 , Elizabeth, 50 , Margaret, 96 , Sir Ralph, 96 , Richard, 50 , Samuel, 120
Harman, Joane, 36 , John, 36 , Katherine, 30 , Roger, 30
Harnehall, 13
Harneys, 153
Harold, Alice, 113 , Robert, 113
Harris, Christopher, 10 , —, 171

INDEX

Harrison, Margaret, 184
Hart, Frideswide, 163, Sir Percival, 163, Winifred, 90
Hartop, Mary, 134, Sir William, 134
Harvey, 36, 116, 156, 190
HARVEY, 36, 116, Adam, 36, Agnes, 37, Alice, 37, 146, Anne, 37, 116, 117, Benjamin, 116, Christian, 36, 37, Cicely, 36, Daniel, 116, Dorothy, 116, 202, Edmond, 48, 65, Edward, 37, Elizabeth 37, 116, 117, Florence, 37, Frances, 37, 129, Sir George, 37, 116, George, 116, Sir Gerard, 116, 206, Gerard, 37, *alias* Smart, Gerard, 116, Gertrude, 117, Henry, 36, Isabel, 37, 48, 65, James, 129, Jane, 36, 37, 117, Joane, 36, Sir John, 36, John, 36, 37, 53, 65, 116, 117, Judith, 116, Julian, 36, Margaret, 36, 37, 48, 65, Martha, 116, Mary, 36, 37, 53, 116, 117, Nathaniel 116, Oliver, 117, Osbert, 36, Richard, 37, Samuel, 116, 202, Stephen, 117, Thomas, 36 65, William, Clarenceux, 72, 81, 94, 123, William, 36, 48, 65, —, 207, 208
Haselden, 115
HASELDEN, 115, Alice, 115, Anthony, 8, Benjamin, 115, Constance, 115, Elizabeth, 8, 115, Hugh, 115, John, 115, Margaret, 115, Martha, 115, Mary, 115, Richard, 115, Robert, 115, Thomas, 115, William, 115, —, 204
Hastings, 21
Hastings, Isabel, 23, Henry, 28, Mary, 28, Sir Ralph, 23, William, 23, —, 204
Hatley, Elizabeth, 145; Joane, 111, William, 145
Hawes, Anne, 29, John, 29, Judith, 85, Margaret, 80, Robert, 71, 80, 85, Thomas, 71.
Hawkins, Lady, 103, —, 206
Hawley, Thomas, Clarenceux, 110
Hawtrey, Sir Philip, 165, Prudence, 165, Sir William, 132, Winifred, 132
Hayes, Sarah, 120, Sir Thomas, 120
Haynes, John, 96, Margaret, 96
Hayward, Anne, 167, Sir Rowland, 167
Haywood, Jane, 176
Hedge, Margaret, 76, Thomas, 76
Heigham, 154
Heigham, Roger, 154
Helder *alias* Spicer, Elizabeth, 119, Joane, 135, Richard, 119, 135

Helder *alias* Squire (? Spicer), Joane, 50
Heming, 179
Heming, Anne, 179, John, 179
Henhull, 67
Henhull, Margaret, 61, Richard, 61
Henley, Magdalen, 46, Sir Walter, 46
Henry VIII, 15, 39, 45
Hinxton, 154
Heriot, Elizabeth, 148
Heron, Alice, 81, Elizabeth, 17, Sir Nicholas, 81, Thomas, 17, 81
Hervey *See* Harvey
Heslerton, Cecilia, 66, Thomas, 66
Heton, Elizabeth, 170, Martin, Bp of Ely, 170
Hewett, 37, 117, 129
HEWETT, 37, 117, Alice, 129, Anne, 38, 78, Arthur, 38, Charles, 117, Dorothy, 37, 38, 97, Edmond, 38, Edward, 117, Elizabeth 38, 98, 117, Francis, 117, Henry, 117, John, 117, Margaret, 37, 38, 117, Martha, 117, Mary, 117, Richard, 78, Robert, 37, 38, 78, 97, 98, 117, Thomas, 37, 117, Sir William, 129, William, 38 117, —, 206. *See* Huet
Hewson, Anne, 102, Thomas, 102
Hibberdine, Cicely, 25, Roger, 25,
Hide *See* Hyde
Higham, 191
Higham, Etheldred, 191, Jane, 159, Thomas, 159
Hill, 3 118
HILL, 118, Alice, 38, Edward, 118, Elizabeth, 118, 177, Henry, 118, Joane, 118, 166, John, 118, Judith, 118, Margery, 3, Martha, 118, Mary, 118, Reynold, 118, Thomas, 118, 177, Ursula, 208, Walter, 208, William, 38
Hillar, —, 182
Hillersden, 174.
HILLERSDEN, 174, Alice, 174, Cicely, 25, Elizabeth, 174, Joane, 174, John, 174, Margaret, 208, Richard, 208, Roger, 25, Sir Thomas, 174, Thomas, 174, —, 207
Hilton, Catherine, 179, Emott, 179, William, 179
Hinde, Sir Francis, 65, Jane, 65, Joane, 190, John, 190,
Hinton, 119
HINTON, 119, Dorothy 119, Frances, 119, 140, George, 119, Mary, 119, Robert, 119, Thomas, 119, 110, —, 206
Hitch, 175,
HITCH, 175, Catherine, 175, Christian, 175, Eleanor, 175,

Jane, 29, 175, John, 29, 175, Richard, 175, Roger, 175, Thomas, 175, William, 175
Hobbs, 155
Hobbs, Robert, 155
Hobby, 67
Hobby, Barbara, 69, William, 69
Hoddesdon, 175
HODDESDON, 175, Alice, 175, Anne, 176, Bridget, 176, Sir Christopher, 175, Christopher, 176, Constance, 175, Edward, 176, Elizabeth, 175, 176, Grace, 176, Henry, 176, Jane, 175, 176, John, 176, Nicholas, 176, Simon, 175, Thomas, 175, 176, Ursula, 175.
Hodgkis, 176
HODGKIS, 176, Allan, 176, Arthur, 177, Charles, 176, Dorothy, 177, Elizabeth, 177, Frances, 176, George, 176, Jane, 176, 177, John, 176, Margaret, 177, Mary, 176, Richard, 176, 177, Thomas, 177, William, 176
Hogshaw, Catherine 179, John, 179, Maude, 179
Holdenby, 22
Holdenby Jane, 22, John, 22
Holland, 13
Holland, David, 165, Elizabeth, 165, Richard, 115
Holman, 148
Holman, Elizabeth, 148, Margery, 148, Nicholas, 148, Simon, 148, William, 148
Holme, Randle, 188, Thomas, Clarenceux, 77
Holt, 186
Holt, Ellen, 186, James, 186
Honywood, Joyce, 136, Robert, 136
Hoo, 155
Hoo, Ellen, 106, Thomas, 106.
Hopkins, Anne, 197
Hopton, Anne, 187, Sir Arthur, 187
Horley, Catherine, 24, Margaret, 24, William, 24
Horne, Joane, 144, Reynold, 144
Horsey, Anne, 136, George, 136
Horsley, Anne, 158, Jason, 158
How, Susan, 75
Howard, Anne, Lady, 51, Charles, Earl of Nottingham, 54, William, Lord, 51,
Huet, Margaret, 89, Thomas, 89
Huggins, Bridget, 30
Hull, George, 9, Jane, 9
Hulso, 67
Hulso, Catherine, 61, Philip, 61
Hume, Elizabeth, 96, Sir Patrick, 96
Humfreville, Elizabeth, 51, Sir Henry, 51.

Humfrey, Margaret, 25, Richard, 25
Hungerford Anthony, 111
Hunt, 38 118, 154
HUNT, 38, 118 Alexander, 72, Alice, 38, Anne, 38, Barbara, 38 Edward, 38, Elizabeth 38, 145, Gregory, 38, James 118, Jane, 38, 118, Joane, 20, 38, 118, Margaret 38, 118, Mary, 38, 118, Roger, 38, 118, Rose, 118, Saxburge, 58, Thomas, 38, 118 William, 38, 118, 145, —, 204
Huntingdon, Earl of, 28
Hurlestone, 177
HURLESTONE, 177, Agnes, 177, Alice, 177, 178, Anne 178 Eleanor 177, Elizabeth, 177, Ellen, 178 Gilbert, 177, Hugh, 177, 178, Humphrey, 177, 178, Isabel, 177, James, 177, John, 177, Margaret 177, 178 208, Mary 178, Maude, 177, Nicholas, 177, Randall, 177, Richard, 177, Robert, 177, Rose, 2, 178, Thomas, 177, Ursula, 178, 208 William, 177
Hussey, Elizabeth, 157, Hubert, 157, Margaret, 41 Thomas, 41
Hutost, 100
Hutton, Rose, 191, Thomas, 191
Huxley, Elizabeth, 174, George, 72, Sir John, 206, 207, John, 174
Hyde, Elizabeth, 106, 170, George, 106, 170, William, 106, 170 —, 110, 207, 208
Hyer, George, 79, Margaret, 79

I

Inglebert, 168
Inglefield, Cicely, 30, Nicholas, 30
Inglethorpe, 13
Insula Robert, 68, Rose, 68
Iplady, Mary, 158, Richard, 158
Ireland, Anne, 16, Henry, 16
Iremonger Edmund, 159, Elizabeth, 84, Grace, 159, John, 84, — 206
Iscomb, Thomasine, 121
Iwardby, Elizabeth, 46, 132, John, 46, 132

J

Jackson Jane, 150
Jacob, 154
Jacob, Abraham, 9, Mary, 9
Jakemon, —, 206
James, Alice, 102
Jekyll, Sir Thomas, 57
Jellibronde 19

Jellibronde Elizabeth, 19
Jemison, Elizabeth, 158, Thomas, 158
Jenkin ap Philip, Rice ap Morgan ap, 53
Jenney, — 4
Jessop, Frances, 183 John, 183
Johnson, 119 154
JOHNSON, 119, Dorothy, 145, Elizabeth, 119 Francis, 119, Isabel 157, John 154 Martha, 197, Mary, 119, Nicholas, 119, Thomas, 119, William, 119, 145, 197, —, 206, 207
Jones, 120
JONES, 120 Anne 120 170, Anne Duppa 120, Catherine, 120, Christian 120 Elizabeth 120, Henry 120 Hester Estington, 120, Hugh, 120, Jane, 120, John 120, Margaret, 120, Margaret Stubbs, 120, Peter, 120, Richard, 120, Robert, 120, Roger, Viscount Ranelagh and Baron of Navan, 120, Sir Roger, 120, Roger, 120, Sarah, 120 Thomas, Archbp of Dublin, 120 Thomas, 120, 170, William, 120
Joy, Anne, 178, Henry 47, 178, Jane, 49, 133, John, 49, 133 Margaret, 47 *See* Gee
Judd, Dorothy, 174, Nicholas, 174
Judg, or *Jug*, 153
Juger, 154
Jurden, Thomas, 115

K

Keeling, Sir John, 205-208, John, 85, Martha, 85
Keldon, 159,
Kelke, Elizabeth, 81, John, 81
Kemp, Ella, 42 Jane, 88, Sir Thomas, 42, William, 88
Kempson, — 206
Kempton, Edward, 184, Elizabeth 184, Katherine, 184
Kendall, — 17
KENT, 178, Charles, 178 Edward, 178, Jane, 178, John, 178, Mary, 178, Thomas, 178, —, 133, 134
Kent, Richard Earl of, 53, —, Earls of, 206
Keyling, —, 204
Keynsham, 121
KEYNSHAM, 121, Alice 121, Anne, 121, Elizabeth 121, Frances, 121, George, 121, Joane 121, John, 121, Richard, 121, Stephen, 121, Thomasine, 121
Kilby, Dorothy, 145
Kinersley, John, 85, Katherine, 85

King Dorothy 33 Elizabeth, 20, 96, 145, George, 96, Philip 20, Saxburge, 38, Thomas, 38, William, 145
Kings, Martha, 194, Robert, 194
Kirby, Judith 133, Thomas, 133
Kirkham, Isabel, 53, Sir Robert, 53
Kirton, 84
Kirton, Allen, 6, 7 Grace, 7, Walter, 7
Knapp, Constance 115, John, 115
Knesworth, 67
Knesworth, Edith, 68, Richard, 68
Knight, Mary, 170, Stephen, 170
Knightley, 67
Knightley, Anne, 61, Elizabeth, 180, Sir Valentine, 61, 180
Kniston, Sir Gilbert, 174 Sir John, 174, Mary, 174
Kunings, Barbara, 88, Thomas, 88
Kymes, Joane, 6

L

Lacey, Albreda, 28, Edmond, Earl of Lincoln, 28, Elizabeth, 120, John, 120 Robert, Earl of Lincoln, 28
Lacon Edward, 185, Elizabeth, 185
Ladd William, 72
Ladington, Alice, 193, Nicholas, 193
Lake 121
LAKE, 121, Agnes, 121, Constance 121, Elizabeth, 121, Livia, 121, Lydia, 121, Mary, 121, Richard, 121, Sarah, 121, Susan, 121, Thomas, 121
Lambert, Mary, 98, 192, William, 98, 192
Lancellott 154
Lancellott, John, 154
Lander, —. 181
Lane, Elizabeth, 158, Francis, 158, Joseph 158, Judith, 135, Mary, 158, Thomas, 158, William 135, 158
Langedeway Mary, 63
Langford, Alice, 144, John, 144, — 206
Langhorne, Agnes, 128, Anne, 128, Benjamin, 128, Elizabeth 107, Richard, 107
Langnorth, 67
Langworth Elias, 60, Joane, 60
Lannor, 156
Lannor, Ralph, 156
Latimer, 40, 44
Latimer, Edith, 41, 44, Sir Nicholas, 41, 44

INDEX

Launcelin, 17, 39, 179
Launcelin, Anne, 39 , Sir Thomas, 39
Larinder, 178
LAVINDER 178 , Anne, 178 , Elizabeth 178 , John, 178 , Margaret, 178 , Mary 178 Richard, 178 Sarah, 178 , Thomas, 178 , William 178
Law Christian, 105 , Matthew, 105
Lawrence Henry, 72 , Humphrey, 72 , Jacob, 109 , Joane, 109 , Richard, 72
Layton, Anne, 127 , Thomas, 127
Leach, Alice, 16 , John, 124 Susan, 124 , Thomas 16
Lecke, Alice, 16 , Thomas 16
Le Despencer, Lady, 11
Lee, Anne 121 , Edmund, 121 Elizabeth, 3 , Sir John, 175 , John, 3 , Ursula, 175
Leech, 67
Leech, Anne, 61 , Elizabeth, 184 , John, 61, 121 184 Thomasine, 121
Legatt 191
Legatt, Dorothy, 191 , John, 191
Leicester, Robert, Earl of, 111
Leigh, 179
LEIGH, 179 , Amy, 179 , Anne, 136, 179 , Elizabeth 37, 131, 179 , Gilbert, 179 , Henry, 179 , Hugh, 179 , Isabel, 37 , Sir John, 179 , John, 37, 97, 179 , Mary, 97, Maude, 179 Philip 179 , Sir Richard, 136 Thomas, Lord, 206 , Sir Thomas, 206 Thomas, 72, 179 , —, 207
Lenox Alexander, Earl of, 181 Donald, 181 , Giltrist, 181 , John, Earl of, 182 , Mateperley, 181 , Parlon, 181
Lenthrop, Jane 55 , Thomas 55
Lenton, Ursula, 108
Lestrange, 40
Leverpoole, Adam, 160 , Catherine, 160 , William, 160
Lewis Clement, 188 , Dorothy 188
Lenson 67
Lewson, Anne, 69 , John, 69
Ley Anne, 9 , Roger, 9 , —, 206
Leyfield, Frances, 163 , Thomas 163
Leylam, Amy 16 , Thomas, 16
Lichfield 8
Lichfield, Isabel, 8 , Maude, 8 , Roger, 8
Lillingston, —, 207
Lilly, Henry, Rougeiose, 71, 158
Lilton, Anne 54 , Sir Rowland, 54
Lily, Dorothy, 111 , Dr Peter, 111

Lincoln, Edmond, Earl of 28 , Robert Earl of, 28
Lindley Magdalen, 46 , Sir Walter, 46
Lions 67
Lions, Elizabeth, 60 , John 60 69 , —, 57 62
Littleton, 24
Litton, Alice, 174 , Sir William 174
Livesay, —, 208
Lizures Albreda, 28 , Robert, Lord 28
Llewelin, Joane 103 , Richard, 103
Lloyd, Mary, 88 , Robert, 88
Locke, Elizabeth 18
Lockey, William, 151
Long, Amy 202 , Gifford, 202
Longports Margery, 69 , Thomas, 69
Longvale 162
Longville Elizabeth, 22 , George, 22 , —, 204
Lord, John, 8 , Margaret, 8
Loring, 12
Loring, Cassandra, 13 , Joane, 13 , Margaret, 14 , Sir Nele 14 , Sir Peter 13 Sir Roger, 13
Loveday, —, 29
Lovell, Anne, 190 , Nicholas, 190
Lovett, Elizabeth 166 , Thomas, 166 , —, 207
Lowdham, 159
Lowdham, Jane, 159 , Sir John, 159
Lowe Elizabeth, 86, 208 , Francis, 208 , Reynes, 86 , Susan, 157
Lowrey, Anne, 107
Lowth, Margaret 157 , Richard, 157
Lucy, 47
Lucy, Catherine, 66 , Sir Godfrey, 66
Ludsup 67
Ludsup, Elizabeth, 69 , William, 69
Luke 17 39, 179
LUKE, 39, 179 , Alice, 93 Anne 37, 39, 108, 179, 180 , Bridget, 39 , Catherine, 180 , Cicely, 39, 83, 94, 198 , Edward, 39 , Elizabeth 18, 39, 95, 96, 180 Humphrey 180 Jane, 39 179 , Sir John, 179 John, 39, 179 180 , Judith, 180 , Margaret 54, 179 , Mary 39, 179, 180 , Nicholas Baron, 18, 37, 39, 95 , Nicholas, 39, 54 179, 180 198 , Sir Oliver, 58, 179, 180, 205 , Oliver, 39, 180 , Paul 39, 83 98, 94, 108 , Sir Samuel 180, 205, 207 , Samuel, 180 , Scudamore, 39 Thomas, 179, 180 , Sir Walter, 39 , Walter 39 , —, 204, 208
Lyose, 190

M

Malcott, Christian, 143
Maliverer, John, 115
Mallet 19
Mallet, — 19
Mallock, Joane, 127 William, 127
Mallory 122
MALLORY, 122 , Anne, 35, 62, 122 , Anthony, 122 Benjamin 122 , Dorothy 122 , Frances, 59, 122 , Francis, 122 Grace, 122 126 John 122 Matthias, 122 , Matthew 122   Nicholas, 122 , Peter 59 122 Ralph, 122, 126 , Sir Richard, 35, 62 Thomas, 122 , William, 122
Malpas, Agnes, 52 , Sir David, 52
Mun, —, 121
Manfield Alice, 24 , Eleanor, 102 , Thomas, 24 102.
Manley, 122, 154
MANLEY, 122 Anthony, 123 , Cicely, 123 , Edward 122 , Francis 123 , James 123 , John, 123, 154 , Mary, 123 , Richard, 123 , Robert, 122, 123 —, 204
Mansell, Afra, 167 , Thomas 167
Mantell 21
Mantell, Henry, 21 , Joane, 21, Maude, 21
Manwaring, — 176
Marchant John, 115
Margett, Anne, 170 , William, 170
Mariett, John, 93 112 , Mary, 112 , Sarah, 93
Markes, —, 176
Markham, Adam, 18 Frances 18 Francis, 132 Gertrude, 136, Mary, 132, Thomas, 136
Mailborough, Agnes, 198 , Duchess of, 208 Henry, 198 , Thomas, 198 , Walter, 198 , —, 207
Marmion 198
Marncy, Lord 65
Marriott Elizabeth, 17 , Richard, 17
Marsh, Cicely 147 Elizabeth, 184 , Frances, 170 John 147 , Mary, 184 Nicholas, 170 Thomas, 184
Martin, 40
MARTIN, 40 , Anne, 40, 176 , Catherine, 10, 40 , Clement, 40 , Crestide 40 , Edward, 8 , Elizabeth, 174 , George 40 , Gilbert, 10, 40 James, 174 , Jane, 40 , John, 40 , Margaret, 8 40 , Martha, 118 , Peter, 118 , Richard, 176 , Robert, 40
Massam, Elizabeth, 25 John, 25
Masters Anne 174 , William 174

225

G G

Masterton, 67
Matthew, David, 53, John, 180 Lettice 30, Mary, 53 180, Sarah, 109 161, Thomas, 30, William, 109, 161
Maudint, 40
Maw, Dr, 115, Martha 115
Mayhew, Anne, 87, Thomas 87
Maynard, Edward, 125, Elizabeth, 125
Mayne Elizabeth 176, Jane 88, Robert, 176, Simon 88
Medwell, Judith, 184 Thomas 134
Mentish, Sir John, Earl of Lenox, 181 182
Meriell, Agnes, 17, Robert, 17
Merry, Dorothy, 37, John, 37, Margaret, 37, Sir Thomas, 91
Merywether, Alice, 167, John, 167
Michael, — 207
Middleton Mary, 184, Sir Thomas 184, —, 207
Midwinter, Joyce, 69, William, 69
Mighton, Joane, 194
Mill John, 115
Millard Sir William, 206
Miller, Dorothy, 97, Edward, 127, Gregory, 127, Joane, 4 80, 127, Sir John 97, Mary, 33 Thomas, 4, 80
Mills, 180
MILLS, 180, Elizabeth, 180, Jane, 79, John, 79 180 Mary, 180 Thomas, 180
Minshull, Catherine, 64, John, 64.
Mitchell, Margaret 136
Mitton, Magdalen, 185, Thomas, 185
Moate, Anne, 77.
Mobson —, 187
Molesworth 84, 159
Molesworth, Joane, 6 Walter, 6
Mollineux, Sir Allan, 179, Anne, 179
Molton, 164
Molton, Cicely, 164 John, 164
Monings, Sir Edward, 117, Mary, 117, —, 167
Monoux, 123
MONOUX, 123, Anne, 123 124, 159, Douglas, 123, Elizabeth, 123, 124, Frances, 124 Sir George, 123, George, 123, 124, Sir Humphrey, 207, Humphrey, 123 124 159, Jane, 124, 159, Lewis, 124 159, Lucy, 123, Margaret, 124, Thomas, 123, 124, Walgrave, 124, William, 123, 124
Montacute, 13
Montagu, Anthony, Viscount, 48, 65
Montgomery, Lord, 182
Monthermer, 13
Montrose, 183
Montrose, Earl of, 183
Moore, 29

MOORE, or MORE 124, Alice, 43 126, Anne, 124, Bridget, 126, Catherine, 189 Dorothy, 42, Elizabeth, 30, Godfrey, 124, Sir Henry, 205, Joane, 3, Sir John, 205, John, 4 126, Judith, 124, Margaret, 124, Richard, 124, Roger, 30, Sidney, 124, Sir St John, 207, Susan, 124, Thomas 42 43, 126, William 124, —, 207
Moorhouse, John 159, Priscilla, 159
Mordaunt 40, 125
MORDAUNT, 40, 125, 180, Agnes, 41, 42, 180, Alice, 41 Anne, 41, 42, 125 140, 141, 181, Audrey, 42, 181, Avice, 41, Sir Charles, 181, 207, Cnarles, 125, Cicely, 125, Dorothy, 42, Edith, 41, 42, 44 Edmund, 41, 42, 141, 181, Edward, 42 181, Ela, 42 Elizabeth, 41, 42, 123, 125, 181, Ellen 41, Ethreldred, 42, Eustace, 41, Frances, 34, George, 12, 80, 125, 140, James, 34, Jane, 42, 125, 181, Joane 41, John Earl of Peterborough, 34, John, Lord 42, 45, 80, 123, Sir John, 41, 44, 125, John, 125 181, Katherine, 80, 125, Lewis, Lord, 123, Lewis, 42, 125, Margaret 41, 42, 125, Mary, 181, Osbert, 41, Osmund, 41, Parnell 125, Robert, 41, Rose, 41, William, 41, 42, 180, 181, Winifred, 42, —, 204
More, 43
Morgan, Mary, 105, 169
Morgan ap Ienkin ap Philip, Rice ap, 53
Morley, Alice, 37, Henry Lord, 53, Nicholas, 37
Morteyne, 12
Morteyne, Joane, 13
Mortimer, 47
Mortimer, Agnes, 79
Morton, Henry, 135, Olive, 135 *See* Travalard
Mosley, Constance, 175, Michael, 175
Moune, Joane, 122
Mountfort, 162
Mountjoy. Lord, 187
Mowbray, Alexander, 173, Elizabeth, 173
Mulsho, Dorothy 94, John, 94
Multon, 47
Munday, Richard, 78, 153
Munden, Elizabeth, 87, Thomas, 87
Muskett John, 186, Mary 186, Robert, 186, Simon, 186
Musterston, Ellen 61, Thomas, 61
Myles, Jane 90, John, 90
Mylles, Joane 4, Thomas, 4

N

Nanscutt, 12
Nanscutt Sir Pierse, 13
Napier, 181
NAPIER, 181, Sir Alexander, 181 183, Alexander, 96, 181, 184, Andrew, 183, Anne, 182 184, Sir Archibald, 183, Archibald 181-184, Arundell, 183, Christian, 185, Christopher, 182, Donald, 181 Edward, 182, 183, Elizabeth, 96, 183, 184, Frances, 183 185, George, 182, Gerard, 183, Grace, 184, James, 182 183 Joane 184, Sir John, 183, 207 John, 182 184, Katherine 182-184, Magdalen, 183, 185, Margaret, 184, Mary, 184, Sir Nathaniel, 183, Nicholas 182, Peter, 181, Richard, 184, *alias* Sandy, Sir Robert, 58, 96, 205, Sir Robert, 96, 183-185, 205, Robert, 182, 183, 185, Sarah, 185 Shelton, 183, Thomas 182, 184, William 182-184, —, 204
Naris, Sir Edward, 116
Navan, Baron of 120
Neale, 43, 125
NEALE, 43, 125, 185, Alice 43, 44, 126, Anne 126, Benjamin, 126, Bridget, 126, Catherine, 43, 44 126, Conquest, 44, Dorothy, 44, Edmond 44, 185 Elizabeth, 44, 97, 126 185, Ellen, 43, 126, 185, Ennis, 126, Frances, 44, 185, George, 44, Goodith, 43, Grace 44, 122, 126 185, Gro —, 192, Henry, 185, Isaac, 126, James, 126, 185 Jane 44, 185 192 John, 43, 44, 97, 125, 126, 185, Joseph, 126, Judith 44, Lacon, 185, Lancelot, 185, Margaret, 185 Mary, 43 44, 126, Noah, 126, Paul, 126, Peter, 126, Raphael, 44, 185, Richard 43, 126, Samuel, 126, Sir Thomas, 158, Thomas, 43, 122, 125, 126, 185, Timothy, 126, Walter, 185, William, 44, — 204
Neatley, Temperance, 2
Nedham Anne, 129, Bridget 132, Eustace, 129, 203, Frances, 203, Jane, 125 John, 125, 132
Needham, 67
Negus, John, 110, Mary, 76, Thomas, 76
Nernute, 116
Nevill 13, 36, 168
Nevill, Alice, 169, Anne, 10, 53 169, Catherine, 168, Ed 18, Jane, 138 169 John, 168, Margaret, 18, Sir Tho-

INDEX.

mas, 138, Thomas, 10, 53, 138, 169, William 10, 53, 168. 169
Newdigate, 153
NEWDIGATE,185, Anne, 20,185, Dorothy, 185 Elizabeth 185, 186, Mary, 186, Sir Robert, 185, 207, Robert 20, 185, William 185
Nenman 126
NEWMAN 126, Anne, 126, Daniel, 126, Margaret 35, 62,174 Mary,126, William, 126
Newnham Anne 69, Margery, 69, William 69
Newport 10
Newport, Elizabeth 4, Jane, 195 John 4, 195, Phillis, 10, Roger 4, William, 10
Newsam, Judith, 140, Thomas, 110
Newton, 127
NEWTON 127 Anne, 127, Dorothy, 127 Edward 127 Elizabeth, 127, Ellen, 127, Frances, 127, Humphrey, 127, Isabel, 127 Joane, 127 John, 7, 84, 127, Mary 7 84 127, Thomas, 127, William, 127
Neyrnute 36
Neyrnute, Joane, 36 Sir John 36, Margaret, 36
Nicholas, Anne, 176, John, 176.
Nicholls 63, 186
NICHOLLS, 63 186, Anne 186, Anthony 186, Bruce, 186, Catherine, 63, Christian,186, Edward 186, Elizabeth 63, 186, Ellen, 186, Ferdinand, 63, Francis 186, George, 63 Grace, 186, Henry, 63, Isabel 186, Joane, 63, John 63 186, Margaret, 186, Mary, 63, 90, 186, Matthew 63 Richard, 186 Robert, 186, Roger, 63, Susanna, 63, Tempest, 186 Thomas, 186, Walter, 63, 186, —, 207
Nodes 127
NODES,127, Agnes 128, Anne, 128, Beatrice, 128, Benjamin, 128, Edmund, 128, Edward,128, Elizabeth, 128, Ellen, 85, 128 George 85, 128, Joane, 127, 128, John 128, Mary, 128 Rose, 128, William 127, 128
Nodham, Dorothy 61
Nokes, Mary, 27, Thomas, 27
Noone 12
Noone, Anne, 11, Edmund, 14
Norbury, 162
Norbury, Anne, 163 Elizabeth, 162, Sir Henry, 163 Jane, 163 Joane, 163, Sir John, 162 163
Norgald, Beatrice, 68, Henry, 68

Norman, Anne 104, 169, William, 104, 169
Norreys, Elizabeth 5, John, 5
Norris, Elizabeth, 162 Sir John, 162
North, Edward, Lord, 6, Margaret, Lady, 6
Northumberland, Dukes of, 203
Norton, 167
NORTON 128, Anne 129,167, Benjamin, 129, Elizabeth, 129, Ellen 129, Graveley, 129 John, 167, Lettice,128 129, Luke, 50 128 Mabel, 81 Martha, 129 Mary 201, Sir Richard, 81 Richard, 129, 201 Susan, 129, Talbott 50, 129, Thomas 128, 129, —, 207
Norton alias Nervile, 128
Noteman, Henry 200 Joane, 200
Nottingham, Charles, Earl of 54
Nutthall, Alice, 178, Richard, 178
Nutting, —, 97

O

Oakley 67
Oakley Elizabeth, 60, Stephen, 60, William 60
Offley, Anne 129, Jane, 166, Richard, 166, Robert, 129, Sir Thomas, 166
Ogilbey Lord, 183
Ogle Mary, 29, Richard, 29
Oldenby, Elizabeth 41, John, 41
Olney, Alice, 66, Avice, 61 John, 66 Sir Robert, 66, Sir William, 41
Ongley Sir Samuel, 206
Onslow, Cicely, 199, Richard, 199
Orlebar, Charles 94, Elizabeth, 94 —, 204, 207
Orlibeare alias Orlingbury Anne 93 Elizabeth 93 George, 93 John 93 Margaret 93, Maude, 93, Richard, 93
Ormerod, Alice, 150
Osborne 129
OSBORNE, 129, Alice, 85 129, Anne, 129, 130, Sir Edward, 129, Edward, 85, 129, 130, 195, Elizabeth, 101, 130, Frances, 129, Sir Hewett. 129, Isabel, 195, James 130, Jane, 129, Sir Peter 205 Peter 101 Richard, 129, Ursula, 130, William, 130 — 127, 204 207
Oulton, Richard 115
Over 187
OVER, 187, Anne 187, Bennett, 187, Edward, 187, Gregory, 187 Henry, 187, James,

187 Jane, 187; John 187, Katherine, 187 Mary, 187, Nicholas, 187, Robert 187, Stephen, 187 Thomas, 187, Timothy 187, William 187
Owen, 32
OWEN, 187, Anne, 187, Benjamin, 188, Sir David, 48 187 David. 188, Dorothy, 187 Elizabeth 48, 65, 188, George York Herald,71,153, Sir Henry, 187, Henry 34, 18 188, Jane, 34 188, Jasper, 188 John, 34 188 Joyce, 187, Levi, 188 Mary, 187, Robert, 188, Roger, 187, Thomas, 187, 188, William, 188
Owen Tudor, 187
Oxenbridge, Anne, 39, William 39
Oxford, John de Vere, Earl of, 14

P

Pabenham, 65, 197
Pabenham Elianora 66, Sir Lawrence, 66
Page, 44
PAGE, 44, Alice, 146, Anne 45, Cicely, 44, 45, Dorothy 45, Elizabeth, 45, 102 Sir Gregory 208 John 44 45, 146, Margaret,45, Mary,45, Richard, 45, Robert, 102, Thomas, 45
Pakingham 154
Palgrave, Frances, 109
Palmer, 130, 168
PALMER, 130, Anne, 169, Bridget 130, Catherine, 168 Dorothy, 130, Elizabeth, 177, Geoffrey, 177, John, 130, 169, May 130, Robert, 130, Thomas, 90, 130, 168, Sir William, 207, William, 130, — 207
Paradine 130
PARADINE, 130, Anne, 131, Dorothy, 131, Elizabeth, 131, George, 130, 131, Mary 131, Matthew, 131, Peter 131 Richard, 131, Robert, 72, 130, 131, Thomas, 71, 131 William 131, —, 207
Parbonc Henry, 115
Paris Joyce, 145, Pair 145
Parker, Alice, 53, Anne, 53, Elizabeth 107, 121 Henry, Lord Morley, 53
Parkinson, 131
PARKINSON,131, Edward 131, Frances 131, James, 131, John, 131, Margery 131, Thomas, 131
Parr 67
Parr, Elizabeth, 69, 180 Lady Mary, 69, Mary, 22, Sir William, Baron of Horton, 69 William, Lord, 22

THE VISITATION OF BEDFORDSHIRE.

Parratt, Elizabeth, 123 ; John, 123 ; Mary, 139 ; Thomas 139
Parris, Bridget, 39 ; Elizabeth 55 ; Robert, 55 ; Thomas, 39, 55
Partington, Anne 106 ; Dr John, 106
Paschall, Elizabeth, 137 ; William, 137 ; — 174
Pashley, Abbot of 181
Paston, Jane, 36 ; William, 36
Patishull, 9, 51 154
Patishull, Isabel, 52 ; John, 52 Mabel 52 ; William, 52
Paveley, 9, 51
Paveley, Isabel, 52 ; John, 52 ;
Pawlett, Sir Amyas, 112 ; Edith, 112 ; Elizabeth, 194 ; William, 194
Payne, 92
Payne Alice, 121 ; Anne, 93 ; Daniel 93 ; Elizabeth, 51 ; Francis 93, Isabel, 93 John, 126 ; Margaret, 93, Mary, 126 ; Robert 51, William, 92 93 ; — 207
Paynell, Joane, 172 ; Ralph 172
Payton Alice 129 ; Elizabeth, 166 Sir John 129 166
Peacock, 84
Peacock, Anne 7, 84 Thomas, 7, 84
Peck, 141
Peck, Anne, 55 ; John, 41 ; Margaret, 41
Peckham, Mary, 163 ; Robert, 163
Peers, Henry, 129, Jane 120
Pence, Dr, 129 ; Elizabeth 129
Pelham, Sir John, 54 ; Judith, 54
Pell Parnell, 125 ; Sir Richard, 96 ; Thomas, 125 ; Ursula, 96
Pelsant Constance, 34
Pemberton, Sir Lewis, 119 ; Mary, 149 ; — 204
Pendred, 64
Pendred Elizabeth 64 ; John, 64 ; Robert 64
Penfold, 153
Penn, 45
PENN 45 , Alice, 45 Dorothy, 45 , Elizabeth, 45 ; Ellen, 45 ; John, 45 Lucy, 45 Margery, 45 ; Mary, 45 ; Robert, 45 , Susan, 45 ; Thomas, 45
Perriam Jane, 192 ; Sir William, Lord Ch Baron 192
Perient, Elizabeth, 106 ; Sir George, 80 106 ; Mary, 80
Perin Elizabeth, 50, 169 ; Sir George 50
Perrott, 12
Perrott, Anne 124 ; Cassander, 13 Reynold, 13 Thomas, 124 *See* Pyrott
Peter, Elizabeth, 33 ; Sir John 33

Peterborough, John, Earl of, 34
Petitit Florence, 12 ; Frances, 12 ; Snach, 12
Petts Sir John, 182
Pever, 12, 154
Pever, Margaret, 14 , Mary, 14 ; Thomas, 14
Philip, Rice ap Morgan ap Jenkin ap 58
Phillips, Sir Edward, 186 ; Elizabeth 186 , Robert, 88
Phillipson Christopher, 161 , Frances, 161
Philpot, —, Somerset Herald, 148
Pichard, 169
Pichard, Margaret 104, 105, 169
Pickering, Sir Gilbert, 208 ; Jane 173 , William 173
Pierpoint, Sir Edmond, 28
Pigott, 46, 116, 132, 154, 172
PIGOTT, 46, 132, 188 , Agnes, 132 , Alice, 132 , Anne, 46, 47, 132, 188 189 , Anthony, 47, Baldwin, 173 , Benjamin, 47, 114 132 188 Bridget, 132 , Catherine, 132, 189, Clement, 47, 188 Dorothy, 173, 188 , Edward 47 Eleanor, 47, 132 , Elizabeth, 46, 132, 188 189 Eustace, 47, 188 , Frances, 132, 188, 189 Francis 47, 53, 132, 189 , George, 47, 188 , Sir Henry, 205 , Henry, 132, Isabel, 46, 189 Jane, 3, 59 188 , Joane, 172, 188 , John, 3, 47 59, 132, 173, 188 189 Judith, 114 132 , Lewis, 47, 189 , Magdalen, 46 Margaret, 24, 47 53, 132 188 , Mary 132 Michael, 47, 172, 188 , Nicholas, 24, 47, Oliver, 47, 132, 188, Randolph, 46 , Richard, 46, 47, 188 , Robert, 46, 47 , Roger 46 , Rose, 47 , Susan, 132 , Talbott, 132 , Sir Thomas, 47, 188 , Thomas, 46 47, 132, 188 , Sir William 46 , William 132 , Winifred, 132, Wyborow 47 , — 207
Pimpe, —, 15
Pitts, 3
Pitts, Anne, 30
Plomer 189
PLOMER 189 Anne, 189 Catherine, 189 Edward 189 Elizabeth 189 Ellen, 189 , George, 189 John, 189 , Margaret, 189 , Mary, 189 , Rose, 189 , Thomas, 189 Sir William, 189, 207 William 189
Pollard, Alice, 54 , Anthony, 54 , Sir John, 54
Poole, 64
POOLL, 64 , Catherine, 64 Edith 52 , Elizabeth, 64 Sir Geoffrey 52 Isabel, 177, John, 64 Margaret, 52

Mary, 64 , Sir Richard, 52 Sir Thomas, 64 Thomas 64, 177, Sir William, 64
Pooley 190
POOLLY, 190 , Alice, 190 , Anne 190 Barbara 190 Catherine, 190 Jane, 190 , Joane 190 , John, 190 , Margaret, 190 , Maude, 190 , Nicholas, 190 , Prudence, 190 , Richard, 190 , Robert, 190 , Rose 190 Simon, 190 , Thomas, 190
Popham, Sir John 202
Popplewell, Elizabeth, 186
Porter, Augustin 100 , Elizabeth, 100 Joane, 151 , 200 , John, 200 William, 65
Portington Judith 134 , William, 134
Potter, Joane 200 , John, 200
Potts Elizabeth, 114 , John, 207 , Mary, 119 , Nicholas, 119 Ralph, 114
Povery, John, 177 , Dorothy, 177
Powell —, 182
Poynes, Elizabeth, 101 , Sir John, 101
Praers, 67
Praers, Hawise, 68 , Henry 68
Prannell —, 57
Pratt, Mary, 92
Prescott, Edward, 142 Gertrude 34 , Mary, 112 , Thomas, 34
Prestoliffe Elizabeth, 188, John, 188
Preux, 39
Price, Catherine 66 Edward, 66 Mary, 117 , Robert, 117, Susan, 106
Pudsey, 46
PUDSEY, 46 , Catherine, 46 Joane 46 , John 46 , Margaret, 46 , Richard, 46 , Thomas, 46 — 57
Pulter, Edward, 170 , Mary, 170
Puttenham 12
Puttenham, Mary 12, 92 , Robert, 12, 92
Pyke, 5 151
Pyke, Anne, 33 , Jane, 6
Pyrott, 40
Pyrott Cassandra 41 , Elizabeth, 41 , Ralph, 41 *See* Perrott

Q

Quadring, Arthur 198 Audrey, 198 , Gabriel 198 , William, 198.
Quatermayne, 24
Quinton, 21
Quinton Lawrence, 22, Margaret, 22 , Sir William, 22
Quitlaw *See* Wheatley

INDEX.

R

Radcliffe, 47, 64 153
RADCLIFFE, 47, 64, Anne, 48 64, 65, Edward, Earl of Sussex, 65, Sir Edward 48, 207, Edward, 48, Elizabeth 48 64 188, Ellen, 65, Frances 48, 65 George, 48, 65 Henry, Earl of Sussex, 48, 65, Humphrey Earl of Sussex, 48, Sir Humphrey, 33 48, 65, 188 Isabel 48, 65, Jane, 65, John Lord Fitzwalter, 48 64 Sir John 48 64, Margaret, 48, 64, Martha, 33, 48, 65, Mary 48 64 65 Robert Lord Fitzwalter 1st Earl of Sussex, 48, 64, Thomas, 48, 65
Radwell, John, 48, Margery, 48, Thomas, 48, 49
Ragon, 21, 67
Ragon, Agnes 22, Elizabeth 22, John 22, Reynold 22
Raleigh, 67
Raleigh, Sir Edward, 69, Mary, 69
Randall Mary, 193 Thomas, 193
Randes, 48, 133
RANDES, 48, 133, Agnes, 49, Alice, 49, Catherine, 49, Cicely, 133, Edmond 19 Edward 49, 133, Elizabeth, 49 Frances 49 133, George, 49, Giles, 133, Jane, 49, 133, Joane, 49, John, 49 133, Judith, 133, Margery, 48, 49, Oliver, 133, Thomas, 48, 49, 133 William, 49, 133
Raneleigh Viscount 120
Ras, Isaac ap 162, Jane, 162
Ratcliffe, Ralph 208
Ravens, —, 207
Rawlen, John 25 103, Margaret 25 103
Rawlins, Elizabeth 133, John, 133
Raymond Margaret, 107, Robert, 107
Raynes, 21, 140
Raynes, Elizabeth, 21, 86, 140, John, 140, Margaret, 189, Mary, 100, Richard, 100, Thomas, 21
Reade, Dorothy, 194, Elizabeth, 66, John, 194, Thomas, 66
Reding, Agnes, 121, George 125, Margaret 125
Ree 67
Ree Elizabeth, 61, Ellen, 61, William, 61.
Reston, Anne, 170, John 170
Reynes, Elizabeth, 8, Joane, 6, Richard 8
Rice Catherine, 53 Sir Griffith, 53
Rice ap Morgan ap Jenkin ap Philip, Isabel, dau of, 53
Rich, 51

Rich, Anne, 47, 188, John, 81, Judith 81 Richard, Lord, 188, Sir Richard, 47, Thomas, 81
Richard, 169
Richard, Margaret, 169
Richardson, Anne, 176, Sir Edward 98, John, 123, Lewis 112, Mary 98, 112, 123
Ridley, Christopher, 189, Mary, 189
Risley, Anne 178, Margaret, 31
Rives Anne, 183, Sir John, 183
Roane, Alice 107, Anthony 107
Roberts Anne, 99, Dr 201, Edward, 99 Elizabeth, 137, 201, Francis, 137, Magdalen, 46
Robinson, Elizabeth, 76, Frances, 166, John 184, Mary 184, Sarah, 76, Susan, 76, William, 76, 166
Roborough, Anne, 79, Henry, 79
Roche, Elizabeth, 22, John, Baron 22
Rocher 163
Rocke, Anne 8, Hugh, 8
Rockley, Elizabeth, 28 Sir Robert, 28
Rodney Anne, 42, John, 42
Rogers, Elizabeth, 18, William, 18
Rolleston 168
Rolt, 133, 134
ROLT, 133 Benjamin, 135, Catherine, 134 Charles 134 Dorothy, 134, Edward, 133-135, Elizabeth, 133 135, Ellen, 134 Frances, 122, Francis, 135, Giles, 135, Henry, 133, 134 Jane 134, 135, John, 133 135 Judith, 133-135 Loa 134, Martha, 134, Mary, 134 135 Muriel, 135, Nathaniel, 135, Rebecca, 134, Richard 134 Samuel, 134, 135, Sarah, 134, Stephen 134, Susanne 135, Theophilus 135, Thomas 133 135, Walter, 122 134, William 133-135, —, 207
Rookes, —, 207
Roos, 197
Rose, Anne 169 John, 169
Rotherham, 8 49, 135, 156, 191
ROTHERHAM, 49, 135, 191, 193 Agnes, 50, 51, 192, 193, Alice, 4 49, 50, 59, 77, 191, 192, Anna, 50, Anne 50 135, 140, 193, Audrey, 49 Catherine, 50 156, 192, Cheney, 51, Cordall 51, Edmond, 50 Edward 50 51, Elizabeth 49-51, 53, 98, 135, 184, 192, Frances, 18, George 49 51, 135, 140, 192 193, Hugh 50, Isaac, 50, Jane, 8, 49-

51, 192, 193, Joane, 50, 135 Sir John, 49, 50 98, 191 192, 207, John, 50, 51 193, Julian, 49, Mary, 49, 135, Nicholas, 51, 192, 193, Olive, 135, Ralph 50, Talbott 50, 129, *alias* Scott Thomas, Archbp of York, 49 191, Sir Thomas, 8 49-51 53, 156, 181 192 Thomas, 4 8, 50 59, 77, 129, 135, 192, 193, Thomas Atwood 193, William 18, 50
Rouse, 154
Rouse, Dorothy, 20, Elizabeth, 174, John 20, 89, Margaret 89 Thomas, 174
Rowe 193
ROWE 193, Alice, 193, Elizabeth, 34 193, Sir Henry, 193, Henry 193, John, 193, Judith, 193, Mary 193, Rebecca 193, Reynold, 193, Robert, 193, Sarah, 193 Sir Thomas 193, Thomas, 193, William, 193
Rowesley, Anne, 171
Rowley 67
Rowley, Elizabeth 61, Lora, 59 157, Margaret 61, Thomas, 157, William 61
Rowlston, Catherine, 29, Thomas 29
Rudall, Dorothy, 1 John, 1
Rudd Edmund 128, Elizabeth, 128, Sarah,134, Thomas, 134.
Ruding, 40
Ruding, Humfrey, 40 Margaret, 40
Rudyard, Sir Benjamin, 186, Elizabeth, 186, Lawrence, 186
Rueborough John, 115
Rufford 27
Rufford Alice, 29, Elizabeth, 142, 173, John, 29, Thomas 142, 173
Rushton, Maude 177
Russell Anne, 182, Sir George, 143, 203, 207, Jane, 38, 118, John, 38, 118 182, Katherine 143
Ruthall, Elizabeth, 88, Margaret, 8 Richard 88, Thomas, 8
Rutter, Reginald, 143
Rydell 154
Ryve, Jane, 44, Marlyon 44

S

Sabcotts, Anne, 14, Sir Guy, 14
Sackville Bridget, 25, Jane, 109, Mildred, 29, Richard, 29, Robert 25 Simon, 109
Sadler, 136
SADLER 136, Anne, 136, 137, Blount, 136, Dorothy, 136, Edward, 136, 137, Edwin

229

137, Elizabeth, 137, Ellen, 136, Frances 137, 208, Gertrude, 136, Grace, 136, Henry, 136, Jane, 136 137, Joyce, 136, Leigh, 137, Margaret 136, Mary 136, Sir Ralph, 136, Ralph, 136, 137 Raphael, 136, Richard, 136, 137 Robert, 136, 137, Sarah 137, Sir Thomas 136 Thomas, 136, 137, Thomas Leigh, 9, 137 208, Ursula, 136, William, 137, —, 207
Salisbury Ambrose, 178, Elizabeth 22, Margaret, 178 Mary, 22, William 22
Sallare, — 15
Samm, Ellen, 147, Thomas, 147
Sams, Elizabeth, 107, William, 107
SANDERSON, 194, Jane, 194, Joane, 194 John 194, Lawrence 194, Susan, 194, William 194
Sandes Edith, 15, William Lord, 15, Sir William, 15
Sandford, 155
Sandford, Francis Rouge Dragon, 122 — Baron of 155
Saudy *See* Napier
Sandys Elizabeth, 97 Golden or Edwin, 207, 208, Henry, 97, Mary, 97, Miles, 97
Sankey, Thomas, 132, Winifred, 132
Sare, Margaret, 7 84, Peter, 7, 84
Sargar, Dorothy 7 Robert 7
Sargeant, Anne, 161 Joyce, 161 William 161
Saunders, 137
SAUNDERS, 137, Anne, 137, Dorothy, 127, Edward, 66, 127, Elizabeth, 137, 175, 183, Ellen, 101 137, Frances, 66, Francis, 137 Isabel, 137 Sir John, 137 John, 137 143, Margery, 45, 148, Mary, 137 178 Sir Nicholas, 183, Richard, 137, Thomas, 45, 101, 137, 178, William, 101 137, —, 33, 171, 207, 208
SAVAGE, 138, Amy 138, Sir Arthur 116 138, 207 Catherine, 18, Douglas 138, Edmund, 138, Francis, 138 Henry, 138, Jane, 138 John 18, 138, Sarah, 138, Sir Thomas 138, William, 138
Sav and Seale, Lord, 37
Saywell 21
Saywell, Henry, 22 Maude 22
Scargill, 116, 172
Scargill Constance, 173, Margaret 116, 173, Sir Robert, 173, Robert, 116, Sir William 173
Scarisbrick, 177
Scarisbrick, Agnes, 177
Scott, Dorothy, 199, George, 199 *See* Rotherham

Scovill 163
Scroggs, 154, 195
SCLOGGS 195, Alexander 154 195, Francis 195, Jane 195 Margaret, 106, Richard, 195 Thomas 154, 195
Scroope, Elizabeth, 52 Lord, 52
Scudamore, Elizabeth 39, Simon, 39
Seckford, Sir Henry, 193, Rebecca, 193 Sarah, 193
Sedgwick, John 150 Martha, 150
See 167
Segar, Sir William, Garter, 78, 85, 98, 120, 127
Sencill, 153
Sewester, Sarah, 138
Sexton Anne, 170 Sir George, 170
Seycoll Anne, 98 William, 98
Seymour Anne 69 David, 69
Sha, Bridget, 25, Robert, 25
Shaa, 190
Shalcross, Elizabeth, 177, James, 177
Sharpe Elizabeth, 83, William, 83
Shaw, Sir John, 30, Julian, 30
Shawler, Elizabeth, 109, Gabriel 109, Jane 109, Michael, 109, Walter, 109
Sheffeld, Anne, 5, Grisell, 75, Lord, 75, Thomas, 5
Sheldon, Prudence 190, Richard 190
Shelley, John 29, Mary 29
Shelton, Anne, 182, Humphrey 182
Sheppard, 138
SHEPPARD or Shepherd, 138, Amphilis, 138, 189, 169, Constance, 86, 109, 139, 169, Elizabeth 139, 169, Francis, 139, John, 139 Margaret 149, Mary 139 Thomas, 86, 138, 139, 169, William, 138, —, 207
Sacrington Sir Henry, 136, Ursula, 136
Sherman Frances, 145, Richard 145
Short, Elizabeth 151, 201
Shotisbroole, 12
Shotisbrooke, Edith, 15, Eleanor, 15, Sir Robert, 15
Shoyswell, John 193, Judith 193
Shrewsbury Anne, dau of Francis Earl of, 163, Countess of 110
Shuckborough, Anne, 197, John 197
Sibthorpe, Anne, 176, Robert, 176
Silvester, Alice, 196
Simcotts —, 204, 207, 208
Simons, 74
Simons, Anne 74, Thomas, 74
Singleturne, 129

Shevington, 67
Skevington, Catherine 61, William 61
Skinner, Anne, 172 Austin 172
Skipwith Elizabeth 3, 59 Joane, 159 Martha 92, William 3 59, 92, 159
Slade, 154
Slade Edward, 49 133, Elizabeth, 55, Jane 133, Joane, 49 John, 55
SLINGSBY, 139, Abiath, 139, Edmund, 139 Hezekiah 139, Mark 139, Robert, 139
Smallman, Alice, 152, 202 Francis, 152, 202
Smalwood, Mary, 186, Thomas, 186
Smart, Gerard, 116
Smith, 67, 139, 146
SMITH, or Smyth, 139, Alice, 35, 62, 190 Andrew, 35 62 Anne 35 69, 125 140, Barbara, 140, Catherine, 146, Christopher, 50 75, 192, Constance, 102, Edward, 72 121, Elizabeth, 45 94, Ellen, 106, Florence, 98, George 102, 125, 139, 140, Jane 50, 102, Jasper, 45, Sir John, 69 John, 95, 190, Judith, 140 159, Lydia, 121, Magdalen 75 Margaret, 46, 140 164 Mary, 34, 95, 139, 140 Mercy 107, 140, Robert, 146, Thomas 7 46, 84, 107, 139, 140, 159 164, Ursula 7, 84, Sir William, 206, Dr William, 94 98, William 139, 140, —, 204
Smithson, Sir Hugh, 203, Sir Jerome 203, May, 203
Smythes Alderman, 138, Sarah, 138, —, 204
Snagg 140
SNAGG 140, Agnes, 50, 192, Anne, 140, 141 181, Charles, 141, Douglas 138, Edward, 208 Elizabeth 89, 140 141, 151, Lewis, 140, Mary 140, 141, Mordaunt, 141, Philip, 140 Ralph, 141, 207, Richard, 141 Robert, 140, Sir Thomas 138, 140, 181 205, Thomas, 50, 140, 141, 181, 192 William, 89, 110, —, 207
Sneycale, William, 43
Snow, 110
Snow Daniel, 111 Edward, 97 111, Elizabeth, 110, Lawrence, 45 Margaret 45, Rebecca 111, Richard, 110 111, Sarah, 97
Soame, Anne, 143, Judith, 75, Sir Stephen 143, Stephen, 75
Somerset, John Duke of, 15, 52, 196, Margaret, Duchess of, 15 52, 156

INDEX. 231

Somery, 153, 154
Soulton, —, 176
Sounde, 67
South, Eleanor, 53, Sir John, 53
Speneer 12, 55, 141, 195
SPENCER, 55, 141, 195, Alice 55, 141, 112, Anne, 39, 55, 141, 196, Christian, 141, 195, 196, Elizabeth, 55, Frances, 195, Isabel, 195, June, 196, Joane 55, Sir John, 11, John, 18, 55, 195, 196, Margaret, 196, Mary 11, 34, 141 196, Nicholas 34, 141, 142, Robert, 55, 141, 195, Rose 18, 55 141 Thomas, 39, 55 71, 141, William, 55, 141, 195, —, 207, 208
Spicer, Anne, 112, Richard, 112, —, 207 *See* Helder, Chamberlain
Spurston, 67
Spurstow, Ellen, 61, John, 61
Squire, 142
SQUIRE, 142, Alice, 141, 142 Elizabeth, 142 Gaius, 141, 142, Joane, 142, Mary, 142, Rowland, 142 Thomas, 142, William, 142, —, 208 *See* Helder
Stacy, Elizabeth 96
Stafford, Elizabeth, 48, 64, 141, Henry, Duke of Buckingham 48, 64 Jane, 138, Margaret 108 Richard, 103, Thomas, 138, Sir William, 141
Stamford, Elizabeth, 37, John, 37, Margaret, 37
Stanley Margaret, 48, 64, —, Earl of Derby 48 64
Stapers, Anne, 184, Richard, 184
Staunton 142
STAUNTON, 142, Anne, 142, Edmund, 142, Elizabeth, 142, Sir Francis, 142 205, Francis, 142, John 142, Mary, 142 Robert, 142, 207, William, 142, —, 208
Staveley, Catherine, 134 Elizabeth, 181, Margaret, 5, Thomas, 5, 134
Sterling, —, 183
Stewart, Allen, Lord Darnley and Earl of Lenox, 181 John, Lord Darnley and Aubeney, Earl of Lenox, 182, John, Lord Darnley, 182, Margaret, 182, Matthew, Lord Darnley and Aubeney, Earl of Lenox, 182, Robert, Earl of Atholl, 182, Robert, 182
St George, Alice, 191, Anne, 191, Dorothy, 191, Elizabeth 191, Etheldred 191 Francis, 191, Sir George 191, Sir Henry, Norroy, 98, 191, John, 62, 174, 191, 192, Mary, 62, 174, 191, Sir Richard, 191, Sir Richard Clarenceux, 71, 90, 101 108 119, 130 144 191, Rose, 191, Thomas, 191 192
St John, 9, 32 51, 54, 55 191
St JOHN 51, 194, Agnes, 52 54 192, Sir Alexander, 194, 205 Alexander 51, 53, 55 Alice, 52-55, Anne, 53, 54, 169 194, Sir Anthony, 194, Anthony, 191, Arabella, 194, Barbara, 194, Beatrice, 51 Sir Beauchamp 194, 205, 207, Catherine, 53, 54 Charles 53, Crestide, 10, 53, Dorothy, 194 Dudley, 194, Edith, 52, Eleanor, 53, Elizabeth, 50 54, 73, 81, 191, 192, 194. Francis, 194 Francis, 54, 194, George, 54, 83, Sir Henry, 194, 205, Henry, 44 51, 54, 112, Isabel, 52, 53, Jane, 44, 53, 55 116, 173, John, Lord, 173, Sir John, 10, 37, 50-55 116 192 John, 54, 169, 194, Judith, 54, 112, 147, 194, Margaret 15 17, 33, 47 52-55, 83, 91 94, 132, 179, 194, Martha 54, 152, 192, 194 202, Mary 26, 37, 32 54, 77, 116, Morris, 53, Nicholas 191, Oliver, Earl of Bolingbroke, 71, 81, 92 96 147, 192 194 Oliver, Lord 33, 47, 91, 132, 152, 179 192 194. Sir Oliver, 15, 52, 54, Oliver, 17, 26, 52 55, 73, 94, Sir Pawlett, 96, Pawlett, 194, Sir Rowland 194, Thomas 54, William, Lord, 173, William, 51, 77, —, Lord, 54, 202, —, 20
St Leger, Sir John, 15 Margaret, 15
Stocke Alice, 82, John, 82
STOCKER, 143 Agnes, 143, Alderman, 143, Anne 184, Barbara, 143, Christian, 143, Elizabeth, 143, Henry, 143, Jane, 143, John, 143, Margaret, 143, Mary 143, Matthew, 184, Oliver, 143, Richard, 143, Thomas, 143 William, 143
Stokes 154
Stokes, Grace, 27, Richard, 27
Stone, 143
STONE, 143, Anne, 143, Barbara, 144, Dorothy, 144 John, 143, Katherine 143, 144, 147, Margaret, 144 Masera, 62, Massy, 55, Richard, 143, 144, 147 William, 35, 62, 143, 141, —, 208
Stonham, 12
Stonham, Elizabeth, 14 Katherine, 14, Mary, 14, Robert, 14
Stonor, 13
Stourton Edith, 15, 52, John, Lord, 15, 52
Strange, 67
Strange, Agnes, 41, Annabel, 60, Anne 41, Elizabeth, 41, Ellen, 29, John, 41, Sir Nicholas, 29, Thomas, 60 *See* Lestrange
Strangways, Giles 42 Jane, 42
Streightley, Anne, 169, Paul, 169
Strickland, 21
Strickland, Mary, 23, Sir Walter 23
Strong Annabella, 60, Isabel, 60, Thomas le 60
Stump, Anne, 189
Sturgeon 51
Sturgeon, Jane, 53
Sturrey, 9, 51
Stutvile, Elizabeth, 185, Thomas 185
STYLE 144, Alice 144, Anne, 110, Edmond, 110, Elizabeth, 144, Joane, 144, Joan, 144, Lora, 134, Mary, 144, Michael 134 Sarah, 144, Thomas, 144
Styles, Margery, 132, Oliver, 132
Sudley, 162
Sumpter, Hester, 76, Simon, 76
Sussex Edward, Earl of 65, Henry, Earl of, 48 65, Humphrey Earl of, 48, Robert, Earl of, 48, 64
Suthill, Sir Henry, 28, Jane, 28
Sutton, Elizabeth, 106, 170, Sir Richard, 106, 170
Swann Muriel, 135, Sir William 135
Swinfin, John, 8 Maude, 8
Symcotts *See* Simcotts
Symons, 104
Symons, Elizabeth, 113, Maude, 104

T

Talbot, Sir John 64, Mary, 64.
Tanner, Anne, 30, Catherine, 158 Thomas, 30
Tansley, John, 28, Margaret, 28
Tape Elizabeth 17, Robert, 17
Tate, Elizabeth, 82, Sir William 82
Tattenhall, Margaret, 164 Thomas, 164
Tattershall, 27
Taverner, 191, 196
TAVERNER 196, Alice, 196, Anne, 196, Frances, 192, Francis 192 Gilbert, 196, Henry, 196, Jane, 192, John 196, Margaret, 152 192, 202, Nicholas, 196, Peter 152 192, 203, Richard 152, 192, 196, Robert, 196, Roger, 196, Silvester 196, Thomas, 196, Warren le, 196, —, 119

Taylard, Eleanor, 22, Elizabeth 38
Taylor, 144, 145
TAYLOR, 144 Anne, 146, Cicely, 145 Clara, 145, Conquest 146, Dorothy, 145, 146, Edmond, 146, Elizabeth, 85, 87, 107 145, 146, Frances, 145, Grace, 184, Hester, 97, 146, Humphrey 115, Isabel 145, Jane, 146, John 142, 145, Joyce 145, Judith, 145, Margaret, 38 145, 146 Martha, 145 Mary, 142, 145 Oliver, 145, Richard, 71, 85 144 145, Robert 87, 97, 145, 146, Samuel, 145, Simon 145, Thomas, 107, 144 146, Ursula 145, 146, Walter, 184, William 145, —, 87 207, 208
Tempest, Anne, 186, Henry, 186
Temple, Edmond, 88, Elizabeth 88, Frances, 74, Sir John, 74, Lettice, 100, Thomas 100
Tennant, James, 169, Jane 169
Teringham *See* Tyringham
Theobald Francis 97, Judith, 97
Thimelby Elizabeth, 97, Richard 97
Thompson, 146
THOMPSON, 146, Agnes, 146, Alice 146, Anne, 147 Auditor 170, Catherine 144, 146, 147, Christian, 186, Dorothy, 146, Elizabeth, 146, 170, Francis, 146, 147 Henry, 146 Jane, 146, Sir John, 144, 147 194, John, 146, 147 Judith, 147, 194, Margery, 146, Mary, 136, Richard, 146 Robert, 146, St John, 144 147, Thomas, 146, William, 146, —, 208
Th orckholme — 183
Thornell, Sir Bryan, 28
Thornhurst, Frances 185, Sir William 185
Thornton Edmund, 76 Martha 76
Thorowgood, Sarah, 79, Thomas, 79
Thrale Elizabeth, 3, George, 3
Throgmorton, Agnes 198 Anne 181 Edith, 26 Gabriel, 198, Goodith, 26, 43, Joane, 87 Mary, 10, Richard, 10 26, 43, Robert, 87, Simon 181
Thynne, Elizabeth, 188, William, 188
Tilton, 117
Tilton, Margery, 37 117
Tingleton, —, 188
Tiptoft, 13
Tiringham *See* Tyringham
Turell Beatrice, 18, Sir Thomas, 18.

Titley, 164
Titley Ardeene, 164, John, 164
Todd, Elizabeth, 134, Richard, 134
Tooke, —, 101
Torrington, Lord, 208
Town Thomas at, 15
Tracy 67
Travalard alias *Morton*, 160
Trayley, 154
Tregonnell, Mary, 52, Sir Richard, 52
Treheron, Alice, 198, Thomas, Somerset Herald, 198
Treowen —, 120
Tresham, 67
Tresham Isabella, 69, John, 198 Richard, 69
Trevor, Lord, 208
Troche, Elizabeth 89, James, 89, William 89
Trogeant, Sir Robert, 21
Trott John, 166, Sir Nicholas, 207, Susan, 166
Thoughton, Grace, 162
Trussell, Isabella, 69, Sir Thomas, 69
Tudor, 187
Tudor Dorothy, 30, Sir Owen, 187 Thomas, 30
Turnell, Anne, 76, Dionisia, 76, Edmund, 76 Hester, 76
Tunstall, Francis, 173 Sir Marmaduke, 173
Turbeville Anne 123, John, 123
Turke, —, 17
Turner, 147
TURNER, 117, Alice 147, Sir Christopher, 205, Christopher, 147, Cicely, 148, Edmund, 147, Elizabeth, 147, 166 Ellen, 147, Henry, 147 Isabel, 147, Margaret 147, Martha 147, Robert 147, Sarah 147, Susan, 147 Thomas, 147 166
Tuthill, Anne 76, Roger, 76
Twinehoe Audrey, 181, William, 181
Twinnhoe, Sir James, 182 Katherine, 182
Tyndall Jane 159, Sir Thomas, 159
Tyringham, 65, 197
TYRINGHAM, 65, 197, Alice, 66, Anne, 66 184 197, Sir Anthony, 127, Anthony 66, Bridget, 197, Catherine 66, Cecilia, 66, Christian, 66, Edmund, 66, 197, Eleanora, 66, Elizabeth, 66, 197, Frances, 66, Francis, 197, George, 197, Godfrey, 66, Isabella, 66, 127, Jane, 197, John, 66 197, Joseph 197, Judith, 197, Margaret, 66, Martha, 197, Mary, 66, 197, Petronilla, 66 Richard, 66, Robert, 197 Roger 66, Sir Thomas, 66, 184, 207, Thomas, 66, 197

U

Umfreville, 9, 51
Underwood, Elizabeth, 101, 149, Michael, 101, 149
Unedall, Dorothy, 1, John, 1
Unter, 116

V

Varney, Sir Richard, 11
Vaughan, Anne, 80, Mary 6, Thomas 6, William, 80
Vaux, 148
VAUX, 148 Alice, 148, Elizabeth, 148 Joane 111, John 148, Margaret 148, Mary, 148, Robert, 118, —, 46, 204, 208
Ventris, 148
VENTRIS 148, Charles, 149, Sir Francis, 148, 149, Henry, 149, Joane, 148, John, 148, 149, Mary, 148, 149, — 204, 208
Vere, 155
Vere, Elizabeth, 42, 125, Guy de 125, Henry, 42 125, John de, Earl of Oxford 14, 155, Katherine de 14
Verney, Elizabeth, 163, Sir Ralph 163
Villers, Ellen, 28 William, 28
Vincent, Anne, 22, William, 22 —, 92
Vinter, 116, 172
Vinter, John 173
Visdeloup, 29
Vites, — 207
Vivonia 67
Vivonia, Helvise 68, Hugh, 68

W

Wade, Ennis, 126, Samuel, 126, Thomas, 126
Wadington, Mary, 29
Waffer, —, 171
Wagstaff 155, 177
Wagstaff, Richard, 155
Wahull alias *Woodhall*, 67, 68
WAHULL *alias* WOODHALL, 68 Agnes 61, 68, 69, Alice, 68 69, Anne, 69, Anthony, Baron, 61, 69, Barbara 69, Beatrice, 68, Dorothy, 69, Edith, 68, Egidius, 69, Eleanor 68, Elizabeth, 68 69, Foulke, Baron, 69, Foulke, 69, Hawise, 68, Isabella 68, 69, Jane, 69, Joane, 69, John Baron, 68 69, John, 69, Joyce, 69, Lawrence 63, Margaret, 68, Mary, 63, 69, Michael, 68, 69, Nicholas, Baron, 69, Nicholas, 68, 69, Richard, 68, Rose 68, Sacrus, 68, Simon, Baron, 68, Simon, 68, Thomas, Baron, 68, 69, Thomas, 69, Walter,

INDEX 233

Baron 68, Walter, 68, William, 68 69
Wake, 116, 172
Wake, Dorothy 23 Sir Ralph, 41 Richard, 23, Rose, 41
Wakeman, —, 182
Walcott Anne 108, Beatrice, 23, Charles 23, Cicely 108, Dorothy 97 Ellis, 97, William 108
Waldron, Mary, 186
Walgrave Anne 123 Anthony, 35, 62, Edward 123, Elizabeth 35, 62, Margaret, 53, Sir William, 53
Walker Anne, 38, Elizabeth, 115, John 38, William, 145
Waller, Anne, 17 Margaret, 163, Mary, 17 Robert 17, Thomas 71, Sir Walter, 163 William 71, —, 207
Wallis, Anne, 59, Beatrice, 17 John 17, 59
Wallop, Elizabeth, 50
Walsh Elizabeth, 124 Thomas 124
Walsingham, Jane, 105
Walter Anne, 17, Mary, 17, Robert, 17
Walton, Bridget, 39, William, 39
Walwyn, Lucy, 162 Roger 162
Wanton, or Wauton, 12, 39, 179, 198
WANTON, Wauton, or Waulton 198, Agnes, 198, Alice, 169, 198 Audrey, 198 Cicely, 39, 198, Elizabeth 25 198 George, 198 John, 198, Mary 38 Nicholas 198, Osbert 198 Sir Thomas, 39, 198, Thomas 38 198, William, 198, —, 14
Ward, Judith, 145 William, 145
Warden, Magdalen, 46
Wardener, —, 15
Wardour, Chedeoke 81, Sir Edward, 81, Mary 81
Warham, Edward, 183, John 183, Katherine, 183
Warre, Amy, 152, 202, Roger, 152, 202
Warren, 27
Warren, Anne, 167, 184 Dorothy 98, Elizabeth, 184, Ella 27, Isabella 164, Joane, 184 John, 167 184, Sir Lawrence, 164, Magdalen, 184 Margaret, 189 Robert, 189, Thomas, 184 William, Earl, 27, 28, William, 71, 98
WARREN alias WALLER, 149, Elizabeth, 149, Mary, 149, Robert 149, Thomas, 149, William 149
Warwick, Earl of, 32.
Wassy, Dorothy, 21
Wath Margaret, 196, Twiford, 196

Watson, 149
WATSON, 149, Agnes 149, Anne, 149, Sir Edward, 100, 131, Frances, 149, George 149, John, 149, Mary, 100, 149 Richard, 100, 149, —, 207
Waverer, —, 207
Webb, Anne, 176, Elizabeth, 73 Joane, 184, Richard, 176, Thomas, 73
Weddell, Lucy, 79, William, 79
Weedon, Grace 176.
Weheathill, Anne, 64, Sir Richard, 64
Welby, Jane, 129, John, 129
Welch Alice, 49
Weldon, William 75
Welford, Alice, 50, Thomas, 50 See Wilford
Wellesford, Alice, 192, Thomas, 192
Wells, 156
Wells, Lady 156, —, 208
Welsh, 197
Wendy Mary, 88, Thomas, 88
Wenlock, 155
Wenlock, Elizabeth, 155, Sir John 155
Wentworth, 12
Wentworth, Anne, 84, Sir Giles, 48 65, Jane 15, John, 34, Margaret, 48, 65, Thomas, Lord, 15
West, Dorothy, 131, 187, Elizabeth 23, John, 23, R,131, Thomas, Lord Delaware, 187
Westcott, 24
Westcott, Christopher 30, Jane 24, Margaret, 30
Weston Isabella, 66, Sir Thomas, 66, William, 155
Wetherhall, Judith, 193
Wettenhall 122
Weyland, 190
Wharton, Anne, 48, 65, Sir Thomas, 48, 65
Wheatley, 2
Wheatley alias Quitlaw Catherine, 2, Elizabeth, 2, Robert 2
Whelton, Maude, 21 Sir Roger, 21
Whitaker, 150
WHITAKER, 150, Alice, 150, Christopher, 150, Edward, 150, Isabel 95 150, James, 150 Jane, 150, John, 95 150 Joyce, 150 Richard, 150 Thomas, 150
White, Alice, 161, Anne 174, 193, Elizabeth, 107, George, 63, John 196, Mary, 196, Richard, 193, Susanna, 63, Thomas 107
Whitebread, Agnes, 149, John, 149, Mary, 151, 201, William, 151 201 — 201
Whitehead, Sir Henry, 102, Katherine, 102

Whitlock 131
Whitlock Henry, 164
Wibbe, John, 10, Margaret, 10
Wickham, Margaret 37, William, 37
Wideville, 67
Wideville Elizabeth, 60, Richard, 60
Wigtoft, Catherine, 22
Wilbraham, Ellen, 164, Thomas 164
Wilford Alice, 4, 59, 77, Thomas, 4 59, 77
Wilkes, 32, 150
WILKES, 150, Edward, 150, Jane 150 Joane, 150, John, 150, Luke 150, Mark, 150 Martha, 150, Mary, 150, Matthew 150 Thomas, 150
Wilkinson Isabel, 145 John 145
William the Conqueror, 27
Williams Edward, 90, Elizabeth 57, 116 Jane, 87 John, Lord, 37, 116 Sir John, 37, Paradise, 90
Williamson, Anne 181, Nicholas, 181, —, 208
Willmott, Frances, 16, Richard, 16
Willoughby, Elizabeth, 16, Mary, 30 127, Philip, 127, Richard, 16, 30
Wilmer, Andrew 148, Mary, 148
Wilson Elizabeth, 9, James, 9
Winch, 154
Winch, Cicely, 199, Dorothy, 199, Elizabeth, 80 180, Ellen, 199 Sir Humphrey, 88, 199 207 Humphrey, 154, 199 John, 80, Judith, 88, 199, Margaret, 199 Onslow, 88, 180 199, William, 80
Windsor, Andrew Lord, 30, Elizabeth 30
Wingate 151 152 191, 199
WINGATE, 151, 152 199, Agnes, 200 202, Alice 152 202, Amy 152 202, Anne, 78 89 151 152 201, 202, Button, 89 151 201, Dorothy, 116, 151, 201, 202, Edmond, 1, 89, 151 152, 200, 201, Edward 2 151, 152 192 200-203, Elizabeth, 89, 151, 152 201, 202 Ellen, 202, Frances 203, Sir Francis 206, Francis, 152, 202, George 54, 78, 116, 152 200, 202 203, Heming 200, Henry, 202, Hester, 152, 202, Jane, 151, 159, 201, 202, Joane, 151, 200 203, John, 151 152, 200, 202, Judith, 202, Lucy, 201, Margaret 152 192, 200, 202 Martha, 54, 202, Mary, 1, 2, 151, 152, 201-203, Nicholas 202, Ralph, 151 152, 201-203, Richard 152, 200, 202,

H H

Robert 151, 152, 200 202
Roger, 89, 151, 159, 201 ;
Thomas 151, 201, William,
151, 200-202 , —, 119, 207,
208
Winn, Margaret, 80 Thomas,
80
Wiseman, Agnes, 202 Anne,
132, 152, 202, Ellen, 202 ,
John, 202 , Thomas, 132 ,
William, 152
Wither, 172
Withers, Margaret, 47 , William, 47
Witton, Alice, 100 , William, 100
Woburn Abbey, 155
Wodden, Amy, 179 , Richard, 179
Wolrich, Rose, 2, 178
Wolsey, Cardinal, 33, 173
Wood, 35
Wood, Anthony, 23 Edward, 167 , Elizabeth 35, 62, 100, 174 , Isabel, 23 , Margaret, 100 , Nicholas 35, 62, 174 , Robert, 100
Woodhall *See* Wahull
Woodville, 21
Woodville, Elizabeth, 22 , Thomas, 22
Wore, 164
Wortley, Ellen, 65 Sir Richard, 65
Wright, Anne, 132 , Edward, 132 , Jane, 10 , Joane, 38, 118 , John, 115 , Mary, 115 , Robert 10 Thomas, 38, 118
Wriothelsey, Thomas, Garter, 110
Wroth, Judith 88 , Margaret, 103 , Sir Thomas, 88 , William, 103
Wroynon, Katherine, 93
Wyant George 207
Wylde, 21
WYLDE, 152 , Agnes, 22 , Dorothy, 152 Sir Edmund, 152 Edmund, 152 , Elizabeth, 22 , George, 152 , Henry, 152 , Thomas, 22 , Walter 152
Wynd, Charles, 128 , Elizabeth, 128
Wyrley, —, 179

Y

Yarway Cicely, 73 William, 73
Yelverton, Sir Christopher, 93 , Henry, 93 , Isabel, 93
Yeomans, Amy, 103, 105 Robert, 103, 105
Yorke, —, 88
Young, Anne, 130 , Elizabeth, 94, 184 , Ellis, 130 , Henry 184 , — 15

Z

Zouche, 147
Zouche, Eleanor, 53 Elizabeth, 52 , Sir John, 53 , William, Lord, 52 , —, Lord, 200

The Harleian Society,

INSTITUTED FOR THE

PUBLICATION OF INEDITED MANUSCRIPTS

RELATING TO

GENEALOGY, FAMILY HISTORY, AND HERALDRY.

The Harleian Society,

INSTITUTED FOR THE

PUBLICATION OF INEDITED MANUSCRIPTS

RELATING TO

GENEALOGY, FAMILY HISTORY, AND HERALDRY.

COUNCIL ROOM—140 WARDOUR STREET, W.

President.
HIS GRACE THE DUKE OF MANCHESTER, K P

Vice-Presidents.
HIS GRACE THE DUKE OF WESTMINSTER, K G
THE MOST NOBLE THE MARQUIS OF BUTE, K T
THE RIGHT HON VISCOUNT MIDLETON
THE RIGHT HON LORD MONSON
THE HON HENRY ROPER-CURZON
SIR HENRY M VAVASOUR, BART F S A
RALPH ASSHETON, Esq

Council.
W PRIDEAUX COURTNEY, Esq
DUDLEY G CARY ELWES, Esq, F S A
SIR JOHN MACLEAN, F S A
W AMHURST TYSSEN AMHERST, Esq, F S A
GEORGE W MARSHALL, Esq, LL D, F S A
J PAUL RYLANDS Esq, F S A
GRANVILLE LEVESON GOWER, Esq, F S A
GEORGE J ARMYTAGE, Esq, F S A
JOSEPH JACKSON HOWARD Esq, LL D, F S A
THOMAS BROOKE, Esq, F S A
THE REV F T COLBY, D D, F S A
CAPT EDWARD ARTHUR WHITE, F S A

Committee for Publication of Parish Registers.
GRANVILLE LEVESON GOWER, Esq, F S A
JOSEPH JACKSON HOWARD, Esq, LL D, F S A
GEORGE J ARMYTAGE, Esq, F S A
CAPT EDWARD ARTHUR WHITE, F S A

Honorary Treasurer.
JOSEPH JACKSON HOWARD, Esq, LL D, F S A,
3 Dartmouth Row, Blackheath, S E

Honorary Secretaries.
GEORGE J ARMYTAGE, Esq, F S A,
Clifton Woodhead, near Brighouse.
*J PAUL RYLANDS, Esq, F S A,
25 Stanley Gardens, Belsize Road, N W

Bankers.
THE LONDON AND COUNTY BANK, 21 Lombard Street, E C

Auditors.
HENRY WAGNER, Esq, F S A
THE REV C J ROBINSON, M A

Hon. Local Secretary for U.S.A.
W H WHITMORE, Esq

* To whom all communications are to be addressed relative to the Society

Rules.

1. This Society shall be called the HARLEIAN SOCIETY.

2. It shall have for its chief object the publication of the Heraldic Visitations of Counties, and any manuscripts relating to Genealogy, Family History, and Heraldry, selected by the Council.

3. The Council shall consist of a President, nine Vice-Presidents, and twelve Members of Council, two of whom shall hold the posts of Secretary and Treasurer, and any four, including the Treasurer or Secretary shall form a quorum. In case of equality of votes, the Chairman to have a casting vote. Any Candidate may be elected with the consent in writing of one Member of the Council, the Treasurer, and the Secretary.

4. Three Members of the Council shall retire in rotation annually, but shall be eligible for re-election.

5. The Annual Subscription shall be One Guinea, paid in advance, and due on the 1st day of January in each year, and new Members shall pay an Entrance Fee of 10s. 6d. in addition to their first Annual Subscription.

6. Members may at their option subscribe Two Guineas per annum, in which case they will be entitled to the publications of the Register Section of the Society.

7. The funds raised by the Society shall be expended in publishing such works as are selected by the Council, but no payment in money shall be made to any person for editing any work for the Society.

8. One volume at least shall be supplied to the Members every year.

9. An Annual Meeting shall be held in the month of January every year, at such time and place as the Council may direct, and due notice shall be sent to the Members of the Society at least a fortnight previously.

10. No work shall be supplied to any Member unless his Subscription for the year be paid; and any Member not having paid his Subscription for two years, having received notice thereof, shall cease to belong to the Society.

11. No copies of the publications of the Society shall be supplied to persons not actually Members, and each Member shall be restricted to a single Subscription.

12. An account of the receipts and expenses of the Society to be made up to the 31st of December in each year, and published with a list of the Members and the Rules of the Society in the following Volume.

13. These Rules shall not be altered except at the Annual Meeting, and three clear weeks' notice must be given to the Secretary of any such intended alteration.

Report for the Year 1884.

During the year twenty-four Members have joined the Society, fifteen have resigned, five have died, and the names of eight have been removed under Rule X.

Three hundred and sixty-eight remain on the Roll of whom one hundred and eighty are subscribers to the Register Section.

The Second Volume of the "Visitation of London, 1633-4," was issued in the Spring.

The "Visitations of Bedfordshire" are complete, and the Index will be printed in a few days.

The 'Visitation of Gloucestershire" has again been delayed by the Editors, but it is hoped it may be ready to follow the Bedfordshire Visitations.

The "Visitation of Dorsetshire in 1623" is ready for the press, and the 'Visitation of Shropshire" is now being transcribed.

The First Volume of the "Registers of St James, Clerkenwell" is now being issued to Members who subscribe to the Register Section. The Second Volume is well advanced.

The "Registers of Christ Church, Newgate Street," have been transcribed.

The Accounts are appended to this Report, and it is hoped they will meet with the Members' approval.

The retiring Members of Council are Mr Brooke, Dr Colby, and Capt White. They offer themselves for re-election.

Harleian Society.

Accounts for the Year ending 31st December, 1884

ORDINARY ACCOUNT

Dr.

	£	s	d
Balance to 31st Dec., 1883	671	6	8
Subscriptions	367	7	6
Books purchased by Members	55	18	6
Dividend on Stock (£532 8s.)	19	11	6
Interest on Deposit (£150)	2	16	7
Balance of London Visitation Illustration Fund	53	2	2
	£1170	**2**	**11**

Cr.

	£	s	d
Messrs Mitchell and Hughes —			
Balance of London Visitation	74	13	3
On account of Gloucestershire and Bedfordshire Visitations	240	0	0
General Printing, Carriage, etc.	16	7	2
Ditto ditto, including Insurance, £8 8s, and Rent of Room, £5	28	17	10
Advertisements	0	11	0
Incidents, Honorary Treasurer and Secretary	20	0	0
Mr Eedes, Dorset Visitation Transcript	4	4	0
Mr E Cleghorn, London Visitation Woodcuts	53	2	2
	227	0	10
Correction of London Visitation Woodcuts	7	0	0
Bedford Visitation, Transcript	6	0	0
	£677	**16**	**3**
Balance	492	6	8
	£1170	**2**	**11**

REGISTER SECTION

	£	s	d		£	s	d
Balance to 31st Dec, 1883	149	10	7	Messrs Mitchell and Hughes:—			
Subscriptions	164	17	0	Binding Registers, etc	15	10	3
Books purchased by Members	15	12	0	Registers of St James, Clerkenwell, Vol I	185	15	1
				Miss Morse, Transcript of Christ Church Registers	15	10	0
				Mr Eedes, Transcript of St James, Clerkenwell, Registers	43	0	0
					259	15	4
				Balance	70	4	3
	£329	19	7		£329	19	7

GENERAL BALANCE.

	£	s	d		£	s	d
To Balance, Ordinary Account	492	6	8	Net Balance in Bank	562	10	11
,, Register Section	70	4	3				
	£562	10	11		£562	10	11

Examined and found correct,
HENRY WAGNER,
CHARLES J ROBINSON

16th January, 1885

JOSEPH JACKSON HOWARD, *Honorary Treasurer*

List of Members, with the Dates of their Election.

Corrected to January 1st, 1885

Those marked (*) are Subscribers to the Register Section

27 Sept 1876	*F WILLIAM ALINGTON, 13 Mitre Court Chambers, Temple, E C
24 Nov 1869	*REGINALD AMES, 2 Albany Terrace, Park Square East, N W
29 Apr 1869	*W AMHURST T AMHERST, M P, F S A (*Council*), Didlington Hall, Brandon
31 Dec 1875	*JOHN AMPHLETT, Clent, Stourbridge
24 Nov 1869	FRANK ANDREW, Chester Square, Ashton-under-Lyne
1 July, 1870	WILLIAM SUMNER APPLETON, Boston, U S A
27 Mar 1869	*GEORGE J ARMYTAGE, F S A (*Hon Secretary*), Clifton Woodhead, near Brighouse
12 Apr 1869	*RALPH ASSHETON (*Vice-President*), Downham Hall, Clitheroe
6 Dec 1870	JOHN ASTLEY, Stoneleigh Terrace, Coventry
5 Oct 1872	ATHENÆUM, Liverpool (W ROSCOE JONES, Librarian)
4 Sept 1880	*Capt T W T ATTREE, R F, Springfield House, Worthing
9 Aug 1884	T A CARLESS ATTWOOD, The Cliff, Malvern Wells
21 Jan 1882	FRANCIS JOSEPH BAIGENT, Winchester
13 June, 1871	*JOHN E BAILEY, F S A Egerton Villa Stretford, Manchester
22 Sept 1869	CHARLES BAKER, F S A, 7 Westbourne Crescent, Hyde Park, W
28 July, 1869	JOSEPH GURNEY BARCLAY, 54 Lombard Street, E C
14 Jan 1879	*The Rev C W BARDSLEY, Vicarage, Ulverston, Lancaster
1 Jan 1883	*Captain H BATHURST, Springhill, Frome, Somerset
4 Nov 1870	JOHN BATTEN, F S A, Aldon, Yeovil
12 June, 1871	*FRANCIS BAYLEY, F S A, 66 Cambridge Terrace, Hyde Park, W
7 June 1877	EDWIN J BEDFORD, 37 Elmore Road, Broomhill, Sheffield
21 Sept 1876	BEDFORD ARCHÆOLOGICAL SOCIETY Bedford (D G C ELWES, Hon Secretary)
11 Aug 1877	WALTON GRAHAM BERRY, Broomfield, Fixby, near Huddersfield
17 June, 1875	SAMUEL BIRCHAM, 46 Parliament Street, S W
13 Dec 1878	THOMAS BIRD, Canons, Romford
9 Mar 1871	*BIRMINGHAM LIBRARY, Union Street, Birmingham (C E SCARSE, Librarian)
24 July, 1883	*BIRMINGHAM CENTRAL FREE LIBRARY, Ratcliffe Place, Birmingham (J MULLINS, Librarian)
31 May, 1879	The Rev C M BLAKE, San Francisco (care of B F Stevens, 4 Trafalgar Square, W C)
24 Apr 1869	F A BLAYDES, Shenstone Lodge, Ashburnham Road, Bedford
1 June, 1869	*The Rev CHARLES W BOASE, Exeter College, Oxford
22 Oct 1874	*REGINALD STEWART BODDINGTON, 15 Markham Square, S W
20 Jan 1871	*BODLEIAN LIBRARY, Oxford

16 Feb 1884 CHARLES NEWPORT BOLTON, Brook Lodge, Waterford
27 July, 1871 *WILLIAM EDWARD BOOLS, 7 Cornhill, E C
26 Jan 1871 Lieut.-Colonel HAWORTH-BOOTH, Hullbank House, Hull
25 Apr 1877 *R C BOSTOCK, Little Langtons, Lower Camden Chislehurst
8 Sept 1874 *BOSTON ATHENÆUM, Boston, U S A (per Trubner and Co, 57 Ludgate Hill)
15 Oct 1875 *BOSTON FREE PUBLIC LIBRARY, Boston, U S A (per Trubner and Co, 57 Ludgate Hill)
20 Jan 1877 *C E B BOWLES, M A, 34 Richmond Terrace Clifton, Bristol
3 Apr 1877 *Miss JULIA BOYD, Voor House, Leamside, Durham
28 July, 1869 *EDMUND M BOYLE, F S A, 14 Hill Street, Berkeley Square, W
12 Sept 1872 EDWARD W BRABROOK F S A, 28 Abingdon Street Westminster, S W
18 May, 1870 +The Rev WILLIAM BREE, The Rectory, Allesley, Coventry
26 Aug 1882 *WILLIAM ERNEST BRENNAND, Blandford, Dorset
13 Aug 1878 +The Hon and Rev Canon BRIDGEMAN, Wigan Hall Wigan
24 Nov 1869 +The Hon and Rev JOHN R O BRIDGEMAN, 89 Harley Street, W
24 Nov 1869 *THOMAS BROOKE F S A (Council), Armitage Bridge Huddersfield
29 Apr 1869 *FRANCIS CAPPER BROOKE, Ufford Place, Woodbridge
4 Nov 1870 *The Rev FREDERICK BROWN, F S A, Fern Bank, Beckenham, Kent
28 Nov 1876 *J R BROWN, F R G S 14 Hilldrop Road, Camden Town, N
19 June, 1869 *PERCY C S BRUERE, Rockville, Lansdown, near Bath
12 June, 1871 C G PRIDEAUX-BRUNE, 10 Grosvenor Gardens, S W
21 May, 1869 *Colonel W E G LYTTON-BULWER, Quebec House, East Dereham
5 Mar 1878 HENRY C J BUNBURY, Barton Hall, Bury St Edmunds
20 Apr 1880 *GEORGE R BURNABY, 128 East 24th Street, New York (care of Cassell, Smith and Co, 80 Fenchurch Street, London E C)
11 June, 1869 *Sir BERNARD BURKE, C B, LL D, Ulster King-of-Arms, The Castle, Dublin
2 May, 1871 *The Most Noble the MARQUIS OF BUTE (Vice-President), 118 Grosvenor Road, S W

20 Nov 1873 *CAMBRIDGE UNIVERSITY LIBRARY, Cambridge (H BRADSHAW, M A, Librarian)
27 Mar 1879 H H SMITH CARINGTON, Brookfield House, Whaley Bridge, Stockport
15 May 1884 R SMITH CARINGTON, St Cloud, near Worcester
5 Feb 1879 WILLIAM FOWLER CARTER, 33 Waterloo Street, Birmingham
24 Mar 1883 *Major TANKERVILLE J CHAMBERLAIN, 80th Reg, Government House, Natal (care of V Holt and Co, 17 Whitehall Place, S W)
1 Sept 1884 *W H C CHAMBERLAINE, Blagden House, Keevil, Trowbridge, Wilts
18 Oct 1870 THOMAS CHAPMAN, F R S, F S A, 25 Bryanston Square, W
12 Apr 1882 *JOHN H CHAPMAN, M A, F S A, 38 St Charles Square, North Kensington, W
21 May, 1878 *THOMAS WILLIAM CHARLTON, Chilwell Hall, Nottingham
18 Oct 1870 +CHETHAM'S LIBRARY, Hunt's Bank Manchester
6 Oct 1881 J W CLAY, Rastrick House near Brighouse
12 Aug 1881 *HOWARD COGHILL, 29 East 39th Street, New York, U S A
11 Sept 1880 H T COGHLAN, 14 Hyde Park Gardens, W
23 June, 1869 B COKAYNE, College of Arms, Queen Victoria Street, E C
23 June, 1869 *G E COKAYNE, F S A, Norroy King-at-Arms, College of Arms, Queen Victoria Street, E C
1 June, 1869 The Rev FREDERIC T COLBY, D D, F S A (Council), Litton Cheney Rectory, Dorchester Dorset

1 Dec 1883	CHARLES F COLE Flintfield, Caterham, Surrey
6 Dec 1870	Major J KYRLE COLLINS, Wiltondale, Ross, Herefordshire
22 Mar 1883	EDWARD CONDER, Elmhurst, Romford, Essex
16 Mar 1874	EDWARD COODE, Polapit Tamar, Launceston
10 Mar 1871	WM HENRY COOKE Q C , F S A , 42 Wimpole Street W
2 Nov 1877	JAMES HERBERT COOKE, F S A Berkeley, Gloucestershire
21 Feb 1882	*Colonel EDWARD H COOPER, 42 Portman Square, W
28 July, 1869	W H COTTELL, Yeolmbridge, Wood Vale, Forest Hill, S E
18 May, 1870	*W PRIDEAUX COURTNEY (Council), Ecclesiastical Commission, 10 Whitehall Place, S W
20 July, 1873	*J C CRABB, Clifton Lodge, Fallowfield, near Manchester
24 June, 1878	*E B CRANE, Worcester, Massachusetts, U S A
10 July, 1884	WILFRID CRIPPS, Farleigh House, Sandgate Kent
12 Aug 1881	*F A CRISP, Inglewood House, Grove Park, Denmark Hill, S E
8 Dec 1883	*TALBOT K CROSSFIELD, 354 Hackney Road, E
23 Nov 1882	*GERY MILNER-GIBSON CULLUM Hardwick House, Bury St Edmunds
28 Apr 1869	*The Hon HENRY ROPER-CURZON (Vice-President), The Ants' Nest, Tonbridge
15 May, 1874	J E CUSSANS, 4 Wyndham Crescent Junction Road N
18 May, 1875	*Lady ELIZABETH CUST 13 Eccleston Square, S W
8 Oct 1874	*Miss CUST, 20 Thurloe Place, South Kensington, S W
2 Dec 1881	J EDWARD K CUTTS, 28 Southampton Street, Strand, W C
20 Nov 1883	*Mrs DALISON, Greetwell Hall Kirton Lindsey, Lincolnshire
5 May, 1874	The Rev JOHN NEALE DALTON, M A F S A , Marlborough House, S W
29 May, 1869	R S LONGWORTH-DAMES, M A 21 Herbert Street, Dublin
18 Mar 1874	*The Rev G H DAVENPORT, Foxley, Hereford
28 July, 1869	*GORDON DAYMAN, St Giles s Oxford
4 Nov 1870	The Rev JOHN BATHURST DEANE, M A , F S A Sion Hill, Bath
27 Dec 1876	*DE BURNARDY BROTHERS, 28 John Street, Bedford Row, W C
25 Aug 1883	*JOHN T DICKINSON, Eastbourne, Prince's Park, Liverpool
31 Dec 1875	The Hon HAROLD A DILLON, F S A , 3 Swan Walk, Chelsea, S W
18 Apr 1878	JOSEPH DODGSON, 33 Park Row Leeds
1 Jan 1879	THOMAS DORMAN, Sandwich, Kent
22 Sept 1869	*ROBERT DOWMAN, 29 Shakspeare Street, Ardwick, Manchester
12 June, 1874	WILLIAM DOWNING, Springfield House, Olton, Acock's Green, Birmingham
4 Oct 1872	*Sir WILLIAM DRAKE, F S A , 46 Parliament Street, S W
9 Nov 1875	*The Rev JOHN INGLE DREDGE, Buckland Brewer, Bideford
10 Jan 1878	*Mrs DUGDALE, Wroxall Abbey, Warwick
1 Nov 1882	*The Rev R E H DUKE, Mark Fryston, South Milford, Yorkshire
22 June 1870	GEORGE F DUNCOMBE, 17 St Stephen s Road, Bayswater, W
17 June 1878	*The Dean and Chapter of DURHAM Chapter Offices, Durham
12 Jan 1872	ROBERT DYMOND, F S A , 1 St Leonard Road, Exeter
18 Apr 1878	JOHN PARSONS EARWAKER, M A , F S A , Pensarn Abergele, North Wales
10 Feb 1883	†The Hon DANIEL C EATON New Haven, Connecticut U S A
18 May, 1870	The EARL OF EGMONT, 26 St James's Place, S W
22 Sept 1869	The Rev HENRY T ELLACOMBE, M A , F S A Clyst St George Rectory, Topsham
28 July, 1869	WILLIAM SMITH ELLIS, 6 Holtham Road, Abbey Road, N W

15 Apr 1869 *DUDLEY G CARY ELWES, FSA (Council), 9 The Crescent, Bedford
22 June, 1870 *V CARY ELWES, FSA, Billing Hall, Billing-road Station, Northampton
18 Oct 1870 WILLIAM ROBERT EMERIS, MA, FSA Louth, Lincolnshire

19 May, 1869 J G FANSHAWE, 2 Halkin Street West, Belgrave Square, SW
19 Jan 1878 HENRY ST CLAIR FEILDEN, Corpus Christi College, Oxford
22 Sept 1869 WILLIAM FENNELL, Wakefield
3 Apr 1877 *RICHARD S FERGUSON, FSA, Lowther Street, Carlisle
3 Nov 1873 Miss FFARINGTON, Worden, Preston
16 June, 1872 J LEWIS FFYTCHE, MA FSA, Thorpe Hall, Louth Lincolnshire
3 Dec 1874 *OSGOOD FIELD, FSA 4 Grosvenor Mansions, Victoria Street, SW
8 Dec 1877 *Colonel THOMAS WM FLETCHER, MA, FRS, FSA, Lawneswood House, Stourbridge
31 Dec 1873 *CECIL G S FOLJAMBE, MP, FSA, 2 Carlton House Terrace, SW
29 Jan 1879 JOHN FOSTER, Town Head Horton in Ribblesdale, Settle
31 Dec 1875 *JOSEPH FOSTER, 21 Boundary Road, St John's Wood, NW
28 Nov 1870 *CHARLES H FOX, MD, The Beeches, Brislington, Bristol
11 June 1884 A W FRANKS, MA, FSA, British Museum, WC
16 Jan 1884 *EDWIN FRESHFIELD, LLD, FSA 5 Bank Buildings, Old Jewry, EC

27 Apr 1871 CLEMENT S BEST GARDNER Eaglesbush, Neath
5 Feb 1883 CHARLES W GEORGE, 24 Aberdeen Terrace, Clifton
17 Apr 1871 *HENRY H GIBBS St Dunstan's Villa, Outer Circle, Regent's Park NW
27 Mar 1872 *JAMES GIBSON Salem Washington County, New York, USA
12 May, 1878 *JOSEPH GILLOW 19 Northwood Road Higngate N
8 Sept 1871 C GOLDING, Colchester
25 Jan 1870 *HENRY GOUGH, Sandcroft, Redhill
12 Apr 1869 *GRANVILLE LEVESON GOWER, FSA (Council), Titsey Place, Limpsfield, Surrey
7 Oct 1882 HENRY GRAY, 25 Cathedral Yard Manchester
22 Sept 1869 *HENRY SYDNEY GRAZEBROOK Treasury Chambers, Whitehall, SW
31 Dec 1881 *JOSEPH J GREEN, Stansted Montfitchet, Bishop's Stortford
16 Dec 1870 BENJAMIN WYATT GREENFIELD, 4 Cranbury Terrace, Southampton
24 Nov 1869 The Rev HENRY THOMAS GRIFFITH, BA Smallburgh Rectory, Norwich
26 May, 1883 Sir WILLIAM GUISE, Bart, Elmore Park, Gloucester
26 July, 1878 *RICHARD H J GURNEY North Repps Hall, Cromer Norfolk
29 Dec 1872 J E A GWYNNE, FSA, FRGS 97 Harley Street, W

29 Apr 1869 EDWARD HAILSTONE, FSA, Walton Hall, Wakefield
12 June, 1882 Mrs HALLIDAY, West View, Torquay, South Devon
10 Aug 1874 *Captain PHILIP HAMOND, care of C A HAMOND, Twyford Hall, Guist, Norfolk
11 Apr 1883 *Sir REGINALD HANSON, MA, FSA, 4 Bryanston Square, W
29 Sept 1880 *THEODORE J HARE, Crook Hall, Chorley
1 Jan 1884 HENRY SEATON HARLAND, FSA Stanbridge, Staplefield, Crawley Sussex

30 Apr 1869   WILLIAM MARSH HARVEY, Goldington Hall, Bedford
17 Apr 1869   *The Rev SAMUEL HAYMAN, M A, The Rectory, Douglas, Cork
22 Feb 1883   C ARTHUR HEAD Hartburn Hall, Stockton-on-Tees
3 June, 1873 *WILLIAM C HEANE, The Lawn, Cinderford, Gloucestershire
14 May, 1869 Lady HEATHCOTE, Hursley Park, Winchester
18 May, 1876 Miss FRANCES MARGERY HEAT, Lostwithiel, Cornwall
22 Sept 1869 JOHN HIRST, Jun, Dobcross, Saddleworth
27 Dec 1879   *HISTORICAL SOCIETY OF PENNSYLVANIA (care of B F Stevens, 4 Trafalgar Square, W C)
1 Jan 1883   RICHARD A HOBLYN 2 Sussex Place Regent's Park, N W
24 Apr 1869   The Ven Archdeacon HOLBECH, Farnborough Banbury
31 Dec 1879   WILLIAM J HOLLWAY, Woodrising, Pinner, Watford
2 Nov 1877   CHARLES G HORNYOLD, Blackmore Park, Great Malvern
16 June, 1872 *ROBERT HOVENDEN, Heathcote, Park Hill Road, Croydon
27 Mar 1869   *JOSEPH JACKSON HOWARD, LL D, F S A (*Hon Treasurer*), 3 Dartmouth Row, Blackheath, S E
4 Nov 1870   *THOMAS HUGHES, F S A, The Groves, Chester
20 Feb 1874   W ESSINGTON HUGHES, 89 Alexandra Road South Hampstead, N W
20 Feb 1879   HULL SUBSCRIPTION LIBRARY, Albion Street, Hull (ALFRED MILNER, Librarian)

11 Dec 1871   *INNER TEMPLE LIBRARY, The Librarian, E C

23 Sept 1872 *WILLIAM JACKSON, F S A, 33 South Castle Street Liverpool
22 July, 1872 *T E JACOBSON, M D, Sleaford, Lincolnshire
9 Feb 1880   *FRANCIS JAMES, 190 Cromwell Road, S W
1 July, 1869 *The Rev EDMUND JERMYN, M A, Forbescourt Dundee, N B
2 Nov 1877   ARTHUR J JEWERS, F S A, Chester Place Mutley, Plymouth
20 Mar 1881   *JOHN JOSEPH JONES Abberley Hall, Stourport
6 Mar 1871   MORRIS C JONES F S A, Gungrog, Welshpool

12 June, 1878 AUGUSTUS KELHAM, 67 Ashburnham Road, Bedford
3 June, 1873 The Rev EDWARD KING, B A, F S A Scot Werrington Vicarage, near Launceston
17 Apr 1880   KING'S INNS LIBRARY Dublin (J M LA BARTE, Librarian)
1 Jan 1879   *Mrs HENRY KINGSLEY 10 Ridgway Place, Wimbledon
31 Dec 1870   *THOMAS C SNEYD KYNNERSLEY, Moor Green, Moseley, Birmingham

30 Dec 1882   *FREDERIC DE HOCHEPIED LARPENT, Barrackpore Bombay
13 Dec 1883   C MILLER LAYTON F S A, Shortlands, Castle Hill Avenue, Folkestone
4 Nov 1870   *THOMAS LAYTON, F S A, Kew Bridge, Middlesex
2 Jan 1871   Sir EDMUND A H LECHMERE, Bart, M P, 13 Bolton Row, Mayfair, W
22 Sept 1869 The Rev F G LEE D C L, F S A All Saints' Vicarage, York Road, Lambeth, S E
27 Dec 1882   *JOSEPH LEETE, Eversden, South Norwood Park, S E
24 Nov 1883   *LEHIGH UNIVERSITY, South Bethlehem, Pennsylvania, U S A (per H Sotheran and Co, 136 Strand, W C)
27 Apr 1874   *STANLEY LEIGHTON, M P, Athenæum Club, 107 Pall Mall, S W
3 Apr 1869   *Mrs LITTLEDALE, 26 Cranley Gardens, S W
2 Sept 1872   *LIVERPOOL FREE PUBLIC LIBRARY, William Brown Street Liverpool (PETER COWELL, Librarian)

8 Sept 1871	The Rev W J LOFTIE, F S A , 3a Sheffield Terrace, Campden Hill, Kensington, W
9 May, 1873	*LIBRARY COMMITTEE OF THE CORPORATION OF THE CITY OF LONDON, Guildhall Library, E C (W H OVERALL, Librarian)
20 Dec 1877	LONDON LIBRARY, 12 St James's Square, S W (ROBERT HARRISON, Librarian)
2 Nov 1877	*WILLIAM LONG, F S A , West Hay, Wrington, Somerset
24 June, 1881	*G B LONGSTAFF, Southfield Grange, Wandsworth, S W
7 Apr 1869	*WILLIAM H DYER LONGSTAFFE, Gateshead
31 Dec 1878	B DE BERTODANO LOPEZ, 22 Chester Terrace, Regent's Park, N W
14 May, 1869	Sir JOHN MACLEAN, F S A (Council), Glasbury House, Richmond Hill, Clifton, Bristol
28 Nov 1870	*The Rev A R MADDISON, Vicars' Court, Lincoln
1 Feb 1879	Mrs MANBY, care of Charles Jenser, Esq , Oakhill, Bath
16 Mar 1874	*MANCHESTER FREE LIBRARY, Manchester (CHARLES W SUTTON, Librarian)
23 June, 1869	His Grace the DUKE OF MANCHESTER (President), 1 Great Stanhope Street, W
10 Apr 1869	*GEORGE W MARSHALL, LL D , F S A (Council), 60 Onslow Gardens, S W
7 Oct 1882	EDMUND STORY-MASKELYNE, Hatt House, Box, Wilts
7 June, 1877	The Rev G S MASTER, West Dean Rectory, Salisbury
20 May, 1869	*WALTER C METCALFE, F S A , 10 Lupus Street, St George's Square, S W
7 May, 1878	*THOMAS TINDAL METHOLD, 7 Ashburn Place, Cromwell Road, South Kensington, S W
24 May, 1869	The Right Hon VISCOUNT MIDLETON (Vice-President), Eaton Square, S W.
20 July, 1878	SAMUEL MILNE MILNE, Calverley House, near Leeds
24 Aug 1870	The Rev JOHN MIREHOUSE, Colsterworth Rectory, Grantham
10 Sept 1877	MITCHELL LIBRARY, Ingram Street East, Glasgow (F P BARRETT, Librarian)
1 Apr 1879	*W J C MOENS, Tweed, near Lymington, Hants
1 Nov 1881	J B M LINGARD-MONK, Belmore, Craneswater Park, Southsea
12 Apr 1869	*The Right Hon LORD MONSON (Vice-President), 29 Belgrave Square, S W
19 Jan 1878	The Rev CECIL MOORE, M A , Lovell Heath Lodge, Charlwood, Crawley, Sussex
18 May, 1870	*Colonel CHARLES THOMAS JOHN MOORE, F S A , Frampton Hall, near Boston
17 June, 1878	Mrs MOORE, Lawneswood House, Stourbridge.
20 Feb 1880	*JOHN MULLINGS, Cirencester
31 Dec 1869	GEORGE J MURRAY, Mytchett Place, Frimley, Surrey
16 Apr 1875	*W MARTIAL MYDDLLTON, 12 Albion Grove, Stoke Newington, N
28 May, 1884	NATIONAL LIBRARY OF IRELAND (care of Hodges, Figgis, and Co , 104 Grafton Street, Dublin)
14 Sept. 1872	NAVAL AND MILITARY CLUB, 94 Piccadilly, W
4 Feb 1884	FRANK NEAME, Luton House, Faversham
24 Jan 1878	The Rev CHARLES NEVE, Oak Road, Woolston, Southampton
7 Sept 1878	*NEW ENGLAND HISTORIC GENEALOGICAL SOCIETY, 18 Somerset Street, Boston, U S A (J WARD DEAN, Librarian), (care of E G Allen, 28 Henrietta Street, Covent Garden, W C)
15 Feb 1879	*NEW YORK STATE LIBRARY, Albany, U S A (care of Stevens and Haynes, Bell Yard, Temple Bar)

30 June, 1873	FREDERICK I NICHOLL, F S A , 120 Harley Street, W
11 Aug 1876	G W NICHOLL, The Ham, Cowbridge, Glamorganshire
8 Sept 1871	J W SPRADLING NICHOLL-CARNE, D C L , St Donat's Castle, Bridgend, Glamorganshire
20 May, 1881	J GAMSON NICHOLSON, 19 St Andrew's Crescent, Cardiff
3 Apr 1874	The Rev C B NORCLIFFE Langton Hall, Malton, Yorkshire
28 May, 1879	J N PYKE NOTT, Bydown, Swymbridge, Barnstaple
7 June, 1875	*NOTTINGHAM FREE PUBLIC LIBRARY (J P BRISCOE, Librarian)
31 Dec 1875	NOTTINGHAM SUBSCRIPTION LIBRARY, Nottingham (W P PHILLIMORE, Hon Secretary)
19 June, 1874	The Rev T R O'FFLAHERTIE, Capel Vicarage, Dorking
20 Feb 1880	JOHN O'HART, Ringsend, Dublin
28 Feb 1877	*HENRY LEIGH ORMSBY, 2 Harcourt Buildings, Inner Temple, E C
28 July, 1869	EVAN ORTNER, 3 St James's Street, S W
6 May, 1871	Sir CHARLES J PALMER, Bart , Dorney Court, Windsor
14 Feb 1880	*Captain JOHN W R PARKER, 19th Foot, The Barracks, Tralee, Kerry, Ireland
24 Feb 1874	MANSFIELD PARKYNS, Woodborough Hall, near Nottingham
7 Sept 1877	*THOMAS W PARR, The Grove, Cossington, Leicester
7 Apr 1869	DANIEL PARSONS, M A , Stuart's Lodge, Malvern Wells
28 July, 1869	D WILLIAMS PATERSON, Newark Valley, New York, U S A
28 May 1884	*W K PAULI Luton, Bedfordshire
28 July, 1869	EDWARD PEACOCK, F S A , Bottesford Manor, Brigg, Lincolnshire
1 Jan 1884	Captain FREDERICK CLINTON PEARCE, Rockford, Illinois, U S A
28 July, 1869	The Rev A J PEARMAN, Merstham, Surrey
1 May, 1871	IRA B PECK, Woonsocket, Rhode Island, U S A
29 Dec 1872	RICHARD LAWRENCE PEMBERTON, Hawthorne Tower, Seaham Harbour, co Durham
22 July, 1875	HUGH PENFOLD, Rustington, Worthing
30 May, 1881	WILLIAM P W PHILLIMORE, M A , 28 Budge Row, Cannon Street, E C
20 May 1881	Mrs PIERCE, Sherbourne House, Leamington
5 Apr 1883	*Sir LIONEL M SWINNERTON PILKINGTON, Bart , Chevet Park, Wakefield
15 Feb 1873	*W DUNCOMBE PINK, 5 King Street, Leigh, Lancashire
18 Apr 1878	The Rev ALFRED STEPHENSON PORTER, M A , The Vicarage, Claines, Worcester
31 Dec 1875	The Rev F J POYNTON, Kelston Rectory, Bath
18 Dec 1878	JOHN EDWARD PRICE, F S A , F R S L , 60 Albion Road, Stoke Newington, N
8 Dec 1877	*Lieut -Col W F PRIDEAUX, 2 Sidlaw Terrace, Bognor
29 July, 1875	*BERNARD QUARITCH, 15 Piccadilly, W
11 May, 1869	The Rev Canon RAINE, York
6 Dec 1870	J R RAINES, Burton Pidsea, Burstwick, near Hull
11 Dec 1874	EVELYN W RASHLEIGH, Menabilly, Cornwall
29 Oct 1875	JONATHAN RASHLEIGH Kilmarth, Par Station, Cornwall
13 Jan 1883	R NORMAN S REDMAYNE, South Dene, Gateshead-on-Tyne
31 Oct 1884	REFORM CLUB, 104 Pall Mall, S W (care of Mr Ridgway, 169 Piccadilly, W)
10 Mar 1874	The Rev O J REICHEL, Sparsholt Vicarage, Challow Station, Great Western Railway, Berks
29 Apr 1871	*SAMUEL RIGBY, Fern Bank, Liverpool Road, Chester
30 Mar 1869	*The Rev C J ROBINSON, M A (*Auditor*) West Hackney Rectory, Stoke Newington, N

11 Sept 1880	*BROOKE ROBINSON, Barford House, Warwick
12 Nov 1883	*W P ROBINSON, care of Messrs L and J B Young and Co, New York (per Trubner and Co, 57 Ludgate Hill, E C)
6 Jan 1883	ARNOLD HENRY ROBSON, The Esplanade, Sunderland
14 Apr 1880	ROCHDALE FREE PUBLIC LIBRARY, Rochdale
27 May, 1869	*The Rev EDWARD ROGERS, M A, Odcombe Rectory, Ilminster
7 Dec 1883	*GEORGE A ROOKE, 12 Bloomsbury Square, W C
12 Sept 1877	W O ROPER, Southfield, Lancaster
1 Jan 1883	*SIMPSON ROSTRON, 1 Hare Court, Temple, E C
3 Dec 1873	J BROOKING ROWE, F S A, Plympton Lodge, Plympton, South Devon
29 Jan 1878	*ROYAL HISTORICAL SOCIETY (P EDWARD DOVE, Secretary), 11 Chandos Street, Cavendish Square, W
20 Jan 1871	ROYAL IRISH ACADEMY, 19 Dawson Street, Dublin
28 May, 1869	ROYAL LIBRARY, Windsor Castle, Windsor
28 July, 1869	The Rev DAVID ROYCE, Netherswell Vicarage, Stow-on-the-Wold
18 May, 1870	*JAMES RUSBY, F R Hist Soc, 18 Oppidans Road, Regent's Park, N W
12 Dec, 1874	EDWARD RUSSELL, Boston, U S A
20 Jan 1871	J PAUL RYLANDS, F S A (Hon Secretary), 25 Stanley Gardens, Belsize Park, Hampstead, N W
31 Dec 1881	*THOMAS GLAZEBROOK RYLANDS, F S A, Highfields, Thelwall, near Warrington
27 July, 1879	*W DE RYTHRE, Riverstown House, Monasterevan, Ireland
24 June 1878	S SUTHERLAND SAFFORD, Parkshot, Richmond, Surrey
3 June, 1873	*General Sir JOHN ST GEORGE, K C B, 22 Cornwall Gardens, Queen's Gate, S W
18 Aug 1873	JOHN EDMUND SANDBACH, Stoodley Hall, Eastwood, Todmorden
12 July, 1881	Mrs LEOPOLD SCARLETT, Parkhurst, Dorking
8 Dec 1877	G D SCULL, Rugby Lodge, 12 Norham Road, Oxford
15 Dec 1883	*WALTER H S SHADWELL, 21 Nottingham Place, Marylebone, W
10 July, 1884	MICHAEL SHEARD, Boothroyd, Birstall, Leeds
18 Feb 1873	*CONINGSBY C SIBTHORP, Canwick Hall, Lincoln
6 Sept 1882	RICHARD SIMPSON, 13 Thurlow Road, Roslyn, Hampstead, N W
29 Jan 1878	*SION COLLEGE LIBRARY, London Wall, E C (Rev W R MILMAN, Librarian)
12 Jan 1871	*ROBERT HARDISTY SKAIFE, 5 Blenheim Place, Holgate Road, York
5 June, 1874	HUBERT SMITH Belmont House, Bridgenorth
10 Nov 1873	*J C C SMITH, H M Probate Court Somerset House, W C
25 Jan 1871	The Rev WALTER SNEYD, 55 Portland Place, W
22 Mar 1871	*SOCIETY OF ANTIQUARIES OF LONDON, Burlington House, W
12 Nov 1883	SOCIETY OF ANTIQUARIES OF NEWCASTLE-UPON-TYNE, The Castle, Newcastle-upon-Tyne
20 Jan 1877	*EDWARD SOLLY, F R S, F S A, Camden House, Sutton, Surrey
7 June, 1872	*SOMERSETSHIRE ARCHÆOLOGICAL SOCIETY, Museum, Taunton
27 Jan 1879	*Rev J H STANNING, Leigh Vicarage, Leigh, Lancashire
21 Dec 1881	*JOHN STANSFELD, Daisy Bank, Meanwood, Leeds
30 May, 1884	The Rev FRANCIS STERRY, Poltimore Rectory, Exeter
10 Oct 1884	EDWARD STONE 5 Finsbury Circus, E C
31 Dec 1875	The Rev HUGH A STOWELL, Breadsall Rectory, Derby
22 Sept 1869	*JOHN SYKES, M D, F S A, Doncaster
28 Dec 1871	*The Rev JAMES TAYLOR, Whicham Rectory, Sylecroft, Cumberland
3 Apr 1876	Mrs G BLUNDELL-THOMPSON, The Grove, Allerton, Liverpool

15 June, 1878	*C H Tindall, Platt Hall, Rusholme, Manchester
15 Dec 1883	*John Tolhurst, F S A , Glenbrook, Beckenham, Kent
23 Dec 1884	George W Tomlinson, F S A , The Elms, Huddersfield
28 Dec 1876	John Tremayne, Heligan, St Austell, Cornwall
1 Jan 1884	*Henry Trethewy, Silsoe, Ampthill, Bedfordshire
16 Mar 1871	*Joseph Herbert Tritton, 36 Queen's Gate Gardens, S W
8 Mar 1881	H J Trotter, 2 Harcourt Buildings, Temple, E C
1 Feb 1876	*Stephen Tucker, Somerset Herald, College of Arms, Queen Victoria Street, E C
19 Jan 1881	Wm Murray Tuke, Saffron Walden
31 Oct 1884	*Wm H Upton, Wallawalla, Washington, U S A
9 Jan 1875	Henry F J Vaughan, 30 Edwardes Square, Kensington, W
10 June, 1869	*Sir Henry M Vavasour, Bart , F S A (Vice-President), 8 Upper Grosvenor Street, W
3 Dec 1874	Colonel P D Vigors, Holloden, Bagenalstown, co Carlow, Ireland
18 Dec 1874	*Henry Wagner, F S A (Auditor), 13 Half Moon Street, Piccadilly, W
23 Feb 1884	*Sir Herewald Wake, Bart , 5 Belgrave Place, Belgrave Square, S W
26 May, 1883	Hubert H Wall, P O Box 19, Flatbush, Long Island, New York, U S A
18 May, 1870	*Edward Waltham, Watcomb House, St Anne's Place, Streatham Hill, S W
2 Jan 1871	The Earl of Warwick, 1 Stable Yard, St James's, S W
28 Feb 1877	*Washington Library of Congress, U S A (care of E G Allen, 28 Henrietta Street, Covent Garden W C)
22 Feb 1883	*A Jas Waterlow, 25 Park Crescent, Portland Place, W
2 Sept 1872	*Watkinson Library, Hartford, Connecticut, U S A (care of E G Allen)
22 June, 1870	Frank G Watney, Landmore, Aghadowey, co Derry
4 Nov 1870	*John Watney, F S A , F R G S , Mercers' Hall, Ironmonger Lane, Cheapside, E C
18 Oct 1884	The Rev F W Weaver, Milton Vicarage, Evercreech, Bath
1 Mar 1871	Archibald Weir, M D , St Mungho's, Great Malvern
18 May, 1870	*W H Weldon, College of Arms Queen Victoria Street, E C
1 Dec 1882	His Grace the Duke of Westminster (Vice-President), Grosvenor House Grosvenor Street, W
22 Sept 1869	Lieut -Colonel Gould Hunter-Weston, F S A , Hunterston, West Kilbride, Ayrshire
2 Oct 1874	Charles A White, New Haven, Connecticut, U S A
1 July, 1876	*Captain Edward Arthur White, F S A (Council), Old Elvet, Durham
17 Nov 1876	*George White, Ashley House, Epsom
28 July, 1869	William H Whitmori, Boston, USA (Hon Local Sec for U S A)
1 May, 1872	The Rev Thomas Whorwood, D D , Willoughby, near Rugby
12 June, 1878	J J Garth Wilkinson, M D , F R G S , 76 Wimpole Street, W
22 Dec 1870	The Rev Augustin Williams, Todenham Rectory, Moreton-in-the-Marsh
24 Apr 1879	Charles Williams, Moseley Lodge, Birmingham
31 Dec 1880	Edward Windeatt, Totnes, Devon
13 Apr 1871	*The Hon Robert C Winthrop, 90 Marlborough Street, Boston, U S A
13 Apr 1880	*Benjamin Winstone, 53 Russell Square, W C
24 Nov 1869	R H Wood, F S A , Penrhos House, Rugby

18 May, 1876	CHARLES H L WOODD, F G S, 34 New Bond Street, W
14 Jan 1884	*The Rev ADOLPHUS F A WOODFORD, M A, 25A Norfolk Crescent, Hyde Park, W
21 Feb 1882	*JOHN WOODGATE, Little Bentley Hall, Colchester
18 May 1870	*Sir ALBERT W WOODS, F S A, Garter King-of-Arms, College of Arms, Queen Victoria Street, E C
10 Mar 1871	*ASHBEL WOODWARD, M D, Franklin, Connecticut, U S A
20 Aug 1878	Dr A E WOOLRYCH, 43 King s Road, Chelsea, S W
7 Oct 1879	*YALE COLLEGE, U S A (care of E G Allen, 28 Henrietta Street, Covent Garden, W C)
23 Feb 1884	LAMBTON YOUNG, 16 Harcourt Terrace, Radcliffe Square, S W

PUBLICATIONS.

VOL
1 — The Visitation of London, in 1568, by Cooke. Edited by J J Howard, Esq, LL D, F S A, and G J Armytage, Esq, F S A
2 — The Visitation of Leicestershire, in 1619, by Lennard and Vincent. Edited by John Fetherston Jun, Esq, F S A
3 — The Visitation of Rutland, in 1618, by Camden. Edited by George J Armytage, Fsq, F S A
4 — The Visitations of Nottingham in 1569 and 1614. Edited by Geo W Marshall, Esq, LL D, F S A
5 — The Visitations of Oxford, 1574 and 1634. Edited by W H Turner, Esq
6 — The Visitation of Devon in 1620. Edited by the Rev F T Colby, D D, F S A
7 — The Visitation of Cumberland in 1615. Edited by John Fetherston, Esq, F S A
                                                           [*The preceding Seven Works are out of Print*]
8 — Le Neve's Catalogue of Knights. Edited by George W Marshall, Esq, LL D, F S A   £1 1 0
9 — The Visitation of Cornwall, 1620. Edited by Col Vivian and Dr H H Drake   £1 1 0
10 — The Registers of Westminster Abbey. Edited by Colonel Chester, D C L, LL D   £1 1 0
11 — The Visitation of Somersetshire in 1623. Edited by the Rev F T Colby, D D, F S A   £1 1 0
12 — The Visitation of Warwickshire. Edited by John Fetherston Esq, F S A   £1 1 0
13 — The Visitations of Essex in 1552, 1558, 1612 and 1634. Part I. Edited by Walter C Metcalfe, Esq, F S A   £1 1 0
14 — The Visitation of Essex, consisting of Miscellaneous Pedigrees, and Berry's Pedigrees Part II. With general Index   £1 1 0
15 — The Visitation of London, 1633-4. Vol I. Edited by J J Howard, Esq, LL D, F S A, and Colonel Chester, D C L, LL D   £1 1 0
16 — The Visitation of Yorkshire in 1564. Edited by the Rev C B Norcliffe, M A   £1 1 0
17 — The Visitation of London, 1633-4. Vol II. Edited by J J Howard Esq, LL D, F S A   £1 1 0
18 — The Visitation of Cheshire in 1580. Edited by J Paul Rylands, Esq, F S A   £1 1 0
19 — The Visitations of Bedfordshire in 1566, 1582, and 1634. Edited by F A Blaydes, Esq   £1 1 0
20 — The Visitation of Dorsetshire, in 1623, by St George and Lennard as Deputies to Camden. Edited by J Paul Rylands, Esq, F S A   [*In the Press*]
21 — The Visitation of Gloucestershire, in 1623, by Chitting and Phillipot as Deputies to Camden. Edited by Sir John Maclean, F S A, and W C Heane, Esq   [*In the Press*]

PROSPECTIVE PUBLICATIONS

The Visitation of Shropshire, in 1584, by Lee as Deputy to Cooke. To be Edited by J Paul Rylands, Esq, F S A
The Registers of Durham Cathedral. To be Edited by Captain White, F S A
The Visitation of Hertfordshire, in 1572, by Cooke. To be Edited by Walter C Metcalfe, Esq, F S A
The Visitations of Worcestershire in 1569 and 1634
The Visitations of Hampshire, in 1530, 1552, 1575, and 1622, by Benolte, Hawley, Cooke, and Philipot as Deputy to Camden. To be Edited by the Rev F W Weaver
The Visitations of Sussex, in 1530, by Benolte, 1574, by Cooke, and 1633, by Philpot and Owen as Deputies to St George and Burrough.
The Book of Peers from 1 Edward I. to 17 Henry VI. To be Edited by Sir John Maclean, F S A
The Visitation of Berkshire, in 1531, by Benolte. To be Edited by Granville Leveson Gower, Esq, F S A
The Visitations of Northamptonshire, in 1566 and 1618, by Harvey and Camden.

      Entrance Fee · Half-a-Guinea.   Annual Subscription · One Guinea

    Members whose Subscriptions are due are requested to forward them to J J Howard, Esq, LL D, Honorary Treasurer, at 3 Dartmouth Row, Blackheath, Kent, who will also receive Subscriptions towards the publication of "Parish Registers"
    Persons wishing to join the Society should apply to J Paul Rylands, Esq, F S A, Hon Sec, 25 Stanley Gardens, Belsize Park, N W
    The Publications of the Society which are in print can be obtained, by Members *only*, at the prices above mentioned, on application to Messrs Mitchell and Hughes, 140 Wardour Street, W

REGISTER SECTION.

PUBLICATIONS

Vol I.—THE REGISTERS OF ST PETER'S, CORNHILL, LONDON   Part I, A D 1538 to 1666   Edited by Granville Leveson Gower, Esq, F S A   £0 10 6

Vol II.—THE REGISTERS OF CANTERBURY CATHEDRAL   Edited by Robert Hovenden, Esq   £0 10 6

Vol III.—THE REGISTERS OF ST DIONIS BACKCHURCH, LONDON   Edited by the late Colonel J L Chester, D C L, LL D   £0 10 6

Vol IV.—THE REGISTERS OF ST PETER'S, CORNHILL, LONDON   Part II, A D 1666 to 1754   Edited by Granville Leveson Gower, Esq, F S A   £0 10 6

Vol V.—THE REGISTERS OF ST MARY ALDERMARY, LONDON   Edited by the late Colonel J L Chester, D C L, LL D   £1 1 0

Vol VI.—THE REGISTERS OF ST. THOMAS APOSTLE, LONDON   Edited by the late Colonel J L Chester, D C L, LL D   £1 1 0

Vol VII.—THE REGISTERS OF ST MICHAEL, CORNHILL, LONDON   Partly Edited by the late Colonel J L Chester, D C L, LL D   £1 1 0

Vol VIII.—THE REGISTERS OF ST ANTHOLIN, BUDGE ROW, AND ST JOHN BAPTIST ON WALLBROOK, LONDON   £1 1 0

Vol IX.—THE REGISTERS OF ST JAMES, CLERKENWELL, LONDON   Vol I   Edited by Robert Hovenden, Esq   £1 1 0

Vol X.—THE REGISTERS OF ST JAMES CLERKENWELL, LONDON   Vol II   Edited by Robert Hovenden, Esq   [*In the Press*

PROSPECTIVE PUBLICATIONS

THE MARRIAGE REGISTER OF ST GEORGE'S HANOVER SQUARE   To be Edited by Granville Leveson Gower, Esq, F S A

THE REGISTERS OF CHRIST CHURCH, NEWGATE STREET, LONDON   To be Edited by the Rev Cecil Moore, M A

THE REGISTERS OF ST SEPULCHRE'S, LONDON

AND MANY OTHERS

The Publications of the Register Section will be supplied to Members on payment of an extra Subscription of One Guinea, and can be obtained, by Members *only*, from Messrs Mitchell and Hughes, 140 Wardour Street, W, at the above Prices

Forms of Application, and all other particulars, may be obtained by applying to J Paul Rylands, Esq F S A, Hon Sec, 25 Stanley Gardens, Belsize Road, N W,